# LINUX
## THE TEXTBOOK

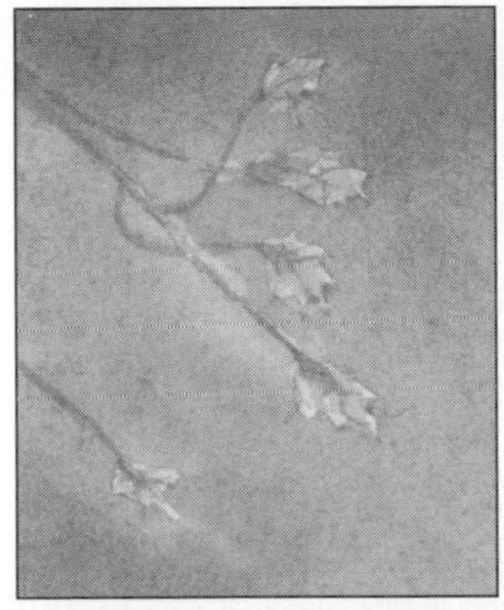
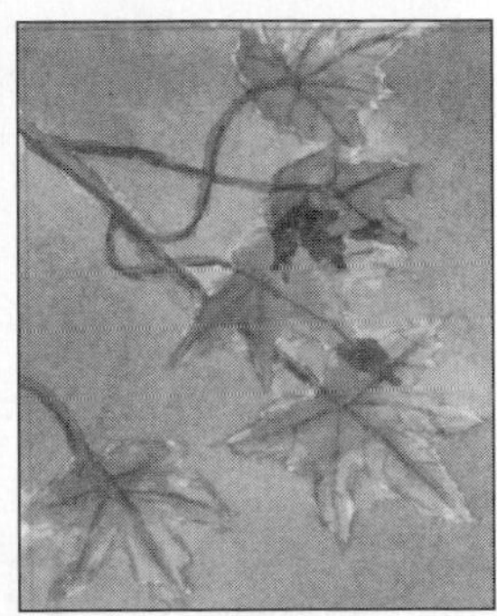

**SYED MANSOOR SARWAR**
University of Portland

**ROBERT KORETSKY**
University of Portland

**SYED AQEEL SARWAR**
GE Capital IT Solutions

Boston San Francisco New York
London Toronto Sydney Tokyo Singapore Madrid
Mexico City Munich Paris Cape Town Hong Kong Montreal

| | |
|---|---|
| Senior Acquisitions Editor | Maite Suarez-Rivas |
| Assistant Editor | Lisa Hogue |
| Composition and Art | Pre-Press Company, Inc. |
| Interior Design | Delgado Design |
| Design Manager | Regina Hagen |
| Production Services | Marilyn Lloyd/Pre-Press Company, Inc. |
| Production Supervisor | Helen Reebenacker |
| Manufacturing Buyer | Caroline Fell |

Access the latest information about Addison-Wesley titles from our Web site: http://www.awl.com/cs.

The programs and applications presented in this book have been included for their instructional value. They have been tested with care, but are not guaranteed for any particular purpose. The publisher does not offer any warrantees or representations, nor does it accept any liabilities with respect to the program or applications.

**Library of Congress Cataloging-in-Publication Data**

Sarwar, Syed Mansoor.
LINUX : the textbook / Syed Mansoor Sarwar, Robert Koretsky, Syed Aqeel Sarwar.—1st ed.
p. cm.
Includes index.
ISBN 0-201-72595-9 (pbk.)
1. Linux. 2. Operating systems (Computers) I. Koretsky, Robert. II. Sarwar, Syed Aqeel. III. Title.

QA76.76.063 S35545 2001
005.4'32—dc21 00-069963



1 2 3 4 5 6 7 8 9 10 MA -030201

## Dedications

To my wife and children.

**S.M.S.**

To my family.

**R.M.K.**

To my parents.

**S.A.S.**

# PREFACE

## THE SUBVERSIVE SOFTWARE SYSTEM

> "Linux is subversive. Who would have thought even five years ago [1991] that a world-class operating system could coalesce as if by magic out of part-time hacking by several thousand developers scattered all over the planet, connected only by the tenuous strands of the Internet?"
>
> Eric Raymond, *The Cathedral and the Bazaar*

Yes, who would have thought that a "subversive " software system, whose forerunner had hardly a foothold in the small computer market, would move into a position to challenge, and by every indication, best the very interests that sought to undermine the freedom of the greatest technological invention of our time? Certainly it didn't happen magically. The Open Source philosophy championed by the UINIX community finally bore fruit, thanks to the proliferation of the Internet, on the very hardware platforms that held the highest promise and empowered the individual user. If UNIX was ultimately for hackers, then LINUX was and is the embodiment of their personal freedom.

This textbook is a testament to the pervasive power of the Internet and to those thousands of individual hackers who saw themselves as a part of a greater whole. The best way to get a real sense of this community is to get on line, follow some or all of the Internet resources listed at the end of selected chapters, and read what the creators of LINUX have to say for themselves. We guarantee that after diligent practice and thoughtful, creative solutions to the problems we pose, you will find the fulfillment that the community of LINUX users share.

## WHY WE WROTE THIS BOOK

LINUX has reached that level of maturity in the computer science and engineering fields, as witnessed by our writing of this textbook, which we felt was long overdue. Together, we have more than 35 years of practical teaching experience at the college level. Our initial concept for this book grew out of our unwillingness to use either the large, intractable LINUX reference sources or the short, "LINUX-for-Idiots" guides to teach meaningful, complete, and relevant introductory classes on the subject. Moreover, a textbook approach, with pedagogy incorporating in-chapter tutorials and exercises, as well as useful problem sets at the end of each chapter, allows us to present all the important LINUX topics for a classroom lecture-laboratory-homework presentation.We can achieve this presentation in a manner that is optimal for learning (i.e., well-thought-out sequencing of topics, well-developed and timely lessons, laboratory work, and homework exercises/problems synchronized with the sequencing of chapters in the book). Additionally, because of the depth and breadth of coverage of these topics, anyone interested in furthering their professional knowledge of the subject matter will also find this textbook useful.

## The Purposes of This Book

Our primary purpose is to describe to readers the LINUX application user's interface (AUI) and to do it in a way that gives the reader insight into the inner workings of the system, along with some important LINUX concepts, data structures, and algorithms. Notable examples are the LINUX file and process concepts and I/O redirection. The secondary purpose of this textbook is to describe some important LINUX software engineering tools for developers of C software and shell scripts. However, we do not describe the LINUX applications programmer's interface (API) in terms of C libraries and LINUX system calls. In writing this textbook we assumed no previous knowledge of LINUX or programming on the part of the reader.

## The Presentation Format

The book is laced with many diagrams and tables, hundreds of in-chapter tutorials and interactive shell sessions, in-chapter exercises, and end-of-chapter problems. A syntax box for every command, tool, and application covered describes the syntax of the command, its purpose, the output produced by the command, and its useful options and features. In addition, every chapter contains a summary of the material covered in the chapter.

## Pathways Through the Text

*If this book is to be used as the main text for an introductory course* in LINUX, all the chapters should be covered, with the possible exception of Chapter 20. If the book is to be used as a companion to the main text in an operating systems concepts and principles course, the coverage of chapters would be dictated by the order in which the main topics of the course are covered but should include Chapters 7, 12, and 13. *For use in a C or Shell programming* course, Chapters 7–20 and relevant sections of Chapters 3–6 would be a great help to students. The extent of coverage of Chapter 20 would depend on the nature of the course—partial coverage in an introductory and full coverage in an advanced course.

## The Design of Fonts

The following typefaces have been used in the book for various types of text items.

| Typeface | Text Type |
|---|---|
| **Boldface Roman** | Keywords |
| **`Boldface Monospace`** | Any character or string typed at the keyboard (commands, shell variables, and user input) |
| `Monospace` | Commands, tools, applications, and their options in the text |
| *Italic* | A word being used as a word and text being emphasized |
| Roman | Everything else, including file pathnames |

The keyboard presses are enclosed in angle brackets (e.g., <Enter> and <Ctrl-D>). The instruction "press <Ctrl-D>" means to hold the <Ctrl> key down while pressing the <D> key. This instruction is also denoted ^D.

## SUPPLEMENTS

A comprehensive and informational Web site containing solutions to the In-Chapter Exercises, source code, and further references and links to other LINUX sites can be found at http://lhotse.up.edu/~koretsky/linux.html. Also, you can link to this site from the Addison Wesley Web Site at www.awl.com/cseng/titles/0-201-72595-9.

Solutions to the problems at the end of each chapter are available exclusively to professors using this book to teach a course. Please contact your local Addison-Wesley sales representative.

We take full responsibility for any errors in this textbook. We would really appreciate if you would send your error reports and comments to us at sarwar@up.edu and koretsky@up.edu. We will incorporate your feedback and fix any errors in subsequent editions.

## ACKNOWLEDGEMENTS

Completing a book of this magnitude in a short time of less than one year is not possible without the help of many. We thank all the individuals at Addison-Wesley who were involved in this project. This is our second book with Maite Suarez-Rivas, the acquisitions editor, and she continues to be an outstanding professional. She supported our idea of the need for a textbook on LINUX and gave invaluable advice for its timely completion. Thank you, Maite! We also convey our sincere gratitude to her crew at Addison-Wesley: Lisa Hogue, Patti Mahtani, Helen Reebenacker, Regina Hagen, and Jarrod Gibbons, for their support and professionalism. Lisa, thank you for providing all round help! Special thanks are extended to Marilyn Lloyd, Project Manager at Pre-Press Company, Inc., for her patience, many excellent suggestions, and outstanding work during the production phase of this book.

Our sincere thanks to the following reviewers who gave valuable feedback, and numerous accurate and insightful comments. Their contribution has certainly enhanced the quality of the final product.

Ronald E. Bass, Austin Community College
Thomas A. Burns, Henry Ford Community College
Simon Gray, Ashland University
Chuck Lesko, Carven Community College
Toshimi Minoura, Oregon State University
Selmer Moen, Minot State University
Gregory B. Newby, University of North Carolina at Chapel Hill
Marianne Vakalis, Franklin University
G. Jan Wilms, Union University, Jackson, Tennessee
Bill Wood, Arizona State University

Last, but not least, many thanks to Dale Frakes of University of Portland School of Engineering Computing Laboratories for his continued support in various capacities. He was always there when we needed him.

## Personal Acknowledgements

**Syed Mansoor Sarwar** Writing two books in two years would have been impossible without the support, understanding, inspiration, and love of my family. My whole family deserves a special thank you. I thank my dear parents for their love and for teaching me who I am. They are my role models in hard work and morality, and I continue to draw strength from their teachings. I thank my wife, Robina, and children, Hassaan and Maham, for their love, understanding, and support, and for allowing me to work long and odd hours to complete this book. Guys, I couldn't have done it without you. So, thank you! I thank my sisters, Rizwana and Farhana, and brothers, Masood, Nadeem, Aqeel, and Nabeel, for their love and friendship. Special thank you to Nadeem and Nabeel for their continued encouragement as I worked on this book. *Muk hondie aiy hoon? Asif out!*

I thank Tom Nelson, my former dean, mentor, and friend, for his encouragement throughout my career at the University of Portland. Thanks also to my friend Shahid Younas of Synplicity and colleagues Aziz Inan and Matthew Kuhn for their support.

Last, but not least, I sincerely thank my coauthors, Bob Koretsky and Aqeel Sarwar, for being such a joy to work with.

**Robert M. Koretsky** I thank my wife Kathe, daughter Tara, and son Cody, for all of the love and support they have given me over the years. I also thank Mansoor Sarwar, for his inspiration and friendship.

**Aqeel Sarwar** I thank Allah, the One who created me, for being kind to me and for teaching me the things I had no knowledge of. I also thank my parents for their personal sacrifices and patience in raising me and for lasting love. I thank my elder brother, Dr. Syed Mansoor Sarwar, for his continued support. I especially thank my brothers, Masood Sarwar, Dr. Nadeem Sarwar, Nabeel Sarwar and my dear sisters Rizwana Sarwar and Dr. Farhana Sarwar for their friendship and love. Finally, I thank my wife, Mamoona, for her support and my son, Mohammad, for just being there.

# TABLE OF CONTENTS

CHAPTER

# 1

# Overview of Operating Systems

**OBJECTIVES**

- To explain what an operating system is
- To describe briefly operating system services
- To describe character and graphical user interfaces
- To discuss different types of operating systems
- To mention what LINUX is

## 1.1 INTRODUCTION

Many operating systems are available today, some general enough to run on any type of computer (from a **personal computer**, or **PC**, to a **mainframe**), and some specifically designed to run on a particular type of computer system such as a **real-time computer system** used to control the movement of a robot. In this chapter, we describe the purpose of an operating system and different classes of operating systems. Before describing different types of operating systems and where LINUX fits in this categorization, we present and describe a layered diagram of a contemporary computer system and discuss the basic purpose of an operating system. We then describe different types of operating systems and the parameters used to classify them. Finally, we identify the class that LINUX belongs to and briefly discuss the different members of the LINUX family.

## 1.2 WHAT IS AN OPERATING SYSTEM?

A computer system consists of various hardware and software resources, as shown in a layered fashion in Figure 1.1. The primary purpose of an operating system is to facilitate easy, efficient, fair, orderly, and secure use of these resources. It allows the users of a computer system to use **application software**—spreadsheets, word processors, Web browsers, e-mail software, and the like. Programmers use **language libraries**, **system calls**, and **program generation tools** (e.g., text editors, compilers, and version control systems) to develop software. Fairness is obviously not an issue if only one user at a time is allowed to use the computer system. However, if multiple users are allowed to use the computer system, fairness and security are two main issues to be tackled by the operating system designers.

Hardware resources include keyboard, display screen, main memory (commonly known as **random access memory**, or **RAM**), disk drive, modem, and **central processing unit (CPU)**. Software resources include applications such as word processors, spreadsheets, games, graphing tools, picture processing tools, and Internet-related tools such as Web browsers. These applications, which reside at the topmost layer in the diagram, form the **application user's interface (AUI)**. The AUI is glued to the operating system **kernel** via the language libraries and the system call interface. The kernel is the part of an operating system where the real work is done. The system call interface comprises a set of functions that can be used by the applications and library routines to start execution of the kernel code for a particular service, such as reading a file. The language libraries and the system call interface comprise what is commonly known as the **application programmer's interface (API)**. The layers in the diagram are shown in an expanded form for the LINUX operating system in Chapter 3, where we also describe them briefly.

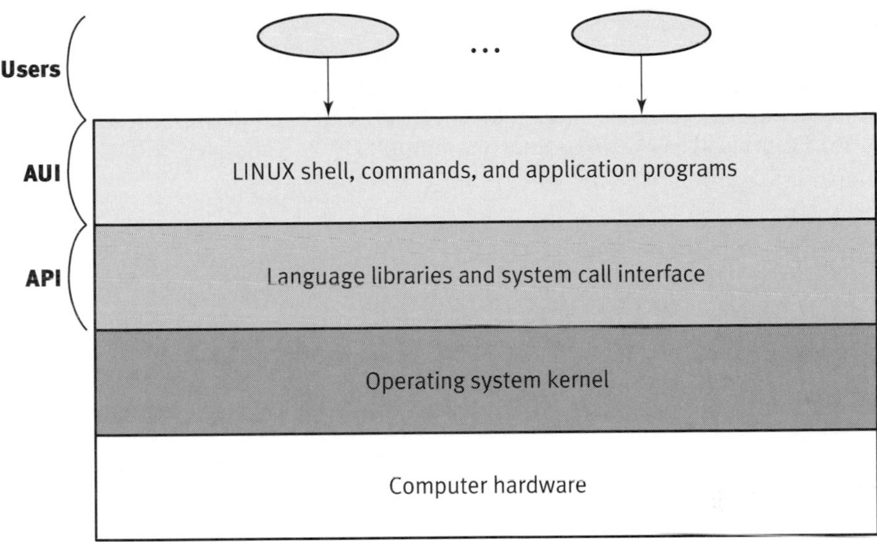


**Figure 1.1** A layered view of a contemporary computer system

There are two ways to view an operating system: top–down and bottom–up. In the bottom–up view, an operating system can be viewed as a piece of software that allocates and deallocates system resources (hardware and software) in an efficient, fair, orderly, and secure manner. For example, the operating system decides how much RAM space is to be allocated to a program before it is loaded and executed. The operating system ensures that only one file is printed on the printer at a time. The operating system also prevents an existing file on the disk from being accidentally overwritten by another file. The operating system further guarantees that, when execution of a program given to the CPU for processing has been completed, the program relinquishes the CPU so that other programs can be executed. Thus the operating system can be viewed as a **resource manager**.

In the top–down view, which we espouse in this textbook, an operating system can be viewed as a piece of software that isolates you from the complications of hardware resources. You therefore do not have to deal with the extremely difficult (impossible for most users) task of interacting with these resources directly. For example, as a user of a computer system, you don't have to write the software that allows you to save your work as a file on a hard disk, use a mouse as a point-and-click device, and print on a particular printer. Also, you do not have to write new software for a new device (e.g., mouse, disk drive, or DVD) that you buy and install in your system. The operating system performs the task of dealing with complicated hardware resources and gives you a simple machine to deal with. This machine allows you to use simple commands to retrieve and save files on a disk, print files on a printer, and play movies on a DVD. In a sense, the operating system provides a **virtual machine** that is much easier to deal with than the real machine.

You can, for example, use a command such as `cp memo letter` to make a copy of the memo file to the letter file on the hard disk in your computer system, without having to worry about the location of the memo and letter files on the disk, the structure and size of the disk, the brand of the disk drive, and the number or name of the disk drive in case your system has multiple drives (floppy, CD-ROM, and one or more hard disks).

## 1.3 OPERATING SYSTEM SERVICES

An operating system provides many services for you. Most of these services are meant to allow you to execute your software, both application programs and program development tools, efficiently and securely. Some services are meant for housekeeping tasks, such as keeping track of the amount of time that you have used the system. The major operating system services therefore provide mechanisms for secure and efficient

- execution of a program,
- input and output operations performed by programs,
- communication between processes,
- error detection and reporting, and
- manipulation of all types of files.

A detailed discussion of these services is outside the scope of this textbook, but we discuss them briefly when they are relevant to the topic being presented.

## 1.4 CHARACTER VERSUS GRAPHICAL USER INTERFACES

In order to use a computer system, you have to give commands to its operating system. An input device such as a keyboard is used to issue a command. If you use the keyboard to issue commands to the operating system, the operating system has a **character user interface**, commonly known as the **commandline user interface (CUI)**. If the primary input device for issuing commands to the operating system is a **point-and-click device** such as a mouse, the operating system has a **graphical user interface (GUI)**. Some operating systems have both character and graphical user interfaces, and you can use either. Some have a CUI as their primary interface but allow you to run software that provides a GUI. Operating systems such as DOS, LINUX, and UNIX have character user interfaces, whereas MacOS, OS/2, and Microsoft Windows have graphical user interfaces.

Although a GUI makes a computer easier to use, it gives you an automated setup with minimal flexibility. A GUI also presents an extra layer of software between you and the task that you want to perform on the computer, thereby making the task slower. In contrast, a CUI gives you control of your computer system and allows you to run application programs any way you want to. A CUI is also more efficient because a minimal layer of software is needed between you and your task on the computer, thereby making doing the task faster. Because many people are accustomed to the graphical interfaces of Nintendo and Web browsers, the character interface presents a new and somewhat challenging style of communicating commands to the computer system. However, most users are able to meet this challenge after a few hands-on sessions. Although LINUX comes with a CUI as its basic interface, it can run software based on the X Window System (Project Athena, MIT) that provides a GUI interface.

Graphical user interface is the hallmark of LINUX systems. Although all LINUX commands are executed under a character user interface, a large number of Internet and software development tools have graphical user interfaces. Most LINUX systems come packaged with a graphical user interface in the form of an X based desktop environment. The most popular desktop environments are the **GNU Network Object Model Environment (GNOME)** and the **K Desktop Environment (KDE)**. GNOME is the default desktop environment for Red Hat LINUX 6.1 and later versions and a new consortium was recently established to promote KDE. We discuss the LINUX GUI in Chapter 21.

## 1.5 TYPES OF OPERATING SYSTEMS

Operating systems can be categorized by the number of users who can use a system at the same time and the number of **processes** (executing programs) that an operating system can run simultaneously. These criteria lead to three types of operating systems.

- *Single-user, single-process systems:* These operating systems allow only one user at a time to use the computer system, and the user can run only one process at a time. Such operating systems are commonly used for PCs. Examples of such operating systems are MacOS, DOS, and Windows 3.1.
- *Single-user, multiprocess systems:* As the name indicates, these operating systems allow a single user to use the computer system, but the user can run multiple processes simultaneously. These operating systems are also used on PCs. Examples of such operating systems are OS/2 and Windows NT Workstation.
- *Multiuser, multiprocess systems:* These operating systems allow multiple users to use the computer system simultaneously, and every user can run multiple processes at the same time. These operating systems are commonly used on computers that support multiple users in organizations such as universities and large businesses. Examples of such operating systems are LINUX, UNIX, and Windows NT Server.

Multiuser, multiprocess systems are used to increase **resource utilization** in the computer system by multiplexing (time sharing) expensive resources such as the CPU. This capability leads to increased system **throughput** (the number of processes finished in unit time). Resource utilization increases because, in a system with several processes, when one process is performing input or output (e.g., reading input from the keyboard, capturing a mouse click, or writing to file on the hard disk), the CPU can be moved from that process to another process—running both processes at the same time. The mechanism of assigning the CPU to another process when the current process is performing I/O is known as **multiprogramming**. Multiprogramming is the key to all contemporary multiuser, multiprocess operating systems. In a single-process system, when the process using the CPU performs I/O, the CPU sits idle because there is no other process that can use the CPU at the same time.

Operating systems that allow users to interact with their executing programs are known as **interactive operating systems**, and the ones that do not are called **batch operating systems**. Batch systems are useful when programs are run without the need for human intervention, such as systems that run payroll programs. The VMS operating system has both interactive and batch interfaces. Almost all well-known contemporary operating systems (LINUX, UNIX, DOS, Windows, etc.) are interactive. LINUX and UNIX also allow programs to be executed in batch mode, with programs running in the background (see Chapter 13 for details of background process execution in LINUX). The multiuser, multiprocess, and interactive operating systems are known as **time-sharing systems**. In time-sharing systems, the CPU is switched from one process to another in quick succession. This method of operation allows all the processes in the system to make progress, giving each user the impression of sole use of the system. Examples of time-sharing operating systems are LINUX, UNIX, and Windows NT Server.

## 1.6 THE LINUX FAMILY

In October 1991, Linus Torvalds, a 21-year-old student at the University of Helsinki, Finland, posted the following message on the comp.os.minix newsgroup.

> I'm doing a (free) operating system (just a hobby, won't be big and professional like GNU) for 386(486) AT clones.

Torvalds's "hobby" eventually became what is known as the LINUX operating system. Although LINUX, a UNIX look-alike, is less than 10 years old, it has revolutionized the PC and Internet world. Millions of computer users around the world use LINUX on their home PCs and office workstations. Initially designed and written for PCs based on Intel CPUs, LINUX now runs on a wide range of platforms, including Alpha, Amiga, Atari, Macintosh, and Sun SPARC.

A few years ago the name LINUX referred to a single operating system, but it is now used to refer to a family of operating systems that are offshoots of the original. They provide different user interfaces and application suites. Some of the members of this family are Caldera, Corel, Debian, Mandrake, Red Hat, Slackware, and SuSE. You can download most of these brands of LINUX free of charge from various Internet sites, or buy them from your local computer store for under $30. In Chapter 2, we give a brief history of the development of the LINUX system.

## SUMMARY

An operating system is software that runs on the hardware of a computer system to manage the system's hardware and software resources. It also gives the user of the computer system a simple, virtual machine that is easy to interact with. The basic services provided by an operating system offer efficient and secure program execution. These services include allowing program execution, I/O operations, communication between processes, error detection and reporting, and file manipulation.

Operating systems are categorized by number of users that can use a system at the same time and the number of processes that can execute on a system simultaneously: single-user single-process, single-user multiprocess, and multiuser multiprocess operating systems. Furthermore, operating systems that allow users to interact with their executing programs (processes) are known as interactive systems, and those that do not are called batch systems. Multiuser, multiprocess, interactive systems are known as time-sharing systems, of which LINUX is a prime example. The purpose of multiuser, multiprocess systems is to increase the utilization of system resources by switching them among concurrently executing processes. This capability leads to higher system throughput, or the number of processes finishing in unit time.

In order to use a computer system, the user issues commands to the operating system. If an operating system accepts commands via the keyboard, it has a character user interface (CUI). If an operating system allows users to issue commands via a point-and-click device such as a mouse, it has a graphical user interface (GUI). Although LINUX comes with a CUI as its basic interface, it can run software based on the X Window System (Project Athena, MIT) that provides a GUI. Most LINUX systems now have both interfaces.

All commercial versions of the LINUX system come bundled with a GUI. A character user interface is used to run LINUX commands and the GUI is used for most of the Internet and program development tools.

## PROBLEMS

1. What is an operating system?
2. What are the three types of operating systems? How do they differ from each other?
3. What is a time-sharing system? Be precise.
4. What are the main services provided by a typical contemporary operating system? What is the basic purpose of these services?

5. List one advantage and one disadvantage each for the commandline interface and the graphical user interface.
6. What is the difference between the commandline and graphical user interfaces? What are the most popular graphical user interfaces for LINUX systems?
7. What comprises the application programmer's interface (API) and application user's interface (AUI)?
8. Name five popular members of the LINUX family. What is the name of your LINUX system?
9. Name six computer platforms on which LINUX can run. What platform does your LINUX run on?

CHAPTER

# 2

# LINUX History

**OBJECTIVES**

- To describe the background that enabled the development of LINUX
- To give details of the development of LINUX by Linus Torvalds
- To give an up-to-date synopsis of the major distributions
- To give a brief history of the LINUX kernel
- To forecast major new directions in operating system development
- To list current Web resources

## 2.1 INTRODUCTION

The Internet is an electronic medium that we are just beginning to understand in terms of how it affects our way of learning and thinking about the world. By this we mean the Internet of information sharing, not the Internet of commercial enterprises. LINUX is a child of the Internet. How can you effectively learn about all aspects of LINUX history? Go to your favorite search engine, type "LINUX history" in the search field, and click on "Go". We provide some general and specific online references to LINUX informational sites in Table 2.1. For example, if you are interested in learning about attempts to standardize LINUX distributions, consult reference 7 in Table 2.1. To read up-to-date articles on every aspect of LINUX, consult reference 2 in Table 2.1.

## 2.2 OPEN SOURCE BACKGROUND

LINUX developed in a manner very similar to the development of UNIX, but with a much more accelerated rate of growth due to the pervasive influences of the Internet. The historical development of LINUX can be traced to a single man, Linus Torvalds. To gain an appreciation of why and how this development took place, we must understand the technical and cultural influences on Torvalds by the open source philosophy of program development. See references 8 and 10 in Table 2.1 for a thorough treatment of the economic, philosophic, and technical issues surrounding open source programming.

As aptly put by a devoted open source programmer, Eric S. Raymond, in *The Cathedral and the Bazaar*, "LINUX is subversive." The development of source code for a major software system by a collectivized process, driven by a nonsecretive sharing of resources is a reaction in large part to the individualized, secretive development of non–open source programming, and an attempt (quite successful in the case of LINUX) to overcome the shortcomings of that process. Whether this was a cultural or an economic reaction, or both, can hardly be determined here. Paraphrasing what has been stated in our previous work, UNIX itself was an academic reaction to proprietary operating systems.

Raymond used the term *cathedral* to describe the secretive, individualized building of a complex structure of code in a large software system. His *bazaar* represents the environment of shared resources. As so aptly put by Raymond (see reference source 9 in Table 2.1),

> The history of UNIX should have prepared us for what we're learning from LINUX (and what I've verified experimentally on a smaller scale by deliberately copying Linus's methods). That is, that while coding remains an essentially solitary activity, the really great hacks come from harnessing the attention and brainpower of entire communities. The developer who uses only his or her own brain in a closed project is going to fall behind the de-

**Table 2.1** Web Resources

| Reference | URL | Description |
|---|---|---|
| 1 | www.ibiblio.org/mdw/index.html | LINUX Documentation Project |
| 2 | www2.LINUXjournal.com | LINUXjournal |
| 3 | www.LINUXhq.com | LINUX HeadQuarters |
| 4 | www.fokus.gmd.de/LINUX/LINUX-distrib.html | LINUX Distributions |
| 5 | www.kernal.org | LINUX Kernel Archives |
| 6 | www.slackware.com | Slackware LINUX Web site |
| 7 | www.LINUXbase.org | LINUX Standard Base |
| 8 | www.gnu.org | GNU/LINUX, an open software project |
| 9 | www.tuxedo.org/~esr/writings/cathedral-bazaar/ | The writings of Eric Raymond |
| 10 | www.opensource.org/history.html | History of the Open Source Initiative |
| 11 | www.memalpha.cx/Linux/Kernel/ | LINUX kernel version history |
| 12 | www.wired.com/wired/archive/5.08/linux.html | Article on Linus Torvalds and LINUX |
| 13 | www.bitkeeper.com/history/history.gif | Graph of the kernel releases |
| 14 | counter.li.org | Statistics and graphs on LINUX use growth rates worldwide |

veloper who knows how to create an open, evolutionary context in which feedback exploring the design space, code contributions, bug-spotting, and other improvements come back from hundreds (perhaps thousands) of people.

Three factors make the bazaar possible. First, there must be a medium that allows source code sharing; for LINUX this is the Internet. Second, there must be a way of organizing the components of the project; for LINUX this is the archive sites, or Internet sites that are repositories of kernel source code, utility source code, and documentation. For a contemporary example of a kernel archive site, see reference 5 in Table 2.1. Third, people must be motivated to participate in a project where there is no measurable reward other than the work itself. This was certainly true for LINUX early on in its development; see Section 2.3. But this factor becomes weakened when many commercially viable releases of the system compete in the same way that proprietary software does. (See Section 2.4.)

More online documentation on open source programming can be found at references 8 and 10 in Table 2.1. An online collection of Eric Raymond's writing can be found at reference 9 in Table 2.1.

## 2.3 LINUS TORVALDS

Linus Torvalds, the "inventor" of the LINUX operating system, is a computer scientist who based his work on a UNIX look-alike called minix. Minix was developed by Andrew S. Tanenbaum, an academic who wanted to teach his students about the internals of a real operating system. He designed minix to run on Intel 8086 microprocessors.

In the summer of 1991, while working on a degree in computer science, Linus Torvalds decided to write the code for his own operating system, which he dubbed LINUX, and posted some initial news about it via a minix newsgroup. His preliminary work implemented **bash** and **gcc**. But he soon solicited and received help from the wider Internet community of open-software supporters, who were waiting for just such an operating system to emerge, particularly some of the programmers participating in the GNU project and the Free Software Foundation efforts. Linus described his earliest efforts as a hobby. The following quote is taken from one of his Web posts of August 25, 1991.

> Hello everybody out there using minix—I'm doing a (free) operating system (just a hobby, won't be big and professional like GNU) for 386(486) AT clones. This has been brewing since April, and is starting to get ready. I'd like any feedback on things people like/dislike in minix, as my OS resembles it somewhat (same physical layout of the file-system (due to practical reasons) among other things). I've currently ported bash(1.08) and gcc(1.40), and things seem to work. This implies that I'll get something practical within a few months, and I'd like to know what features most people would want. Any suggestions are welcome, but I won't promise I'll implement them :-)

Why was he so successful, and why did this system proliferate and flourish? As stated by Eric Raymond

> Linus's innovation wasn't so much in doing quick-turnaround releases incorporating lots of user feedback (something like this had been UNIX-world tradition for a long time), but in scaling it up to a level of intensity that matched the complexity of what he was developing. In those early times (around 1991) it wasn't unknown for him to release a new kernel more than once a *day!* Because he cultivated his base of co-developers and leveraged the Internet for collaboration harder than anyone else, this worked.

Contrast this with the release history of most commercial software, developed in a cathedral environment. LINUX releases came fast and furious between 1991 and 1994, and debugging those releases and adding to the systems functionality became a masterful job of software engineering.

More online documentation about Linus Torvalds can be found at reference 12 in Table 2.1.

## 2.4 LINUX DISTRIBUTIONS

As of this writing, there are over 250 varieties of LINUX, used on a very wide spectrum of hardware platforms, from large 64-bit processor architectures and Internet servers to tiny embedded processors, and even in wristwatches. Table 2.2 lists the major LINUX distributions, along with some of the important minimum features of each.

More online documentation for LINUX distributions can be found at references 4 and 7 in Table 2.1.

## 2.5 KERNEL HISTORY

The first of the LINUX kernels, V0.01, was released to the public in September 1991. The size of the tar.gz-archive for this kernel was 71KB. This version of the kernel only ran on Intel 80386 processors on a PC architecture. It contained rudiments of a virtual memory subsystem and very few device drivers. The file system was the same one used with the minix OS. There was no networking capability.

The first stable release V1.0 of the kernel was in March 1994. The latest (stable) release, V2.4.2, was made available in Febuary 2001. The size of the tar.gz-archive for the latest stable version of the kernel was 24.1MB. This latest version runs on many diverse architectures, including Intel x86, SPARC, Alpha, Ultra, M68k, and Power PC. There are hundreds of drivers and many supported file systems. The network support in this kernel is a model of what network support should be.

More online documentation for LINUX kernel history can be found at references 5, 11, and 13 in Table 2.1.

**Table 2.2** Major LINUX Distributions

| Feature | Caldera | Corel | Debian | Mandrake | Red Hat | Slackware | SuSE |
|---|---|---|---|---|---|---|---|
| KDE | Yes | Yes | Yes | Yes | Yes | Yes | Yes |
| GNOME | Yes | Yes | Yes | Yes | Yes | Yes | Yes |
| Disk[1] [3] | 300 | 800 | 64 | 400 | 500 | 50 | 140 |
| RAM | 32 | 24 | 12 | 24 | 32 | 16 | 16 |
| Install[2] [3] | C, net, H | C, net, H | C, net, H | C, net, H | C, net, H | C, net, H | C, net, H |

[1] Disk in MB without GUI.
[2] C = CD installation, net = network installation, H = hard disk installation.
[3] Minimum requirements for these systems as of this writing.

## 2.6 POPULARITY OF LINUX

It is estimated that 20 million people around the world use LINUX. This user community is growing rapidly and is presently spread over 200 countries, from Greenland to Antarctica and Mauritania to Russia. Browse the counter.li.org Web site for more information on the worldwide use of LINUX.

## 2.7 FUTURE DEVELOPMENTS

As of this writing, several distributions of LINUX are implemented on the newest class of 64-bit architecture processors, the Intel Itanium and AMD Sledgehammer. We expect this trend to continue. More importantly, the offering of LINUX as the standard preinstalled operating system on new computers, whatever their hardware configuration, which is just now beginning, will no doubt accelerate in the future as consumers realize the advantages of LINUX's stability and highly customizable environment.

GUI window management systems, such as GNOME and KDE, will mature to the point where they offer more graphical functionality than competing operating systems. For example, desktop management will become more sophisticated and functional, with data sharing possible between applications in a manner similar to what is currently available in competing operating systems.

The biggest area of future development for LINUX is in applications. For example, Sun's StarOffice suite of personal productivity software rivals and even surpasses the capabilities of similar products found on competing operating systems. It is obvious that the open source approach will engender growth in the development of applications for LINUX in the future.

## 2.8 WEB RESOURCES

Table 2.1 lists Web sites that can provide further general and specific information on the topics presented in this chapter. These Web resources are current as of this writing and an up-to-date listing may be found on the Web page for this textbook.

## SUMMARY

The history of LINUX is grounded in a specific model of program development, the open source model. LINUX was developed by Linus Torvalds in 1991. We have provided an up-to-date synopsis of the major distributions of LINUX now available from various sources. We have given a brief history of the LINUX kernel and shown how it grew to its current state. We have also attempted to forecast major new directions in operating system development And finally, we have provided a list of current Web resources that the reader should consult to gain further insight into the topics and issues discussed in this chapter.

## PROBLEMS

1. What are the current stable release designation and latest release designation of the LINUX kernel? (*Hint:* See online reference source 5 in Table 2.1.)
2. Browse some of the major computer manufacturers' online product offerings, and list the companies and their models that offer LINUX as the preinstalled operating system. Do not include specialty Web server machines.
3. Read Eric Raymond's *The Cathedral and the Bazaar* (listed as reference 9 in Table 2.1), and summarize the difference between development environments for software.
4. Go to the LINUX Documentation Project Web site, as listed in reference 1 in Table 2.1, and read their "Manifesto." Describe the purpose of the project in your own words. Print out the FAQs, HOWTOs, and man page documents for later reference.
5. Go to the LINUXjournal Web site (see reference 2 in Table 2.1), and click on the search button at the top of the page. You can enter any search criteria subject you want pertaining to LINUX, and you will get a listing of articles that are pertinent to this subject. Search for articles on Linus Torvalds. How many are there?
6. Go to the Web site listed as reference 4 in Table 2.1. What is the name of the French distribution of Slackware LINUX?
7. Write a brief summary of the history of the minix operating system, with references to as many online documents as you can find.
8. Browse the counter.li.org Web site and write down how many people around the world are using LINUX. How many countries is the LINUX community spread over? Write down the names of the three countries that have the most number of LINUX users.

CHAPTER

# 3

# Getting Started

## OBJECTIVES

- To give an overview of the structure of a contemporary system hardware
- To describe briefly the structure of the LINUX operating system
- To explain the logon and logoff procedures
- To detail some important system setups
- To list some useful commands for the beginner
- To cover the commands and operators `cp`, `echo`, `exit`, `hostname`, `ls`, `man`, `mv`, `read`, `passwd`, `set`, `setenv`, `telnet`, `uname`, `whatis`, `whereis`, `who`, and `whoami`

## 3.1 INTRODUCTION

As we mentioned previously, a computer system consists of several hardware and software components (also called resources). In this chapter we describe the structure of a contemporary computer system and its most important and visible components. We also describe briefly the structure of the LINUX operating system, including the purpose of each component and the operations performed by the main part of the LINUX operating system, called the LINUX *kernel*. We then explain the login and logout procedures and introduce some simple but important LINUX commands. One useful feature of the LINUX operating system is its online manual, which you can search to view the description of any command, utility, tool, or application. One of the commands described in this chapter allows you to browse the online LINUX manual.

## 3.2 COMPUTER SYSTEM HARDWARE

The hardware of a contemporary computer system consists of several subsystems, including main/primary memory, one or more CPUs, secondary storage devices (floppy and hard disk drives), and input/output (I/O) devices (CD-ROM drive, keyboard, scanner, printer, and mouse). Figure 3.1 shows schematically how these subsystems are connected. A brief description of each subsystem follows.

### 3.2.1 MAIN/PRIMARY STORAGE

The main memory is a storage place that comprises a number of storage locations, with each location having an address. The size of a location is typically 1 byte. A **byte** (abbreviated B) is made up of 8 bits, and a **bit** is the smallest unit of storage that can store a 1 or a 0. The address of a location is a positive integer, with the

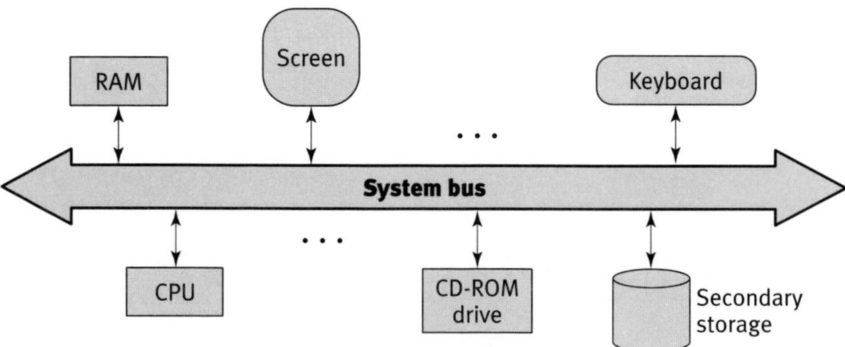


**Figure 3.1** Diagram of a typical computer system

first location having an address 0. Each location can be randomly accessed by specifying its address. Figure 3.2 shows the logical view of a RAM with $2^N$ locations. If $N$ is 10, the RAM size is $2^{10}$ = 1024, also known as 1K (K for kilo) locations. If $N$ is 20, the RAM size is $2^{20}$ = 1024*1024, also known as 1M (M for mega) locations. If $N$ is 30, the RAM size is $2^{30}$ = 1024*1024*1024, also known as 1G (G for giga, or billion) locations. (Note use of the asterisk for the multiplication symbol.)

The purpose of main storage is to store executing programs, or processes. This storage place is also called the *volatile* storage place because, when the power to the computer system is turned off, it loses whatever is stored in it. Typical personal computer systems today contain 128MB of RAM, and typical multiuser time-sharing systems contain about 512MB to 1GB of RAM. The speed at which a memory location can be accessed is known as the RAM **access time**. Today, typical RAMs have access times of 10 to 60 nanoseconds. A **nanosecond** is $10^{-9}$ seconds.

### 3.2.2 Central Processing Unit (CPU)

The CPU is the brain of a computer system. This subsystem executes your programs by fetching them from the RAM, one instruction at a time. Most of the CPUs in today's computers can execute only one program at a time. The speed at which a CPU can execute instructions is dictated by its clock speed. Today's CPUs typically operate at 800M or more cycles per second. By the time this textbook is available, CPUs with clock speeds of 1.5G– 2G cycles per second will be available. One cycle per second is also known as 1 Hertz (Hz).

Every CPU has its own language, called its **instruction set**. A CPU can understand instructions only in its own instruction set, which is usually a superset of its predecessors made by the same company. Thus most CPUs made by the same company can also execute programs written for their predecessors.

A CPU is functionally divided into two parts: a **control unit** and an **execution unit** (also called the *arithmetic and logic unit*, or *ALU*). The purpose of the

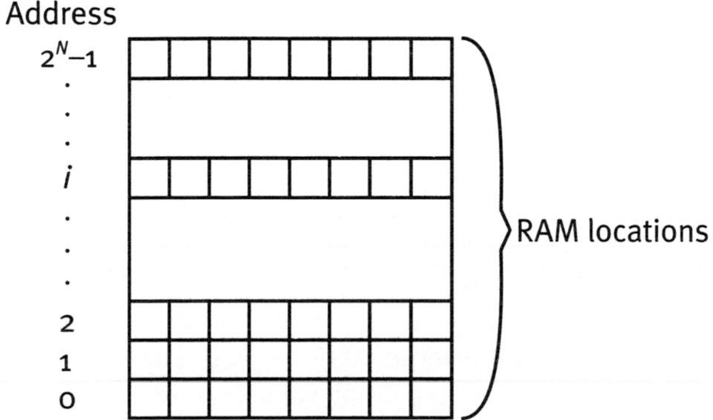


**Figure 3.2** Logical structure of RAM with $2^N$ locations

control unit is to interact with the devices in the computer system (memory, keyboard, disk, display monitor, etc.) via the **controllers** (electronic circuitry) in these devices. The control unit also fetches a program instruction from the main memory and decodes it to determine whether the instruction is valid. If the instruction is valid, the control unit orchestrates execution of the instruction by the execution unit, by delivering the appropriate sequence of control signals. Thus the purpose of the CPU is to fetch, decode, and execute program instructions. A CPU contains a number of storage locations that it uses as scratch pads. These storage locations are called the CPU **registers**. The number of registers in a CPU varies from a few to a few hundred. Each register has the same size—typically *32 or 64 bits* for contemporary CPUs.

### 3.2.3 Disk

A disk is a storage place that contains all the computer system's programs and applications. It is a nonvolatile storage place that retains its contents even if the power to the computer is turned off. Disks are read and written in terms of **sectors**. Typical disks have a sector size of 512B. Most hard disks allow read and write operations in multiple sectors, known as a **cluster**. Cluster size is typically 1, 2, 4, or 8 sectors. Today's PCs use disk drives with storage capacities of 10–40GB. Typical multiuser network-based systems use 512GB hard disk storage space. The speed of a disk drive is dictated by its latency and seek times. The **latency time** for a disk is dictated by the speed at which the drive can spin (the unit used is rotations per minute, or rpm), and the **seek time** is governed by the speed at which the head can move (laterally). A typical disk drive has a latency time of a few milliseconds and a seek time of 8 milliseconds. A **millisecond** is $10^{-3}$ second.

### 3.2.4 Bus

A *bus* is a set of parallel wires used to carry information in the form of bits from one subsystem in a computer to another. Each wire carries a single bit. The bus size therefore is measured in bits. A **system bus** consists of three types of buses: data bus, address bus, and control bus. The **data bus** is used to carry data from one subsystem to another. For example, it carries instructions for an executing program from the main memory to the CPU and the results of some computation from the CPU to the main memory. The **address bus** carries the address of a main memory location that has to be written to or read from. The **control bus** carries the control information, such as read or write instruction from the CPU to the main memory. The sizes of these buses in a computer system are dictated by the type of CPU. Typical data and address bus sizes today are 32 to 64 bits.

Before a command (application/program/tool/utility) starts execution, it resides on disk in the form of an executable program (a *binary* program or a *shell script*). When the user types a command line and hits the <Enter> (or <Return>) key (or points and clicks the application icon in a graphical user interface) to run the application, the **loader program** reads the application from the disk and loads it into the main memory. It then sets the internal state of the CPU so that it knows the location of the program's first instruction. The control unit of the CPU then

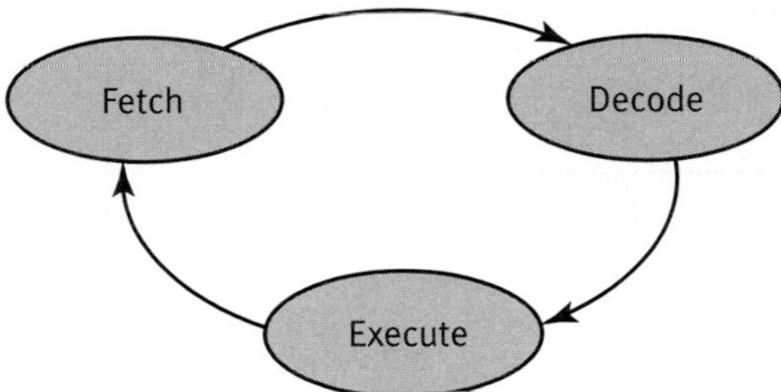


**Figure 3.3** The machine cycle

fetches the first program instruction and decodes it to determine whether the instruction is a valid instruction for the CPU. If the control unit finds that the instruction is valid, it gives it to the execution unit, which executes the instruction. The fetch, decode, and execute operations form a **machine cycle**, as shown in Figure 3.3. The CPU remains in this cycle until either the program finishes and terminates gracefully or produces an error (exception) and terminates abnormally. The CPU then becomes idle and stays in this state until it starts execution of another user or system program or an I/O device needs the CPU's service.

### 3.2.5 I/O Devices

A contemporary computer system also has several input and output devices that allow the user to run commands and applications, supply inputs, and capture outputs. Commonly used I/O devices are the keyboard, mouse, display monitor, printer, plotter, scanner, tape drive, CD-ROM drive and DVD drive.

## 3.3 LINUX SOFTWARE ARCHITECTURE

Figure 3.4 shows a layered diagram for a LINUX-based computer system, identifying the system's software components and their logical proximity to the user and hardware. We briefly describe each software layer from the bottom up.

### 3.3.1 Device Driver Layer

The purpose of the device driver layer is to interact with various hardware devices. It contains a separate program for interacting with each device, such as the hard disk driver, floppy disk driver, CD-ROM driver, keyboard driver, mouse driver, DVD driver, and display driver. These programs execute on behalf of the LINUX kernel when a user command or application needs to perform a hardware-related operation such as a file read (which translates to one or more disk reads). The user doesn't have direct access to these programs and therefore can't execute them as commands.

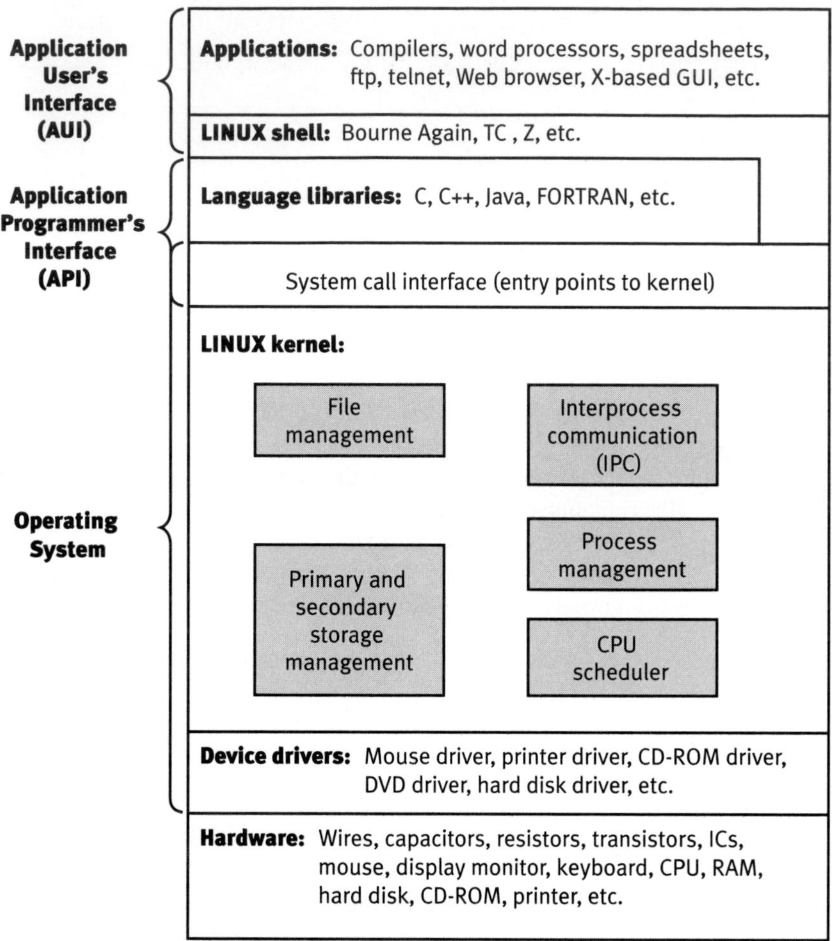


**Figure 3.4** The software architecture of the LINUX operating system

## 3.3.2 The LINUX Kernel

The LINUX kernel layer contains the actual operating system. Some of the main functions of the LINUX kernel are listed in Figure 3.4.

### Process Management

The kernel manages processes in terms of creating, suspending, and terminating them, and maintaining their states. It also provides various mechanisms for processes to communicate with each other and schedules the CPU to execute multiple processes simultaneously in a time-sharing system. Interprocess communication

(IPC) is the key to today's client–server-based software that is the foundation for Internet applications such as the Netscape Navigator. The LINUX system provides several IPC mechanisms/channels, but the following are most often used.

- *Pipe:* A pipe can be used as an IPC channel by two or more related processes running on the same computer. Typically, these processes have a parent–child or sibling relationship. A pipe is a temporary channel that resides in the main memory and is created by the kernel usually on behalf of the parent process.
- *Named pipe:* A named pipe (also known as *FIFO*) is a permanent communication channel that resides on the disk and can be used for IPC by two or more related or unrelated processes that are *running on the same computer*.
- *BSD socket:* A BSD socket is also a temporary channel that allows two or more processes in a network (or on the Internet) to communicate, although they can also be used by processes on the same computer. Sockets were originally a part of the BSD UNIX only, but they are now available on almost every UNIX and LINUX system. Internet software such as Web browsers, ftp, telnet, and electronic mailers are implemented by using sockets.

A detailed description of these mechanisms is beyond the scope of this textbook.

### File Management

The kernel also manages files and directories (also known as *folders*). It performs all file-related tasks, such as file creation and removal, directory creation and removal, and file and directory attribute maintenance. A file operation usually requires manipulation of a disk. In a multiuser system a user must never be allowed to manipulate a disk directly because it contains files belonging to other users and user access to a disk poses a security threat. Thus only the kernel may perform all file-related operations, such as file removal. Also, only the kernel may decide where and how much space to allocate to a file.

### Main Memory Management

Main Memory Management allocates and deallocates RAM in an orderly manner so that each process gets enough space to execute properly. It also ensures that part or all of the space allocated to a process does not belong to some other process. The space allocated to a process in the memory for its execution is known as its **process address space**. The kernel maintains areas in the main memory that are free to be used so that, when a program is to be loaded in the main memory, adequate space can be allocated. It also records where all the processes reside in the memory so that, when a process tries to access main memory space that does not belong to it, the kernel can terminate the process and give a meaningful message to the user. When a process terminates, the kernel deallocates the space allocated to the process and puts this space back in the free space pool so that it can be reused.

#### Disk Management

The kernel is also responsible for maintaining free and used disk space and for the orderly and fair allocation and deallocation of disk space. It decides where and how much space to allocate to a newly created file. Also, the kernel performs **disk scheduling**, deciding which request to serve next when multiple requests (for file read, write, etc.) arrive for the same disk.

In addition, the kernel performs several other tasks for fair, orderly, and safe use of the computer system. These tasks include managing the CPU, printers, and other I/O devices. The kernel ensures that no user process takes over the CPU forever, that multiple files are not printed on a printer simultaneously, and that a user cannot terminate another user's process.

### 3.3.3 The System Call Interface

The system call interface layer contains *entry points* into the kernel code. Because all system resources are managed by the kernel, any user or application request that involves access to any system resource must be handled by the kernel code. But user processes must not be given open access to the kernel code for security reasons. So that user processes can invoke (start) the execution of kernel code, LINUX provides several gates or function calls, known as *system calls*. Tens of system calls allow the user to manipulate processes, files, and other system resources. These calls are well tested and most of them have been used for several years, so their use poses much less of a security risk than if any user code were allowed to perform the task.

### 3.3.4 Language Libraries

A **library** is a set of prewritten and pretested functions available to programmers for use with the software that they develop. The availability and use of libraries saves time because programmers do not have to write these functions from scratch. This layer contains libraries for several languages, such as C, C++, Java, and FORTRAN. For the C language, for example, there are several libraries, including a string library (which contains functions for processing strings, such as a function for comparing two strings), and a math library (which contains functions for mathematical operations, such as a finding the cosine of an angle).

As we mentioned in Chapter 1, the libraries and system calls layers form what is commonly known as the application programmer's interface (API). In other words, programmers who write software in a language such as C can use library and system calls in their codes.

### 3.3.5 LINUX Shell

The LINUX shell is a program that starts running when you log on and interprets the commands that you enter. We discuss this topic in detail later in this chapter and in Chapters 4 and 13.

### 3.3.6 Applications

The applications layer contains all the applications (tools, commands, and utilities) that are available for your use. A typical LINUX system contains hundreds of applications; we discuss the most useful and commonly used applications throughout this textbook. When an application that you're using needs to manipulate a system resource (e.g., reading a file), it needs to invoke some kernel code that performs the task. An application can get the appropriate kernel code to execute in one of two ways: (1) by using a proper library function and (2) by using a system call. Library calls constitute a higher level interface to the kernel than system calls, which makes library calls a bit easier to use. However, all library calls eventually use system calls to start execution of appropriate kernel code. Therefore the use of library calls results in slightly slower execution. A detailed discussion of library and system calls is beyond the scope of this textbook, but we briefly describe a few library and system calls in later chapters.

The user can use any command or application that is available on the system. As we mentioned in Chapter 1, this layer is commonly known as the application user's interface (AUI).

## 3.4 LOGGING ON AND LOGGING OFF

The LINUX system is a multiprocess, multiuser, and interactive computing environment. *Multiprocess* means that a user can start and run several computational processes or programs at once. *Multiuser* means many users can be using the same system at the same time; this makes logon and logoff necessary, because each individual user must identify and differentiate him- or herself on the system when he or she enters via logon and leaves via logoff. One of the most important differences between LINUX and other operating systems is that LINUX was originally designed for a networking environment, where a single computer is connected to a larger computing environment composed of many computers, which adds to the complexity and mandatory nature of the logon and logoff procedure. In addition, LINUX can be run on a standalone computer, such as a PC, but identification of the individual user via logon is still mandatory, because of the access privileges the user is given at logon. For example, certain users need administrative privileges to maintain system integrity and performance, and other users just need to be able to run applications and store files on the standalone computer.

There are two approaches to logging on and logging off a LINUX system: a **text-based interface** or a **graphical user interface (GUI)**. In this section, we explain the methods of logging on and logging off using a text-based interface. Chapter 21 explains using a GUI and gaining access to the system via graphical logon, and exiting via graphical logoff.

A text-based interface logon uses three basic methods, or combinations of two or more of them. Variations are affected by the system setup of any single component. The basic methods are as follows.

1. **Local area network (LAN) connection**: Loosely stated, the LAN connection is a modern variation of the traditional terminals connected to a mainframe configuration, such as a VT-100 terminal connected to a Sun workstation using an RS-232 line. In any LAN system the terminal has little or no compute power—it acts as a dumb **graphical server**—and the computer (the component that does have compute power) can serve many such terminals. The terminal is connected via a high-speed communications link to a single computer or multiple computers that are all interconnected with a LAN, and the terminal is the user's interface to the operating system running on the single or multiple computers. This method could also be called intranet login. (See Chapter 21.) A variation of this method involves using a LINUX workstation with compute power to log in to a LINUX server.
2. **Internet connection**: The Internet method is similar to LAN login, except that the network is a federation of LANs and **wide area networks (WANs)**, usually the Internet. In its simplest form, a remote, standalone computer, via software such as Windows Telnet for the PC or NCSA Telnet for Macintosh, connects to a LINUX system over a high-speed telecommunications link. The telnet software then becomes the graphical server, allowing the user to log in and use a remote computer or system that is running LINUX. This method could also be called *Internet log-in*. A variation of this method involves using the LINUX `telnet` command to establish a connection between a LINUX machine acting as a telnet client and a LINUX machine acting as a telnet server. The LINUX `telnet` command is covered in Chapter 14. A variation on this method not covered in this textbook is the use of SLIP/PPP to dial in to a host computer over a telecommunications line.
3. **Standalone connection**: In the standalone method a computer that is not hooked up to a LAN, intranet, or the Internet is dedicated to a single user who logs on to use LINUX on that hardware platform only. In fact, the previous two methods, when used with a text-based interface, eventually look and feel exactly like an interaction with LINUX in this method.

A combination of the three methods could work as follows. The user sits at a standalone computer that is networked to other computers via a LAN, boots up, and sees the LINUX **login prompt**. The user logs in to this standalone machine, then enables the LAN connection on this standalone computer. The user then types in the LINUX `telnet` command to log in to a remote host on the intranet, which is also running LINUX, and works with the operating system there. Finally, the user "telnets" from the LAN to a remote site on the Internet and logs in to a computer in a remote location—perhaps even in another country—and works with LINUX on that computer. All of these computers are running LINUX.

If you use telnet to connect to a LINUX system and you are a beginner, it is a good idea to write down the exact steps involved in making the telnet connection. Be sure to note all details of the connection procedure, including any preference changes, as explicitly as possible. If you forget any of the steps, you can always refer to your written instructions to help you to make your telnet connection. This process may even preempt any printed login handouts your instructor has prepared for you, because you will write down the procedure in a subjective way that is meaningful to you, as long as it is correct and complete.

When using any of the three methods or a combination of them to connect to a LINUX system, identifying yourself to the system is your first task. Doing so involves typing in a valid **username**, or **login name**, consisting of a string of valid characters, associated with a **userid** given to you by your system administrator. For our purposes, we use the terms *username, login name*, and *userid* interchangeably. You then must type in a valid **password** for that username. See Section 3.7.1 for information about changing your password. Depending on how your system administrator has set up your particular installation, the login prompt may appear on the screen of the terminal or computer that you sit in front of, similar to Figure 3.5. Items enclosed in brackets [ ] in Figure 3.5 are system-dependent, and may or may not appear during your login procedure.

Note that in this chapter we use <Enter> or <↵> to indicate either the <Enter> or <Return> key. In the remainder of the book, when we ask you to type or use a command, we assume that you will press the <Enter> key because the shell does not start interpreting your command until you do so, but we will no longer show either <Enter> or <↵>.

At the `login:` prompt, you type in your username and press the <Enter> key. At the `password:` prompt you type in your assigned password, then press the <Enter> key. Depending on your system setup, you may be asked to type in both the kind of display that you are sitting in front of and the kind of terminal that you want to use during this session. Both may have defaults assigned, for which you can signify acceptance of by pressing the <Enter> key after the display and terminal prompts. An optional message may appear on your screen from the system administrator, announcing news or important information.

```
login: your username ↵

password: your password ↵

[display=default] ↵

[terminal=default] ↵

[message from the file /etc/motd]

$
```

**Figure 3.5** Text-based login screen on a typical LINUX computer

When you are starting out, you should write down your username and password, and save them in a secure place in case you forget them. *And don't lose that piece of paper!*

After you successfully log in to your LINUX computer, a **shell** prompt, such as the `$` (% for Tcsh) character, will appear on the screen, as in Figure 3.5. The shell prompt is simply a message from the computer system telling you that it is ready to accept typed input on the **command line** that directly follows the prompt.

The general syntax, or structure of a singe command as it is typed on the command line is as follows:

```
$ command [[-]option(s)] [option argument(s)] [command argument(s)]
```

where:

**$** is the shell prompt from the computer

anything enclosed in [ ] is not always needed

**command** is the name of the valid LINUX command for that shell in lowercase letters

**[-option(s)]** is one or more modifiers that change the behavior of command

**[option argument(s)]** is one or more modifiers that change the behavior of -option(s)

**[command argument(s)]** is one or more objects that are affected by command.

Note that a space separates the words *command, option, option argument,* and *command argument,* but no space is necessary between multiple options or multiple option arguments. Note also that the order of multiple options or option arguments is irrelevant. A space character is optional between the option and the option argument. *Always press the <Enter> key to submit the command to the shell for interpretation.*

Following are examples of the ways that a single command can be typed, along with options and arguments, on the command line.

```
$ ls
$ ls -la
$ ls -la m*
$ lpr -Pspr -n 3 proposal.ps
```

The first item contains only the command. The second contains the command `ls` and two options, `l` and `a`,which modify the behavior of the command. The third contains the command `ls`, two options, `l` and `a`, and a command argument, `m*`, which the command "works" on. The fourth contains the command `lpr`, two options, `P` and `n`, two option arguments, `spr` and `3`, which the options "work on", and a command argument, `proposal.ps`. These items are case sensitive. In the fourth item there is a space between one option and its argument, but no space between the other option and its argument.

You will be able to type commands on the command line displayed in the console window. LINUX systems use this text-based form of interaction between each user and the computer system, wherein each user can concurrently type commands using proper syntax. The operating system interprets the command line contents and takes actions based on the content of the command. We discuss the details of shells and how commands are interpreted in Chapters 4 and 13.

The procedure for logging off the computer, or leaving the system properly, is as important as the procedure for logging in. To log off, at the shell prompt, on a blank line press and hold down the <Ctrl> key while pressing the <D> key on the keyboard. You will then be logged off the system for the current session with the computer, and the login prompt shown in Figure 3.5 will reappear on the screen, allowing you to log on for another session. If you initiated your connection with the LINUX system via the **`telnet`** command, your telnet connection closes at this point. We refer to pressing and holding down the <Ctrl> key while pressing the <D> key as <Ctrl-D> or <^D> in this textbook. We use text type with brackets for the keyboard keys to indicate that you are to press (type) them, and we use boldface monospace type for commands and strings of characters that you are to type.

If you start a new shell during your session and do not exit that shell before logging off, LINUX will prompt `Not login shell`, and you will not be able to log off immediately. In this case, press <^D> and the new shell will terminate. If you start more than one shell and do not exit the shells before you log off, you will have to use the <^D> for each nonterminated shell before you can log off. On some systems, you must type **`exit`** on the command line to terminate a shell process. In either case, you will then be able to use the logoff procedure to leave the system properly. To practice logging on and logging off, do Problem 9 at the end of this chapter.

## 3.5 CORRECTING COMMAND LINE TYPING MISTAKES

When you are typing commands on the command line in a LINUX system, you may need to correct typing mistakes before you press <Enter>. Table 3.1 lists some

**Table 3.1** Important Control Key Combinations

| Key Combination | Purpose |
|---|---|
| <Backspace> or <Ctrl-H (^H)> | Erases the previous character and moves the cursor to the previous character position. |
| <Ctrl-U (^U)> | Erases the entire current line and moves the cursor to the beginning of the current line. |
| <Ctrl-C (^C)> | Terminates the current command and moves the cursor to the beginning of the next line. |

important keys or key combinations that can be used to correct mistakes. For each key combination, as is the case with <^D>, press and hold down the <CTRL> key while pressing the second key. The table assumes you are running the default Bash shell. A more complete description of command line editing can be found in Chapter 5, Section 5.6.

## 3.6 SOME IMPORTANT SYSTEM SETUPS

The properties and appearance of the console window and the environment within which the commands are interpreted are established by the system administrator for a typical computer user. The environmental settings are controlled by **environment variables**, which obtain or are set to their default when you log on. The environment controls which shell, or command line interpreter, you use when you type in commands or execute other important operations. In this textbook, we assume you are running one of the popular shells, either the Bourne Again shell (abbreviated Bash), the Z shell (abbreviated Zsh), or the TC shell (abbreviated Tcsh).

To find the default setting of an individual environment variable (e.g., the environment variable that controls the shell that you are running), type **`echo $SHELL`** and press <Enter>. The system replies by showing on the screen the path to the shell that you are running by default. To view a list of the default environment variable settings in Bash, type **`set`** and press <Enter>. The settings of the Bash environment variables will appear on screen. To see a list of the environment variable default settings in Zsh, or Tcsh, type **`setenv`** at the shell prompt and press <Enter> on the keyboard. You will see a screen display showing the settings of the Zsh or Tcsh environment variables.

You can easily change these environment variable settings for the duration of one login session or for every subsequent session. You should not change several of the environment variables, particularly if you are a beginner with LINUX. For a list of environment variables that you can safely change, see Table 4.3.

To set an environment variable for the current session in Bash, type **`Variable=Setting`** and press <Enter>. *Variable* is a valid environment variable, and *Setting* is a valid setting for that environment variable.

To set an environment variable for the current session in Zsh or Tcsh, type **`setenv Variable Setting`** and press <Enter>. *Variable* is a valid environment variable, and *Setting* is a valid setting for that environment variable.

To set an environment variable for all subsequent sessions, you must edit the **configuration file** for the shell that you are running by using a text editor, change the environment variable setting of interest, and save the changes you make in that configuration file in the editor. Table 3.2 lists various LINUX shells and the names of the primary and/or secondary configuration files for those shells in your home directory; the tilde (~) represents your home directory on LINUX systems.

Always make copies of your default configuration files with the **`cp`** command before attempting to edit them to change environment variables. For example, to

**Table 3.2** Shell Configuration Files

| LINUX Shell | Name of the Configuration File(s) |
|---|---|
| Bash (Bash) | ~/.bashrc, ~/.bash_profile, /etc/profile* |
| TC (Tcsh) | ~/.cshrc, ~/.login |
| Z (Zsh) | ~/.zshrc |

**Note:* Do not attempt to edit this file!

make a backup copy of your .cshrc file, type **`cp .cshrc .cshrc_bak`**, then press <Enter>. After this command executes, you will have two identical files, one named .cshrc and another named .cshrc_bak. That way, if you make a mistake while editing .cshrc, you can revert to the .bak version of the file, using the **`mv`** command, as follows. After you have left the text editor, type **`rm .cshrc`** then press <Enter>. Next type **`mv .cshrc_bak .cshrc`** and press <Enter>. Your old .cshrc file is now reinstalled; mv has renamed it from .cshrc_bak to .cshrc. If you mess up both the original and the backup, you will have to get a new .cshrc file from the system administrator!

These changes in your environment variables will take effect after you next log on and will remain in effect for every subsequent session. See Chapter 4 for instructions on how to change your environment variables in the appropriate configuration file for a shell.

The following In-Chapter Exercises ask you to change one of your environmental variables so you can see the effects of the change. The exercises assume you are running Bash; if you are running another shell, substitute the syntax for that shell for the syntax shown. For further practice in setting environment variables, see Problem 10 at the end of this chapter.

## IN-CHAPTER EXERCISES

**3.1.** At the shell prompt, type **`echo $LINES`** and press <Enter>. The system gives you a message that shows the number of lines visible in the console window. How many are visible in your console window?

**3.2.** At the shell prompt, type **`set`** and press <Enter>. The system displays a list of environment variables and their current settings. What are the settings for each of the variables shown?

**3.3.** At the shell prompt, type **`echo $PS1`** and press <Enter>. How does the system respond?

**3.4.** At the shell prompt, type **`PS1=%`** and press <Enter>. How does your screen display differ ?

## 3.7 SOME USEFUL COMMANDS FOR THE BEGINNER

For the beginner, several indispensable commands, including those described in the preceding sections, make using the LINUX system easy and productive. Some of these commands allow you to control the behavior of the system by changing your working environment, as shown in Section 3.6. Other commands display important systemwide information for you.

### 3.7.1 CHANGING YOUR PASSWORD

To maintain the general security of your system and, in particular, to keep your files secure on the system, you should change your initial password. Then perform a password change regularly to ensure that no unauthorized person can gain access to your system. Limit your password by making it easy to remember, not a word in any dictionary in any language, at least six characters long, and a mix of uppercase and lowercase letters, numbers, and punctuation marks.

To change your password, use the **passwd** command, as shown, where **your_username** is your login name. Recall that the ↵ symbol means you should press the <Enter> key on the keyboard.

```
$ passwd ↵
Changing password for your_username
old password: Your current password ↵
new password: Your new password ↵
retype new password: Your new password ↵
Changing password for your_username.
$
```

You now have a new password. If you are running LINUX over a network, you may have to use the `yppasswd` or `nispasswd` command instead of the `passwd` command to change your password on all the computers to which you have access on the network.

### 3.7.2 GETTING HELP

To get help in using all the LINUX commands and their options, go to the *LINUX Reference Manual Pages*. The pages themselves are organized into eight sections, according to the topic described and the topics that are applicable to the particular system. Table 3.3 lists the sections of the manual and what they contain. Most users find the pages they need in Section 1. Software developers mostly use library and system calls and thus find the pages they need in Sections 2 and 3. Users who work on document preparation get the most help from Section 7. Administrators mostly need to refer to pages in Sections 1, 4, 5, and 8.

The manual pages comprise multipage, specially formatted, descriptive documentation for every command, system call, and library call in LINUX. This format

**Table 3.3** Sections of the LINUX Manual

| Section | Describes |
|---|---|
| 1 | User commands |
| 2 | System calls |
| 3 | Language library calls (C, FORTRAN, etc.) |
| 4 | Devices and network interfaces |
| 5 | File formats |
| 6 | Games and demonstrations |
| 7 | Environments, tables, and macros for `troff` |
| 8 | System maintenance–related commands |

consists of seven general parts: name, synopsis, description, list of files, related information, errors/warnings, and known bugs. You can use the **man** command to view the manual page for a command. Because of the name of this command, the manual pages are normally referred to as LINUX *man pages*. When you display a manual page on the screen, the top-left corner of the page has the command name with the section it belongs to in parentheses, as in `ls (1)`. The following is a brief description of the **man** command.

Syntax:

**man [options] [-s section] command-list**
**man -k keyword-list**

**Purpose:** First Syntax: Display *LINUX Reference Manual Pages* for commands in "command-list," one screenful at a time

Second Syntax: Display summaries of commands related to keywords in "keyword-list"

**Output:** Manual pages one screen at a time

**Commonly used options/features:**

| | |
|---|---|
| `-k` keyword-list | Search all man pages for summaries of keywords in keyword-list and display them; can be very slow—specify a section to narrow down the search area |
| `-S` sec_num | Search section number "sec_num" for manual pages and display them |

The command used to display the manual page for the **passwd** command is

```
$ man passwd ↵
```

The manual page for the **passwd** command now appears on the screen, as shown in Figure 3.6. Because they are multipage text documents, the manual pages for each topic take more than one screenful of text to display their entire contents. To see one screenful of the manual page at a time, press the space bar on the keyboard. To quit viewing the manual page, press the <Q> key.

What do you see onscreen when you run the **passwd** command on your system? Pressing the <Q> key returns you to the shell prompt.

Now type the command

```
$ man pwd ↵
```

If more than one section of the man pages has information on the same word and you are interested in the man page for a particular section, you can use the **-S** option. The following command line therefore displays the man page for the read system call and not the man page for the shell command **read**.

```
$ man -S2 read ↵
```

You can specify the section number without the **-S** option. On such systems, `man 2 read` displays the manual page for the read system call. The command `man -S3 fopen fread strcmp` displays man pages for three C library calls: fopen, fread, and strcmp.

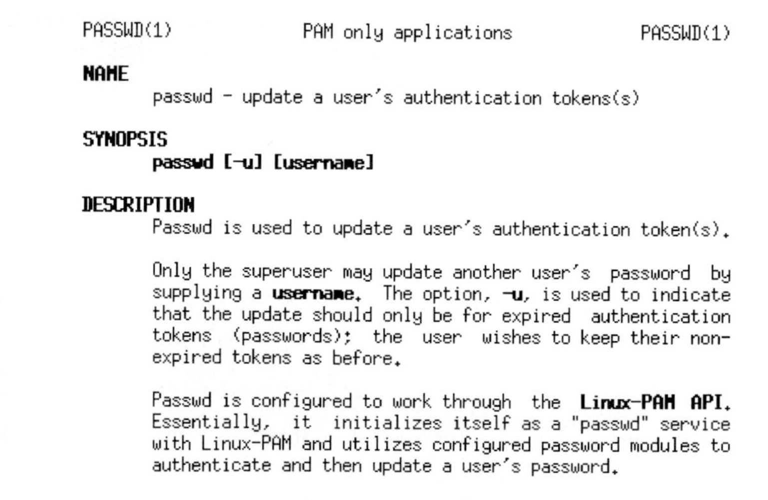

```
PASSWD(1)              PAM only applications              PASSWD(1)

NAME
       passwd - update a user's authentication tokens(s)

SYNOPSIS
       passwd [-u] [username]

DESCRIPTION
       Passwd is used to update a user's authentication token(s).

       Only the superuser may update another user's  password  by
       supplying a username.  The option, -u, is used to indicate
       that the update should only be for expired  authentication
       tokens  (passwords);  the  user  wishes to keep their non-
       expired tokens as before.

       Passwd is configured to work through  the  Linux-PAM API.
       Essentially,  it  initializes itself as a "passwd" service
       with Linux-PAM and utilizes configured password modules to
       authenticate and then update a user's password.
```

**Figure 3.6** *Manual Pages* first screen display for the passwd command

Another example of using the **man** command includes typing the command with the **-k** option, thereby specifying a keyword that limits the search. The search then yields man page headers from all the man pages that contain just the keyword reference. This option is very useful when you don't remember the name of the command you need information about but know the topic that the command deals with. For example, typing **man -k passwd** may yield the following on-screen output on our system. (Output on your system may be a bit different.)

```
$ man -k passwd
chpasswd(8)   -     update password file in batch
gpasswd(1)    -     administrate the /etc/group file
mkpasswd(8)   -     update passwd and group database files
nwpasswd(8)   -     change password for a Netware user
passwd(5)     -     password file
yppasswd(1)   -     NIS password update clients
$
```

To get a short description of what any particular LINUX command does, you can use the whatis command. Following is an illustration of how to use whatis.

```
$ whatis man ↵
man(1)         -format and display the online manual pages
man(7)         -macro to format man pages
man.config(5) -configuration data for man
$
```

You can also obtain short descriptions of more than one command by entering multiple arguments to the **whatis** command on the same command line, with spaces between each argument. Following is an illustration of this method.

```
$ whatis login set setenv ↵
login(1)     -sign on
set(1)       -set runtime parameters for session
set(n)       -read and write variables
setenv(1)    -change or add an environment variable
$
```

The following In-Chapter Exercises ask you to use the **man** command and the **whatis** command and to note their characteristics.

**IN-CHAPTER EXERCISES**

**3.5.** Use the **man** command with the **-k** option to display abbreviated help on the **man** command. Doing so will give you a screen display similar to that obtained with the **whatis** command, but it will show all apropos command names that contain the string man. Note the list of commands, their names, and their brief descriptions. Also use the **man -k** command to display information about commands that deal with sorting.

**3.6.** Use the **whatis** command to find brief descriptions of the commands shown in Exercise 3.5 and note the differences. Then use the **man** command with no options to view the manual pages for the same commands and again note the essential differences in them.

The **whereis** command allows you to search along certain prescribed paths to locate utility programs and commands, such as shell programs. For example, if you type **whereis tcsh** and press <Enter>, you will see a list of the paths to the TC shell program files themselves. Note that the paths to a built-in or *internal command* cannot be found with the **whereis** command. We provide more information about internal and external shell commands in Chapter 13.

### 3.7.3 Finding Out Who You Are and What the Name of Your LINUX System Is

When you first log on, being able to view a display of information about your userid, the computer or system you have logged onto, and the operating system on that computer is useful. These tasks can be accomplished with the **whoami** command, which displays your userid on the screen; the **hostname** command, which displays the name of the host computer you have logged into; and the **uname** command, which displays information about the operating system running on the computer. The following session shows how our system responded to these commands when we typed them at the command line.

```
$ whoami ↵
bobk
$ hostname ↵
upibmg:egr.up.edu
$ uname ↵
Linux
$
```

The output of the **hostname** command shows that we were logged onto a computer called upibmg on the network with the name egr.up.edu. We present a detailed discussion of networks and internetworks in Chapter 14.

The following In-Chapter Exercises give you the chance to use the **whoami**, **who**, and **hostname** commands to obtain the information just described.

**IN-CHAPTER EXERCISES**

**3.7.** Use the **whoami** command to find your username on the system that you're using. Then use the **who** command to see how your username is listed, along with other users of the same system. What is the onscreen format of each user's listing that you obtained with the **who** command? Try to identify the information in each field on the same line as your username.

**3.8.** Use the **hostname** command to find out what host computer you are logged onto. Can you determine from this list whether you are using a standalone computer or a networked computer system? Explain how you can tell the difference by looking at the list that the **hostname** command gives you.

## SUMMARY

A computer system consists of several hardware and software components. The primary hardware components of a typical computer system include a central processing unit (CPU), main memory (commonly known as RAM), disk drive(s), a keyboard, a mouse, a display screen, a bus, and several other input/output (I/O) devices. The software components of a typical LINUX system consist of several layers: applications, shell, language libraries, system call interface, LINUX kernel, and device drivers. The kernel is the main part of the LINUX operating system and performs all the tasks that deal with allocation and deallocation of system resources. The shell and applications layers comprise what is commonly known as the application user's interface (AUI). The language libraries and the system call interface comprise the application programmer's interface (API).

A computer using the LINUX operating system can run many programs for the same user at the same time (multiprocess and multitasking). It can also support many different users at once (multiuser and time-sharing). To operate in a multiuser environment, a user must log on and log off the system, in order to maintain the security of the system and the integrity of the files of all the users. LINUX uses a text-based command user interface, which allows typing commands on a command line. These commands must be typed in the proper syntax. Table 3.4 lists the commands introduced in this chapter that are most useful for the beginner.

**Table 3.4** Useful Commands for the Beginner

| Command | What It Does |
|---|---|
| <Ctrl-D> | Allows you to leave the computer properly. |
| `cp` | Allows you to copy files. |
| `echo $SHELL` | Displays the shell that you are currently running. |
| `exit` | Ends a shell that you have started. |
| `hostname` | Displays the name of the host computer that you are logged on to. |
| `login` | Allows you to log on to the computer with a valid username/password pair. |
| `ls` | Allows you to display names of files and directories. |
| `man` | Allows you to view a manual page for a command or topic. |
| `mv` | Allows you to move or rename files. |
| `passwd` | Allows you to change your password on the computer. |
| `set` | Allows you to see and change environmental variables in bash. |
| `setenv` | Allows you to see and change environmental variables in tcsh. |
| `telnet` | Allows you to log on to a computer on a network or the Internet. |
| `uname` | Displays information about the operating system running the computer. |
| `whatis` | Allows you to view a brief description of a command. |
| `whereis` | Displays the path(s) to commands and utilities in certain key directories. |
| `who` | Displays information about the users currently using your system. |
| `whoami` | Displays your username. |

## PROBLEMS

1. What is the purpose of main memory?
2. What do the terms *bit* and *byte* mean? What do the storage units kilo, mega, and giga signify?
3. What is the purpose of the central processing unit? What comprises a machine cycle?
4. What is a bus and what is its purpose in a computer system? What are the sizes of the data, address, and control buses in your computer? (*Hint*: Read the user's manual for the CPU in your computer or visit the home page of the CPU manufacturer on the Internet.)
5. What is an operating system kernel? What are the primary tasks performed by the LINUX kernel?

6. What is a system call? What is the purpose of the system call interface?
7. What comprise AUI and API?
8. Give the sequence of events that take place when you type a command line and press <Enter> before the command executes. Be precise.
9. If you access a LINUX system with the **telnet** command, write down the exact step-by-step procedure you go through to log on and log off. Include as many descriptive details as possible in this procedure so that if you forget how to log on, you can always refer back to this written procedure.
10. Log on to your LINUX computer system and note the shell prompt being used. Most probably, which shell is it for? How can you identify a particular shell by the prompt displayed onscreen? How can you change the shell prompt? Experiment with changing the shell prompt to some other character, such as > or + .
11. What is your initial username/password pair? What is the name of the computer system that you are logging on to? What command did you use?
12. Give several examples of bad passwords, that is, passwords that you should not use, and explain why they are bad.
13. Using the proper terminology (e.g., command, option, option argument, and command argument), identify the constituent parts of the following LINUX single commands.

    ```
    ls -la *.exe
    lpr -Pwpr
    chmod g+rwx *.*
    ```

14. View the man pages for each of the useful commands listed in Table 3.4. Which part of the man pages is most descriptive for you? Which of the options shown on each of the man pages is most useful for beginners? Explain.
15. How many users are logged onto your system at this time? What command did you use to find out?
16. Determine the name of the operating system that your computer runs. What command did you use to find out?
17. Give the command line for displaying manual pages for the socket, read, and connect system calls. What is the command line for displaying the manual page for the Bash command **read**?

CHAPTER

# 4

# LINUX Shells

## OBJECTIVES

- To explain what a LINUX shell is
- To describe briefly some commonly used shells
- To discuss briefly some more useful commands for the beginner
- To discuss briefly the shell metacharacters
- To cover the commands and operators `#`, `"`, `$`, `&`, `'`, `( )`, `*`, `[ ]`, `^`, `` ` ``, `{}`, `|`, `;`, `<`, `>`, `?`, `/`, `\`, `!`, `%`, `~`, `alias`, `biff`, `cal`, `cat`, `cd`, `lpr`, `ls`, `mesg`, `mkdir`, `move`, `pg`, `pwd`, `rmdir`, `talk`, `unalias`, `uptime`, and `write`

## 4.1 INTRODUCTION

When you log on, the LINUX system starts running a program that acts as an interface between you and the LINUX kernel. This program, called the LINUX *shell*, executes the commands that you have typed in via the keyboard. When a shell starts running, it gives you a prompt and waits for your commands. When you type a command and press <Enter>, the shell interprets your command and executes it. If you type a nonexistent command, the shell so informs you, redisplays the prompt, and waits for you to type the next command. Because the primary purpose of the shell is to interpret your commands, it is also known as the LINUX **command interpreter**. The Bourne Again shell (Bash), TC shell (Tcsh), and Z shell (Zsh) are the most popular LINUX shells. We focus on Bash and Tcsh in this book.

A shell command can be *internal (built-in)* or *external*. The code to execute an internal command is part of the shell process, but the code to process an external command resides in a file in the form of a binary executable program file or a shell script. (We describe in detail how a shell executes commands in Chapter 13.) Because the shell executes commands entered from the keyboard, it terminates when it finds out that it cannot read anything else from the keyboard. You can so inform your shell by pressing <^D> at the beginning of a new line. As soon as the shell receives <^D>, it terminates and logs you off the system. The system then displays the `login:` prompt again, informing you that you need to log on again in order to use it.

The shell interprets your commands by assuming that the first word in a command line is the name of the command that you want to execute. It assumes that any of the remaining words starting with a hyphen (-) are options and that the rest of them are the command arguments. After reading your command line, it determines whether the command is an internal or external command. It processes all internal commands by using the corresponding code segments that are within its own code. To execute an external command, it searches several directories in the **file system structure** (see Chapter 7), looking for a file that has the name of the command. It then assumes that the file contains the code to be executed and runs the code. The names of the directories that a shell searches to find the file corresponding to an external command are stored in the shell variable `PATH` (or `path` in the TC shell). Directory names are separated by colons in the Bash shell and by spaces in the TC shell. The directory names stored in the variable form what is known as the **search path** for the shell. You can view the search path for your variable by using the `echo $PATH` command in Bash and the `echo $path` command in the TC shell. The following is a sample run of this command under the Bourne Again and TC shells, respectively. Note that in the Bourne Again shell the search path contains the directory names separated by colons and that in the TC shell the directory names are separated by spaces.

```
$ echo $PATH
/usr/sbin:/usr/X11/include/X11:.:/users/faculty/sarwar/bin:/usr/ucb
:/bin:/usr/bin:/usr/include:/usr/X11/lib:/usr/lib:/etc:/usr/etc:/usr
/local/bin:/usr/local/lib:/usr/local/games:/usr/X11/bin
$
% echo $path
/usr/sbin /usr/X11/include/X11 . /users/faculty/sarwar/bin /usr/ucb
/bin /usr/bin /usr/include /usr/X11/lib /usr/lib /etc /usr/etc /usr
/local/bin /usr/local/lib /usr/local/games /usr/X11/bin
%
```

The `PATH` (or `path`) variable is defined in a **hidden file** (also known as a **dot file**) called .profile or .login in your home directory. If you can't find this variable in one of those files, it is in the **start-up file** (also a dot file) specific to the shell that you're using. (See Section 4.2.4 for more details.) You can change the search path for your shell by changing the value of this variable. To change the search path temporarily for your current session only, you can change the value of `PATH` at the command line. For a permanent change, you need to change the value of this variable in the corresponding dot file. In the following example, the search path has been augmented by two directories, ~/bin and . (current directory). Moreover, the search starts with ~/bin and ends with the current directory.

```
$ PATH=~/bin:$PATH:.
$
```

You can determine your login shell by using the `echo $SHELL` command, as described in Chapter 3. Each shell has several other environment variables set up in a hidden file associated with it. We describe these files in Section 4.2 and present a detailed discussion of LINUX files in Chapter 7.

## 4.2 VARIOUS LINUX SHELLS

Every LINUX system comes with a variety of shells. There are several LINUX shells available, with Bash, TC, and Z shells being the most common. When you log on, one particular type of shell starts execution. This shell is known as your **login shell**. The usual default login shell is Bash. The system administrator of your computer system decides what your login shell is. If you want to change your default login shell, you can do so by running a corresponding command available on your system. For example, if your default login shell is Bash, but you want it to be the TC shell every time you log on, you can make it so by using the `tcsh` or `chsh` command.

### 4.2.1 Various Shell Programs

As we mentioned in Section 4.1, essentially a shell is an **interpreted program**, which might give you a hint about why there are so many different shells. Programs have a tendency to evolve and grow with time, depending on the needs of the users, and shell programs are typical of this evolution. Table 4.1 lists the most common shells, their location on the system, and the program names of those shells. Note that the locations shown here are typical for most systems; consult your instructor or system administrator if you can't find the location shown for a shell on your system, or use the `whereis` command, as shown in Chapter 3.

### 4.2.2 Which Shell Suits Your Needs?

Most shells perform very similar functions, and knowing the exact details of how they do so is important in deciding which shell to use for a particular task. These functions are interactive command use, the control of command input and output, and programming. A graphical representation of the functionality of common LINUX shells is given in Figure 4.1. Also, some shells are better in shell programming than others. Thus choosing a shell is a matter of preference and need. The Bourne Again shell has more advanced programming features than the TC shell, and both are equally powerful in their interactive use. Bash is, therefore, the shell of choice on LINUX-based systems. You can use the `sh` and `csh` commands to run Bourne and C shells, respectively. However, on most LINUX systems, these commands run Bash and Tcsh, respectively, because /bin/sh and /bin/csh are symbolic links (see Chapter 11) to /bin/bash and /bin/tcsh, respectively. The Bourne Again and TC shells have very similar features; some of their similarities and dissimilarities are summarized in Table 4.2. The popular LINUX shells have similar built-in, or internal, commands, as noted in Table 4.3. See the LINUX Command Appendix for a description of the command syntax and the arguments for these commands.

**Table 4.1** Shell Locations and Program Names

| Shell | Location on System | Program (Command) Name |
|---|---|---|
| Bourne | /bin/sh | sh |
| Bourne Again | /bin/bash | bash |
| C shell | /bin/csh | csh |
| TC shell | /bin/tcsh | tcsh |
| Korn shell | /bin/ksh | ksh |
| Z shell | /bin/zsh | zsh |

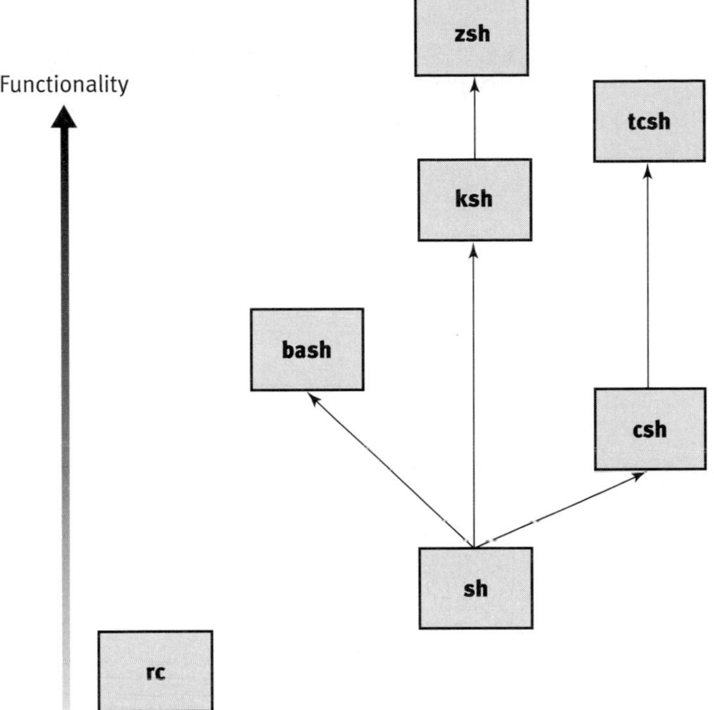


**Figure 4.1** Shell families and their relative functionalities

### 4.2.3 Various Ways to Change Your Shell

As we mentioned in Section 4.1, you can easily determine what your default shell is by typing `echo $SHELL` on the command line when you first log on to your computer system. Why would you want to change your default shell, or for that matter, even use an additional shell? You may want the greater functionality of another shell. For example, your default shell might be Bash. A friend of yours offers you a neat and useful TC shell script that allows you to take advantage of the TC shell programming capabilities, a script that would not work if run under Bash. You can run this script by running the TC shell at the same time you are running Bash. Because LINUX is a multiprocess operating system, more than one command line interpreter can be active at a time. That doesn't mean that a single command will be interpreted multiple times; it simply means that input, output, and errors are hooked into whatever shell process has control over them currently. (See Chapter 13 for more information about process and shell command input/output.)

You can change your shell in one of three ways: (1) by changing to a new default for every subsequent login session on your system; (2) by creating additional shell sessions running on top of, or concurrent with, the default shell; and (3) by changing your shell for only the current login session. The premise of all three of

**Table 4.2** Shell Similarities and Disimilarities

| Functional Element | Bash | Tcsh |
|---|---|---|
| Output redirection | > | > |
| Append to file | >> | >> |
| Input redirection | < | < |
| Pipe output | \| | \| |
| Run in background | & | & |
| Multiple commands | ; | ; |
| Multicharacter match | * | * |
| One character match | ? | ? |
| Repeat command x | !x | !x |
| Execute in subshell | () | () |
| Substitute output | ` ` | ` ` |
| Character quote | \ | \ |
| Change directory | cd | Cd |
| Display output | echo | Echo |
| Run a new shell | exec | Exec |
| Prompt | $ | % |
| Force redirection | >\| | > ! |
| Variable assignment | var = value | set var = value |
| Set environment variable | export var = value | setenv var value |
| Number of arguments | $# | $#argv |

**Table 4.3** Some Useful Shell Built-In Commands

| Bash Syntax | Tcsh Syntax | Description |
|---|---|---|
| `alias name=com` | `alias name com` | Equate name with a command. |
| `bind key:function` | `bindkey key command` | Bind a key to a command. |
| `cd dir` | `cd dir` | Change working directory to dir. |
| `echo string` | `echo string` | Write string to standard output. |
| `eval command` | `eval command` | Execute command. |
| `history lines` | `history n` | Print a command history of *n* lines. |
| `jobs` | `jobs` | List all running jobs. |
| `kill id#s` | `kill id#s` | Stop process identification numbers. |
| `logout` | `logout` | Exit a login shell. |
| `pwd` | `pwd` | Display present working directory. |
| `set arg1 arg2` | `set var=value` | Set variables to values. |
| `wait` | `wait` | Pause in execution until all child processes terminate. |

these methods is that you have confirmed that the shell you want to change to is available on your system, as detailed in Section 4.2.1. An additional way of seeing what shells are available on your system is to type **chsh –l** . You will then be shown the contents of the /bin/shells file, which lists the paths to the available shells on your system. Whether or not these shells are indeed available to you for execution is determined by the system administrator on your system.

To change your default shell, after you have logged on type **chsh** and press <Enter>. Depending on your system, you will be asked for your login password and be prompted for the name of the shell you want to change to. Type the complete path to the shell you want to change to; for example, **/bin/tcsh** to change to the TC shell. To create or run additional shells on top of your default shell, simply type the name of the shell program, as shown in Table 4.1, on the command line whenever you want to run that shell. The following session illustrates this method. In this session, your default shell is the Bourne Again shell, which uses $ as the shell prompt. Your objective is to change to the TC shell, which shows % as the shell prompt.

```
$ echo $SHELL
/bin/bash
$ tcsh
% ps
PID    TTY    TIME    CMD
1025   pts/0  00:00:00      bash
1041   pts/0  00:00:00      tcsh
1048   pts/0  00:00:00      ps
%
```

The first command line in this session allows you to determine what your default shell is. The system shows you that this default is set at Bash. The second command line allows you to run the TC shell at the same time as Bash. The fourth line shows that you have been successful, because the `ps` command has listed your current processes, or programs that you are running as `bash`, `tcsh`, and the `ps` command itself. If the TC shell were not available on your system, or were inaccessible to you, you would get an error message after line 3. If your search path does not include /bin, you either have to type **/bin/tcsh** in place of **tcsh** or include /bin in your shell's search path and then use the `tcsh` command.

In order to terminate or leave this new, temporary shell and return to your default login shell, press <Ctrl-D> on a blank line. If this way of terminating the new shell does not work, type **exit** on the command line and press <Enter>. This exits the new shell, and the default shell prompt will appear on the display.

You can also change your shell by using the **exec** command. For example, if you have determined that your current shell is Bash and you want to change to the TC shell, simply type **exec /bin/csh** on the command line, and you will be running the TC shell instead of Bash.

The following In-Chapter Exercises ask you to determine whether various shells are available on your system by using the **whereis** command and to read the *Manual Pages* for them by using the **man** command.

## IN-CHAPTER EXERCISES

**4.1.** Using the **whereis** command as described in Chapter 3, verify the locations of the various shells listed in Table 4.1. Are all of these shells available on your system? Where are they located if they are not found at the locations shown in Table 4.1?

**4.2.** Using the **man** command as described in Chapter 3, read the *Manual Pages* for each of the shells listed in Table 4.1 that you have on your system.

### 4.2.4 Shell Start-up Files and Environment Variables

The actions of each shell, the mechanics of how it executes commands and programs, how it handles command and program I/O, and how it is programmed are affected by the setting of certain environment variables, which we mentioned briefly in Section 3.6. Each LINUX system has an initial system start-up file, usually in /etc/profile. This file contains the initial settings of important environment variables for the shell and some other utilities. In addition, there are hidden files, or dot files, for specific shells, which are executed when you start a particular shell. These, also known as **shell start-up files**, are found in a user's home directory (signified by a ~) as ~/.profile, or in a particular shells' profile or login file in each user's home directory. For example, Bash profile and login files are usually named ~/.bash_profile or ~/.bash_login. These hidden files are initially configured by the system administrator for secure use by all users. Table 4.4 lists some important environment variables common to Bash and TC shells; if the TC shell variable name that performs the same function is different, it follows the Bash name.

**Table 4.4** Shell Environment Variables

| Environment Variable | What It Affects |
|---|---|
| **CDPATH** | The alias names for directories accessed with the `cd` command |
| **EDITOR** | The default editor you use in programs such as the e-mail program `elm` |
| **ENV** | The path along which LINUX looks to find configuration files |
| **HOME** | The name of the user's home directory, when the user first logs in |
| **MAIL** | The name of the user's system mailbox file |
| **PATH** | The directories that a shell searches to find a command or program |
| **PS1, prompt** | The shell prompt that appears on the command line |
| **PWD, cwd** | The name of the current working directory |
| **TERM** | The type of console terminal the user is using |

When you log on and your login shell is Bash, it first executes commands in the /etc/profile file, if this file exists. It then searches for the ~/.bash_profile, ~/.bash_login, or ~/.profile file, in this order, and executes commands in the first of these that is found and is readable. When a login Bash exits, it executes commands in the ~/.bash_logout file.

When you start an interactive Bash shell, it executes commands in the ~/.bashrc file, if this file exists and is readable. When started non-interactively to run a shell script (see Chapters 15 and 16), Bash looks for the environment variable BASH_ENV to find out the name of the file to be executed.

If your shell is a TC shell, it executes commands in the /etc/csh.cshrc or /etc/.cshrc file, if it exists and is readable. A login shell then executes commands in the /etc/csh.login file, if it exists. Every shell (login or non-login) then executes commands in the ~/.tcshrc file (or the ~/.cshrc file if ~/.tcshrc does not exist), followed by reading the ~/.history file. A login shell then executes commands in the ~/.login and ~/.cshdirs files. When a login TC shell exits, it executes commands in the /etc/csh.logout and ~/.logout files, if they exist and are readable. Table 4.5 shows the names of some important startup files and when they are executed.

The following In-Chapter Exercises allow you to view the settings of your environment variables. They assume you are initially running Bash. If you aren't, change to that shell as shown in Section 4.2.3 before doing the Exercises.

**IN-CHAPTER EXERCISES**

**4.3.** At the shell prompt, type **set**, then press <Enter>. What do you see on your screen display? Identify and list the settings for all the environment variables shown. shown.

**4.4.** At the shell prompt, type **exec /bin/csh** and press <Enter>. Then type **setenv** and press <Enter>. Identify and list the settings for all the environment variables shown.

**Table 4.5** Shell Startup Files for Bash and TC Shells

| File | What It Does |
|---|---|
| /etc/profile | Executes automatically at login |
| ~/.bash_profile, ~/.bash_login, ~/.profile | Executes automatically at login |
| ~/.bashrc | Executes automatically at shell login |
| ~/.bash_logout | Executes automatically at logout |
| ~/.bash_history | Records last session's commands |
| /etc/passwd | Source of home directories for ~name abbreviations |
| ~/.cshrc or ~/.tcshrc | Executes at each shell startup |
| ~/.login | Executed by login shell after .cshrc (or .tcshrc) at login |
| ~/.cshdirs | Executes after tcsh .login |
| ~/.logout | Executes at logout from csh or tcsh |

In addition to the shells, several other programs that have their own hidden files. These files are used to set up and configure the operating environment within which these programs execute. We discuss these hidden files in Chapters 5 and 6. They are called hidden files because when the names of files contained in the user's home directory are listed—for example, with the `ls -l` command and option (see Chapter 7)—these files do not appear on the list. The hidden file names always start with a dot (.) such as .profile.

## 4.3 SOME USEFUL GENERAL-PURPOSE COMMANDS

In this section we briefly discuss some useful general-purpose commands. More detailed descriptions of most of these commands are presented in Chapter 7 and beyond. The purpose of the discussion here is to help you become more comfortable with the LINUX system and prepare you to go through Chapters 5 and 6 with relative ease.

### 4.3.1 Creating and Displaying Directories

The LINUX operating system allows users to give a hierarchical structure to their files and directories. In Chapter 7 we describe details of this structure. We discuss file-related commands in Chapters 7 through 12 but introduce some of them here for your use in Chapters 5 and 6.

You can determine your current working directory by using the **pwd** (print working directory) command. The commands that create and remove directories are **mkdir** (make directory) and **rmdir** (remove directory), respectively. The **mkdir dir1** command creates a directory called **dir1** in the current working directory. You can change your current working directory by using the **cd** (change directory) command. The command to display the contents of (names of files and directories in) a directory is **ls** (list). It can be run with several options. When executed without any arguments, the **ls** command displays the names of all the files, except the dot files, and directories in the current working directory. The **-a** option can be used to display the names of the dot files as well. With the **-C** option, the **ls** command displays output in multicolumn sorted order. The following session shows some examples of the **cd**, **ls**, **mkdir**, **pwd**, and **rmdir** commands. The commands **cd linuxbook** and **cd examples** can be combined into a single **cd linuxbook/examples** command. Again, note the case specific format of the commands. **.** stands for the current directory and **..** stands for the parent of the current directory (more in Chapter 7).

```
$ pwd
/home/faculty/sarwar
$ ls
ece231
ece345
```

```
ece441
ece445
ece446
personal
linuxbook
$ ls -C
ece231 ece345 ece441 ece445 ece446 personal linuxbook
$ ls -aC
. .. .cshrc .login ece231 ece345 ece441 ece445 ece446
personal linuxbook
$ cd linuxbook
$ cd examples
$ pwd
/home/faculty/sarwar/linuxbook/examples
$ ls -C
chapter1 chapter2 chapter3 chapter4
$ mkdir dir1
$ ls -C
chapter1 chapter2 chapter3 chapter4 dir1
$ cd dir1
$ pwd
/home/faculty/sarwar/linuxbook/examples/dir1
$ cd ..
$ rmdir dir1
$ ls -C
chapter1 chapter2 chapter3 chapter4
$ cd ~
$ ls -C linuxbook/examples
chapter1 chapter2 chapter3 chapter4
$
```

### 4.3.2 Displaying Files

The commands for displaying files are `cat` and `more`. The `cat` command displays all the contents of one or more files at one time, and the `more` command displays file contents one screen at a time. You need to press the <space bar> to display the next page. Thus the `cat sample` command displays the contents of the sample file. The `more sample phones` command displays the contents of the sample file a screenful at a time, followed by a display of the contents of the phones file the same way. The `pg` command is similar to the `more` command. These commands should only be used to display text files.

### 4.3.3 Printing Files

We discuss commands related to printing and printer control in detail in Chapter 9 but briefly describe here the commands needed to print files. You can print files by using the `lpr` command. In the following session the first command line is used to print the sample file on the spr printer. Note that with the `lpr` command, you need to use the `-P` option to specify the printer to print on and the `-n` option to specify the number of copies to print. The second command prints three copies of the sample file on the same printer. Ask your instructor the name of the printer that you can send your files to for printing

```
$ lpr -P spr sample
$ lpr -P spr -n 3 sample
$
```

### 4.3.4 Displaying a Calendar

The command to display a calendar for a year or a month is `cal`. A brief description of the command follows.

Syntax: **cal [[month] year]**

**Purpose:** Display calendar

The optional parameter "month" can be between 1 and 12, and "year" can be 0 to 9999. If no argument is specified, the command displays the calendar for the current month of the current year. If only one parameter is specified, it is taken as the year. Thus the `cal 3 2000` command displays the calendar for March 2000. The command `cal 1991` displays the calendar for the year 1991, the year the LINUX operating system was born.

### 4.3.5 One-Way Real-Time Messaging

You can use the `write` command to send a message to another user who is currently logged on to the system. The syntax and a brief description of the command follow.

Syntax:

**write username [terminal]**

**Purpose:** Write on the terminal of the user with login name "username". The user must currently be logged on to the system.

The example presented in Figure 4.2 illustrates the use of this command. The `who` command is used to determine whether the person to whom you want to write is logged on. In this case, both sender (sarwar) and receiver (bobk) are logged on to the computer (upibm7). The receiver's screen is garbled with the message, but no harm is caused to any work that the user may be doing. Under the shell, pressing <Enter> does the trick of resetting the screen, and inside the vi editor (discussed in Chapter 5), the screen can be reset by pressing <Ctrl-R>.

### 4.3.6 Notification of and Permission for Electronic Communication

You can use the `biff` command to let the system know whether you want to be notified of a newly arriving e-mail message immediately. The system notifies you by a beep on your terminal. You can use the command `biff y` to enable notification and `biff n` to disable notification. When the `biff` command is used without an argument, it displays the current setting, `n` or `y`.

You can use the `mesg` command to enable or disable real-time one-way messages and chat requests from other users with the `write` and `talk` commands, respectively (see Chapter 14). The `mesg y` command permits others to initiate communication with you by using the `write` or `talk` command. If you think that you are being bothered too often with `write` or `talk`, you can turn off the permission by executing the `mesg n` command. When you do so, a user who runs a `write` or `talk` command gets the message `Permission denied`. When the `mesg` command is used without an argument, it returns the current value of permission, `n` or `y`.

### 4.3.7 Creating Pseudonyms for Commands

The `alias` command can be used to create **pseudonyms** (nicknames) for commands. The command has one syntax in Bash and another in the TC shell, both of which follow.

Syntax:

**alias [ name [=string] ... ]** **Bash shell**
**alias [ name [string] ]** **TC shell**

**Purpose:** Create pseudonym "string" for the command "name".

**Sender's (sarwar's) Screen**

```
$ who
bobk      upibm7:ttyC2    Jul  6 13:47 :34
deborahs  upibm7:ttyp0    Jul  6 08:53 :17
dfrakes   upibm7:ttyp1    Jul  6 12:10 :55
khan      upibm9:ttyp1    Jul  6 11:49
kuhn      upibm22:ttyp0   Jul  6 09:03 :12
oster     upibm7:ttyC6    Jul  6 10:28 :06
sarwar    upibm7:ttyp0    Jul  6 08:33 :05
$ write bobk ttyC2
Bob,

How is Chapter 5 coming along? I am working
through some useful commands for Chapter 4. Any
progress on the issue of picture formats? I
talked to Lisa today regarding the conversion
process and will brief you on that tomorrow.

Take care,

Mansoor
^d
```

**Receiver's (bobk's) Screen**

```
$
Message fom sarwar@upibm7.egr.up.edu on ttyp0
at 14:26 ...
Bob,

How is Chapter 5 coming along? I am working
through some useful commands for Chapter 4.
Any progress on the issue of picture formats?
I talked to Lisa today regarding the
conversion process and will brief you on that
tomorrow.

Take care,

Mansoor
EOF
```

**Figure 4.2** An illustration of the `write` command

When you use the **alias** command to create pseudonyms, you have created **aliases**. Pseudonyms are usually created for commands, but they can also be used for other items, such as naming e-mail groups (see Chapter 6). Both the Bash and TC shells allow you to create aliases from the command line.

Command aliases can be placed in a system start-up file, the ~/.profile file, or the ~/.login file, but they are typically placed in a shell start-up file; the .bashrc file (Bash) and the .cshrc file (TC shell). The ~/.profile or ~/.login file executes when

**Table 4.6** Some Useful Aliases

| Bash | Tcsh |
|---|---|
| `alias dir='ls -la \!*'` | `alias dir 'ls -la \!*'` |
| `alias rename='mv \!*'` | `alias rename 'mv \!*'` |
| `alias spr='lpr -Pspr \!*'` | `alias spr 'lpr -Pspr \!*'` |
| `alias ls='ls -C'` | `alias ls 'ls -C'` |
| `alias ll='ls -ltr'` | `alias ll 'ls -ltr'` |
| `alias more='pg'` | `alias more 'pg'` |

you log on, and the ~/.cshrc or ~/.bashrc file executes every time you start Tcsh or Bash. Table 4.6 lists some useful aliases to put in one of these files. If set in your environment, these aliases allow you to use the names **dir**, **rename**, **spr**, **ls**, w, **ll**, and **more** as commands, substituting them for the actual commands given in quotes. The \!* string is substituted by the actual parameter passed to the **dir** command. For example, when you use the **dir** command, the shell actually executes the **ls -la** command. Thus for the **dir linuxbook** command, the shell executes the **ls -la linuxbook** command.

When you use the **alias** command without any argument, it lists all the aliases set. The following session illustrates the use of this command with the Bash and TC shells.

```
$ alias
dir='ls -la \!*'
rename='mv \!*'
spr='lpr -Pspr \!*'
ls='ls -C'
ll='ls -ltr'
more='pg'
$
```

Running the same command with the TC shell produces the following output.

```
% alias
dir     ls -la \!*
rename mv \!*
spr     lpr -Pspr \!*
ls      ls -C
ll      ls -ltr
```

```
more    pg
%
```

You can use the **unalias** command to remove one or more aliases from the alias list. You can use the **-a** option to remove all aliases from the alias list.

The first of the two **unalias** commands in the following session removes the alias for **ls**, and the second removes all of the aliases from the alias list. Note that the output of the first **alias** command does not contain an alias for the **ls** command after the **unalias ls** command has been executed. Use of the second **alias** command produces no output because the **unalias -a** command removes all the aliases from the alias list.

```
$ unalias ls
$ alias
dir='ls -la \!*'
rename='mv \!*'
spr='lpr -Pspr \!*'
ll='ls -ltr'
more='pg'
$ unalias -a
$ alias
$
```

### 4.3.8 Displaying System Up Time

You can use the **uptime** command to display system up time (the duration of time the system has been running since it was last booted) and some other useful statistics, such as the number of users currently logged onto the system. The command doesn't require any parameters. The following example shows the output of the command.

```
$ uptime
11:39AM up 7:04, 11 users, load average: 0.08, 0.12, 0.17
$
```

In the following In-Chapter Exercises, use the **write**, **alias**, **uptime**, and **cat** (or **more**) commands to reinforce their semantics.

## IN-CHAPTER EXERCISES

**4.5.** Use the **write** command to communicate with a friend who is logged on to the system.

**4.6.** Use the **alias** command to display the nicknames (aliases) of commands in your system.

**4.7.** Use the **uptime** command to determine how long your system has been up and running and how many users are currently using the system.

**4.8.** Display the contents of the /etc/passwd file on your system to determine how many users can log on to the system.

## 4.4 SHELL METACHARACTERS

Most of the characters other than letters and digits have special meaning to the shell. These characters are called **shell metacharacters** and cannot be used in shell commands as literal characters without specifying them in a particular way. Thus try not to use them in naming your files. Also, when these characters are used in commands, no space is required before or after them. However, you can use spaces before and after a shell metacharacter for clarity. Table 4.7 contains a list of the shell metacharacters and their purpose.

The shell metacharacters allow you to specify multiple files in multiple directories in one command line. We describe the use of these characters in subsequent chapters, but we give some simple examples here to explain the meanings of some commonly used metacharacters: *, ?, ~, and [ ]. The ? character is a wildcard character that matches any single character and * matches zero or more characters. The ?.txt string can be used for all the files that have a single character before .txt such as a.txt, G.txt, @.txt, and 7.txt. The [0–9].c string can be used for all the files in a directory that have a single digit before .c such as 3.c and 8.c. The lab1\ /c string stands for lab1/c. Note the use of backslash (\) to quote (escape the special meaning of) the slash character (/). The following command prints the names of all the files in your current directory that have two-character long file names and an .html extension, with the first character being a digit and second being an uppercase or lowercase letter. The printer on which these files are printed is spr.

```
$ lpr -Pspr [0-9][a-zA-Z].html
$
```

Note that **[0–9]** means any digit from 0 through 9 and **[a–zA–Z]** means any lowercase or uppercase letter.

**Table 4.7** Shell Metacharacters

| Metacharacter | Purpose | Example |
|---|---|---|
| New Line | To end a command line | |
| space | To separate elements on a command line | ls /etc |
| Tab | To separate elements on a command line | ls    /etc |
| # | To start a comment | # This is a comment line |
| “ | To quote multiple characters but allow substitution (Chapter 15) | “$file”.bak |
| $ | To end line and dereference a shell variable | $PATH |
| & | To provide background execution of a command (Chapter 13) | command & |
| ‘ | To quote multiple characters | ‘$100,000’ |
| () | To execute a command list in a subshell | (command1; command2) |
| * | To match zero or more characters | chap*.ps |
| [ ] | To insert wildcards | [a-s] or [1,5-9] |
| ^ | To begin a line and negation symbol | [^3-8] |
| ` | To substitute a command | PS1=`command` |
| { } | To execute a command list in the current shell | {command1; command2} |
| \| | To create a pipe between commands | command1 \| command2 |
| ; | To separate commands in sequential execution | command1; command2 |
| < | To redirect input for a command | command < file |
| > | To redirect output for a command | command > file |
| ? | To substitute a wildcard for exactly one character | lab.? |
| / | To be used as the root directory and as a component separator in a pathname | /usr/bin |
| \ | To escape/quote a single character; used to quote <New Line> character to allow continuation of a shell command on the following line | command arg1 \ arg2 arg3 \? |
| ! | To start an event specification in the history list and the current event | !!, !4 |
| % | The TC shell prompt, or the starting character for specifying a job number (Chapter 13) | % or %3 |
| ~ | To name home directory | ~/.profile |

## SUMMARY

When you log on to a LINUX computer, the system runs a program called a shell that gives you a prompt and waits for you to type commands, one per line. When you type a command and hit <Enter>, the shell tries to execute the command, assuming that the first word in the command line is the name of the command. A shell command can be built-in or external. The shell has the code for executing a built-in command, but the code for an external command is in a file. To execute an external command, the shell searches several directories, one by one, to locate the file that contains the code for the command. If the file is found, it is executed if it contains code (binary or shell script). The names of the directories that the shell searches to locate the file for an external command comprise what is known as the search path. The search path is stored in a shell variable called ***PATH*** (for the Bourne Again shell) or ***path*** (for the TC shell). You can change the search path for your shell by adding new directory names in ***PATH*** or deleting some existing directory names from it.

Several shells are available for you to use. These shells differ in terms of convenience of use at the command line level and features available in their programming languages. The most commonly used shells in LINUX-based systems are the Bourne Again and TC. The Bourne Again shell is the superset of the Bourne shell and has an excellent programming language and rich command-level interface. The TC shell has several of the interactive features that Bash does but its programming features are less powerful.

There are several hundred commands, utilities, and tools in a typical LINUX system. Some of the most useful for a beginner are **mkdir** (make directory), **rmdir** (remove directory), **cd** (change directory), **ls** (list name of files in a directory), **pwd** (print name of the current/working directory), **lpr** (print files), **cat** (display files at one time), **more** (display files a screenful at a time), **pg** (display files a screenful at a time), **cal** (display calendar), **write** (one-way real-time messaging), **biff** (e-mail notification enable/disable), **mesg** (real-time communication enable/disable), **alias** (nicknaming existing commands), **unalias** (remove an alias—a nickname—from the alias list), and **uptime** (displaying system up time).

Certain characters, called shell metacharacters, have special meaning to the shell. Because the shell treats them in special ways, they should not be used in file names. If you must use them in commands, you need to quote them so that the shell will treat them literally.

## PROBLEMS

1. What is a shell? What is its purpose?
2. What are the two types of shell commands? What are the differences between them?
3. Give names of three LINUX shells. Which are the most popular? What is a login shell?
4. What do you type in to terminate the execution of a shell? How do you terminate the execution of your login shell?
5. What shells do you think are "supersets" of other shells? In other words, which shells have other shells' complete command sets plus their own? Can

you find any commands in a subset shell that are not in a superset shell? Refer to Figure 4.1.

6. What is the search path for a shell? What is the name of shell variable that is used to maintain it for the Bourne Again and TC shells? Where (in which file) is this variable typically located?
7. What is the search path set to in your environment? How did you find out? Set your search path so that your shell searches your current and your ~/bin directories while looking for a command that you type. In what order does your shell search the directories in your search path? Why?
8. What are hidden files? What are the names of the hidden files that are executed when you log on to a LINUX system?
9 What is a shell start-up file? What is the name of this file for the TC shell? Where (which directory) is this file stored?
10. What important features of each shell, as discussed on the manual pages for that shell, seem to be most important for you as a new, intermediate, or advanced user of LINUX? Explain the importance of these features to you in comparison to the other shells available and their features.
11. Suppose that your login shell is a TC shell. You received a shell script that runs with the Bourne Again shell. How would you execute it? Clearly write down all the steps that you would use.
12. Create a directory called linux in your home directory. What command line did you use?
13. Give a command line for displaying the files lab1, lab2, lab3, and lab4. Can you give two more command lines that do the same thing? What is the command line for displaying the files lab1.c, lab2.c, lab3.c, and lab4.c? (*Hint:* Use shell metacharacters.)
14. Give a command line for printing all the files in your home directory that start with the string `memo` and end with `.ps` on a printer called "upmpr". What command line did you use?
15. Give the command line for nicknaming the command `who -H` as `w`. Give both Bourne Again and TC shell versions. Where would you put this command line so that it executes every time you log on? Where would you put it if you want it to execute every time you start a new shell?
16. Run the `man ls > ~/linux/ls.man` on your system. This command will put the man page for the `ls` command in the ls.man file in your ~/unix directory. Give the command for printing two copies of this file on a printer in your lab. What command line did you use?
17. What is the `mesg` value set to for your environment? If it is on, how would you turn off your current session? How would you set it permanently?
18. What does the command `lpr -Pqpr [0-9]*.jpg` do? Explain your answer.

CHAPTER

# 5

# Editing Text Files

## OBJECTIVES

- To explain the utility of editing text files
- To show that `pico` is the editor of choice for creating short, simple files
- To show how `vi` has the capabilities of a word processor
- To show that `emacs` can be customized
- To show how to do graphical editing, using `XEmacs`.
- To cover the commands and primitives `cp`, `emacs`, `ls`, `pico`, `pwd`, `sh`, `vi`, and `who`

## 5.1 INTRODUCTION

By now, it should be clear that LINUX is a **text-driven operating system**. Therefore, to do useful things such as execute multiple commands from within a script file, or write e-mail messages, or create C language programs, you must be familiar with one or perhaps many ways of entering text into a file. In addition, you must also be familiar with how to edit existing files efficiently, that is, to change their contents or otherwise modify them in some way. Text editors also allow you simply to view a file's contents, similar to the `more` command (see Chapter 3) so that you can perhaps identify the key features of the file. For example, a file without any extension, such as foo (rather than foo.eps) might be an Encapsulated PostScript file that you can identify with a valid PostScript header at the start of the file. That header can be viewed with a text editor.

The editors that we consider here are all **full-screen display editors**. That is, in the console window or terminal screen that you are using to view the file, you are able to see a portion of the file, which fills most or all of the screen display. You are also able to move the **cursor**, or point, to any text that you see in this full screen display. That material is usually held in a temporary storage area in computer memory, called the **editor buffer**. If your file is larger than one screen in size, the buffer contents change as you move the cursor through the file. The difference between a file, which you edit, and a buffer is crucial. For text editing purposes, a file is stored on disk as a sequence of data. When you edit that file, you edit a copy that the editor creates, which is in the editor buffer. You make changes to the contents of the buffer—and can even manipulate several buffers at once—but when you save the buffer, you write a new sequence of data to the disk, thereby saving the file.

Another important operational feature of all the editors discussed in this chapter is that their actions are based on **keystroke commands**, whether they are single key presses or combinations of keys *pressed* simultaneously or sequentially. Because the primary input device in LINUX is the keyboard, the correct syntax of keystroke commands is mandatory. But this method of input, once you have become accustomed to it, is as efficient or even more efficient than mouse/GUI input. Keystrokes also are more flexible, giving you more complete and customizable control over editing actions. Generally, you should choose the editor that you are most comfortable with, in terms of the way you prefer to work with the computer. However, your choice of editor also depends on the complexity and quantity of text creation and manipulation that you want to do. Practically speaking, the more powerful editors such as `vi` and `emacs` are capable of handling complex editing tasks. But to take advantage of that power, you have to learn the commands that are needed to perform those tasks and how they are implemented—and retain that knowledge. The text editing functions common to the text editors that we cover here are listed in Table 5.1, along with a short description of each function.

**Table 5.1** Common Functions of LINUX Text Editors

| Function | Description |
|---|---|
| Cursor movement | Moving the location of the insertion point or current position in the buffer |
| Cut or copy, paste | "Ripping out" text blocks or duplicating text blocks, reinserting ripped or duplicate blocks |
| Deleting text | Deleting text at a specified location or in a specified range |
| Inserting text | Placing text at a specified location |
| Opening, starting | Opening an existing file for modification, beginning a new file |
| Quitting | Leaving the text editor, with or without saving the work done |
| Saving | Retaining the buffer as a disk file |
| Search, replace | Finding instances of text strings, replacing them with new strings |

## 5.2 HOW TO DO SHORT AND SIMPLE EDITS BY USING THE pico EDITOR

The **pico** LINUX text editor allows you to do simple editing on small text files efficiently. Its user interface is friendly and simple, compared to the editors that we cover later in this chapter. The **pico** editor is distributed free with the pine e-mail system, so if you cannot access the program by typing **pico** at the shell prompt, ask your system administrator where your shell can locate it. Then set your search path to include that location, as described in Chapter 4.

### 5.2.1 CREATING THE TEXT OF AN E-MAIL MESSAGE WITH THE pico TEXT EDITOR

Example: pico Text Editor shows how to create and save a small e-mail message with the **pico** text editor. In the example at the beginning of Chapter 6, you will

**Example: pico Text Editor**

**Step 1:** At the shell prompt, type **pico** and press <Enter>.

**Step 2:** The pico screen display appears similar to Figure 5.1.

**Step 3:** On the first blank line in the text area, type **Subject: My first file** and press <Enter>.

**Step 4:** Type **Dear Me: This is what the first file I created with pico looks like.**

**Step 5:** Hold down the <Ctrl> and <X> keys on the keyboard at the same time, and when prompted to enter a file name, type **first.txt**, then press <Enter>.

**Step 6:** Hold down the <Ctrl> and <X> keys at the same time, to exit pico.

use this file as the body of an e-mail message that can be sent with the LINUX `mail` command.

## 5.2.2 How to Start, Save a File, and Exit

For small text files, such as short e-mail messages or shell scripts, the **`pico`** editor is easily and quickly learned. As apparent in Figure 5.1, it has a straightforward screen display that has two main parts: a text area, where you can enter and change text by typing, and a keystroke command area at the bottom of the screen, which shows valid keystroke commands. The general methods of starting **`pico`** from the command line are as follows.

Syntax:

**pico [options] [file]**

**Purpose:** Allows you to edit a new or existing text file

**Output:** With no options or file(s) specified, you are placed in the pico program and can begin to edit a new buffer.

**Commonly used options/features:**

| | |
|---|---|
| **-h** | List valid command line options. |
| **-m** | Enable mouse functionality in a GUI environment. |
| **-o** dir | Set the operating directory. Only files within *dir* are accessible. |

To edit a new buffer, type **`pico`** at the shell prompt and press <Enter>. The program begins, and you will see a screen display similar to that shown in Figure 5.1. You are immediately in text-entry mode, and whatever you type will appear in the text area of the **`pico`** screen display. Note that, to the left of each keystroke command listed at the bottom of the screen, there are two characters (e.g., `^O` next to `WriteOut` and `^X` next to `Exit`). Recall that the first character (the caret) tells you to hold down the <Ctrl> key on your keyboard while holding down the next character (the letter key) to execute the command (e.g., writeOut, or save a file, or eXit from `pico`).

To save at any point, hold down the <Ctrl> and <O> keys at the same time. A prompt appears near the bottom of the screen, asking you to type in a filename to which the current text body will be saved. Type in a name, as shown in Figure 5.2. Anytime you want to save the text that you have entered, use <Ctrl-O> to confirm the filename that the text will be saved to. Then press <Enter>, and the current text will be saved to the filename that you specify. You should save your file at

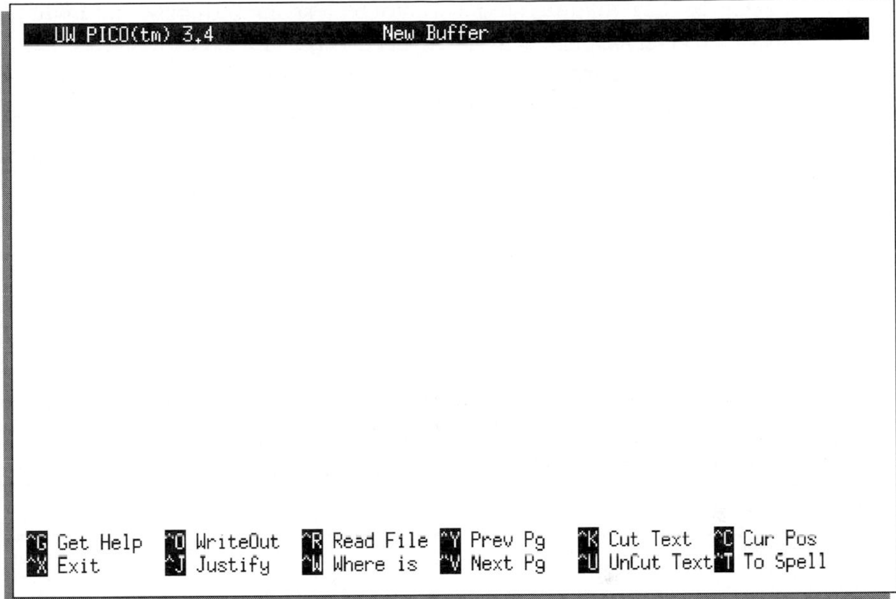


**Figure 5.1** First `pico` screen display

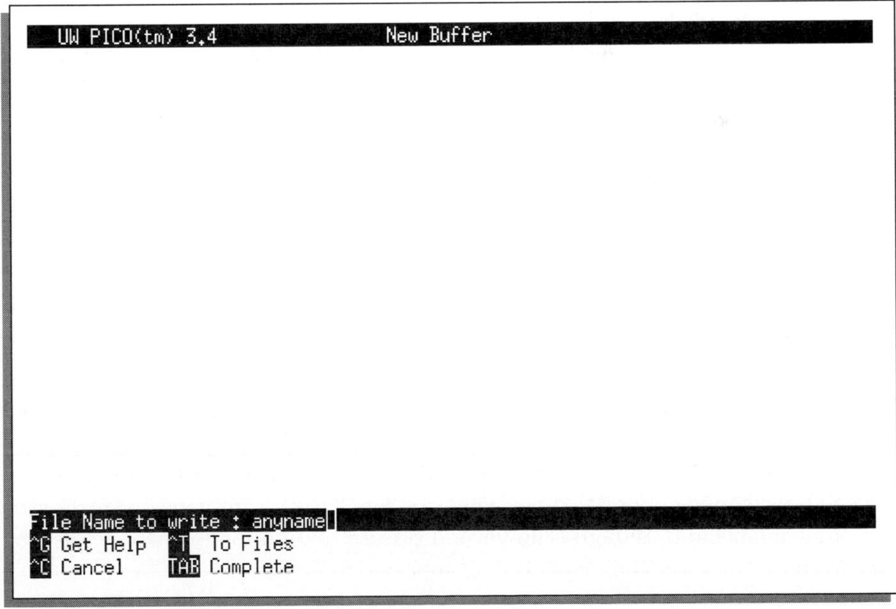


**Figure 5.2** Saving a file with a name in `pico`

least once every 15 to 20 minutes so that you don't lose more than that amount of work if the system crashes.

To exit **pico**, hold down the <Ctrl> and <X> keys at the same time. If you have made any changes in the text since the last time you saved the file, you can type <Y> to save the changes.

Practice Session 5.1 gives you the chance to use these commands to enter and save text and exit from **pico**.

### Practice Session 5.1

**Step 1:** At the shell prompt, type **pico** and press <Enter>.

**Step 2:** In the text area of the `pico` screen, place the cursor on the first line and type

**This is text that I have entered on a line in the pico editor.**

Use the <Delete> and <arrow> keys to correct any typing errors you make.

**Step 3:** Press <Enter > three times.

**Step 4:** Type **This is a line of text three lines down from the first line**.

**Step 5:** Hold down the <Ctrl> and <O> keys at the same time (<Ctrl-O> or <^O>).

**Step 6:** At the prompt `File Name to Write:` type **linespaced** and then press <Enter>.

**Step 7:** Hold down the <Ctrl> and <X> keys at the same time (<Ctrl-X> or <X>) to return to the shell prompt.

**Step 8:** At the shell prompt, type **more linespaced** and press <Enter>.

### 5.2.3 General Keystroke Commands and Cursor Movement

In addition to the **WriteOut** and **Exit** commands mentioned in Section 5.2.2, **pico** has some general basic text editing features, as summarized in Table 5.2.

For example, to read the Help pages while in **pico**, hold down the <Ctrl> and <G> keys at the same time. Then move down through the Help pages by holding down the <Ctrl> and <V> keys at the same time. To move up through the pages hold down the <Ctrl> and <Y> keys at the same time. Although **pico** is a basic text editor, fortunately it has useful features such as search and cut and paste. Advanced text editing options that you might be familiar with from a word processor are not available in it, though. The **vi** and **emacs** text editors, which we discuss shortly, have those capabilities.

**Table 5.2** Keystroke Commands and Their Actions in pico

| Keystroke Command | Action |
|---|---|
| ‹^Shift 6› | Begins to mark a section of text for cutting out text |
| ‹^C› | Reports the current cursor position as line # and character # |
| ‹^G› | Allows access to `pico` Help text |
| ‹^J› | Justifies the selected text, similar to wordwrap in a word processor |
| ‹^K› | Cuts the selected text |
| ‹^O› | Writes out, or saves, the current text to a file |
| ‹^R› | Reads in text from a file and pastes the text at the current cursor position |
| ‹^T› | Checks spelling |
| ‹^U› | Pastes the current line of text |
| ‹^V› | Scrolls one page down in the Help pages |
| ‹^W› | `Whereis` (allows you to search for a string of characters) |
| ‹^X› | `Exit` (pico allows you to save any changes before exiting) |
| ‹^Y› | Scrolls one page up in the Help pages |

Table 5.3 shows how to move the cursor to different positions in the file quickly and easily. Along with using the <arrow> keys on the keyboard, these keystroke commands are quick and efficient ways of positioning text.

The following In-Chapter Exercises ask you to evaluate some of the results obtained in Practice Session 5.1.

**Table 5.3** Important Cursor Movement Keystroke Commands in `pico`

| Keystroke Command | Action |
|---|---|
| ‹^F› | Moves the cursor forward a character |
| ‹^B› | Moves the cursor backward a character |
| ‹^P› | Moves the cursor to the previous line |
| ‹^N› | Moves the cursor to the next line |
| ‹^E› | Moves the cursor to the end of the current line |
| ‹^V› | Moves the cursor to the next page of text |
| ‹^Y› | Moves the cursor to the previous page of text |

**IN-CHAPTER EXERCISES**

**5.1.** After finishing Step 8 in Practice Session 5.1, what did you see on the screen?

**5.2.** Edit the file named linespaced that you created in Practice Session 5.1, and use the appropriate keystroke commands to position the cursor at the beginning and ending character of each line of text. Use the <^C> command to locate each character position as you use the cursor movement commands. How many characters are in the file? The beginning of each line is what percent of the total file?

## 5.2.4 Cutting, Pasting and Searching

A useful function to have in even a basic text editor is the ability to cut and paste sections of text. In `pico`, to cut a section of text out and paste it back in at another location, you must do the following.

1. Mark the beginning of the text section that you want to cut out by holding down the <Ctrl> key and *both* the <Shift> and <6> keys at the same time. Note that the boundary of the selected text will start at the left edge of the current character under the cursor.
2. Then move the cursor (using the <arrow> keys on the keyboard) to a point *one character beyond* the end of the text you want to cut out. Note that the selected text will end at the left edge of the current character under the cursor, thus leaving that character out of the selection.
3. Hold down the <Ctrl> and <K> keys at the same time to cut out the marked text.
4. Use the <arrow> keys to move the cursor to where you want to insert the text that you just cut. Hold down the <Ctrl> and <U> keys at the same time to paste in the text after the cursor location.

Practice Session 5.2 lets you edit the file that you created in Practice Session 5.1 by using the commands presented in the preceding list.

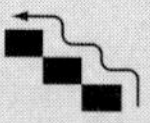

**Practice Session 5.2**

**Step 1:** At the shell prompt, type **`pico linespaced`** and press <Enter>. The line-spaced file you created in Practice Session 5.1 appears in the `pico` screen.

**Step 2:** Position the cursor at the beginning of the fourth line, at the character `T` in the word `This`, using the <arrow> keys on the keyboard.

### Practice Session 5.2 (cont.)

**Step 3:** Hold down the <Ctrl> and both the <Shift> and <6> keys at the same time.

**Step 4:** Move the cursor with the <right arrow> key on the keyboard until you have highlighted the entire fourth line, including the period. The cursor should be one character to the right of the period at the end of the line.

**Step 5:** Hold down the <Ctrl> and <K> keys at the same time. This action cuts the line of text out of the current "buffer," or file that you are working on.

**Step 6:** Position the cursor with the <arrow> keys at the beginning of the second line of the file, directly under the line that reads `This is text that I have entered on a line in the` **`pico`** `editor.`

**Step 7:** Hold down the <Ctrl> and <U> keys at the same time. This action pastes the former fourth line into the second line of the file.

**Step 8:** Use the <arrow> keys on the keyboard to position the cursor at the third line of the file.

**Step 9:** Hold down the <Ctrl> and <U> keys on the keyboard at the same time. This action pastes the former fourth line into the third line of the file.

**Step 10:** Now change the wording of lines 2 and 3 so that they read as shown in Figure 5.3. How many lines are there in this file now, as far as `pico` is concerned?

**Step 11:** Hold down the <Ctrl> and <O> keys at the same time.

**Step 12:** At the prompt `File Name to Write:` type **`linespaced2`** and press <Enter>.

**Step 13:** Hold down the <Ctrl> and <X> keys at the same time to return to the shell prompt.

**Step 14:** At the shell prompt, type **`more linespaced2`** and press <Enter>. What do you see on screen? How many lines does the `more` command show in this file?

To get some further practice with `pico`, do Problems 1 through 3 at the end of this chapter.

## 5.3 OBTAINING MORE CONTROL BY USING THE `vi` EDITOR

The `vi` LINUX text editor has almost all the features of a word processor and tremendous flexibility in creating text files. It is significantly more complex than `pico`, but it gives you the ability to work on much larger files.

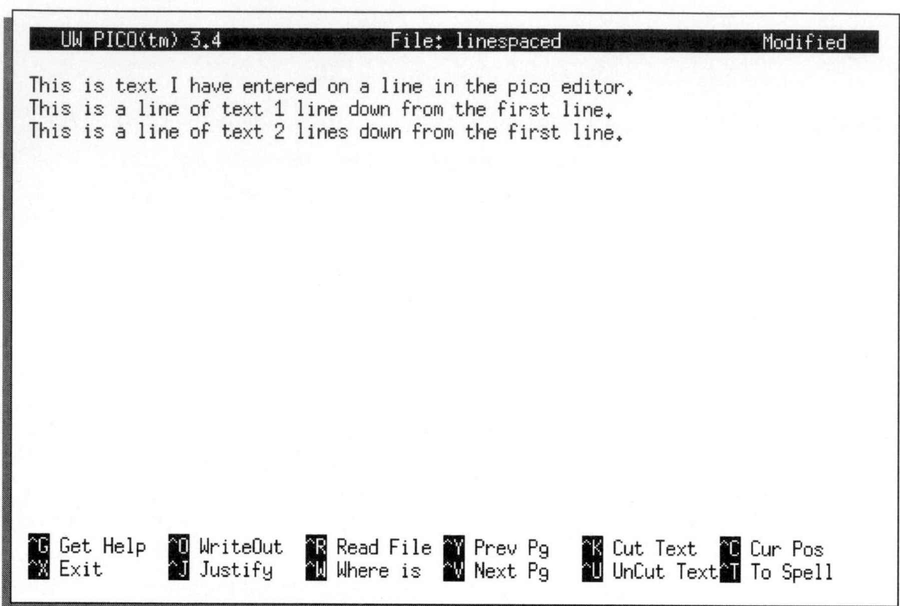


**Figure 5.3** Cut and pasted linespaced text in `pico`

As we mentioned in Section 5.1, the notion of a buffer as a temporary storage facility for the text that you are editing is very useful and important in **vi**. The **main buffer**, sometimes referred to as the *editing buffer*, or the *work buffer*, is the main repository for the body of text that you are trying to create or to modify from some previous permanently archived file on disc. The **general purpose buffer** is where your most recent "ripped-out" (cut/copied text) is retained. **Indexed buffers** allow you to store more than one temporary string of text.

### 5.3.1 Shell Script File

Example: **vi** Text Editor shows how to create a *script* file, or collection of LINUX commands that are executed in sequence, and then execute the script. We present more about shell programming and script files in Chapters 15 through 18. For this example, we assume that you are running Bash. If you are running some other shell by default, go back to Chapter 4 and review how to identify and change shells. And don't worry too much if you mess up in Steps 2, 3, and 4; you can go through the rest of the script file discussion and then come back to this example after you've learned some of the editing commands.

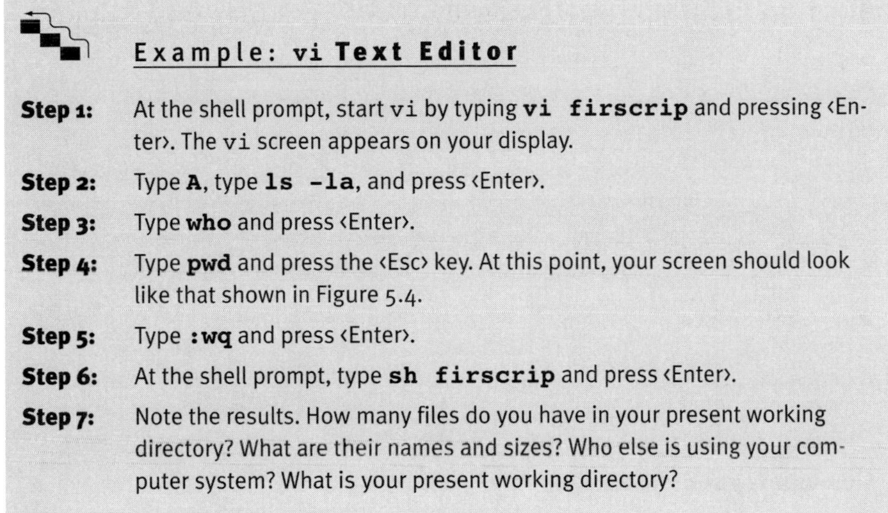

## Example: vi Text Editor

**Step 1:** At the shell prompt, start `vi` by typing **`vi firscrip`** and pressing ‹Enter›. The `vi` screen appears on your display.

**Step 2:** Type **`A`**, type **`ls -la`**, and press ‹Enter›.

**Step 3:** Type **`who`** and press ‹Enter›.

**Step 4:** Type **`pwd`** and press the ‹Esc› key. At this point, your screen should look like that shown in Figure 5.4.

**Step 5:** Type **`:wq`** and press ‹Enter›.

**Step 6:** At the shell prompt, type **`sh firscrip`** and press ‹Enter›.

**Step 7:** Note the results. How many files do you have in your present working directory? What are their names and sizes? Who else is using your computer system? What is your present working directory?

**Figure 5.4** LINUX vi screen with example script file

## 5.3.2 How to Start, Save a File, and Exit

When you need to do LINUX text editing that gives you as much functionality as a typical word processor, you can use the `vi` text editor. To start `vi` from the command line, use the following general syntax.

Syntax:

**vi [options] [file(s)]**

**Purpose:** Allows you to edit a new or existing text file(s)

**Output:** With no options or file(s) specified, you are placed in the vi program and can begin to edit a new buffer.

**Commonly used options/features:**

| | |
|---|---|
| **+n** | Begin to edit file(s) starting at line *n*. |
| **+/exp** | Begin to edit at the first line in the file matching string *exp*. |

The operations that you perform in `vi` fall into two general categories: **Command mode operations**, which consist of key sequences that are commands to the editor to take certain actions, and **Insert mode operations**, which allow you to input text. The general organization of the `vi` text editor and how to switch modes are illustrated in Figure 5.5. For example, to change from the command mode, which you are in when you first enter the editor, to the insert mode, type a valid command, such as <A>, to append text at the end of the current line. Certain commands that are prefixed with the **:** , **/**, **?**, or **:!** characters, are echoed or shown to you on the last line on the screen and must be terminated by pressing <Enter>. To change from Insert mode to Command mode, press the <Esc> key. The keystroke commands that you execute in `vi` are case-sensitive—for example, uppercase <A> appends new text after the last character at the end of the current line, whereas lowercase <a> appends new text after the character the cursor is on.

In Example: `vi` Text Editor, at Step 2, typing <A> took `vi` out of Command mode (which is what `vi` starts in by default) and placed it in one of the forms of Insert mode. In other words, anything that you typed at the keyboard was appended as text on the first line in the text area of the editor. When you pressed the <Esc> key in Step 4, `vi` was taken out of the Insert mode and was put back into Command

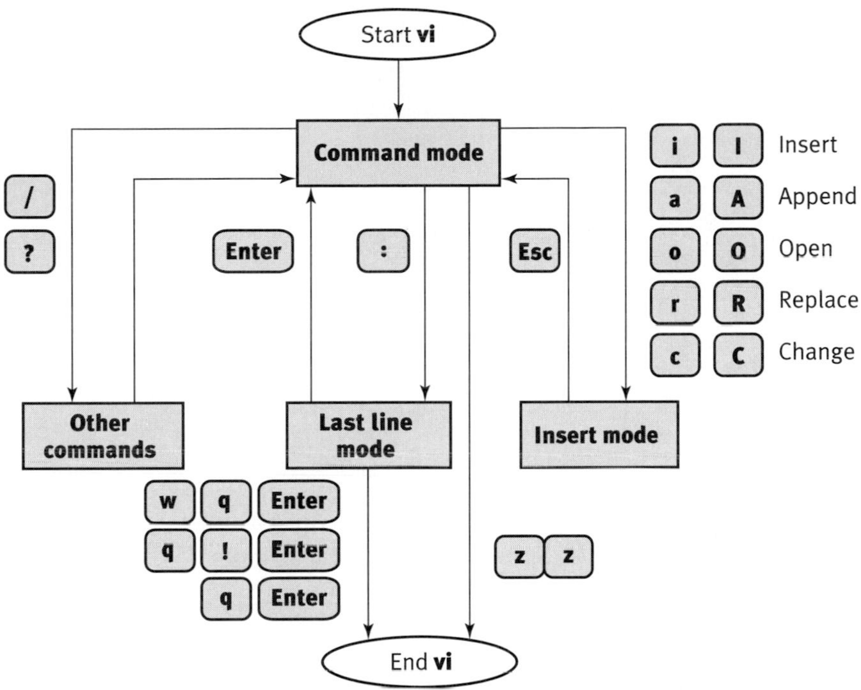


Figure 5.5 Operating modes of the `vi` text editor

mode. When you typed **:** in Step 5, it was a valid command mode prefix character for the two commands that followed. When you typed **wq** after the **:**, `vi` interpreted those commands as write out or save the file, and quit the editor.

To start `vi`, at the shell prompt, type **vi** and press <Enter>. The `vi` display appears on your screen, as shown in Figure 5.6. You are now in the Command mode. To enter Insert mode, type **A**; you are now able to insert text on the first line of the file. After entering text, you can press the <Esc> key to enter Command mode. From Command mode, you can save the text that you just inserted to a file on disk by typing **:w filename** and pressing <Enter>, where filename is the name of the file you want to save the text to. To quit the editor, type **:q**.

## 5.3.3 The Format of a vi Command and the Modes of Operation

In either Command or the Insert mode, the generic syntax of keystrokes is

**[#1] operation [#2] target**

**Figure 5.6** The `vi` start-up screen

where

anything enclosed in **[ ]** is optional;

**#1** is an optional number, such as 5, specifying how many operations are to be done;

**operation** is what you want to accomplish, such as deleting lines of text;

**#2** is an optional number, such as 5, specifying how many targets are affected by the operation; and

**target** is the text that you want to do the operation on, such as an entire line of text.

Note that, if the current line is the target of the operation, the syntax for specifying the target is the same as the syntax of the operation—for example **dd** deletes the current line. Also, a variation on this generic syntax are cursor movement commands, whereby you can omit the numbers and operation and simply move the cursor by word, sentence, paragraph, or section. Table 5.4 lists some specific examples of this generic syntax and variations used in both Command and Insert modes.

**Table 5.4** Examples of `vi` Command Syntax

| Command | Action |
|---|---|
| `5dw` | Deletes five words, starting at the current cursor position |
| `7dd` | Deletes seven lines, starting at the current line |
| `7o` | Opens seven blank lines after the current line |
| `7O` | Opens seven blank lines before the current line |
| `c2b` | Changes back two words |
| `d7,14` | Deletes lines 7 through 14 in the buffer |
| `1G` | Puts the cursor on the first line of the file |
| `10yy` | Yanks (copies) the next (starting with the current line) 10 lines into a temporary buffer |

As we stated previously, you enter **`vi`** in command mode. When you want to use Insert Mode instead of command mode, press a valid key to accomplish the change. Some of these keys are shown in Table 5.5.

After inserting text, you can edit the text, move the cursor to a new position in the buffer, and save the buffer and exit the editor, all from within Command mode. When you want to change from Insert mode to Command mode, press the <Esc> key. The general commands that are useful in Command mode are shown in Table 5.6, with those executed from the status line prefaced with a colon(**:**).

**Table 5.5** Important Keys for the Insert Mode

| Key | Action |
|---|---|
| <a> | Appends text after the character the cursor is on |
| <A> | Appends text after the last character of the current line |
| <c> | Begins a change operation, allowing you to modify text |
| <C> | Changes from the cursor position to the end of the current line |
| <i> | Inserts text before the character the cursor is on |
| <I> | Inserts text at the beginning of the current line |
| <o> | Opens a blank line below the current line and puts the cursor on that line |
| <O> | Opens a blank line above the current line and puts the cursor on that line |
| <R> | Begins overwriting text |
| <s> | Substitutes single characters |
| <S> | Substitutes whole lines |

**Table 5.6** Important Commands for the Command Mode

| Command | Action |
|---|---|
| `d` | Deletes words, lines, etc. |
| `u` | Undoes the last edit |
| `p` | Pastes (inserts) the yanked or deleted line(s) after the current line |
| `P` | Pastes (inserts) the yanked or deleted line(s) before the current line |
| `:r filename` | Reads and inserts the contents of the file filename at the current cursor position |
| `:q!` | Quits `vi` without saving the buffer |
| `:wq` | Saves the buffer and quits |
| `:w filename` | Saves the current buffer to filename |
| `:w! filename` | Overwrites filename with the current text |
| `ZZ` | Quits `vi`, saving the file only if changes were made since the last save |

Practice Session 5.3 lets you continue editing the file you created in Practice Session 5.1 by using the commands presented in Tables 5.5 and 5.6.

## Practice Session 5.3

**Step 1:** At the shell prompt, type **`vi firstvi`** and press <Enter>.

**Step 2:** Type **`A`**, type **`This is the first line of a vi file`**, and press <Enter>.

**Step 3:** Type **`This is the line of a vi file`** and press <Enter>.

**Step 4:** Type **`is the 3r line of a vi`**.

**Step 5:** Press the <Esc> key.

**Step 6:** Type **`:w`** and press <Enter>. Your screen display should look similar to Figure 5.7.

**Step 7:** Use the <arrow> keys to position the cursor on the character `l` in the word line on the second line of the file.

**Step 8:** Type **`i`** and then **`2nd_`**.

**Step 9:** Press the <Esc> key.

## Practice Session 5.3 (cont.)

**Step 10:** Use the <arrow> keys to position the cursor anywhere on the third line of the file.

**Step 11:** Type **`I`** and then **`This_`**.

**Step 12:** Press the <Esc> key.

**Step 13:** Use the <arrow> keys to position the cursor on the character `r` in `3r` on this line.

**Step 14:** Type **`a`** and then **`d`**.

**Step 15:** Press the <Esc> key.

**Step 16:** Type **`A`** and then **`_file`**.

**Step 17:** Press the <Esc> key on the keyboard. Your screen display should look similar to Figure 5.8.

**Step 18:** Type **`:wq`** to return to the shell prompt.

```
This is the first line of a vi file.
This is the line of a vi file.
is the 3r line of a vi
~
~
~
~
~
~
~
~
~
~
~
~
~
~
~
~
~
~
~
~
"firstvi" 3 lines, 91 characters written
```

**Figure 5.7** Saved file firstvi

```
This is the first line of a vi file.
This is the 2nd line of a vi file.
This is the 3rd line of a vi file.
~
~
~
~
~
~
~
~
~
~
~
~
~
~
~
~
~
~
~
~
```

Figure 5.8 Final form of file firstvi

The following In-Chapter Exercises ask you to apply some of the operations you learned about in the previous Practice Sessions.

**IN-CHAPTER EXERCISES**

**5.3.** With `vi` you begin editing a file that you created yesterday. You want to save a copy of it with a different filename while still in `vi`, but you don't want to quit this editing session. How do you accomplish this result in `vi`?

**5.4.** What happens if you accomplish five operations in `vi` and then type **5u** when in command mode?

## 5.3.4 Cursor Movement and Editing Commands

In Command mode several commands accomplish cursor movement and text editing tasks. Table 5.7 lists important cursor movement and keyboard editing commands. As we've already shown, character-at-a-time or line-at-a-time moves of the cursor can be accomplished easily with the <arrow> keys.

**Table 5.7** Cursor Movement and Keyboard Editing Commands

| Command | Action |
|---|---|
| ‹1G› | Moves the cursor to the first line of the file |
| ‹G› | Moves the cursor to the last line of the file |
| ‹0› (zero) | Moves the cursor to the first character of the current line |
| ‹Ctrl-G› | Reports the position of the cursor in terms of line number and column number |
| ‹$› | Moves the cursor to the last character of the current line |
| ‹w› | Moves the cursor forward one word at a time |
| ‹b› | Moves the cursor backward one word at a time |
| ‹x› | Deletes the character at the cursor position |
| ‹dd› | Deletes the line at the current cursor position |
| ‹u› | Undoes the most recent change |
| ‹r› | Replaces the character at the current cursor location with what is typed next |

Practice Session 5.4 lets you continue editing the file you created in Practice Session 5.1 by using commands presented in Table 5.7.

## Practice Session 5.4

**Step 1:** At the shell prompt, type `vi firstvi`, and press ‹Enter›.

**Step 2:** Type **G**. The cursor moves to the last line of the file.

**Step 3:** Hold down the ‹Ctrl› and ‹G› keys at the same time. On the last line of the screen display, `vi` reports the following: `"firstvi" line 3 of 3 --100%-- col 1`. This is a report of the buffer that you are editing, the current line number, the total number of lines in the buffer, the percentage of the buffer that this line represents, and the current column position of the cursor.

**Step 4:** Type **o**. A new line opens below the third line of the file.

**Step 5:** Type **`This is the 5th line of a vi file.`**

**Step 6:** Type **0** (zero). The cursor moves to the first character of the line you just typed in.

**Step 7:** Type **$**. The cursor moves to the last character of the current line.

**Step 8:** Type **O**. A new line opens above the current fourth line.

**Step 9:** Type **`This is the 44th line of a va file.`**

**Step 10:** Use the ‹arrow› keys to position the cursor over the first 4 in 44 on this line.

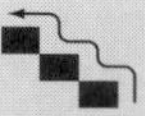

### Practice Session 5.4 (cont.)

**Step 11:** Type **x**.

**Step 12:** Use the <arrow> keys to position the cursor over the a in va on this line.

**Step 13:** Type **r** and then type **i**.

**Step 14:** Type **dd**.

**Step 15:** Type **:wq** to go back to the shell prompt.

**Step 16:** At the shell prompt, type **more firstvi** and press <Enter>.

How many lines with text on them does more show in this file?

## 5.3.5 Yank and Put (Copy and Paste) and Substitute (Search and Replace)

Every word processor is capable of copying and pasting text as well as searching for old text and replacing it with new text. Copying and pasting are accomplished with the vi commands **yank** and **put**. In general, you use **yank** and **put** in sequence and move the cursor (with any of the cursor movement commands) only between yanking and putting. Some examples of the syntax for **yank** and **put** are given in Table 5.8.

The simple vi form of search and replace are accomplished using the **substitute** command. This command is executed from the last line of the screen

**Table 5.8** Examples of the Syntax for the yank and put Commands

| Command Syntax | What It Accomplishes |
|---|---|
| y2W | Yanks two words, starting at the current cursor position, going to the right |
| 4yb | Yanks four words, starting at the current cursor position, going to the left |
| yy or Y | Yanks the current line |
| p (lowercase) | Puts the yanked text after the current cursor position |
| P (uppercase) | Puts the yanked text before the current cursor position |
| 5p | Puts the yanked text in the buffer five times after the current cursor position |

display, where you preface the command with a colon (**:**) and terminate the command by pressing <Enter>. The format of the `substitute` command as it is typed on the status line is

**:[range]s/old_string/new_string[/option]**

where

anything enclosed in **[ ]** is not mandatory;

**:** is the colon prefix for the status line command;

**range** is a valid specification of lines in the buffer (if omitted, the current line is the range);

**s** is the syntax of the substitute command;

**/** is a delimiter for searching;

**old_string** is the text you want to replace;

**/** is a delimiter for replacement;

**new_string** is the new text; and

/option is a modifier, usually g for global, to the command.

Note that the grammar of `old_string` and `new_string` can be extremely explicit and complex, and takes the form of a **regular expression**. (We present more information on the formation of regular expressions in Chapter 10.) Some examples of the syntax for the `substitute` command are given in Table 5.9.

Practice Session 5.5 shows you how to use the `vi` commands `yank` and `put` to copy and paste. It also allows you to do individual and multiple searches and replace text with the `vi substitute` command.

**Table 5.9** Examples of the Syntax for the `substitute` Command

| Command Syntax | What It Accomplishes |
|---|---|
| `:s/john/jane/` | Substitutes the word *jane* for the word *john* on the current line, only once |
| `:s/john/jane/g` | Substitutes the word *jane* for every word *john* on the current line |
| `:1,10s/big/small/g` | Substitutes the word *small* for every word *big* on lines 1–10 |
| `:1,$s/men/women/g` | Substitutes the word *women* for every word *men* in the entire file |

Practice Session 5.5 lets you create a new text file and manipulate the text in it using the commands and operations presented in Tables 5.8 and 5.9.

## Practice Session 5.5

**Step 1:** At the shell prompt, type **`vi multiline`** and press <Enter>.

**Step 2:** Type **`A`** and then type **`Windows is the operating system of choice for everyone.`**

**Step 3:** Press the <Esc> key. You have left the insert mode and are now in the command mode.

**Step 4:** Press the <0> (zero) key. The cursor moves to the first character of the first line.

**Step 5:** Type **`yy`**. This action yanks, or copies, the first line to a special buffer.

**Step 6:** Type **`7p`**. This action puts, or pastes, the first line seven times, creating seven new lines of text containing the same text as the first line. The cursor should now be on the first character of the eighth line.

**Step 7:** Type **`1G`**. This action puts the cursor on the first character of the first line in the buffer.

**Step 8:** Hold down the <Shift> and <;> keys at the same time. Doing so places a colon (**`:`**) in the status line at the bottom of the `vi` screen display, allowing you to type a command.

**Step 9:** Type **`s/everyone/students/`** and press <Enter>. The word `everyone` at the end of the first line is replaced with the word `students`.

**Step 10:** Use the <arrow> key to position the cursor on the first character of the second line.

**Step 11:** Type **`:s/everyone/computer scientists/`** and press <Enter>.

**Step 12:** Repeat Steps 8 through 10 on the third through eighth lines of the buffer, substituting the words `engineers`, `system administrators`, `web servers`, `scientists`, `networking`, and `mathematicians` for the word `everyone` on each of those six lines.

**Step 13:** Type **`:1,$s/Windows/LINUX/g`** and press <Enter>. You have globally replaced the word `Windows` on all eight lines of the file with the word `LINUX`. Correct?

To get some further practice with **`vi`**, do Problems 8 through 11 at the end of this chapter.

### 5.3.6 SETTING THE vi ENVIRONMENT

You can use any of several environment options to customize the behavior of the **vi** editor. These options include specifying maximum line length and automatically wrapping the cursor to the next line, displaying line numbers as you edit a file, and displaying the mode that **vi** is in at any time. You can use full or abbreviated names for most of the options. Some of the most important and useful options are summarized in Table 5.10.

You can set these options by using the the **:set** command (i.e., using the **set** command in the Last Line Mode). Thus, after the **:set shomode** command has been executed, **vi** displays the current mode at the right bottom of the screen. Similarly, after the **:set nu** command has been executed, **vi** displays the line numbers for all the lines in the file. When the **:set ai** command has been executed, the next line is aligned with the beginning of the previous line. This useful feature allows you to easily indent source codes that you compose with **vi**. Pressing <^D> on a new line moves the cursor to the previous indentation level.

When you set the environment options within a **vi** session, the options are set for that session only. If you want to customize your environment permanently, you need to put your options in the .exrc file in your home directory. You can use the set command to set one or more options in the .exrc file as in

```
$ cat .exrc
set wm=5 shm nu ic
$
```

The wm=5 option sets the wrap margin to 5. That is, each line will be up to 75 characters long. The **ic** option allows you to search for strings without regard to the

**Table 5.10** Important Environment Options for vi

| Option | Abbreviation | Purpose |
|---|---|---|
| **autoindent** | **ai** | Aligns the new line with the beginning of the previous line |
| **ignorecase** | **ic** | Ignores the case of a letter during the search process (with a / or the ? command) |
| **number** | **nu** | Displays line numbers when a file is being edited; line numbers are not saved as part of the file |
| **scroll** | | Sets the number of lines to scroll when the ^D command is used to scroll the vi screen up |
| **showmode** | **smd** | Displays the current vi mode in the bottom right corner of the screen |
| **wrapmargin** | **wm** | Sets the wrap margin in terms of the number of characters from the end of the line, assuming a line length of 80 characters |

case of a character. Thus, after this option has been set, the `/Hello/` command searches for strings hello and Hello.

### 5.3.7 Executing Shell Commands from Within vi

At times you will want to execute a shell command and wish that you could do it without quitting `vi` and then restarting it. You can do so in Command Mode by preceding the command with **`:!`**. Thus, for example, typing **`:! pwd`** would display the pathname of your current directory, and typing **`:! ls`** would display the names of all the files in your current directory. After executing a shell command, `vi` returns to its Command Mode.

## 5.4 GETTING MAXIMUM CONTROL BY USING THE emacs EDITOR

The **`emacs`** editor is the most complex and customizable of the LINUX text editors, and it gives you the most freedom, flexibility, and control over the way that you edit text files. But along with that freedom a more complex command structure.

Some terms common to both **`vi`** and **`emacs`** *do not* have the same meaning. For example, **`emacs`** has major modes of operation, such as LISP Mode and C Mode, but they are for formatting text rather than allowing you to switch between actions in the editor, as do **`vi`** Command and Insert modes. The keystroke command syntax itself in **`emacs`** is different and more complex than in **`vi`**, involving prefix characters. The **`emacs`** concepts of *point* and *cursor location* are also more refined and specific than in **`vi`**. In **`emacs`** the point is the location in the buffer where you are currently doing your editing; the point is assumed to be at the left edge of the cursor, or always between characters or white space (what you enter into a text file when you press the space bar). This difference becomes an important issue when you want to use the cut/copy/paste operations. In **`vi`** *yanking* removes text from the main buffer, or cutting/copying, whereas in **`emacs`** *yanking* is more like pasting into the main buffer. The notion of a buffer is exactly the same in **`emacs`** as it is in **`vi`**.

### 5.4.1 DOS Aliases

The following example shows how to create a file to define aliases, or command name substitutes, that allow you to type DOS command names at the LINUX shell prompt to execute some of the common LINUX file maintenance operations you learned in Chapter 3. Again, as in the example in Section 5.3, we assume that you are running the Bash; if you are running another shell, review Chapter 4 to find out how to change shells. In Problem 8 at the end of this chapter, we ask you to insert this file at the end of your .bashrc file so that, at login, these DOS aliased commands will be available. (See Chapters 3 and 4 to review your environment and shell setups.)

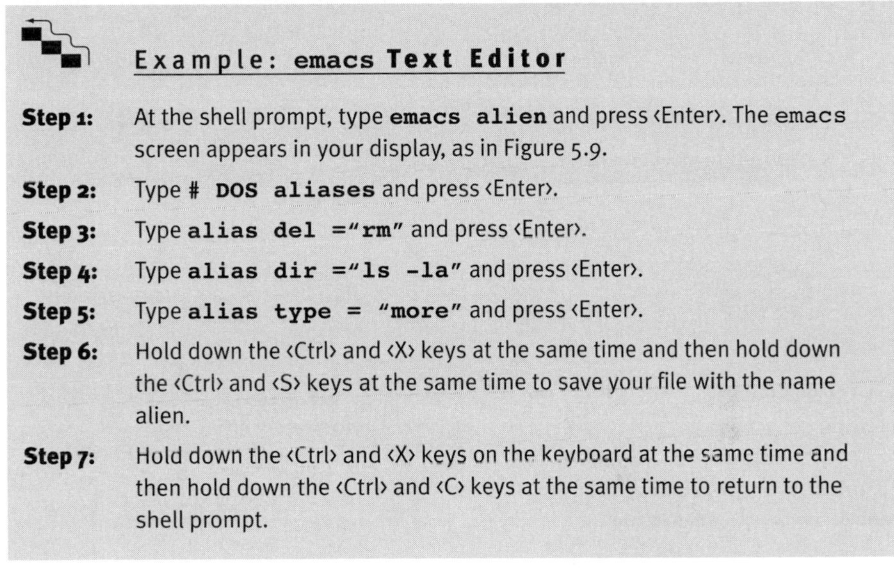

### Example: emacs **Text Editor**

**Step 1:** At the shell prompt, type **`emacs alien`** and press ‹Enter›. The emacs screen appears in your display, as in Figure 5.9.

**Step 2:** Type **`# DOS aliases`** and press ‹Enter›.

**Step 3:** Type **`alias del ="rm"`** and press ‹Enter›.

**Step 4:** Type **`alias dir ="ls -la"`** and press ‹Enter›.

**Step 5:** Type **`alias type = "more"`** and press ‹Enter›.

**Step 6:** Hold down the ‹Ctrl› and ‹X› keys at the same time and then hold down the ‹Ctrl› and ‹S› keys at the same time to save your file with the name alien.

**Step 7:** Hold down the ‹Ctrl› and ‹X› keys on the keyboard at the same time and then hold down the ‹Ctrl› and ‹C› keys at the same time to return to the shell prompt.

**Figure 5.9** First emacs screen display

## 5.4.2 How to Start, Save a File, and Exit

As we previously stated, **emacs** has the most functions and features, and is the most customizable, of the LINUX text editors. To start **emacs** from the command line, use the following general syntax.

Syntax:

**emacs [options] [file(s)]**

**Purpose:** Allows you to edit a new or existing text file(s)

**Output:** With no options or file(s) specified, you are placed in the **emacs** program and begin to edit a new buffer.

**Commonly used options / features:**

| | |
|---|---|
| **+n** | Begin to edit file(s) starting at line number **n**. |
| **-nw** | Run without opening a window, which is useful in a GUI environment. |

The emacs Editor is a full-screen display editor, with which you use keystroke commands prefixed with either the <Ctrl> key or a "META" key—in our case the <Esc> key. The typical screen is composed of a large text entry area, wherein you can type text immediately, and a small area at the bottom of the screen, known as the *mode line*, where editor information and prompts are displayed. (See Figure 5.9.) The most important commands in **emacs** are listed in Table 5.11.

**Table 5.11** Important emacs Commands

| Command | Action |
|---|---|
| <Ctrl-X>+<Ctrl-C> | Exits emacs |
| <Ctrl-G> | Cancels the current command or command operations |
| <Ctrl-X>+<Ctrl-W> | Saves a buffer that has never been saved before |
| <Ctrl-X>+<Ctrl-S> | Saves the buffer |
| <Ctrl-X>+<U> | Undoes the last edit and can be used multiple times if necessary |
| <Ctrl-H> | Gets Help documentation |
| <Ctrl-X I> | Inserts text from a file at the current cursor position |
| <Ctrl-X 1> | Deletes all windows but this one (useful in Help documentation) |

**Table 5.12** Important **emacs** Cursor Movement and Editing Commands

| Command | Action |
|---|---|
| ‹Esc-‹› | Moves cursor to the beginning of the buffer |
| ‹Esc-›› | Moves cursor to the end of the buffer |
| ‹Ctrl-A› | Moves cursor to the beginning of the current line |
| ‹Ctrl-E› | Moves cursor to the end of the current line |
| ‹Esc-F› | Moves cursor forward one word at a time |
| ‹Esc-B› | Moves cursor backward one word at a time |
| ‹Ctrl-D› | Deletes the character at the cursor |
| ‹Esc-D› | Deletes the word at the cursor |
| ‹Esc-Delete› | Deletes the word before the cursor |
| ‹Ctrl-K› | Deletes from the cursor to the end of the current line |
| ‹Ctrl-Y› | Puts back into the buffer what has been deleted |

### 5.4.3 Cursor Movement and Editing Commands

In addition to general-purpose commands, **emacs** has some important cursor movement and editing commands that allow you to move quickly and easily around the text and to make changes. These commands are listed in Table 5.12.

Practice Session 5.6 lets you create a new text file by using the commands presented in Tables 5.11 and 5.12.

#### Practice Session 5.6

**Step 1:** At the shell prompt, type **emacs alien** and press ‹Enter›. The file that you created in the example at the beginning of this section is loaded into the buffer, and your screen display should look similar to the one shown in Figure 5.10 .

**Step 2:** Using the ‹arrow› keys, position the cursor to the right of the quote (") character at the end of the third line.

**Step 3:** Press ‹Enter›.

**Step 4:** Type **alice dir/w= "ls"**

**Step 5:** Hold down the ‹Ctrl› and ‹A› keys at the same time. The cursor moves to the beginning of the line.

**Step 6:** Hold down the ‹Esc› and ‹D› keys at the same time. The word `alice` has been cut from the buffer.

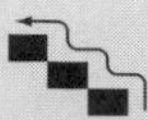

## Practice Session 5.6 (cont.)

**Step 7:** Type **alias**.

**Step 8:** Hold down the ‹Esc› and ‹B› keys at the same time. The cursor moves to the beginning of the word alias.

**Step 9:** Position the cursor with the arrow keys on the keyboard at the beginning of the first blank line, below the line that reads alias type =**"more"**.

**Step 10:** Hold down the ‹Ctrl› and ‹Y› keys at the same time. The cut word alice has been put back into the buffer at the start of the line.

**Step 11:** Use the ‹arrow› keys to position the cursor at the end of the word alice if it is not there already.

**Step 12:** Use the ‹Delete› or ‹Back Space› key to delete the letters *c* and *e* from the word alice.

**Step 13:** Type **as copy ="cp"**.

**Step 14:** Hold down the ‹Ctrl› and ‹X› keys at the same time and then hold down the ‹Ctrl› and ‹W› keys at the same time.

**Step 15:** At the Write file: prompt, erase anything on the line with the ‹Back Space› key, type **~/alien2**, and press ‹Enter›. Your screen display should now look similar to the one shown in Figure 5.11.

**Step 16:** Hold down the ‹Ctrl› and ‹H› keys at the same time and then press the **A** key. The minibuffer area shows a prompt for you to obtain Help. Hold down the ‹Ctrl› and ‹G› keys at the same time. Doing so cancels your Help request.

**Step 17:** Hold down the ‹Ctrl› and ‹X› keys at the same time and then hold down the ‹Ctrl› and ‹C› keys at the same time to quit emacs and return to the shell prompt.

### 5.4.4 Keyboard Macros

The emacs text editor contains a simple function that allows you to define **keyboard macros**, or collections of keystrokes that can be recorded and then accessed at any time. This capability allows you to define repetitive multiple keystroke operations as a single command and then execute that command at any time—as many times as you want. The keystrokes may include emacs commands and other keyboard keys. A macro may also be saved with a name, or even be saved to a file, for use during subsequent emacs editing sessions. Table 5.13 shows a list of some of the most important keyboard macro commands.

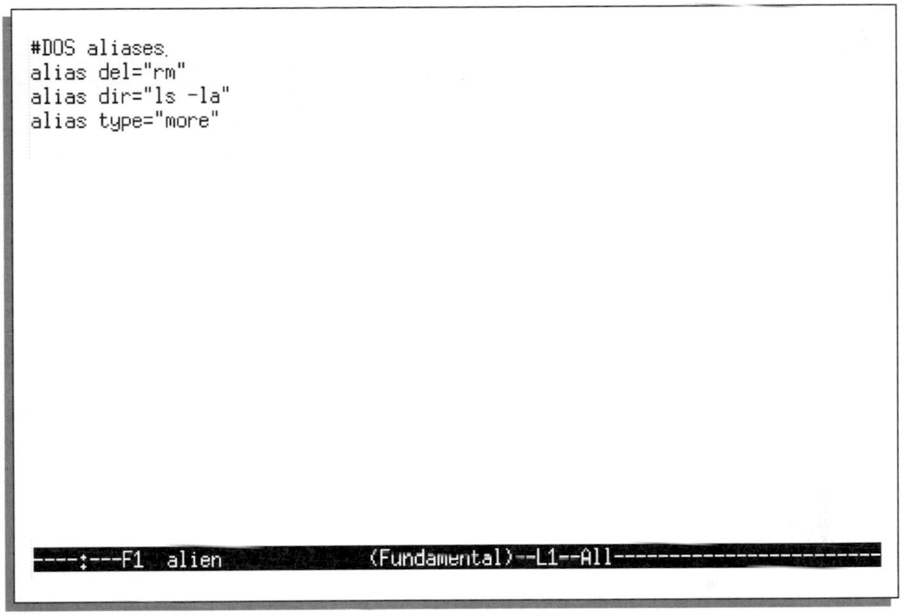

```
#DOS aliases
alias del="rm"
alias dir="ls -la"
alias type="more"

----:---F1  alien            (Fundamental)--L1--All-----------------------
```

**Figure 5.10** The emacs display of the file alien

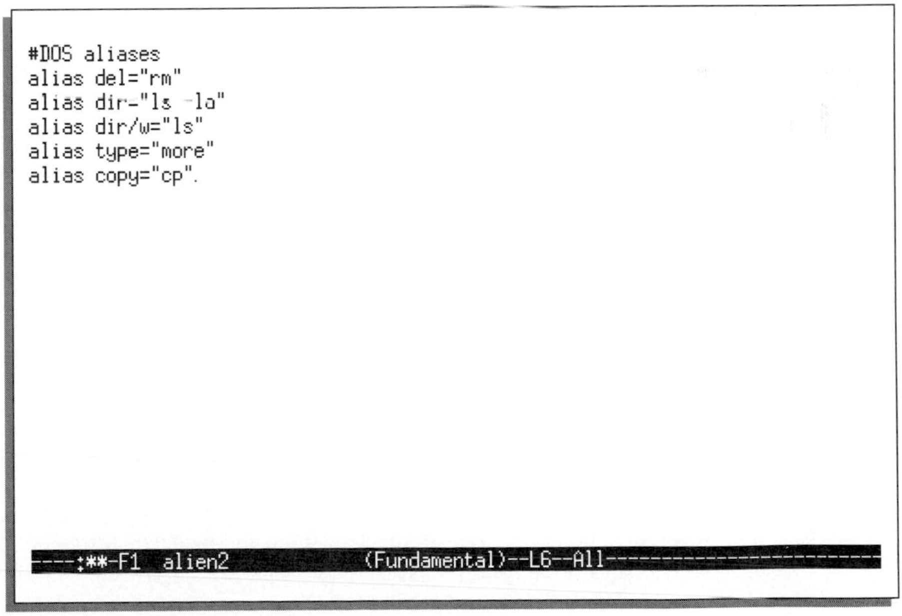

```
#DOS aliases
alias del="rm"
alias dir="ls -la"
alias dir/w="ls"
alias type="more"
alias copy="cp"

----:**-F1  alien2           (Fundamental)--L6--All-----------------------
```

**Figure 5.11** The file alien2 after the buffer contents have been saved

**Table 5.13** Important Keyboard Macro Commands

| Keystrokes | Action |
|---|---|
| <Ctrl-X (> | Begins the macro definition |
| <Ctrl-X )> | Ends the macro definition |
| <Ctrl-X E> | Executes the last keyboard macro defined |
| <Esc-X name-last-kyd-macro Enter> | Names the last macro created |
| <Esc-X name> | Repeats the named macro name |

Practice Session 5.7 lets you create a new text file using the commands presented in Table 5.13.

## Practice Session 5.7

**Step 1:** At the shell prompt, type **`emacs datafile`** and press <Enter>. The `emacs` screen appears on your display.

**Step 2:** Hold down the <Ctrl> and <X> keys on the keyboard at the same time and then hold down the <Shift> and <9> keys at the same time. These actions begin your keyboard macro definition. If you make a mistake anywhere in subsequent steps, simply hold down the <Ctrl> and <G> keys at the same time to cancel the current macro definition.

**Step 3:** Type **`1 2 3 4 5 6 7 8 9 10`** and press <Enter>.

**Step 4:** Hold down the <Ctrl> and <X> keys at the same time and then hold down the <Shift> and <0> (zero) keys at the same time. These actions end your macro definition.

**Step 5:** Hold down the <Ctrl> and <X> keys at the same time and then press the <E> key. Doing so replays the macro that you just defined, placing another line of the numbers 1–10 in the buffer.

**Step 6:** Repeat Step 5 eight more times so that your display looks similar to that shown in Figure 5.12.

**Step 7:** Hold down the <Ctrl> and <X> keys at the same time and then hold down the <Ctrl> and <S> keys at the same time. These actions save the buffer to the file datafile.

**Step 8:** Hold down the <Ctrl> and <X> keys at the same time and then hold down the <Ctrl> and <C> keys at the same time to exit from `emacs`.

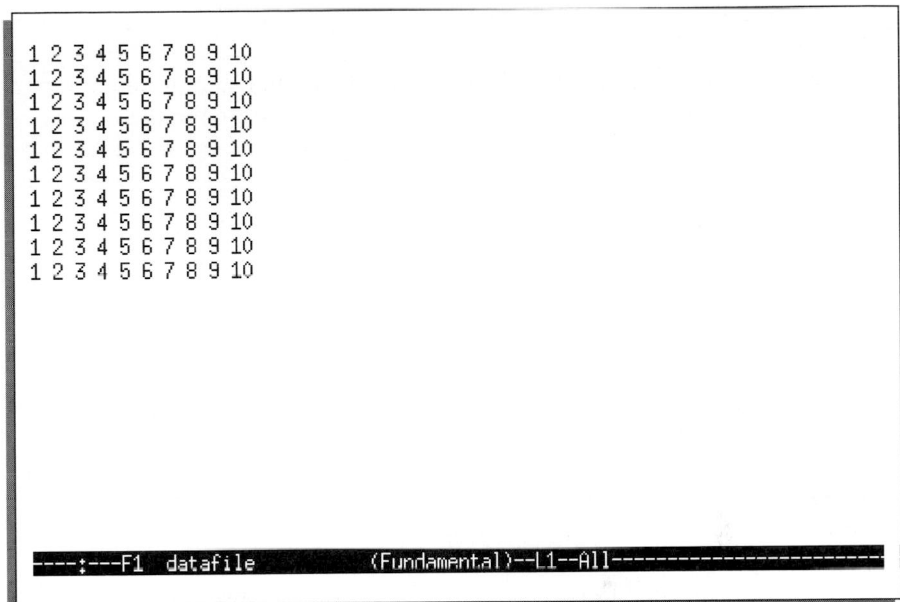


**Figure 5.12** The file datafile with 10 rows of data

## 5.4.5 Cut or Copy and Paste and Search and Replace

As we mentioned previously, every word processor has the capability to cut or copy text and then paste that text back into the document, and to search for old text and replace it with new text. Because `emacs` operations are text-activated, whereby you use sequences of keystrokes to execute commands, cutting or copying and pasting are fairly complex operations. They are accomplished with the **Kill Ring**, whereby text is held in a buffer by killing it and is then restored to the document at the desired position by yanking it. Global search and replace are somewhat less complex and are accomplished by either an unconditional replacement or an interactive replacement.

The **Mark** is simply a placeholder in the buffer. For example, to cut three words from a document and then paste them back at another position, move Point before the first word you want to cut and press <Esc-D> three times. The three words are then cut to the Kill Ring. Because the Kill Ring is a **FIFO** buffer, you can now move Point to where you want to restore the three words and press <Ctrl-Y>. The three words are yanked into the document in the same order, left-to-right, that they were cut from the document.

To copy three words of text and then paste them back at another position, you must set Mark by positioning Point after the three words and then pressing

<Ctrl-@> at that position. Then reposition Point before the three words; you have now defined a **Region** between Point and Mark. There is only one Mark in the document. Press <Esc-W> to send the text between Point and Mark to the Kill Ring, but the text is *not* blanked from the screen display. To restore the three words at another position, move Point there and press <Ctrl-Y>. The three words are restored at the new position. Table 5.14 gives the important **kill** and **yank** commands for **emacs**.

Global search and replace can be either unconditional, where every occurrence of old text you want to replace with new text is replaced without prompting, or it can be interactive, where you are prompted by **emacs** before each occurrence of old text is replaced with new text. Also, the grammar of replacement can include regular expressions, which we do not cover here (see Chapter 10).

For example, to replace the word *men* unconditionally with the word *women* from the current position of Point to the end of the document, press <Esc-x>, type **replace-string**, and press <Enter>. You are then prompted for the old string. Type **men** and press <Enter>. You are next prompted for the new string. Type **women** and press <Enter> on the keyboard. All occurrences are replaced with no further prompts.

To accomplish an interactive replacement, simply press <Esc-x>, type **query-replace**, and then press <Enter>. You can then input old and new strings, but you are given an opportunity at each occurrence of the old string to replace it or not to replace it with the new string. Table 5.15 shows the actions that you can take while in the midst of an interactive search and replace. Practice Session 5.8 contains further examples of copying and pasting and global search and replace, both unconditional and interactive. Your objective will be to type in one line of text, copy it into the Kill Ring, and paste it into the document seven times. Then, you are to modify the contents of the original line and each pasted line by using both interactive search and replace and unconditional search and replace.

**Table 5.14** Important emacs Kill and Yank Commands

| Command | Action |
|---|---|
| ‹Ctrl-Delete› | Kills the character at the cursor |
| ‹Esc-D› | Kills characters from the cursor to the end of the current word |
| ‹Ctrl- U 1› ‹Ctrl-K› | Kills characters from the cursor forward to the end of the line |
| ‹Esc-W› | Copies the Region to the Kill Ring, but does not blank the text from the document |
| ‹Ctrl-W› | Kills the Region |
| ‹Ctrl-Y› | Pastes the most recent text in the Kill Ring into the document at Point |

**Table 5.15** Interactive Search and Replace Actions

| Key | Search and Replace Action |
|---|---|
| ‹**Delete**› | Do not make this replacement, keep searching. |
| ‹**Enter** (or ‹**Return**›) | Do not continue replacements; quit now. |
| ‹**space bar**› | Do this replacement and then continue searching. |
| **,** (comma) | Make this replacement, display the replacement, and prompt for another command. |
| **.** (period) | Make this replacement and then end searching. |
| **!** (exclamation mark) | Replace this and all the remaining occurrences unconditionally. |

## Practice Session 5.8

**Step 1:** At the shell prompt, type **`emacs osfile`** and press ‹Enter›.

**Step 2:** Type **`Windows is the operating system of choice for everyone.`**

**Step 3:** Press ‹Ctrl-@› . The Mark is now set at the end of the line you typed in Step 2. Highlight the whole first line with the cursor.

**Step 4:** Press the ‹Esc› key and then the ‹W› key. This action copies the Region to the Kill Ring.

**Step 5:** Position the cursor at the beginning of the second line in the buffer, which should be blank.

**Step 6:** Press ‹Ctrl-Y›. The first line of text is now pasted into the second blank line.

**Step 7:** Repeat Steps 5 and 6 six more times so that you now have eight lines of text in the buffer, all containing the text `Windows is the operating system of choice for everyone.`

**Step 8:** Position the cursor on the `W` in `Windows` on the first line of the buffer.

**Step 9:** Save the buffer at this point with ‹Ctrl-X Ctrl-S›.

**Step 10:** Press the ‹Esc› key and then the ‹X› key. Then type **`query-replace`** and press ‹Enter›. These actions begin an interactive search and replace. The prompt `Query replace:` appears.

**Step 11:** Type **`everyone`** and press ‹Enter›. The prompt `with:` appears.

**Step 12:** Type **`students`** and press ‹Enter›. The prompt `Query replacing everyone with students : (? for help)` appears.

**Step 13:** Pressing the ‹space bar› on the keyboard replaces the word `everyone` on the first line with the word `students`, and the prompt `Query replacing everyone with students : (? for help)` appears again.

**Practice Session 5.8 (cont.)**

**Step 14:** Press <Enter>. The prompt `Replaced 1 occurrence` appears.

**Step 15:** Position the cursor over the `e` in the word `everyone` on the second line of the buffer.

**Step 16:** Repeat Steps 10 through 14, interactively replacing the word `everyone` each time it appears with the words `computer scientists`, `engineers`, `system administrators`, `web servers`, `scientists`, `networking`, and `mathematicians` on lines 2 through 8 of the buffer.

**Step 17:** Position the cursor on the `W` in `Windows` on the first line of the buffer.

**Step 18:** Press the <Esc> key and then the <X> key. Then type **`replace-string`** and press <Enter>. These actions begin an unconditional search and replace. The prompt `replace string:` appears.

**Step 19:** Type **`Windows`** and press <Enter>. The prompt `Replace string Windows with:` appears.

**Step 20:** Type **`LINUX`** and press <Enter>. The prompt `Replaced 8 occurrences` appears. This is a fact.

**Step 21:** Save the buffer with <Ctrl-X Ctrl-S> and print it using the facilities available on your computer system.

The following In-Chapter Exercises ask you to apply some of the operations you learned about in the previous practice sessions.

## IN-CHAPTER EXERCISES

**5.5.** Run **`emacs`** and define keyboard macro commands that automatically delete

- every other word in a line of unspecified length
- every other line in a file of unspecified length
- every other word and every other line in a file of unspecified length with lines of unspecified length

**5.6.** Write a keyboard macro, as shown in Section 5.4.4, to do everything shown in Steps 10 through 14 of Practice Session 5.8.

To get some further practice with **`emacs`**, do Problems 12 through 14 at the end of this chapter.

## 5.5 HOW TO DO GRAPHICAL EDITING BY USING XEMACS

Most people install LINUX along with a window management system, such as GNOME or KDE, and, in turn, will be using a window manager such as Sawfish, so that they can use a graphical version of the emacs text editor known as XEmacs. XEmacs is similar to emacs and has all of the functionality. In this section, we use the graphical user interface of XEmacs to accomplish many of the tasks commonly done in a LINUX text editor, summarized in Table 5.1. We use the text-based interface of the text editors in the previous sections. A combination of text-based and graphical methods, tailored to the needs of the individual user, is best when approaching the creation and editing of text for diverse kinds of documents, such as e-mail, program source code, and manuscripts. Keyboard input of text is still the primary way that text is entered into such documents. For the sake of expediency, keyboard commands are also a valid way of formatting the text contained in such documents.

### 5.5.1 EDITING DATA FILES WITH XEMACS

The following example demonstrates the use of XEmacs to do some further editing of the data file created in Section 5.4.4. Depending on which window management system you are using, you may be able to graphically launch the XEmacs program. For example, under GNOME version 1.2, if you installed the XEmacs package when you installed LINUX, you can launch XEmacs by making the Panel cascading menu choices Programs>Editors>XEmacs.

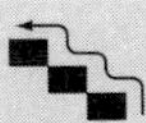

**Example: XEmacs buttons**

**Step 1:** Launch XEmacs. A new window should open on screen, and your screen display should look similar to Figure 5.13. Identify the following components of the XEmacs screen:

a. a menu bar of pull-down choices
b. toolbar buttons to do common editing tasks
c. the buffer display
d. the mode line (very similar to emacs run in a terminal window).

**Step 2:** Left-click on the Open button. An emacs "scratch" window should open on screen, allowing you to specify the path to the file you want to open. At the `Find file:` prompt that appears in this window, leave the ~/ specification and type **`datafile`**. Then left-click on the OK button in the emacs scratch window. The datafile should be opened and appear in the main buffer window, as shown in Figure 5.14.

## Example: XEmacs buttons

**Step 3:** Position the cursor in the main buffer window at the 1 at the beginning of the tenth line of data by left-clicking on the 1. Be careful not to left-click on the space that separates the 1 and the 2.

**Step 4:** Click and hold down the left-most mouse button over the character 1 and drag the mouse so that the entire tenth line is highlighted and the cursor is after the 0 in 10.

**Step 5:** Left-click on the Copy button at the top of the screen. The text is unhighlighted.

**Step 6:** Position the cursor at the beginning of the eleventh line. Left-click on the Paste button at the top of the screen. The entire row of numbers from the tenth row has been pasted into the eleventh line.

**Step 7:** Left-click on the Save button at the top of the screen. You have just saved the contents of the buffer to your home directory.

**Step 8:** From the File pull-down menu, select Exit XEmacs. The XEmacs window closes.

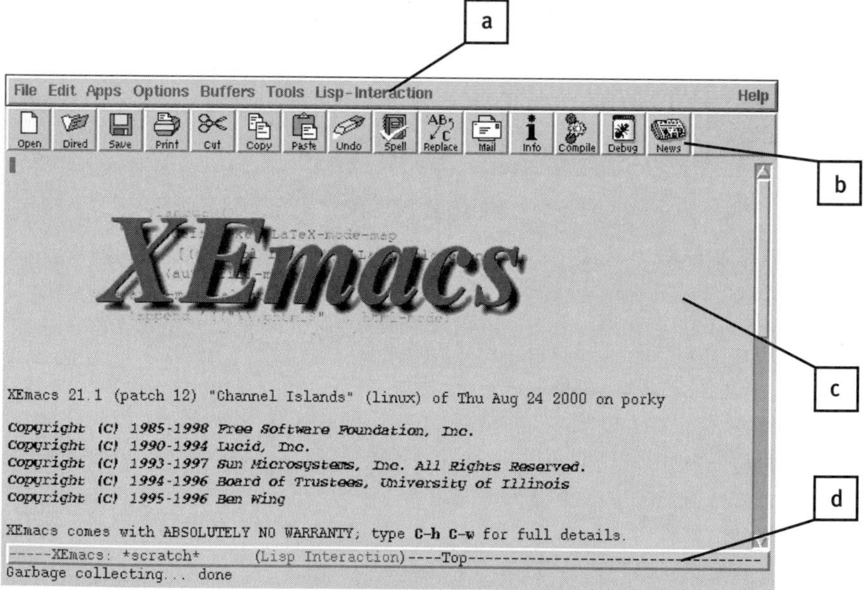


**Figure 5.13** The layout of the first XEmacs screen display

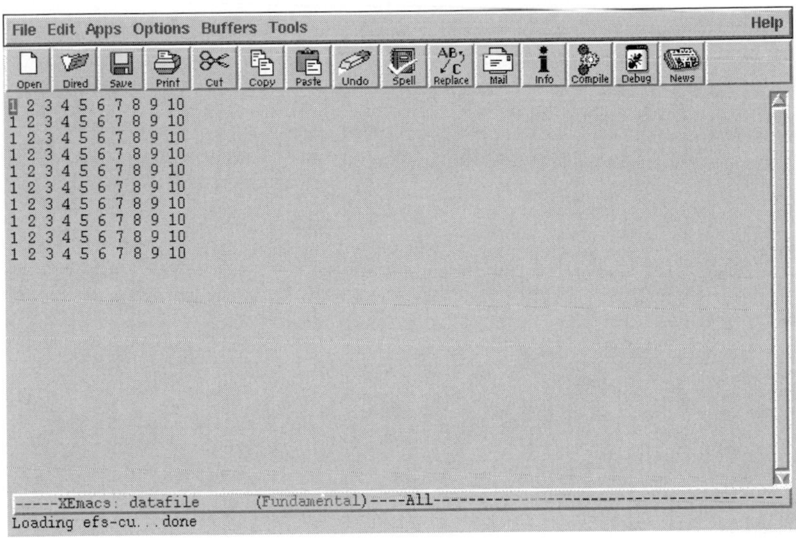


**Figure 5.14** Initial display of datafile in XEmacs

## 5.5.2 XEmacs Menus and Buttons

A brief description of the pull-down menu headings is given in Table 5.16. A brief description of the toolbar buttons is given in Table 5.17

**Table 5.16** XEmacs Pull-Down Menu Choices Described

| Pull-Down Menu | Description |
|---|---|
| File | Open and save/saveas files and buffers |
| Edit | Cut, copy, paste, search/replace, and undo |
| Apps | Read e-mail, send e-mail, browse the Web |
| Options | Customization of editing and appearance |
| Buffers | List open buffers |
| Tools | Execute LINUX commands |
| Lisp-Interaction | Run Lisp from within emacs |
| Help | Help on basics and keystroke commands |

**Table 5.17** XEmacs Toolbar Button Descriptions

| Toolbar Button | Brief Description |
|---|---|
| Open | Open a file |
| Dired | Edit a directory, allowing you to view and manipulate files |
| Save | Save the current buffer |
| Print | Print the current buffer |
| Cut | Kill a Region |
| Copy | Copy a Region |
| Paste | Paste from the clipboard |
| Undo | Undo an edit |
| Spell | Check spelling |
| Replace | Search and replace |
| Mail | Read e-mail |
| Info | Documentation |
| Compile | Start a compilation |
| Debug | Start a debugger |
| News | Read news |

### 5.5.3 How to Start, Save a File, and Exit

As illustrated in the Example: XEmacs Buttons, GUI interactivity in emacs improves your dialog with the computer. In doing Practice Session 5.9, which simply repeats Practice Session 5.6, notice your increase in performance and efficiency when you use a purely graphical text editor. Of course, entering text into a file in most cases is done via the keyboard. Practice Session 5.9 lets you continue editing the file alien, which you created in the Example: Emacs Text Editor by using XEmacs.

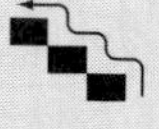

#### Practice Session 5.9

**Step 1:** Launch XEmacs as shown in the Example: XEmacs Buttons. A new window should open on screen, and your screen display should look similar to Figure 5.13. *Note*: At this point, if you wanted to begin a new file, you would use <Ctrl-X>+<Ctrl-F> to visit or open that file, type its new name on the mode line, and press <Enter>. This opens a new buffer, which you could save as a new text file. Also, it is possible to launch XEmacs from the shell prompt in an Xterminal window by typing **`xemacs filename`** and pressing <Enter>, where *filename* is the name of a file you want to edit.

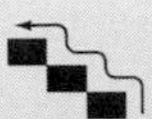

## Practice Session 5.9 (cont.)

**Step 2:** Left-click on the Open button. An emacs scratch window should open on screen, allowing you to specify the path to the file you want to open. At the `Find file:` prompt, leave the ~/ specification and type **`alien`**. Then left-click on the OK button in the emacs scratch window. The file alien should appear in the main buffer window. The cursor should be over the # sign, which is the first character in line 1. If you make the pull-down menu choice Buffers at this point, what open buffers appear in the list that pulls down? They should be scratch and alien. Scratch is a temporary buffer you can use for notes and Lisp evaluation.

**Step 3:** Position the cursor, using the mouse and left mouse button, to the right of the " character at the end of the third line.

**Step 4:** Press <Enter> to open a blank line; the cursor should be at the beginning of the line.

**Step 5:** Type **`alice dir/w="ls"`**.

**Step 6:** Position the cursor, using the mouse and the left mouse button, at character `a` in `alice`.

**Step 7:** Hold down the left mouse button and move the mouse so that the word `alice` and the `d` character in `dir` are highlighted. Then left-click on the Cut button in the button bar at the top of the screen. The word `alice` is cut from the buffer. The new first character on line four is `d`.

**Step 8:** Position the cursor, using the mouse and left mouse button, over the first letter `a` in `alias` at the beginning of the third line.

**Step 9:** Position the cursor, using the mouse and left mouse button, at the beginning of the first blank line in the buffer, below the line that reads `alias type="more"`. If for some reason there is no blank line in the buffer below the fifth line, create one with the <Enter> key as you did in Steps 3 and 4.

**Step 10:** Left-click on the Paste button. The cut word `alice` has been put back in the buffer at the start of the line.

**Step 11:** Position the cursor, using the mouse and left mouse button, at the space character after the word `alice`, just after the character e.

**Step 12:** Use the <Delete> or <Back Space> key to delete the letters `c` and `e` from the word `alice`.

**Step 13:** Type **`as copy="cp"`** . Your screen display should look like the one shown in Figure 5.15.

### Practice Session 5.9 (cont.)

**Step 14:** Left-click on the Save button. This overwrites your old version of the file alien with the changes you have made. At this point, if you had wanted to save the modified buffer with a new name, you would have made the File Save As menu choice.

**Step 15:** From the File pull-down menu, make the Exit XEmacs choice.

## 5.6 COMMAND LINE EDITING

Bash provides the GNU command line editing interface implemented through the use of a package called the **Readline library**. This interface provides useful command line editing facilities. You can use most of the editing features of `emacs` or `vi` to perform tasks such as moving and changing text, manipulating the history list, yanking text, and pasting text. The default editor for command line editing is `emacs`, but you can change it to the `vi` editor. Once you have manipulated a command line, you can hit `<Enter>` to execute the command; you don't have to move the cursor to the end of the command line.

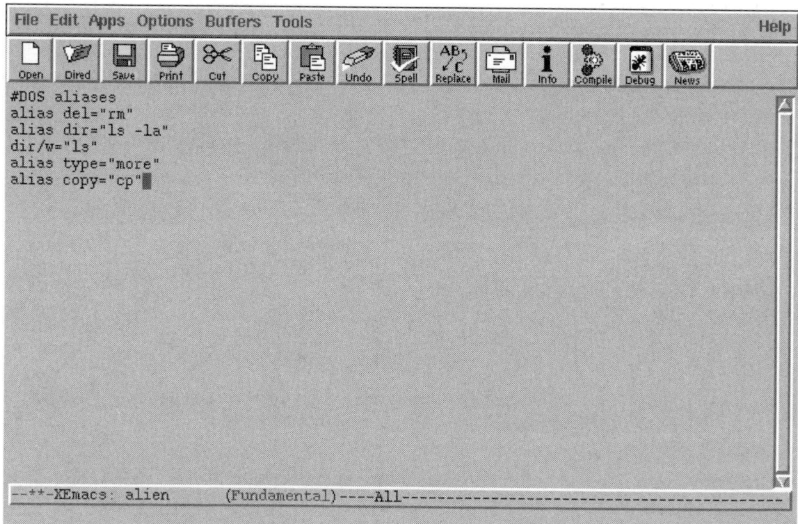


**Figure 5.15** File alien after being edited in XEmacs

The command line editing features provided by the Readline library are controlled by the contents of the .inputrc file, which is usually located in your home directory. In this file, the lines beginning with # are comments and the lines beginning with $ are conditional constructs. The rest of the lines are for key bindings for commands and variables settings. Variables can be assigned values by using the `set` command. The following is the syntax for setting the value of a variable.

**`set variable value`**

Table 5.18 lists some important Readline variables and their purpose.

Thus the Readline variable *`editing-mode`* can be set to `vi` by using the `set editing-mode vi` command. After this command has executed, `vi` becomes your command line editor. The same task can also be performed by using the `set -o vi` command. Either of these commands can be executed interactively or placed in the .inputrc file. In order to switch back to the emacs mode, you can execute the `set -o emacs` command.

A number of Readline line commands can be bound to key sequences and are, therefore, called the bindable Readline commands. You can use the `bind -v` command to display the current key bindings. You can change the current bindings by making appropriate changes in the ~/.inputrc file, if it exists. On some systems, .inputrc is found in the /etc directory. On our version of LINUX, Mandrake release 6.1 (Helios), it is found in the /etc/skel directory. In Red Hat LINUX version 7.0, it is found in the /etc directory as inputrc. You can use the `find /etc -name .inputrc -print` command to find its location on your system.

There are several categories of the general-purpose command line editing commands. Some of these commands have been discussed already and are summarized in Table 5.19.

**Table 5.18** Important Readline Variables

| Variable | Purpose |
|---|---|
| editing-mode | Can be set to emacs or vi. The setting determines the key bindings used by Readline for command line editing. The default value of the variable is emacs. |
| expand-tilde | If set to 'on', Readline performs tilde expansion whenever it tries to expand a word. The default value of this variable is 'off'. |
| keymap | This variable dictates the keymap for keybinding commands. It can be set to emacs, emacs-ctlx, emacs-meta, emacs-standard, vi, vi-command, or vi-insert. The settings emacs and emacs-standard are the same, as are vi and vi-command. The value of the *`editing-mode`* variable also affects the keymap. |
| Mark-directories | If the variable is set to 'on' (the default value), the completed directory names have a slash (/) appended to them. |

**Table 5.19** Commonly Used Bindable Readline Commands

| Command | Purpose |
|---|---|
| **Moving the Cursor in the Command Line** | |
| <Esc-b> | Move the cursor to the previous word |
| <Esc-f> | Move the cursor to the next word |
| <^a> | Move the cursor to the start of the line |
| <^b> | Move the cursor to the previous character position |
| <^e> | Move the cursor to the end of the line |
| <^f> | Move the cursor to the next character position |
| <^l> | Clear the screen and display the line at the top of the screen |
| **Manipulating the Command History List** | |
| <Enter> | Add the line to the history list; if it was already in the history list, then restore the history line to its original state |
| <Esc-<> | Move to the first line in the history list |
| <Esc->> | Move to the last line of the history list (i.e., the current command line) |
| <^n> | Go to the next command in the history list |
| <^p> | Go to the previous command in the history list |
| **Manipulating Text in the Command Line** | |
| <Esc-c> | Capitalize the word at the current cursor position; do not move the cursor |
| <Esc-l> | Convert the word at the current cursor position to lowercase; do not move the cursor |
| <Esc-t> | Swap the word in front of the current cursor position to the one behind it and move the cursor over the new next word |
| <Esc-u> | Convert the word at the current cursor position to uppercase; do not move the cursor |
| <^d> | Delete the character under the cursor |
| <^q> or <^v> | Insert the next character typed to the line verbatim (This is how control characters such as ^u are inserted.) |
| <^t> | Swap the character before the cursor with the one after it and move the cursor over to the next position |
| **Typing Text in the Command Line** | |
| <Tab> | Try to complete the text before the cursor |
| <Esc-?> | List of possible completions of the text before the cursor |

**Table 5.19** *(continued)*

| **Deleting/Killing and Yanking Text from the Command Line** | |
|---|---|
| ‹Esc-Del› | Delete the word before the cursor |
| ‹Esc-d› | Delete the text from the current cursor position to the end of the current word (or the next word if the cursor is between words) |
| ‹Esc-y› | If the previous command was ‹^y› or ‹Esc-y›, rotate the Kill Ring and yank the new top at the cursor position |
| ‹^k› | Delete the text from the current cursor position to the end of command line |
| ‹^x› | Delete the text from the current cursor position to the beginning of command line |
| ‹^u› | Delete the text from the current cursor position to the beginning of command line and save the text in Kill Ring |
| ‹^w› | Delete the word before the cursor and save it in a buffer called Kill Ring |
| ‹^y› | Yank the top of the Kill Ring at the current cursor position |
| **Miscellaneous Tasks** | |
| ‹Esc-^› | Perform history expansion on the current command line |
| ‹Esc-~› | Perform tilde (~) expansion on the current word |
| ‹Esc-r› | Undo all the changes made to the current line |
| ‹^-› or ‹^x› ‹^u› | Undo the previous change made to the line |
| ‹^e› | If in the vi editing mode, switch to the emacs mode |
| ‹^g› | Abort the current line and ring the terminal bell |

One of the commonly used commands is accessed by pressing the <Tab> key, which is used for completing the text before the cursor. There are several types of completions: command completion, filename completion, and variable completion. The type of completion applied depends on when you are typing. Pressing the <Tab> key results in your shell completing the command, filename, or variable for you. If there are multiple choices, your shell beeps at you. If you press <Tab> a second time and your shell is Bash, the shell displays the list of possible commands, filenames, or variables whose names start with the characters that you have typed and redisplays the partial command for you to complete typing. This allows you to complete your task or terminate the command with <^c>. The following Bash session illustrates how you can use these features.

```
$ ls /usr/i<Tab><Tab>
i386-glibc20-linux include
i486-linux-libc5 info
$ ls /usr/include/sys
```

```
[ output of the ls /usr/include/sys command ]
$ loca<Tab><Tab>
local locale localedef locate
$ locate socket.h
/usr/include/bits/socket.h
/usr/include/sys/socket.h
...
/usr/i386-glibc20-linux/include/linux/socket.h
/usr/i386-glibc20-linux/include/sys/socket.h
$ l
Display all 691 possibilities? (y or n)n
$ l<^c>
$
```

## SUMMARY

In this chapter we covered the four most useful text editors that LINUX offers. They are useful because LINUX is a text-driven operating system. Useful operations, such as editing script files, writing e-mail messages, or creating C language programs, are done with text editors. A full-screen display editor shows a portion of a file that fills most or all of the screen display. The cursor, or Point, can be moved to any of the text shown in the screen display. Editing a file involves editing a copy that the editor creates, called a buffer. Keystroke commands are the primary way of interacting with these editors. The editor(s) used should fit the user's personal criteria. The most important functions that are common to these LINUX text editors are cursor movement, cutting, copying, and pasting, deleting text, inserting text, opening an existing file, starting a new file, quitting, saving, and search and replace. All of these functions are available in a GUI environment editor, XEmacs.

## PROBLEMS

1. Despite the availability of fancy and powerful word processors, why is text editing still important?
2. List 10 commonly used text editing operations.
3. What are the four most popular text editors in LINUX? Which one is your favorite? Why?
4. What is an editor buffer?

5. Run **pico** on your system. Create and edit a block of text that you want to be the body of an e-mail message explaining the basic capabilities of the **pico** editor. For example, part of your message might describe the three most important keystroke commands in **pico**, devoting one line of description to each command. Try not to type more than 15 to 20 lines of text into the file. Then save the file with **^O** as first.txt. Use the **mail** command in Chapter 6 to send this message to yourself.
6. Run **pico** and create a file with three lines of text in it. Then, use the cut and paste features of **pico** to duplicate the three lines so that the file contains nine lines of text. How do you copy a line of text from one place to another in **pico**? Save this file as prob6.
7. Run **pico** and use the keystroke commands **^G**, **^V**, and **^Y** to find out how to position the cursor *without* using the <arrow> keys. Then, use the **^R** command to read the text from the file prob6 that you created in Problem 6. Position the cursor within this new file, using only the keystroke commands that you learned from the Help text.
8. Run **vi** on your system and create a Bash shell script file that contains the lines

   **echo $SHELL**

   **chsh -l**

   Then save the file as **sheller** and quit **vi**. At the shell prompt, type **bash sheller** and press <Enter>. The screen display is a list of the current shell and the contents of a LINUX file that contains other shells available on your system. Review the material in Chapter 4 on the various shells and their uses (if necessary).
9. Run **vi** on your system. Create and edit a block of text that you want to be the body of an e-mail message explaining the basic capabilities of the **vi** editor. For example, part of your message might describe the difference between the insert and command modes. This file can be at least one page long, or 45 to 50 lines of text. Then save the file as vi_doc.txt. Use the **mail** command in Chapter 6, insert the body of text in an e-mail message, and send it to yourself.
10. Run **vi** on your system and write definitions in your own words, without looking at the textbook, for
    a. full screen display editor
    b. file versus buffer
    c. keystroke commands
    d. text file versus binary file

    Then refer back to the relevant sections of this chapter to check your definitions. Make any necessary corrections or additions. Re-edit the file to incorporate any corrections or additions that you made and then print out the file using the print commands available on your system.

11. Edit the file that you created in Problem 10, and change the order of the text of your definitions to (d), (a), (c), and (b), using the `yank`, `put`, and `D` or `dd` commands. Print out the file using the print commands available on your system.
12. This problem assumes that you are running the Bash shell. Before you begin, be sure to back up your .bashrc file by using the `cp` command described in Chapter 3. To do so, type **`cp .bashrc .bashrc_bak`** and press<Enter>. If for any reason you destroy the contents of the .bashrc file while doing this problem, you can restore the original by typing **`cp .bashrc_bak .bashrc`** and pressing <Enter>. Use `emacs` to edit the .bashrc file in your home directory and then use the <Ctrl-X I> command to insert the file alien2 at the bottom of the buffer. Save the buffer, exit `emacs`, and log off your computer system. Log on to your computer system again so that the new .bashrc is in effect and test each of the DOS aliases that are in alien2 by typing them at the shell prompt, with their proper arguments (if necessary).
13. You can edit more than one file at a time in `emacs`, where each of the files' contents are being held in different buffers. Experiment by first using the `cp` command at the shell prompt to make a copy of the file datafile that you created in Practice Session 5.7. Name this copy datafile2. Use `emacs` to open both files with the command <Ctrl-X>+<Ctrl-F> and switch between buffers with <Ctrl-X B>. Then edit both of them at the same time and cut and paste three or four lines of each between the two, using <Ctrl-@>, <Ctrl-W>, and <Ctrl-Y>. *Don't save your changes to the file datafile.*
14. Write a keyboard macro, as described in Section 5.4.4, to do everything shown in Steps 10 through 16 of Practice Session 5.8.
15. Repeat Problem 13, using XEmacs. This time, make two copies of the datafile, named datafilex and datafilexx. Open all three files and, using the multiple-buffer capability of an XEmacs, cut and paste among the files with the mouse/GUI. Again, as in Problem 13, *don't save your changes to the file datafile.*
16. While you're in XEmacs, send an e-mail message to one of your friends, composing the message body from within XEmacs.

CHAPTER

# 6

# Electronic Mail

## OBJECTIVES

- To describe basic e-mail concepts and their specific implementations on a LINUX system.
- To illustrate the effective use of a line display e-mail system—the LINUX `mail` command
- To show how elm, a full-screen display e-mail system, is more advantageous than a line-display e-mail system
- To show further capabilities of a full-screen display e-mail system with `pine`
- To show the basics of KDE Kmail
- To cover the commands and primitives `cd`, `elm`, `mail`, `mkdir`, `pine`, and `rm`

## 6.1 INTRODUCTION

This section describes what is common to the electronic mail (e-mail) systems on LINUX. The fundamental concept of e-mail is to give you the ability to communicate via some permanent record medium on your own computer system with other users, or with users on other systems over an intranet or the Internet. Other forms of communication that can also be facilitated by the computer include audio and video, which are fundamentally transitory media. Because LINUX systems are text-based, they accommodate the e-mail medium most successfully.

One of the most important structural parts of an e-mail message is the **message header**. It usually appears at the top of the message text, called the **message body**, and contains some standard or universal blank fields that you fill in as you write a message. The purpose of the message header is to help in the automated delivery of e-mail by your local e-mail program and by the various mail handling programs on your system or on the network(s) to which your system is linked. The most important of these fields are

- the `To:` field, which contains the e-mail address(es) of the recipient(s)
- the `From:` field, which contains the e-mail address of the originator of the message
- the `Cc:` field, which contains the address(es) of any additional recipient(s)
- the `Attch:` field, which lists any attachments that might accompany the message, usually in the form of external files
- the `Subject:` field, which indicates the subject or purpose of the message

Basically, two kinds of attachments can accompany an e-mail message. The simplest kind is a text file, which contains only ASCII text. It can be part of the message body or in a separate file along with the message. Of course a binary, non-human readable file can be converted with the :LINUX **uuencode** utility into an ASCII text file for attachment to an e-mail message. Then, at the recipient's end, the **uudecode** utility will translate the ASCII text back into binary. We present more information about this method in Chapter 10. The more prevalent kind of attachment in contemporary e-mail is supported by **Multimedia Internet Mail Standard (MIME)**, which defines various multimedia content types and subtypes for attachments. In particular, digital images(.jpeg), audio files(.mp3), and movie files(.mpeg) can be transported via e-mail attachment, even on dissimilar e-mail systems, if the systems are MIME compliant. All the e-mail systems that we examine here are capable of attaching text easily, but only `pine` can attach multimedia files to e-mail messages easily.

Going hand in hand with the basic concept of e-mail as a permanent record is the notion of a **folder**, or subdirectory, into which you can place that record in some organized and logical fashion. You can create a variety of folders based on who you send e-mail to (the recipients) or who you get e-mail from (the sender). Similar to paper mail, an e-mail correspondent is someone with whom you have a dialog by exchanging e-mail messages. The messages themselves are simply files stored archivally in those folders or awaiting further disposition. The most common form of disposition of e-mail messages is deletion. Further disposition might be forwarding a message, or passing it along for its information content. Another form of disposition might be replying to the sender and giving a response to the message. Forwarding and replying can also be a multiple operation, with more than one destination for retransmission. The process of sending a message to one recipient but at the same time sending copies of this original message to others is called sending carbon copies (abbreviated cc). Finally, e-mail can be disposed of by printing it on paper, using the printing facilities of your system.

The proper form of an e-mail address underpins the entire system of electronic mail. On the LINUX **local host computer system** (see Chapter 14) that you are logged on to—and on which you have a username—your e-mail address is your username. When you send mail and specify a username as the recipient, either on the command line or in the To: field of the e-mail message header, that username can be resolved to a valid local host e-mail address with the aid of the LINUX system. When you want to send e-mail over the Internet, the e-mail address relies on the **Internet Domain Name System** for its basic form.

Being able to maintain a list of frequent correspondents is also a fundamental part of any e-mail system. That way, as in a paper address book, you can quickly route e-mail messages by looking up recipients' addresses automatically in an electronic address book functionally attached to your e-mail program.

An important basic feature of e-mail on a LINUX system is a **system mailbox file**, usually in the directory **/usr/spool/mail**, and messages that people send you are stored in that file. When you log onto the system and have messages in that system mailbox, you are notified on the screen that `you have mail`. When you read your mail, with the `mail` command for example, the `mail` program reads your system mailbox and informs you of the individual messages in it. You may then dispose of the messages that you have already read, or they are saved for further disposition in a folder (e.g., **mbox**). Figure 6.1 shows schematically the components of the e-mail dialog, whereby a sender's message is composed by a mail program, the mail system(s) handle the transfer of the message on the same computer or over a network, the system mailbox contains incoming messages, the recipient's `mail` program handles the incoming message, and it is disposed of either in the recipient's collection of folders or by being deleted.

There are two categories of e-mail systems for LINUX systems. The `mail` program described in Section 6.2 is a **line display e-mail system**, which means that you can only edit one line at a time when you are composing an e-mail message.

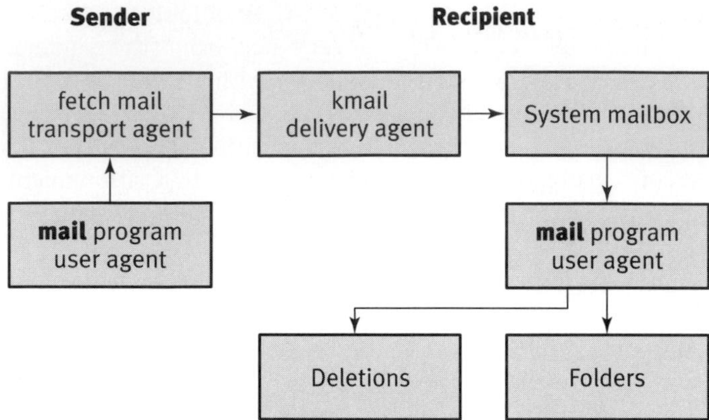


**Figure 6.1** Components of the e-mail dialog

The `elm`, `pine`, and `K-mail` programs, described later in this chapter, are **full-screen display e-mail systems**, which means that you can edit any text you see on a single-screen display, as you would on a word processor. Recall that, in Chapter 5, all the LINUX text editors you worked with were full-screen display editors.

Table 6.1 lists and briefly describes the common e-mail functions found in the LINUX e-mail systems that we cover in this chapter.

**Table 6.1** E-Mail Functions Common to LINUX E-Mail Systems

| Function | Description |
|---|---|
| aliases (addressbook) | Allows the user to define a list of frequent correspondents' e-mail addresses |
| attachments | Allows the sender to attach either text or multimedia files to a message |
| cc | Allows the sender to specify recipients of copies of a message |
| deleting | Allows the sender to dispose of messages by deleting them from the system mailbox |
| forwarding | Allows the sender to pass a received message to a new recipient quickly |
| reading | Allows the recipient to read incoming messages |
| replying | Allows the recipient to reply immediately to a current or disposed message |
| saving in folders | Allows the recipient to dispose of messages in a logical directory structure for e-mail |
| sending | Allows the user to send messages |

## 6.2 HOW TO USE THE LINUX `mail` COMMAND EFFECTIVELY

The easiest and quickest e-mail system to use on LINUX systems is the `mail` program.

### 6.2.1 Sending and Reading E-mail with the LINUX `mail` Command

Example: `mail` Command demonstrates how to use the LINUX `mail` command to send and read an e-mail message. The body of the e-mail message was created in `pico` as Problem 5 at the end Chapter 5. If you haven't done that problem, use your favorite LINUX text editor to create a block of text that explains the basic capabilities of the text editor. Save the file as first.txt, then proceed with the example.

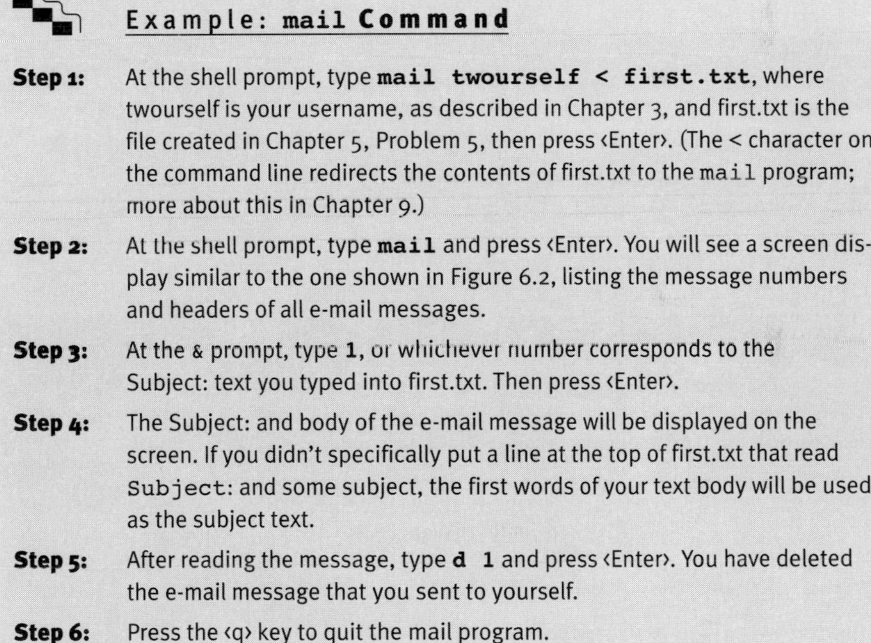

**Example: mail Command**

**Step 1:** At the shell prompt, type **`mail twourself < first.txt`**, where twourself is your username, as described in Chapter 3, and first.txt is the file created in Chapter 5, Problem 5, then press ‹Enter›. (The < character on the command line redirects the contents of first.txt to the `mail` program; more about this in Chapter 9.)

**Step 2:** At the shell prompt, type **`mail`** and press ‹Enter›. You will see a screen display similar to the one shown in Figure 6.2, listing the message numbers and headers of all e-mail messages.

**Step 3:** At the & prompt, type **`1`**, or whichever number corresponds to the Subject: text you typed into first.txt. Then press ‹Enter›.

**Step 4:** The Subject: and body of the e-mail message will be displayed on the screen. If you didn't specifically put a line at the top of first.txt that read `Subject:` and some subject, the first words of your text body will be used as the subject text.

**Step 5:** After reading the message, type **`d 1`** and press ‹Enter›. You have deleted the e-mail message that you sent to yourself.

**Step 6:** Press the ‹q› key to quit the mail program.

```
[bobk@localhost bobk]$ mail
Mail version 8.1 6/6/93.  Type ? for help.
"/var/spool/mail/bobk": 4 messages 1 unread
    1 MAILER-DAEMON@localh  Tue Jun 29 19:24  12/520   "DON'T DELETE THIS MES"
    2 bobk@localhost.local  Mon May 24 19:11  18/488   "My second elm message"
    3 bobk@localhost.local  Tue May 25 16:39  21/638   "Re: My second elm mes"
>U  4 bobk@localhost.local  Tue Jun 29 19:24  19/606   "Message to myself"
&
```

**Figure 6.2** Screen display when the `mail` program is first run

## 6.2.2 Sending E-Mail with the `mail` Command

Next, we briefly describe the `mail` command.

Syntax:

**mail [options] [recipient(s)]**

**Purpose:** Allows you to send and receive e-mail

**Output:** With no options or recipients specified, you are placed in the mail program and a list of message headers appears on your screen display.

**Commonly used options/features:**

***For sending mail:***

| | |
|---|---|
| **-s** | A `Subject:` line is included in the message header for all recipients. |
| **-c** add | A carbon copy is sent to address *add*. |
| **-b** add | A blind carbon copy is sent to address *add*. |

***For reading mail:***

| | |
|---|---|
| **-h** | A screen display of message headers is shown first. |
| **-P** | All messages are displayed with full headers. |

The mail program commonly runs at the command line in one of two ways. In the first way, you are sending e-mail; first, type **mail** at the shell prompt, followed by options and option arguments if necessary, then type an e-mail address or addresses. Next type in the body of the e-mail message, one line at a time. When you press <Ctrl-D> at the beginning of a blank line, the e-mail message is sent. In the second way, you are reading mail; first, type **mail** at the shell prompt, then press <Enter>. If you have undisposed or new e-mail messages in the system mailbox, a list of message headers appears on screen, showing you some information about each undisposed message. You may then type in commands to read and dispose of your messages. If you have no e-mail in the system mailbox, you get a reply from LINUX: `No mail for username`, where username is your username on the computer system you are logged on to.

You may also send e-mail on a LINUX system in one of two ways when using the `mail` command. If you want to use the `mail` command to send an e-mail message to someone on your system, you can type the `mail` command and one or more usernames of the recipients to whom you want to send the e-mail message. Recall from Chapter 3 that your username identifies you on your LINUX computer system. Users on your system have system mailboxes in **/var/spool/mail** or **/usr/spool/mail**. When you include a recipient on the command line, that recipient's username is resolved to an address, or location in the file structure of the computer system that your mail message will be sent to. (For more information on the LINUX file system structure, see Chapter 7.)

If you want to use the `mail` command to send an e-mail message to someone *not* on your system, presuming that your system is connected to the Internet in some way, you must know the valid Internet address of the recipient, which usually takes the form

**username@hostname.domain_name...** ,

where

**username** is the name that identifies that recipient on the system he or she is on

**hostname** is the computer on which the recipient has a username

**domain_name...** are valid Internet domain names

Of course, you can also specify the complete Internet address of someone who is on your computer system. This brings up the question of how you can find out what a person's Internet address is. The simplest way is to ask that person! But mechanisms are available on the Internet for finding a person's e-mail address, and we explore them in Chapter 14.

Some valid ways of specifying the recipient for the `mail` command—for someone on your system or on the Internet—are shown in Table 6.2.

**Table 6.2** Examples of Valid Recipient E-Mail Addresses

| Recipient Specification | Meaning |
|---|---|
| johnb | A valid username for someone with a mailbox on a user's computer system |
| johnb@egr | Username and hostname specified for someone on a user's computer system |
| johnb@egr.yoyodyne.com | Username@hostname.domain_name.domain_name for someone on the Internet |

The following In-Chapter Exercises ask you to use the Internet and your e-mail system to discover some important facts about extra e-mail addresses.

## IN-CHAPTER EXERCISES

**6.1.** In what ways can you find a person's e-mail address by using Internet searches? Which have you found to be most successful?

**6.2.** What happens when you specify a nonexistent Internet address in an e-mail message? Does the e-mail system response allow you to resend the message without recomposing it once you have found the correct address?

Some helpful command line options can be used to customize the execution of the `mail` program when you are sending mail. Several of them are given in Table 6.3.

If you execute the `mail` program and specify recipient(s), you are in the `mail` program composing the body of a message to the recipient(s). First, type a subject at the **`Subject:`** field prompt. Then, type the body of the mail message. Finally, signify that you have finished composing the message by pressing <Ctrl-D> with the cursor on a blank line. Practice Session 6.1 gives you the opportunity to use the `mail` program.

**Table 6.3** Command Line Options Used with the `Mail` Program

| Option | Action |
|---|---|
| **-t** | Prints a To: field in the message header, with recipient name(s) |
| **-s** "string with spaces" | Allows specifying the Subject: field on the command line |
| **-c** | Sends carbon copies to a list of recipients |
| **-v** | Gives full details of delivery on the screen (verbose mode) |

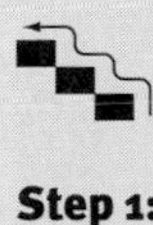

## Practice Session 6.1

**Step 1:** At the shell prompt, type **`mail twourself`**, where twourself is your username; then press ‹Enter›.

**Step 2:** At the `Subject:` prompt, type **`Thru mail`** and press ‹Enter›.

**Step 3:** Type **`This is a quick single-line mail message sent using the mail command.`** Then press ‹Enter›.

**Step 4:** Hold down the ‹Ctrl› and ‹D› keys at the same time on a blank line.

**Step 5:** If you get a `Cc:` prompt, press ‹Enter›. Entering valid e-mail addresses here allows you to send carbon copies of this e-mail message to others.

**Step 6:** You are back at the shell prompt, having successfully sent another e-mail message to yourself.

In Practice Session 6.2, you use options to customize your `mail` command.

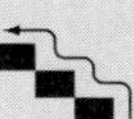

## Practice Session 6.2

**Step 1:** At the shell prompt, type **`mail -vs "wowie" twourself`**, where twourself is your username; then press ‹Enter›.

**Step 2:** Type **`Look at these options, will you?`** and press ‹Enter›.

**Step 3:** Hold down the ‹Ctrl› and ‹D› keys at the same time on a blank line.

**Step 4:** If you get a `Cc:` prompt, press ‹Enter›.

**Step 5:** You now get a display of messages on the screen similar to

```
twourself . . .     Connecting to local . . .
twourself . . .     Sent
```

Then you are back at the shell prompt. After a short time, you may hear your computer bell beep, and the message
`You have new mail in /var/spool/mail/twourself`
appears on screen, notifying you of the delivery of an e-mail message to your mailbox.

### 6.2.3 Reading E-Mail with `Mail`

If you execute the **`mail`** program, specify no options or recipients, and have been sent mail, a list of message headers appears on your screen. In this list, by default, each message has a number, ordered sequentially by arrival time. You are then placed in the `mail` program, and the command line prompt in `mail` is the & character. At the & prompt, several useful commands with arguments are presented that you can use when you want to read mail that you have been sent; they are listed in Table 6.4.

Practice Session 6.3 allows you to read the mail messages you sent to yourself in Practice Sessions 6.1 and 6.2 and to dispose of them in different ways.

## Practice Session 6.3

**Step 1:** At the shell prompt, type **`mail`** and press ‹Enter›.

**Step 2:** If you get the onscreen message `No mail for twourself`, where twourself is your username, go back to Section 6.2.2 and complete the two Practice Sessions.

**Step 3:** You should see a header list, similar to the following.

```
>N 1 twourself@hostname.domain_name date time size
"Thru mail"
N 2 twourself@hostname.domain_name date time size
"wowie"
&
```

**Step 4:** At the & prompt, type **`t 1`** and press ‹Enter›. The header and contents of message #1 appear on your screen. This was the Practice Session 6.1 e-mail message.

**Step 5:** At the & prompt, type **`p 2`** and press ‹Enter›. The header and contents of message #2 appear on your screen. This was the Practice Session 6.2 e-mail message.

**Step 6:** At the & prompt, type **`d 1`** and press ‹Enter›. Message #1 is deleted.

**Step 7:** At the & prompt, type **`s 2 savops`** and press ‹Enter›. The `mail` program gives you back the message "savops" [New file]. You have just saved message #2 in a file named savops.

**Step 8:** At the & prompt, type **`q`** and press ‹Enter› to return to the shell prompt.

**Step 9:** At the shell prompt, type **`more savops`** and press ‹Enter›. The contents of the savops file is displayed on your screen. Does the message header contain the same Subject**:** entry you saw on your screen in Step 5?

**Step 10:** At the shell prompt, type **`rm savops`** and press ‹Enter›. Is this message still available to you if you go back into the `mail` program?

**Table 6.4** Commands in `Mail` for Reading and Disposing of Incoming Messages

| Command | Name | Action |
|---|---|---|
| <-> (hyphen) | | Shows the contents of the previous message on the screen |
| <?> | Help | Shows a helpful summary of commands on the screen |
| <r #> | Reply | Replies to the originator of the message # |
| <d #> | Delete | Deletes the message # |
| <t #> | Type | Shows the contents of message # on the screen |
| <n> | Next | Goes to the next message # and shows its contents on the screen |
| <p #> | Print | Shows the contents of message # on the screen |
| <q> | Quit | Terminates the `mail` command and returns the user to the shell prompt |
| <s #> filename | Save | Saves the message # in *filename* |

## 6.2.4 Saving Messages in Folders

In Section 6.2.3, we showed you how to enter commands at the mail & prompt to view and dispose of your messages; Practice Session 6.3 showed you how to dispose of a message sent to you by using the **s** (save) command. In this section we show you how to organize your mail messages into folders, or subdirectories, containing information that is related in some way. Where was the mail message in Practice Session 6.3 saved to? A logical way of organizing your mail messages is to dispose of them into specific folders named for the recipient or sender of the message. Folders for mail messages can be subdirectories of your main directory or subdirectories of a mail subdirectory. Review Chapter 4 on how to create subdirectories, and then if you want more information on the subject, look ahead to Chapter 7.

For example, if you get a large quantity of e-mail from user johnbigboote, you can save any of the messages that come from that sender in a folder named johnb. One way to do so is first to create a subdirectory named johnb under your main directory with the **mkdir** command (see Chapter 3). Then, when you are in the **mail** program and the most current mail message from user johnbigboote is message #7, type

```
& s 7 ~/johnb/johns_latest
```

and press <Enter>. This command saves message #7 in the subdirectory johnb with the name johns_latest. You may also set the default mail subdirectory by changing your .mailrc file. See Problem 7 at the end of this chapter for a further exploration of this technique. Practice Session 6.4 lets you create a subdirectory under your main directory, run the `mail` program, and dispose of a mail message by saving it to that subdirectory. We have assumed that your present working directory is your main directory. If needed, repeat Practice Session 6.2.

## Practice Session 6.4

**Step 1:** At the shell prompt, type **`mkdir incoming`** and then press <Enter>.

**Step 2:** Type **`mail`** and press <Enter>.

**Step 3:** At the & prompt, type **`s # ~/incoming/saveops2`**, where # is the message number of the message with `Subject: wowie`; then press <Enter>. The `mail` program gives you back the message

`"/home/twourself/incoming/saveops2" [New file]`

**Step 4:** At the & prompt, type **`q`** and press <Enter> to go back to the shell prompt.

**Step 5:** At the shell prompt, type **`cd incoming`** and press <Enter>. Doing so changes your present working directory to be incoming.

**Step 6:** At the shell prompt, type **`more saveops2`** and press <Enter>. What appears on the screen?

**Step 7:** At the shell prompt, type **`cd`** and press <Enter>. Doing so changes your present working directory to be your main directory.

**Step 8:** At the shell prompt, type **`mail -f incoming/saveops2`** and press <Enter>. You are back in the `mail` program, and the message headers list appears on your screen. What does the **`-f`** command line option do when you are reading mail?

### 6.2.5 Replying to and Forwarding Messages—and Including Attachments

You may often need to dispose of your e-mail messages by replying to the sender or by forwarding the message that you received to someone else. These facilities are available in `mail` via the use of the `reply` command, and the `~f` command.

When you are reading e-mail, the `reply` command is available at the mail & prompt. For example, if you want to reply to a message from bobk@localhost whose message number is 3 and whose Subject: was tilde escapes, the following session shows how you would proceed.

```
& r 3
To: bobk@localhost.localdomain
Subject: tilde escapes
```

**Type in your reply here**

<Ctrl-D>

`Cc:` Press <Enter>.

The reply is sent.

Note that the To: and Subject: fields of the reply are automatically supplied by `mail`, as you are replying to the message with that subject sent by that sender.

Forwarding a message can be accomplished by including the message that you want to forward in the body of a new message that you are currently sending with `mail`. To do so, use a `tilde(~) escape` command, meaning that you use the ~ character as a prefix to a special command that lets you escape from typing text into the message body. For example, suppose that you want to forward a message that you know is message number 7 in your system mailbox. While you are composing a message, on a blank line type **`~f 7`** and press <Enter>. That message will be included as part of the message that you are currently sending when you press <Ctrl-D> on a blank line.

Being able to include an attached file with your e-mail message is very convenient. You can attach a file in one of two ways. The first way makes use of another tilde escape command, the `mail ~r` command. For example, if a file named reports exists in your home directory, and you currently are in `mail` sending a message, on a blank line type **`~r reports`** and press <Enter>. That file will be included as part of the message that you are sending currently when you press <Ctrl-D> on a blank line. The second way of sending a file to one or more recipients is to use the < output redirection character. (For more information on input and output redirection, see Chapter 12.) For example, to send a file named statistics in your home directory to the recipient aliceb@byu.edu, at the shell prompt type `mail aliceb@byu.edu < statistics` and press <Enter>. The file will be sent as the e-mail message. To send the file to multiple recipients, simply include multiple addresses as arguments to the `mail` command.

### 6.2.6 `Mail` ALIASES

If you frequently correspond with one person or several people via e-mail, having a list of their e-mail addresses stored in the `mail` program is very useful. That way, whenever you want to send e-mail to one or more of these people, you can use the internal address list rather than having to retrieve them from some external source. For example, you might frequently send e-mail to a person who has a long e-mail address that is difficult to memorize. So, instead of trying to remember that address whenever you want to compose a new e-mail message and send it to that person, you can simply store the address in the `mail` program and recall it whenever you want to insert the address in the message header. If you frequently send messages to the same group of people but don't want to type each recipient's e-mail address, you can send a message to the group. To do so, compile a list of e-mail addresses of the group and give it a name. Then, simply insert that name in the To: or Cc: field of the message and have the group name converted automatically to the individuals' e-mail addresses. This method is very efficient if the group has a large number of members—say, 50 or 100.

The address list facility is available in the `mail` program with the use of aliases. Recall that aliases are abbreviated substitutes for much longer and complex text, such as a command (see Section 4.3.7), an e-mail address, or many e-mail addresses. You can use aliases to send messages to an individual or group of recipients in one of two ways. The first way involves using the `alias` command at the mail `&` prompt. Doing so establishes an abbreviation for the current session of `mail`. For example, if you want to send a message to johnbigboote@yoyodyne.com, at the `&` prompt you could proceed by typing **`alias jb johnbigboote@yoyodyne.com`** and press <Enter>. Then you could type **`m jb`** and again press <Enter>. The `mail` program now allows you to enter a mail message and send it. To include multiple addresses in the definition of the alias, simply type multiple addresses after the alias name, such as **`alias gp bobk billg aliceb@byu.edu maryk`**. You can now use the alias gp in place of the addresses bobk, billg, aliceb@byu.edu, and maryk.

The second way to use aliases to send messages involves editing the .mailrc file in your home directory with a text editor of your choice and adding the alias definitions to that file so that `mail` will be configured with those aliases every time you run it. For example, if you add the following lines to your .mailrc file, you will be able to use the same aliases just defined for a single session in all subsequent sessions you have with `mail`.

**alias jb johnbigboote@yoyodyne.com**

**alias gp bobk billg aliceb@byu.edu maryk**

To get some further practice with the `mail` command, do Problems 8 and 9 at the end of this chapter.

## 6.3 elm—A FULL-SCREEN DISPLAY E-MAIL SYSTEM

The `elm` system is a full-screen display e-mail system that displays a menu of relevant commands onscreen at all times. In addition, it displays the context-sensitive options available to you when you are performing functions in the `elm` program. It allows you to run the text editor `vi` while you are composing an e-mail message body, letting you take advantage of the full-screen editing capabilities while you are writing.

### 6.3.1 Sending a Message in `elm`

Example: `elm` Program shows how to create and send an e-mail message with `elm`. We have assumed that you are running the Bash shell and that your .profile file contains the following line.

```
set TERM = VT100 ; export TERM
```

If you're running the TC shell, at the shell prompt type **`setenv TERM vt100`** and then press <Enter>. Review the general-purpose commands in Chapter 4 if you don't know which shell you're running. We also have assumed that you have some familiarity with the `vi` text editor (see Chapter 5).

**Example: `elm` Program**

**Step 1:** At the shell prompt, type **`elm formyself`**, where formyself is your username on this computer system (see Chapter 3); then press ‹Enter›.

**Step 2:** If this is the first time you have run `elm`, a message appears on your screen asking whether you want `elm` to set up a .elm directory under your main directory. Type **`Y`**.

**Step 3:** In the `Subject:` field, type **`My first elm message`** and press ‹Enter›.

**Step 4:** In the `Copies to:` field, press ‹Enter›, which puts you in the `vi` editor.

**Step 5:** Type **`A`** to put you in `vi` insert mode.

**Step 6:** Type **`This is a line of text in my first elm e-mail message.`**

**Step 7:** Use the `vi Esc :wq` sequence of commands to make your changes and exit `vi`, returning to the `elm` program.

**Step 8:** Type **`s`** to return to the shell prompt and send your e-mail message.

### 6.3.2 Sending E-Mail with `elm`

After you have done Example: `elm` Program, it should be apparent that `elm`, a screen-display e-mail system, is easier to use and much more friendly than a line-display e-mail system, such as `mail`. It is friendly in the sense that you can make changes in the text of the e-mail message with the more advanced commands of a full-screen display text editor. In addition, `elm` has a user interface style that (a) puts a menu of useful commands on the screen when you need to make a choice, (b) gives you full-screen control over the cursor's position, and (c) lets you use simple keystrokes to execute the `elm` command. The following is a brief description of the command to run the `elm` program.

Syntax:

## elm [options] [option arguments][recipient(s)] [< attachment]

**Purpose:** Allows you to send and receive e-mail

**Output:** With no options or recipient(s) specified, you are placed in the `elm` program and a list of message headers appears on your screen display if you have undisposed mail in the system mailbox.

**Commonly used options/option arguments:**

***To send mail:***

**-s** subject Specifies a *subject* of the message

***To receive mail:***

**-z** Do not run `elm` if no mail is in the system mailbox.

**-f** folder Have `elm` start by reading from *folder*.

The `elm` program is commonly run from the command line in one of three ways. The first way is

```
$ elm -s subject address
```

Here, the **-s** option signifies that a subject of the message is supplied as subject. The address can be either a valid e-mail address or an alias, or the abbreviated substitute for the full address. There are two types of aliases in `elm`: individual, which contains only a single e-mail address; and group, which contains multiple e-mail addresses.

The second way is

```
$ elm -s subject address < attachment
```

Although this way is similar to the first, the redirect operator < signifies that a file will be sent along with the message as an attachment. The format of what is transmittable as an attachment in `elm` is somewhat limited in comparison to other mail programs.

The third way is

```
$ elm
```

When you type `elm` at the shell prompt—with no options or recipients specified—`elm` displays an **Index screen**, similar to the one shown in Figure 6.3, which is characteristic of its user interface.

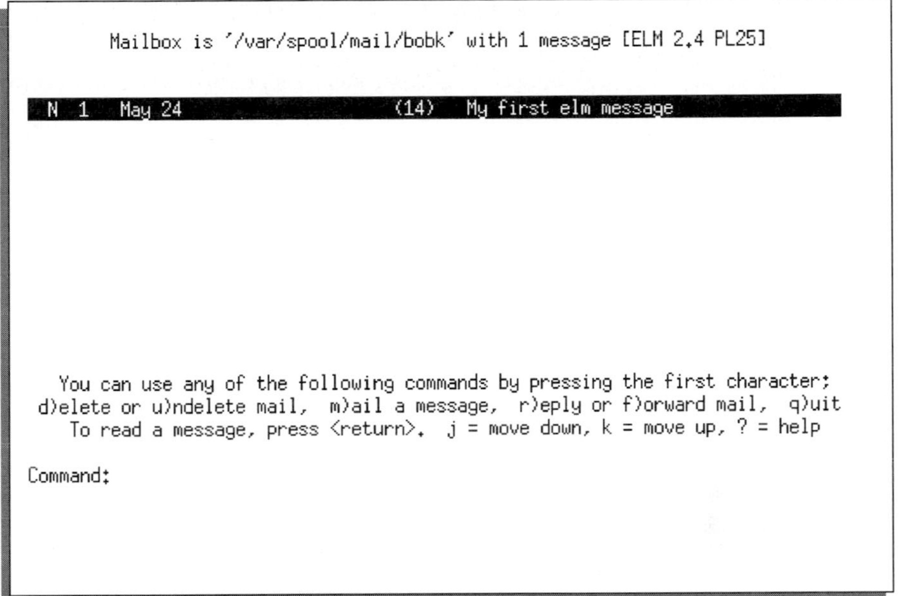
Mailbox is '/var/spool/mail/bobk' with 1 message [ELM 2.4 PL25]
N 1 May 24 (14) My first elm message
You can use any of the following commands by pressing the first character;
d)elete or u)ndelete mail, m)ail a message, r)eply or f)orward mail, q)uit
To read a message, press <return>. j = move down, k = move up, ? = help
Command:

**Figure 6.3** First `elm` screen display

Note the three parts of the **`elm`** Index screen display.

1. The **`elm`** program displays a message list at the top of the screen, telling you what is in your system mailbox. The e-mail message that you sent to yourself in Example: `elm` Program is shown, with the subject listed as **`My first elm message`**.
2. A suggested list of valid commands is given near the bottom of the screen, helpful reminders about what you can do next.
3. A command prompt **`Command:`** at the bottom of the screen allows you to proceed by typing the letter of a valid command.

At this point, from the Index screen, you can delete or undelete messages, mail a message, reply to a message, forward a message, quit **`elm`**, or read a message. If there is mail in your system mailbox, it would appear in the list at the top of the Index screen display. If that message is the current message, an arrow (->) points to it or it is highlighted, as in Figure 6.3.

The following is a general step-by-step procedure for sending mail with **`elm`**, starting from the Index screen.

1. Type **`m`**. A prompt **`Send the message to:`** appears on screen, allowing you to enter the recipient(s) name(s). If you want to specify more than one recipient, separate their usernames or Internet addresses with commas (**`,`**).

2. A prompt `Subject of message:` appears, allowing you to enter a subject for the message.
3. A prompt `Copies to:` appears, allowing you to send copies to other recipients.
4. You are placed in the `vi` text editor where you can compose the body of your e-mail message.
5. Exit `vi` with the **Esc :wq** sequence of commands.
6. Dispose of the message by typing **s** to send it.
7. You are then back at the Index screen and the `Command:` prompt.

Practice Session 6.5 allows you to send an e-mail message to yourself and to practice using the `elm` user interface. We have assumed that you have some familiarity with the `vi` text editor (see Chapter 5).

## Practice Session 6.5

**Step 1:** At the shell prompt, type **elm** and press <Enter>. The `elm` Index screen appears on your display, similar to that shown in Figure 6.3.

**Step 2:** Type **m** to mail a new message. The prompt `Send the message to:` appears at the bottom of the screen.

**Step 3:** Type **youruserid**, where youruserid is your username on the computer system; then press <Enter>. The prompt `Subject of message:` appears at the bottom of the screen.

**Step 4:** Type **My second elm message** and press <Enter>. The prompt `Copies to:` appears.

**Step 5:** Press <Enter> to be put in the `vi` text editor.

**Step 6:** Type **A** to enter the `vi` insert mode.

**Step 7:** Type **This is a line of text in my second elm e-mail message.**

**Step 8:** Use the **Esc :wq** sequence of commands for `vi` to write out your changes and exit `vi`. You will be back in the `elm` program, and choices for editing, sending, or abandoning this e-mail message appear at the bottom of the screen.

**Step 9:** Type **s** to send it.

**Step 10:** You are back at the Index screen, at the `Command:` prompt. A message at the bottom of the screen reads `Mail sent!`

**Step 11:** Type **q** to quit **elm**. A message may be displayed at the bottom of the screen, asking you to dispose of `Read message`. Type **n** to retain the message and to return to the shell prompt.

## 6.3.3 Reading E-Mail in `elm`

To read e-mail messages with `elm`, type **`elm`** at the shell prompt, with no options or recipients specified. Then, `elm` displays the Index screen, as shown previously. At this point, from the Index screen you can read a message that appears in the message list or dispose of messages in the list, by using the options shown at the bottom of the Index screen. The following is a general step-by-step procedure for reading mail with `elm`, starting from the Index screen.

1. Press <Enter> when the message in the list that you want to read is the current message.
2. The header and contents of that message appear on the screen. If the message is longer than one screenful of text, for most systems pressing the <space bar> on the keyboard lets you see one screenful of text at a time. When you see the last screenful of the message, the prompt `Command('i' to return to index):` appears, allowing you to dispose of the message in one of several different ways.
3. Type **`i`** at this point to return to the Index screen and the `Command:` prompt.

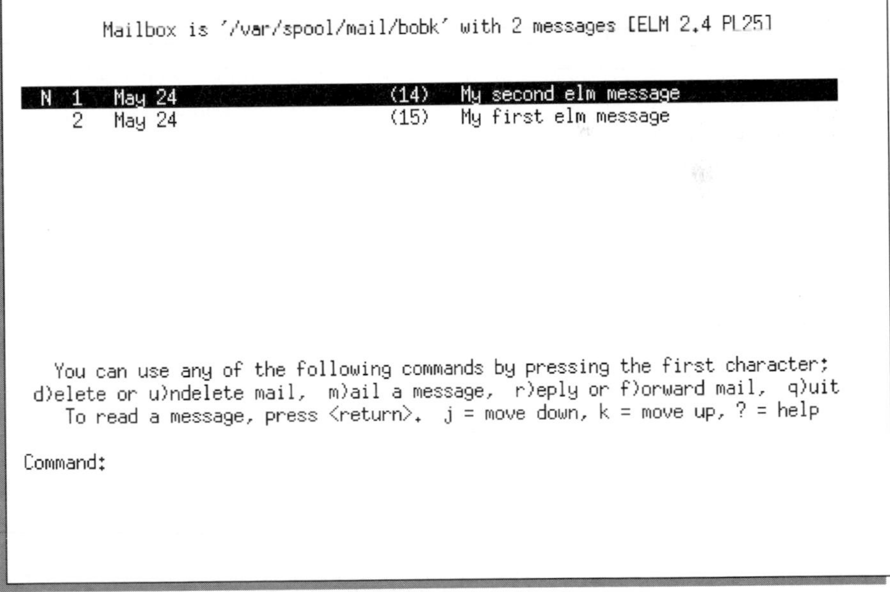

Mailbox is '/var/spool/mail/bobk' with 2 messages [ELM 2.4 PL25]
N 1 May 24 (14) My second elm message
2 May 24 (15) My first elm message
You can use any of the following commands by pressing the first character;
d)elete or u)ndelete mail, m)ail a message, r)eply or f)orward mail, q)uit
To read a message, press <return>. j = move down, k = move up, ? = help
Command:


**Figure 6.4** The `elm` Index screen with new mail

Practice Session 6.6 allows you to read the e-mail message you sent to yourself in Practice Session 6.5 and to practice the commands that let you dispose of your messages.

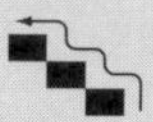

## Practice Session 6.6

**Step 1:** At the shell prompt, type **`elm`** and press <Enter>. Your screen looks like that in Figure 6.4. You are on the `elm` index screen.

**Step 2:** The current message should be the message that you sent to yourself in Practice Session 6.5. If it isn't, use the <arrow> keys (or the <J> and <K> keys) on the keyboard to highlight the message that shows `Subject: My second elm message`.

**Step 3:** Press <Enter>.

**Step 4:** The message text and header from Practice Session 6.5 appear on the screen. Also the prompt `Command ('i' to return to index):` appears at the bottom of the screen. For a list of essential commands that you could type at this point, see Table 6.5.

**Step 5:** Type **`?`**. A prompt `Help for key:` appears.

**Step 6:** Type **`?`**. You now can view the Help pages, which show a list of `elm` commands activated by keystroke.

**Step 7:** Press the <space bar> on the keyboard, reading through the keystroke commands one screenful at a time. After reading, at the `Command:` prompt press <Enter> to redisplay the current message. The `Command:` prompt remains at the bottom of the screen.

**Step 8:** Type **`s`**. The prompt `Save message to: =username` appears. Here, `elm` has supplied the name of a folder in which you can save this message. Note that the folder name is the same as the username of the sender, which should be your username.

**Step 9:** Type **`i`** to return to the Index screen.

**Step 10:** Type **`q`**. The prompt `Delete message (y/n)` appears. Type **`n`**.

**Step 11:** The prompt `Move read messages to "received" folder (y/n)` appears. Type **`n`** to return to the shell prompt.

### 6.3.4 Forwarding and Replying to an E-Mail Message in `elm`

Two extremely common events that occur in e-mail correspondence are forwarding messages and replying to messages. For example, let's say that you receive a message from Johnb, which has some information in it that would be of interest to Jillb. Rather than retype all the information into a new e-mail message to send to

**Table 6.5** Essential `elm` Commands

| Command | Action |
|---|---|
| ‹?› | Gets help on commands |
| ‹a› | Creates an alias for an e-mail address |
| ‹d› | Deletes this message |
| ‹f› | Forwards this message |
| ‹i› | Returns to the Index screen |
| ‹q› | Quits `elm` |
| ‹r› | Replies to the current message |
| ‹s› | Saves the current message in a folder |

Jillb, you simply forward Johnb's message to Jillb. Also, while reading Johnb's message, you can formulate a quick reply, without having to dispose of the current message. Practice Session 6.7 shows you how to perform these two operations in `elm`.

## Practice Session 6.7

**Step 1:** At the shell prompt, type **`elm`** and press ‹Enter›. The `elm` Index screen appears on your display.

**Step 2:** Make the current message the message you sent to yourself in Practice Session 6.5. If it isn't already the current message, use the ‹arrow› keys (or the ‹J› and ‹K› keys) to highlight the message that shows `Subject: My second elm message`.

**Step 3:** Press ‹Enter› to read this message. Remember: At this point you are only reading the message as it has been retained; you are *not* editing it. The prompt `Command('i' to return to index)` is at the bottom of the screen.

**Step 4:** Type **`f`**. The prompt `Edit outgoing message?(y/n)` appears. Type **`n`**. The prompt `Send message to:` appears.

**Step 5:** Type **`username`**, where username is your username on your LINUX system or your valid Internet address; then press ‹Enter›. The prompt `Subject of message: My second elm e-mail message (fwd)` appears.

**Step 6:** Press ‹Enter›. The prompt `Copies to:` appears.

**Step 7:** Press ‹Enter›. A prompt now appears allowing you to `e)dit message`, `edit h)eaders`, `s)end it`, or `f)orget it`.

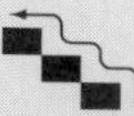

## Practice Session 6.7 (cont.)

**Step 8:** Type `f` to forget it and go back to the `Command:` prompt. If you had typed `s`, you would have forwarded the message to the recipient.

**Step 9:** Type `r`. The prompt `Copy message? (y/n)` appears.

**Step 10:** Type `y`. The prompt `Subject of message: Re: My second elm message` appears.

**Step 11:** Press <Enter>. The prompt `Copies to:` appears.

**Step 12:** Press <Enter>. You are now in the `vi` editor. The `vi` screen contains the body of the message to which you are replying. Leave it in there. At this point you could type in the body of a reply.

**Step 13:** Exit `vi` with the `Esc :wq` sequence of keystrokes. A prompt now appears allowing you to `e)dit message`, `edit h)eaders`, `s)end it`, or `f)orget it`.

**Step 14:** Type `s` and press <Enter> to refresh your view of the current message.

**Step 15:** Type `I`. You are back at the Index screen. Note that you have a new message in the message list at the top of the screen. You just replied to a message that you sent to yourself.

**Step 16:** Type `q`. The prompt `Move read messages to "received" folder (y/n)` appears.

**Step 17:** Type `n`. You are back at the shell prompt.

The following In-Chapter Exercises ask you about your use of the `elm` program.

## IN-CHAPTER EXERCISES

**6.3.** As you can see in Steps 6 and 7 of Practice Session 6.7, `elm` gives you control over whom you send a reply to. Many e-mail systems allow you to reply to a message and send the reply to *all* the correspondents who received the original message, regardless of who they were. Is this good or bad? Why?

**6.4.** How does `elm` differentiate between the new text in the reply and the original message text? What is contained in the reply to the message that you sent to yourself in Practice Session 6.7?

### 6.3.5 Saving Messages in Folders

In Practice Session 6.6, you were able to dispose of an e-mail message by saving it in a folder with a default name supplied by **elm**. That method is similar to the way that you disposed of messages with the LINUX **mail** program in Section 6.2.4. The **elm** program has a facility that allows you to organize your e-mail by folders, which you can create from within **elm**. This option is available when you type **s** on the **elm** command line to save e-mail messages. If you are on the Index screen and have highlighted a message, after you type **s**, **elm** prompts **Save message to: =username**, where username is that of the sender. If you type **?** and press <Enter>, you get help in the form of options for saving the current message, as shown in Table 6.6. The **elm** program creates a default folder in your home directory named Mail, in which it saves your messages. It can also create folders for sent and received mail messages. In addition, if you enter **=***, **elm** will list all the folders in your Mail folder.

### 6.3.6 elm Aliases

If you frequently correspond with one person or several people via e-mail, having a list of their e-mail addresses stored in the **mail** program is very useful. That way, whenever you want to send e-mail to one or more of these people, you can use the internal address list rather than having to retrieve them from some external source. For example, you might frequently send e-mail to a person who has a long e-mail address that is difficult to memorize. So, instead of trying to remember that address whenever you want to compose a new e-mail message and send it to that person, you can simply store the address in the **mail** program and recall it whenever you want to insert the address in the message header. If you frequently send messages to the same group of people but don't want to type each recipient's e-mail address, you can send a message to the group. To do so, compile a list of e-mail addresses of the group and give it a name. Then simply insert that name in

**Table 6.6** Options for Saving elm E-Mail Messages

| If You Enter | elm Will Save Your Message to |
|---|---|
| filename | a folder named *filename* in your home directory. |
| =filename | a folder named *filename* in your Mail folder. |
| ! | your incoming mailbox folder. |
| > | your "received" mail folder. |
| < | your "sent" mail folder. |
| . (period) | the previous folder you used for saving a message. |
| @alias | the default folder for alias (see Section 6.3.6 for a description of alias). |

the To: or Cc: field of the message and have the group name converted automatically to the individuals' e-mail addresses. This method is very efficient if the group has a large number of members—say, 50 or 100.

The `elm` facility that handles such tasks is aliases. As in Section 6.3.2, a common way of running `elm` from the command line includes specifying either an address or an alias as the argument to the command. In `elm`, there are two types of aliases: individual, which contains only a single e-mail address; and group, which contains multiple e-mail addresses.

So, if you want to send a message to a recipient whose e-mail address is complex and difficult to remember, you can create an alias for this recipient. You can use either of two methods. To use the first method, create an aliases.text file in your .elm subdirectory and then place the alias for the recipient in that file, using the text editor of your choice. The aliases.text file must be formatted properly. Then, run `elm`'s **newalias** utility program from the command line to activate the alias in `elm`. In the second method (which is preferable), use the `alias` command from the `elm` command line to achieve the same results. When you type `a` at the `elm` command line, the `elm` Alias screen appears, as illustrated in Figure 6.5.

Table 6.7 shows the actions of each of the alias subcommands in `vi` in creating, maintaining, and using `elm` aliases. Note that, if you add a new alias with the `a` or `n` subcommand, you must first leave the Alias screen with the `r` subcommand

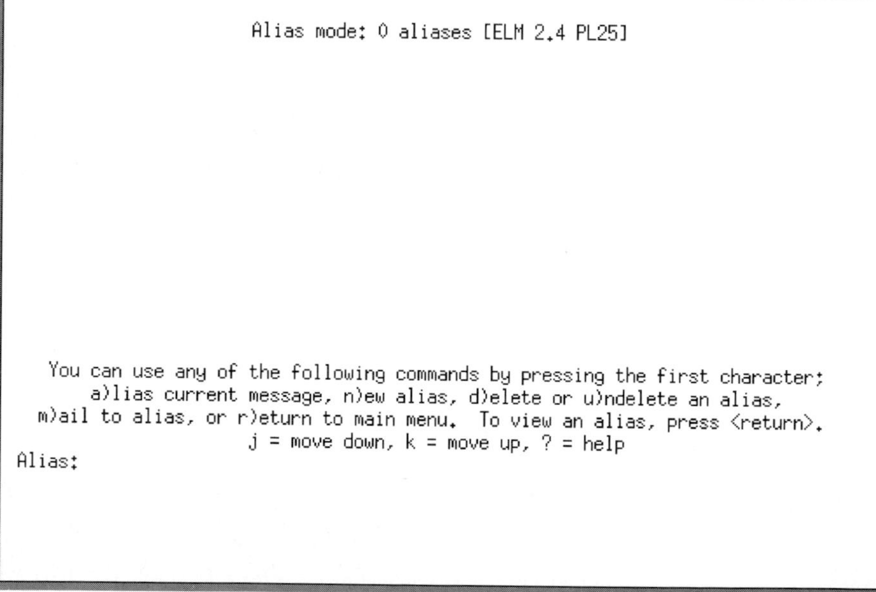

Alias mode: 0 aliases [ELM 2.4 PL25]
You can use any of the following commands by pressing the first character;
a)lias current message, n)ew alias, d)elete or u)ndelete an alias,
m)ail to alias, or r)eturn to main menu. To view an alias, press <return>.
j = move down, k = move up, ? = help
Alias:


**Figure 6.5** The `elm` Alias screen

**Table 6.7** The `elm` `Alias` Subcommands

| Subcommand | Action |
|---|---|
| `a` | If an e-mail message from someone the recipient wants to create an alias for is the current message, this subcommand creates an alias from the address of that sender. The recipient supplies the alias name. |
| `n` | This subcommand creates a new alias, based on a name and address(es) the user types in. |
| `d` | This subcommand deletes an already defined alias. |
| `u` | This subcommand undeletes an alias the user deleted during the current session. |
| `m` | This subcommand allows a user to send a message to the current alias highlighted on the alias screen. |
| `r` | This subcommand returns the user to the Main Menu. |

before the new aliases can be placed in the alias database for **`elm`**, enabling you to use them.

To create an individual alias, use the **`n`** subcommand and follow the prompts that appear onscreen. Be sure to enter the proper e-mail address when asked for it. You create group aliases with the **`n`** subcommand in the same way you create individual aliases, except that when you are prompted for an e-mail address, type in the group of addresses, separating them with commas.

To get some further practice with the **`elm`** program, do Problems 10 through 13 at the end of this chapter.

## 6.4 pine—ANOTHER FULL-SCREEN DISPLAY E-MAIL SYSTEM

The **`pine`** system is probably the most extensive and friendly e-mail program available for LINUX. It has a complete set of functions, extensive help options online, and handles the common functions of e-mail optimally.

### 6.4.1 Sending an E-Mail Message by Using pine with an Attachment Created in vi

Example: **`pine`** System shows how to send an e-mail message and an attached text file with **`pine`**. We have assumed that you did Problem 9 at the end of Chapter 5, creating the file vi_doc.txt with the **`vi`** text editor. If you have *not* done so, before you start this example, create a text file using the **`vi`** text editor—or a text editor of your choice—that contains a short explanation (100–150 words) of the capabilities of **`vi`** or the text editor you chose. Then, save the text as vi_doc.txt in your main directory, exit **`vi`** or other text editor, and proceed with the example.

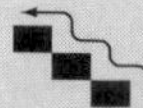

## Example: pine System

**Step 1:** At the shell prompt, type **pine** and press <Enter>.

**Step 2:** The pine Main Menu screen, similar to the one shown in Figure 6.6, appears. The highlighted menu choice is `L Folder List - Select a folder to view.`

**Step 3:** Type **C** to compose a message. The pine Compose Message screen, similar to the one shown in Figure 6.7, appears.

**Step 4:** In the To: field, type your login name and press <Enter>.

**Step 5:** Use the <down arrow> key to move the cursor to the Attchmnt: field.

**Step 6:** Type **vi_doc.txt** and press <Enter>. This file should be in your main directory.

**Step 7:** Use the <down arrow> to move the cursor to the Subject: field.

**Step 8:** Type **Attachments**.

**Step 9:** Use the <down arrow> to move the cursor to the `Message Text` area of the screen display.

**Step 10:** Type **This e-mail message contains an attached text file I created with vi.**

**Step 11:** Press <Ctrl-X>; pine asks for confirmation.

**Step 12:** Typing **y** sends your e-mail message and returns you to the pine Main Menu display.

**Step 13:** Type **Q** and then **Y** to return to the shell prompt.

## IN-CHAPTER EXERCISES

**6.5.** In the Example: pine System, how would you have specified the name of the attachment if you had wanted to attach a file from a subdirectory under your home directory instead of a file from your home directory?

**6.6.** In that same example, what would have happened if you had specified a nonexistent e-mail address in the To: field? Although it might be difficult for pine running on your system to check the validity of an Internet e-mail address, do you think that it could do so? How should it respond before you send that message?

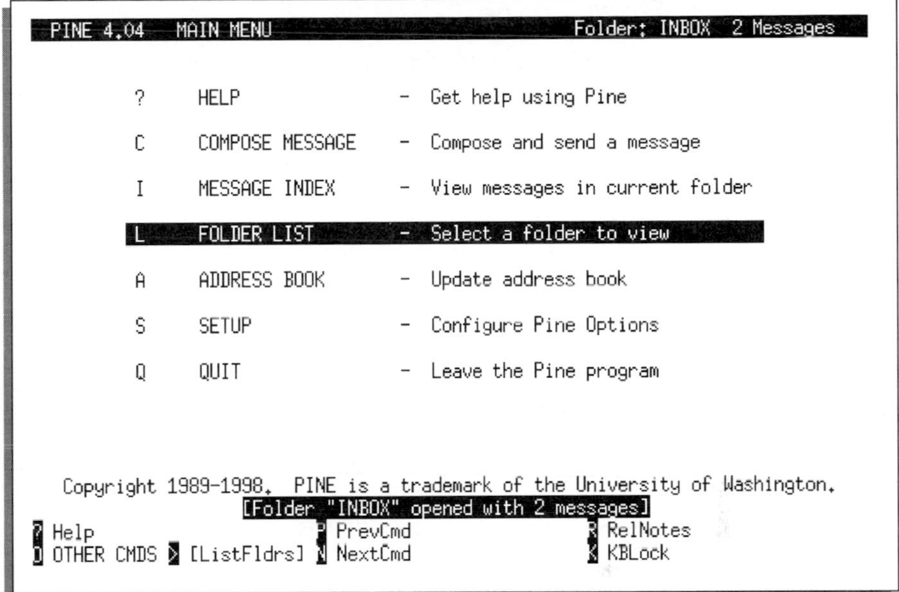


**Figure 6.6** The pine Main Menu screen

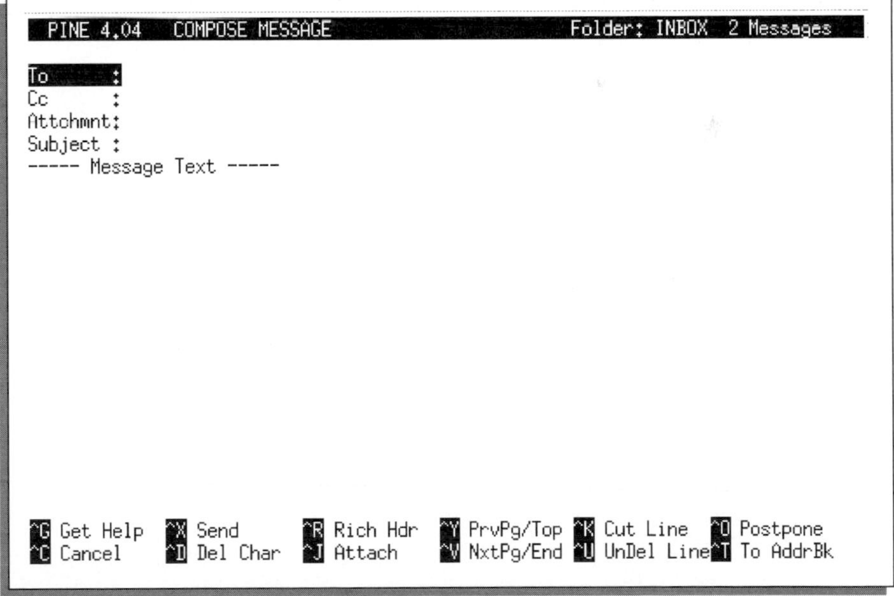


**Figure 6.7** The pine Compose Message screen

## 6.4.2 Sending E-Mail with pine

The **pine** program is an Internet e-mail and news-reading program that is freely distributed for LINUX systems by the University of Washington. It is a screen-display e-mail system, which allows you to use keystroke combinations, similar to **emacs** and **vi**, to execute commands. It presents a menu of available commands at all times at the bottom of the screen and also has extensive online help. Figures 6.6 and 6.7 show **pine**'s typical user interface format. The following is a brief description of the command used to run the **pine** program.

Syntax:

**pine [options] [recipient(s)]**

**Purpose:** Allows you to send and receive e-mail

**Output:** With no options or recipients specified, you are placed in the **pine** program and the **pine** Main Menu appears on screen.

**Commonly used options/features:**

***To send mail:***

| | |
|---|---|
| **-signature-file**=file | Set new signature file to *file*. |
| **recipient** | Go directly to the Compose Message screen with **To:** field set to recipient. |

***To receive mail:***

| | |
|---|---|
| **-i** Inbox | Go directly to the Inbox, bypassing the Main Menu. |

The quickest way to send an e-mail message to someone with **pine** is to type **pine recipient**, where recipient is a valid username of someone on your LINUX system, or a valid Internet address, and press <Enter>. When you run **pine** this way, the Compose Message screen appears immediately on your display, with the To: field already filled in with the recipient's address. The following is a general step-by-step procedure for sending mail with **pine**, starting from the Compose Message screen.

1. Press <Enter>, because the recipient's address has already been entered in the To: field. Unfortunately, the only way of verifying that the recipient's

address is correct is to send the e-mail message; if you get a returned-to-sender response, you can try again.

2. Type in entries for the Cc:, Attchmnt:, and Subject: fields, pressing <Enter> after typing each entry. If you change your mind or make a mistake in any of these fields, simply use the <up arrow> or <down arrow> key to reposition the cursor in a field and then correct or redo the entry. You can also use the <arrow> keys and reposition the cursor to change the entries in any of these fields at any time before you send the message.
3. When the cursor is in the Message Text field, type the message body. You can cancel sending this message by pressing <Ctrl-C> at the same time. Then, `pine` will prompt you to confirm your cancellation. If you type **y**, you will exit `pine` and return to the shell prompt. A file dead.letter will be created, which you can then delete with the `rm` command.
4. When you have finished composing the message body, press <Ctrl-X>. Then, `pine` will prompt you to confirm sending the message. If you type **y**, the message is sent and you exit `pine`.

Practice Session 6.8 helps you send e-mail with `pine`.

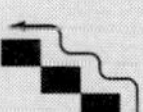

## Practice Session 6.8

**Step 1:** At the shell prompt, type **`pine recipient`**, where recipient is a valid username on your LINUX system, or a valid Internet address, and press <Enter>. The pine Compose Message screen appears on your display, with the To: field already filled in.

**Step 2:** Use the <down arrow> key to place the cursor in the Cc: field.

**Step 3:** Type **`your_username`**, where your_username is your username on the LINUX system you are now logged on to, and press <Enter>.

**Step 4:** Use the <down arrow> key to place the cursor in the Subject: field.

**Step 5:** Type **`My 2nd pine e-mail!1`** and press <Enter>. The cursor is now in the message text area of the Compose Message screen.

**Step 6:** Type **`Pine is a really neat and easy to use e-mail program.`** and press <Enter>. Your screen display should now look something like that shown in Figure 6.8.

**Step 7:** Press <Ctrl-X>. The prompt `Send message?` appears.

**Step 8:** Type **y** to send your message, exit `pine`, and return to the shell prompt.

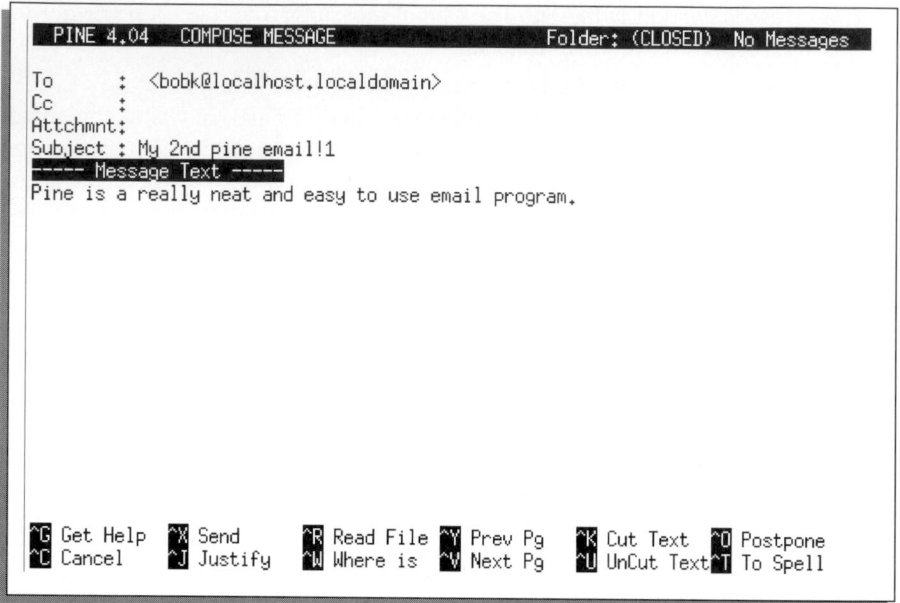


**Figure 6.8** Compose Message screen showing My 2nd `pine` e-mail

## 6.4.3 Reading E-Mail with `pine`

The **`pine`** program features an extensive set of facilities for message reading and disposal. In Practice Session 6.7, you sent a copy of the e-mail message to yourself. To read that message, you can use the following general step-by-step procedure for reading mail with `pine`.

1. At the shell prompt, type **`pine`** and press <Enter>. The `pine` Main Menu screen appears on your display, as shown in Figure 6.6, with the Folder List menu option highlighted.
2. Press <Enter> or press <**L**>. The Folder List screen appears on your display, with the Inbox folder highlighted. If the Inbox folder is not highlighted, use the <arrow> keys on the keyboard to highlight the Inbox folder.
3. Press <Enter>. The Message Index screen appears on your display, with a list of messages displayed. To view the contents of one of these messages, use the <down arrow> or <up arrow> key to highlight that message.
4. Press <Enter> to display the header and body of that message onscreen.
5. At this point, you can dispose of the message, read other messages by returning to the Message Index screen, or return to the `pine` Main Menu screen and quit.

Practice Session 6.9 gives you the opportunity to read e-mail with **pine**.

## Practice Session 6.9

**Step 1:** At the shell prompt, type **pine** and press <Enter>. The pine Main Menu screen appears on your display, similar to the one shown in Figure 6.6, with the Folder List menu choice highlighted.

**Step 2:** Press <Enter>. The Folder List screen appears on your display, with the Inbox folder highlighted.

**Step 3:** Press <Enter>. The Message Index screen appears on your display.

**Step 4:** If the message from Practice Session 6.7 is not highlighted, use the <up arrow> or <down arrow> key to highlight that message in this list. If it is not in the list, go back to Practice Session 6.7 and redo those steps.

**Step 5:** Press <Enter> when the Practice Session 6.7 message is highlighted. The Message Text screen appears on your display.

**Step 6:** When you have read the message text, press the letter **o** key on the keyboard, which gives you access to other commands. Another menu of keystroke commands appears at the bottom of the Message Text screen.

**Step 7:** Type **M**. The pine Main Menu screen appears on your display.

**Step 8:** Type **Q**, and pine prompts `Really quit pine?`

**Step 9:** Type **Y** to exit pine and go back to the shell prompt.

## 6.4.4 Disposing of E-Mail in Folders in pine

As you become a frequent user of e-mail on a LINUX system, you will soon need to organize the e-mail you receive and send, in some logical structure. As we discussed with regard to the **mail** command and **elm** earlier in this chapter, this structure will be implemented in LINUX as directories, subdirectories, and files. In fact, directories, subdirectories, and the messages they contain are all simply files in the file structure of the LINUX system. A subdirectory, or folder, useful for storing e-mail messages handled by **pine**, is just a special kind of file that enables **pine** to separate easily the messages stored in it. This capability is similar to the concept that your system mailbox is just a larger file that a **mail** program reads and then separates into messages, or smaller files, that can be read and disposed of individually.

The **pine** program has a facility for organizing your messages in groups of folders, similar to the folders you worked with in **mail** and **elm**. When you first run **pine**, it creates three folders in one collection for you: an Inbox folder, for storing your most recently received messages, a Sent Mail folder, for storing messages that you send to other recipients, and a Saved Mail folder, for storing messages that you save. The name of this collection in terms of your directory structure depends on your system and `pine` configuration, but they are generally created by `pine` initially as **~/mail**. By default, when you take some action to dispose of a message, it goes into this collection.

You can create any number of folder collections in which you can dispose of messages. In addition, you can add, delete, or change folders and their contents in each collection. Of course, within the default collection, you can add, delete, or change folders—which is probably what most users of `pine` will do in managing their messages. Then you can save messages to specific folders. Practice Session 6.10 allows you to add a folder and then move a message from your Inbox folder to the newly created folder.

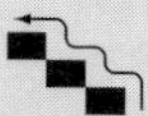

## Practice Session 6.10

**Step 1:** At the shell prompt, type **`pine -I`** and press <Enter>. The Message Index screen for your Inbox folder appears on your display immediately because you have specified the `i` option on the command line.

**Step 2:** Press <Shift-,>. This action yields the < character, telling `pine` to go to the Folder List screen, where all the folders in your default collection are displayed. These folders should include Inbox, Sent Mail, and Saved Mail. Inbox will be highlighted.

**Step 3:** Press the <A> key. A prompt `Folder name to add:` appears.

**Step 4:** Type **myown** and press <Enter>. On the Folder List screen, a new folder name, myown, appears.

**Step 5:** Using the <arrow> keys, highlight Inbox on the Folder List screen. Then press <Enter>. The Folder Index screen for the Inbox folder appears on your display.

**Step 6:** Use the <arrow> keys to highlight one of the messages in the list, perhaps `Subject: My first elm message`.

**Step 7:** Press the <O> key to get access to other commands.

**Step 8:** Press the <S> key to save this message. `The prompt SAVE #1 to folder [saved-messages]:` appears.

**Step 9:** Type **myown** and press <Enter>. The prompt `[Message 1 copied to folder "myown" and deleted]` appears. Note that, in the status field of the Message Index screen for the Inbox folder, a `D` now appears to the left of the message that you just saved in the new folder myown, signifying that this message has been deleted.

**Step 10:** Press <Shift-,>, telling `pine` to go to the folder list screen.

**Step 11:** Use the <arrow> keys to highlight the folder name myown. Then press <Enter>.

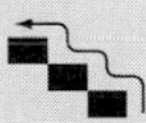

**Practice Session 6.10 (cont.)**

**Step 12:** The Message Index screen for the folder myown appears on your display. It contains a list of the files that you saved to this folder in Steps 6 through 9.

**Step 13:** Press the ‹M› key to return to the `pine` Main Menu screen.

**Step 14:** Press the ‹Q› key. The prompt `Expunge the 1 deleted message from "INBOX"?` appears.

**Step 15:** Press the ‹Y› key to confirm the deletion of this file from your Inbox folder.

## 6.4.5 Using the pine Address Book

If you frequently correspond with one person or several people via e-mail, having a list of their e-mail addresses stored in the **e-mail** program is very useful. That way, whenever you want to send e-mail to one or more of these people, you can use the internal address list rather than having to retrieve them from some external source. For example, you might frequently send e-mail to a person who has a long e-mail address that is difficult to memorize. So, instead of trying to remember that address whenever you want to compose a new e-mail message and send it to that person, you can simply store the address in the **e-mail** program and recall it whenever you want to insert the address in the message header. If you frequently send messages to the same group of people but don't want to type each recipient's e-mail address, you can send a message to the group. To do so, compile a list of e-mail addresses of the group and give it a name. Then, simply insert that name in the To: or Cc: field of a message and have the group name converted automatically to the individuals' e-mail addresses. This method is very efficient if the group has a large number of members—say, 50 or 100.

The `pine` program includes a feature that handles such tasks—and many more similar tasks—known as the Address Book. Address Book entries can be of two general types: aliases, which associate a nickname with a single e-mail address; or distribution lists, which associate a single nickname with a group of e-mail addresses. With the `pine` Address Book, you can use aliases or distribution lists for automatic insertion in the **To:** field of the Compose Message screen. You can also compose a message with the **To:** field of the message header being automatically filled in with an alias or distribution list's e-mail address(es). Finally, you can have more than one Address Book.

You can activate the Address Book by selecting Address Book on the `pine` Main Menu screen. When you make this menu choice, the Address Book screen appears on your display, as shown in Figure 6.9. This screen in `pine` allows you to add, delete, and edit entries in your Address Book. Table 6.8 contains a summary of the actions of each menu choice on the Address Book screen.

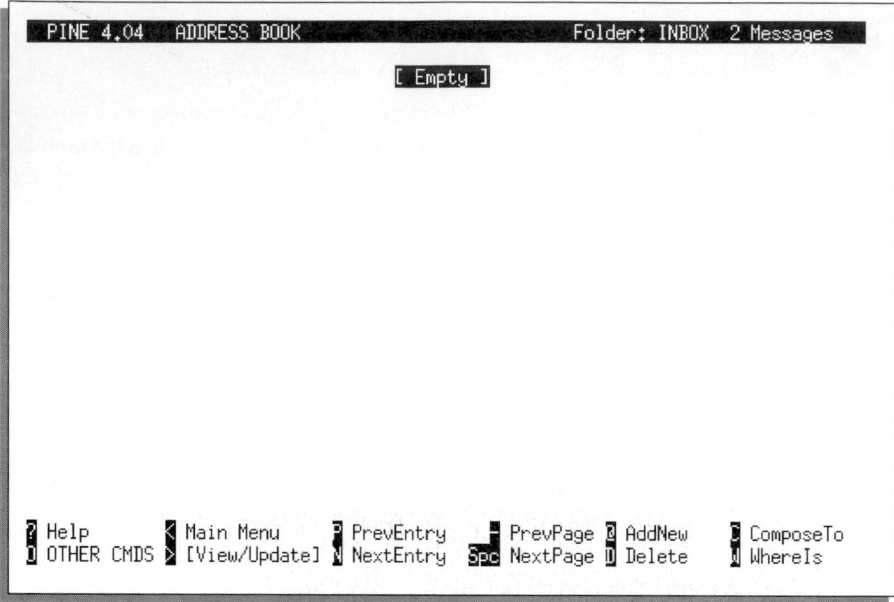


Figure 6.9 The `pine` Address Book screen

**Table 6.8** The `pine` Address Book Menu Choices

| Menu Choice | Action |
|---|---|
| **?** Help | Gives screen displays of Help on the Address Book |
| ‹ Main Menu | Returns the user to the Main Menu screen |
| **P** PrevEntry | Goes to the previous entry in the Address Book |
| - PrevPage | Goes to the previous page of the Address Book |
| **@** AddNew | Adds a new Address Book entry |
| **C** ComposeTo | Composes a new e-mail message supplying the current Address Book entry in `To:` field |
| **O** Other CMDS | Allows the user to apply additional `pine` commands, such as `Index`, `Print`, `Save`, `Forward`, `List Folders`, and `Quit Pine` |
| › [View/Update] | Edits a selected entry in the Address Book (e.g., to change e-mail addresses) |
| **N** NextEntry | Goes to the next entry in the Address Book |
| **SpaceBar** NextPage | Goes to the next page of the Address Book |
| **D** Delete | Deletes an entry in the Address Book |
| **W** Whereis | Searches for a word or name in the Address Book |

Practice Session 6.11 shows you how to add a new entry (a distribution list) to your `pine` Address Book for a group of your friends to whom you would frequently like to send e-mail. We have assumed that you are currently running the `pine` program.

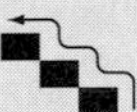

## Practice Session 6.11

**Step 1:** From the `pine` Main Menu screen, select `Address Book`. Your screen display will look similar to the one shown in Figure 6.9.

**Step 2:** Type **`@`**. Your screen display will now look similar to the one shown in Figure 6.10. The cursor should be in the Nickname field of this screen, allowing you to start a new entry by adding a nickname for the new distribution list entry. Note that, any time during the next five steps you want to edit any of the entries that you have made in any of the fields, you can simply use the <arrow> keys to reposition the cursor over the entry and change the entry (or delete it).

**Step 3:** Type **buds** and press <Enter>.

**Step 4:** In the Fullname: field, type **`My friends`** and press <Enter>. This entry will be included in the message header if you put the distribution list nickname in the To: or Cc: field when you are composing a message.

**Step 5:** In the Fcc: field, type `""` (two double quotes) and press <Enter> to signify that you don't want any file copies associated with this entry.

**Step 6:** In the Comment: field, type **`My best buddies`** and press <Enter>.

**Step 7:** In the Addresses: field, type in the e-mail addresses of some of your friends, being sure to separate the addresses with commas—for example, `bobk@ucsd.edu, sarwar@umich.edu`, etc. You have now finished making a distribution list entry. If necessary, go back over the field entries and check them to see that they are correct, particularly the e-mail addresses.

**Step 8:** Press <Ctrl-X>. At the prompt `Exit and Save changes?` type **`Y`**. This action causes you to save the entry, leave the Address Book Add screen, and return to the Address Book screen. Note that the Address Book screen now shows one highlighted, or selected, entry with three fields. The first field is the nickname, the second is the full name, and the third contains the e-mail addresses.

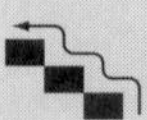

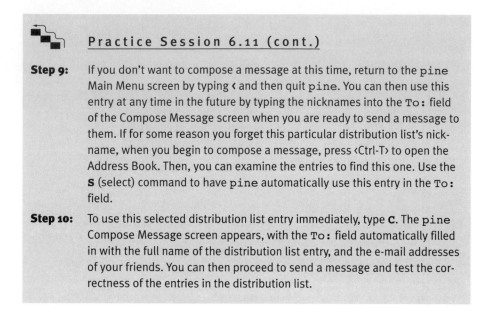

## Practice Session 6.11 (cont.)

**Step 9:** If you don't want to compose a message at this time, return to the `pine` Main Menu screen by typing **<** and then quit `pine`. You can then use this entry at any time in the future by typing the nicknames into the `To:` field of the Compose Message screen when you are ready to send a message to them. If for some reason you forget this particular distribution list's nickname, when you begin to compose a message, press <Ctrl-T> to open the Address Book. Then, you can examine the entries to find this one. Use the **S** (select) command to have `pine` automatically use this entry in the `To:` field.

**Step 10:** To use this selected distribution list entry immediately, type **C**. The `pine` Compose Message screen appears, with the `To:` field automatically filled in with the full name of the distribution list entry, and the e-mail addresses of your friends. You can then proceed to send a message and test the correctness of the entries in the distribution list.

To get more practice with the Address Book, and with `pine`, do Problems 8 and 9 at the end of this chapter.

PINE 4.04 ADDRESS BOOK (Add) Folder: INBOX 2 Messages
Nickname :
Fullname :
Fcc :
Comment :
Addresses :
Fill in the fields just like you would in the composer.
To form a list, just enter multiple comma-separated addresses.
It is ok to leave fields blank. Press "^X" to save the entry, "^C" to cancel.
If you want to use quotation marks inside the Fullname field, it is best
to use single quotation marks; for example: George 'Husky' Washington.
^G Get Help ^X eXit/Save ^R RichView ^Y PrvPg/Top ^K Cut Line
^C Cancel ^D Del Char ^V NxtPg/End ^U UnDel Line ^T To AddrBk

**Figure 6.10** The `pine` Address Book Add Entry screen

### 6.4.6 A Summary of `pine` Commands

The following tables present summaries of the important operations of **`pine`**. Table 6.9 contains operations that may be executed while you are reading and disposing of messages. Table 6.10 contains operations that you may execute while composing a message. Table 6.11 contains general **`pine`** operations. Table 6.12 contains Folder Index screen commands. Table 6.13 contains Address Book commands.

**Table 6.9** Message Disposition Commands

| Command | Description |
|---|---|
| <D> | Deletes the current message |
| <E> | Saves the current message as a plain text file in the default folder |
| <F> | Forwards the current message |
| <R> | Replies to the current message |
| <S> | Saves the current message in a folder |
| <U> | Undeletes the current message |
| <Y> | Prints the current message with a default print command |

**Table 6.10** General Message Composition Commands

| Command | Description |
|---|---|
| <Ctrl-C> | Cancels the message being composed and writes it to dead.letter |
| <Ctrl-G> | Gets online help that is context-sensitive |
| <Ctrl-L> | Refreshes the screen contents |
| <Ctrl-O> | Postpones the sending message being composed |
| <Ctrl-T> | Invokes the spell checker |
| <Ctrl-X> | Sends the message being composed |

**Table 6.11** General `pine` Commands

| Command | Description |
|---|---|
| <?> | Shows the Help screen for this screen menu |
| <C> | Composes a new message using the Compose Message screen display |
| <L> | Goes to the Folder List screen display |
| <M> | Returns to the Main Menu screen display |
| <O> | Shows all other available commands for this screen menu |
| <Q> | Quits `pine`, allowing disposal of deleted messages |

**Table 6.12** Folder Index Screen Commands

| Command | Description |
|---|---|
| ‹F› | Forwards the currently selected message |
| ‹J› | Jumps to a specific message Address Book |
| ‹N› | Moves to the next message |
| ‹P› | Moves to the previous message |
| ‹space bar› | Shows the next screenful of messages |
| ‹W› | Searches for a specific folder |

**Table 6.13** Address Book Commands

| Command | Description |
|---|---|
| ‹-› | Moves to the previous page of the current Address Book |
| ‹A› | Adds a new entry to the current Address Book |
| ‹C› | Composes a message to the current entry in this Address Book |
| ‹D› | Deletes the selected entry from the current Address Book |
| ‹N› | Moves to the next address |
| ‹P› | Moves to the previous address |
| ‹space bar› | Moves to the next page of the current Address Book |
| ‹T› | Takes address to another Address Book |
| ‹V› | Views/edits the selected entry in the current Address Book |
| ‹X› | Exports the current entry to a file |
| ‹Y› | Prints the current Address Book |

## 6.5 GRAPHICAL E-MAIL WITH KMAIL

In addition to text-based e-mail systems, LINUX supports Kmail. What really differentiates Kmail as a LINUX e-mail system from the other e-mail systems we have used so far in this chapter is that almost everything that was done previously by using text-based commands and operations can be accomplished graphically in Kmail. Kmail is very similar to Netscape Messenger, used to send and receive e-mail in the Netscape Communicator browser.

The common functions found in Table 6.14 are all accomplished in Kmail via mouse point-and-click operations. The only typing the user need do is for the message body itself and necessary parameter changes or text specifications in the in-

**Table 6.14** Message Status Flags in the Header Pane

| Status Flag (Appearance) | What It Means |
|---|---|
| New: (red dot, message colored red) | The message has been received for the first time and is unread. |
| Unread: (green dot, message colored blue) | The message has already been retrieved off the server at least once, but has not been read yet. |
| Read: (dash) | The message has been read. |
| Replied: (blue U-turn arrow) | A reply has been composed to this message. |
| Queued: (envelope) | The message has been queued in the Outbox to be sent later. |
| Sent: (angled envelope) | The message has been sent. |

put fields of various menus or command windows in the Kmail graphical environment. As mentioned in Chapter 5, a combination of keyboard entry of text and graphical operations, suited to the needs of the individual user, is the best approach to take with both text editing and e-mail.

### 6.5.1 Starting Out with Kmail

The following Example: Kmail assumes that you are connected to a network, that you know your e-mail address, and that your instructor or system administrator can provide you with e-mail server information. It also assumes that you are running the KDE window management system as the front-end to your LINUX operating system. More information on KDE can be found in Chapter 21.

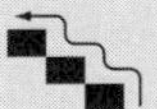

**Example: Kmail**

**Step 1:** Create a signature file in your home directory with your favorite text editor, such as XEmacs, as shown in Chapter 5. A signature file contains informational text that you want to include as part of all e-mail messages you send. Save this file as ksig.sig.

**Step 2:** Launch Kmail Mail by left-clicking on the Mail Client button (at the extreme right-corner of the panel on the Kdesktop) or by making the launcher pop-up menu choice Internet> Mail Client. Note: when you run Kmail for the first time, it creates a Mail directory containing the files inbox, outbox, sent-mail, and trash in your home directory. A Settings window also appears, in which you must enter some initial information so Kmail will be able to properly retrieve and send your messages. To begin sending and receiving email you will only have to change the settings in the Identity and Network tabs.

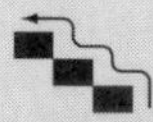

## Example: Kmail (cont.)

**Step 3:** If it is not already the current tab, click on the Identity tab in the Settings window. Fill in the E-mail Address and Reply-to Address fields with your e-mail address. Specify the path to your signature file, ksig.sig in the Signature File field by clicking on the browse button (...) if necessary.

**Step 4:** Click on the Network tab in the Settings window. In the Sending Mail block, choose SMTP and fill in the Server field with the name and domain of your e-mail server. Get this information from your instructor or systems administrator.

**Step 5:** To set up an account so you can receive mail, press the Add... button in the Incoming Mail block of the Settings window.

**Step 6:** You will be prompted for the type of account. Select POP3; then press OK.

**Step 7:** The Configure Account window appears. Fill in the Name field to name your account, and the Login, Password, and Host fields with your login name, password, and hostname. Get this information from your instructor or systems administrator. You should also check the box Delete mail from server so as to not leave your mail on the server. The account's mailbox should be set to inbox. Finally, make the OK choice in the Configure Account window. A new account should now appear in the Incoming Mail block. *Note*: If at this point, you get error messages, you have not configured the network settings properly. Go back and readjust the settings, starting at Step 4. Get help from your instructor or systems administrator if necessary.

**Step 9:** Close the Settings window by left-clicking on the X in the upper-right corner. The Message Reader window should now be displayed on the screen, similar to Figure 6.11.

**Step 10:** From the pull-down menu in the Message Reader window, choose File › New Composer. A Composer window will appear, allowing you to compose a new e-mail message.

**Step 11:** In the To: field, type your e-mail address.

**Step 12:** In the subject field, type **`My first Kmail e-mail message!`** and press <Enter>. Notice that in the title bar of the Composer window, that subject is now displayed.

**Step 13:** You can now add text to the body of the e-mail message. Type **`Kmail is cool!`** in the main (the largest) block of the Composer window.

**Step 14:** From the pull-down menu in the Composer window, choose Attach › Append Signature. If the Choose Signature File window appears, select the file ksig.sig that you created in Step 1 and click on the OK button. Whatever you input into ksig.sig from Step 1 will now be appended to the message body after the line `Kmail is cool!`

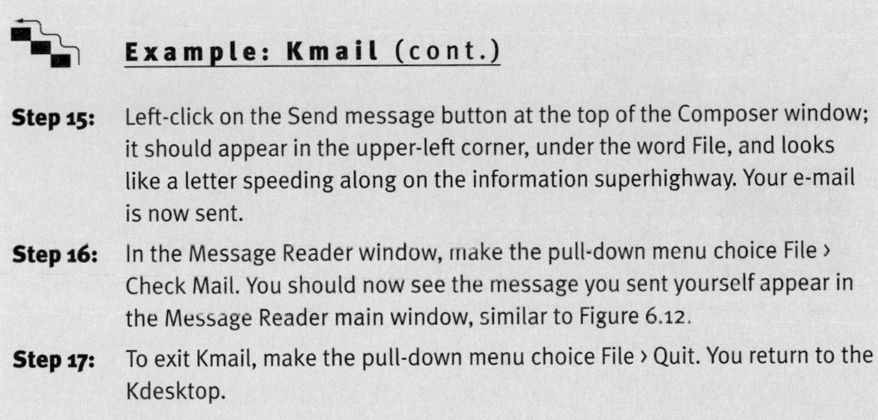

**Example: Kmail (cont.)**

**Step 15:** Left-click on the Send message button at the top of the Composer window; it should appear in the upper-left corner, under the word File, and looks like a letter speeding along on the information superhighway. Your e-mail is now sent.

**Step 16:** In the Message Reader window, make the pull-down menu choice File › Check Mail. You should now see the message you sent yourself appear in the Message Reader main window, similar to Figure 6.12.

**Step 17:** To exit Kmail, make the pull-down menu choice File › Quit. You return to the Kdesktop.

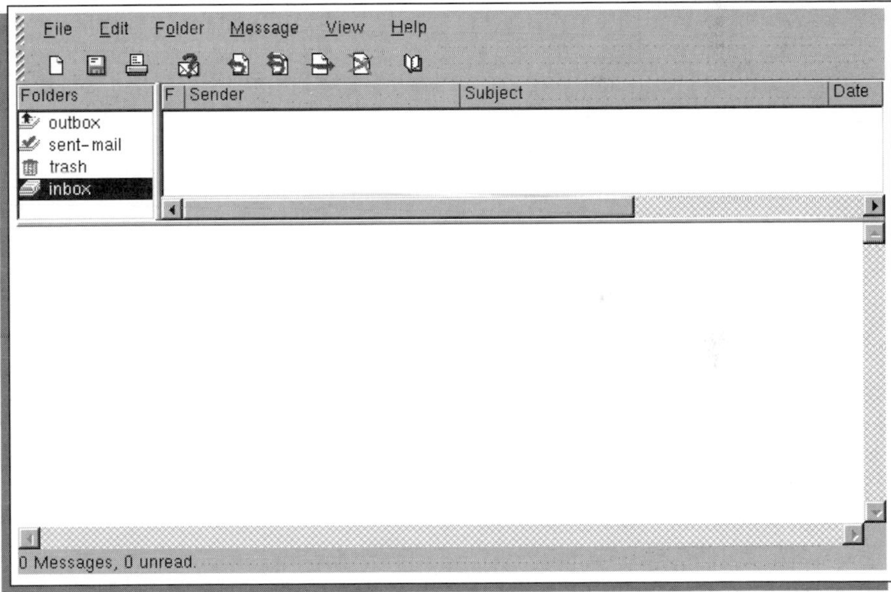


**Figure 6.11** Message Reader window in Kmail

## 6.5.2 Reading E-Mail in Kmail

When you launch the Kmail program, the Message Reader window opens. It has three major "panes": the Folders pane, the Header pane and the Message pane.

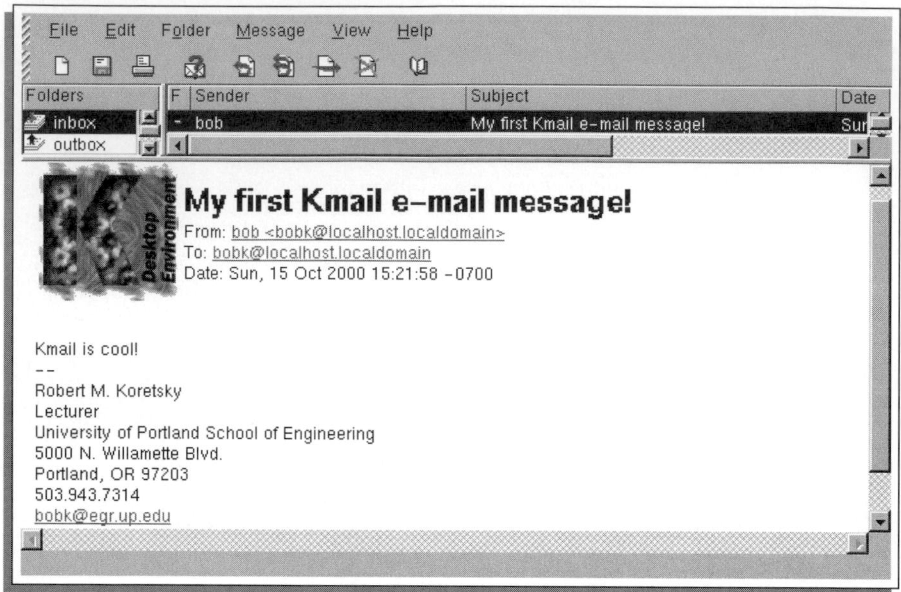


**Figure 6.12** First Kmail e-mail message

1. The Folders pane (upper left) shows your available message folders. To view the contents of a folder, simply click on it.
2. The Header pane (upper right) lists e-mail message header information, including message status flags (F), sender, subject, and the date the message was sent for the messages in the currently selected folder. Click on a header to select that message and display it in the Message pane. See Table 6.14 for a list of the meaning of the message status flags. You can also select a series of messages by clicking on one message, holding down the <SHIFT> key, and clicking on another message. The two messages will be selected, along with all the messages in between. You can sort the messages by clicking on the column that you want to sort.
3. The Message pane is the main area of the window. To scroll through the message, use the scroll bar at the right of the Message pane.

## IN-CHAPTER EXERCISES

**6.7.** Launch Kmail and examine the Header pane. What appears in it? What is (are) the status of message(s) shown?

**6.8.** In the Folders pane, click on the sent-mail folder. What appears in the Headers pane? What is (are) the status of the message(s) shown? What appears in the Message pane?

The following Practice Session gives you further practice in reading e-mail with Kmail and disposing of e-mail messages. If you are not running Kmail, launch it now.

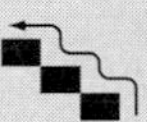

## Practice Session 6.12

**Step 1:** In the Message Reader window, in the Folders pane, click on the sent-mail folder icon, then click on `Subject: My first Kmail e-mail message!`

**Step 2:** Press the ‹D› key. The message is deleted from the sent-mail folder.

**Step 3:** Click on the trash folder icon, then click on the message `Subject: My first Kmail e-mail message!`

**Step 4:** Press the ‹D› key. The message is deleted from the trash folder.

**Step 5:** Click on the inbox folder icon, then click on the message `Subject: My first Kmail e-mail message!`

**Step 6:** Left-click on the Forward button at the top of the Message pane. It looks like a blue arrow over a white page. The Composer window opens on screen, with `Fwd: My first Kmail e-mail message!` listed in the title bar of that window, as well as in the subject line. The message body of that message is also shown in the Message pane.

**Step 7:** In the To: field, type your e-mail address. Click on the Subject: field, erase whatever is in there using the ‹backspace› key, and type **`Forwarded first Kmail message`**.

**Step 8:** Left-click on the send button at the upper left of the Composer window. You are returned to the Message Reader window. At the extreme bottom-left corner, a line of text appears telling you that Kmail is done sending messages. In the Header pane, what is the status flag showing for the message `My first Kmail e-mail message!`? Refer back to Table 6.14.

**Step 9:** Depending on the speed of your system, a new message header appears in the Header pane. The subject of this message should be `Forwarded first Kmail message`. what is the status flag showing for this message? Refer back to Table 6.14.

**Step 10:** Click on the new message in the Header pane. Notice that the status flag changes from a red button to a dash, meaning it is now a read message. Delete ,`My first Kmail e-mail message!` and `Forwarded first Kmail message`. How did you accomplish this deletion? Delete these messages from the trash folder and the sent-mail folder. Exit Kmail by choosing File › Quit from the pull-down menu at the top of the Message Reader window.

### 6.5.3 Sending E-Mail in Kmail

To send new e-mail messages in Kmail, you use the Composer window. Open the Composer window by clicking on the Compose New Message button in the upper-left corner of the Mail Reader window, or by choosing File > New Composer (keyboard shortcut <CTRL>+N) from the pull-down menu.
If you have not indicated the location of your signature file and you have Automatically Append Signature checked in the Composer tab of the Settings dialog, you will be prompted for the location of your signature file before the Composer window opens. See Figure 6.13.

Notice the components of this window: pull-down menus at the top, speed button bar, header fields for the message, and a large pane to contain the body of the e-mail message. To send a new message, fill in the blank header fields correctly in the Composer window. Following are some useful operations you can perform to compose a new message.

1. To use the Address Book: The buttons to the right of the To: and Cc: field boxes, the ones with ellipses (...) in them, allow you to use Address Book entries to fill in these fields, if you have any Address Book entries. You can easily add, edit, or delete entries in your Address Book by clicking on the Open address Book button at the top of the Composer window or by choosing File > Address Book from the pull-down menu. An Address Book Manager window opens, allowing you to add, edit, or delete entries to your Address Book.

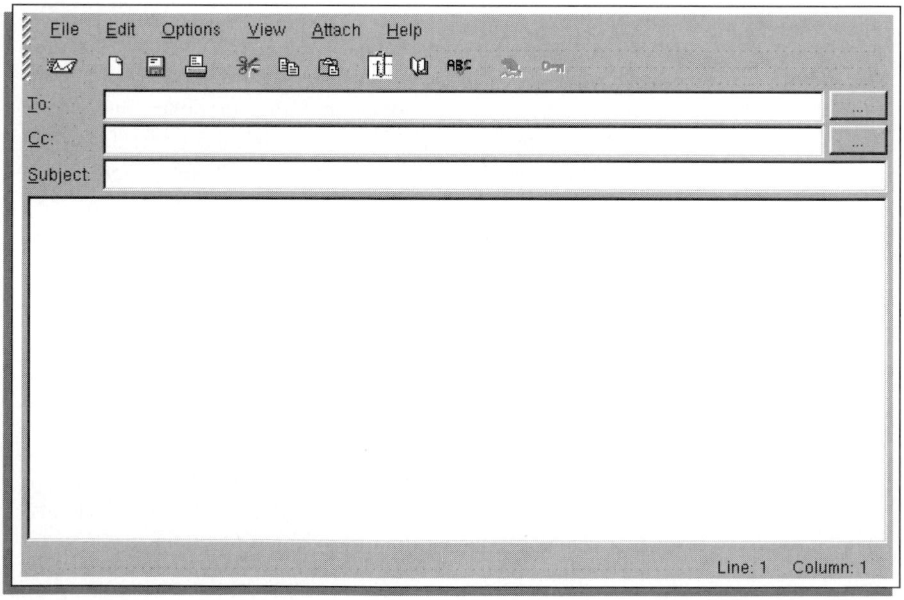

**Figure 6.13** Kmail Composer window

2. If you want to add a Bcc: field (send blind carbon copies) to the display, choose View > Bcc from the pull-down menu. Make sure there is a check next to the box next to Bcc.
3. To include files as attachments, click on the Attach File button (it looks like a piece of paper with a large paper clip over it) at the top of the Composer window. The Message Part Properties window appears on screen, allowing you to change encoding, mime-typeset. When you choose OK in the Message Part Properties window, your file is attached to the message you are composing, and you see a new pane open below the main message pane.
4. You can use the Spellchecker button (it looks like the letters ABC with a check over the letters) to verify that your message uses proper spelling.
5. To access the Help function, press the function key <F1>. Help documentation opens in its own window on screen.
6. You can use the pull-down menu choice Attach > Insert File to insert text from a file in one of your directories directly into the message body at the cursor location in the message body. If you have copied text onto the Kdesktop clipboard in another window by highlighting the text, the button Paste Clipboard Contents will paste whatever is on the clipboard into your message wherever the cursor is positioned in the message body.

To get practice with these facilities when composing a new e-mail message, do Practice Session 6.13.

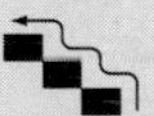

## Practice Session 6.13

**Step 1:** Use your favorite text editor, such as XEmacs, to compose a short description of the Kmail Composer window buttons. Save the file as buttons in your home directory.

**Step 2:** If you are not already in Kmail, launch the program now. In the Message Reader window, click on the Compose New Message button. Your screen display should look similar to Figure 6.13.

**Step 3:** Click on the Open Address Book button at the top of the Composer window. In the Address Book Manager window that opens, type your e-mail address into the line above the bottom row of buttons, then click on the Add button. You have added your own e-mail address to your Address Book. Click on the OK button to close the Address Book Manager window.

**Step 4:** To the right of the To: field, click on the button with the ellipses (...) in it. The Address Book window opens. Click on your e-mail address, then click on OK. Your e-mail address is added into the To: field of this new message.

**Step 5:** In the Subject: field, type **`My second Kmail e-mail message!`**

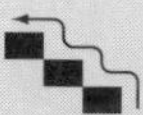

**Practice Session 6.13 (cont.)**

**Step 6:** If you have created the signature file from Example: Kmail and it was not automatically appended to this message, make the pull-down menu choice Attach › Append Signature. Whatever is in your file ksig.sig will be appended into the body of the e-mail message, leaving just one blank line at the top of the message body.

**Step 7:** Click on the Attach File button at the top of the Composer window. In the Attach File window that opens on screen, click on the file named buttons shown in your home directory, the one you created in Step 1. Then click on OK in the Attach File window. The Message Part Properties window opens, and you can click on the OK button in that window. Notice that a new pane opens below the main message body pane, showing you some information about the attachment you just made to this message.

**Step 8:** In the main message body pane, type **`Find attached a plain text file describing the buttons found at the top of the Kmail Composer window`**. Then press Enter on the keyboard.

**Step 9:** Click on the Send message button. The Composer window closes. The e-mail message is delivered, in an amount of time dependent on your system.

**Step 10:** In the Message Reader window, choose File › Check Mail. In the Header pane, a new message is shown; the body of the message is shown in the Message pane.

**Step 11:** If necessary, scroll to the bottom of the message body. Click on the Buttons icon. In a short time, the Kedit text editor window opens on screen, showing you the contents of the buttons file. From within this text editor window, save or print this file if you desire. Quit Kedit by choosing File › Exit from the pull-down menu.

**Step 12:** In the Message Reader window, delete the message `My second Kmail e-mail message!` by clicking the Delete Message button when the message header is highlighted in the Header pane. Delete it from the sent-mail folder and the trash folder as well.

**Step 13:** Quit Kmail by holding down the ‹CTRL› and ‹Q› keys at the same time.

## 6.5.4 Simple Filtering of E-Mail into Folders

It is very useful to be able to sort your e-mail into folders for reading and disposition. This is particularly true if you receive many messages in a day and want to be able to organize them. The Kmail facility known as filtering, which allows you to apply criteria to e-mail messages and sort them automatically into folders that you specifically create for such purposes. For example, suppose that you are getting a lot of mail from a particular sender and wish to have that sender's e-mail automatically stored in a folder all by itself as soon as it comes in. This can be accomplished in two easy steps.

1. Create a folder for storage of the messages using the Message Reader window pull-down menu choice Folder > Create. In the New Folder window that opens, type new folder name in the Name: field, then click OK to close this window.
2. Design a filter using the Message Reader window pull-down menu choice File > Filter. In the Filter Rules window that opens, select the criteria for filtering and the action(s) to be taken when e-mail from this particular sender arrives in your Kmail Inbox folder.

That's it! Now everything sent from that sender will automatically go to the designated folder whenever you check your e-mail with File > Check Mail. Of course, designing the criteria for sorting can be complex if you have several logically dependent criteria, but this simple, two-step model shows you how you can achieve the automated process. To get some experience in designing a simple filter criteria, do Practice Session 6.14.

## Practice Session 6.14

**Step 1:** Launch Kmail if you are not already running the program.

**Step 2:** In the Message Reader window, choose Folder › Create. The New Folder window appears on screen.

**Step 3:** In the Name: field of the New Folder window, type **me**, then click the OK button. This creates a new empty folder under your Mail directory named me. In fact, you can now see this folder name appear in the Folders pane on your screen (scroll down to it if necessary).

**Step 4:** In the Message Reader window, choose File › Filter. The Filter Rules window appears, similar to Figure 6.14. The letters A thru G in that figure refer to the fields you will fill in in the following steps.

**Step 5:** In the left-most pane of the Filter Rules window, an empty filter appears as a ‹›:. It should be highlighted as shown in Figure 6.14 (A); if it is not, click on it.

**Step 6:** The three fields at the top of the Filter Rules window to the right of the highlighted empty filter should be filled in as follows, from left to right: Make the pull-down choice From for the first field (B); leave the Contains choice in the second field (C); in the third field (D) type your complete e-mail address (Note: These are the matching criteria fields, which allow you to design criteria for sorting the messages).

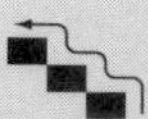

## Practice Session 6.13 (cont.)

**Step 7:** The eight smaller panes in the middle of the window are the actions fields (Note: These are the fields that specify an action to be done on messages that meet the criteria from Step 6). In the top one (E), make the pull-down menu choice Transfer. A new field opens to the right of your transfer action field at letter F. From the pull-down menu choose the folder me in this field.

**Step 8:** In the second action field from the top (G), choose Skip Rest. Click on the OK button at the bottom of the Filter Rules window. You have now designed a new filter for use on sorting, or disposing of, new e-mail that arrives in your Inbox.

**Step 9:** To test this filter, open a new Composer window by clicking on the Compose new message button in the Message Reader window.

**Step 10:** Send an e-mail message to yourself, as you did in Practice Session 6.13, but this time make the subject Automatic Sort 1. Contents of the message are up to you.

**Step 11:** Send the message from the Composer window.

**Step 12:** In the Message Reader window, choose File › Check Mail from the pull-down menu. The e-mail message that you sent to yourself in Step 11 is now in the folder me, not in the Inbox. where else can you see this new message? How can you tell in what other folders the message has been retained? To complete this Practice Session, delete the new e-mail message from the three locations it occupies, as well as the folder me.

## SUMMARY

The most fundamental concept of e-mail is to give you the ability to communicate via some permanent record medium on your own local computer system with other users or with users on other systems over an intranet or the Internet. LINUX systems are text-based, therefore they accommodate the e-mail medium very successfully. Similar to paper mail, an e-mail correspondent is someone who you have a dialogue with by sending and receiving e-mail messages. If you initiate the e-mail message, you are the sender. A recipient is someone to whom e-mail is addressed.

What an e-mail address is, or what the proper form of an e-mail address is, underpins the entire system of e-mail. When you wish to send e-mail over the Internet, the e-mail address relies upon the Internet Domain Name System for its basic form. The System Mailbox file, usually in the directory /usr/spool/mail, is

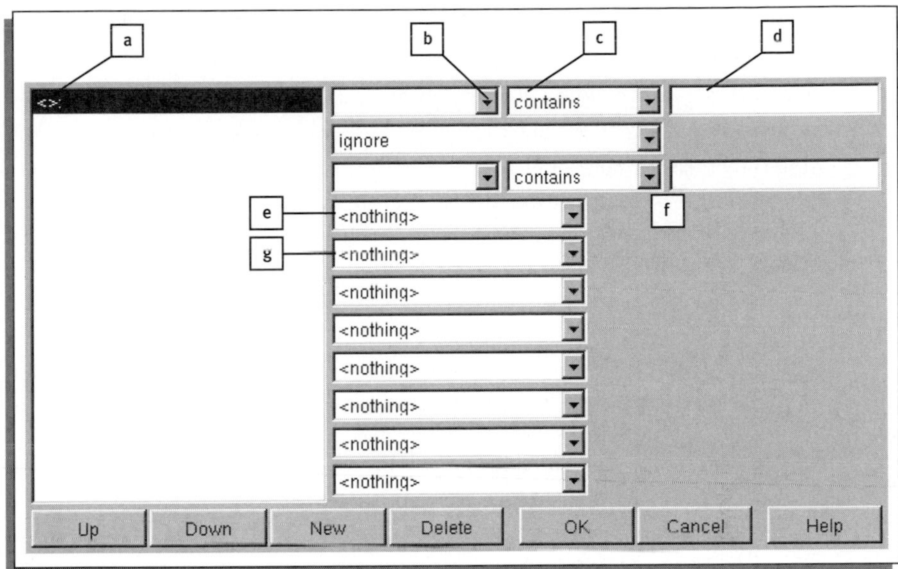


**Figure 6.14** Kmail Filter Rules window components

where messages you receive are held. There are two categories of e-mail system for LINUX systems: line-display e-mail systems, in which you can only edit one line at a time when you are composing an e-mail message, and full-screen display e-mail systems, in which you can edit any text you see on a single screen display.

The most important functions common to the LINUX mail programs described in this chapter are aliases (Address Book), attachments, carbon copy, deleting, forwarding, reading, replying, saving in folders, and sending. There is a variant of the full-screen e-mail system for LINUX that uses the XFree86 graphical user interface. The most typical of these X-based e-mail systems is Kmail, an application found on the K Desktop. Kmail gives you a graphical way of executing all the functions common to LINUX e-mail.

In conclusion, Kmail gives you the capability to graphically accomplish all of the important e-mail functions. To follow up on the Practice Sessions, you should go on to the Problems at the end of this chapter that deal with Kmail.

## PROBLEMS

1. What is the purpose of e-mail? Name the three most commonly used LINUX utilities for e-mail.
2. What is the difference between an e-mail message body and attachment?

3. List five operations that can be performed while you are using an e-mail utility.
4. What is a local host?
5. On a LINUX system, where (in which directory) are your incoming e-mail messages saved?
6. Using the editor of your choice from Chapter 5, compose an e-mail message addressed to a friend on your LINUX system and send it by using the `mail` command. In addition, edit your .mailrc file and add an alias for this recipient so that you can use this alias every time you want to e-mail that friend.
7. We assumed that you successfully completed Example: `mail` Command and Practice Session 6.4 in Section 6.2.
   a. Using the editor of your choice from Chapter 5, create or edit a file named .mailrc under your main directory and type the line **set folder=incoming** in it.
   b. Save the file and exit the editor.
   c. With the present working directory set at your main directory, at the shell prompt type **`mail`** and press <Enter>. What appears on your screen? Quit the mail program if necessary.
   d. With the present working directory set at your main directory, at the shell prompt type **`mail -f +saveops2`** and press <Enter>. What appears on your screen? Why? Quit the mail program.
   e. With the present working directory set at your main directory, at the shell prompt type **`mail -f saveops2`** and press <Enter>. What appears on your screen? Why? Can you run the mail program when there is no mail in the system mailbox for you?
8. Using the `mkdir` command, create subdirectories either under your main directory or under a mail subdirectory that would be used to save messages from your friends. Name each of these subdirectories with the usernames of your friends or with nicknames. Then, when you get incoming mail, read the messages with the `mail` command and save the messages in the appropriate subdirectories. When you want to reread or further dispose of the messages, use what you discovered in Problem 7.
9. What are e-mail aliases? Why are they needed? How do you create them for the `mail` command?
10. Are any e-mail systems available to you on your LINUX system in addition to mail, pine, or elm? If there are, what are their names? How can you find out what mail systems are available on your particular LINUX system, without asking the system administrator? If you find another system, compare its ease of use to the mail program. You may want to use that system in place of mail.
11. Compose an e-mail message addressed to another user on your system and then send it by using the elm program. Additionally, create an individual alias in elm for this user with the alias subcommand **n**. Then, whenever you need to send the same user a new e-mail message, you can use this alias.

12. When you did Practice Session 6.6, Step 8, where was the message saved to? Was it saved to your main directory? What LINUX commands can you use to help you locate this file and the directory it is in? Review Section 4.3 to help you answer these questions. Assuming that you have done Problem 3, when you get e-mail from other users, use elm to save their messages in the folders you created there. That way, when you use elm you can read, reply, and dispose of e-mail messages sent to you by using the same folders that you access when you use the `mail` command. In elm, how do you save to the same folders you created with mail?

13. When you receive e-mail from another user on your system or from someone over the Internet, use elm to forward that message to several friends for whom you have created a group alias in elm.

14. Compose an e-mail message addressed to another user on your system and then send it by using pine.

15. The pine program allows you to reconfigure the way that you interact with it, via the Setup Menu. Run pine, and at the Main Menu screen type **s**. The Setup Menu appears at the bottom of the Main Menu screen. Type **c** to access the Configuration Setup Menu. You can review the pages of the Configuration Menu by pressing the **-** (hyphen) key to go to a previous page and the <space bar> to go to the next page. When features need to be set or unset, using the <X> key activates or deactivates the feature of interest. When options need to be typed, type in valid options. Use the information given in Table 6.14 to reconfigure your pine program to take advantage of these useful operating characteristics.

16. Can you read e-mail messages composed in pine using Kmail? How?

17. The Kmail GUI is most similar to what other user e-mail interface that you are familiar with?

18. If the K Desktop is not installed on your system, what other GUI e-mail programs can you use with the Desktop that you have installed? Are they as easy to use as what is described in Kmail in this chapter?

19. After completing the Practice Sessions and In-Chapter Exercises found in Chapter 21. XFree86, how does the Kmail interface change when you change the style of the window manager?

CHAPTER

# 7

# Files and File System Structure

## OBJECTIVES

- To explain the LINUX file concept
- To discuss various types of files supported by LINUX
- To describe attributes of a file
- To explain the notion of pathnames
- To explain the user view of the LINUX file system
- To describe the user's interface to the LINUX file system—browsing the file system
- To discuss representation of a file inside the LINUX system
- To describe how a LINUX file is stored on the disk
- To explain the concept of standard files in LINUX
- To cover the commands and primitives `~`, `.`, `..`, `/`, `PATH`, `cat`, `more`, `cd`, `dirs`, `echo`, `file`, `ls`, `mkdir`, `popd`, `pushd`, `pwd`, `rmdir`, `ypcat`

## 7.1 INTRODUCTION

Most computer system users work mostly with the file system structure. While using a computer system, a user is constantly performing file-related operations: creating, reading, writing/modifying, or executing files. Therefore the user needs to understand what a file is in LINUX, how files can be organized and managed, how they are represented inside the operating system, and how they are stored on the disk. In this chapter the description of file representation and storage is somewhat simplistic owing to the introductory nature of the book. More details on these topics are available in books on operating system concepts and principles and in books on LINUX internals. All references to a file system in this textbook are to the **local file system**. The description of the LINUX network file system (NFS) is beyond the scope of this textbook, but we refer to it briefly in Chapter 14.

## 7.2 THE LINUX FILE CONCEPT

One of the many remarkable features of the LINUX operating system is the concept of files used in it. This concept is simple, yet powerful and results in a uniform view of all system resources. In LINUX, a file is a sequence of bytes. Period. Thus everything, including a network interface card, a disk drive, a keyboard, a printer, a simple/ordinary (text, executable, etc.) file, or a directory is treated as a file because they all deal with sequences of bytes. As a result, all input and output devices are treated as files in LINUX, as described under file types and file system structure.

## 7.3 TYPES OF FILES

LINUX supports five types of files:

- simple/ordinary file
- directory
- symbolic (soft) link
- special file (device)
- named pipe (FIFO)

### 7.3.1 Simple/Ordinary File

Simple/ordinary (or ordinary for short) files are used to store information and data on a secondary storage device, typically a disk. An ordinary file can contain a source program (in C, C++, Java, etc.), an executable program (applications such as compilers, database tools, desktop publishing tools, graphing software, etc.), PostScript code, pictures, audio, graphics, and so on. LINUX does not treat any one of these files any differently from another. It does not give any structure or attach any meaning to a file's contents because every file is simply a sequence of bytes. Meanings are attached to a file's contents by the application that uses or processes the file. For example, a C program file is no different to LINUX than an html file for a Web page or a file for a video clip. However, these files are treated differently by a C compiler (e.g., cc), a Web browser (e.g., Netscape Navigator), and a video player (e.g., RealPlayer).

You can name files by following any convention that you like to use; LINUX doesn't impose any naming conventions on files of any type. File names can be up to 255 letters in LINUX. Although you can use any characters for file names, we strongly recommend that nonprintable characters, white spaces (spaces and tabs), and shell metacharacters (described in Chapter 4) not be used because they are difficult to deal with as part of a file name. You can give file names any of your own or application-defined extensions, but the extensions mean nothing to the LINUX system. For example, you can give an .exe extension to a document and a .doc extension to an executable program. Some applications require extensions, but others do not. For example, all C compilers require that C source program files have a .c extension, but not all Web browsers require an .html extension for files for Web pages. Some commonly used extensions are given in Table 7.1.

### 7.3.2 Directory

A directory contains the names of other files and/or directories (we use the terms *directory* and *subdirectory* interchangeably). In some systems terms such as *folder*, *drawer*, or *cabinet* are used for a directory. A directory file in any operating system consists of an array of directory entries, although contents of a

**Table 7.1** Commonly Used Extensions for Some Applications

| Extension | Contents of File |
|---|---|
| .bmp | Bit-mapped picture file |
| .c | C source code |
| .C, .cpp | C++ source code |
| .gif | Graphics/picture file |
| .html | File for a Web page |
| .o | Object code |
| .ps | PostScript code |
| .Z | Compressed |

directory entry vary from one system to another. In LINUX, a directory entry has the structure shown in Figure 7.1.

The **inode number** is 4 bytes long and is an index value for an array on the disk. An element of this array, known as an **index node** (more commonly called an **inode**) contains file attributes such as file size (in bytes). The LINUX kernel allocates an inode whenever a new file is created. Thus every unique file in LINUX has a unique inode number. We discuss the details of an inode and how it is used by the kernel to access file contents (on the disk) later in this chapter.

### 7.3.3 Link File

We formally discuss the concept of a **link** in LINUX under file sharing in Chapter 11. A **link file** is created by the system when a symbolic link is created to an existing file. The link file points to the existing file, allowing you to rename an existing file and share it without duplicating its contents. Symbolic links are a creation of BSD UNIX but are presently available on all flavors of LINUX.

### 7.3.4 Special File (Device)

A special file is a means of accessing hardware devices, including the keyboard, hard disk, CD-ROM drive, DVD driver, tape drive, and printer. Each hardware device is associated with at least one special file—and a command or an application accesses a special file in order to access the corresponding device. Special files are divided into two types: **character special files** and **block special files**. Character special files correspond to **character-oriented devices**, such as a keyboard, and block special files correspond to **block-oriented devices**, such as a disk.

Special files are typically placed in the /dev directory (see Section 7.4). This directory contains at least one file for every device connected to the computer. Applications and commands read and write peripheral device files in the same way that they read or write an ordinary file. That capability is the main reason that input and output in LINUX is said to be device independent. Some special files are fd0 (for floppy drive 0), hda (for hard drive a), lp0 (line printer 0), and tty (for teletype terminal). Various special devices simulate physical devices and are therefore known as **pseudo devices**. These devices allow you to interact with a LINUX system without using the devices that are physically connected to the system. These devices are becoming more and more important because they allow

| Inode number | File name |
|---|---|

**Figure 7.1** Structure of a directory entry

use of a LINUX system via a network or modem or with virtual terminals in a window system such as the X Window System (see Chapter 21).

### 7.3.5 Named Pipe (FIFO)

LINUX has several mechanisms that enable processes to communicate with each other. These mechanisms, which are the key to the ubiquitous client–server software paradigm, are called **interprocess communication (IPC) mechanisms** (commonly known as *IPC primitives*). The three commonly used primitives are called **pipes**, **named pipes** (also called *FIFOs*), and **sockets**. A detailed description of these primitives is beyond the scope of this textbook, but we briefly mention the purpose of each so that you can appreciate the need for each mechanism and understand the need for FIFOs.

A pipe is an area in the kernel memory (a kernel buffer) that allows two processes to communicate with each other, provided that the processes are running on the same computer system and are related to each other; typically, the relationship is parent-child. A FIFO is a file (of named pipe type) that allows two processes to communicate with each other if the processes are on the same computer; but the processes do not have to be related to each other. A socket is a data structure in the kernel memory that can be used by processes on different computers to communicate with each other; the computers can be on a network (intranet) or on the Internet. We illustrate the use of pipes and FIFOs at the command level in Chapter 12. Discussion of LINUX IPC primitives at the application development level is beyond the scope of this textbook, but you can learn about them from any book on LINUX TCP/IP network programming.

## 7.4 FILE SYSTEM STRUCTURE

Three issues are related to the file system structure of an operating system. The first is how files in the system are organized from a user's point of view. The second is how files are stored on the secondary storage (usually, a hard disk). The third is how files are manipulated (read, written, etc.).

### 7.4.1 File System Organization

The LINUX file system is structured hierarchically (like an upside-down tree). Thus the file system structure starts with one main directory, called the **root directory**, and can have any number of files and subdirectories under it, organized in any way desired. This structure leads to a parent-child relationship between a directory and its subdirectories/files. A typical LINUX system contains hundreds of files and directories, organized as shown in Figure 7.2.

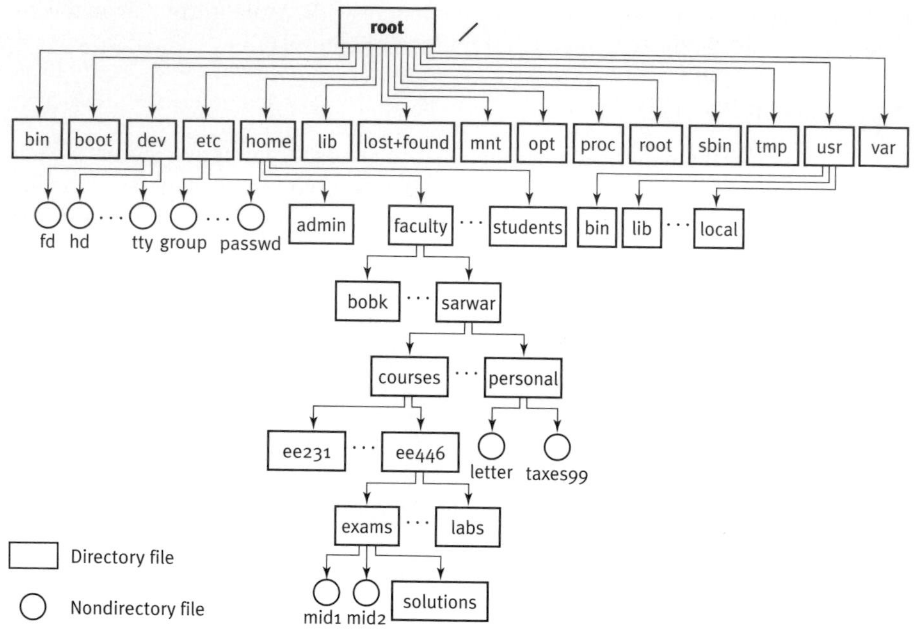


**Figure 7.2.** A typical LINUX file system structure

## 7.4.2 Home and Present Working Directories

When you log on, the LINUX system puts you in a specific directory, called your **home/login directory**. For example, the directory called sarwar in Figure 7.2 is the home directory for the user with login sarwar. As we mentioned in Chapter 4, while using the Bourne Again or TC shell you can specify your home directory by using the tilde (~) character. The directory that you are in at any particular time is called your **present working directory** (also known as your *current directory*). The present working directory is also denoted **.** (pronounced *dot*). The parent of the present working directory is denoted **..** (pronounced *dotdot*).

Later in this chapter, we describe commands that you can use to determine your home and present working directories. We also identify commands that you can use to interact with the LINUX file system in general.

## 7.4.3 Pathnames: Absolute and Relative

A file or directory in a hierarchical file system is specified by a **pathname**. Pathnames can be specified in three ways: (1) starting with the root directory, (2) starting with the present working directory, and (3) starting with the user's home directory. When a pathname is specified starting with the root directory, it is called an **absolute pathname** because it can be used by any user from anywhere in the file system structure. For example, /home/faculty/sarwar/courses/ee446 is the absolute pathname for the ee446 directory under sarwar's home directory. The absolute pathname for the file called mid1 under sarwar's home directory is /home/faculty/sarwar/courses/ee446/exams/mid1.

Pathnames starting with the present working directory or a user's home directory are called relative pathnames. When the user sarwar logs on, the system puts him into his home directory, /home/faculty/sarwar. While in his home directory, sarwar can specify the file mid1 (see Figure 7.2) by using a relative pathname ./courses/ee446/exams/mid1 or courses/ee446/exams/mid1. Sarwar (or anyone else) in the directory ee446 can specify the same file with the relative pathname **exams/mid1**. The owner (or anyone logged on as the owner) of the mid1 file can also specify it from anywhere in the file structure by using the pathname ~/courses/ee446/exams/mid1 or $PATH/courses/ee446/exams/mid1.

A typical LINUX system has several disk drives that contain user and system files, but as a user, you don't have to worry about which disk drive contains the file that you need to access. In LINUX, multiple disk drives and/or disk partitions can be mounted on the same file system structure, allowing their access as directories and not as named drives A:, B:, C:, and so on, as in MS-DOS and Microsoft Windows. Files and directories on these disks and/or partitions can be accessed by specifying their pathnames as if they were part of the file structure on one disk/partition. Doing so gives a unified view of all the files and directories in the system, and you don't have to worry about remembering the names of drives and files (and directories) they contain.

## 7.4.4 Some Standard Directories and Files

Every LINUX system contains a set of standard files and directories organized according to the **File System Standard** (**FSSTND**) proposed in 1994. The standard directories contain some specific files. We describe briefly the purpose of each directory.

### Root Directory ( / )

The root directory is at the top of the file system hierarchy and is denoted by a slash ( / ). It contains some standard files and directories, and, in a sense, it is the master cabinet that contains all drawers, folders, and files.

### /bin

Also know as the binary directory, the /bin directory contains binary (executable) images of most essential LINUX commands for system administrators and users. All of the files in this directory are either executable files or symbolic links to executable files in some other directories. Some of the general-purpose commands in this directory are `bash`, `cat`, `chmod`, `cp`, `date`, `echo`, `kill`, `ln`, `ls`, `mail`,

**mkdir**, **more**, **mv**, **ps**, **pwd**, **rm**, **rmdir**, **sh**, **stty**, **su**, **tcsh**, **uname**, and **vi**. Some of the commands in this directory have been added for system restoration. These files include **tar**, **gzip**, **gunzip**, and **zcat**. The /bin directory also contains some of the necessary networking commands. These commands include **domainname** (or **nisdomainname**), **hostname**, **netstat**, and **ping**. The /usr/bin directory contains most of the user commands.

### /boot

The /boot directory contains all the files needed to boot the LINUX system, including the binary image of the LINUX kernel. (Some systems store the configuration files and kernel map in some other directories.) The kernel file name is vmlinux (or vmlinuz), followed by the version and release information. For example, on Red Hat LINUX 6.1, the kernel is in the /boot/vmlinux-2.2.5-15 file.

### /dev

The /dev directory, which is also known as the device directory, contains files corresponding to the devices (terminals, disk drives, CD-ROM drive, tape drive, modem, printer, etc.) connected to the computer. These files are also known as special files, and are divided into two groups: **character special files** and **block special files**. The character special files correspond to devices that perform character-oriented I/O such as a keyboard. The block special files correspond to devices that perform I/O in terms of blocks or chunks of bytes such as a disk drive. Some of the files in this directory are cdrom (CD-ROM drive), console (the console), fd (floppy drive), hd (hard disk or a partition on a hard disk), isdn (ISDN connection), lp (line printer), midi (midi interface), pty (pseudoterminal), ram (RAM disk), and tty (terminal). A system may have several devices of each type; for example, 10 hard disks or partitions, 20 terminals, 100 pseudoterminals, and 2 RAM disks. For example, on a network-based system that the first two authors use at work, there are a total of 2,361 files in the /dev directory. The Red Hat 6.1 LINUX created 2,248 files in this directory by default, including 136 for hard disk drives/partitions and 17 for RAM disks.

### /etc

The /etc directory contains host-specific files and directories. These files and directories contain system configuration files; the /etc. directory does not contain any binaries. The files in this directory are primarily for the use of the system administrator only; however, an average user has read permission for most of these files. Some of the general files and directories in this directory are X11, bashrc, csh.login, crontab, group, inittab, lilo.conf, linuxconf, localtime, motd, passwd, pine.conf, profile, securetty, shells, skel, syslog.conf, ttytype, and zshrc. The X11 directory contains the configuration files for the X Window System. Some of the networking-related files and directories in /etc are exports, ftpusers, gateways, host.conf, hosts, hosts.allow, hosts.deny, hosts.equiv, hosts.lpd, httpd, inetd.conf, inputrc, lynx.cfg, mail, mail.rc, networks, news, printcap, protocols, rc.d, resolv.conf, rpc, services, snmp, and uucp. Discussion of most of the files in this directory is beyond the scope of this textbook. However, we do discuss some of these files in Chapters 13 through 18. We briefly discuss the /etc/passwd file toward the end of this section.

### /home

The /home directory contains users' home directories. The setup for this file differs from host to host. On small systems, this directory contains the home directories for the users, such as /home/bobk. On large systems where home directories are shared by hosts by using the NFS protocol, the user home directories are usually subdivided into many groups of users such as /home/admin, /home/faculty, /home/staff, and /home/students. There are local variations to this scheme. At the University of Portland system, which the first two authors use, there are 43 subdirectories under /home that contain users' home directories, each containing home directories for administration, staff, students, and faculty belonging to various departments.

### /lib

The /lib directory contains a collection of related object image files for a given language in a single file called an **archive**. A typical LINUX system contains libraries for C, C++, and FORTRAN. The archive files for one of these languages can be used by applications developed in that language. This allows software developers to use the prewritten and pretested functions in their software. The library images in the /bin directory are needed to boot the system and run some commands. In particular, it contains the standard C library /lib/libc.so.*, the math library libm.so.*, the shared dynamic linker /lib/ld/so, and some other shared libraries that are used by the commands in /bin and /sbin. The /lib/modules directory contains loadable kernel modules. Most of the remaining libraries are stored in the /usr/lib directory, but /lib contains all essential libraries.

### /lost+found

The /lost+found directory contains all the files on the system not connected to any directory. These files are found by a LINUX tool, fsck (file system check), which system administrators use to check a file system. System administrators decide the fate of the files in this directory.

### /mnt

The /mnt directory is primarily used by system administrators to mount file systems temporarily by using the `mount` command. This directory on our system contains the cdrom, disk, and floppy mount points. Thus mounting of a device, such as a CD-ROM drive, allows you to access the files on a CD-ROM as files under the /mnt/cdrom directory.

### /opt

The /opt directory is used to install add-on software packages. The programs to be invoked by the users for a package should be located in the /opt/package_name/bin directory, where package_name is the name of the installed package. The manual pages for the package are located in the /opt/package_name/man directory.

### /proc

The /proc directory contains process and system information.

### /root

The /root directory is used on many LINUX systems as the home directory of the root account. This directory is completely protected from the normal users.

### /sbin

The directories /sbin, /usr/sbin, and /usr/local/sbin contain system administration tools, utilities, and general root-only commands. Some of the general root-only commands in /sbin are `getty`, `init`, `update`, `mkswap`, `swapon`, and `swapoff`. The commands for halting the system are `halt`, `reboot`, and `shutdown`. The utilities for file system management are `fdisk`, `fsck`, `fsck.ext2`, `fsck.minix`, `mkfs`, `mkfs.ext2`, `mkfs.minix`, `mkfs.msdos`, and `mkfs.vfat`. The minimum set of networking commands in /sbin are `ifconfig` and `route`.

### /tmp

Used by several commands and applications, the /tmp directory contains temporary files. You can use this directory for your own temporary files as well. All the files in this directory are deleted periodically so that the disk (or a partition of disk) doesn't get filled with temporary files. The life of a file in the /tmp directory is set by the system administrator and varies from system to system, but it is usually only a few minutes. On most systems the **sticky bit** (Section 8.6.3) is set for /tmp so that only the owner of a file can remove a file in it.

### /usr

The /usr directory is one of the largest sections of the LINUX file system. It contains read-only data that can be shared between various hosts. On most LINUX systems, /usr contains at least the following subdirectories: X11R6, bin, doc, games, include, lib, local, man, sbin, share, src, and tmp. Table 7.2 gives a brief description of what these directories contain.

**Table 7.2** Main Subdirectories in /usr

| Subdirectory | Contents |
|---|---|
| X11R6 | The X Window system, version 11 release 6, and files related to it |
| bin | Most of the user commands and interpreters such as perl, python, and tcl. |
| doc | Documentation for various tools, utilities, libraries, applications, and interpreters such as cc, gcc, Xfree86, GNOME, Mesa, and Zsh. |
| games | Executables for games and educational software |
| include | C/C++ header files and directories that contain some specific header files, such as header files needed for writing network applications (/usr/include/netdb, /usr/include/netinet, etc.), GNU C++ header files (/usr/include/g++), and system-specific header files (/usr/include/sys) |
| lib | Object files, libraries, and internal binaries (not to be executed directly by users or shell scripts). Some subdirectories such as gcc-lib, gnome-libs, netscape, perl5, tcl8.0, and xemacs contain libraries for specific tools or applications. |
| local | Software (binaries and data) installed locally by the system administrator to be shared between hosts. Most systems contain the following directories under this directory: bin, doc, etc, games, lib, man, sbin, share, and src. |
| man | The manual pages for the LINUX commands, utilities, tools, and applications |
| sbin | Any nonessential commands and tools used by the system administrator and daemons (see Chapter 13) |
| share | Read-only architecture independent data files— that is, data files that can be shared by various platforms (Pentium, Alpha, Sparc, etc.) for a given OS |
| src | The source code for LINUX and package management software (e.g., RPM: Red Hat Package Management) |
| tmp | A symbolic link to /tmp |

### /var

The /var directory contains the variable data—that is, data that keep changing while the system is running. This data is maintained in several subdirectories but the discussion of most of the these subdirectories is beyond the scope of this textbook. One of these directories, /var/spool/mail, contains your incoming mail. When you read your new mail, it comes from a file in this directory set aside to contain your incoming mail. Once you have read the mail, it is put in a file in your home directory called mbox. The /var/yp directory contains maps for the NIS database.

### /etc/passwd

The /etc/passwd file contains one line for every user on the system and describes that user. Each line has seven fields, separated by colons. The following is the format of the line.

```
login_name:dummy_or_encrypted_password:user_ID:group_ID:user_info:home_
directory:login_shell
```

The login_name is the login name by which the user is known to the system and is what the user types to log in. The dummy_or_encrypted_password field contains the dummy password x (or *) or an encrypted version of the password. If dummy passwords are stored in the /etc/passwd file, the encrypted passwords are stored in /etc/shadow. The user_ID is an integer between 0 and 65535 assigned to the user; 0 is assigned to the super-user and 1 through 99 are reserved. The group_ID identifies the group that the user belongs to and is an integer between 0 and 65535, with 0 through 99 reserved. The user_info field contains information about the user, typically the user's full name. The home_directory field contains the absolute pathname for the user's home directory. The last field, login_shell, contains the absolute pathname for the user's login shell. The command corresponding to the pathname specified in this field is executed by the system when the user logs on. Back-to-back colons mean that the field value is missing, which is sometimes done with the user_info field. The following line from the /etc/passwd file on our system is for the user davis. In this line, the login name is davis, the password field contains x, the user ID is 134,

```
davis:x:134:105:James A Davis:/home/faculty/davis:/bin/bash
```

the group ID is 105, the personal information is the user's full name, James A Davis, the home directory is /home/faculty/davis, and the login shell is /bin/bash.

You can display the password and group information on your system by using the `cat` or `more` command, as in `cat /etc/passwd` or `cat /etc/group`. If password information for computers on your local area network is maintained in a Network Information Service "NIS" database/maps, you can display this information by using the `ypcat` command. On our local area network, there are several NIS maps that are used to maintain various types of information, including password information, user group information, internet services information, and information about hosts on the network. In the following session, we use the `ypcat -x` command to display the nicknames for the NIS maps on our system. We use the remaining two commands to display the password and group information maintained in NIS databases passwd.byname and group.byname (we use the nicknames for these maps).

```
$ ypcat -x
Use "ethers"    for map "ethers.byname"
Use "aliases"   for map "mail.aliases"
Use "services"  for map "services.byname"
```

```
Use "hosts"     for map "hosts.byaddr"
Use "networks"  for map "networks.byaddr"
Use "group"     for map "group.byname"
Use "passwd"    for map "passwd.byname"
$ ypcat passwd
scoluken:QYdGTxZWZpTgg:5330:139:Scott Lukenbaugh, CS:/usr2.y/scoluken:/bin/csh
kyljohns:L5IE0OX0IzxmY:5236:139:Kyle Johnson, CS:/usr2.y/klyjohns:/bin/csh
miclahou:CNcW0kv0rk09k:5132:139:Michael Lahoud, EE:/usr2.r/miclahou:/bin/csh
pauoster:GLxBfKcYhnWyE:5019:118:Paul Osterhout:/usr1.j/pauoster:/bin/csh
carmittl:fv15nAmlG8Pt2:4707:139:Cary Mittelmark, EE:/usr2.i/carmittl:bin/csh
mohalhaj:SQ3EhWxPCfY8U:3949:139:Mohammad Al-Hajri:/usr2.c/mohalhaj:/bin/csh
mahalsaf:.h0.JOUucCDJg:5363:139:Ahmad Al Saffar, ME:/usr2.w/mohalsaf:/bin/csh
colgross:WSmDaDXH9wNvo:4563:139:Colleen Gross, EGR:/usr2.m/colgross:/bin/csh
chrseage:Zw5RQbDpbhodc:4228:139:Chrystal Seager:/usr2.d/chrseage:/bin/csh
...
$ ypcat group
studente:*:139:
studenta:*:154:
operator:*:5:
labaides:*:114:
daemon:*:1:daemon,cron,uucp,nobody,sroot,sysadmin,uupvax
alumni:*:184:steveo,robertf,matth,janetw,fuadm,dand,omers,aarone,pauln,bobbyd,tr
iend,annp,kimn,stevew,sallyt,mohsene,rons,kayf,jeffg
faculty:*:152:
staff:*:10:
guest:*:131:guest
games:*:136:games
...
$
```

The following In-Chapter Exercises give you practice in browsing the file system on your LINUX system, and help you understand the format of the /etc/passwd file.

## IN-CHAPTER EXERCISES

**7.1.** Go to the /dev directory on your system and identify one character special file and one block special file.

**7.2.** View the /etc/passwd file on your system to determine your user ID.

## 7.5 NAVIGATING THE FILE STRUCTURE

Now we describe some useful commands for browsing the LINUX file system, creating files and directories, determining file attributes, determining the absolute pathname for your home directory, determining the pathname for the present working directory, and determining the type of a file. The discussion is based on the file structure shown in Figure 7.2 and the username sarwar.

### 7.5.1 DETERMINING THE ABSOLUTE PATHNAME FOR YOUR HOME DIRECTORY

When you log on, the system puts you in your home directory. You can find the full pathname for your home directory by using the `echo` and `pwd` commands. The following is a brief description of the `echo` command.

Syntax: **echo [options] [string]**

**Purpose:** Send "string" to the display screen; "string" can contain white spaces and terminates with newline

**Output:** 'string'

**Commonly used options/features:**

| | |
|---|---|
| `-E` | Don't interpret \-escape characters |
| `-e` | Enable interpretaion of the \-escape characters. Some of the commonly used escape characters are:<br>`\c` Send line without newline<br>`\t` Tab character<br>`\\` Backslash<br>-n Don't output the trailing newline |

With no argument, the command displays a blank line on the screen. You can determine the absolute pathname of your home directory by using the `echo` command, as in

```
$ echo $HOME
/home/faculty/sarwar
$
```

*HOME* is a shell variable (a placeholder) that the shell uses to keep track of your home directory. We discuss shell variables and the **echo** command in detail in Chapters 15 through 18.

Another way to display the absolute pathname of your home directory is to use the **pwd** command. You use this command to determine the absolute pathname of the directory you are currently in; it doesn't require any arguments. When you log on, the LINUX system puts you in your home directory. You can use the **pwd** command right after logging on to determine the absolute pathname of your home directory. The command doesn't take any parameter, as in

```
$ pwd
/home/faculty/sarwar
$
```

### 7.5.2 Browsing the File System

You can browse the file system by going from your home directory to other directories in the file system structure and displaying a directory's contents (files and subdirectories in the directory), provided that you have the *permissions* to do so. (We cover file security and permissions in detail in Chapter 8.) For now, we show how you can browse your own files and directories by using the **cd** (change directory) and **ls** (list directory) commands. The following is a brief description of the **cd** command.

Syntax: **cd [directory]**

**Purpose:** Change the present working directory to "directory", or to the home directory if no argument is specified

The shell variable *PWD* is set after each execution of the **cd** command. The **pwd** command uses the value of this variable to display the present working directory. After getting into a directory, you can view its contents (the names of files or subdirectories in it) by using the **ls** command. On the next page is a brief description of this command. The **cd** and **ls** commands are two of the most heavily used LINUX commands.

If the command is used without any argument, it displays the names of files and directories in the present working directory. The following session illustrates how the **ls** and **cd** commands work with and without parameters. The **pwd** command displays the absolute pathname of the current directory. With the exception of hidden files, the **ls** command displays the name of all the files and directories in the current directory. The **cd courses** command is used to make the courses directory the current directory. The **cd ee446/exams** command makes the ee446/exams the current directory. The `ls ~` and `ls $HOME` commands display the names of the files and directories in the home directory. The **cd** command (without any argument) takes you back to your home directory. In other words, it makes your home directory your current directory.

Syntax:

**ls [options] [pathname-list]**

**Purpose:** Send the names of the files in the directories and files specified in "pathname-list" to the display screen

**Output:** Names of the files and directories in the directory specified by "pathname-list", or the names only if "pathname-list" contains file names only

**Commonly used options/features:**

| | |
|---|---|
| `-F` | Display / after directories, * after binary executables, and @ after symbolic links |
| `-a` | Display name of all the files, including hidden files ., .., etc. |
| `-i` | Display inode number |
| `-l` | Display long list that includes access permissions, link count, owner, group, file size (in bytes), and modification time |

```
$ pwd
/home/faculty/sarwar
$ ls
courses   personal
$ cd courses
$ ls
ee231   ee446
$ cd ee446/exams
$ pwd
/home/faculty/sarwar/courses/ee446/exams
$ ls
mid1  mid2
$ ls ~
```

```
courses   personal
$ ls $HOME
courses   personal
$ cd
$ ls
courses   personal
$
```

We demonstrate the use of the `ls` command with various flags in the remainder of this chapter and other chapters of the book.

In a typical LINUX system, you are not allowed to access all the files and directories in the system. In particular, you are not allowed to access many important files and directories related to system administration and to other users' files and directories. However, you have permissions to read a number of directories and files. The following session illustrates that we have permissions to go to and list the contents of, among many other directories, the / and /usr directories.

```
$ cd /usr
$ ls
bin  lib  local
$ cd /
$ ls
bin boot dev etc home lib lost+found mnt opt proc root
sbin tmp usr var
$ cd
$ ls /usr
bin  lib  local
$
```

Without any flag, the `ls` command does not show all the files and directories; in particular, it does not display the names of hidden files. Examples of these files include ., .., .addressbook, .bashrc, .cshrc, .exrc, .login, .mailrc, and .profile. We have already discussed the **.** and **..** directories. The purposes of some of the more important hidden files is summarized in Table 7.3.

You can also display the names of the hidden files by using the `ls` command with the **-a** option. The following command line is an example.

```
$ ls -a
.  ..  .addressbook  .bashrc  .bash_history  .cshrc  .exrc
.login  .pinerc  .profile  courses  personal
$
```

**Table 7.3** Some Important Hidden Files and Their Purposes

| File Name | Purpose |
|---|---|
| . | Present working directory |
| .. | Parent of the present working directory |
| .addressbook | Address Book for `pine` |
| .bash_history | History list from the previous bash sessions |
| .bashrc | Setup for Bourne Again shell |
| .cshrc | Setup for C shell |
| .exrc | Setup for `vi` |
| .login | Setup for shell if C shell is the login shell; executed at login time |
| .mailrc | Setup and Address Book for `mail` and `mailx` |
| .profile | Setup for shell if Bourne or Korn shell is the login shell; executed at login time |

You can use shell metacharacters when specifying multiple files or directory parameters to the **ls** command. For example, the command **ls /usr/*** displays the names of all the files in the /usr directory and in the directories in /usr.

#### Tilde Expansion

As stated earlier ~ stands for your home directory in the Bash and TC shells. Any occurrence of ~ in a command line is expanded to the full pathname for your home directory, as shown in the following examples.

```
$ echo ~
/home/faculty/sarwar
$
```

When a ~ precedes a user's login name, it is substituted by the full pathname for that user's home directory. The following session illustrates this point with two examples. The **echo ~kuhn** command is used to display the full pathname for kuhn's home directory and the **cd ~kuhn/share** command is used to change the directory to the share directory under kuhn's home directory.

```
$ echo ~kuhn
/home/faculty/kuhn
$ cd ~kuhn/share
/home/faculty/kuhn/share
$
```

The tilde expansion not supported by the TC shell is **~-** (the previous directory). Thus the **cd ~-** command changes the directory to your previous directory. In the following shell session, the **ls ~-/time*.h** command displays all the files under /usr/include/sys that start with the string time and end with .h, and the **cd ~-** command makes /usr/include/sys your new current directory.

```
$ cd /usr/include/sys
$ pwd
/usr/include/sys
$ cd /dev
$ pwd
/dev
$ ls ~-/time*.h
/usr/include/sys/time.h  /usr/include/sys/times.h
/usr/include/sys/timeb.h /usr/include/sys/timex.h
$ cd ~-
$ pwd
/usr/include/sys
$
```

### 7.5.3 Creating Files

While working on a computer system, you need to create files and directories: files to store your work and directories to organize your files better. You can create files by using various tools and applications, such as editors, and directories by using the `mkdir` command. In Chapter 5 we discussed various editors (`pico`, `vi`, `emacs`, and `XEmacs`) that you can use to create files containing plain text. You can create nontext files by using various applications and tools, such as a compiler that translates source code in a high-level language (e.g., C) and generates a file that contains the corresponding executable code.

### 7.5.4 Creating and Removing Directories

We briefly discussed the `mkdir` and `rmdir` commands in Chapter 4. Here, we cover these commands fully. You can create a directory by using the `mkdir` command. The following is a brief description of this command.

Syntax: **mkdir [options] dirnames**

**Purpose:** Create directories specified in "dirnames"

**Commonly used options/features:**

| | |
|---|---|
| `-m` MODE | Create a directory with the given access permissions (see Chapter 8) |
| `-p` | Create parent directories that don't exist in the pathnames specified in "dirnames" |

Here, "dirnames" are the pathnames of the directories to be created. When you log on, you can use the following command to create a subdirectory, called memos, in your home directory. You can confirm the creation of this directory by using the `ls -F` command, as in

```
$ mkdir memos
$ ls -F
courses/   memos/  personal/
$
```

Similarly, you can create a directory called test_example in the /tmp directory by using

```
$ mkdir /tmp/test_example
$
```

While in your home directory, you can create the directory professional and a subdirectory letters under it by using the **mkdir** command with the **-p** option, as in

```
$ mkdir -p professional/letters
$
```

You can use the `rmdir` command to remove an empty directory. If a directory isn't empty, you must remove the files and subdirectories in it before removing it. For removing nonempty directories, you need to use the `rm` command with the `-r` option (see Chapter 9). Using `*` with `rm` is especially dangerous because, unless your system administrator has done regular backups, the files are really gone! The following is a brief description of the `rmdir` command.

Syntax:

**rmdir [options] dirnames**

**Purpose:** Remove the empty directories specified in "dirnames"

**Commonly used options/features:**

| | |
|---|---|
| `-p` | Remove empty parent directories as well |

The following command removes the letters directory from the present working directory. If letters isn't empty, the `rmdir` command displays the error message `rmdir: letter: Directory not empty` on the screen. If letters is a file, the command displays the error message `rmdir: letters: Path component not a directory`.

```
$ rmdir letters
$
```

The following command removes the directories letters from your present working directory and memos from your home directory.

```
$ rmdir letters ~/memos
$
```

If the ~/personal directory contains only one subdirectory, called diary, and it is empty, you can use the following command to remove both directories.

```
$ rmdir -p ~/personal/diary
$
```

### 7.5.5 Manipulating the Directory Stack

While working under a Bash or TC shell, if you need to access certain directories frequently, you can store their pathnames in a fashion that allows you to change directory and access them quickly. The storage structure used to maintain the pathnames of these directories is called a **stack**. The use of this structure allows you to **push** and **pop** directory pathnames just like you push and pop a stack of plates in a cafeteria: the last plate placed (pushed) on the stack is the first one to be picked (popped). The topmost directory on the stack is your current directory.

You can use the `dirs` command to display the contents of your directory stack. With this command, the stack is displayed left to right, with the first (leftmost) pathname being for the directory at the top of stack—always for your current directory. At the top of the next page is a brief description of the `dirs` command.

The entries on the directory stack (pathnames) are numbered, with the element at the top of the directory stack numbered 0 and the subsequent elements numbered sequentially. The `dirs -v` command can be used to show the stack entries with index numbers. The following session shows that the pathname at the top of the directory stack is ~/linuxbook/chapters, followed by ~/courses. Note that the `dirs -l` command can be used to display the directory stack with absolute pathnames for the directories on it. The `dirs -l -v` command is used to show the absolute pathnames of the stack entries with index numbers. Figure 7.3 shows the snapshot of the stack.

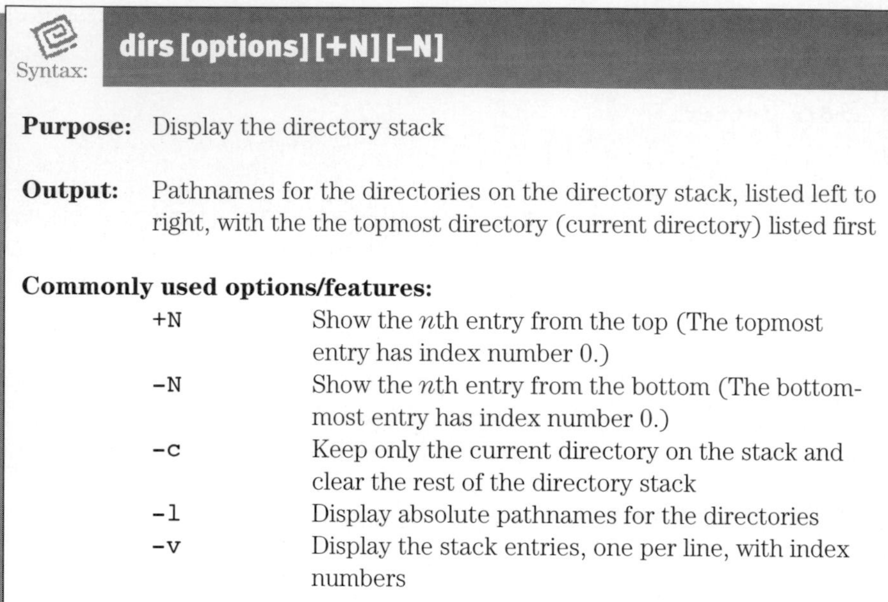

Syntax:

**dirs [options] [+N] [–N]**

**Purpose:** Display the directory stack

**Output:** Pathnames for the directories on the directory stack, listed left to right, with the the topmost directory (current directory) listed first

**Commonly used options/features:**

| | |
|---|---|
| `+N` | Show the *n*th entry from the top (The topmost entry has index number 0.) |
| `-N` | Show the *n*th entry from the bottom (The bottom-most entry has index number 0.) |
| `-c` | Keep only the current directory on the stack and clear the rest of the directory stack |
| `-l` | Display absolute pathnames for the directories |
| `-v` | Display the stack entries, one per line, with index numbers |

```
$ dirs
~/linuxbook/chapters ~/courses
$ dirs -l
/home/faculty/sarwar/linuxbook/chapters
/home/faculty/sarwar/courses
$ dirs -l -v
0 /home/faculty/sarwar/linuxbook/chapters
1 /home/faculty/sarwar/courses
$
```

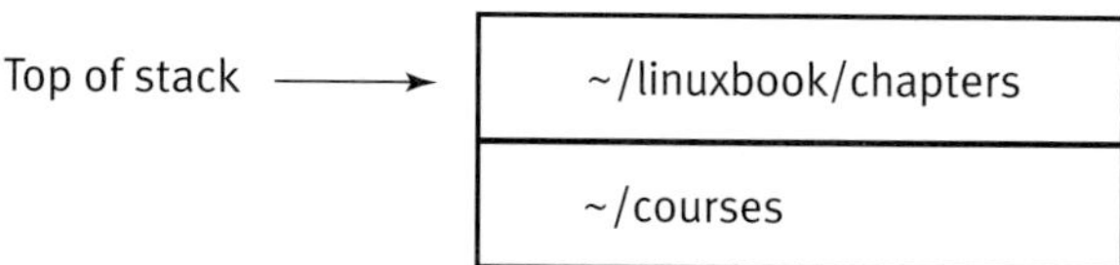


**Figure 7.3** Snapshot of the directory stack

The **pushd** command can be used to push a directory pathname at the top of the directory stack. The output of this command is the new state of the directory stack.

Syntax:

**pushd [–n] [directory]**
**pushd [–n] [+N] [–N]**

**Purpose:** First syntax: Push 'directory' on the directory stack; without any argument, swap the top two entries on the stack

Second syntax: Rotate the stack to bring the *n*th entry to the top of stack

**Output:** The current state of the directory stack; that is, the pathnames of all the directories on the stack, with the topmost entry listed first

**Commonly used options / features:**

| | |
|---|---|
| `+N` | Rotate the stack to bring the *n*th entry from the top to the top of stack (The topmost entry has index number 0.) |
| `-N` | Rotate the stack to bring the *n*th entry from the bottom to the top of stack (The bottommost entry has index number 0.) |
| `-n` | Don't make the new directory the current directory |

When executed without an argument, the **pushd** command swaps the top two elements (pathnames) of the stack. In the following session, the first **pushd** command is used to push the ~/unixbook directory on the stack and the second **pushd** command is used to swap the top two elements of the stack. The **pwd** command is used to show that after a pushd command has executed, the directory next to the top of the stack has become the new current directory and the previous current directory is next to the top of the stack. Figure 7.4 shows the directory stack before and after the execution of the two **pushd** commands.

```
$ pushd ~/unixbook
~/unixbook ~/linuxbook/chapters ~/courses
$ pushd
~/linuxbook/chapters ~/unixbook ~/courses
$ pwd
/home/faculty/sarwar/linuxbook/chapters
$
```

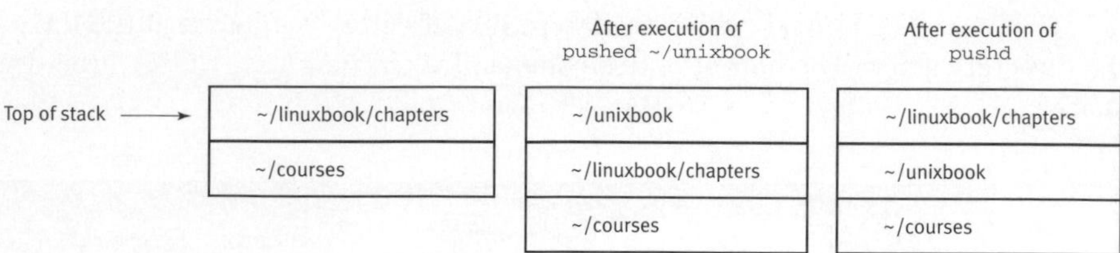


**Figure 7.4** Snapshots of the directory stack after execution of the `pushd ~/unixbook` and `pushd` commands

You can rotate the directory stack to bring any entry at the top (and make it your current directory) by passing its index number, preceded by a plus sign, as an argument to **pushd**. When you precede an index number with a negative sign, the stack entries are numbered starting with the bottommost element. The following session illustrates the use of **pushd** with parameters. The **pushd +2** command is used to rotate the directory stack to bring the second entry (the ~ directory) to the top of stack. The **pushd -n /tmp** command is used to push /tmp on the directory stack, keeping /usr/include as the current directory.

```
$ pwd
/etc
$ dirs -v
0 /etc
1 ~
2 /usr/include
3 /bin
$ pushd +2
/usr/include /bin /etc ~
$ pushd -n /tmp
/usr/include /tmp /bin /etc ~
$ dirs -v
0 /usr/include
1 /tmp
2 /bin
3 /etc
4 ~
$ pwd
/usr/include
$
```

The **popd** command can be used to remove an entry from the directory stack. The following is a brief description of this command.

Syntax:

## popd [-n] [+N] [-N]

**Purpose:** Remove an entry from the directory stack and **cd** to the new top of stack; without an argument, remove the entry at the top of stack

**Output:** The current state of the directory stack—that is, the pathnames of all the directories on the stack with the topmost entry listed first

**Commonly used options/features:**

| | |
|---|---|
| `+N` | Remove entry number *n* from the directory stack (The topmost entry has index number 0.) |
| `-N` | Remove entry number *n* from the directory stack (The bottommost entry has index number 0.) |
| `-n` | Don't make the new directory the current directory |

The **popd** command in the following example removes ~/courses from the directory stack, leaving ~/linuxbook/chapters at the top of stack. Thus the new current directory is ~/linuxbook/chapters.

```
$ dirs
~/courses  ~/linuxbook/chapters  ~/unixbook
$ popd
~/linuxbook/chapters ~/unixbook
$ pwd
/home/faculty/sarwar/linuxbook/chapters
$
```

Any element (pathname) from the directory stack can be removed by executing the **popd** command with the element's number, preceded by a plus sign, as its argument. In the following session, the **popd +1** command is used to remove the second element from the directory stack (recall that the top element is numbered 0). The **dirs** command is used to display the current directory stack.

```
$ dirs
~/linuxbook/chapters ~/unixbook ~/personal
$ popd +1
~/linuxbook/chapters ~/personal
$
```

If the **pushd** (or **popd**) command is passed a negative number as an argument, the numbers are counted from the bottom of stack (i.e., the bottom element is numbered 0). Thus **pushd -3** puts the third element from the bottom of the stack at the top and makes it the current directory. If you specify a number for a nonexistant element as an argument to a **pushd** or **popd** command, the command will display an appropriate error message and terminate. For example, if you have two directories on the directory stack and execute **pushd +4**, you will get the error message **pushd: Stack contains only 2 directories** under Bash and **pushd: Directory stack not that deep** under the TC shell.

The following session illustrates the use of **popd** with the **-n** option. Notice that with this option, the **popd** command removes the second entry (the entry next to the top of stack) from the stack and does not change your current directory.

```
$ dirs -v
0 /bin
1 /etc
2 /usr/include
$ popd -n
/bin /usr/include
$ dirs -v
0 /bin
1 /usr/include
$ pwd
/bin
$
```

### 7.5.6 Determining File Attributes

You can determine the attributes of files by using the **ls** command with various options. The options can be used together, and their order doesn't matter. For example, you can use the **-l** option to get a long list of a directory that gives the attributes of files, such as the owner of the file, as in

```
$ ls -l
drwxr-x---  2  sarwar  faculty  512  Apr 23 09:37  courses
drwxr-----  1  sarwar  faculty  12   May 01 13:22  memos
drwx------  1  sarwar  faculty  163  May 05 23:13  personal
$ ls -l ~/courses/ee446/exams
-rwxr--r--  1  sarwar  faculty  163  Mar 16 11:10  mid1
-rwxr--r--  1  sarwar  faculty  163  Apr 11 14:34  mid22
drwxrwxrwx  1  sarwar  faculty  163  May 12 23:44  solutions
$
```

**Table 7.4** Summary of the Output of the `ls -l` Command (fields are listed left to right)

| Field | Meaning |
|---|---|
| First letter of first field | File type: – ordinary file<br>b block special file<br>c character special file<br>d directory<br>l link<br>p named pipe (FIFO) |
| Remaining letters of first field | Access permissions for owner, group, and others |
| Second field | Number of links |
| Third field | Owner's login name |
| Fourth field | Owner's group name |
| Fifth field | File size in bytes |
| Sixth, seventh, and eighth fields | Date and time of last modification |
| Ninth field | File name |

The information displayed by the `ls -l` command is summarized in Table 7.4. In the preceding two uses of `ls -l`, courses, memos, personal, and solutions are directories, and mid1 and mid2 are ordinary files. (We discuss access permissions and user types in Chapter 8.) The owner of the files is sarwar, who belongs to the group faculty. The values of the remaining fields are self-explanatory.

You can use the `ls` command with the `-i` option to determine the inode numbers of files. The following example of its use shows that the inode numbers for courses, memos, and personal are 12329, 22876, and 12487, respectively.

```
$ ls -i
12329 courses   22876 memos 12487 personal
$
```

The `ls -al` command displays the long list of all the files in a directory, as in

```
$ ls -al ~/courses/ee446/exams
drwxr-x---  1  sarwar   faculty  512   Mar 16 08:24  .
drwxr-x---  1  sarwar   faculty  512   Jan 29 13:27  ..
-rwxr--r--  1  sarwar   faculty  1863  Mar 16 11:10  mid1
-rwxr--r--  1  sarwar   faculty  459   Apr 11 14:34  mid22
drwxrwxrwx  1  sarwar   faculty  512   May 12 23:44  solutions
$
```

You can use the **-F** option to identify directories, executable files, and symbolic links. The **ls -F** command displays an asterisk (*) after an executable file, a slash (/) after a directory, and an at symbol (@) after a symbolic link (discussed in Chapter 11), as in

```
$ ls -F ~
bin/  courses/  demo@  a.out*  personal/
$
```

You are encouraged to read the online man pages for the **ls** command on your system, or see Appendix B for a concise description of the command.

By using the shell metacharacters, you can specify a particular set of files and directories. For example, the following command can be used in TC shell to display the long lists for all the files in the ~/courses/ee446 directory that have the .c extension and start with the string lab followed by zero or more characters, with the condition that the first of these characters cannot be 5. You can replace the ^ character with the ! character under Bash.

```
$ ls -l ~/courses/ee446/lab[^5]*.c
...
$
```

Similarly, the following command can be used to display the inode numbers and names of all the files in your current directory that have four-character-long names and an html extension. The file names must start with a letter, followed by any two characters, and end with a digit from 1 through 5.

```
$ ls -i [a-zA-Z]??[1-5].html
...
$
```

The following command under TC shell displays the names of all the files in the home directory that do not start with a digit and that end with .c or .C. In other words, the command displays the names of all the C and C++ source program files that do not start with a digit. Again, you can replace the ^ character with the ! character under Bash.

```
$ ls ~/ [^0-9]*.[c,C]
...
$
```

### Brace Expansion

Taken from the C shell, a brace expansion allows you to specify a list of comma-separated strings enclosed in braces to be substituted between a **preamble** and a **postamble**, which are optional. This results in a list of filenames consisting of each string in the list sandwiched between the preamble and postamble. In the following session, the `wc` command (See Chapter 9) is used to display, in lines of code, the sizes of the C source files mash.c, matrix.c, and qsort.c in the ./programs/ee446 directory. The `mkdir` command is used to create the BashSessions and TcshSessions directories in the current directory, and the `ls -l` command is used to confirm their creation. Note that the use of square brackets does not work in this case, as shown by the last two commands of the session.

```
$ wc -l ./programs/ee446/{mash,matrix,qsort}.c
   915 ./programs/ee446/mash.c
    73 ./programs/ee446/matrix.c
   139 ./programs/ee446/qsort.c
  1127 total
$ mkdir {Bash,Tcsh}Sessions
$ ls -l
total 2
drwx------ 2 sarwar faculty 512 Oct 8 22:11 BashSessions
drwx------ 2 sarwar faculty 512 Oct 8 22:11 TcshSessions
$ mkdir my[Bash,Tcsh]Sessions
$ ls -l
total 3
drwx------ 2 sarwar faculty 512 Oct 8 22:11 BashSessions
drwx------ 2 sarwar faculty 512 Oct 8 22:11 TcshSessions
drwx------ 2 sarwar faculty 512 Oct 18 14:43 my[Bash,Tcsh]Sessions
$
```

Brace expansion not only works for files, it can also be used to generate arbitrary strings by enclosing them in double quotes. For example, the following `echo` command is used to generate a greeting message for John and Cindy Doe. Note the use of double quotes inside the braces and in the postamble.

```
$ echo Hello, {John,"and Cindy"}" Doe"!
Hello, John Doe and Cindy Doe!
$
```

## 7.5.7 Determining the Type of a File's Contents

Because LINUX does not support types of ordinary files and extensions, you can't determine what a file contains simply by looking at its name. However, you can find the type of a file's contents by using the **`file`** command. Mostly, this command is used to determine whether a file contains text or binary data. Doing so is important because text files can be displayed on the screen, whereas displaying binary files can freeze your terminal, as it may interpret some of the binary values as control codes. The command has the following syntax.

Syntax:

**file [options] file-list**

**Purpose:** Attempt to classify files in "file-list"

**Commonly used options/features:**

`-f` FILE    Use FILE as a file of "file-list"

The following session shows a sample run of the command. In this case, types of the contents of all the files in the root directory are displayed.

```
$ file /*
all.backup: POSIX tar archive
bin:         directory
boot:        directory
dev:         directory
etc:         directory
home:        directory
lib:         directory
lost+found:  directory
mnt:         directory
opt:         directory
proc:        directory
root:        directory
sbin:        directory
tmp:         directory
usr:         directory
var:         directory
$
```

Some more classifications that the `file` command displays are English text, C program text, Bourne Again shell script text, empty, nroff/troff, perl command text, PostScript, sccs, setuid executable, and setgid executable.

The following In-Chapter Exercises familiarize you with the `echo`, `cd`, `ls`, and `file` commands and the formats of their output.

**IN-CHAPTER EXERCISES**

**7.3.** Right after you log on, run `echo ~` to determine the full pathname of your home directory.

**7.4** Practice the use of `dirs`, `popd`, and `pushd` commands as discussed in Section 7.5.5.

**7.5.** Use the `cd` command to go to the /usr/bin directory on your system and run the `ls -F` command. Identify two symbolic links and five binary files.

**7.6.** Run the `ls -l` command in the same directory and write down sizes (in bytes) of the `find` and `make` commands.

**7.7.** Run the `file /etc/*` command to identify types of all the files in this directory.

## 7.6 FILE REPRESENTATION AND STORAGE IN LINUX

As we mentioned before, the attributes of a file are stored in a data structure on the disk, called *inode*. At the time of its creation, every file is allocated a unique inode from a list (array) of inodes on the disk, called the **i-list**. The LINUX kernel also maintains a table of inodes, called the **inode table**, in the main memory for all open files. When an application opens a file, an inode is allocated from the inode table. The i-list and inode table are indexed by a file's inode number. The inode number is used to index the inode table, allowing access to the attributes of an open file. When a file's attributes (e.g., file size) change, the inode in the main memory is updated; disk copies of the inodes are updated at fixed intervals. For files that are not open, their inodes reside on the disk. Some of the contents of an inode are shown in Figure 7.5.

The 'link count' field specifies the number of different names the file has within the system. The 'file mode' field specifies what the file was opened for (read, write, etc.). The 'user ID' is the ID of the owner of the file. The 'access permissions' field specifies who can access the file for what type of operation (discussed in detail in Chapter 8). The 'file's location on disk' is specified by a number of direct and indirect pointers to **disk blocks** containing file data.

A typical computer system has several disk drives. Each drive consists of a number of platters with top and bottom surfaces. Each surface is logically divided

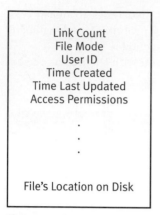

Link Count
File Mode
User ID
Time Created
Time Last Updated
Access Permissions
.
.
.
File's Location on Disk

**Figure 7.5** Contents of an inode

into concentric circles called *tracks*, and each track is subdivided into fixed size portions called sectors. Tracks at the same position on both surfaces of all platters comprise a cylinder. Disk I/O takes place in terms of one sector, also called a disk block. The address of a sector is a four-dimensional address comprising the disk number, cylinder number, track number (surface number), sector number. This four-dimensional address is translated to a *linear* (one-dimensional) block number, and most of the software in LINUX uses block addresses because they are relatively easy to deal with. These blocks are numbered with sector 0 of the outermost cylinder at the topmost surface (i.e., the topmost track of the outermost cylinder) assigned block number 0. The block numbers increase through the rest of the tracks in that cylinder, through the rest of the cylinders on the disk, and then through the rest of the disks. The diagram shown in Figure 7.6 is a logical view of a disk system consisting of an array of disk blocks. File space is allocated in clusters of two, four, or eight 512-byte disk blocks.

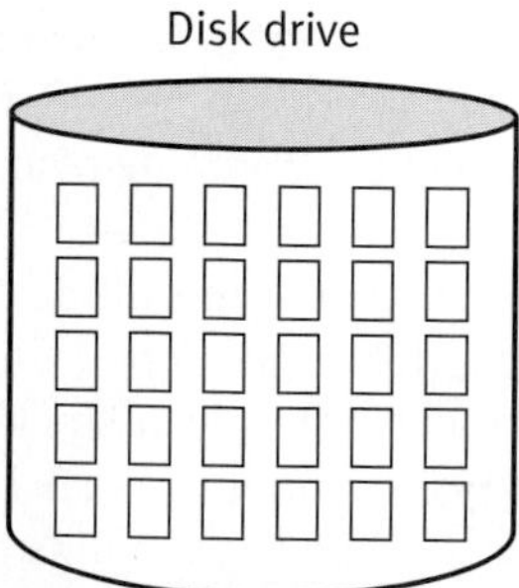


**Figure 7.6** Logical view of a disk drive—an array of disk blocks

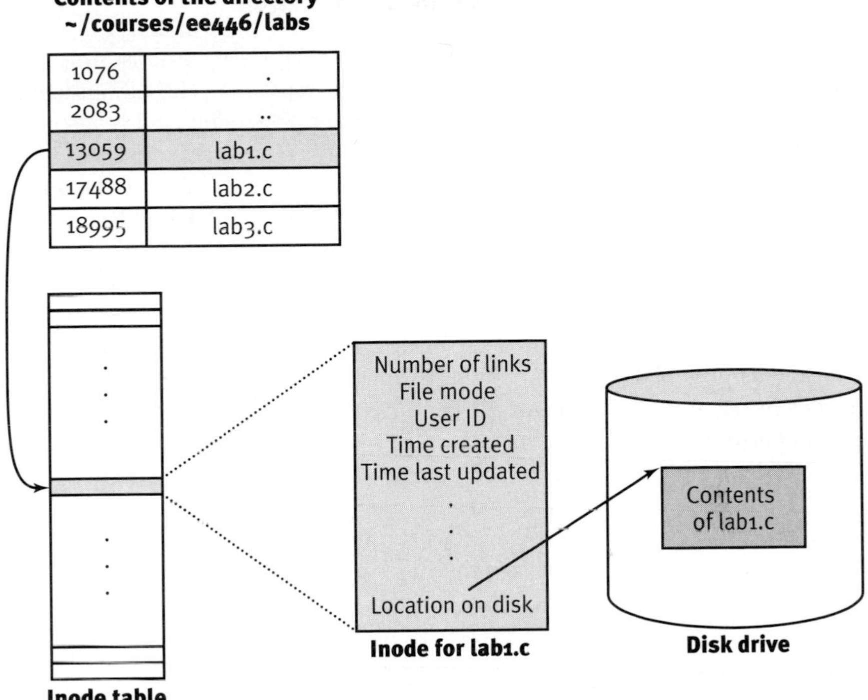


**Figure 7.7.** Relationship between the file lab1.c in a directory and its contents on disk

Figure 7.7 shows how an inode number for an open file can be used to access that file's attributes, including the file's contents, from the disk. It also shows contents of the directory ~/courses/ee446/labs and how the LINUX kernel maps the inode of the file lab1.c to its contents on disk. As we discussed before and as shown in the diagram, a directory consists of an array of entries <inode #, filename>. Accessing (reading or writing) the contents of lab1.c requires use of its inode number to index the in-memory inode table to get to the file's inode. The inode, as we stated before, contains, among other things, the location of lab1.c on the disk.

The inode contains the location of lab1.c on the disk in terms of the numbers of the disk blocks that contain the contents of the file. The details of how exactly a LINUX file's location is specified in its inode and how it is stored on the disk are beyond the scope of this textbook. Such details are available in any book on LINUX internals.

## 7.7 STANDARD FILES AND FILE DESCRIPTORS

When an application needs to perform an I/O operation on a file, it must first open the file and then issue the file operation (read, write, seek, etc.). LINUX automatically opens three files for every command it executes. The command reads input from one of these files, and sends its output and error messages to the other two files. These files are called standard files: **standard input (stdin) files**, **standard output (stdout) files**, and **standard error (stderr) files**. By default, these files are attached to the terminal on which the command is executed. That is, the shell makes the command input come from the terminal keyboard and its output and error messages go to the monitor screen (or the console window in case of a telnet session or an xterm in a LINUX system running the X Window System, as discussed in detail in Chapter 21). These default files can be changed to other files by using the **redirection operators**: < for input redirection and > for output and error redirection.

A small integer, called a **file descriptor**, is associated with every open file in LINUX. The integer values 0, 1, and 2 are the file descriptors for stdin, stdout, and stderr, respectively, and are also known as standard file descriptors. The kernel uses file descriptors to perform file operations (e.g., file read), as illustrated in Figure 7.8. The kernel uses a file descriptor to index the per process **file descriptor table** to get a pointer to the systemwide **file table**. The file table, among other things, contains a pointer to the file's inode in the inode table. Once the inode for the file has been accessed, the required file operation is performed by accessing appropriate disk block(s) for the file by using the direct and indirect pointers, as described in Section 7.6.

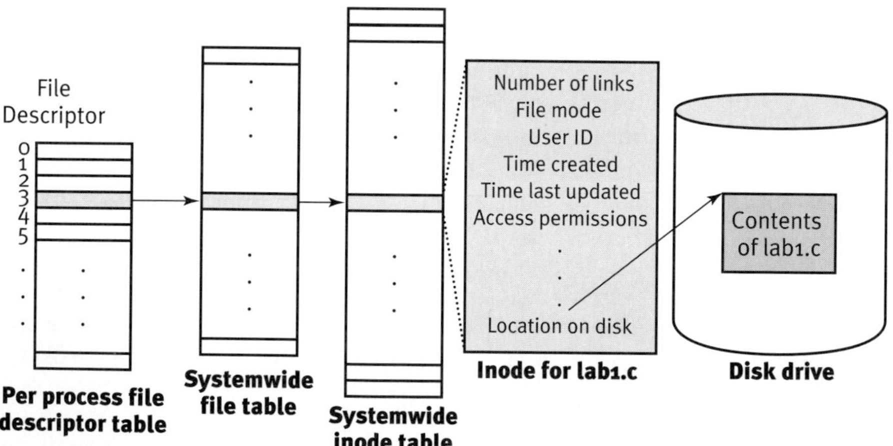


Figure 7.8 Relationship between a file descriptor and contents of the file on disk

Recall that every device, including a terminal, is represented by a file in LINUX. The diagram shown in Figure 7.9 depicts the relationship between a file and its file descriptor. Here, we assume that files lab1.c and lab2.c are open for some file operations (say, file read) and have descriptors 3 and 4, respectively, that the kernel associated with the files when they were opened. We have described the details of this relationship in the preceding paragraph and in Section 7.6, in terms of a file table, inode table, and storage of the file on disk; also see Figures 7.7 and 7.8.

The LINUX system allows standard files to be changed to alternate files for a single execution of a command, including a shell script. This concept of changing standard files to alternate files is called input, output, and error redirection.

We address input, output, and error redirection in detail in Chapter 12. We have briefly mentioned the standard files and file descriptors here because most LINUX commands that take input get it from standard input, unless it comes from a file (or list of files) that is passed to the command as a command line argument. Similarly, most LINUX commands that produce output send it to standard output. This information is important for proper understanding and use of commands in the remaining chapters.

## 7.8 END OF FILE (eof) MARKER

Every LINUX file has an **end-of-file (eof)** marker. The commands that read their input from files, read the eof marker when they reach the end of a file. For files that can be stored, the value of the eof marker is not a character; it is usually a small negative integer such as −1. The <Ctrl-D> on a new line is the LINUX eof marker when the input file is a keyboard. That's why commands such as `cat`, while reading input from the keyboard (see Chapter 9), terminate when you press <Ctrl-D> on a new line. The eof marker is inserted in a file by the editor used to create the file.

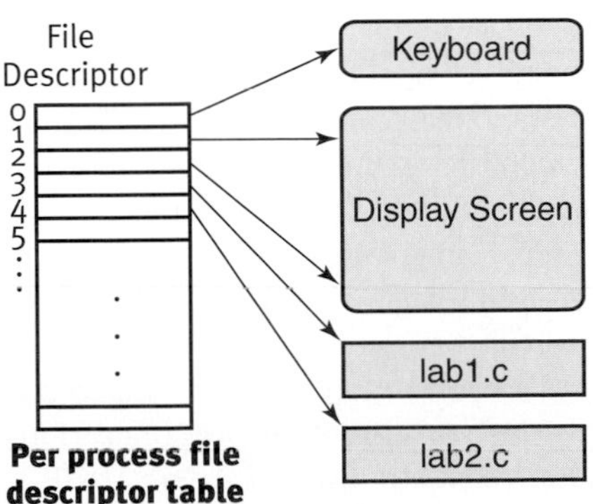


**Figure 7.9** Relationship of a file descriptor and the corresponding file

## SUMMARY

In LINUX, a file is a sequence of bytes. This simple, yet powerful, concept and its implementation lead to everything in the system being a file. LINUX supports five types of files: ordinary file, directory, symbolic link, special file (device), and named pipe (also known as FIFO). No file extensions are supported for files of any type, but applications running on a LINUX system can require their own extensions.

Every file in LINUX has several attributes associated with it, including file name, owner's name, date last modified, link count, and the file's location on disk. These attributes are stored in an area on the disk called an inode. When files are opened, their inodes are copied to a kernel area called the inode table for faster access of their attributes. Every file in a directory has an entry associated with it that comprises the file's name and its inode number. The kernel accesses an open file's attributes, including its contents, by reading the file's inode number from its directory entry and indexing the inode table with the inode number.

The LINUX file structure is hierarchical, with a root directory and all the files and directories in the system being under it. Every user has a directory, called the user's home directory, that he or she gets into when logging on to the system. Multiple disk drives and/or disk partitions can be mounted on the same file system structure, allowing their access as directories and not as named drives A:, B:, C:, and so on, as in MS-DOS and Microsoft Windows. This approach gives a unified view of all the files and directories in the system, and users don't have to worry about remembering the names of drives and the files (and directories) that they contain.

Directories (primarily) can be created and removed under the user's home directory. The file structure can be navigated by using various commands (**mkdir**, **rmdir**, **cd**, **ls**, **dirs**, **pushd**, **popd**, etc.). The name of a file in the system can be specified by using its absolute or relative pathname. An absolute pathname starts with the root directory and a relative pathname starts with a user's home directory or present working directory. You can maintain a directory stack by using the **dirs**, **pushd**, and **popd** commands. This allows you to switch between various directories quickly.

LINUX automatically opens three files for every command for it to read input from, and send its output and error messages to. These files are called standard input (stdin), standard output (stdout), and standard error (stderr). By default, these files are attached to the terminal on which the command is executed; that is, the command input comes from the terminal keyboard, and the command output and error messages go to the terminal's screen display. The default files can be changed to other files by using redirection primitives: < for input redirection, and > for output and error redirection.

The kernel associates a small integer with every open file. This integer is called the file descriptor. The kernel uses file descriptors to perform operations (e.g., read) on the file. The file descriptors for stdin, stdout, and stderr are 0, 1, and 2, respectively.

Every LINUX file has an end-of-file (eof) marker, which is a small negative integer such as −1. The eof marker is <Ctrl-D> if a command reads input from the keyboard.

## PROBLEMS

1. What is a file in LINUX?
2. Does LINUX support any file types? If so, name them. Does LINUX support file extensions?
3. What is a directory entry? What does it consist of?
4. What are special files in LINUX? What are character special and block special files? Run the `ls /dev | wc -w` command to find the number of special files your system has.
5. What is meant by interprocess communication? What three mechanisms (primitives) does LINUX provide for interprocess communication?
6. Draw the hierarchical file structure, similar to the one shown in Figure 7.2, for your LINUX machine. Show files and directories at the first two levels. Also show where your home directory is, along with files and directories under your home directory.
7. Give three commands that you can use to list the absolute pathname of your home directory.
8. Write down the line in the /etc/passwd file on your system that contains information about your login. What are your login shell, user ID, home directory, and group ID? Does your system contain the encrypted password in the /etc/passwd or /etc/shadow file?
9. What would happen if the last field of the your line in the /etc/passwd file were replaced with /bin/date? Why?
10. What are the inode numbers of the root and your home directories on your machine? Give the commands that you used to find these inode numbers.
11. Create a directory, called memos, in your home directory. Go into this directory and create a file memo.james by using one of the editors we discussed in Chapter 5. Give three pathnames for this file.
12. Give a command line for creating a subdirectory personal under the memos directory that you created in Problem 11.
13. Make a copy of the file memo.james and put it in your home directory. Name the copied file temp.memo. Give two commands for accomplishing this task.
14. Draw a diagram like that shown in Figure 7.7 for your memos directory. Clearly show all directory entries, including inode numbers for all the files and directories in it.

15. Give the command for deleting the memos directory. How do you know that the directory has been deleted?
16. Why does a shell process terminate when you press <Ctrl-D> at the beginning of a new line?
17. Give a command line to display the types of all the files in your ~/linux directory that start with the word chapter, are followed by a digit 1, 2, 6, 8, or 9, and end with .eps or .prn.
18. Give a command line to display the types of all the files in the personal directory in your home directory that do not start with letters a, k, G, or Q and the third letter in the name is not a digit and not a letter (uppercase or lowercase).

CHAPTER

# 8

# File Security

**OBJECTIVES**

- To describe the three protection and security mechanisms that LINUX provides
- To describe the types of LINUX file users
- To discuss the basic operations that can be performed on a LINUX file
- To explain the concept of file access permissions/privileges in LINUX
- To discuss how a user can determine access privileges for a file
- To describe how a user can set and change permissions for a file
- To cover the commands and primitives ?, ~, *, `chmod`, `ls -l`, `ls -ld`, and `umask`

## 8.1 INTRODUCTION

Although a time-sharing system offers great benefits, protecting the hardware and software resources in it is a challenge. These resources include the I/O devices, CPU, main memory, and the secondary storage devices that store user files. We have limited the scope of this chapter to protecting a user's files from unauthorized access by other users. LINUX provides three mechanisms for protecting your files.

The most fundamental scheme for protecting user files is to give every user a login name and a password, allowing a user to use a system (see Chapter 3). To prevent others from accessing your files, only you should know the password for your computer account. The second scheme protects individual files by converting them to a form that is completely different from the original version by means of encryption. You can use this technique to protect important files so that the contents of these files cannot be understood even if someone somehow gains access to them on the system. The third file protection scheme protects your files by associating **access privileges** with them so that only a subset of users can access these files for a subset of file operations. In this chapter we describe all three mechanisms but focus primarily on the third scheme.

## 8.2 PASSWORD-BASED PROTECTION

The first mechanism that allows you to protect your files from other users is the login password. Every user of a LINUX-based computer system is assigned a login name (a name by which the user is known to the LINUX system) and a password. Both the login name and password are assigned by the system administrator and are required for a user to use a LINUX system. All login names are public knowledge and can be found in the /etc/passwd file. A user's password, however, is given to that user only. This prevents users from accessing each other's files. Users are encouraged to change their passwords frequently by using the `passwd` command (see Chapter 3). On some networked systems, you may have to use the `yppasswd` or `nispasswd` command to change your password on all the network's computer systems. Consult your instructor about the command that you need to use on your particular system. Login names can be changed by the system administrator only.

The effectiveness of this protection scheme depends on how well protected a user's password is. If someone knows your password, that person can log on to the system as you and access your files. There are primarily three ways of discovering a user's password: (1) you (the owner of an account) inform others of your password; (2) guessing a user's password; and (3) discovering a user's password by using a brute force method. You must never let anyone else know your password under any circumstances, but you should also change your password regularly as a further precaution. You should also use "good" passwords to make it difficult for others to guess your password. A good password is one that is a mixture of letters, digits, and punctuation marks; is difficult to guess; and is easy to memorize. Never write your password on a piece of paper, and never use birthdays or names of close relatives or friends as passwords. Names of characters from *Star Wars* movies also make bad passwords!

In the brute force method, someone tries to learn your password by trying all possible passwords until the right one is found. Guessing someone's password is a time-consuming process and is commonly used by hackers. The brute force method can be made more time-consuming by the use of longer passwords and passwords that consist of letters, digits, and punctuation marks. To illustrate the significance of using a more complex password, consider a system that requires an eight-character password consisting of decimal digits only. It would allow a maximum of $10^8$ (100 million) passwords that the brute force method would have to go through in the worst case. If the same system requires passwords to consist of a mixture of digits and uppercase letters (a total 36 symbols—10 digits and 26 uppercase letters), the password space would comprise $36^8$ (about 2.8 trillion) passwords. If the system requires passwords to consist of a mixture of digits, uppercase letters, and lowercase letters, the password space would comprise $62^8$ (about 218 trillion) passwords. You get the idea.

The following In-Chapter Exercise asks you to figure out how to change your password on your system.

**IN-CHAPTER EXERCISE**

**8.1.** In some LINUX systems you are not allowed to change your password. Does your system allow you to change your password? If so, change your password. What command did you use?

## 8.3 ENCRYPTION-BASED PROTECTION

In the second protection scheme, a software tool is used to convert a file to a form that is completely different from its original version. The transformed file is called an **encrypted file**, and the process of converting a file to an encrypted file is called **encryption**. The same tool is used to perform the reverse process of transforming the encrypted file to its original form, called **decryption**. You can use this technique to protect your most important files so that their contents cannot be understood even if someone can somehow gain access to them. Figure 8.1 illustrates these processes. You can use the LINUX library call `crypt` to encrypt and decrypt your files.

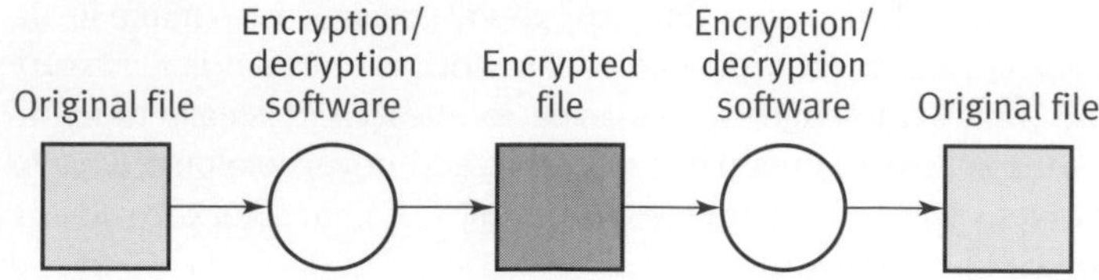


**Figure 8.1** The process of encryption and decryption

## 8.4 PROTECTION BASED ON ACCESS PERMISSION

The third type of file protection is provided by a mechanism that prevents users from accessing each others' files when they are not logged on as a file's owner. As file owner, you can attach certain **access rights** to your files that dictate who can and cannot access them for various types of file operations. This scheme is based on the types of users, the types of access permissions, and the types of operations allowed on a file under LINUX. Without such a protection scheme, users can access each others' files because the LINUX file system structure (see Figure 7.2) has a single root from which all the files in the system hang.

### 8.4.1 Types of Users

Every user in a LINUX system belongs to a group of users, as assigned by the system administrator when the user is allocated an account on the system. A user can belong to multiple groups, but a typical LINUX user belongs to a single group. All the groups in the system and their memberships are listed in the file /etc/group (see Figure 7.2). This file contains one line per group, with the last field of the line containing the login names of the group members. A user of a file can be the owner of the file (known as the **user** in LINUX terminology) or someone who belongs to the same **group** that the owner of the file does or some other users (known as **others**—everyone else who has an account on the system), which comprise the three types of users of a LINUX file. As the owner of a file you can specify who can access it.

Every LINUX system has one special user who has access to all of the files on the system, regardless of the access privileges on the files. This user, commonly known as the **superuser**, is the administrator of the computer system. The login name for the superuser is **root**, and the user ID is 0.

### 8.4.2 Types of File Operations/Access Permissions

In LINUX, three types of access permissions/privileges can be associated with a file: read (r), write (w), and execute (x). The **read permission** allows you to read the file, the **write permission** allows you to write to or remove the file, and the **execute permission** allows you to execute (run) the file. The execute permission should be set for executable files only (files containing binary codes or shell scripts), as setting it for any other type of file doesn't make any sense.

The read permission for a directory allows you to read the contents of the directory. Thus the `ls` command can be used to list its contents. The write permission for a directory allows you to create a new directory entry in it or to remove an existing entry from it. The execute permission for a directory allows you to search for a directory but not to read from or write to it. Thus, if you don't have execute permission for a directory, you can't use the `ls -l` command to list its contents or use the `cd` command to make it your current directory. The same is true if any component in a directory's pathname does not contain execute permission. We demonstrate these aspects of the search permission on directories in Section 8.5.1.

With three types of file users and three types of permissions, a LINUX file has nine different types of permissions associated with it, as shown in Table 8.1. As we stated in Chapter 7, access privileges are stored in a file's inode.

The value of X can be 1 (for permission allowed) or 0 (permission not allowed). Therefore 1 bit is needed to represent a permission type, and a total of 3 bits are needed to indicate file permissions for one type of user (user, group, or others). In other words, a user of a file can have one of the eight possible types of permissions for a file. These eight 3-bit values can be represented by octal numbers from 0 through 7, as shown in Table 8.2; 0 means no permissions, and 7 means all (read, write, and execute) permissions.

The total of 9 bits needed to express permissions for all three types of file users results in possible access permission values of 000 through 777 (in octal) for file permissions. The first octal digit specifies permissions for the owner of the file, the second digit specifies permissions for the group that the owner of the file belongs to, and the third digit specifies permissions for everyone else. A bit value of 0 for a permission is also denoted dash (-), and a value of 1 is also denoted r, w, or x, depending on the position of the bit according to the table. Thus a permission value of 0 in octal (no permissions allowed) for a user of a file can be written as --- and a permission of 7 (all three permissions allowed) can be denoted rwx.

## 8.5 DETERMINING AND CHANGING FILE ACCESS PRIVILEGES

We now describe how you can determine the access privileges for files and directories and how you can change them to enhance or limit someone's access to your files.

**Table 8.1** Summary of File Permissions in LINUX

| | Permission Type | | |
|---|---|---|---|
| **User Type** | **Read (r)** | **Write (w)** | **Execute (x)** |
| User (**u**) | X | X | X |
| Group (**g**) | X | X | X |
| Others (**o**) | X | X | X |

**Table 8.2** Permission Values

| r | w | x | Octal Value | Meaning |
|---|---|---|---|---|
| 0 | 0 | 0 | 0 | No permission |
| 0 | 0 | 1 | 1 | Execute-only permission |
| 0 | 1 | 0 | 2 | Write-only permission |
| 0 | 1 | 1 | 3 | Write and execute permissions |
| 1 | 0 | 0 | 4 | Read-only permission |
| 1 | 0 | 1 | 5 | Read and execute permissions |
| 1 | 1 | 0 | 6 | Read and write permissions |
| 1 | 1 | 1 | 7 | Read, write, and execute permissions |

### 8.5.1 Determining File Access Privileges

You can use the `ls` command with the `-l` or `-ld` option to display access permissions for a list of files and/or directories. The following is a brief description of the `ls` command with the two options.

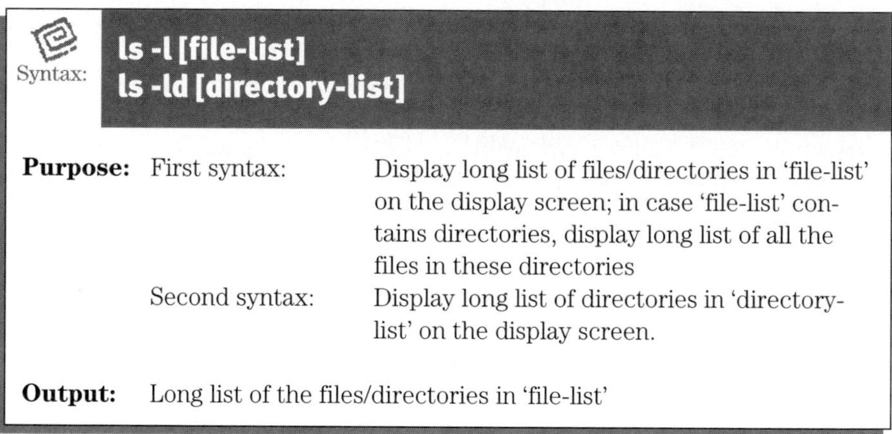

Syntax:

**ls -l [file-list]**
**ls -ld [directory-list]**

**Purpose:** First syntax: Display long list of files/directories in 'file-list' on the display screen; in case 'file-list' contains directories, display long list of all the files in these directories

Second syntax: Display long list of directories in 'directory-list' on the display screen.

**Output:** Long list of the files/directories in 'file-list'

If no 'file-list' is specified, the command gives long lists for all the files (except hidden files) in the present working directory. Add the `-a` option to the command line to include the hidden files in the display.

Consider the following session.

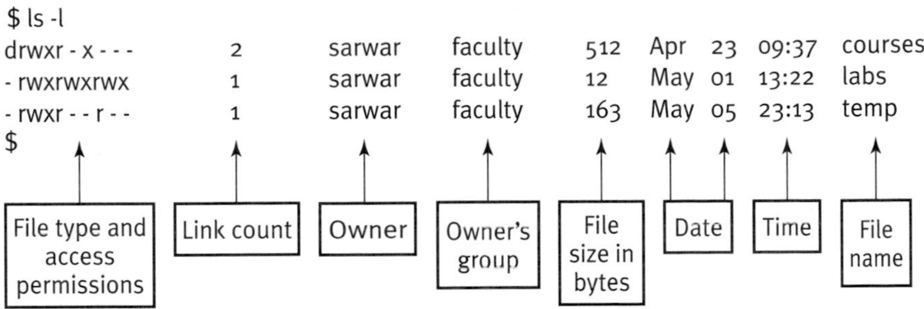


The left-most character in the first field of the output indicates the file type (**d** for directory and **-** for ordinary file). The remaining nine characters in the first field show file access privileges for user, group, and others, respectively. The second field indicates the number of hard links (discussed in Chapter 11) to the file. The third field gives the owner's login name. The fourth field gives the owner's group name. The fifth field gives the file's size (in bytes). The sixth, seventh, and eighth fields give date and time of the file's creation (or last update). The last field gives the file's name. Table 8.3 shows who has what type of access privileges for the three files in this session: courses, labs, and temp. Note that the x permission means search for courses (a directory) and execute for labs and temp (ordinary files).

If an argument of the `ls -l` command is a directory, the command displays the long lists of all the files and directories in it. You can use the `ls -ld` command to display long lists of directories only. When executed without an argument this command displays the long list for the current directory, as shown in the first command in the following session. The second and third commands show that when the `ls -ld` command is executed with a list of directories as its arguments, it displays the long lists for those directories only. If an argument to the `ls -ld` command is a file, the command displays the long list for the file. The fourth command, `ls -ld pvm/*`, displays the long lists for all the files and directories in the pvm directory.

**Table 8.3** Permissions for Access to `courses`, `labs`, and `temp`

| | Access Permissions | | |
|---|---|---|---|
| **File Name** | **User** | **Group** | **Other** |
| `courses` | Read, write, and search | Read and search | No permission |
| `labs` | Read, write, and execute | Read, write, and execute | Read, write, and execute |
| `temp` | Read, write, and execute | Read | Read |

```
$ ls -ld
drwx--x--x  2 sarwar faculty   11264 Jul 8 22:21 .
$ ls -ld ABET
drwx------  2 sarwar faculty     512 Dec 18 1997 ABET
$ ls -ld ~/myweb/Images courses/ee446
drwx------  3 sarwar faculty     512 Apr 30 09:52 courses/ee446
drwx--x--x  2 sarwar faculty    2048 Dec 18 1997 /home/faculty/sarwar/myweb/Images
$ ls -ld pvm/*
drwx------  3 sarwar faculty     512 Dec 18 1997 pvm/examples
drwx------  2 sarwar faculty    1024 Oct 27 1998 pvm/qsort
-rw-------  1 sarwar faculty    1606 Jun 19 1995 pvm/Book_PVM
-rw-------  1 sarwar faculty    7639 Sep 11 1998 pvm/Jim_Davis
$
```

### 8.5.2 Changing File Access Privileges

You can use the **chmod** command to change access privileges for your files. The following is a brief description of the command.

Syntax: **chmod [options] octal-mode file-list**
**chmod [options] symbolic-mode file-list**

**Purpose:** Change/set permissions for files in 'file-list'

**Commonly used options/features:**

| | |
|---|---|
| -R | Recursively descend through directories changing/setting permissions for all the files and subdirectories under each directory |
| -f | Force specified access permissions; no error messages are produced if you are the file's owner |

The *symbolic mode*, also known as *mode control word*, has the form <who><operator><privilege>, with the possible values for *who*, *operator*, and *privilege* shown in Table 8.4.

Note that u, g, or o can be used as a privilege with the = operator only. Multiple values can be used for *who* and *privilege* such as ug for the who field and rx for the privilege field. Some useful examples of the **chmod** command and their purposes are listed in Table 8.5. Recall that the execute permission means search for directories.

**Table 8.4** Values for Symbolic Mode Components

| Who | Operator | Privilege |
|---|---|---|
| **u** User | **+** Add privilege | **r** Read bit |
| **g** Group | **–** Remove privilege | **w** Write bit |
| **o** Other | **=** Set privilege | **x** Execute/search bit |
| **a** All | | **u** User's current privileges |
| **ugo** All | | **g** Group's current privileges |
| | | **o** Others' current privileges |
| | | **l** Locking privilege bit |
| | | **s** Sets user or group ID mode bit |
| | | **t** Sticky bit |

**Table 8.5** Examples of the `chmod` Commands and Their Purposes

| Command | Purpose |
|---|---|
| `chmod 700 *` | Sets access privileges for all the files (including directories) in the current directory to read, write, and execute for the owner, and provides no access privilege to anyone else |
| `chmod 740 courses` | Sets access privileges for courses to read, write, and execute for the owner and read-only for the group, and provides no access for others |
| `chmod 751 ~/courses` | Sets access privileges for ~/courses to read, write, and execute for the owner, read and search for the group, and search-only permission for others |
| `chmod 700 ~` | Sets access privileges for the home directory to read, write, and execute for the owner, and no privileges for anyone else. (The authors use this command for their home directories; they do not trust anyone when it comes to security of their files, and they stop everyone at the main gate.) |
| `chmod u=rwx courses` | Sets owner's access privileges to read, write, and execute for courses and keeps the group's and others' privileges to their present values |
| `chmod ugo-rw sample`<br>or<br>`chmod a-rw sample` | Does not let anyone read or write sample |
| `chmod a+x sample` | Lets everyone execute sample |
| `chmod g=u sample` | Makes sample's group privileges match its user (owner) privileges |
| `chmod go= sample` | Removes all access privileges for the group and others for sample |

The following session illustrates how access privileges for files can be determined and set. The **chmod** commands are used to change (or set) access privileges, and the `ls -l` (or `ls -ld`) commands are used to show the effect of the **chmod** commands. After the **chmod 700 courses** command has been executed, the owner of the courses file has all three access privileges for it, and nobody else has any privileges. The **chmod g+rx courses** command adds the read and execute access privileges to the courses file for the group. The **chmod o+r courses** command adds the read access privilege to the courses file for others. The **chmod a-w *** command takes away the write access privilege from all users for all the files in the current directory. The **chmod 700 [l-t]*** command sets the access permissions 700 for all the files that start with letters l through t, as illustrated by the output of the last `ls -l` command, which shows access privileges for the files labs and temp changed to 700.

```
$ cd
$ ls -l
drwxr-x---   2  sarwar  faculty  512   Apr 23 09:37  courses
-rwxrwxrwx   1  sarwar  faculty  12    May 01 13:22  labs
-rwxr--r--   1  sarwar  faculty  163   May 05 23:13  temp
$ chmod 700 courses
$ ls -ld courses
drwx------   2  sarwar  faculty  512   Apr 23 09:37  courses
$ chmod g+rx courses
$ ls -ld courses
drwxr-x---   2  sarwar  faculty  512   Apr 23 09:37  courses
$
$ chmod o+r courses
$ ls -ld courses
drwxr-xr--   2  sarwar  faculty  512   Apr 23 09:37  courses
$ chmod a-w *
$ ls -l
dr-xr-x---   2  sarwar  faculty  512   Apr 23 09:37  courses
-r-xr-xr-x   1  sarwar  faculty  12    May 01 13:22  labs
-r-xr--r--   1  sarwar  faculty  163   May 05 23:13  temp
$ chmod 700 [l-t]*
$ ls -l
dr-xr-x---   2  sarwar  faculty  512   Apr 23 09:37  courses
-rwx------   1  sarwar  faculty  12    May 01 13:22  labs
```

```
-rwx------   1  sarwar  faculty  163   May 05 23:13  temp
$
```

The access permissions for all the files and directories under one or more directories can be set by using the **chmod** command with the **-R** option. In the following session, the first command sets access permissions for all the files and directories under the directory called courses to 711 recursively. The second command sets access permissions for all the files and directories under ~/personal/letters to 700.

```
$ chmod -R 711 courses
$ chmod -R 700 ~/personal/letters
$
```

If you specify access privileges with a single octal digit in a **chmod** command, it is used by the command to set the access privileges for 'others'; the access privileges for 'user' and 'group' are both set to 0 (no access privileges). If you specify two octal digits in a **chmod** command, the command uses them to set access privileges for 'group' and 'others'; the access privileges for 'user' are set to 0 (no privileges). In the following session, the first **chmod** command sets 'others' access privileges for the **courses** directory to 7 (**rwx**). The second **chmod** command sets 'group' and 'others' access privileges for the personal directory to 7 (**rwx**) and 0 (**---**), respectively. The **ls -l** command shows the results of these commands.

```
$ chmod 7 courses
$ chmod 70 personal
$ ls -l
d------rwx  2 sarwar  faculty  512 Nov 10 09:43 courses
d---rwx---  2 sarwar  faculty  512 Nov 10 09:43 personal
drw-------  2 sarwar  faculty  512 Nov 10 09:43 sample
$
```

Let's now look at what the read, write, and execute permissions mean for directories. As we stated before, the read permission on a directory allows you to read the directory's contents. Recall that the contents of a directory are the names of files and directories in it, that the write permission allows you to create a file in the directory or remove an existing file or directory from it, and that the execute permission for a directory is permission for searching the directory. In the following session, write permission for the courses directory has been turned off. Thus you cannot create a subdirectory ee345 in this directory by using the **mkdir** command. Similarly, as you do not have search permission for the personal directory you cannot use the **cd** command to get into (change directory to) this directory. If the sample directory had a subdirectory for which the execute permission was turned on, you still could not change directory to it because search permission for sample is turned off. Finally, because read permission for the personal directory is turned off, you cannot display the names of files and directories in it by using the **ls** command.

```
$ chmod 600 sample
$ chmod 500 courses
$ chmod 300 personal
$ ls -l
dr-x------  2 sarwar  faculty  512 Nov 10 09:43 courses
d-wx------  2 sarwar  faculty  512 Nov 10 09:43 personal
drw-------  2 sarwar  faculty  512 Nov 10 09:43 sample
$ mkdir courses/ee345
mkdir: Failed to make directory "courses/ee345"; Permission denied
$ cd sample
sample: Permission denied
$ ls -l personal
personal unreadable
$
```

The following In-Chapter Exercises ask you to use the **chmod** and **ls -ld** commands to see how they work, and to enhance your understanding of LINUX file access privileges.

## IN-CHAPTER EXERCISES

**8.2.** Create three directories called courses, sample, and personal by using the **mkdir** command. Set access permissions for the sample directory so that you have all three privileges, users in your group have read access only, and the other users of your system have no access privileges. What command did you use?

**8.3.** Use the **chmod o+r sample** command to allow others read access to the sample directory. Use the **ls -ld sample** command to confirm that 'others' have read permission for the directory.

**8.4.** Use the session preceding these exercises to understand fully how the read, write, and execute permissions work for directories.

### 8.5.3 DEFAULT FILE ACCESS PRIVILEGES

When a new file or directory is created, LINUX sets its access privileges based on the argument of the **umask** command. The following is a brief description of the command.

Syntax:

**umask [mask]**

**Purpose:** Set access permission bits on newly created files and directories to 1, except for those bits that are set to 1 in the 'mask'

The argument of the **umask** command is a **bit mask**, specified in octal, which identifies the protection bits that are to be turned off when a new file is created. The access permission value for a file is computed by the expression

file access permission = default permissions − mask

where 'mask' is the argument of the **umask** command and 'default permissions' are 777 for an executable file or directory and 666 for a text file. (Symbolic links are always created with 777 access privileges, and device files are created with permissions specified in the **mknod** command.) Therefore, if the **umask 013** command is executed, file access privileges for the newly created executable files and directories are set to (777 − 013) − 764. Thus every new executable file or directory has its access privileges set to **rwxrw-r--**. The mask value of 777 disallows any access to newly created files and directories because all the bits in the mask (777) are set. In other words, the access privileges for the newly created executable files and directories are set to (777 − 777) = 000.

A commonly used mask value is 022, which sets the default access privileges for newly created executable files and directories to (777 − 022) = 755 and for text files to (666 − 022) = 644. The authors of this textbook prefer a mask value of 077 so that their files are always created with full protection in place, that is, full access permissions for the owner and no permissions for anyone else. Recall that you can change access privileges for files on an as-needed basis by using the **chmod** command. In the following session, we use the **umask**, **touch**, and **ls -l** commands to show how the **umask** command affects the file permissions of the newly created files. The **touch** command without an argument can be used to create an empty file. The foo file created after the permissions mask has been set to 022 has its permissions set to 644, and the bar file and foobar directory created after the permissions mask has been set to 077 have their access privileges set to 600.

```
$ umask 022
$ touch foo
$ umask 077
$ touch bar
$ mkdir foobar
$ ls -l foo bar foobar
-rw------- 1 sarwar faculty 0   Nov 5 16:16 bar
-rw-r--r-- 1 sarwar faculty 0   Nov 5 16:16 foo
drw------- 2 sarwar faculty 512 Nov 5 16:16 foobar
$
```

The **umask** command is normally placed in a system startup file ~/.profile, ~/.login, or /etc/profile. It may also be placed in a shell startup file such as ~/.cshrc, /etc/zshrc, /etc/bashrc, /etc/csh.cshrc, /etc/skel/.bashrc, /etc/skel/.bash_profile, or /etc/skel/.zshrc.

When the command is executed without an argument, it displays the current value of the bit mask, as in

```
$ umask
777
$
```

The following In-Chapter Exercise asks you to use the **umask** command to determine the current file protection mask.

**IN-CHAPTER EXERCISE**

**8.5.** Run the **umask** command without any argument to display the current value of the bit mask.

## 8.6 SPECIAL ACCESS BITS

In addition to the nine commonly used access permissions bits described in this chapter (read, write, and execute for user, group, and others), three additional bits are of special significance. These bits are known as the **set-user-ID (SUID) bit**, **set-group-ID (SGID) bit**, and **sticky bit**.

## 8.6.1 The Set-User-ID (SUID) Bit

We've previously shown that the external shell commands have corresponding files that contain binary executable codes or shell scripts. The programs contained in these files are not special in any way in terms of their ability to perform their tasks. Normally, when a command executes, it does so under the access privileges of the user who issues the command, which is how the access privileges system described in this chapter works. However, a number of LINUX commands need to write to files that are otherwise protected from users who normally run these commands. An example of such a file is /etc/passwd, the file that contains a user's login information (see Chapter 7). Only the superuser is allowed to write to this file to perform tasks such as adding a new login and changing a user's group ID. However, LINUX users normally are allowed to execute the **passwd** command to change their passwords. Thus, when a user executes the **passwd** command, the command changes the user password in the /etc/passwd file on behalf of the user who runs this command. The problem is that we want users to be able to change their passwords, but at the same time they must not have arbitrary write access to the /etc/passwd file to keep information about other users in this file from being compromised.

As we stated before, when a command is executed, it runs with the privileges of the user running the command. Another way of stating the same thing is that, when a command runs, it executes with the "effective user ID" of the user running the command. LINUX has an elegant mechanism that solves the problem stated in the preceding paragraph—and many other similar security problems—by allowing commands to change their "effective user ID" and become privileged in some way. This mechanism allows commands such as **passwd** to perform their work, yet not compromise the integrity of the system. Every LINUX file has an additional pro tection bit, called the SUID bit, associated with it. If this bit is set for a file containing an executable program for a command, the command takes on the privileges of the owner of the file when it executes. Thus, if a file is owned by 'root' and has its SUID bit set, it runs with superuser privileges and this bit is set for the **passwd** command. Thus, when you run the **passwd** command, it can write to the /etc/passwd file (replacing your existing password with the new password), even though you do not have access privileges to write to the file.

Several other LINUX commands require 'root' ownership and SUID bit set because they access and update operating system resources (files, data structures, etc.) that an average user must not have permissions for. Some of these commands are **lp**, **mail**, **mkdir**, **mv**, and **ps**. Another use of the SUID bit can be made by the authors of a game software that maintains a scores file. When the SUID bit is set for such software, it can update the scores file when some user plays the game, although the same user cannot update the scores file by explicitly writing to it.

The SUID bit can be set by the **chmod** command by using octal or symbolic mode, according to the following syntaxes.

Syntax:

**chmod 4xxx file-list**
**chmod u+s file-list**

Here, 'xxx' is the octal number that specifies the read, write, and execute permissions, and the octal digit 4 (binary 100) is used to set the SUID bit. When the SUID bit is set, the execute bit for the user is set to 's' if the execute permission is already set for the user; otherwise it is set to 'S'. The following session illustrates use of these command syntaxes. The first `ls -l cp.new` command is used to show that the execute permission for the cp.new file is set. The `chmod 4710 cp.new` command is used to set the SUID bit. The second `ls -l cp.new` command shows that the **x** bit value has changed to `s` (lowercase). The following two **chmod** commands are used to set the SUID and execute bits to 0. The `ls -l cp.new` command is used to show that execute permission has been taken away from the owner. The `chmod u+s cp.new` command is used to set the SUID bit again, and the last `ls -l cp.new` command shows that the bit value is `S` (uppercase) because the execute bit was not set before the SUID bit is set.

```
$ ls -l cp.new
-rwx--x---  1  sarwar    faculty  12  May 08 20:00   cp.new
$ chmod 4710 cp.new
$ ls -l cp.new
-rws--x---  1  sarwar    faculty  12  May 08 20:00   cp.new
$ chmod u-s cp.new
$ chmod u-x cp.new
$ ls -l cp.new
-rw---x---  1  sarwar    faculty  12  May 08 20:00   cp.new
$ chmod u+s cp.new
$ ls -l cp.new
-rwS--x---  1  sarwar    faculty  12  May 08 20:00   cp.new
$
```

Although the idea of the SUID bit is sound, it can compromise the security of the system if not implemented correctly. For example, if the permissions of any Set-UID program are set to allow write privileges to others, you can change the program in this file or overwrite the existing program with another program. Doing so would allow you to execute your (new) program with superuser privileges.

### 8.6.2 The Set-Group-ID (SGID) Bit

The SGID bit works in the same manner that SUID bit does, but it causes the access permissions of the process to take the group identity of the group to which the owner of the file belongs. This feature is not as dangerous as the SGID feature because most privileged operations require superuser identity regardless of the current group ID. The SGID bit can be set by using either of the following two command syntaxes.

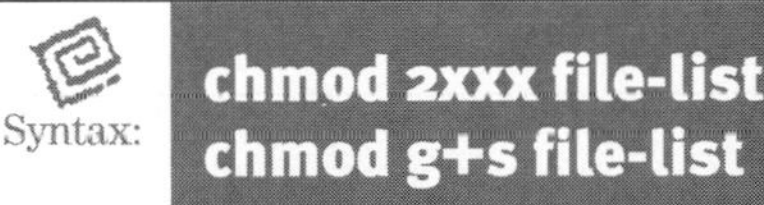


**chmod 2xxx file-list**
**chmod g+s file-list**

Here, 'xxx' is the octal number specifying the read, write, and execute permissions, and the octal digit 2 (binary 010) specifies that the SGID bit is to be set. When the SGID bit is set, the execute bit for the group is set to 's' if the group already has the 'execute' permission; otherwise it is set to 'S'. The following session illustrates the use of these command syntaxes. The command `chmod 2751 cp.new` sets the SGID bit for the cp.new file and sets its access privileges to 751 (rwxr-x--x). The rest of the commands are similar to those in Section 8.6.1.

```
$ ls -l cp.new
-rwxr-x--x  1   sarwar   faculty  12   May 08 20:00   cp.new
$ chmod 2751 cp.new
$ ls -l cp.new
-rwxr-s--x  1   sarwar   faculty  12   May 08 20:00   cp.new
$ chmod g-s cp.new
$ chmod g-x cp.new
$ ls -l cp.new
```

```
-rwxr----x 1   sarwar   faculty  12   May 08 20:00   cp.new
$ chmod g+s cp.new
$ ls -l cp.new
-rwxr-S--x 1   sarwar   faculty  12   May 08 20:00   cp.new
$
```

You can set or reset the SUID and SGID bits by using a single **chmod** command. Thus the command **chmod ug+s cp.new** can be used to perform this task on the cp.new file. You can also set the SUID and SGID bits along with the access permissions bits (read, write, and execute) by preceding the octal number for access privileges by 6 because the left-most octal digit 6 (110) specifies that both the SUID and SGID bits be set. Thus the command **chmod 6754 cp.new** sets the SUID and SGID bits for the cp.new file and its access privileges to 750.

## 8.6.3 The Sticky Bit

The last of the 12 access bits, the sticky bit, can be set to ensure that an unprivileged user may not remove or rename files of other users in a directory. You must be the owner of a directory or have appropriate permissions to set the sticky bit for it. It is commonly set for shared directories that contain files owned by several users.

Originally, this bit was designed for the UNIX system to inform the kernel that the code segment of a program is to be shared or kept in the main memory or the swap space owing to frequent use of the program. Thus, when this bit is set for a program, the system tries to keep the executable code for the program (process) in memory after it finishes execution—the processes "stick around in the memory." If for some reason, memory space occupied by this program is needed by the system for loading another program, the program with the sticky bit on is saved in the **swap space** (a special area on the disk used to save processes temporarily). That is, if the sticky bit is set for a program, the program is either kept in memory or on the swap space after it finishes its execution. When this program is executed again, with the program code in memory, program execution starts right away. If the program code is on the swap space, the time needed for loading it is much shorter than if it were stored on disk as a LINUX file. The advantage of this scheme, therefore, is that, if a program with the sticky bit on is executed frequently, it is executed much faster.

This facility is useful for programs such as compilers, assemblers, and editors, and commands such as **ls** and **cat**, which are frequently used in a typical computer system environment. Care must be taken that not too many programs have this bit set, or system performance will suffer because of lack of free space, with more and more space being used by the programs whose sticky bit is set. This historical use of the sticky bit is not needed in newer UNIX systems and LINUX systems, because they use virtual memory systems that do not remove the most recently used pages or segments of recently executed processes. The sticky bit is now used to ensure that someone other than the owner of a directory cannot remove a file under the directory even if he or she has write permission for the directory. The person with write permission for the directory can still create files and/or directories under this directory. This allows you to put an extra security wall around your shared directories.

The sticky bit can be set by using either of the following command syntaxes.

Syntax:

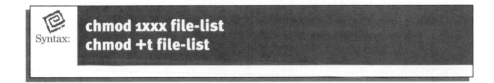

**chmod 1xxx file-list**
**chmod +t file-list**

Here, 'xxx' is the octal number specifying the read, write, and execute permissions, and the octal digit 1 (binary 001) specifies that the sticky bit is to be set. When the sticky bit is set, the execute bit for 'others' is set to 't' if 'others' already has execute permission; otherwise it is set to 'T'. The following session illustrates the use of these syntaxes. The `chmod 1775 testSticky` command sets the sticky bit for the testSticky directory and sets its access privileges to 775. The rest of the command lines are similar to those explained in Sections 8.6.1 and 8.6.2 and need not be explained further.

```
$ chmod 1775 testSticky
$ ls -l
total 1
drwxrw-r-t 2 sarwar faculty 512 Oct 28 12:24 testSticky
$ chmod 760 testSticky
$ chmod +t testSticky
$ ls -l
total 1
drwxrw---T 2 sarwar faculty 512 Oct 28 12:24 testSticky
$
```

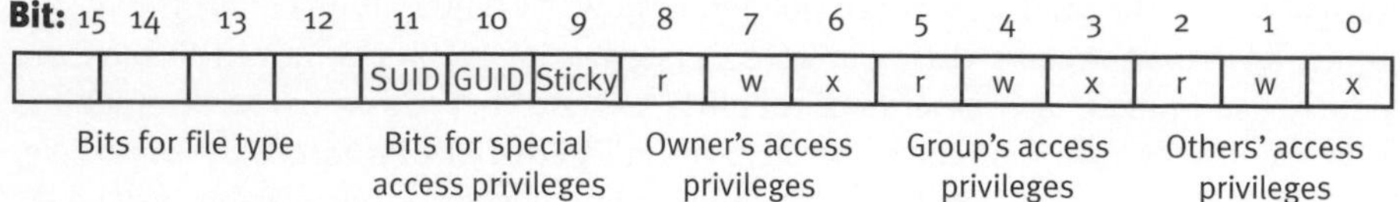


**Figure 8.2** Position of file type and access privilege bits for LINUX files

## 8.7 FILE PERMISSIONS AND TYPES

The file permissions and types are stored together in a 16-bit location: the lower 9 bits for file access privileges, the next 3 bits for special permission bits (SUID, SGID, and Sticky bits), and the uppermost 4 bits for file type, as shown in Figure 8.2. Further discussion of the bits used to specify file type is beyond the scope of this textbook. You can find values of all access and file types bits in the /usr/include/sys/stat.h file and a detailed discussion on this topic in a book on LINUX programming.

## SUMMARY

A time-sharing system has to ensure protection of one user's files from unauthorized (accidental or malicious) access by other users of the system. LINUX provides several mechanisms for this purpose, including one based on access permissions. Files can be protected by informing the system what type of operations (read, write, and execute) are permitted on the file by the owner, group (the users who are in the same group as the owner), and others (everyone else on the system). These nine commonly used access permissions are represented by bits. This information is stored in the inode of the file. When a user tries to access a file, the system allows or disallows access based on file's access privileges stored in the inode.

Access permissions for files can be viewed by using the `ls -l` command. When used with directories, this command displays attributes for all the files in the directories. The `ls -ld` command can be used to view access permissions for directories. The owner of a file can change access privileges on it by using the `chmod` command. The `umask` command allows the user to specify a bit mask that informs the system of access permissions that are disabled for the user, group, and others. When a file is created by the LINUX system, it sets access permissions for the file according to the specification given in the `umask` command. In a typical system, the access permissions for a new executable file or directory are set to (777 − mask) and to (666 − mask) for a text file.

LINUX also allows three additional bits—the set-user-ID (SUID), set-group-ID (SGID), and sticky bits—to be set. The SUID and SGID bits allow the user to execute commands such as `passwd`, `ls`, `mkdir`, and `ps` that access important

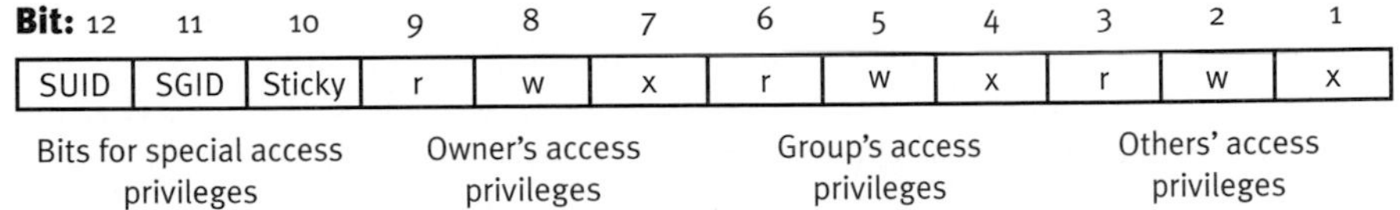


**Figure 8.3** Position of access privilege bits for LINUX files as specified in the `chmod` command

system resources to which access is not allowed otherwise. The sticky bit can be set for a directory to ensure that an unprivileged user may not remove or rename files of other users in that directory. Only the owner of a directory, or someone else having appropriate permissions, can set the sticky bit for the directory. It is commonly set for shared directories that contain files owned by several users. Historically, the sticky bit has served another purpose. It can be set for frequently used utilities so that LINUX keeps them in the main memory or on a fixed area on the disk, called the swap space, after their use. This feature makes subsequent access to these files much faster than if they were to be loaded from the disk as normal files.

The Linux system stores a file's type and its permissions in a 16-bit location, as shown in Figure 8.2. The final format of the 12 access permissions bits, as used in the `chmod` command, is shown in Figure 8.3.

## PROBLEMS

1. What are the three basic file protection schemes available in LINUX?
2. List all possible two-letter passwords comprising digits and punctuation letters.
3. If a computer system allows six-character passwords comprising a random combination of decimal digits and punctuation marks, what is the maximum number of passwords that a user will have to try with the brute force method of breaking into a user's account? Why?
4. What is the maximum number of passwords that can be formed if a system allows digits, uppercase and lowercase letters, and punctuation marks to be used. Assume that passwords must be 12 characters long.
5. How does file protection based on access permissions work? Base your answer on various types of users of a file and the types of operations they can perform. How many permission bits are needed to implement this scheme? Why?
6. How do the read, write, and execute permissions work in LINUX? Illustrate your answer with some examples.

7. Create a file test1 in your present working directory and set its access privileges to read and write for yourself, read for the users in your group, and none to everyone else. What command did you use to set privileges? Give another command that would accomplish the same thing.
8. The user sarwar sets access permissions to his home directory by using the command `chmod 700 $HOME`. If the file cp.new in his home directory has read permissions to 777, can anyone read this file? Why or why not? Explain your answer.
9. What is the effect of each command? Explain your answers.
   a. `chmod 776 ~/lab5`
   b. `chmod 751 ~/lab?`
   c. `chmod 511 *.c`
   d. `chmod 711 ~/*`
   e. `ls -l`
   f. `ls -ld`
   g. `ls -l ~/personal`
   h. `ls -ld ~/personal`
10. What does the execute permission mean for a directory, a file type for which the execute operation makes no sense?
11. What `umask` command should be executed to set the permissions bit mask to 037? With this mask, what default access privileges are associated with any new file that you create on the system? Why? Where would you put this command so that every time you log onto the system this mask is effective?
12. Give a command line for setting the default access mode so that you have read, write, and execute privileges, your group has read and execute permissions, and all others have no permission for a newly created executable file or directory. How would you test it to be sure that it works correctly?
13. Give `chmod` command lines that perform the same tasks that the `mesg n` and `mesg y` commands do. (*Hint:* Every hardware device, including your terminal, has an associated file in the /dev directory.)
14. What are the purposes of the set-user-ID (SUID), set-group-ID (SGID), and sticky bits?
15. Give one command line for setting all three special access bits (SUID, SGID, and sticky) for the file cp.new. (*Hint:* Use the octal mode.)
16. In a LINUX system, the `cat` command is owned by root and has its SUID bit set. Do you see any problems with this setup? Explain your answer.
17. Some LINUX systems do not allow users to change their passwords with the `passwd` command. How is this restriction enforced? Is it a good or bad practice? Why?
18. How many bits are used by LINUX to store a file's type and permissions? Show the arrangement of these bits.

CHAPTER

# 9

# Basic File Processing

## OBJECTIVES

- To discuss how to display contents of a file
- To explain copying, appending, moving/renaming, and removing/deleting files
- To describe how to determine the size of a file
- To discuss commands for comparing files
- To describe how to combine files
- To discuss printer control commands
- To cover the commands and primitives `>`, `>>`, `^`, `~`, `[ ]`, `*`, `?`, `cat`, `cp`, `diff`, `head`, `less`, `lpc`, `lpq`, `lpr`, `lprm`, `lptest`, `ls`, `more`, `mv`, `nl`, `pg`, `pr`, `rm`, `tac`, `tail`, `uniq`, and `wc`

## 9.1 INTRODUCTION

In this chapter we describe how some basic file operations can be performed in LINUX. These operations are primarily for nondirectory files, although some are applicable to directories as well. (We previously discussed the most commonly used directory operations in Chapter 7.) When discussing these operations, we also describe related commands and give examples to illustrate how these commands can be used to perform the needed operations.

## 9.2 VIEWING CONTENTS OF TEXT FILES

Files are viewed to identify their contents. Several LINUX commands can be used to view contents of text files on the display screen. These commands differ from each other in terms of the amount of the file displayed, the portion of file contents displayed (initial, middle, or last part of the file), and whether the file's contents are displayed a screen or page at a time. Recall that you can view only those files for which you have read permission. In addition, you must have search (execute) permissions for all the directories involved in the pathname of the file to be displayed.

### 9.2.1 VIEWING COMPLETE FILES

You can display the complete contents of one or more files on screen by using the `cat` command. However, because the command does not display file contents a screen or page at a time, you see only the last page of a file that is larger than one page in size. The following is a brief description of the `cat` command.

Syntax: **cat [options] [file-list]**

**Purpose:** Concatenate/display the files in 'file-list' on standard output (screen by default)

**Output:** Contents of the files in 'file-list' displayed on the screen, one file at a time

**Commonly used options/features:**

| | |
|---|---|
| `-E` | Display $ at the end of each line |
| `-n` | Put line numbers with the displayed lines |
| `--help` | Display the purpose of the command and a brief explanation of each option |

Here, 'file-list' is an optional argument that consists of pathnames for one or more files, separated by spaces. For example, the following command displays the contents of the student_records file in the present working directory. If the file is larger than one page, the file contents quickly scroll off the display screen.

```
$ cat student_records
John    Doe     ECE    3.54
Pam     Meyer   CS     3.61
Jim     Davis   CS     2.71
Jason   Kim     ECE    3.97
Amy     Nash    ECE    2.38
$
```

The following command displays the contents of files lab1 and lab2 in the directory ~/courses/ee446/labs. The command does not pause after displaying the contents of lab1.

```
$ cat ~/courses/ee446/labs/lab1 ~/courses/ee446/labs/lab2
[ contents of lab1 and lab2 ]
$
```

As we discussed in Chapter 4, shell metacharacters can be used to specify file names. The contents of all the files in the current directory can be displayed by using the **cat *** command. The **cat exam?** command displays all the files in the current directory starting with the string exam and followed by one character. The contents of all the files in the current directory starting with the string lab can be displayed by using the **cat lab*** command.

As is indicated by the command syntax, the file-list is an optional argument. Thus, when the **cat** command is used without any arguments, it takes input from standard input one line at a time and sends it to standard output. Recall that, by default, standard input for a command is the keyboard and standard output is the display screen. Therefore, when the **cat** command is executed without an argument, it takes input from the keyboard and displays it on the screen one line at a time. The command terminates when the user presses <Ctrl-D>, the LINUX eof, on a new line. Again, the boldface text is typed by the user.

```
$ cat
This is a test.
This is a test.
In this example, the cat command will take input from stdin (keyboard)
In this example, the cat command will take input from stdin (keyboard)
stdout (screen). So, this is not how this command is normally used. It
stdout (screen). So, this is not how this command is normally used. It
```

```
is commonly used to display the one line at a time and send it to the
is commonly used to display the one line at a time and send it to the
contents of a user file on the screen.
contents of a user file on the screen.
<Ctrl-D>
$
```

We can use the **tac** (reverse of **cat**) command to display files in the reverse order.

At times you will need to view a file having line numbers. You typically need to do so when, during the software development phase, a compilation of your source code results in compiler errors having line numbers associated with them. The LINUX utility `nl` allows you to display files having line numbers. Thus the `nl student_records` command displays the lines in the student_records file with line numbers, as shown in the following session. The same task can also be performed by using the `cat -n student_records` command.

```
$ nl student_records
        1  John   Doe    ECE  3.54
        2  Pam    Meyer  CS   3.61
        3  Jim    Davis  CS   2.71
        4  Jason  Kim    ECE  3.97
        5  Amy    Nash   ECE  2.38
$
```

Also, if you need to display files with a time stamp and page numbers, you can use the `pr` utility. It displays file contents as the `cat` command does, but it also partitions the file into pages and inserts a header for each page. The page header contains today's date, current time, file name, and page number. The `pr` command, like the `cat` command, can display multiple files, one after the other. The following session illustrates a simple use of the `pr` command.

```
$ pr student_records

May 26 12:34 1999  student_records Page 1

John     Doe      ECE    3.54
Pam      Meyer    CS     3.61
Jim      Davis    CS     2.71
Jason    Kim      ECE    3.97
Amy      Nash     ECE    2.38
$
```

You can print files with line numbers and a page header by connecting the `nl`, `pr`, and `lpr` command. We discuss this method in Chapter 12.

### 9.2.2 Viewing Files One Page at a Time

If the file to be viewed is larger than one page, you can use the **`more`** or **`less`** command, also known as the **LINUX pagers**, to display the file screenful at a time. We discuss these commands one by one. The following is a brief description of the `more` command.

Syntax:

**more [options] [file-list]**

**Purpose:** Concatenate/display the files in 'file-list' on standard output a screenful at a time

**Output:** Contents of the files in 'file-list' displayed on the screen one page at a time

**Commonly used options/features:**

| | |
|---|---|
| `+/`*`str`* | Start two lines before the first line containing *str* |
| `-nN` | Display *N* lines per screen/page |
| `+N` | Start displaying the contents of the file at line number *N* |

When run without 'file-list', the **`more`** command, like the **`cat`** command, takes input from the keyboard one line at a time and sends it to the display screen. If a 'file-list' is given as an argument, the command displays the contents of the files in 'file-list' one screen at a time. To display the next screen, press the <space bar>. To display the next line in the file, press <Enter> (or <Return>). At the bottom left of a screen, the command displays the percentage of the file that has been displayed up to that point. To return to the shell, press the <Q> key.

The following command displays the file sample in the present working directory a screenful at a time.

```
$ more sample
[contents of sample]
$
```

The following command displays contents of the files sample, letter, and memo in the present working directory a screenful at a time. The files are displayed in the order they occur in the command.

```
$ more sample letter memo
[contents of sample, letter, and memo]
$
```

The following command displays the contents of the file param.h in the directory /usr/include/sys one page at a time with 20 lines per page.

```
$ more -n20 /usr/include/sys/param.h
[contents of /usr/include/sys/param.h]
$
```

The following command displays, one page at a time, the contents of all the files in the present working directory that have the .c extension (files containing C source codes).

```
$ more ./*.c
[contents of all .c files in the current directory]
$
```

The `less` command can also be used to view a file page by page. It is similar to the `more` command but is more efficient and has many features that are not available in `more`. It has support for many of the `vi` command mode commands. For example, it allows forward and backward movement of file contents one or more lines at a time, redisplaying the screen, and forward and backward string search. It also starts displaying a file without reading all of the file, which makes it more efficient than the `more` command or the `vi` editor for large files. The following is a brief description of the `less` command.

Syntax:

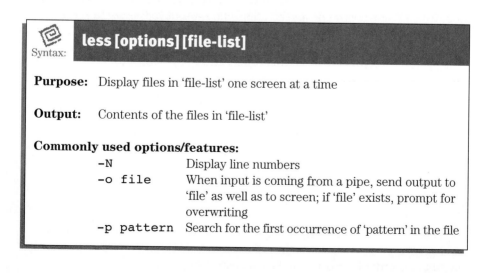

**less [options] [file-list]**

**Purpose:** Display files in 'file-list' one screen at a time

**Output:** Contents of the files in 'file-list'

**Commonly used options/features:**

| | |
|---|---|
| `-N` | Display line numbers |
| `-o file` | When input is coming from a pipe, send output to 'file' as well as to screen; if 'file' exists, prompt for overwriting |
| `-p pattern` | Search for the first occurrence of 'pattern' in the file |

While you are viewing a file with the **less** command, you can use a number of commands to browse through the file and perform other operations on it. A number of **vi** command mode commands are supported by **less**. Some useful commands are listed in Table 9.1.

Most of the options of the **less** command can be changed, while **less** is executing, by using the – command. Options can also be specified in the environment variable *LESS*. This way you don't have to type the options every time you run **less**. In order to do this, you need to use the **sentenv** command under the TC shell and the shell variable assignment statement and the **export** command under the Bash shell (see Chapters 15 and 17). For example, under the Bash shell, you can put the following lines in the system startup or Bash startup file.

**Table 9.1** Some Useful less Commands

| Command | Purpose |
|---|---|
| <space>, f, <Ctrl-F>, <Ctrl-V> | Scroll forward one screenful |
| <Enter>, e, j, <Ctrl-E>, <Ctrl-J>, <Ctrl-N> | Scroll forward one line (default) |
| d, <Ctrl-D> | Scroll forward half screen |
| b, <Ctrl-B>, <Esc-V> | Scroll back one screen |
| y, k, <Ctrl-K>, <Ctrl-P>, <Ctrl-Y> | Scroll back one line |
| u, <Ctrl-U> | Scroll back half screen |
| r, <Ctrl-L>, <Ctrl-R> | Redraw screen |
| /pattern | Find the next occurrence of 'pattern' starting with the second line displayed. The '!' character can be used before 'pattern' to search for lines not containing 'pattern'. The '@' character can be used before 'pattern' to start a search with the first line in the file. |
| ?pattern | Like /pattern, but search backward. The special characters '!' and '@' can be used just as they are used with /pattern. |
| n | Repeat the last pattern search in the forward direction |
| N | Repeat the last pattern search in the backward direction |
| :n | Read in the next file in 'file-list' |
| :N | Read in the previous file in 'file-list' |
| :x | Read in the first file in 'file-list' |
| q, :q, :Q, ZZ | Quit |
| !command | Run the shell command 'command' under *$SHELL* or sh |

```
LESS="-N -o less_log"
export LESS
```

Under the TC shell, the command

```
setenv LESS "-N -o less_log"
```

can be used to perform the same task. Because the environment variables are parsed before the command line, the options specified in the command line override the options specified in the ***LESS*** variable.

In the following session, we use the `less` command to display the bash.man file and use `!ps` to execute the shell command `ps` while the `less` command is still running. The `q` command is used to quit `less`. The `-N` option is used to display lines in the bash.man file with line numbers.

```
$ less -N bash.man
      1
      2
      3
      4 BASH2(1)                                        BASH2(1)
      5
      6
      7 NAME
      8        bash2 - GNU Bourne-Again SHell
      9
     10 SYNOPSIS
     11        bash2 [options] [file]
     12
     13 COPYRIGHT
     14        Bash is Copyright (C) 1989-1999 by the Free
     15        Software Foundation, Inc.
     16
     17 DESCRIPTION
     18        Bash is an sh-compatible command language
     19        interpreter that executes commands read from
     20        the standard input or from a file. Bash also
     21        incorporates useful features from the
     22        Korn and C shells (ksh and csh).
```

```
     23
     24        Bash is intended to be a conformant
     25        implementation of the
!ps
  PID TTY          TIME CMD
29181 pts/3 00:00:00 csh
29214 pts/3 00:00:00 bash
29894 pts/3 00:00:00 less
29916 pts/3 00:00:00 csh
29936 pts/3 00:00:00 ps
!done (press RETURN)
:q
$
```

### 9.2.3 Viewing the Head or Tail of a File

Having the ability to view the **head** (some lines from the beginning) or **tail** (some lines from the end) of a file is useful in identifying the type of data stored in the file. For example, the head operation can be used to identify a PostScript file or an uuencoded file, which have special headers. (We discuss encoding and decoding of files in Chapter 10.) The LINUX commands for displaying the head or tail of a file are `head` and `tail`. The following is a brief description of the `head` command.

Syntax:

**head [option] [file-list]**

**Purpose:** Display the beginning portions (head) of files in 'file-list'; the default head size is 10 lines.

**Output:** Heads of the files in 'file-list' displayed on the display screen

**Commonly used options/features:**

| | |
|---|---|
| `-N` | Display first *N* lines |

Without any option and the 'file-list' argument, the command takes input from standard input (the keyboard by default). The following session illustrates use of the `head` command.

```
$ head sample
[first 10 lines of sample]
$ head sample memo1 phones
[first 10 lines each of sample, memo1, and phones]
$ head -5 sample
[first 5 lines of sample]
$
```

The first command shows the first 10 lines of the file sample. The third command displays the first 5 lines of sample. The output of the second command is the first 10 lines of the files sample, memo1, and phones.

The following command, which displays the first 10 lines of the file otto, shows that the file is a PostScript file. The output of the command gives additional information about the file, including the name of the software used to create it, the total number of pages in the file, and the page orientation. All of this information is important to know before the file is printed.

```
$ head otto
%!PS-Adobe-3.0
%%BoundingBox: 54 72 558 720
%%Creator: Mozilla (NetScape) HTML->PS
%%DocumentData: Clean7Bit
%%Orientation: Portrait
%%Pages: 1
%%PageOrder: Ascend
%%Title: Otto Doggie
%%EndComments
%%BeginProlog
$
```

Similarly, the following command shows that data is a **uuencoded file** and that, when uudecoded (see Chapter 10), the original file will be stored in the file data.99.

```
$ head -4 data
begin 600 data.99
M.0I$3T4L($IO92!#.B`@,#`P.3`P.3H@0T4Z(“`@(“`@(“!34CH@9&]E,4!S
M;6EL92YC;VTZ(#4P,RXR,C(N,C(R,CH@-3`S+C,S,RXS,S,S"E-A<G=A<BP@
M4WEE9"!-.C`P,#$P-34Z144Z4U(Z<V%R=V%R0'5P+F5D=3HU,#,N,3$Q+C$R
$
```

The `tail` command is used to display the last portion (tail) of one or more files. It is useful to ascertain, for example, that a PostScript file has a proper end or that a uuencoded file has the required **end** on the last line. The following is a brief description of the command.

Syntax:

**tail [options] [file-list]**

**Purpose:** Display the last portions (tails) of the files in 'file-list'; the default tail size is 10 lines

**Output:** Tails of the files in 'file-list' displayed on the monitor screen

**Commonly used options/features:**

| | |
|---|---|
| `-f` | Follow growth of the file after displaying the last line of a file, and display lines as they are appended to the file. This option is terminated by pressing <Ctrl-C>. |
| `±n` | Start $n$ lines from the beginning of the file for $+n$, and $n$ lines before the end of file or $n$ units before the end of file for $-n$. By default, $-n$ is $-10$. |
| `-r` | Display lines in reverse order (last line first) |

Like the `head` command, the `tail` command takes input from standard input if no 'file-list' is given as argument. The following session illustrates how the `tail` command can be used with and without options.

```
$ tail sample
… last 10 lines of sample …
$ tail -5 sample
… last 5 lines of sample …
$ tail +8 sample
… all the lines in sample starting with line number 8 …
$ tail -5r sample
… last 5 lines of sample displayed in reverse order …
$
```

The first command displays the last 10 lines of sample, and the second command displays the last 5 lines of sample. The third command displays all the lines in the sample file, starting with line 8. The last command displays the last 5 lines in reverse order (the last line of the file is the first displayed).

The following commands show that files otto and data have proper PostScript and uuencoded tails.

```
$ tail -5 otto
8 f3
( ) show
pagelevel restore
showpage
%%EOF
$
$ tail data
M;W4@:&%V90IN;W0@=')I960@;W5T(&9O<B!L;VYG('1I;64N("!(;W=E=F5R
M+"!T;R!B92!S=6-C97-S9G5L+"!Y;W4@;75S="!T<@I(96QL;RP@5V]R;&0A
"(0H`
`

end
$
```

The **-f** option of the **tail** command is very useful if you need to see the tail of a file that is growing. This situation occurs quite often when you are running a simulation program that takes a long time to finish (several minutes, hours, or days) and you want to see the data produced by the program as it is generated. It is convenient to do if your LINUX system runs X Window System (see Chapter 21). In an X environment, you can run the **tail** command in an xterm (a console window) to monitor the newly generated data as it is generated and keep doing your other work concurrently. The following command displays the last 10 lines of the sim.data file and displays new lines are they are appended to the file. The command can be terminated by pressing <Ctrl-C>.

```
$ tail -f sim.data
… last 10 lines of sim.data …
… more data as it is appended to sim.data …
```

### 9.2.4 Displaying the NIS Database

As described in Section 7.4, the **ypcat** command can be used to display a NIS database map. For example, you can use the **ypcat passwd** command to display password-related information about the login names on the screen. Similarly, you can display all system-wide aliases with the **ypcat aliases** command. You can use the **ypcat -x** command to display names of the NIS maps maintained on your system and their nicknames.

In the following In-Chapter Exercises, you are asked to use the **cat**, **head**, **more**, **pr**, and **tail** commands to display different parts of text files, with and without page titles and numbers.

## IN-CHAPTER EXERCISES

**9.1.** Insert the student_records file used in Section 9.2.1 in your current directory. Add to it 10 more student records. Display the contents of this file by using the `cat student_records` and `cat -n student_records` commands. What is the difference between the outputs of the two commands?

**9.2.** Display the student_records file by using the `more` and `pr` commands. What command lines did you use?

**9.3.** Display the /etc/passwd file two lines before the line that contains your login name. What command line did you use?

**9.4.** Give commands for displaying the first line and the last seven lines of the student_records file.

## 9.3 COPYING, MOVING, AND REMOVING FILES

In this section, we describe commands for performing copy, move/rename, and remove/delete operations on files in a file structure. The commands discussed are `cp`, `mv`, and `rm`.

### 9.3.1 COPYING FILES

The LINUX command for copying files is `cp`. The following is a brief description of the command.

Syntax: **cp [options] file1 file2**

**Purpose:** Copy 'file1' to 'file2'. If 'file2' is a directory, make a copy of 'file1' in this directory

**Commonly used options/features:**

| | |
|---|---|
| `-i` | If destination exists, prompt before overwriting |
| `-p` | Preserve permissions and modification times |
| `-r` | Recursively copy files and subdirectories |

You must have permission to read the source file ('file1') and permission to execute (search) the directories that contain 'file1' and 'file2'. In addition, you must have write permission for the directory that contains 'file2' if it does not exist already. If 'file2' exists, you don't need the write permission to the directory that contains it but you must have the write permisson for 'file2'. If the destination file ('file2') exists by default, it will be overwritten without informing you if you have permission to write to the file. To be prompted before an existing file is overwritten you need to use the -i option. If you don't have permission to write to the destination file, you'll be so informed. If you don't have permission to read the source file, an error message will appear on your screen.

The following command line makes a copy of temp in temp.bak. The **ls** commands show the state of the current directory before and after execution of the **cp** command. Figure 9.1 shows the same information in pictorial form.

```
$ ls
memo   sample  temp
$ cp temp temp.bak
$ ls
memo   sample  temp   temp.bak
$
```

The command returns an error message if temp does not exist or if it exists but you do not have permission to read from it. The command also returns an error message if temp.bak exists and you do not have permission to write to it. The following session illustrates these points. The first error message is reported because the letter file does not exist in the current directory. The second error message is reported because you do not have permission to read the sample file. The last command reports an error message because temp.bak exists and you do not have write permission for it.

```
$ ls -l
-rwxr----- 1 sarwar  faculty  371 Nov 17 21:57 memo
```

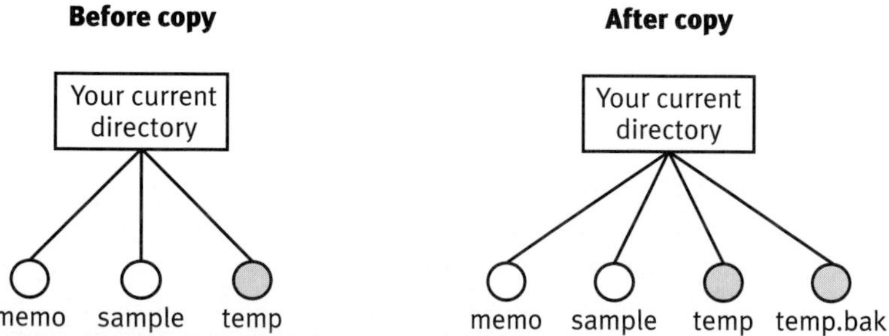


**Figure 9.1** State of the current directory before and after the temp file is copied to temp.bak

```
--wxr----- 1 sarwar  faculty  164 Nov 17 22:22 sample
-r-xr----- 1 sarwar  faculty  792 Nov 17 10:57 temp
-r-xr----- 1 sarwar  faculty  792 Nov 17 23:01 temp.bak
$ cp letter letter.bak
cp: cannot access letter
$ cp sample sample.new
cp: cannot open sample: Permission denied
$ cp memo temp.bak
cp: cannot create temp.bak: Permission denied
$
```

The following command makes a copy of the .profile file in your home directory and puts it in the .profile.old file in the ~/sys.backups subdirectory. This command works regardless of the directory you are in when you run the command because the pathname starts with your home directory. You should execute this command before changing your run-time environment (as specified in the ~/.profile file) so that you have a backup copy of the previous working environment in case something goes wrong when you set up the new environment. The command produces an error message if ~/.profile does not exist, you do not have permission to read it, the ~/sys.backups directory does not exist or you do not have execute (search) and write permissions for it, or .profile.back exists but you do not have permission to read it.

```
$ cp ~/.profile ~/sys.backups/.profile.bak
$
```

The following command copies all the files in the current directory, starting with the string lab to the directory ~/courses/ee446/backups. The command also prompts you for overwriting if any of the source files already exist in the backups directory. In this case (in which multiple files are being copied), if backups is not a directory, or it does not exist, an error message is displayed on the screen informing you that the target must be a directory.

```
$ cp -i lab* ~/courses/ee446/backups
$
```

If you want to copy a complete directory to another directory, you need to use the `cp` command with the `-r` option. This option recursively copies files and subdirectories from the source directory to the destination directory. It is a useful option that you can use to create backups of important directories periodically. Thus the following command recursively copies the ~/courses directory to the ~/backups directory.

```
$ cp -r ~/courses ~/backups
$
```

### 9.3.2 Moving Files

Files can be moved from one directory in a file structure to another. This operation in LINUX may result in simply renaming a file if it is on the same file system. The renaming operation is equivalent to creating a hard link (see Chapter 11) to the file, followed by removing/deleting (see Section 9.3.3) the original file. If the source and destination files are on different file systems, the move operation results in a physical copy of the source file to the destination, followed by removal of the source file. A **filesystem** is a directory hierarchy with its own root stored on a disk or disk partition, mounted under (glued to) a directory. The files and directories in the filesystem are accessed through the directory under which they are mounted. The command for moving files is `mv`. The following is a brief description of the command.

Syntax:

**mv [options] file1 file2**
**mv [options] file-list directory**

**Purpose:** First syntax: Move 'file1' to 'file2' or rename 'file1' as 'file2'
Second syntax: Move all the files in 'file-list' to 'directory'

**Commonly used options/features:**

| | |
|---|---|
| `-f` | Force the move regardless of the permissions of the destination file |
| `-i` | Prompt the user before overwriting the destination |

You must have write and execute access permissions to the directory that contains the existing file ('file1' in the description), but you do not need read, write, or execute permission to the file itself. Similarly, you must have write and execute access permissions to the directory that contains the target file ('file2' in the description), execute permission for every directory in the pathname for 'file2', and write permission to the file if it already exists. If the destination file exists, by default it is overwritten without informing you. If you used the `-i` option, you are prompted before the destination file is overwritten.

The following command moves temp to temp.moved. In this case the temp file is renamed temp.moved. The `mv` command returns an error message if temp does not exist, or you do not have write or execute permission for the directory it is in. The command prompts you for moving the file if temp.bak already exists but you do not have write permission for it.

```
$ mv temp temp.moved
$
```

The following command moves temp to the backups directory as the temp.old file. Figure 9.2 shows the state of your current directory before and after the temp file is moved.

```
$ mv temp backups/temp.old
$
```

The following command is a sure move; you can use it to force the move, regardless of the permissions for the target file—temp.moved in this case.

```
$ mv -f temp temp.moved
$
```

The following command moves all the files and directories (excluding hidden files) in dir1 to the dir2 directory. The command fails, and an error message appears on your screen if dir2 is not a directory, it does not exist, or you do not have write and execute permissions for it.

```
$ mv dir1/* dir2
$
```

After the command is executed, dir1 contains hidden files only; the `ls-a` command can be used to confirm this status.

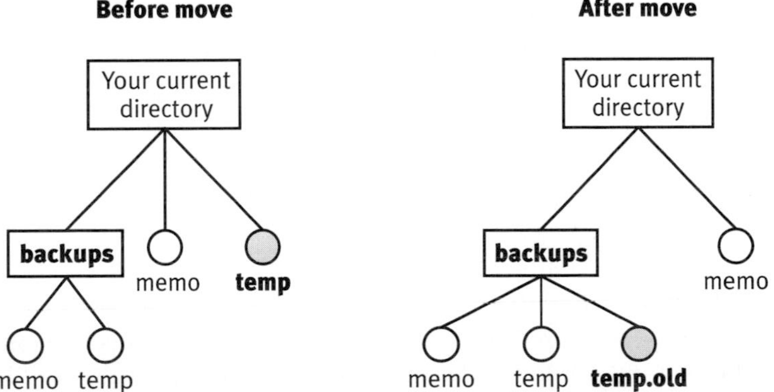


**Figure 9.2** Current directory before and after execution of the `mv temp backups/temp.old` command

### 9.3.3 Removing/Deleting Files

When files are not needed any more, they should be removed from a file structure to free up some disk space to be reused for new files and directories. The LINUX command for removing (deleting) files is `rm`. The following is a brief description of the command.

Syntax:

**rm [options] file-list**

**Purpose:** Remove files in 'file-list' from the file structure (and disk)

**Commonly used options/features:**

| | |
|---|---|
| `-f` | Force remove regardless of the permissions for 'file-list' |
| `-i` | Prompt the user before removing the files in 'file-list' |
| `-r` | Recursively remove the files in the directory, which is passed as an argument. This action removes everything under the directory, so be sure that you want to do so before using this option. |

If files in 'file-list' are pathnames, you need the search (execute) permissions for all the directory components in the pathnames and write and search permissions for the last directory (that contains the files to be deleted), but you do not need to have read or write permission to the files themselves. If you run the command from a terminal and do not have the write permission for the file to be removed, the command displays your access permissions for the file and prompts you for an action.

The following command lines illustrate use of the `rm` command to remove one or more files from various directories.

```
$ rm temp
$ rm backups/temp.old
$ rm -f phones grades ~/letters/letter.john
$ rm ~/dir1/*
$
```

The first command removes temp from the current directory. The second command removes the temp file from the current directory and the temp.old file from the backups directory. Figure 9.3 shows the semantics of this command. The third command removes the files phones grades and ~/letters/letter.john regardless of their access permissions. The fourth command removes all the files from ~/dir1 directory; the directories are not removed.

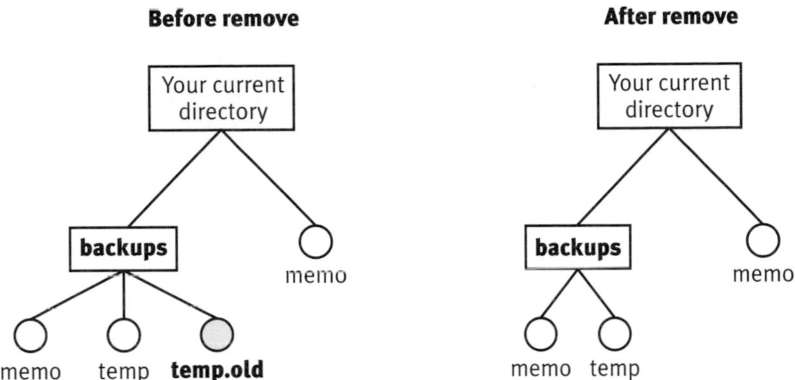


**Figure 9.3** Current directory before and after execution of the `rm temp backups/temp.old` command

Let's consider the following commands that use some shell metacharacter features.

```
$ rm [kK]*.prn
$ rm [a-kA-Z]*.prn
$
```

The first command removes all the files in current directory that have the .prn extension and names starting with k or K. The second command removes all the files in the current directory that have the .prn extension and names starting with a lowercase letter from a through k or an uppercase letter.

In Chapter 7, we talked about removing directories and showed that the `rmdir` command can be used to remove only the empty directories. The `rm` command with the `-r` option can be used to remove nonempty directories recursively. Thus the following command recursively removes all the files and subdirectories in your home directory. This command is one of the commands that you must *never* execute unless you really know its consequences—the loss of all the files and directories in your home directory, that is, everything you own on the system!

```
$ rm -r ~
$
```

You should generally combine the `-i` and `-r` options to remove a directory (~/personal in this case), recursively, as shown in the following command. The `-i` option is for interactive removal, and when you use this option, the `rm` command prompts you before removing a file.

```
$ rm -ir ~/personal
rm: examine files in directory /home/faculty/sarwar/personal (y/n)? y
rm: remove /home/faculty/sarwar/personal/John.11.14.99 (y/n)? y
rm: remove /home/faculty/sarwar/personal/Tom.2.24.99(y/n)?
...
$
```

### 9.3.4 Determining File Size

You can determine the size of a file by using one of several LINUX commands. The two commands commonly used for this purpose are `ls -l` and `wc`. We described the `ls -l` command in Chapter 8, where we used it to determine the access permissions for files. We revisit this command here in the context of determining file size.

As we mentioned before, the `ls -l` command displays a long list of the files and directories in the directory (or directories) specified as its argument. You must have read and execute permissions for a directory to be able to run the `ls` command on it successfully; no permissions are needed on the files in the directory to be able to see the list. The command gives output for the current directory if none is specified as an argument. The output of this command has nine fields, and the fifth field gives file sizes in bytes (see Section 8.5). In the following command, the size of the lab2 file is 163 bytes.

```
$ ls -l lab2
-r-xr--r--  1   sarwar    faculty   163   May 16 23:46  lab2
$
```

This command also displays the size of directory files. You can use it to get the sizes of multiple files by specifying them in the command line and separating them by spaces. For example, the following command displays long lists for files lab1 and lab2.

```
$ ls -l lab1 lab2
-r-xr--r--  1   sarwar    faculty   163   May 16 23:46  lab1
-r-xr--r--  1   sarwar    faculty   709   Apr 23 11:15  lab2
$
```

The following command uses the shell metacharacter * to display long lists for all the files in the ~/courses/ee446 directory.

```
$ ls -l ~/courses/ee446/*
... output of the command ...
$
```

Whereas `ls -l` is a general-purpose command that can be used to determine most of the attributes of one or more files, including their sizes in bytes or characters, `wc` is a special-purpose command that displays only file sizes. The following is a brief description of the `wc` command.

Syntax:

**wc [options] file-list**

**Purpose:** Display sizes of the files in 'file-list' as number lines, words, and characters

**Commonly used options/features:**

| | |
|---|---|
| `-c` | Display only the number of characters |
| `-l` | Display only the number of lines |
| `-w` | Display only the number of words |

The output of the command for every file is a line with four fields: line count, word count, character count, and file name. The command does not work with directories. The following session illustrates use of this command.

```
$ wc sample
       4       44      227 sample
$
```

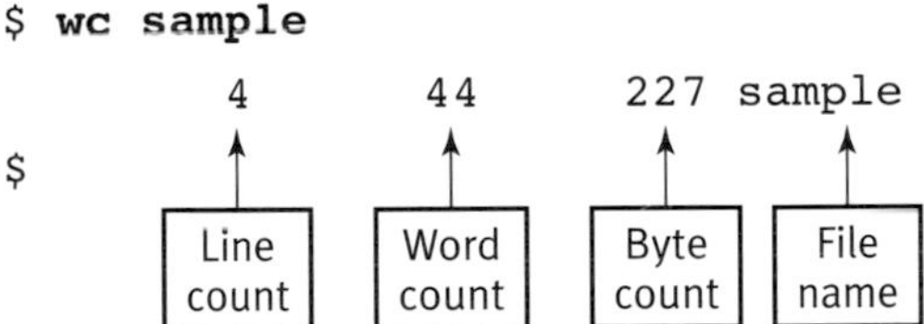

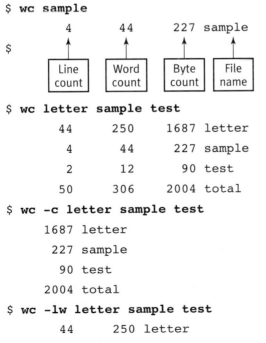

```
$ wc letter sample test
      44      250     1687 letter
       4       44      227 sample
       2       12       90 test
      50      306     2004 total
$ wc -c letter sample test
    1687 letter
     227 sample
      90 test
    2004 total
$ wc -lw letter sample test
      44      250 letter
       4       44 sample
```

```
        2       12 test
       50      306 total
$
```

The first command displays the number of lines, words, and characters in the file sample in the present working directory. Thus the size of sample is 4 lines, 44 words, and 227 bytes. The second command displays the same information for the files letter, sample, and test in the present working directory. The last line in the output of this command also displays the total for all three files. The third command displays the number of characters in letter, sample, and test. The last command shows that multiple options can be used in a single command; in this case the output is the number of words and letters for the three files in the command line.

As we stated before, the **wc** command cannot be used to display the size of a directory and returns an error message when used with a directory argument, as in

```
$ wc /etc/uucp
wc: /etc/uucp: Is a directory
       0        0        0 /etc/uucp
$
```

The **wc** command can be used with shell metacharacters such as * and ?. The following command displays sizes of all the files in the directory /usr/include/sys.

```
$ wc /usr/include/sys/*
… output of the command …
$
```

## 9.4 APPENDING TO FILES

By *appending to a file* we mean putting new data at the end of the contents of the file. If the file does not exist, it is created to contain the new data. The append operation is useful when an application or a user needs to augment a file by adding data to it. The following command syntax is used to append one or more files, or keyboard input, at the end of a file.

Syntax: **cat [file-list] ›› destination-file**

**Purpose:** Append the contents of the files in 'file-list' at the end of 'destination-file'

The >> operator is the LINUX *append* operator. We discuss the >>, <, and > operators in detail in Chapter 12. There we describe how input of your commands can be read as input from a file instead of the keyboard and how output and error messages of your commands can be redirected from the terminal (or console widow) to files. In this chapter, we use these operators only to describe how you can append new data at the end of the current contents of a file and how you can combine the contents of multiple files and put them in one file.

The following session illustrates how the append operation works. The **cat sample >> temp** command appends the contents of sample at the end of temp. The **cat** commands before and after this command show the contents of the files involved. The command syntax can be used to append multiple files to a file, as shown in the command **cat memo1 memo2 memo3 >> memos.record**. This command appends the contents of the memo1, memo2, and memo3 files at the end of the memos.record file.

```
$ cat temp
This is a simple file used to illustrate the working
of append operation. The new data will be appended
right below this line.
$ cat sample
These are the new data that will be appended at the
end of the test file.
$ cat sample >> temp
$ cat temp
This is a simple file used to illustrate the working
of append operation. The new data will be appended
right below this line.
These are the new data that will be appended at the
end of the test file.
$ cat memo1 memo2 memo3 >> memos.record
$
```

Without the optional 'file-list' argument (see the command description), the command can be used to append keyboard input at the end of 'destination-file'. The following command takes input from the keyboard and appends it to a file called test.letter. The command terminates when you press <Ctrl-D> on a new line.

```
$ cat test.letter
John Doe
12345 First Lane
Second City, State 98765
```

```
$ cat >> test.letter
November 14, 2000

Dear John:

This is to inform you ...
...
<Ctrl-D>

$ cat test.letter
John Doe
12345 First Lane
Second City, State 98765

November 14, 2000

Dear John:

This is to inform you ...
...
$
```

## 9.5 COMBINING FILES

The following command syntax can be used to combine multiple files into one file.

Syntax: **cat [file-list] › destination-file**

**Purpose:** Combine the files in 'file-list' and put them in 'destination-file'

The 'destination-file' is overwritten if it already exists. If you do not have write permission for the 'destination-file', the command displays an error message informing you that you do not have permission to write to the file.

The following session illustrates how this command works. Without the optional 'file-list' argument, you can use the command to put keyboard input in 'destination-file'. Thus this command syntax can be used to create a new file whose contents are what you enter from the keyboard until you press <Ctrl-D> on a new line.

```
$ ls -l
-r-xr--r--  1  sarwar  faculty  1687  Jan 10 11:26 memo1
-r-xr--r--  1  sarwar  faculty  1227  Feb 19 14:37 memo2
-r-xr--r--  1  sarwar  faculty  790   Apr 23 15:46 memo3
-r--------  1  sarwar  faculty  9765  Jan 15 22:11 memos.old
$ wc memo?
       44   250   1687 memo1
       34   244   1227 memo2
       12   112    790 memo3
       90   606   3704 total
$ cat memo1 memo2 memo3 > memos.new
$ wc memos.new
       90   606   3704 memos.new
$ cat memo1 memo2 memo3 > memos.old
memos.old: Permission denied.
$
```

The `ls -l` command is used to view permissions for the files. The `wc memo?` command displays the sizes of all the files in the current directory that start with the string memo and have one more letters after this string. The third command combines the contents of the memo1, memo2, and memo3 files and puts them in the memos.new file, in the order they appear in the command. This command is equivalent to `cat memo? > memos.old`. You can also do the same task by using the following command sequence.

```
$ cat memo1 > memos.new
$ cat memo2 >> memos.new
$ cat memo3 >> memos.new
$
```

The command `wc memos.new` is used to confirm that the memos.new file has the same number of lines, words, and characters as the three memo files combined. Execution of the `cat memo1 memo2 memo3 > memos.old` command shows that you do not have permission to write to memos.old.

The following In-Chapter Exercises have been designed to give you practice using the `cp`, `mv`, `ls -l`, `wc`, and `cat` commands and the operator for appending to a file.

## IN-CHAPTER EXERCISES

**9.5.** Copy the .profile (or .login) file in your home directory to a file .profile.old (or .login.old) in a directory called backups, also in your home directory. Assume that you are in your home directory. What command did you use?

**9.6.** Create a directory called new.backups in your home directory and move all the files in the backups directory to new.backups. What commands did you use?

**9.7.** Display the size in bytes of a file lab3 in the ~/ece345 directory. What command did you use?

**9.8.** Give a command for appending all the files in the ~/courses/ece446 directory to a file called BigBackup.ece446 in the ~/courses directory.

## 9.6 COMPARING FILES

At times you will need to compare two versions of a program code or some other document to find out where they differ from each other. You can use the `diff` command to perform this task. The command compares two files and displays differences between them in terms of commands that can be used to convert one file to the other. The following is a brief description of the command.

Syntax:

**diff [options] [file1] [file2]**

**Purpose:** Compare 'file1' with 'file2' line by line and display the differences between them as a series of commands that can be used to convert 'file1' to 'file2' or vice versa. Read from standard input if - is used for 'file1' or 'file2'

**Commonly used options/features:**

| | |
|---|---|
| `-b` | Ignore trailing (at the end of lines) white spaces (blanks and tabs), and consider other strings of white spaces equal |
| `-e` | Generate and display a script for the ed editor that can be executed to change 'file1' to 'file2' |
| `-h` | Do fast comparison (the `-e` option cannot be used) |

The 'file1' and 'file2' arguments can be directories. If 'file1' is a directory, **diff** searches it to locate a file named 'file2' and compares it with 'file2' (the second argument). If 'file2' is a directory, **diff** searches it to locate a file named 'file1' and compares it with 'file1' (the first argument). If both arguments are directories, the command compares all pairs of files in these directories that have the same names.

The **diff** command does not produce any output if the files being compared are the same. When used without any options, the **diff** command produces a series of instructions for you to convert 'file1' to 'file2' if the files are different. The instructions are `a` (add), `c` (change), and `d` (delete) and are described in Table 9.2.

The following session illustrates a simple use of the **diff** command.

```
$ cat Fall_OH
Office Hours for Fall 2001

Monday
        9:00 - 10:00 A.M.
        3:00 - 4:00 P.M.

Tuesday
        10:00 - 11:00 A.M.

Wednesday
        9:00 - 10:00 A.M.
        3:00 - 4:00 P.M.

Thursday
        11:00 - 12:00 A.M.
        2:00 - 3:00 P.M.
        4:00 - 4:30 P.M.
```

**Table 9.2** File Conversion Instructions Produced by `diff`

| Instruction | Description for Changing 'file1' to 'file2' |
|---|---|
| L1**a**L2,L3<br>> lines L2 through L3 | Append lines L2 through L3 from 'file2' after line L1 in 'file1' |
| L1,L2**c**L3,L4<br>< lines L1 through L2 in file1<br>---<br>> lines L3 through L4 in file2 | Change lines L1 through L2 in 'file1' to lines L3 through L4 in 'file2' |
| L1,L2**d**L3<br>< lines L1 through L2 in 'file1' | Delete lines L1 through L2 from 'file1' |

```
$ cat Spring_OH
Office Hours for Spring 2002

Monday
        9:00 - 10:00 A.M.
        3:00 - 4:00 P.M.

Tuesday
        10:00 - 11:00 A.M.
        1:00 - 2:00 P.M.

Wednesday
        9:00 - 10:00 A.M.

Thursday
        11:00 - 12:00 A.M.
$ diff Fall_OH Spring_OH
1c1
< Office Hours for Fall 2001
---
> Office Hours for Spring 2002
8a9
>       1:00 - 2:00 P.M.
12c13
<       3:00 - 4:00 P.M.
---
>
15,16d15
<       2:00 - 3:00 P.M.
<       4:00 - 4:30 P.M.
$
```

The instruction `1c1` asks you to change the first line in the Fall_OH file (`Office Hours for Fall 2001`) to the first line in the Spring_OH file (`Office Hours for Spring 2002`). Similarly, the instruction `12c13` asks you to change line 12 in Fall_OH (`3:00 - 4:00 P.M.`) to a blank line (note that nothing is given after the `>` symbol). The `8a9` instruction asks you to append line 9 in Spring_OH after line 8 in Fall_OH. The `15,16d15` instruction asks you to delete lines 15 and 16 from Fall_OH.

The following session illustrates use of the `-e` option with the `diff` command and how the output of this command can be given to the `ed` editor in order to make Fall_OH the same as Spring_OH. The command is used to show you what the output of the command looks like. The second command (with > diff.script) is used to save the command output (the `ed` script) in the diff.script file. The `cat` command is used to convert the diff.script file into a complete working script for the `ed` editor by adding two lines containing `w` and `q`. As we stated previously, this command terminates with <Ctrl-D>. Finally, the `ed` command is run to change the contents of Fall_OH, according to the script produced by the `diff -e` command, and make it the same as Spring_OH. The last command, `diff Fall_OH Spring_OH`, is run to confirm that the two files are the same.

```
$ diff -e Fall_OH Spring_OH
15,16d
12c

.
8a
     1:00 - 2:00 P.M.
.
1c
Office Hours for Spring 2002
.
$
$ diff -e Fall_OH Spring_OH > diff.script
$ cat > diff.script
w
q
<Ctrl-D>
$ ed Fall_OH < diff.script
216
183
$ diff Fall_OH Spring_OH
$
```

Most systems have a command called `diff3` that can be used to do a three-way comparison, that is, compare three files.

The **zdiff** and **zcmp** commands can be used to compare compressed files (see Chapter 10). The **zdiff** command uncompresses the files and passes them to the **diff** command, along with any options. The **zcmp** command uncompresses the files and passes them to the **cmp** command, along with any options. If one or both files are uncompressed, they are simply passed to the **diff** (or **cmp**) command. If only one file (say file1) is passed as an argument, then file1 and the uncompressed version of file1.gz are compared. In the following session, we show the use of the two commands with one and two arguments. The **zdiff bash.man.gz** command is used to compare the uncompressed bash.man.gz and bash.man.

```
$ ls –l bash.man*
-rw-------   1 sarwar      72501  Nov 20 12:24 bash.man.gz
-rw-------   1 sarwar      284064 Nov 22 11:22 bash.man
$ zdiff bash.man bash.man.gz
$ zdiff bash.man.gz
$ cp bash.man.gz bash.man.backup.gz
$ zdiff bash.man.gz bash.man.backup.gz
$ zdiff bash.man.gz tcsh.man.gz
4c4
< BASH2(1)                                                  BASH2(1)
---
> TCSH(1)                                                    TCSH(1)
8c8,9
<         bash2 - GNU Bourne- Again Shell
---
>         tcsh - C shell with file name completion and command line
>         editing
11c12,13
<         bash2 [options] [file]
---
>         tcsh [-bcdefFimnqstvVxX] [-Dname[=value]] [arg ...]
>         tcsh -l
13,16d14
< COPYRIGHT
<         Bash is Copyright (C) 1989–1999 by the Free Software Foun-
<         dation, Inc.
<
```

```
18,21c16,29
<        Bash is an sh-compatible command language interpreter that
<        executes commands read from the standard input or from a
<        file. Bash also incorporates useful features from the
<        Korn and C shells (ksh and csh).
---
>        tcsh is an enhanced but completely compatible version of
<Ctrl-C>
$ zcmp bash.man bash.man.gz
$ zcmp bash.man.gz
$ cp bash.man.gz bash.man.backup.gz
$ zcmp bash.man.gz bash.man.backup.gz
$ zcmp bash.man.gz tcsh.man.gz
- /tmp/tcshman.gz.779 differ: char 4, line4
$
```

## 9.7 REMOVING REPEATED LINES

You can use the `uniq` command to remove all but one copy of successive repeated lines in a file. In other words, the command is designed to work on sorted files. (We discuss sorting in Chapter 10.) The following is a brief summary of the command.

Syntax:

**uniq [options] [+N] [input-file] [output-file]**

**Purpose:** Remove repetitious lines from the sorted 'input-file' and send unique (nonrepeated) lines to 'output-file'. The 'input-file' does not change. If no 'output-file' is specified, the output of the command is sent to standard output. If no 'input-file' is specified, the command takes input from standard input

**Commonly used options/features:**

| | |
|---|---|
| `-c` | Precede each output line by the number of times it occurs |
| `-d` | Display the repeated lines |
| `-u` | Display the lines that are not repeated |

The following session illustrates how the **uniq** command works. The **cat** command is used to show the contents of the sample file. The **uniq sample** command shows that only consecutive duplicate lines are considered duplicate. The **uniq -c sample** command shows the line count for every line in the file. The **uniq -d sample** command is used to output repeated lines only. Finally, the **uniq -d sample outfile** sends output of the command to the outfile file. The **cat** command is used to show contents of outfile.

```
$ cat sample
This is a test file for the uniq command.
It contains some repeated and some nonrepeated lines.
Some of the repeated lines are consecutive, like this.
Some of the repeated lines are consecutive, like this.
Some of the repeated lines are consecutive, like this.
And, some are not consecutive, like the following.
Some of the repeated lines are consecutive, like this.
The above line, therefore, will not be considered a repeated
line by the uniq command, but this will be considered repeated!
line by the uniq command, but this will be considered repeated!
$ uniq sample
This is a test file for the uniq command.
It contains some repeated and some nonrepeated lines.
Some of the repeated lines are consecutive, like this.
And, some are not consecutive, like the following.
Some of the repeated lines are consecutive, like this.
The above line, therefore, will not be considered a repeated
line by the uniq command, but this will be considered repeated!
$ uniq -c sample
 1 This is a test file for the uniq command.
 1 It contains some repeated and some nonrepeated lines.
 3 Some of the repeated lines are consecutive, like this.
 1 And, some are not consecutive, like the following.
 1 Some of the repeated lines are consecutive, like this.
 1 The above line, therefore, will not be considered a repeated
 2 line by the uniq command, but this will be considered repeated!
```

```
$ uniq -d sample
Some of the repeated lines are consecutive, like this.
line by the uniq command, but this will be considered repeated!
$ uniq -d sample out
$ cat out
Some of the repeated lines are consecutive, like this.
line by the uniq command, but this will be considered repeated!
$
```

In the following In-Chapter Exercises, you will use the **diff** and **uniq** commands to appreciate the tasks they perform.

**IN-CHAPTER EXERCISES**

**9.9.** Duplicate the interactive sessions given in Section 9.6 to appreciate how the **diff** command works.

**9.10.** Give a command to remove all but one occurrence of the consecutive duplicate lines in a file called Phones in the ~/personal directory. Assume that you are not in your home directory.

## 9.8 PRINTING FILES AND CONTROLLING PRINT JOBS

We briefly discussed the LINUX commands for printing files in Chapter 4. In this section, we cover file printing fully, including commands related to printing and printer control. These commands include commands for printing files, checking the status of print requests/jobs on a printer, and canceling print jobs.

### 9.8.1 LINUX Mechanism for Printing Files

The process of printing files is similar to the process of displaying files; in both cases the contents of one or more files are sent to an output device. In the case of displaying output the output device is a display screen, whereas in the case of printing output the output device is a printer. Another key difference results primarily from the fact that every user has an individual display screen but that many users share a single printer on a typical LINUX (or any time-sharing) system. Thus,

**Table 9.3** List of Commands Related to Printing

| Command | Purpose |
|---|---|
| `lpr` | Submits a file for printing |
| `lpq` | Shows the status of print jobs for one or more printers |
| `lprm` | Removes/purges one or more jobs from the print queue |
| `lpc` | Activates the printer control program |
| `lptest` | Generates ripple pattern for testing the printer |

when you use the `cat` or `more` command to display a file, the contents of the file are immediately sent to the display screen by LINUX. However, when you print a file, its contents are not immediately sent to the printer because the printer may be busy printing some other file (yours or some other user's). To handle multiple requests a **first-come first-serve (FCFS) mechanism** places a print request in a queue and processes the request in its turn when the printer is available.

LINUX maintains a queue of print requests, called the **print queue**, associated with every printer in the system. Each request, also called a **job**, is assigned a number, called **job ID**. When you use a command to print a file, the system makes a temporary copy of your file, assigns a job ID to your request, and puts the job in the print queue associated with the printer specified in the command line. When the printer finishes its current job, it is given the next job from the front of the print queue. Thus your job is processed when the printer is available and your job is at the head of the print queue.

The work of maintaining the print queue and directing print jobs to the right printer is performed by a LINUX process called the **printer spooler**, or **printer daemon**. This process, called **lpd**, starts execution in the background when the system boots up, and waits for your print requests. We discuss daemons in Chapter 13, but for now, you can think of a daemon as a process that runs but you are not aware of its presence as it does not interact with the terminal.

Table 9.3 contains a list of the printing-related commands for LINUX. The last two commands, `lpc` and `lptest`, are normally used by the superuser—the system administrator.

### 9.8.2 Printing Files

As shown in Table 9.3, you can print files by using the `lpr` command. The following is a brief description of this command.

Syntax:

**lpr [options] file-list**

**Purpose:** Submit a print request to print the files in 'file-list'

**Commonly used options/features:**

| | |
|---|---|
| `-#` N | Print *N* copies of the file(s) in 'file-list'; default is one copy |
| `-P` ptr | Submit the print request for the 'ptr' printer |
| `-T` title | Print 'title' on a banner page |
| `-m` | Send mail after printing is complete |
| `-p` | Format the output by using the `pr` command |

The following session shows how to use the `lpr` command with and without options. The first `lpr` command sends the print request for printing the sample file on the default printer. The second command sends the request for printing the sample file on the spr printer. The third command prints three copies of the sample and phones files on the qpr printer.

```
$ lpr sample
$ lpr -P spr sample
$ lpr -P qpr -# 3 sample
$
```

You can use the following command to print the sample file with the header information on every page produced by the `pr` command. The vertical bar ( | ) is called the pipe symbol, and is discussed in detail in Chapter 12.

```
$ pr sample | lpr
$
```

You can perform the same task with the `lpr -p sample` command. You can print a file with line numbers and a pr header on each page by using the following command. You can also perform the same task with the `nl sample | lpr -p` command.

```
$ nl sample | pr | lpr
$
```

### 9.8.3 Finding the Status of a Print Request

The following is a brief description of the **lpq** command, which can be used to display the status of print jobs on a printer.

Syntax:

**lpq [options]**

**Purpose:** Display the status of print jobs on a printer

**Commonly used options/features:**

| | |
|---|---|
| `-P` printer-list | Display the status of print jobs on the printers specified in 'printer-list' |
| `-l` | Display the status of print jobs on the default printer for the `lpr` command in a long format |

The most commonly used option is `-P`. In the following session, the first command is used to display the status of print jobs on the mpr printer. The output of the command shows that four jobs are in the printer queue: jobs 3991, 3992, 3993, and 3994. The active job is at the head of print queue. When the printer is ready for printing, it will print the active job first. The second command shows that the qpr printer does not have any job to print.

```
$ lpq -Pmpr
mpr is ready and printing
Rank    Owner    Job     Files            Total Size
active  sarwar   3991    mail.bob         1056 bytes
1st     sarwar   3992    csh.man          93874 bytes
2nd     davis    3993    proposal1.nsa    2708921 bytes
3rd     tom      3994    memo             8920 bytes
$ lpq -Pqpr
no entries
$
```

### 9.8.4 Canceling Print Jobs

At times you may suddenly realize that you have submitted the wrong file for printing and want to cancel your print request.

The LINUX command for performing this task is `lprm`. The following is a brief description of the command.

Syntax:

**lprm [options] [jobID-list] [user(s)]**

**Purpose:** Cancel print requests that were made by using the `lpr` commands, that is, remove these jobs from the print queue. The jobs IDs in 'jobID-list' are taken from the output of the `lpq` command

**Commonly used options/features:**

| | |
|---|---|
| `-` | Remove all the jobs owned by 'user' |
| `-P` ptr | Specify the print queue for the 'ptr' printer |

The following `lprm` commands show how print jobs can be removed from a printer. The first command removes print job 3991 from the mpr printer and the second removes all print jobs for the user sarwar from the mpr printer.

```
$ lprm -Pmpr 3991
3991 dequeued
$ lprm -Pmpr sarwar
3997 dequeued
3998 dequeued
$
```

When run without an argument, the `lprm` command removes the job that is currently active, provided it is one of your jobs. You cannot remove others' print jobs from a printer.

The following In-Chapter Exercises have been designed to give you practice using the printing-related commands.

## IN-CHAPTER EXERCISES

**9.11.** How would you print five copies of the file memo on the printer ece_hp1? Give the command to perform this task.

**9.12.** After submitting the two requests, you realize that you really wanted to print five copies of the file letter. How would you remove the print jobs from the print queue? Give the command to perform this task.

## SUMMARY

The basic file operations involve displaying (all or part of) a file's contents, renaming a file, moving a file to another file, removing a file, determining a file's size, comparing files, combining files and storing them in another file, appending new contents (which may come from another disk file, keyboard, or output of a command) at the end of a file, and printing files. LINUX provides several utilities that can be used to perform these operations.

The `cat` and `more` commands can be used to display all the contents of a file on the display screen. The > symbol can be used to send outputs of these commands to other files, and the >> operator can be used to append new contents at the end of a file. The `cat` command sends file contents as continuous text, whereas the `more` and `less` commands send them in the form of pages. Furthermore, the `more` and `less` commands have several useful features, such as displaying a page that contains a particular string. The `pg` command is similar to the `more` command. The `less` command is the most powerful of the three and has the most features.

The `head` and `tail` commands can be used to display the initial or end portions (head or tail) of a file. These helpful commands are usually used to find out the type of data contained in a file, without using the `file` command (see Chapter 7). In addition, the `file` command cannot decipher contents of all the files.

A copy of a file can be made in another file or directory by using the `cp` command. Along with the > operator, the `cat` command can also be used to make a file copy, although there are differences between using the `cp` and `cat >` commands for copying files (see Chapter 12). A file can be moved to another file by using the `mv` command. Depending on whether the source and destination files are on the same file system, its use may or may not result in actual movement of file data from one location to another. If the source and destination files are on the same file system, the file data are not moved and the source file is simply linked to the new place (destination). If the two files are on different file systems, an actual copy of the source file is made at the new location and the source file is removed (unlinked) from the current directory. Files can be removed from a file structure by using the `rm` command. This command can also be used to remove directories recursively.

The size of a file can be determined by using the `ls -l` or `wc` command; both give file size in bytes. In addition, the `wc` command gives number of lines and words in the file. Both commands can be used to display the sizes of multiple files by using the shell metacharacters *, ?, [ ], and ^.

The `diff` command can be used to display differences between two files. The command, in addition to displaying the differences between the files, displays useful information in the form of a sequence of commands for the `ed` editor that can be used to make the two files the same. The `zdiff` and `zcmp` commands can be used to compare compressed files. The `uniq` command can be used to remove all but one occurrence of successive repeated lines. With the **-d** option, the command can be used to display the repeated lines.

The `lpr` command can be used for printing files on a printer. The `lpq` command can be used for checking the status of all print jobs (requests) on a printer (waiting, printing, etc.). The `lprm` command can be used to remove a print job from a printer queue so that the requested file is not printed.

## PROBLEMS

1. List 10 operations that you can perform on LINUX files.
2. Give a command line for viewing the sizes (in lines and bytes) of all the files in your present working directory.
3. What does the `tail -10r ../letter.John` command do?
4. Give a command for viewing the size of your home directory. Give a command for displaying the sizes of all the files in your home directory.
5. Give a command for displaying all the lines in the Students file, starting with line 25.
6. Give a command for copying all the files and directories under a directory courses in your home directory. Assume that you are in your home directory. Give another command to accomplish the same task, assuming that you are not in your home directory.
7. Repeat Problem 6, but give the command that preserves the modification times and permissions for the file.
8. What do the following commands do?
   a. `rm -f ~/personal/memo*.doc`
   b. `rm -f ~/linuxbook/final/ch??.prn`
   c. `rm -f ~/linuxbook/final/*.o`
   d. `rm -f ~/courses/ece446/lab[1-6].[cC]`
9. Give a command line for moving files lab1, lab2, and lab3 from the ~/courses/ece345 directory to a newlabs.ece345 directory in your home directory. If a file already exists in the destination directory, the command should prompt the user for confirmation.
10. Give a command to display the lines in the ~/personal/Phones directory that are not repeated.
11. Refer to In-Chapter Exercise 9.9. Give a sequence of commands to save the sequence of commands for the **ed** editor and use them to make sample and example the same files.
12. You have a file in your home directory called tryit&. Rename this file. What command did you use?

13. Give a command for displaying attributes of all the files starting with a string prog, followed by zero or more characters and ending with a string .c in the courses/ece345 directory in your home directory.
14. Refer to Problem 13. Give a command line if file names have two English letters between prog and .c. Can you give another command line to accomplish the same task?
15. Give a command line for displaying files got|cha and M*A*S*H a screenful at a time.
16. Give a command line for displaying the sizes of files that have the .jpg extension and names ending with a digit.
17. What does the `rm *[a-zA-Z]??[1,5,8].[^p]*` command do?
18. Give a command to compare the files sample and example in your present working directory. The output should generate a series of commands for the `ed` editor.
19. Give the command for producing 10 copies of the report file on the ece_hp3 printer. Each page should contain a page header produced by the `pr` command.
20. Give the command for checking the status of a print job with job ID ece_hp3-8971. How would you remove this print job from the print queue?

CHAPTER

# 10

# Advanced File Processing

## OBJECTIVES

- To discuss the formation and use of regular expressions
- To explain file compression and how it can be performed
- To explain the sorting process and how files can be sorted
- To discuss searching for commands and files in the LINUX file structure
- To describe searching files for expressions, strings, and patterns
- To describe how database-type operations of cutting and pasting fields in a file can be performed
- To discuss encoding and decoding of files
- To explain command history
- To cover the commands and primitives >, ~, !, `crypt`, `cut`, `egrep`, `fc`, `fgrep`, `find`, `grep`, `gunzip`, `gzexe`, `gzip`, `history`, `paste`, `pcat`, `sort`, `uuencode`, `uudecode`, `whereis`, `which`, `zcat`, `zcmp`, `zdiff`, `zegrep`, `zfgrep`, `zforce`, and `zgrep`

## 10.1 INTRODUCTION

In this chapter we describe some of the more advanced file processing operations and show how they can be performed in LINUX. But, before describing these operations, we discuss the important topic of **regular expressions**, which are a set of rules that can be used to specify one or more items in a single character string (sequence of characters). While discussing the operations, we also describe their related commands and give examples to illustrate how these commands can be used to perform the needed operations.

## 10.2 REGULAR EXPRESSIONS

While using some of the LINUX commands and tools, you will need to be able to specify a set of items by using a single character string, similar to the use of shell metacharacters. Regular expressions allow you to do just that; that is, they are a set of rules that you can use to specify one or more items, such as words in a file,

**Table 10.1** Regular Expression Operators and Their Support by LINUX Tools

| Name | Operator | Example of Usage | Meaning | Supported by |
|---|---|---|---|---|
| Alternation | \| | x\|y\|z | x, y, or z | awk, egrep |
| Any character | . | /L..e/ | Love, Live, Lose,... | All |
| Beginning of string | ^ | ^x | A line starting with an x | All |
| Concatenation | | xyz | xyz | All |
| End of string | $ | x$ | A line ending with an x | All |
| Escape sequence | \ | * | * | ed, sed, vi |
| Grouping | ( ) or \( \) | (xy)+ | xy, xyxy, xyxyxy,... | All |
| Optional | ? | xy? | x, xy | awk, egrep |
| Repetition (0 or more times) | * | xy* | x, xy, xyy, xyyy,... | All |
| Repetition (1 or more times) | + | xy+ | xy, xyy, xyyy,... | awk, egrep |
| Set | [ ]<br>[^] | /[Hh]ello/<br>/[^A-KM-Z]ove/ | Hello, hello<br>Love | All |

by using a single character string. Some of the commonly used tools that allow the use of regular expressions are **awk**, **ed**, **egrep**, **grep**, **sed**, and **vi**, but the level of support for regular expressions isn't the same for all these tools. Whereas **awk** and **egrep** have the best support for regular expressions, **grep** has the weakest.

Table 10.1 lists the regular expression operators, their names, examples of usage, their meanings, and the tools that support them. The regular expression operators overlap with shell metacharacters, but you can use single quotes around them to prevent the shell from interpreting them. The word *All* in the last column means that all the tools mentioned support the corresponding operator.

Table 10.2 lists some commonly used regular expressions in the **vi** editor and their meanings. Needless to say, regular expressions are used in the **vi** commands. We discuss examples for **grep** and **egrep** in Section 10.6.

In Table 10.3 we list some examples of the **vi** commands that use regular expressions and their meaning. Note that these commands are used when you are in **vi**'s command mode.

**Table 10.2** Examples of Regular Expressions for vi and Their Meaning

| Regular Expression | Meaning | Examples |
|---|---|---|
| /^Yes/ | A line starting with the string **Yes** | **Yes**...<br>**Yes**terday...<br>**Yes**teryear...<br>etc. |
| /th/ | Occurrence of the string **th** anywhere in a word | **th**e, **th**ere, pa**th**, ba**th**ing,... |
| /:$/ | A line ending with a colon | ...the following**:**<br>...below**:**<br>etc. |
| /[0-9]/ | A single digit | 0, 1,..., 9 |
| /[a-z][0-9]/ | A single lowercase English letter followed by a single digit | a0, a1,..., b0, b1,..., z0, z1..., z9 |
| /*.c/ | Any word that ends with .c (all C source code files) | lab1.c, program1.c, client.c, server.c,... |
| /[a-zA-Z ]*/ | Any string composed of letters (uppercase or lowercase) and spaces; no numbers and punctuation marks | All strings without numbers and punctuation marks such as 767-N. |

**Table 10.3** Some Commonly Used vi Commands Illustrating the Use of Regular Expressions

| Command | Meaning |
|---|---|
| `/ [0-9] /` | Does forward search for a single stand-alone digit character in the current file; digits that are part of strings are not identified. |
| `?*.c[1-7]?` | Does backward search for words or strings in words that end with .c, followed by a single digit between 1 and 7 |
| `:1,$s/:$/./` | Searches the whole file and substitutes colon (:) at the end of a line with a period (.) |
| `:.,$s/^[Hh]ello /Greetings /` | From the current line to the end of file, substitutes the words *Hello* and *hello*, starting a line with the word *Greetings* |
| `:1,$s/^ *//` | Eliminates one or more spaces at the beginning of all the lines in the file |

In the following In-Chapter Exercises, you will use regular expressions in the `vi` editor to appreciate their power.

**IN-CHAPTER EXERCISES**

**10.1.** Create a file that contains the words UNIX, LINUX, Windows, and DOS. Be sure that some of the lines in this file end with those words. Replace the string Windows with LINUX in the whole document as you edit it with the `vi` editor. What command(s) did you use?

**10.2.** As you edit the document in Exercise 10.1, in `vi`, run the command `:1,$s /DOS\./LINUX\./gp`. What does the command do to the document?

## 10.3 COMPRESSING FILES

Reduction in the size of a file, known as **file compression**, has both space and time advantages. A compressed file takes less disk space, less time to transmit from one computer to another in a network or Internet environment, and less time to copy. Compression takes time, but, if a file is to be copied or transmitted several times, the time spent compressing the file could be just a fraction of the total time saved. In addition, if the compressed file is to be stored on a secondary storage device (e.g., disk) for a long time, the savings in disk space is considerable. One consequence of compression is that the compressed file is not readable, but, this is not a problem because the process is fully reversible and a compressed file can be converted back to its original form.

The LINUX operating system has several commands for compressing and decompressing files, and for performing various operations on compressed files.

These commands include the traditional UNIX commands for compressing and decompressing files, **compress** and **uncompress**, and the GNU tools **gzexe**, **gzip**, **gunzip**, **zcat**, **zcmp**, **zforce**, **zmore**, and **zgrep**. We describe the GNU tools here; we do not discuss the **compress** and **uncompress** commands because the corresponding GNU commands (**gzip** and **gunzip**) are better.

### 10.3.1 The `gzip` Command

The `gzip` command can be used to compress files. The command reads the contents of files that are passed to it as parameters, analyzes their contents for repeated patterns, and then substitutes a smaller number of characters for these patterns by using **Lempel-Ziv coding**. A compressed file's contents are altogether different from the original file. The compressed file contains nonprintable control characters, so a compressed file displayed on the screen is a bunch of control characters, or garbage. The compressed file is saved in a file that has the same name as the original file, with an extension .gz appended to it. The compressed files retain the access/modification times, ownership, and access privileges of the original files. The original file is removed from the file structure. The following is a brief description of the `gzip` command.

Syntax:

**gzip [options] [file-list]**

**Purpose:** First syntax: Compress each file in 'file-list' and store it in filename.gz, where 'filename' is the name of the original file; if no file is specified in the command line or if - is specified, take input from stdin

**Commonly used options/features:**

| | |
|---|---|
| `-N` | Control compression speed (and compression ratio) according to the value of *N*, with 1 being fastest and 9 being slowest; slow compression compresses more |
| `-c` | Send output to stdout; input files remain unchanged |
| `-d` | Uncompress a compressed file |
| `-f` | Force compression of a file when its .gz version exists, or it has multiple links, or input file is stdin |
| `-l` | For compressed files given as arguments, display sizes of uncompressed and compressed versions, compression ratio, and uncompressed name |
| `-r` | Recursively compress files in the directory specified as argument |
| `-t` | Test integrity of the compressed files specified as arguments |
| `-v` | Display compression percentage and the names of the compressed files |

With no file argument or with - as an argument, the **gzip** command takes input from standard input (keyboard by default), which allows you to use the command in a pipeline (see Chapter 12). We normally use the command with one or more files as its arguments.

### 10.3.2 The gunzip Command

The **gunzip** command can be used to perform the reverse operation and bring compressed files back to their original forms. The **gzip -d** command can also perform this task. With the **gunzip** command, the **-N**, **-c**, **-f**, **-l**, and **-r** options work just like they do with the **gzip** command.

The following session shows the use of the two commands with and without arguments. We use the **man bash > bash.man** and **man tcsh > tcsh.man** commands to save the manual page for the Bourne Again and TC shells in the bash.man and tcsh.man files, respectively. The **gzip bash.man** command is used to compress the bash.man file and the **gzip –l bash.man.gz tcsh.man.gz** command is used to display some information about the compressed and uncompressed versions of the bash.man and tcsh.man files. The **gzip bash.man.gz** command is used to show that **gzip** does not compress an already compressed file that has a .gz extension. If a compressed file does not have the .gz extension, **gzip** will try to compress it again. The **gunzip bash.man.gz** command is used to decompress the compressed file bash.man.gz file. The **gzip –d bash.man.gz** command can be used to perform the same task. The **ls –l** commands have been used to show that the modification time, ownership, and access privileges of the original file are retained for the compressed file.

```
$ man bash > bash.man
$ ls -l bash.man
-rw------- 1 sarwar  faculty  284064 Nov 20 12:24 bash.man
$ gzip bash.man
$ ls -l bash.man.gz
-rw------- 1 sarwar  faculty  72501 Nov 20 12:24 bash.man.gz
$ gzip bash.man tcsh.man
$ gzip -l bash.man.gz tcsh.man.gz
compressed uncompr. ratio uncompressed_name
   72501   284064   74.4% bash.man
   73790   261316   71.7% tcsh.man
  146291   545380   73.1% (totals)
$ gzip bash.man.gz
gzip: bash.man.gz already has .gz suffix — unchanged
$ gunzip bash.man.gz
```

```
$ ls -l bash.man
-rw------- 1 sarwar faculty 284064 Nov 20 12:24 bash.man
$ gzip -v bash.man tcsh.man
bash.man:                74.4% -- replaced with bash.man.gz
tcsh.man:                71.7% -- replaced with tcsh.man.gz
$
```

### 10.3.3 THE gzexe COMMAND

The `gzexe` command can be used to compress executable files. An executable file compressed with the `gzexe` command remains an executable file and can be executed by using the name of the executable file. This is not the case if an executable file is compressed with the `gzip` command. Therefore, an executable file is compressed with the `gzexe` command in order to save disk space and network bandwidth if the file is to be transmitted from one computer to another, for example, via e-mail over the Internet. The following is a brief description of this command.

Syntax:

**gzexe [options] [file-list]**

**Purpose:** Compress the executable files given in 'file-list'. Backup files are created in filename~ and should be removed after the compressed files have been successfully created

**Commonly used options/features:**

`-d` Decompress compressed files

The following session illustrates the use of the `gzexe` command. Note that when the executable file banner is compressed with the `gzexe` command, a backup of the original file is created in banner~. After the banner file has been compressed, it can be executed as an ordinary executable file. The `gzexe -d banner` command is used to decompress the compressed file banner. The backup of the compressed version is saved in the banner~ file.

```
$ file banner
banner: ELF 32-bit LSB executable, Intel 80386, version 1,
dynamically linked (uses shared libs), not stripped
$ banner datafile 10
[ output of the banner command ]
$ gzexe banner
banner:                  58.0%
```

```
$ ls -l banner*
-rwx------ 1 sarwar faculty 5239  Nov 19 11:45 banner
-rwx------ 1 sarwar faculty 10881 Nov 19 11:44 banner~
$ banner datafile 10
[ output of the banner command ]
$ gzexe -d banner
$ ls -l banner*
-rwx------ 1 sarwar faculty 10881 Nov 19 11:48 banner
-rwx------ 1 sarwar faculty 5239  Nov 19 11:45 banner~
$
```

### 10.3.4 The zcat Command

Converting the compressed file back to the original and then displaying it is a time-consuming process because file creation requires disk I/O. If you only want to view the contents of the original file, you can use the LINUX command `zcat` (the `cat` command for compressed files) that displays the contents of files compressed with `compress` or `gzip`. The command uncompresses a file before displaying it. The original file remains unchanged. The `zmore` command can be used to display the compressed files one screenful at a time. When no file or – is given as a parameter, these commands read input from stdin. Both commands allow you to specify one or more files as parameters. The following is a brief description of the `zcat` command.

Syntax:

**zcat [options] [file-list]**

**Purpose:** Concatenate compressed files in 'file-list' in their original form and send them to stdout; if no file is specified, take input from stdin.

**Commonly used options/features:**

- `-h` Display help information
- `-r` Operate recursively on subdirectories
- `-t` Test integrity of compressed files

In the following session, the `gzip` command is used to compress the bash.man file and store it in the bash.man.gz file. When the `more` command is used to display the compressed file, garbage is displayed on the screen. The `zmore` command is used to display the contents of the original file. We did not use the `zcat` command because bash.man is a large, multipage file.

```
$ gzip bash.man
$ more bash.man.gz
:bash.manÔý{µ?ÿ;¾i)Ä²¦ '¤i         Ð
MJá´9ÉXÙÓH¡âÛkÖ}¯}YIÝç÷<újË3û°öÚëú]o½õÖïî?ÞýÝ£;Pü¼úüê·
Pzë3ê3ûÕýO«OVß?5ÃÅÝú¤Þä3¯êßõ»Íª=1Þt«úñïÛÅâ-·WÿVý
OëoæÝ¢}úÖ[ªü.´óeõ%¼ÞIõÉï«ß?©h#¿AÔÝP?è×Wîüb[=8®
üê¿urçW¿úU}vUo/ÚúãMÛÖûùö2ÙÀoýnu¢-
ÌïuR?ZMOßzë£ê#"úæ.¡{è~¡Àd¬ãêw6z@3ªùi¿\Cg¶ÍjV/Õù®9oënµm7ëM
         ÿãj¶ÚZûªî¶íPë+ðÓ¦mfõ|Ó/iÃ¾m63hb½ÛÖýÿÔh
5¿ùn·Ív·Áo¨ìB[zVýñYÕ?«6ÏªU£V=¨                ¸d§É°ÅÐÃóÓ~3î7
                         ØÓ¡>zQ½ÐÆá/ÓjÊ¿ÃÒWç¼µ3zÛ×gmÝÀWó~3ÜÖÝr½h
jKP÷s?G>¬¿øüñ£¿Ö±{ê2~Ò÷0zX·ÓnPMùÅú®¿î7/ºÕ1¶ðÉ¦ß-ë;·oÿìô.
©Éo§£ÇGDL3uÜ
^L×[´'ÓfÓLqÑH®¸aèÎWLFøXïíªî¶¼Ê/ûíìÛê¶6oxVmi7;ØÐgÕyýhÎSÓG¸
5lú`üó*"m5|yæ]!
>¢Ãakèç;\Ø·fsÊ[£ñä
$ zmore bash.man.gz
------> bash.man.gz <------
BASH2(1)
NAME
     bash2 - GNU Bourne-Again SHell
SYNOPSIS
     bash2 [options] [file]
COPYRIGHT
     Bash is Copyright (C) 1989-1999 by the Free Software
     Foundation, Inc.
DESCRIPTION
     Bash is an sh-compatible command language interpreter
     that executes commands read from the standard input
     or from a file. Bash also incorporates useful
     features from the Korn and C shells (ksh and csh).
$
```

### 10.3.5 Renaming Files

The `zforce` command allows you to rename gzipped files that don't have the .gz extension to filenames with the .gz extension. It does not work on all LINUX systems.

It is important to note that the LINUX commands for compressing and uncompressing have nothing to do with the `zip` and `unzip` utilities (or variant of these such as `pkzip` and `pkunzip`) that were created originally for DOS to pack (archive) and unpack (unarchive) multiple compressed files in to one file. They can be used for this purpose under LINUX also, although there are several other LINUX utilities such as `tar` (see Chapter 19) that can be used together with `gzip` or `compress` commands to perform the same task.

In the following In-Chapter Exercises, you will get practice using the `gzip`, `gunzip`, `zmore`, and `zcat` commands.

## IN-CHAPTER EXERCISES

**10.3.** Create the bash.man file used in this section. Use the `gzip` command to compress the file. What command line did you use?

**10.4.** Display the compressed version of the bash.man file on the display screen. What command line did you use? What command is needed to display the file one screen at a time?

**10.5.** Give the command line for uncompressing the compressed file generated in Exercise 10.3. Where does the uncompressed (original) file go?

## 10.4 SORTING FILES

**Sorting** means ordering a set of items according to some criteria. In computer jargon it means ordering a set of items (e.g., integers, a character, or strings) in ascending (the next item is greater than or equal to the current item) or descending order (the next item is less than or equal to the current item). So, for example, a set of integers {10, 103, 75, 22, 97, 52, 1} would become {1, 10, 22, 52, 75, 97, 103} if sorted in ascending order and {103, 97, 75, 52, 22, 10, 1} if sorted in descending order. Similarly, words in a dictionary are listed in ascending order. Thus the word *apple* appears before the word *apply*.

Sorting is a commonly used operation, performed in a variety of software systems. Systems in which sorting is used include

- words in a dictionary
- names of people in a telephone directory
- airline reservation systems that display arrival and departure times for flights sorted according to flight numbers at airport terminals
- names of people displayed in a pharmacy with ready prescriptions
- names of students listed in class lists coming from the registrar's office

The sorting process is based on using a field, or portion of each item, known as the **sort key**. The items in a list are compared (usually two at a time) by using their key fields to determine the position of each item in the sorted list. Which field is used as the key depends on the items to be sorted. If the items are personal records (e.g., student employee records), last name, student ID, and social security number are some of the commonly used keys. If the items are arrival and departure times for the flights at an airport, flight number and city name are commonly used keys.

The LINUX `sort` utility can be used to sort items in text (ASCII) files. The following is a brief description of this utility.

Syntax:

**sort [options] [file-list]**

**Purpose:** Sort lines in the ASCII files in 'file-list'

**Output:** Sorted file to standard output

**Commonly used options/features:**

| | |
|---|---|
| `-b` | Ignore leading blanks |
| `-d` | Sort according to usual alphabetical order: ignore all characters except letter, digits, and then blanks |
| `-f` | Consider lowercase and uppercase letters to be equivalent |
| `+n1[-n2]` | Specify a field as the sort key, starting with `+n1` and ending at `-n2` (or end of line if `-n2` is not specified); field numbers start with 0. |
| `-r` | Sort in reverse order |

If no file is specified in 'file-list', `sort` takes input from standard input. The output of the `sort` command goes to standard output. By default, the `sort` utility takes each line, starting with the first column to be the key. In other words, it rearranges the lines of the file, that is, strings separated by the newline character, according to the contents of all the fields, going from left to right. The following session illustrates the use of the `sort` utility with and without some options. The students file contains the items (student records, one per line) to be sorted. Each line contains four fields; first name, last name, e-mail address, and phone number. Each field is separated from the next by one or more space characters.

```
$ cat students
John Johnsen     john.johnsen@tp.com   503.555.1111
Hassaan Sarwar   hsarwar@k12.st.or     503.444.2132
David Kendall    d_kendall@msnbc.org   229.111.2013
John Johnsen     jjohnsen@psu.net      301.999.8888
Kelly Kimberly   kellyk@umich.gov      555.123.9999
Maham Sarwar     msarwar@k12.st.or     713.888.0000
```

```
Jamie Davidson  j.davidson@uet.edu    515.001.2932
Nabeel Sarwar   nsarwar@xyz.net       434.555.1212
$ sort students
David Kendall   d_kendall@msnbc.org   229.111.2013
Hassaan Sarwar  hsarwar@k12.st.or     503.444.2132
Jamie Davidson  j.davidson@uet.edu    515.001.2932
John Johnsen    jjohnsen@psu.net      301.999.8888
John Johnsen    john.johnsen@tp.com   503.555.1111
Kelly Kimberly  kellyk@umich.gov      555.123.9999
Maham Sarwar    msarwar@k12.st.or     713.888.0000
Nabeel Sarwar   nsarwar@xyz.net       434.555.1212
$
```

Note that the lines in the students file are sorted in ascending order by all characters, going from left to right (the whole line is used as the sort key). The following command sorts the file by using the whole line, starting with the last name—the second field (field number 1)—as the sort key.

```
$ sort +1 students
Jamie Davidson  j.davidson@uet.edu    515.001.2932
John Johnsen    jjohnsen@psu.net      301.999.8888
John Johnsen    john.johnsen@tp.com   503.555.1111
David Kendall   d_kendall@msnbc.org   229.111.2013
Kelly Kimberly  kellyk@umich.gov      555.123.9999
Hassaan Sarwar  hsarwar@k12.st.or     503.444.2132
Maham Sarwar    msarwar@k12.st.or     713.888.0000
Nabeel Sarwar   nsarwar@xyz.net       434.555.1212
$
```

The following command sorts the file in reverse order by using the phone number as the sort key and ignoring leading blanks (spaces and tabs). The `+3` option specifies the phone number to be the sort key (as phone number is the last field), the `-r` option informs the `sort` utility to display the sorted output in reverse order, and the `-b` option asks the sort utility to ignore the leading white spaces between fields.

```
$ sort +3 -r -b students
Maham Sarwar    msarwar@k12.st.or     713.888.0000
Kelly Kimberly  kellyk@umich.gov      555.123.9999
```

```
Jamie Davidson   j.davidson@uet.edu    515.001.2932
John Johnsen     john.johnsen@tp.com   503.555.1111
Hassaan Sarwar   hsarwar@k12.st.or     503.444.2132
Nabeel Sarwar    nsarwar@xyz.net       434.555.1212
John Johnsen     jjohnsen@psu.net      301.999.8888
David Kendall    d_kendall@msnbc.org   229.111.2013
$
```

The `-b` option is important if fields are separated by more than one space and the number of spaces differs from line to line, as is the case for the students file. The reason is that the space character is "smaller" (in terms of its ASCII value) than all letters and digits, and not skipping blanks will generate unexpected output. The sort keys can be combined, with one being the primary key and others being secondary keys, by specifying them in the order of preferences (the primary key occurring first). The following command sorts the students file with the last name as the primary key and the phone number as the secondary key.

```
$ sort +1 -2 +3 -b students
Jamie Davidson   j.davidson@uet.edu    515.001.2932
John Johnsen     jjohnsen@psu.net      301.999.8888
John Johnsen     john.johnsen@tp.com   503.555.1111
David Kendall    d_kendall@msnbc.org   229.111.2013
Kelly Kimberly   kellyk@umich.gov      555.123.9999
Hassaan Sarwar   hsarwar@k12.st.or     503.444.2132
Maham Sarwar     msarwar@k12.st.or     713.888.0000
Nabeel Sarwar    nsarwar@xyz.net       434.555.1212
$
```

The primary key is specified as `+1 -2`, meaning that the key starts with the last name (`+1`) and ends before the email address field (`-2`) starts. The secondary key starts at the phone number field (`+3`) and ends at the end of line. As no field follows the phone number, it alone comprises the secondary key. For our file, however, the end result will be the same as for the command `sort +1 students` because the first John Johnsen's e-mail address is "smaller" than the second's.

## 10.5 SEARCHING FOR COMMANDS AND FILES

At times you will need to find whether a particular command or file exists in your file structure. Or, if you have multiple versions of a command, you might want to find out which one executes when you run the command. We discuss three commands that can be used for this purpose: `find`, `whereis`, and `which`.

### 10.5.1 THE find COMMAND

You can use the **find** command to search a list of directories that meet the criteria described by the expression (see command description) passed to it as an argument. The command searches the list of directories recursively; that is, all subdirectories at all levels under the list of directories are searched. The following is a brief description of the command.

Syntax:

**find directory-list expression**

**Purpose:** Search the directories in 'directory-list' to locate files that meet the criteria described by the 'expression' (the second argument). The expression comprises one or more criteria (see the examples)

**Output:** None unless it is explicitly requested in 'expression'

**Commonly used criteria in 'expression':**

| | |
|---|---|
| **-exec** CMD | The file being searched meets the criteria if the command 'CMD' returns 0 as its exit status (true value for commands that execute successfully); 'CMD' must terminate with a quoted semicolon, that is, \; |
| **-inum** N | Search for files with inode number *N* |
| **-links** N | Search for files with *N* links |
| **-name** pattern | Search for files that are specified by the 'pattern' |
| **-newer** file | Search for files that were modified after 'file' (i.e., are newer than 'file') |
| **-ok** CMD | Like **-exec**, except that the user is prompted first |
| **-perm** octal | Search for files if permission of the file is 'octal' |
| **-print** | Display the pathnames of the files found by using the rest of the criteria |
| **-size** ±N[c] | Search for files of size *N* blocks. *N* followed by 'c' can be used to measure size in characters; +*N* means size > *N* blocks and –*N* means size < *N* blocks. |
| **-user** name | Search for files owned by the user name or ID 'name' |
| \( expr \) | True if **expr** is true; used for grouping criteria combined with OR or AND. |
| ! expr | True if **expr** is false |

More criteria are presented in Appendix A. You can use `[ -a ]` or a space to logically AND, and `-o` to logically OR two criteria. Note that at least one space is needed before and after a bracket, `[` or `]`, and before and after `-o`. A complex expression can be enclosed in parentheses, `\(` and `\)`. The following are some illustrative examples.

The most common use of the `find` command is to search one or more directories for a file, as shown in the first example. Here, the command searches for the Pakistan.gif file in your home directory and displays the pathname of the directory that contains it. If the file being searched occurs in multiple directories, the pathnames of all the directories are displayed.

```
$ find ~ -name Pakistan.gif -print
/home/faculty/sarwar/myweb/Pakistan.html
$
```

The next command searches the /usr/include directory recursively for a file named socket.h and prints the absolute pathname of the file.

```
$ find /usr/include -name socket.h -print
/usr/include/sys/socket.h
$
```

You may want to know the pathnames for all the hard links (discussed in Chapter 11) to a file. The following command recursively searches the /usr and . (present working directory) directories for all the files that have an inode number 258072 and prints the absolute pathnames of all such files.

```
$ find /usr . -inum 258072 -print
/home/faculty/sarwar/myweb/LinuxTcpIP
$
```

The following command searches the present working directory for files that have the name core or have extensions .ps or .o, displays their absolute pathnames, and removes them from the file structure. Parentheses are used to enclose a complex criterion. Be sure that you use spaces before and after `\(` and `-o`. The command does not prompt you for permission to remove; in order to be prompted, replace `-exec` with `-ok`.

```
$ find . \( -name core -o -name '*.ps' -o -name '*.o' \) -print -exec rm {} \;
… output of the command …
$
```

## 10.5.2 THE whereis COMMAND

You can use the **whereis** command to find out whether your system has a particular command and, if it does, where it is in the file structure. You typically need to get such information when you are trying to execute a command that you know is valid but that your shell can't locate because the directory containing the executable for the command isn't in your search path (see Chapters 4 and 7). Under these circumstances, you can use the **whereis** command to find the location of the command and update your search path. The command not only gives you the absolute pathname for the command that you are searching for, but also the absolute pathname for its manual page if it is available on your system. The following is a brief description of the command.

Syntax:

**whereis [options] [file-list]**

**Purpose:** Locate binaries (executables), source codes, and manual pages for the commands in 'file-list'

**Output:** Absolute pathnames for the files containing binaries, source codes, and manual pages for the commands in 'file-list'

**Commonly used options/features:**

| | |
|---|---|
| -b | Search for binaries (executables) only |
| -m | Search for manual page on |
| -s | Search for source code only |

The following examples illustrate use of the **whereis** command. The first command is used to locate the **whereis** command. The second command is used to locate the executable file for the **cat** command. The last command locates the information for the **find**, **compress**, and **tar** commands.

```
$ whereis ftp
ftp: /usr/bin/ftp.expect /usr/bin/ftp /usr/bin/ftp.sh /usr/man/man1/ftp.1.bz2
$ whereis -b cat
cat: /bin/cat
$ whereis find compress tar
find: /usr/bin/find /usr/man/man1/find.1.bz2 /usr/man/mann/findn
compress: /usr/bin/compress  /usr/man/man1/compress.1.bz2
tar: /bin/tar  /usr/include/tar.h /usr/man/man1/tar.1.bz2
$
```

In the outputs of these commands, the directories /bin and /usr/bin contain the executables for commands, the directory /usr/man contains several subdirectories that contain various sections of the LINUX online manual, and the /usr/include directory contains **header files**.

### 10.5.3 THE `which` COMMAND

In a system that has multiple versions of a command, the **`which`** utility can be used to determine the location (absolute pathname) of the version that is executed by the shell that you are using when you type the command. When a command doesn't work according to its specification, the **`which`** utility can be used to determine the absolute pathname of the command version that executes. A local version of the command may execute because of the way the search path is set up in the ***`PATH`*** variable (see Chapters 4 and 7). And, the local version has been broken due to a recent update in the code; perhaps, it does not work properly with the new libraries that were installed on the system. The **`which`** command takes a command list (actually a file list for the commands) as argument and returns absolute pathnames for them to standard output.

In the following In-Chapter Exercises, you will get practice using the `find`, `sort`, and `whereis` commands as well as appreciate the difference between the `find` and `whereis` commands.

**IN-CHAPTER EXERCISES**

**10.6.** Give a command for sorting the students file by using the whole line starting with the e-mail address.

**10.7.** Give a command for finding out where the executable code for the `traceroute` command is on your system.

**10.8.** You have a file called Phones somewhere in your directory structure but you don't remember where it is. Give the command to locate it.

## 10.6 SEARCHING FILES

LINUX has powerful utilities for file searching that allow you to find lines in text files that contain a particular expression, string, or pattern. For example, if you have a large file that contains the records for a company's employees, one per line, and want to search the file for line(s) containing information on John Johnsen. The utilities that allow file searching are `grep`, `egrep`, and `fgrep`. The following is a brief description of these utilities.

Syntax:

**grep [options] pattern [file-list]**
**egrep [options] [string] [file-list]**
**fgrep [options] [expression] [file-list]**

**Purpose:** Search the files in 'file-list' for given pattern, string, or expression; if no 'file-list', take input from standard input

**Output:** Lines containing the given pattern, string, or expression on standard output

**Commonly used options:**

| | |
|---|---|
| `-c` | Print the number of matching lines only |
| `-i` | Ignore the case of letters during the matching process |
| `-l` | Print only the names of files with matching lines |
| `-n` | Print line numbers along with matched lines |
| `-s` | Useful for shell scripts, this option suppresses error messages (the 'return status' is set to 0 for success and nonzero for no success—see Chapter 15) |
| `-v` | Print nonmatching lines |
| `-w` | Search for the given pattern as a string |

Of the three, the `fgrep` command is the fastest but most limited; `egrep` is the slowest but most flexible, allowing full use of regular expressions; and `grep` has reasonable speed and is fairly flexible in terms of its support of regular expressions. In the following sessions, we illustrate the use of these commands with some of the options shown in the description. We use the same students file in these sessions that we used in describing the `sort` utility in Section 10.4. We display the file by using the `cat` command.

```
$ cat students
John Johnsen     john.johnsen@tp.com    503.555.1111
Hassaan Sarwar   hsarwar@k12.st.or      503.444.2132
David Kendall    d_kendall@msnbc.org    229.111.2013
John Johnsen     jjohnsen@psu.net       301.999.8888
Kelly Kimberly   kellyk@umich.gov       555.123.9999
Maham Sarwar     msarwar@k12.st.or      713.888.0000
Jamie Davidson   j.davidson@uet.edu     515.001.2932
```

```
Nabeel Sarwar   nsarwar@xyz.net       434.555.1212
$
```

The most common and simple use of the `grep` utility is to display the lines in a file containing a particular string, word, or pattern. In the following session, we display those lines in the students file that contain the string sarwar. The lines are displayed in the order they occur in the file.

```
$ grep sarwar students
Hassaan Sarwar     hsarwar@k12.st.or  503.444.2132
Maham Sarwar       msarwar@k12.st.or  713.888.0000
Nabeel Sarwar      nsarwar@xyz.net    434.555.1212
$
```

The `grep` command can be used with the `-n` option to display the output lines with line numbers. In the following session, the lines in the students file containing the string sarwar are displayed with line numbers.

```
$ grep -n sarwar students
2:Hassaan Sarwar  hsarwar@k12.st.or  503.444.2132
7:Maham Sarwar    msarwar@k12.st.or  713.888.0000
8:Nabeel Sarwar   nsarwar@xyz.net    434.555.1212
$
```

You can use the `grep` command to search a string in multiple files with regular expressions and shell metacharacters. In the following session, `grep` searches for the string "include" in all the files in the present working directory that end with .c (C source files). Note that the access permissions for server.c were set so that `grep` couldn't read it—the user running the command didn't have read permission for the server.c file.

```
$ grep -n include *.c
client.c: 21: #include   <stdio.h>
client.c: 22: #include   <ctype.h>
client.c: 23: #include   <string.h>
lab1.c: 13: #include     <stdio.h>
grep: can't open server.c
$
```

You can also use the `grep` command with the `-l` option to display the names of files in which the pattern occurs. However, it does not display the lines that contain the pattern. In the following session, the ~/States directory is assumed to contain one file for every state in the United States and this file to contain the names of all the cities in the state (e.g., Portland). The `grep` command therefore displays the names of files that contain the word *Portland*, that is, the names of states that have a city called Portland.

```
$ grep -l Portland ~/States
Maine
Oregon
$
```

The following command displays the lines in the students file that start with letters A through H. In the command, ^ specifies the beginning of a line.

```
$ grep '^[A-H]' students
Hassaan Sarwar  hsarwar@k12.st.or     503.444.2132
David Kendall   d_kendall@msnbc.org   229.111.2013
$
```

The following command displays the lines from the students file that contain at least eight consecutive lowercase letters.

```
$ grep '[a-z]\{8\}' students
John Johnsen    jjohnsen@psu.net      301.999.8888
Jamie Davidson  j.davidson@uet.edu    515.001.2932
$
```

The following command displays the lines that contain a word *starting* with the word (string) Ke. Note that \< is used to indicate start of a word. Single quotes are used in '\<Ke' to ensure that shell does not interpret any letter in the pattern as a shell metacharacter.

```
$ grep '\<Ke' students
David Kendall   d_kendall@msnbc.org   229.111.2013
Kelly Kimberly  kellyk@umich.gov      555.123.9999
$
```

The string \> is the end of the word *anchor*. Thus the following command displays the lines that contain words that end with net. If we replace the string net with the string war, what would be the output of the command?

```
$ grep 'net\>' students
John Johnsen        jjohnsen@psu.net      301.999.8888
Nabeel Sarwar       nsarwar@xyz.net       434.555.1212
$
```

In the following command, the regular expression "Kimberly|Nabeel" is used to have **egrep** display the lines, and their numbers, that contain either *Kimberly* or *Nabeel*. Note that the regular expression uses the pipe symbol ( | ) to logically OR the two strings.

```
$ egrep -n "Kimberly|Nabeel" students
6:Kelly Kimberly    kellyk@umich.gov      555.123.9999
8:Nabeel Sarwar     nsarwar@xyz.net       434.555.1212
$
```

You can use the **-v** option to display the lines that do not contain the string specified in the command. Thus the following command produces all the lines that do *not* contain the words *Kimberly* and *Nabeel*.

```
$ grep -v "Kimberly|Nabeel" students
John Johnsen        john.johnsen@tp.com   503.555.1111
Hassaan Sarwar      hsarwar@k12.st.or     503.444.2132
David Kendall       d_kendall@msnbc.org   229.111.2013
John Johnsen        jjohnsen@psu.net      301.999.8888
Maham Sarwar        msarwar@k12.st.or     713.888.0000
Jamie Davidson      j.davidson@uet.edu    515.001.2932
$
```

The following command displays the lines in the students file that start with letter J. Note the use of ^ to indicate the beginning of a line.

```
$ egrep "^J" students
Jamie Davidson      j.davidson@uet.edu    515.001.2932
John Johnsen        jjohnsen@psu.net      301.999.8888
```

```
John Johnsen       john.johnsen@tp.com  503.555.1111
$
```

The following command displays the lines in the students file that start with letters J or K. Note that ^J and ^K represent lines starting with the letters J and K.

```
$ egrep "^J|^K" students
Jamie Davidson     j.davidson@uet.edu   515.001.2932
John Johnsen       jjohnsen@psu.net     301.999.8888
John Johnsen       john.johnsen@tp.com  503.555.1111
Kelly Kimberly     kellyk@umich.gov     555.123.9999
$
```

The `zgrep` command can be used to search compressed files. The command uncompresses `compress`'ed or `gzip`'ed files and passes them to the `grep` command along with any command line arguments. Multiple files can be passed as arguments to the command. The `zegrep` and `zfgrep` commands can be used to invoke the `egrep` and `fgrep` commands, respectively, instead of the `grep` command. The shell environment variable ***GREP*** can be set to any of the three grep-family commands (`grep`, `egrep`, and `fgrep`) to be invoked when `zgrep` is used. Thus, if ***GREP*** is set `egrep`, the execution of the `zgrep` command invokes the `egrep` command, and not the `grep` command.

In the following In-Chapter Exercises, you will use the commands of the `grep` family to understand their various characteristics.

## IN-CHAPTER EXERCISES

**10.9.** Give a command for displaying the lines in the ~/Personal/Phones file that contain the words starting with the string "David".

**10.10.** Give a command for displaying the lines in the ~/Personal/Phones file that contain phone numbers with area code 212. Phone numbers are stored as xxx-xxx-xxxx, where x is a digit from 0 through 9.

**10.11.** Display the names of all the files in your home directory that contain the word "main" (without quotes).

## 10.7 CUTTING AND PASTING

You can process files that store data in the form of tables in LINUX by using the `cut` and `paste` commands. A table consists of lines, each line comprises a record, and each record has a fixed number of fields. Fields are usually separated by tabs or spaces, although any field separator can be used. The `cut` command allows you to cut one or more fields of a table in one or more files and send them to standard output. In other words, you can use the `cut` command to slice a table vertically in a file across field boundaries. The following is a brief description of the command.

Syntax:

**cut -blist [-n] [file-list]**
**cut -clist [file-list]**
**cut -flist [-dchar] [-s] [file-list]**

**Purpose:** Cut out fields of a table in a file

**Output:** Fields cut by the command

**Commonly used options/features:**

| | |
|---|---|
| `-b` list | Treat each byte as a column and cut bytes specified in the 'list' |
| `-c` list | Treat each character as a column and cut characters specified in the 'list' |
| `-d` char | Use the character 'char' instead of the <Tab> character as field separator |
| `-f` list | Cut fields specified in the 'list' |
| `-n` | Do not split characters (used with `-b` option) |
| `-s` | Do not output lines that do not have the delimiter character |

Here, 'list' is a comma-separated list with - used to specify a range of bytes, characters, or fields. The following sessions illustrate some of the commonly used options and features of the `cut` command. In this section we use the file student_addresses, whose contents are displayed by the `cat` command.

```
$ cat student_addresses
John   Doe    jdoe@xyz.com     312.111.9999  312.999.1111
Pam    Meyer  meyer@uop.uk     666.222.1212  666.555.1212
Jim    Davis  jamesd@aol.com   713.999.5555  713.413.0000
```

```
Jason Kim    j_kim@up.org     434.000.8888  434.555.2211
Amy   Nash   nash@state.gov   888.111.4444  888.827.3333
$
```

The file has five fields numbered 1 through 5, from left to right: first name, last name, e-mail address, home phone number, and work phone number. Although we could have used any character as the field separator, we chose the <Tab> character to give a columnar look to the table and the output of the following **cut** and **paste** commands. You can display a table of first and last names by using the **-f** option. Note that **-f1,2** specifies the first and the second fields of the student_addresses file.

```
$ cut -f1,2 student_addresses
John    Doe
Pam     Meyer
Jim     Davis
Jason   Kim
Amy     Nash
$
```

We generated a table of names (first and last) and work phone numbers by slicing the first, second, and fifth fields of the table in the student_addresses file.

```
$ cut -f1,2,5 student_addresses
John    Doe     312.999.1111
Pam     Meyer   666.555.1212
Jim     Davis   713.413.0000
Jason   Kim     434.555.2211
Amy     Nash    888.827.3333
$
```

To generate a table of names and e-mail addresses, we used the following command. Here, **-f1-3** specifies fields 1 through 3 of the student_addresses file.

```
$ cut -f1-3 student_addresses
John    Doe     jdoe@xyz.com
Pam     Meyer   meyer@uop.uk
```

```
Jim     Davis   jamesd@aol.com
Jason   Kim     j_kim@up.org
Amy     Nash    nash@state.gov
$
```

We recommend that you run this command on your machine to determine whether the desired output is produced. If the desired output is not produced, you have not used the <Tab> character as the field separator for some or all of the records. In such a case, correct the table and try the command again.

In the preceding sessions we have used the default field separator, the <Tab> character. Depending on the format of your file, you can use any character as a field separator. For example, as we discussed in Chapters 3 and 7, the /etc/passwd file uses the colon character (:) as the field separator. You can therefore use the `cut` command to extract information such as the login name, real name, group ID, and home directory for a user. Because the real name, login name, and home directory are the fifth, first, and sixth fields, respectively, the following command can be used to generate a table of names of all users, along with their login IDs and home directories.

```
$ cut -d: -f5,1,6 /etc/passwd
root:root:/root
bin:bin:/bin
daemon:daemon:/sbin
adm:adm:/var/adm
lp::/var/spool/lpd
...
mysql:MySQL server:/var/lib/mysql
...
$
```

Note that the **-d** option is used to specify **:** as the field separator, and it is also displayed as the field separator in the output of the command.

The `paste` command complements the `cut` command; it concatenates files horizontally (the `cat` command concatenates files vertically). Hence, this command can be used to paste tables columnwise. The following is a brief description of the command.

Syntax:

**paste [options] file-list**

**Purpose:** Horizontally concatenate files in 'file-list'; use standard input if - is used as a file

**Output:** Files in 'file-list' pasted (horizontally concatenated)

**Commonly used options/features:**

| | |
|---|---|
| `-d` list | Use 'list' characters as line separators; <Tab> is the default character |

Consider the file student_records that contains student names (first and last), major, and current GPA.

```
$ cat student_records
John   Doe    ECE  3.54
Pam    Meyer  CS   3.61
Jim    Davis  CS   2.71
Jason Kim     ECE  3.97
Amy    Nash   ECE  2.38
$
```

We can combine the two tables horizontally and generate another by using the following command. Note that the output of the `paste` command is displayed on the display screen and is not stored in a file. The resultant table has seven fields.

```
$ paste student_records student_addresses
John    Doe    ECE  3.54  John    Doe    312.999.1111
Pam     Meyer  CS   3.61  Pam     Meyer  666.555.1212
Jim     Davis  CS   2.71  Jim     Davis  713.413.0000
Jason   Kim    ECE  3.97  Jason   Kim    434.555.2211
Amy     Nash   ECE  2.38  Amy     Nash   888.827.3333
$
```

Suppose that you want to use student_addresses and student_records tables to generate and display a table that has student names, majors, and home phone numbers. You may do so in one of two ways. When you use the first method, you `cut` appropriate fields of the two tables, put them in separate files with fields in the order you want to display them, `paste` the two tables in the correct order, and remove the tables. The following session illustrates this procedure and its result. Note that the new table is not saved as a file when the following commands are executed. If you want to save the new table in a file, use the `paste table1 table2 > students_table` command. The students_table contains the columns of table1 and table2 (in that order) pasted together.

```
$ cut -f1-3 student_records > table1
$ cut -f4 student_addresses > table2
$ paste table1 table2
John    Doe     ECE  312.111.9999
Pam     Meyer   CS   666.222.1212
Jim     Davis   CS   713.999.5555
Jason   Kim     ECE  434.000.8888
Amy     Nash    ECE  888.111.4444
$ rm table1 table2
$
```

The procedure just outlined is expensive in terms of space and time because you have to execute four commands, generate two temporary files (table1 and table2), and remove these files after the desired table has been displayed. You can use a different method to accomplish the same thing with the following command.

```
$ paste student_records student_addresses | cut -f1-3,7
John    Doe     ECE  312.111.9999
Pam     Meyer   CS   666.222.1212
Jim     Davis   CS   713.999.5555
Jason   Kim     ECE  434.000.8888
Amy     Nash    ECE  888.111.4444
$
```

Here, you first combine the tables in the two files into one table with nine columns by using the `paste student_records student_addresses` command and then display the desired table by using the `cut -f1-3,7` command. Clearly, this second method is the preferred way to accomplish the task because no temporary files are created and only one command is needed. If you want to save the resultant table in the students_table file, use the command `paste student_records student_addresses | cut -f1-3,7 > students_table`.

## 10.8 ENCODING AND DECODING

In Chapter 6 we discussed electronic mail and various LINUX utilities that can be used to send and receive e-mail. E-mail messages are transported in clear (plain) text, and some e-mail systems are fussy about certain characters contained in the body of the message, such as the tilde character (~) in the first column for the `mail` and `mailx` utilities. This is a serious problem for mail systems, such as `mail`, that do not have convenient support for attachments when you need to attach items such as pictures or executable programs (binaries). The sender can use the **uuencode** utility to convert a file to be mailed to a format that contains readable ASCII characters only, with a letter in the first column. The receiver can use the **uudecode** utility to convert the uuencoded file to the original format. In this section we discuss these two utilities, beginning with a brief description of them expressed as commands.

The **uuencode** command sends the encoded (ASCII) version of the file to standard output. The command takes input from standard input if no 'source-file' is specified in the command. The output has 'decode_label' in the header (first line) of the ASCII version.

Syntax:

**uuencode [source-file] decode_label**

**Purpose:** Encode 'source-file' from binary to ASCII

**Output:** The encoded version of 'source-file' to standard output

**Commonly used options/features:**
None

Syntax:

**uudecode [option] [encoded-file]**

**Purpose:** Decode 'encoded-file' from ASCII to binary

**Output:** The binary version of 'encoded-file' to a file called 'decode_label', the second parameter of the **uuencode** command

**Commonly used options/features:**

| | |
|---|---|
| `-p` | Send the binary version of the uuencoded file to standard output |

The **uudecode** utility recreates the original binary file from the uuencoded (ASCII) file and puts it in a file called decode_label. With the **-p** option, the command sends the binary version to standard output. This option uses the **uudecode** command in a pipeline (see Chapter 12). Both the **uuencode** and **uudecode** commands retain the original files that they translate.

The diagram shown in Figure 10.1 illustrates the process of uuencoding and uudecoding.

You can redirect the output to a file by using the > symbol, as shown in the `uuencode a.out alarm.out > sarwar.out` command in the following session. When you do so, the encoded output goes to the file sarwar.out with a decode_label of alarm.out.

```
$ more a.out
  À _ _ @ D* @
Ô"àÂ@
@@#  ã¿h®ã"^L@K  \@K ¢ OÂ ^ a
                                  Kè `Â dâ h¤®âH  à@4 Ò d à
$ uuencode a.out alarm.out > sarwar.out
$ head sarwar.out
begin 700 alarm.out
M@0,!"P (   "      ,   " @      "\$" T .@0)(#H$25
M*B "E *@!)0"0 H7  0U"+@N ,   C" &((@)  0*  0! 0  "@$
M !  "- 0  $  )&<(Z @0 ( $  !  @! 0  )WCOV@O  (KA7B
M*!$  B0$B(,0  2Y(0( "L$ (D@.@7$  $N4$" @@*(@(!* $\!
MPA.@7H"@80L2@ !+ 0  .@#H&#" Z!DX@.@:*0% &2!( 1+P "*X5XDB0
M$" E! @!1<@ "6$N "F! %D  #2:$" IA ") " !32 Z!DE! @!Q<@
M "6$N 2F! %D  "N:$ 4+P "*X5XG01  (D!(B&T  ".2$" JA
M",(#H&B D ! H "R\  BN%>)(D 3 $I(0 !&4$" '%R  )82X!*8$ 5
M0  %YH0( #" Z!PH 3 >8CH'SJ(Z" [".@A ,  C" &((PB.@B , !#"
$ uudecode sarwar.out
$ more alarm.out
```

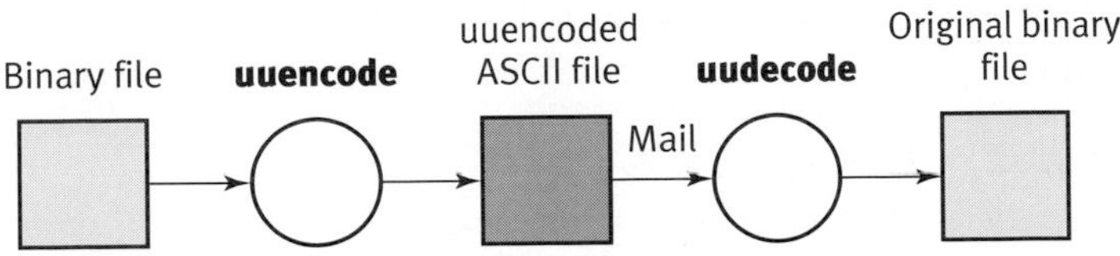


**Figure 10.1** The process of uuencoding and uudecoding

```
  À _ _ @ D* @
Ô"àÂ@
@@#  ã¿h®â"^L@K  \@K ¢ OÂ ^ a
                                         Kè `Â dâ h¤®âH  à@4 Ò d à
$
```

Note the label alarm.out on the first line of the uuencoded file sarwar.out. The **uudecode** command translates the file sarwar.out and puts the original in the file alarm.out. As expected, a.out and alarm.out contain the same data. If you want to recreate the original file in a.out, use a.out as the label in the **uuencode** command, as in **uuencode a.out a.out > sarwar.out**. The **uudecode sarwar.out** command produces the original binary file in the a.out file.

The output generated by **uuencode** is about 35% *larger* than the original file. Thus, for efficient use of the network bandwidth, you should compress binary files before uuencoding them and uncompress them after uudecoding them. Doing so is particularly important for large picture files or files containing multimedia data such as movies.

## 10.9 COMMAND HISTORY

The commands (also called events) that you type at your terminal are saved in a history list. The shell variable ***HISTSIZE*** can be set to a number to specify the number of commands to save in the history list. The default value is 500. When you log on, the history list is initialized from a history file. The ***HISTFILE*** shell variable can be set to the pathname of your history file; the default file is ~/.bash_history. When you log out (or exit a Bash or TC shell), the history list is saved in the history file. The history list is either appended to the history file if the histappend shell option is set; otherwise the history file is overwritten. The number of lines in the history file is limited to the value of the ***HISTFILESIZE*** shell variable. If ***HISTFILESIZE*** is not set to any value, there is no limit and the whole history list is saved. The **set** command can be used to determine the values of the above shell variables used for maintaining the command history, as follows.

```
$ set
...
HISTFILE=/users/faculty/sarwar/.bash_history
HISTFILESIZE=500
HISTSIZE=500
...
$
```

You can manipulate the history list by using the built-in commands **history** and **fc**. The **fc** command is a Bash command and is not available in the TC shell. The following is a brief description of the **history** command.

Syntax: **history [options] [filename]**

**Purpose:** Display or manipulate the history list

**Commonly used options/features:**

| | |
|---|---|
| `N` | Display only the last *N* lines in the history list |
| `-a [filename]` | Append the history lines entered since the beginning of the current shell session to the history file; 'filename', if specified, is used as the history file |
| `-c` | Clear the history list |
| `-w [filename]` | Write the current history list to the history file (overwriting the current contents of the history file) ; 'filename', if specified, is used as the history file. |

The following session shows the use of the **history** command with and without arguments. The first command shows the complete history list, including the current command. The second command shows the last four lines in the history list. The third command clears the history list, and the last command is used to confirm that the history list has been cleared.

```
$ history
  ...
  242 ls
  243 man history
  244 cat ~/.bash_history | nl
  245 ps
  246 history
$ history 4
  244 cat ~/.bash_history | nl
  245 ps
  246 history
  247 history 4
```

```
$ history -c
$ history
  1 history
$
```

If the history list is long and you want to display it one screen at a time, you can use the `history | more` command. We discuss the | operator (called the pipe operator) in detail in Chapter 12.

The Bash command **fc** (fix command) allows you to edit and execute commands in the history list. The following is a brief description of the command.

Syntax:

**fc [-e ename] [-lnr] [first] [last]**
**fc -s [pat=rep] [command]**

**Purpose:** First syntax: Edit and execute commands in the history list or display commands in the history list

Second syntax: Replace every occurrence of 'pat' by 'rep' in the command selected by the 'command' argument and execute it (skip the editing phase)

**Commonly used options/features:**

| | |
|---|---|
| `-e ename` | Edit commands by using the 'ename' editor |
| `-l` | Display the command history list with line numbers |
| `-r` | Display the command history list with line numbers in the reverse order (used with the `-l` option) |

The first command syntax can be used to select commands from 'first' to 'last' from the history list. The parameters 'first' and 'last' may be numbers for the commands in the history list or strings to identify the most recent occurrence of a command beginning with the strings. If 'last' is not specified, it is set to 'first' and if 'first' is not specified, it is set to the last command for editing and –16 for displaying (i.e., the last 17 commands in the history list are displayed). You can specify the editor of your choice by using the **-e** option ('ename' is the name of the editor). If you don't specify an editor, the **fc** command uses the value of the *FCEDIT* variable (if it is set), or the value of the *EDITOR* variable if set, or the **vi** editor if the variables are not set. When you have edited the commands and exit the editor, the commands are executed sequentially, one by one. Without an argument, the **fc** command allows you to edit the last command with the **vi** editor and execute it. The **fc –l** command can be used to display the last 17 lines in the current history list with line numbers. The **–n** option can be used with the **–l** option to display commands in the history list without line numbers. The **–r** option can be used with the **–l** option to display commands in the history list in the reverse order with line numbers.

The following session shows the use of the **fc** command with and without arguments. The first command shows the complete history list, including the current command. The second command allows you to edit and execute commands at lines 245 through 247; as soon as you exit the editor (**vi** in this case), the modified commands are executed one by one. The **fc -l man hist** command displays the most recent commands, starting with the string "man" through the most recent command that begins with "hist". The last command, **fc -s cpr=wpr 247**, executes the command number 247 after substituting "cpr" with "wpr".

```
$ fc -l
   ...
242     ls
243     man history
244     cat ~/.bash_history | nl
245     ps
246     history
247     lpr -Pcpr lab4.c
248     fc -l
$ fc 245 247
ps
history
lpr -Pcpr lab4.c
~
~
~
~
~
~
```

```
:q!
ps
PID TTY          TIME CMD
10720 pts/0     00:00:00 csh
11374 pts/0     00:00:00 bash
11376 pts/0     00:00:00 ps
history
    ...
    242  ls
    243  man history
    244  cat ~/.bash_history | nl
    245  ps
    246  history
    247  lpr -Pcpr lab4.c
    248  fc -l
lpr -Pcpr lab4.c
$ fc -l man hist
243      man history
244      cat ~/.bash_history | nl
245      ps
246      history
$ fc -s cpr=wpr 247
lpr -Pwpr lab4.c
$
```

The **history expansion** feature of Bash allows you to take words from the history list and insert them into the current command line, and makes it easy for you to repeat previously executed commands and fix errors in the previous commands. These history features are borrowed from the C shell. History expansion is introduced by the **!** character, except when it is followed by a space, tab, (, =, or end of line. In order to perform history expansion, you first select a line (command) from the history list (the selected command is called an *event*), select words from the line that are to be acted on, and apply an operation (called a *modifier*) on the selected words. The events are selected by using event designators. Some of the commonly used event designators and their meaning are listed in Table 10.4.

| Table 10.4 | Commonly Used Event Designators for History Expansion | | |
|---|---|---|---|
| Event Designator | Meaning | Example | |
| !N | The event is the command at line *N* in the history list | !10 | The command at line 10 in the history list |
| !-N | The event is the command at the line *N* lines before the current line | !-6 | The command 6 lines back |
| !! | The event is the previous command | !! | The last command that you executed |
| !string | The event is the most recent command starting with "string" | !grep | The most recent command starting with the string "grep" (most likely the last grep command) |
| !?string[?] | The event is the most recent command containing "string"; if end of line follows "string", the trailing ? is not needed | !?cut? | The most recent line that contains the string "cut" |

The following session shows the use of some commonly used event designators to invoke commands from the history list. The `!!` command is used to execute the last command; the `!?~?` command is used to execute the most recent command that contains ~; the `!?courses?` command executes the most recent command that contains the string courses; the `!75` command executes command number 75 in the history list, and the `!ma` command executes the last command that starts with the string `ma` (i.e., the `make clean` command).

```
$ history | tail -10
      69    10:26   cd courses/ee345/2000/prog4
      70    10:26   ps
      71    10:26   echo This is a test
      72    10:26   cd ~
      73    10:27   cd courses/ee345/2000/prog4
      74    10:27   make clean
      75    10:27   ls -al
      76    10:27   history | tail 10
      77    10:27   history
      78    10:27   history | tail -10
```

```
$ !!
history | tail -10
     70 10:26   ps
     71   10:26   echo This is a test
     72   10:26   cd ~
     73   10:27   cd courses/ee345/2000/prog4
     74   10:27   make clean
     75   10:27   ls -al
     76   10:27   history | tail 10
     77   10:27   history
     78   10:27   history | tail -10
     79   10:27   history | tail -10
$ !?~?
cd ~
$ !?courses?
cd courses/ee345/2000/prog4
$ !75
ls -al
total 88
drwx------ 4 sarwar 1024 Nov 22 10:10 .
drwx------ 4 sarwar 512 Nov 20 08:33 ..
-rw------- 1 sarwar 0 Nov 10 08:37 .lastlogin
-rwx------ 1 sarwar 11080 Nov 10 08:52 a.out
-rw------- 1 sarwar 659 Nov 3 08:23 algorithm
drwx------ 2 sarwar 512 Nov 19 11:49 backup
...
$ !ma
make clean
rm *.o
$
```

The words in a selected command are numbered with the first word (the command name) numbered 0 and subsequent words numbered one higher than the previous. Thus the word following the command name (an option or argument) is numbered 1. A word designator can be used to identify the desired word(s) from the selected command/event. A colon (:) is used between an event designator and a word designator. For the word designators ^, $, *, -, and %, the colon (:) is not required. Table 10.5 lists some of the commonly used word designators.

**Table 10.5** Commonly Used Event Designators for History Expansion

| Word Designator | Meaning | Example | |
|---|---|---|---|
| 0 | Word 0 (i.e., the command name) | | |
| N | The *N*th word | 3 | The third word |
| ^ | Word 1 (i.e., the word following the command name) | ^ | The word is lab1.c if the selected command is `cc lab1.c –o lab1` |
| $ | The last word in the selected command | $ | The word is lab1 if the selected command is `cc lab1.c –o lab1` |
| * | All of the words in the selected command except the first word (in other words, all command options and arguments without the command name) | * | The words lab1.c, \|, nl, \|, pr, lpr, and -Pwpr if the selected command is `cat lab1.c \| nl \| pr \| lpr -Pwpr` |
| N1-N2 | The range of words numbering *N*1 through *N*2; -*N*2 is equivalent to 0-*N*2; *N** is *N*-$ and *N*- is *N*-$ without the last word | 1-3 | The words (or letters) lab1.c, \|, and nl if the selected command is `cat lab1.c \| nl \| pr \| lpr –Pwpr` |
| | | 6* | The words \|, lpr, and –Pwpr if the previous command is selected |
| | | 6- | The words \| and lpr if the previous command is selected |

After selecting an event and words in the selected event, you can apply one or more operations on the selected words by using a sequence of operators, known as modifiers. A modifier is preceded by a colon (:). Table 10.6 lists some commonly used modifiers.

The following session shows how some of the commonly used event designators and modifiers can be used for history expansion. The **`chmod`** command is used to set access privileges for courses/ee345/2000/prog4 (the second argument for event 73) to 700. The same task can also be performed by replacing **`!73:2`** with **`!73:$`** (the $ designates the last command line argument for a selected event). The **`!echo:0-3`** command is used to execute the command number 73 with three arguments (excluding the word *test*). The **`!73:0-3`** command performs the same task. In the **`lpr -Pwpr !73:1/main.c`** command, **`!73:1`** stands for the second word in command number 73 in the command history (i.e., ~/courses/ee345/2000/prog4), and in the **`!76:2 -15 !73:1/main.c`** command, **`!76:2`** stands for the third word in command number 76 in the command

**Table 10.6** Commonly Used Modifiers for History Expansion

| Modifier | Meaning | Example |
|---|---|---|
| e | Remove all except the suffix of the form '.suffix' | |
| h | Keep only the head of a pathname | |
| p | Print the new command, but do not execute it | |
| r | Remove the suffix of the form '.siffix' | |
| t | Keep only the tail of a pathname | |
| s/existing/new/ | Substitute 'new' for the first occurrence of 'existing'; if & appears in 'new' it is replaced by 'existing'; a backslash (\) can be used to quote '&' | |
| g | Apply the modifications over the entire event (command line); used with s and &, as in gs/Window/LINUX/ | |

history (i.e., the word *tail*). The `!71:s/a test/fun!/` command results in the execution of command number 71 in the history list after substituting the string "a test" with the string "fun!". The last command in the session results in the execution of the last history command after replacing the string "fun" with the string "it folks".

```
$ history | tail -10
     69   10:26   cd /usr/include
     70   10:26   ps
     71   10:26   echo This is a test
     72   10:26   ls -li stdio.h
     73   10:27   cd ~/courses/ee345/2000/prog4
     74   10:27   make clean
     75   10:27   ls -al
     76   10:27   history | tail 10
     77   10:27   history
     78   10:27   history | tail -10
$ chmod 700 !73:1
$ !echo:1-3
echo This is a
This is a
$ !71:0-3
echo This is a
This is a
```

```
$ lpr -Pwpr !73:1/main.c
lpr -Pwpr ~/courses/ee345/2000/prog4/main.c
$ !76:2 -15 !73:1/main.c
tail -15 ~/courses/ee345/2000/prog4/main.c
[ last 15 lines of the file
~/courses/ee345/2000/prog4/main.c ]
$ !71:s/a test/fun!/
echo This is fun!
This is fun!
$ ^fun^it folks
echo This is it folks!
This is it folks!
$
```

The following In-Chapter Exercises have been designed to give you practice using the **history** and **fc** commands and the history expansion commands to reinforce the command history features supported by the Bash and TC shells.

**IN-CHAPTER EXERCISES**

**10.12** Try all the sessions used in this section on your system.

**10.13** Execute the **lpr** command again after replacing the wpr printer with the jpr printer. Show two versions of the command, one that uses the s/old/new/ format and the second that uses the ^old^new format.

## SUMMARY

Several advanced file processing operations have to be performed from time to time. These operations include compressing and uncompressing, sorting, searching for files and commands in the file structure, searching files for certain strings or patterns, performing databaselike operations of cutting fields from a table or pasting tables together, transforming non-ASCII files to ASCII, and encrypting and decrypting files. Several tools are available in the LINUX operating system that can be used to perform such tasks.

Some of these tools have the ability to specify a set of items by using a single character string. This is done by using a set of nondigit and nonletter characters and a set of rules called regular expressions. The utilities that allow the use of regular expressions are **awk**, **ed**, **egrep**, **grep**, **sed**, and **vi**. In this chapter, we described regular expressions and their use in **vi**, **egrep**, and **grep**.

The **compress** and **gzip** commands can be used to compress files, with **gzip** being the more flexible and powerful of the two. The **uncompress**, **gunzip**, and **gzip -d** commands can be used to uncompress files compressed with the **compress** and **gzip** commands, respectively. The **gzexe** command can be used to compress executable (executable) files and the **gzexe -d** command can be used to uncompress them. Files compressed with **gzexe** can be executed without explicitly uncompressing them. The **zcat** and **zmore** commands can be used to display compressed files without explicitly uncompressing them.

The **sort** command can be used to sort text files. Each line comprises a record with several fields, and the number of fields in all the lines is the same. Text files can be processed like tables by using the **cut** and **paste** commands, that allow cutting of columns in a table and pasting of tables, respectively. The **sort**, **cut**, and **paste** commands can be combined via a pipeline (see Chapter 12) to generate tables based on different sets of criteria.

The **find** and **whereis** commands can be used to search the LINUX file structure to determine locations (absolute pathnames) of files and commands. The **find** command, in particular, is very powerful and lets you search for files based on several criteria, such as file size. The **which** command can be used to determine which version of a command executes, in case there are several versions available on a system.

LINUX provides a family of powerful utilities for searching text files for strings, expressions, and patterns. These utilities are **grep**, **egrep**, and **fgrep**. Of the three, **fgrep** is the fastest, but most limited; **egrep** is the most flexible, but slowest of the three; and **grep** is the middle of the road utility—reasonably fast and fairly flexible. The **zegrep**, **zfgrep**, and **zgrep** commands can be used to uncompress compressed files and pass them to **egrep**, **fgrep**, and **grep** commands respectively, along with any command line arguments.

The **uuencode** and **uudecode** utilities are useful in a system when users want to e-mail non-ASCII files such as multimedia files but the mailing system doesn't allow attachments. The **uuencode** utility can be used to transform a non-ASCII file into an ASCII file, and **uudecode** can transform the ASCII file back into the original non-ASCII version. The **uuencode** utility is therefore used by the sender before sending a non-ASCII file, and **uudecode** is used by the receiver of a uuencoded file to convert it back to the original form.

## PROBLEMS

1. List five file processing operations that you consider advanced.
2. What are regular expressions?
3. Give the **vi** command for replacing all occurrences of the string "DOS" with the string "LINUX" in the whole document that is currently being edited. What are the commands for replacing all occurrences of the strings "DOS" and "Windows" with the string "LINUX" from the lines that start or end with these strings in the document being edited?

4. Give the **vi** command for deleting all four-letter words starting with B, F, b, and f in the file being edited.

5. Give the **vi** command for renaming all C source files in a document to C++ source code files. Note: C source files end with .c and C++ source files end with .C.

6. What is file compression? What do the terms *compressed files* and *decompressed files* mean? What commands are available for performing compression and decompression in LINUX? Which are the preferred commands? Why?

7. Take three large files in your directory structure; a text file, a PostScript file, and a picture file, and compress them by using the **compress** command. Which file was compressed the most? What was the percentage reduction in file size? Compress the same file by using the **gzip** command. Which resulted in better compression, **compress** or **gzip**? Uncompress the files by using **uncompress** and **gunzip** commands. Show your work.

8. What is sorting? Give an example to illustrate your answer. Name four applications of sorting. Name the LINUX utility that can be used to perform sorting.

9. Go to the http://cnn.com/weather Web site and record the high and low temperatures for the following major cities in Asia: Kuala Lumpur, Karachi, Tokyo, Lahore, Manila, New Delhi, and Jakarta. In a file called asiapac.temps construct an ASCII table comprising one line per city in the order: city name, high temperature, and low temperature. The following is a sample line.
   Tokyo 78 72
   Give commands to perform the following operations.
   a. Sort the table by city name.
   b. Sort the table by high temperature.
   c. Sort the table by using the city name as the primary and low temperature as the secondary key.

10. For the students file in Section 10.4, give a command to sort the lines in the file by using last name only as the sort key.

11. What commands are available for file searching? State the purpose of each.

12. Give the command that searches your home directory and displays pathnames of all the files created after the file /etc/passwd.

13. Give a command that searches your home directory and removes all PostScript and .gif files. The command must take your permission (prompt you) before removing a file.

14. On your LINUX system, how long does it take to find all the files that are larger than 1,000 bytes in size? What command(s) did you use?

15. What does the command **grep -n '^' student_addresses** do? Assume that student_addresses is the same file we used in Section 10.7.

16. Give the command that displays lines in student_addresses that start with the letter K or have letter J in them. The output of the command should also display line numbers.
17. What do the following commands do?
    a. `grep '/^[A-H]/' students`
    b. `grep '/^[A,H]/' students`
18. Give a command that displays names of all the files in your ~/courses/ece446 directory that contain the word LINUX.
19. Give a command that generates a table of user names for all users on your system, along with their personal information. Extract this information from the /etc/passwd file.
20. Use the tables student_addresses and student_records to generate a table in which each row contains last name, work phone number, and GPA.
21. Say that you have a picture file campus.bmp that you would like to e-mail to a friend. Give the sequence of commands that are needed to convert the file to ASCII form, reduce its size, and encrypt it before e-mailing it.
22. You need to find out which startup files contain the umask command that sets your default file permissions mask. Assume that the files that may contain this command can only be in your home directory, the /etc directory, or the /etc/skel directory. Furthermore, any file in your home directory and some files in the /etc/skel directory that may contain this command is a dot (hidden) file. What command would you use for this purpose?
23. What is the concept of command history in LINUX (under the Bash and TC shells)? What is a history file? Give the full pathname for the history file on your system.
24. How many commands can be saved in your history file? How did you find out? Give the command lines to display the first 15 and last 15 commands in your history file.
25. What is the command line to edit history commands 10 through 15 and execute them? Try this command on your system. What history command can be used to execute the last command that used the C compiler (`cc` or `gcc`)?

CHAPTER

# 11

# File Sharing

## OBJECTIVES

- To explain different ways of sharing files
- To discuss the LINUX schemes and commands for implementing file sharing
- To describe LINUX hard and soft (symbolic) links in detail and discuss their advantages and disadvantages
- To cover the commands and primitives `*`, `~`, `ln`, `ln -f`, `ln -s`, `ls -i`, `ls -l`, and `symlinks`

## 11.1 INTRODUCTION

When a group of people work together on a project they need to share information. If the information to be shared is on a computer system, group members have to share files and directories. For example, authors of a book or software engineers working on a software project need to share files and directories related to their project. In this chapter, we discuss several ways to implement file sharing in a computer system. The discussion of file sharing in this chapter focuses on how a file can be accessed from various directories by various users in a LINUX system. Under the topic of "version control" in Chapter 20 we address how members of a team can work on one or more files simultaneously without losing their work.

Several methods can be used to allow a group of users to share files and directories. In this chapter we describe duplicate shared files, common login for members of a team, setting appropriate access permissions on shared files, common group for members in a team, and sharing via links. All these methods can be used to allow a team of users to share files and directories in a LINUX system. Although we describe each of these techniques, the chapter is dedicated primarily to a discussion of sharing via links in a LINUX-based computer system.

## 11.2 DUPLICATE SHARED FILES

The simplest way of sharing files is to make copies of these files and give them to all team members. The members can put these copies anywhere in their own accounts (directory structures) and manipulate them in any way they desire. This scheme works well if members of the team are to work on the shared files sequentially, but it has obvious problems if team members are to work on these files simultaneously. In the former case, team members work on one copy of the shared files one by one and complete the task at hand. In the latter case, because the members work on their own copies, the copies become inconsistent and no single copy of the shared files reflects the work done by all the team members. This outcome defeats the purpose of sharing.

## 11.3 COMMON LOGIN FOR MEMBERS OF A TEAM

With common login, the system administrator creates a new user group comprising the members of a team and gives them a new account to which they all have access; that is, they all know the login name and password for the account. All the files and directories created by any team member under this account are owned by the team and everyone has access to them.

It is a simple scheme that works quite well, particularly in situations in which the number of teams is small and teams are stable; that is, they stay together for long periods of time. Such is the case for teams of authors writing a book or programming teams working on large software projects that take several months to finish. However, this scheme also has a couple of drawbacks. First, team members have to use a separate account for their current project and cannot use their regular accounts to access shared files and directories. Second, the system administrator has to create a new account for every new team formed in the organization. Having to do so could create a considerable amount of extra work for the administrator if the duration of projects is short and new teams are formed for every new project. The scheme could be a real headache for the system administrator in a college environment, for example, where student teams are formed to work on class projects, resulting in a large number of teams every semester or quarter.

## 11.4 SETTING APPROPRIATE ACCESS PERMISSIONS ON SHARED FILES

Team members could decide to put all shared files under one member's account, and have the access permissions on these files set so that all team members can access them. This scheme works well if *only* this team's members form the user group (recall the discussion of owner, group, and others in Chapter 8) because, if the group has other users in it, they will also have access to the shared files. For example, suppose that two professors, Art Pohm and Jim Davis, belong to the user group 'faculty'. They decide to put their shared files in Davis's account but set the group access permissions to read, write, and execute for all shared files. All the professors in the user group 'faculty' then will have the same access permissions to these files, which poses security problems. In particular, if the information to be shared is a small portion of total amount of information residing in a member's account (say, two ordinary files out of tens of files and directories that the member owns), the risk of opening the door to all users in a group is too high and a better technique must be used.

## 11.5 COMMON GROUP FOR MEMBERS OF A TEAM

Instead of putting shared files in one user's account, the system administrator could create a new user group consisting of the members of the team only. All team members get individual logins and set access permissions for their files so that they are accessible to other team/group members. This file-sharing scheme is effective and is used often, particularly in conjunction with some version control mechanism.

## 11.6 FILE SHARING VIA LINKS

As we described in Chapter 7, the attributes of a LINUX file are stored in its inode on disk. When a file is opened, its inode is copied into the main memory, allowing speedy access to its contents. In this section, we describe how the use of an inode results in a mechanism that allows you to access a file from various directories by specifying the file name only. System administrators commonly use this scheme to allow access to some files and directories through various directories. Thus, for example, all the files for executable commands can be accessed via the /bin or /usr/bin directories.

A **link** is a way to establish a connection between the file to be shared and the directory entries of the users who want to have access to this file. Thus, when we say that a file has *N* links, we mean that the file has *N* directory entries. The links therefore aid file sharing by providing different access paths to files to be shared. The level of sharing, however, is controlled by setting appropriate access permissions for these files. You can create links to files to which you do not have any access, but that gets you nowhere. Hence file sharing via links is accomplished first by creating access paths to shared files by establishing links to them and then by setting appropriate access permissions on these files.

LINUX supports two types of links: **hard links** and **soft/symbolic links**. Both types are created by using the `ln` command. In the remainder of this chapter we discuss methods of creating both types of links and their internal implementation in the LINUX system.

### 11.6.1 Hard Links

A hard link is a pointer to the inode of a file. When a file is created in LINUX, the system allocates a unique inode to the file and creates a directory entry in the directory in which the file is created. As we discussed before, the directory entry comprises an ordered pair (inode #, filename). The inode number for a file is used to access its attributes, including contents of the file on disk for reading or writing (changing) them (see Chapter 7). Suppose that you create a file Chapter3 in your present working directory and the system allocates inode number 52473 to this file. Therefore the directory entry for this file is (52473, Chapter3).

If we assume that the present working directory previously contained files Chapter1 and Chapter2, its logical structure is shown in Figure 11.1(a). The new file has been highlighted with a gray shade. Figure 11.1(b) shows contents of the disk block that contains the present working directory. The connection between this directory entry and the file's contents is shown in Figure 11.1(c). The inode number in file Chapter3's directory entry is used to index an inode table in the main memory in order to access that file's inode. The inode contains attributes of Chapter3, including its location on disk.

In LINUX, you can create a link to a file by using the `ln` command. This command allows you to give another name to Chapter3 in the same directory that contains the file—or in some other directory. A brief description of the `ln` command follows.

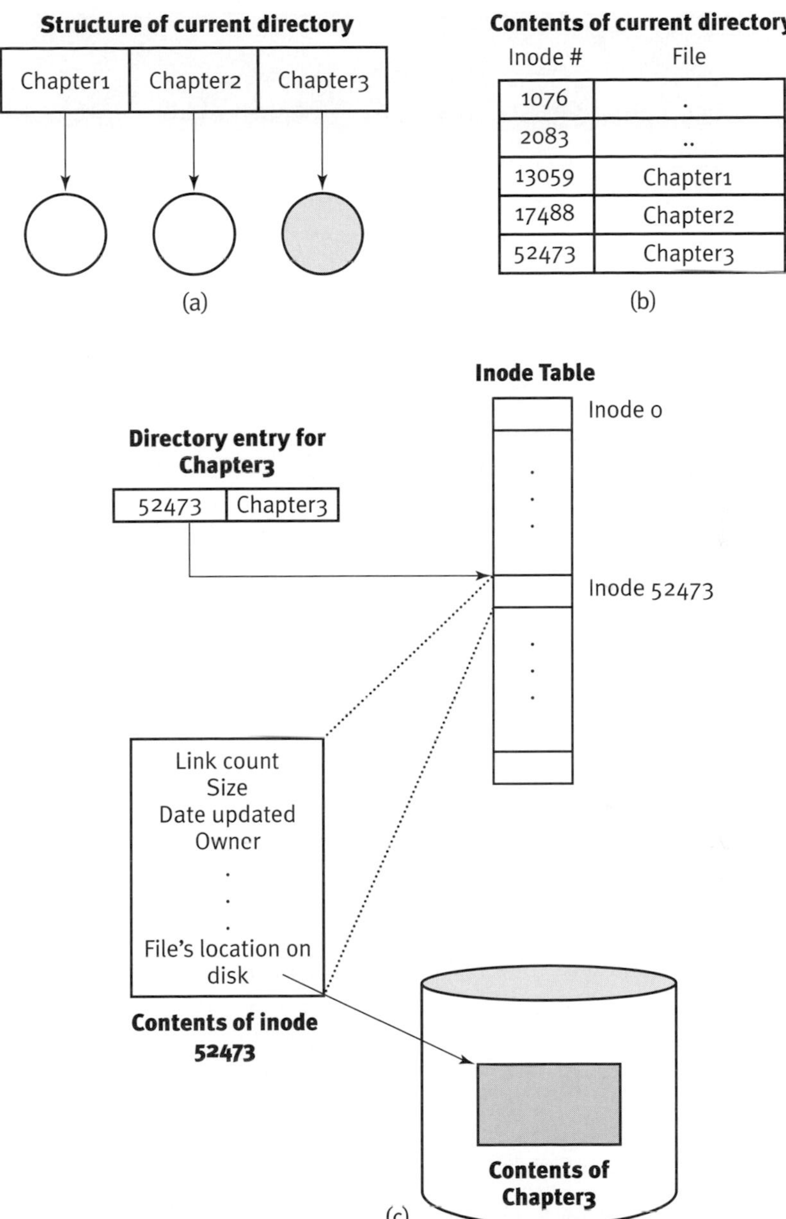


**Figure 11.1** (a) Logical structure of current directory; (b) contents of current directory; and (c) relationship among a directory entry, inode, and file contents

Syntax:

**ln [options] existing-file new-file**
**ln [options] existing-file-list directory**

| | | |
|---|---|---|
| **Purpose:** | First syntax: | Create a hard link to 'existing-file' and name it 'new-file' |
| | Second syntax: | Create hard links to the ordinary files in 'existing-file-list' in 'directory'; links have the same names as the original file. |

**Commonly used options/features:**

| | |
|---|---|
| `-f` | Force creation of link; don't prompt if 'new-file' already exists |
| `-n` | Don't create the link if 'new-file' already exists |
| `-s` | Create a symbolic link to 'existing-file' and name it 'new-file' |

The `ln` command without any option creates a hard link to a file provided the user has execute permission for all the directories in the path leading to the file (the last component of the pathname). The following session illustrates how the `ln` command can be used to create a hard link in the same directory that contains 'existing-file'. The only purpose of this example is to illustrate how the `ln` command is used; it isn't representative of how you would establish and use hard links in practice.

```
$ ls -il
13059 -rwx------  1 sarwar  faculty   398 Mar 11 14:20 Chapter1
17488 -rwx------  1 sarwar  faculty  5983 Jan 17 11:57 Chapter2
52473 -rwx------  1 sarwar  faculty  9352 May 28 23:09 Chapter3
$ ln Chapter3 Chapter3.hard
$ ls -il
13059 -rwx------  1 sarwar  faculty   398 Mar 11 14:20 Chapter1
17488 -rwx------  1 sarwar  faculty  5983 Jan 17 11:57 Chapter2
52473 -rwx------  2 sarwar  faculty  9352 May 28 23:09 Chapter3
52473 -rwx------  2 sarwar  faculty  9352 May 28 23:09 Chapter3.hard
$
```

The `ls -il` command shows the attributes of all the files in the present working directory, including their inode numbers. The command `ln Chapter3 Chapter3.hard` creates a hard link to the file Chapter3; the name of the hard link is Chapter3.hard. The system creates a new directory entry (52473, Chapter3.hard) for Chapter3 in the present working directory. Thus you can refer to Chapter3 by accessing Chapter3.hard as well because both names point to the same file on disk. The second `ls -il` command is used to confirm that Chapter3.hard and Chapter3 are two names for the same file, as both have the same inode number, 52473, and hence the same attributes. Therefore, when a hard link is created to Chapter3, a new pointer to its inode is established in the directory where the link (Chapter3.hard, in this case) resides, as illustrated in Figure 11.2.

Note that the output of the `ls -il` command also shows that both files Chapter3 and Chapter3.hard have link counts of 2 each. Thus, when a hard link is created to a file, the link count for the file increments by 1. That is, the same file exists in the file structure with two names. When you remove a file that has multiple hard links, the LINUX system decrements the link count (in file's inode) by 1. If the resultant link count is 0, the system removes the directory entry for the file, releases the file's inode for recycling, and deallocates disk blocks allocated to the file so that they can be used to store other files and/or directories created in the future. If the new link count is not 0, only the directory entry for the removed file is deleted; the file contents and other directory entries for the file (hard links) remain intact. The following session illustrates this point.

```
$ rm Chapter3
$ ls -il
13059 -rwx------ 1 sarwar  faculty   398 Mar 11 14:20 Chapter1
17488 -rwx------ 1 sarwar  faculty  5983 Jan 17 11:57 Chapter2
52473 -rwx------ 1 sarwar  faculty  9352 May 28 23:09 Chapter3.hard
$
```

This session clearly shows that removing Chapter3 results in the removal of the directory entry for this file but that the file still exists on disk and is accessible via Chapter3.hard. This link has the inode number and file attributes that Chapter3 had, except that the link count, as expected, has been decremented from 2 to 1.

The following `ln` command can be used to create a hard link called memo6.hard in the present working directory to a file ~/memos/memo6. The `ls -il` command is used to view attributes of the file ~/memos/memo6 before the hard link to it is created.

```
$ ls -il ~/memos/memo6
83476 -rwx------ 1 sarwar faculty 1673 May 29 11:22 /home/faculty/sarwar/memos/memo6
$ ln ~/memos/memo6 memo6.hard
$
```

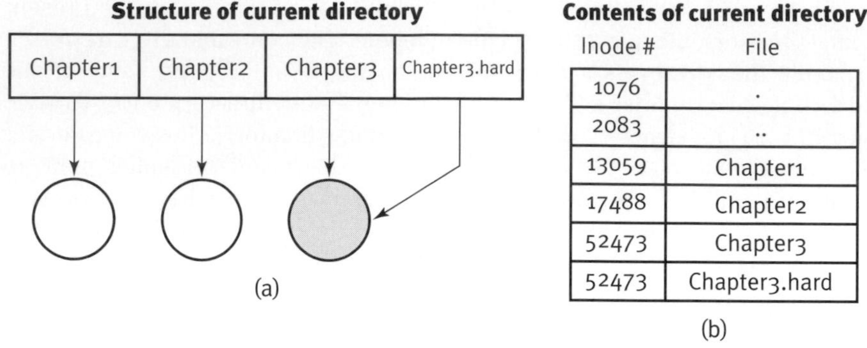


| Inode # | File |
|---|---|
| 1076 | . |
| 2083 | .. |
| 13059 | Chapter1 |
| 17488 | Chapter2 |
| 52473 | Chapter3 |
| 52473 | Chapter3.hard |

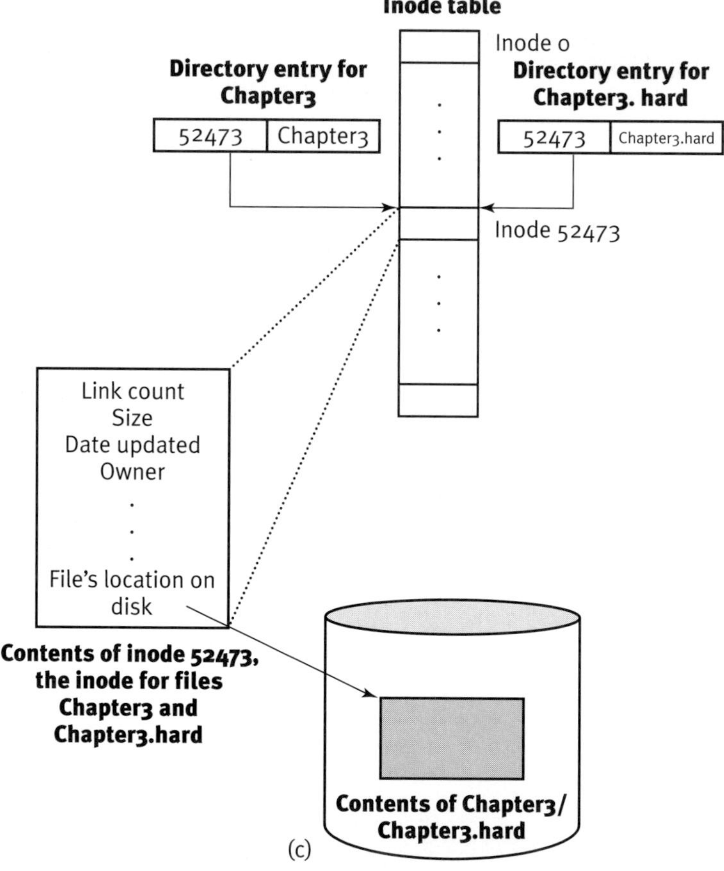


**Figure 11.2** Establishing a hard link: (a) logical structure of current directory; (b) contents of current directory; and (c) hard link implementation by establishing a pointer to inode of the file

After executing the `ln` command, you can run the `ls -il` command to confirm that both files (~/memos/memo6 and memo6.hard) have the same inode number and attributes.

```
$ ls -il ~/memos/memo6
83476 -rwx------- 2 sarwar faculty 1673 May 29 11:22 /home/faculty/sarwar/memos/memo6
$ ls -il memo6.hard
83476 -rwx------- 2 sarwar faculty 1673 May 29 11:22 memo6.hard
$
```

The output shows two important things: first, the link count is up by 1, and second, both files are represented by the same inode, 83476. Figure 11.3 illustrates the hard link.

In the following session, the `ln` command creates hard links to all nondirectory files in the directory ~/linuxbook/examples/dir1. The hard links reside in the directory ~/linuxbook/examples/dir2 and have the names of the original files in the dir1 directory. The second argument, dir2, must be a directory, and you must have execute and write permissions to it. Note that the link counts for all the files in dir1 and dir2 are 2. The `-f` option is used to force creation of hard link in case any of the files f1, f2, or f3 already exists in the ~/linuxbook/examples/dir2 directory.

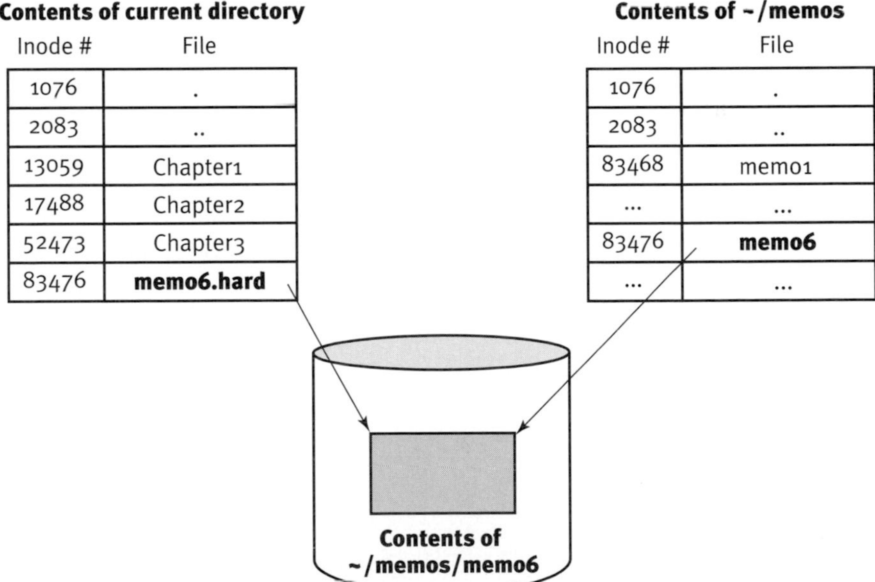

Contents of current directory
Inode #
File
1076
.
2083
..
13059
Chapter1
17488
Chapter2
52473
Chapter3
83476
memo6.hard
Contents of ~/memos
Inode #
File
1076
.
2083
..
83468
memo1
...
...
83476
memo6
...
...
Contents of
~/memos/memo6


**Figure 11.3** Pictorial representation of hard link between ~/memos/memo6 and memo6.hard in the current directory

```
$ cd linuxbook/examples
$ more dir1/f1
Hello, World!
This is a test file.
$ ls -l dir1
-rw-------  1 sarwar  faculty   35 Jun 22 22:21 f1
-rw-------  1 sarwar  faculty   35 Jun 22 22:21 f2
-rw-------  1 sarwar  faculty   35 Jun 22 22:22 f3
$ ln -f ~/linuxbook/examples/dir1/* ~/linuxbook/examples/dir2
$ ls -l dir1
-rw-------  2 sarwar  faculty   35 Jun 22 22:21 f1
-rw-------  2 sarwar  faculty   35 Jun 22 22:21 f2
-rw-------  2 sarwar  faculty   35 Jun 22 22:22 f3
$ ls -l dir2
-rw-------  2 sarwar  faculty   35 Jun 22 22:21 f1
-rw-------  2 sarwar  faculty   35 Jun 22 22:21 f2
-rw-------  2 sarwar  faculty   35 Jun 22 22:22 f3
$ more dir2/f1
Hello, World!
This is a test file.
$
```

You can run the following `ln` command to create a hard link in your home directory to the file /home/faculty/sarwar/linuxbook/examples/demo1. The hard link appears as a file demo1 in your home directory. If demo1 already exists in your home directory, you can overwrite it with the `-f` option. If demo1 exists in the home directory and you don't use the `-f` option, an error message is displayed on the screen informing you that the demo1 file exists. You must have execute permission for the directories in the pathname /home/faculty/sarwar/linuxbook/examples/demo1, and demo1 must be a file.

```
$ ln -f /home/faculty/sarwar/linuxbook/examples/demo1 ~
$
```

The user sarwar can run the following command to create a hard link demo1 in a directory dir1 in bob's home directory that points to the file /home/faculty/sarwar/linuxbook/examples/demo1. The name of the link in bob's directory is demo1, the same as the original file. Figure 11.4 shows the establishment of the link.

```
$ ln -f /home/faculty/sarwar/linuxbook/examples/demo1 /home/faculty/bob/dir1
$
```

The user sarwar must have execute permission for bob's home directory and execute and write permission to dir1 (the directory in which the link is created). The user bob must have proper access permissions to demo1 in sarwar's directory structure to access this file. Thus, if sarwar and bob are in the same user group and bob needs to be able to edit demo1, sarwar must set the group access privileges for the file to read and write. Then, bob can edit demo1 by using, for example, the `vi demo1` command from his home directory.

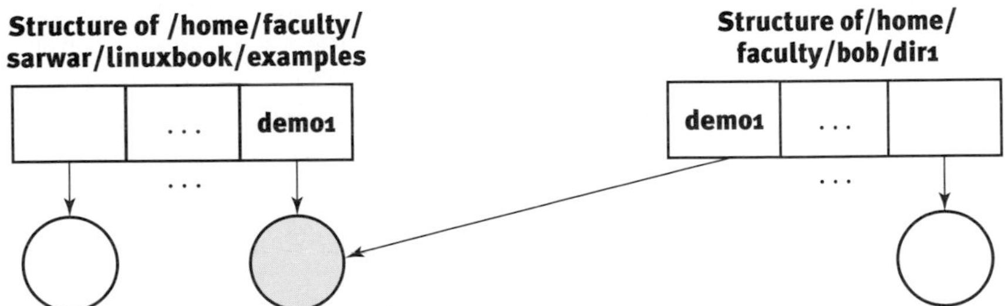


**Figure 11.4** A hard link between /home/faculty/sarwar/linuxbook/examples/demo1 and /home/faculty/bob/dir1

The following command accomplishes the same task. Remember that sarwar runs this command.

```
$ ln -f ~/linuxbook/examples/demo1 /home/faculty/bob/dir1
$
```

You can run the following `ln` command to create hard links to all nondirectory files in your ~/linuxbook/examples directory. The hard links reside in the directory linuxbook/examples in user john's home directory and have the names of the original files. The user john must first create the linuxbook directory in his home directory and the examples directory in his linuxbook directory. You must have execute permission for john's linuxbook directory and execute and write permission for his examples directory.

```
$ ln -f ~/linuxbook/examples/* /home/faculty/john/linuxbook/examples
$
```

### 11.6.2 Drawbacks of Hard Links

Hard links are the traditional way of gluing the file system structure of a LINUX system, which comprises several file systems. Hard links, however, have some problems and limitations that make them less attractive to the average user.

The first problem is that hard links cannot be established between files that are on different file systems. This inability is not an issue if you are establishing links between files in your own directory structure, with your home directory as the top-level directory, or with files in another user's directory structure which is on the same file system as yours. However, if you want to create a hard link between a file (command) in the /bin directory and a file in your file structure, it most likely will not work because on almost all systems the /bin directory and your directory structure reside on different file systems. The following command illustrates this point. In this example, we try to give the name `del` to the LINUX command `rm` which resides in the directory /bin. Because the `rm` command is in one file system and our directory structure is in another, LINUX doesn't allow us to create a hard link, del, between a file in the current directory and /bin/rm.

```
$ ln /bin/rm del
ln: cannot create hard link 'del' to '/bin/rm': Invalid
cross-device link
$
```

This problem also shows up when a file with multiple links is moved to another file system. The following session illustrates this point. The `ls -il` command shows that Chapter3 and Chapter3.hard are hard links to the same file (they have the same inode number). The **mv** command is used to move the file Chapter3 to the /tmp directory, which is on a different file system than the one that currently contains Chapter3 (and Chapter2). Notice that, after the **mv** command is executed, the link count for Chapter2 and /tmp/Chapter3 is 1 each and that the files have different inodes (/tmp/Chapter3 has inode 6 and Chapter3.hard has the same old inode 52473). The `ln` command cannot link /tmp/Chapter3 to temp.hard because the two files are in different file systems.

```
$ ls -il
13059 -rwx------ 1 sarwar  faculty   398 Mar 11 14:20 Chapter1
17488 -rwx------ 1 sarwar  faculty  5983 Jan 17 11:57 Chapter2
52473 -rwx------ 2 sarwar  faculty  9352 May 28 23:09 Chapter3
52473 -rwx------ 1 sarwar  faculty  9352 May 28 23:09 Chapter3.hard
$ mv Chapter3 /tmp
$ ls -il /tmp
    6 -rwx------ 1 sarwar  faculty  9352 May 29 11:57 Chapter3
$ ls -il Chapter3.hard
52473 -rwx------ 1 sarwar  faculty  9352 May 28 23:09 Chapter3.hard
$ ln /tmp/Chapter3 temp.hard
ln: temp.hard: Cross-device link
$
```

The second problem is that only a superuser can create a hard link to a directory. The `ln` command gives an error message when a nonsuperuser tries to create a hard link to a directory myweb, as in

```
$ ln ~/myweb myweb.hard
/home/faculty/sarwar/myweb is a directory
$
```

The third problem is that some editors remove the existing version of the file that you are editing and put the new versions in new files. When that happens, any hard links to the removed file do not have access to the new file, defeating the purpose of linking (file sharing). Fortunately, none of the commonly used editors do so. Thus all the text editors discussed in Chapter 5 (**pico**, **vi**, **emacs**, and **Xemacs**) are safe to use.

In the following In-Chapter Exercises, you will use the `ln` and `ls -il` commands to create and identify hard links, and to verify a serious limitation of hard links.

**IN-CHAPTER EXERCISES**

**11.1.** Create a file Ch11Ex1 in your home directory that contains this problem. Establish a hard link to this file, also in your home directory, and call the link Ch11Ex1.hard. Verify that the link has been established by using the `ls -il` command. What field in the output of this command did you use for verification?

**11.2.** Execute the `ln /tmp ~/tmp` command on your LINUX system. What is the purpose of the command? What happens when you execute the command? Does the result make sense? Why or why not?

### 11.6.3 Soft/Symbolic Links

Soft/symbolic links take care of all the problems inherent in hard links and are therefore used more often than hard links. They are different from hard links both conceptually and in terms of how they are implemented. They do have a cost associated with them, which we discuss in Section 11.6.4, but they are extremely flexible and can be used to link files across machines and networks.

You can create soft links by using the `ln` command with the `-s` option. The following session illustrates the creation of a soft link.

```
$ ls -il
13059 -rwx------ 1 sarwar  faculty   398 Mar 11 14:20 Chapter1
17488 -rwx------ 1 sarwar  faculty  5983 Jan 17 11:57 Chapter2
52473 -rwx------ 2 sarwar  faculty  9352 May 28 23:09 Chapter3
52473 -rwx------ 1 sarwar  faculty  9352 May 29 23:09 Chapter3.hard
$ ln -s Chapter3 Chapter3.soft
$ ls -il
13059 -rwx------ 1 sarwar  faculty   398 Mar 11 14:20 Chapter1
17488 -rwx------ 1 sarwar  faculty  5983 Jan 17 11:57 Chapter2
52473 -rwx------ 1 sarwar  faculty  9352 May 29 12:09 Chapter3
52479 lrwxrwxrwx 1 sarwar  faculty     8 May 29 12:09 Chapter3.soft -> Chapter3
$
```

The `ln -s Chapter3 Chapter3.soft` command is used to create a symbolic link to the file Chapter3 in the present working directory, and the symbolic link is given the name Chapter3.soft. The output of the `ls -il` command shows a number of important items that reveal how symbolic links are implemented and how they are identified in the output. First, the original file (Chapter3) and the link file (Chapter3.soft) have different inode numbers: 52473 for Chapter3 and 52479 for Chapter3.soft, which means that they are *different* files. Second, the original file is of ordinary file type - (ordinary file) and the link file is of link type l (link file). Third, the link count field is 1 for both files, which further indicates that the two files are different. Fourth, the file sizes are different: 9352 bytes for the original file and 8 bytes file the link file. Last, the name of the link file is followed by -> Chapter3, the pathname for the file that Chapter3.soft is a symbolic link to; this is specified as the first argument in the `ln -s` command. The pathname of the existing file is content of the link file, which also explains the size of the link file (there are eight characters in the word Chapter3). Figure 11.5 shows the logical file structure of the current directory, directory entries in the current directory, and a diagram that shows that Chapter3 and Chapter3.soft are truly separate files and that the link file contains the pathname of the file to which it is a link.

In summary, when you create a symbolic link, a new file of type link is created. This file contains the pathname of the existing file as specified in the `ln -s` command. When you make a reference to the link file, the LINUX system sees that the type of the file is link and reads the link file to find the pathname for the actual file to which you are referring. For example, for the `cat Chapter3.soft` command, the system reads the contents of Chapter3.soft to get the name of the file to display (Chapter3 in this case) and send its contents to standard output. Hence, you see the contents of Chapter3 displayed.

You can create soft links across file systems, as illustrated by the following session. Here, the file Chapter3 is copied from one file system (that contains this file) to another that contains the /tmp directory. Then, the command `ln -s /tmp/Chapter3 temp.soft` is used to create a symbolic link to the copied file. The command works without any problem, establishing a symbolic link to /tmp/Chapter3 in temp.soft. Note that inode numbers for the two files are different, indicating that the two files are separate; temp.soft contains the pathname to the file for which it is a symbolic link, /tmp/Chapter3. Recall that in Section 11.6.1 a similar call to establish a hard link between /tmp/Chapter3 and temp.hard failed.

```
$ cp Chapter3 /tmp
$ ln -s /tmp/Chapter3 temp.soft
$ ls -il /tmp/Chapter3 temp.soft
    6 -rwx------  1 sarwar  faculty 7119 May 29 12:36 /tmp/Chapter3
52497 lrwxrwxrwx  1 sarwar  faculty   13 May 29 12:37 temp.soft -> /tmp/Chapter3
$
```

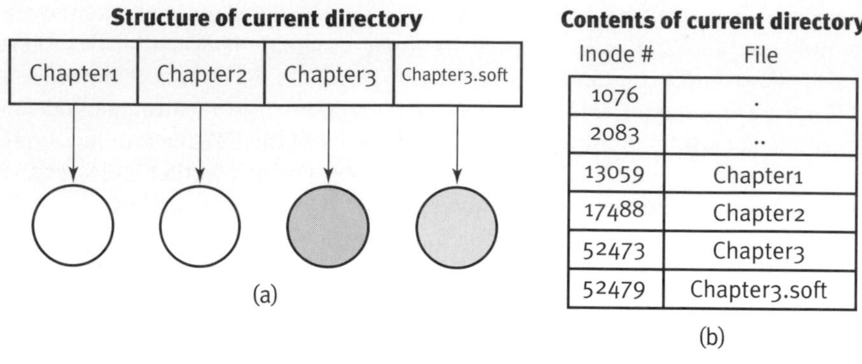


| Inode # | File |
|---|---|
| 1076 | . |
| 2083 | .. |
| 13059 | Chapter1 |
| 17488 | Chapter2 |
| 52473 | Chapter3 |
| 52479 | Chapter3.soft |

**Inode table**

Inode 0

**Directory entry for Chapter3**

| 52473 | Chapter3 |
|---|---|

**Directory entry for Chapter3. hard**

| 52479 | Chapter3.soft |
|---|---|

Inode 52473

Inode 52479

Link count
Size
Date updated
Owner
.
.
.
File's location on disk

**Contents of inode 52473, the inode for file Chapter3**

**Chapter3.soft**

**Contents of Chapter3**

Link count
Size
Date updated
Owner
.
.
.
File's location on disk

**Contents of inode 52479, the inode for file Chapter3.soft**

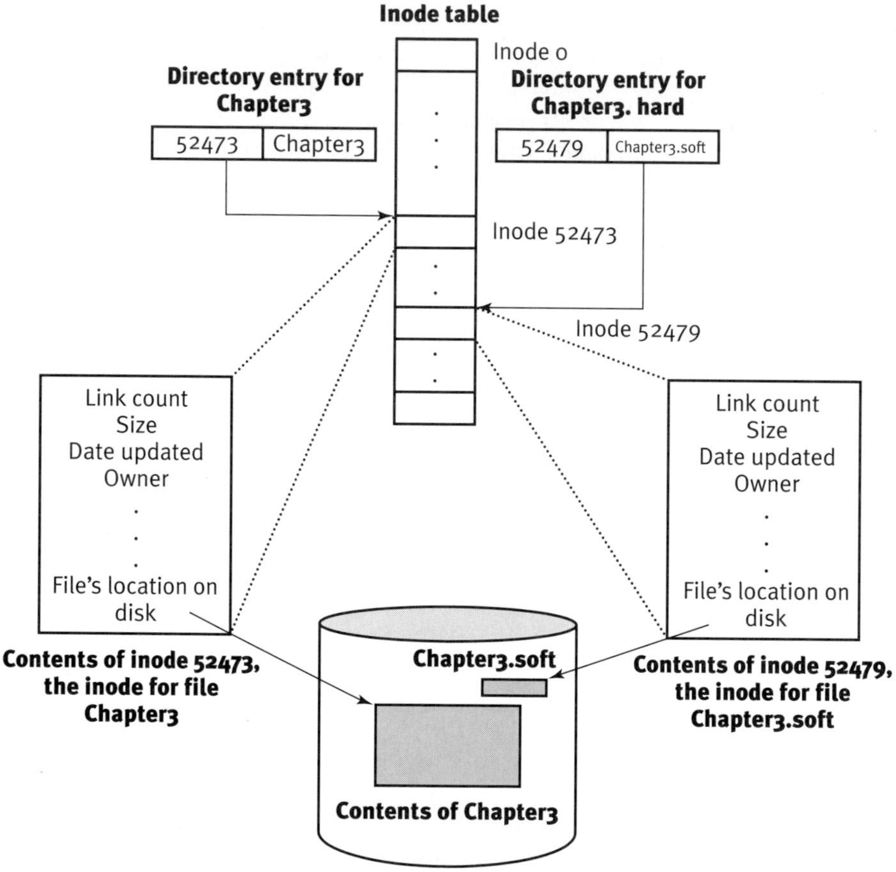

Figure 11.5 Establishing a soft link: (a) logical structure of the current directory; (b) contents of the current directory; and (c) soft link implementation by establishing a "pointer" to (pathname of) the existing file in the link file

The following session shows how symbolic links can be created to all the files, including directory files, in a directory. The `ln -sf ~/linuxbook/examples/dir1/* ~/linuxbook/examples/dir2` command creates soft links to all the files in a directory called ~/linuxbook/examples/dir1 and puts them in the directory ~/linuxbook/examples/dir2. You must have execute and write permissions for the dir2 directory, and execute permission to all the directories in the pathname. The `-f` option is used to force creation of the soft link in case any of the files f1, f2, or f3 already exist in ~/linuxbook/examples/dir2.

```
$ cd ~/linuxbook/examples
$ more dir1/f1
Hello, World!
This is a test file.
$ ls -l dir1
-rw-------   1 sarwar  faculty    35 Jun 22 22:21 f1
-rw-------   1 sarwar  faculty    35 Jun 22 22:21 f2
-rw-------   1 sarwar  faculty    35 Jun 22 22:22 f3
$ ln -sf ~/linuxbook/examples/dir1/* ~/linuxbook/examples/dir2
$ ls -l dir2
lrwxrwxrwx 1  sarwar  faculty 38 Jun 22 22:54 f1 -> /home/faculty/sarwar/linuxbook/examples/dir1/f1
lrwxrwxrwx 1  sarwar  faculty 38 Jun 22 22:54 f2 -> /home/faculty/sarwar/linuxbook/examples/dir1/f2
lrwxrwxrwx 1  sarwar  faculty 38 Jun 22 22:54 f3 -> /home/faculty/sarwar/linuxbook/examples/dir1/f3
$ more dir2/f1
Hello, World!
This is a test file.
$
```

You can run the following command to create a symbolic link in your home directory to the file /home/faculty/sarwar/linuxbook/examples/demo1. The soft link appears as a file called demo1 in your home directory. If demo1 already exists in your home directory, you can overwrite it with the `-f` option. If demo1 exists in the home directory and you don't use the `-f` option, an error message is displayed on the screen informing you that the demo1 file exists. You must have execute permission for the directories in the pathname /home/faculty/sarwar/linuxbook/examples/demo1, and demo1 must be a file.

```
$ ln -sf /home/faculty/sarwar/linuxbook/examples/demo1 ~
$
```

The user sarwar can run the following command to create a soft link called demo1 in a directory dir1 in bob's home directory that points to the /home/faculty/sarwar/linuxbook/examples/demo1 file. Figure 11.6 shows how the soft link is established.

The user sarwar must have execute permission for bob's home directory, and execute and write permission for dir1 (the directory in which the soft link is created). The user bob must have proper access permissions for demo1 in sarwar's directory structure to access this file. Thus, if sarwar and bob are in the same user group and bob needs to be able to edit memo1, sarwar must set the group access privileges on the file to read and write. The user bob can then edit demo1 by using, for example, the `vi demo1` command from his home directory.

```
$ ln -sf /home/faculty/sarwar/linuxbook/examples/demo1 /home/faculty/bob/dir1
$
```

The following command accomplishes the same task. Remember that sarwar runs this command.

```
$ ln -sf ~/linuxbook/examples/demo1 /home/faculty/bob/dir1
$
```

You can run the following `ln` command to create soft links to all the files, including directory files, in your ~/linuxbook/examples directory. These soft links

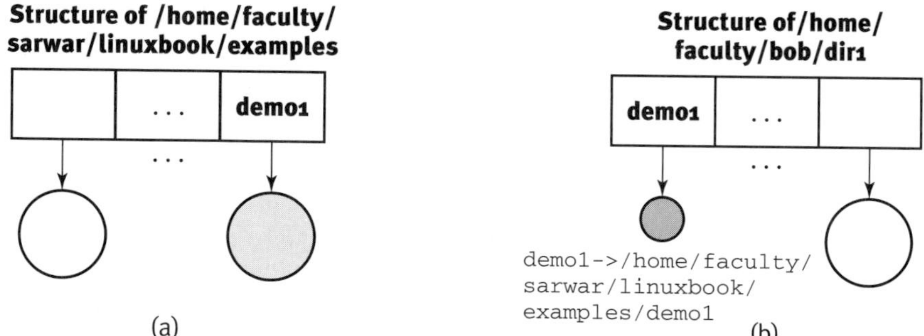


**Figure 11.6** A soft link between (a) /home/faculty/sarwar/linuxbook/examples/demo1 and (b) /home/faculty/bob/dir1

```
$ ln -sf ~/linuxbook/examples/* /home/faculty/john/linuxbook/examples
$
```

reside in the directory called linuxbook/examples in john's home directory and have the names of the original files. The user john must create the linuxbook directory in his home directory and the examples directory in his linuxbook directory. You must have execute permission for john's linuxbook directory and execute and write permission for his examples directory.

### 11.6.4 Types of Symbolic Links

The symbolic links are categorized as absolute, dangling, lengthy, messy, other_fs, and relative, depending on how the target of the link is displayed when you list symbolic links on the screen. You can find the type of a symbolic link by using the `symlinks` command (see Section 11.7).

An **absolute link** is one whose target is specified with an absolute pathname (i.e., a pathname starting with the root (/) directory). A **dangling link** is one for which the target of the link does not currently exist. This can occur for links whose target has been removed or moved elsewhere in the file system or when a file system has been mounted at other than its customary **mount point** (e.g., when the root file system that is normally mounted at / is mounted at /mnt after booting the system from alternative media). A **lengthy link** is a link that uses "../" more than necessary in the pathname for the target of the link (e.g., /bin/vi -> ../bin/vim). These are only detected when you use the `symlinks` command (see Section 11.7) with the `-s` option. A **messy link** contains unnecessary slashes or dots in the path. You can clean the lengthy and messy links by using the `symlinks` command with the `–c` option. An **other_fs link** is one whose target currently resides on a different file system from the file system where `symlinks` was run. A **relative link** is one that was created with its target's path specified relative to the directory in which the link resides. When you browse the LINUX file structure, you'll notice that most of the links are absolute or relative. Occasionally, you will find messy links, and rarely you will find lengthy links.

### 11.6.5 Pros and Cons of Symbolic Links

As we mentioned earlier, symbolic links don't have the problems and limitations of hard links. Thus symbolic links can be established between files across file systems and to directories. Also files that symbolic links point to can be edited by any kind of editor without any ill effects, provided that the file's pathname doesn't get changed—that is, the original file isn't moved.

Symbolic links do have a problem of their own that isn't associated with hard links: If the file that the symbolic link points to is moved from one directory to another, it can no longer be accessed via the link. The reason is that the link file contains the pathname for the original location of the file in the file structure. The following session illustrates this point. Suppose that temp.soft is a symbolic link to the file /tmp/Chapter3. The **mv** command is used to move /tmp/Chapter3 to the present working directory. The `cat` command fails because the soft link still points to the file with pathname /tmp/Chapter3. This result is quite logical but is still a drawback; in hard links the `cat` command would not fail so long as the moved file stays within the same file system.

```
$ mv /tmp/Chapter3 .
$ cat temp.soft
temp.soft: No such file or directory
$
```

Some other drawbacks of the symbolic links are that LINUX has to support an additional file type (the link type) and a new file has to be created for every link. Creation of the link file results in space overhead for an extra inode and disk space needed to store the pathname of the file to which it is a link. Symbolic links also result in slow file operations because, for every reference to the file, the link file has to be opened and read in order for you to reach the actual file. The actual file is then processed for reading or writing, requiring an extra disk read to be performed if a file is referenced via a symbolic link to the file.

In the following In-Chapter Exercises, you will use the `ln -s` and `ls -il` commands to create and identify soft links, and to verify that you can create soft links across file systems.

## IN-CHAPTER EXERCISES

**11.3.** Establish a soft link to the file Ch11Ex1 that you created in Exercise 11.1. Call the soft link Ch11Ex1.soft. Verify that the link has been established. What commands did you use to establish the link and verify its creation?

**11.4.** Execute the `ln-s /tmp ~/tmp` command on your LINUX system. What is the purpose of the command? What happens when you execute the command? Does the result make sense? Why or why not?

## 11.7 SEARCHING FOR SYMBOLIC LINKS

You can search directory hierarchies for symbolic links by using the `symlinks` command. Here is a brief description of this command.

Syntax:

**symlinks [options] directory-list**

**Purpose:** Search the directories in 'directory-list' for symbolic links and display information about them

**Output:** Listing of symbolic links

**Commonly used options/features:**

| | |
|---|---|
| `-c` | Convert absolute links to relative links, except for links across filesystems |
| `-d` | Delete dangling links |
| `-r` | Recursively search the directories in 'directory-list' |
| `-s` | Detect lengthy links as well |
| `-v` | Search for relative links as well |

The information displayed by the command specifies whether a link is absolute, dangling, lengthy, messy, other_fs (to another filesystem), or relative. In the following session, the `symlinks` command is used to display information about all symbolic links in the /bin directory. The following session shows the output of the `symlinks` command with and without options.

```
$ symlinks /bin
absolute: /bin/sh -> /bin/bash
absolute: /bin/fsconf -> /bin/linuxconf
absolute: /bin/lpdconf -> /bin/linuxconf
absolute: /bin/netconf -> /bin/linuxconf
absolute: /bin/userconf -> /bin/linuxconf
absolute: /bin/xconf -> /bin/linuxconf
absolute: /bin/pidof -> /sbin/killall5
```

```
messy: /bin/zsh -> ..//usr/bin/zsh-3.1.6
$ symlinks -v /bin
absolute: /bin/sh -> /bin/bash
relative: /bin/bsh -> ash
relative: /bin/awk -> gawk
relative: /bin/csh -> tcsh
relative: /bin/red -> ed
absolute: /bin/fsconf -> /bin/linuxconf
absolute: /bin/lpdconf -> /bin/linuxconf
absolute: /bin/netconf -> /bin/linuxconf
absolute: /bin/userconf -> /bin/linuxconf
absolute: /bin/xconf -> /bin/linuxconf
relative: /bin/dnsdomainname -> hostname
relative: /bin/domainname -> hostname
relative: /bin/nisdomainname -> hostname
relative: /bin/ypdomainname -> hostname
absolute: /bin/pidof -> /sbin/killall5
relative: /bin/ex -> vi
relative: /bin/rvi -> vi
relative: /bin/rview -> vi
relative: /bin/view -> vi
messy: /bin/zsh -> ..//usr/bin/zsh-3.1.6
$ symlinks -rvs /bin /lib
absolute: /bin/sh -> /bin/bash
...
messy: /bin/zsh -> ..//usr/bin/zsh-3.1.6
relative: /lib/ld-linux.so.2 -> ld-2.1.1.so
...
relative: /lib/libreadline.so -> libreadline.so.4.0
$
```

## SUMMARY

Any of several techniques can be used to allow a team of users to share LINUX files and directories. Some of the most commonly used methods of file sharing are duplicating the files to be shared and distributing them among team members, establishing a common account for team members, setting appropriate permissions on the files to be shared, setting up a LINUX user group for the team members, and establishing links to the files to be shared files in the directories of all team members. File sharing via hard and soft links is the main topic of this chapter. The issue of simultaneous access of shared files by team members is not discussed here (see Chapter 20).

Hard links allow you to refer to an existing file by another name. Although hard links are the primary mechanism used by LINUX to glue the file structure, they have several shortcomings. First, an existing file and its links must be in the same file system. Second, only a superuser can create hard links to directories. Third, moving a file to another file system breaks all links to it.

Soft links can be used to overcome the problems associated with hard links. When a soft link to a file is created, a new file is created that contains the pathname of the file to which it is a link. The type of this file is link. Soft links are expensive in terms of the time needed to access the file and the space overhead of the link file. The time overhead during file access occurs because the link file has to be opened in order for the pathname of the actual file to be read, and only then does the actual read take place. The space overhead is caused by the link file that contains the pathname of the original file.

Hard and soft links are established with the `ln` command. For creating soft links, the `-s` option is used with the command. The `ls -il` command is used to identify (or confirm establishment of) links. The first field of the output of this command identifies the inode numbers for the files in a directory, and all hard links to a file have the same inode number as the original file. The first letter of the second field represents file type ('l' for soft link), and the remaining specify file permissions. The third field identifies the number of hard links to a file. Every simple file has one hard link at the time it is created. The last field identifies file names; a soft link's name is followed by - > filename, where filename is the name of the original file. The `-f` option can be used to force the creation of a link, that is, to overwrite an existing file with the newly created link.

The `symlinks` command is used to search directory hierarchies for symbolic links and display information about them, including the type of each link.

## PROBLEMS

1. What are the five methods that can be used to allow a team of users to share files in LINUX?
2. What is a link in LINUX? Name the types of links that LINUX supports. How do they differ from each other?
3. What are the problems with hard links?
4. Remove the file Ch11Ex1 that you created in In-Chapter Exercise 11.1. Display the contents of Ch11Ex1.hard and Ch11Ex1.soft. What happens? What

command did you use for displaying the files? Does the result make sense? Why or why not?

5. Search the /usr/bin directory on your system and identify three links in it. Write down the names of these links. Are these hard or soft links? How do you know?
6. While in your home directory, can you establish a hard and soft link to /etc/passwd on your system? Why? What commands did you use? Are you satisfied with the results of the command execution?
7. Every LINUX directory has at least two hard links. Why?
8. Can you find the number of hard and soft links to a file? If so, what command(s) do you need to use?
9. Suppose that a file called shared in your present directory has five hard links to it. Give a sequence of commands to display absolute pathnames of all of these links. (*Hint:* Use the `find` command.)
10. Create a directory, dir1, in your home directory and three files, f1, f2, and f3, in it. Ask a friend to create a directory, dir2, in his or her home directory, with dir1.hard and dir1.soft as its subdirectories. Create hard and soft links to all the files in your dir1 in your friend's ~/dir2/dir1.hard and ~/dir2/dir1.soft directories. Give the sequence of commands that you executed to do so.
11. For Problem 10, what are the inode numbers of the hard links and soft links? What command did you use to determine them? What are the contents of the link (both hard and soft) files? How did you get your answers?
12. What are the pros and cons of symbolic links?
13. Clearly describe how file sharing can be accomplished by using links (hard and soft) in LINUX. In particular, do you need to do anything other than establishing links to the files to be shared?
14. Describe various types of symbolic links. Give one example of each type.
15. What command line will you use to search the directory hierarchy ~/bin and display information about all symbolic links in it?

C H A P T E R

# 12

# Redirection and Piping

**OBJECTIVES**

- To describe the notion of standard files—standard input, standard output, and standard error files—and file descriptors
- To describe input and output redirection for standard files
- To discuss the concept of error redirection and appending to a file
- To explain the concept of pipes in LINUX
- To describe how powerful operations can be performed by combining pipes, file descriptors, and redirection primitives
- To explain error redirection in TC shell
- To cover the commands and primitives &, |, <, >, >>, `cat`, `diff`, `grep`, `lp`, `more`, `pr`, `sort`, `stderr`, `stdin`, `stdout`, `tee`, `tr`, `uniq`, `wc`

## 12.1 INTRODUCTION

All computer software (commands) performs one or more of the following operations: input, processing, and output; a typical command performs all three. The question for the operating system is: Where does a shell command (internal or external) take its input from, where does it send its output to, and where are the error messages sent to? If the input is not part of the command code (i.e., data within the code in the form of constants or variables), it must come from an outside source. This outside source is usually a file, although it could be an I/O device such as a keyboard or a network interface card. Command output and error messages can go to a file as well. In order for a command to read from or write to a file, it must first open the file.

There are default files where a command reads its input and sends its output and error messages. In LINUX, these files are known as standard files for the command. The input , output, and errors of a command can be redirected to other files by using file redirection facilities in LINUX. This allows us to connect several commands together to perform a complex task that cannot be performed by a single existing command. We discuss the notion of standard file and redirection of input, output, and error in LINUX in this chapter.

## 12.2 STANDARD FILES

In LINUX, three files are automatically opened by the kernel for every command for the command to read input from, and send its output and error messages to. These files are known as standard input (stdin), standard output (stdout), and standard error (stderr). By default, these files are associated with the terminal on which the command executes. More specifically, the keyboard is standard input and the display screen (or the console at which you are logged in) is standard output and standard error. Therefore every command, by default, takes its input from the keyboard, and sends its output and error messages to the display screen (or the console window), as shown in Figure 12.1. Recall our explanation of the per process file descriptor table in Chapter 7. In the remainder of this chapter, we use the terms *monitor screen*, *display screen*, *console window*, and *display window* interchangeably.

## 12.3 INPUT REDIRECTION

Input redirection is accomplished by using the less-than symbol (<). This syntax is used to detach the keyboard from the standard input of 'command' and attach

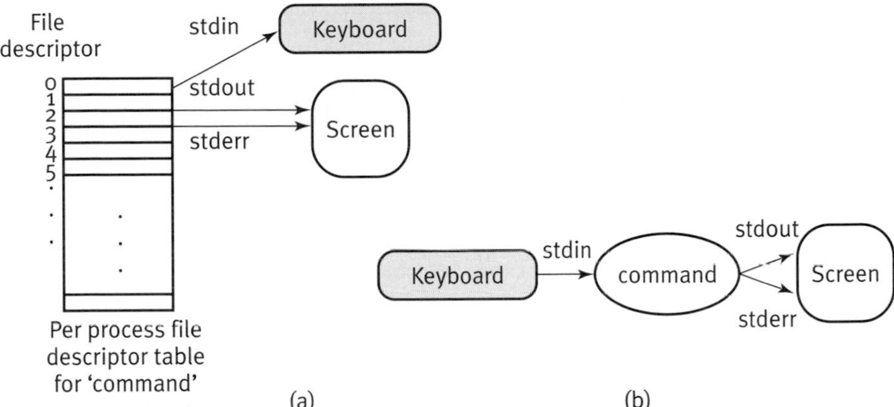


**Figure 12.1** Standard files and file descriptors: (a) file descriptors; (b) semantics of a command execution

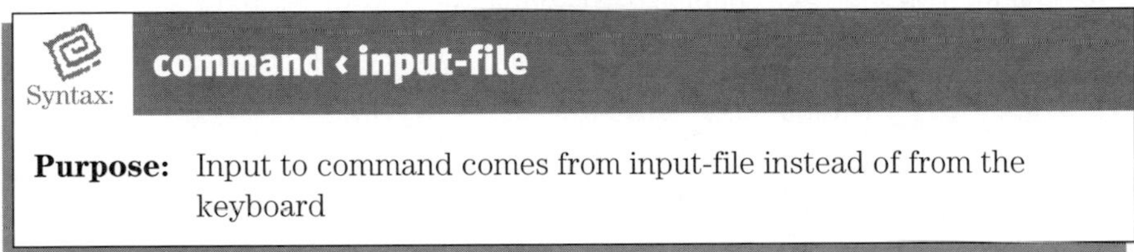

Syntax: **command < input-file**

**Purpose:** Input to command comes from input-file instead of from the keyboard

input-file to it. Thus, if 'command' reads its input from standard input, this input will come from input-file not the keyboard attached to the terminal on which the command is run. The semantics of the command syntax are shown in Figure 12.2. Note that the 'command' input comes from the input-file.

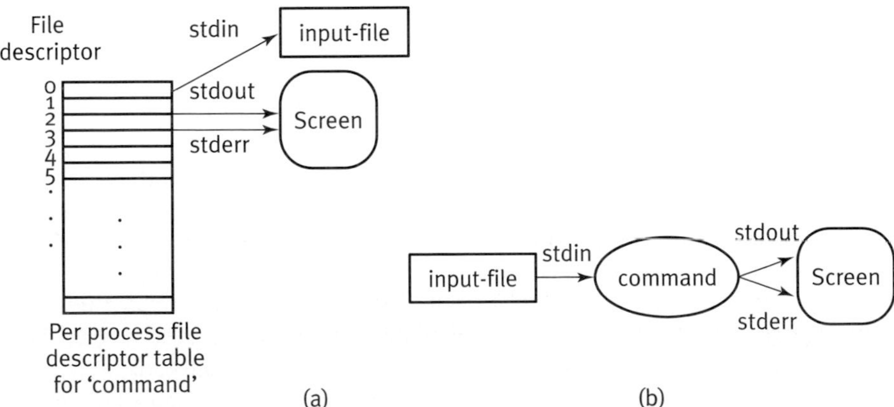


**Figure 12.2** Input redirection: (a) file descriptors and standard files for 'command'; (b) semantics of input redirection

For example, the command `cat < tempfile` takes its input from tempfile (as opposed to the keyboard because standard input for `cat` has been attached to tempfile) and sends its output to the display screen. So, effectively, the contents of tempfile are displayed on the monitor screen. This command is different from `cat tempfile`, in which tempfile is passed as a command line argument to the `cat` command; the standard input of `cat` doesn't change. However, the end result is the same.

Similarly, in `grep "John" < Phones`, the `grep` command takes its input from the Phones file in the current directory, not from the keyboard. The output and error messages of the command go to the display screen. Again, this command is different from `grep "John" Phones`, in which Phones is passed as an argument to `grep`; the standard input of `grep` doesn't change and is still the keyboard attached to the terminal on which the command executes. However, the end result is the same.

The `cat` and `grep` commands take input from the standard input if they aren't passed files as arguments from the command line. The `tr` command takes input from the standard input only and sends its output to standard output. The command doesn't work with a file as a command line argument. Thus input redirection is often used with the `tr` command, as in `tr -s ' ' ' ' < Bigfile`. When this command is executed, it substitutes multiple spaces in Bigfile with single spaces.

## 12.4 OUTPUT REDIRECTION

Output redirection is accomplished by using the greater-than symbol (>).

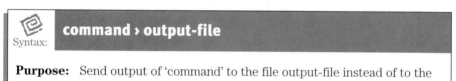

Syntax:

**command › output-file**

**Purpose:** Send output of 'command' to the file output-file instead of to the monitor screen

This syntax is used to detach the display screen from the standard output of 'command' and attach output-file to it. Thus, if 'command' writes/sends its output to standard output, the output goes to output-file, not the monitor screen attached to the terminal on which the command runs. The error messages still go to the display screen, as before. The semantics of the command syntax are shown in Figure 12.3.

Let's consider the `cat > newfile` command. Recall that the `cat` command sends its output to standard output, which is the display screen by default. This command syntax detaches the display screen from standard output of the `cat` command and attaches newfile to it. The standard input of `cat` remains attached to the keyboard. Thus, when this command is executed, it creates a file called newfile whose contents are whatever you type on the keyboard until you hit `<Ctrl-D>` in the first column of a new line. If newfile exists, by default it is overwritten.

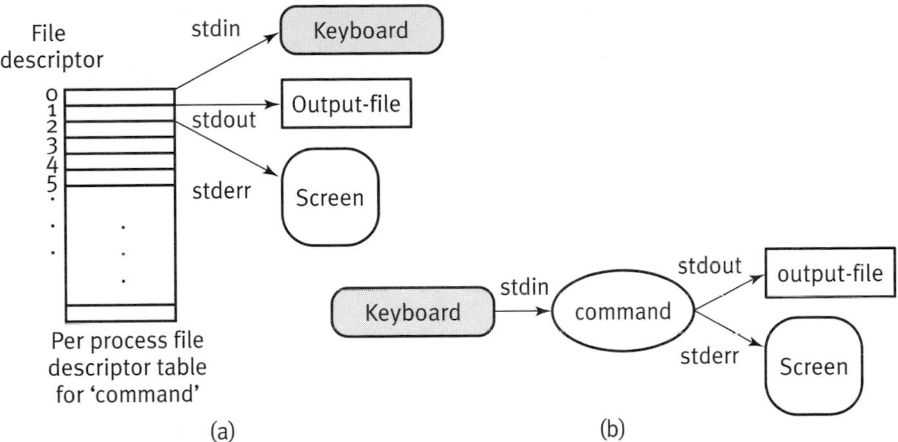


**Figure 12.3** Output redirection: (a) file descriptors and standard files for 'command'; (b) semantics of output redirection

Similarly, the command `grep "John" Phones > Phone_John` sends its output (lines in the Phones file that contain the word "John") to a file called Phone_John, as opposed to displaying it on the monitor screen. The input for the command comes from the Phones file. The command terminates when `grep` encounters the eof character in Phones.

In a network environment, the following command can be used to sort datafile, residing on the computer called the client, that you are currently logged onto on the computer called server. If your environment doesn't allow execution of the `rsh` (remote shell) command, you can try using the `ssh` (secure shell) command. Figure 12.4 illustrates the semantics of this command.

```
$ rsh server sort < datafile
$
```

This command is a good example of how multiple computers can be used to perform various tasks concurrently in a network environment. It is a useful command if your computer (call it client) has a large file, datafile, to be sorted and you don't want to make multiple copies of the file on various computers on the network to

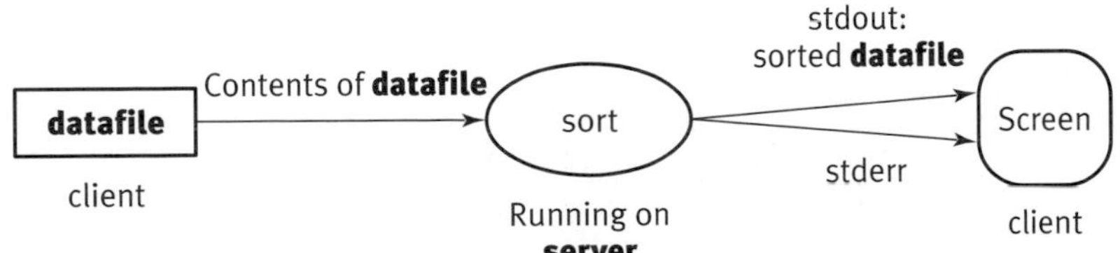


**Figure 12.4** Semantics of the `rsh server sort < datafile` command run on 'client'

prevent inconsistency in them. This command allows you to perform the task. Such commands also are useful if server has specialized LINUX tools that you are allowed to use but not allowed to make copies of on your machine. (See Chapter 14 for network-related LINUX commands and utilities.) We have used this example to illustrate the power of the LINUX I/O redirection feature, not to digress on computing in a network environment.

## 12.5 COMBINING INPUT AND OUTPUT REDIRECTION

Input and output redirections can be used together, according to the syntax given in the following command description.

Syntax: **command < input-file > output-file**
**command > output-file < input-file**

**Purpose:** Input to 'command' comes from input-file instead of the keyboard, and the output of 'command' goes to output-file instead of the display screen

When this syntax is used, 'command' takes its input from input-file (not from the keyboard attached to the terminal) and sends its output to output-file (not to the display screen), as shown in Figure 12.5.

In the command line `cat < lab1 > lab2`, the `cat` command takes its input from the lab1 file and sends its output to the lab2 file. The net effect of this command is that a copy of lab1 is created in lab2. Therefore this command line is equivalent to `cp lab1 lab2`, if lab2 does not exist. If lab2 is an existing file, the two commands have different semantics. The `cat < lab1 > lab2` command truncates lab2 (sets its size to zero and read/write pointer to the first byte position) and overwrites it by the contents of lab1. Because lab2 is not re-created, its attributes (e.g., access permissions and link count) aren't changed. In case of the `cp lab1 lab2` command, not only are the data in lab1 copied into lab2, but also

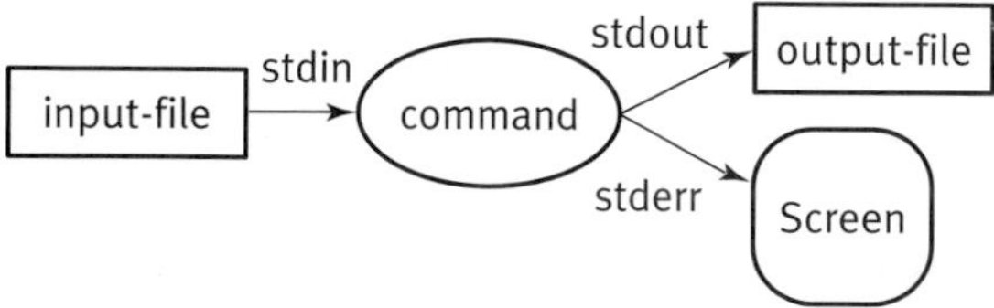


**Figure 12.5** Combined use of input and output redirection

its attributes from its inode are copied into the inode for lab2. Thus the **cp** command results in a true copy (data and attributes) of lab1 into lab2.

In the following In-Chapter Exercises, you will practice the use of input and output direction features of LINUX.

**IN-CHAPTER EXERCISES**

**12.1.** Write a shell command that counts the number of characters, words, and lines in a file called memo in your present working directory and shows these values on the display screen. Use input redirection.

**12.2.** Repeat Exercise 12.1, but redirect output to a file called counts.memo. Use I/O redirection.

## 12.6 I/O REDIRECTION WITH FILE DESCRIPTORS

As we described it in Section 7.7, the LINUX kernel associates a small integer number with every open file, called the file descriptor for the file. The file descriptors for standard input, standard output, and standard error are 0, 1, and 2, respectively. The Bash and POSIX shells allow you to open files and associate file descriptors with them; the TC shell doesn't allow the use of file descriptors. The other descriptors usually range from 3 through 19 and are called user-defined file descriptors. We discuss details of shell-based file I/O in Section 12.13. In the following sections, we describe I/O and error redirection under the Bash and POSIX shells. We discuss the TC shell syntaxes and give examples toward the end of this chapter under separate sections.

By making use of file descriptors, standard input and standard output can be redirected in the Bash and POSIX shells by using the `0<` and `1>` operators, respectively. Therefore, **cat 1> outfile**, which is equivalent to **cat > outfile**, takes input from standard input and sends it to outfile; error messages go to the display screen. Similarly, `ls -l foo 1> outfile` is equivalent to `ls -l foo > outfile`. The output of this command (the long listing for foo) goes into a file called outfile, and error messages generated by it go to the display screen.

The file descriptor 0 can be used as a prefix with the < operator to explicitly specify input redirection from a file. In the command shown, the input to the **grep** command is the contents of tempfile in the present working directory.

```
$ grep "John" 0< tempfile
... command output ...
$
```

## 12.7 REDIRECTING STANDARD ERROR

The standard error of a command can be redirected by using the 2> operator (associating the file descriptor for the standard error with the > operator) as follows.

Syntax:

**command 2> error-file**

**Purpose:** Error messages generated by 'command' and sent to stderr are redirected to error-file

With this syntax, 'command' takes its input from the keyboard, sends its output to the monitor screen, and any error messages produced by 'command' are sent to error-file. The semantics of the command syntax are shown in Figure 12.6. Command input may come from a file passed as a command line argument.

The command `grep "John" Phones 2> error.log` takes input from the Phones file, sends output to the display screen, and any error message produced by `grep` go to a file error.log. If error.log exists, it is overwritten; otherwise it is created. The following example shows how standard error of `ls -l` can be redirected to a file.

```
$ ls -l foo 2> error.log
... long listing for foo if no errors ...
$
```

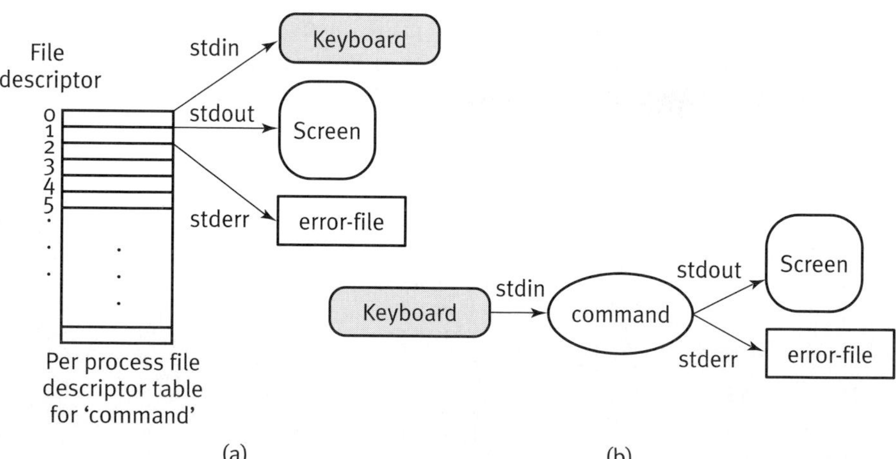


**Figure 12.6** Error redirection: (a) file descriptors and standard files for 'command'; (b) semantics of error redirection

The output of `ls -l foo` goes to the display screen, and error messages go to error.log. Thus, if foo does not exist, the error message `ls: foo: No such file or directory` goes into the error.log file, as shown.

```
$ ls -l foo 2> error.log
$ cat error.log
ls: foo: No such file or directory
$
```

Keeping standard error attached to the display screen and not redirected to a file is useful in many situations. For example, when the `cat lab1 lab2 lab3 > all` command is executed to concatenate files lab1, lab2, and lab3 into a file called all, you would want to know whether any of the three input files are nonexistent or you don't have permission to read any of them. In this case, redirecting the error message to a file doesn't make much sense because you want to see the immediate results of the command execution.

## 12.8 REDIRECTING stdout AND stderr IN ONE COMMAND

Standard output and standard error can be redirected to the same file. One obvious way to do so is to redirect stdout and stderr to the same file by using file descriptors with the > symbol, as in the following command. In this case, the input of the `cat` command comes from the lab1, lab2, and lab3 files, its output goes to the cat.output file, and any error message to the cat.errors file, as shown in Figure 12.7. Note that, although not shown in Figure 12.7(b), files lab1, lab2, and lab3 have file descriptors assigned to them when they are opened by the `cat` command for reading. The command produces an error message if any one of the three lab files doesn't exist or you don't have read permission for any file.

```
$ cat lab1 lab2 lab3 1> cat.output 2> cat.errors
$
```

The following command redirects stdout and stderr of the `cat` command to the cat.output.errors file. Thus the same file (cat.output.errors) contains the output of the `cat` command, along with any error messages that may be produced by the command.

```
$ cat lab1 lab2 lab3 1> cat.output.errors 2>&1
$
```

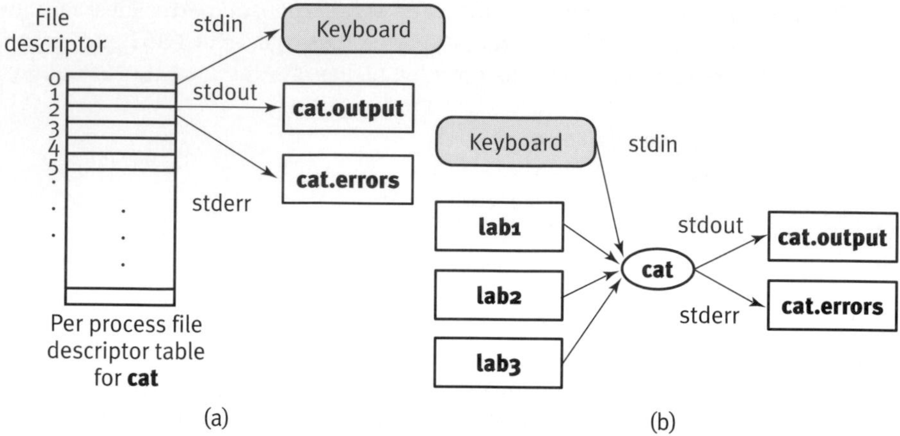


**Figure 12.7** Error redirection: (a) file descriptors and standard files for `cat lab1 lab2 lab3 1> cat.output 2> cat.errors` (b) semantics of the `cat` command

In this command, the string `2>&1` tells the command shell to make descriptor 2 a duplicate of descriptor 1, resulting in error messages going to the same place that the command output goes to. Similarly, the string `1>&2` can be used to tell the command shell to make descriptor 1 a duplicate of descriptor 2. Thus the following command accomplishes the same task. Figure 12.8 shows the semantics of the two commands.

```
$ cat lab1 lab2 lab3 2> cat.output.errors 1>&2
$
```

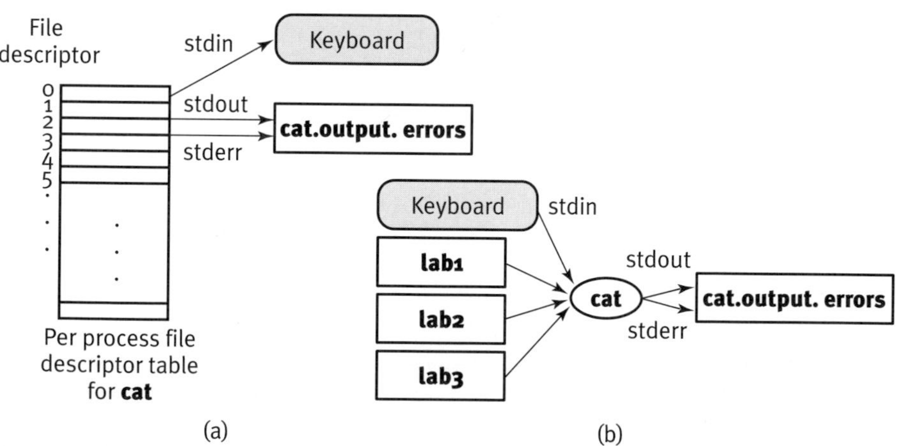


**Figure 12.8** Error redirection: (a) file descriptors and standard files (b) semantics of the `cat lab1 lab2 lab3 1> cat.output.errors 2>&1` and `cat lab1 lab2 lab3 2> cat.output.errors 1>&2` commands

The evaluation of the command line content for file redirection is left to right. Therefore redirections must be specified in left to right order if one notation is dependent on another. In the preceding command, first stderr is changed to the file cat.output.errors, and then stdout becomes a duplicate of stderr. Thus the output and errors for the command both go to the same file, cat.output.errors.

The following command therefore does *not* have the effect of the two commands just discussed. The reason is that, in this command, stderr is made a duplicate of stdout *before* output redirection. Therefore stderr becomes a duplicate of stdout (the display screen at this time) first and then stdout is changed to the file cat.output.errors. Thus the output of the command goes to cat.output.errors and errors go to the display screen. The sequence shown in Figure 12.9 illustrates the semantics of this command.

```
$ cat lab1 lab2 lab3 2>&1 1> cat.output.errors
$
```

## 12.9 REDIRECTING stdin, stdout, AND stderr IN ONE COMMAND

Standard input, standard output, and standard error can be redirected in a single command according to the following syntax.

Syntax:

**command 0< input-file 1> output-file 2> error-file**

**Purpose:** Input to 'command' comes from input-file instead of the keyboard, output of 'command' goes to output-file instead of the display screen, and error messages generated by 'command' are sent to error-file

The file descriptors 0 and 1 aren't required because they are the defaults values. The semantics of this command syntax are shown in Figure 12.10. Evaluation of the command line content for file redirection is left to right, so the order of redirection *is* important. Consider the following command syntaxes. For the first command, if input-file is not found, the error message is sent to the display screen because stderr hasn't been redirected yet. For the second command, if input-file is not found the error message goes to error-file because stderr has been redirected to this file.

The following `sort` command sorts lines in a file called students and stores the sorted file in students.sorted. If the `sort` command fails to start because the students file doesn't exist, the error message goes to the display screen, not to the

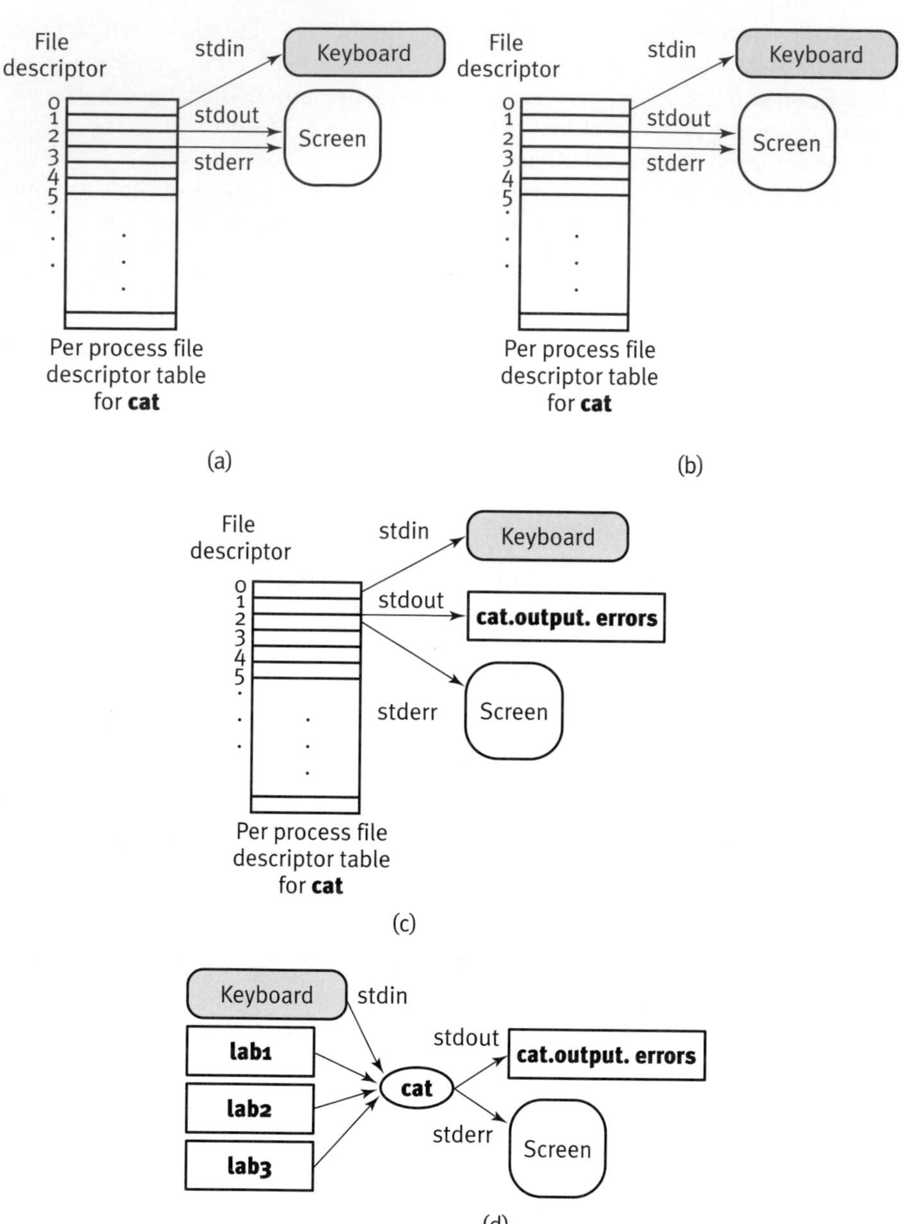


**Figure 12.9** Output and error redirection: (a) file descriptors and standard files for the `cat` command; (b) standard files after `cat lab1 lab2 lab3 2>&1`, with no change in stdout and stderr; (c) standard files after `cat lab1 lab2 lab3 2>&1 1> cat.output.errors`; and (d) command semantics

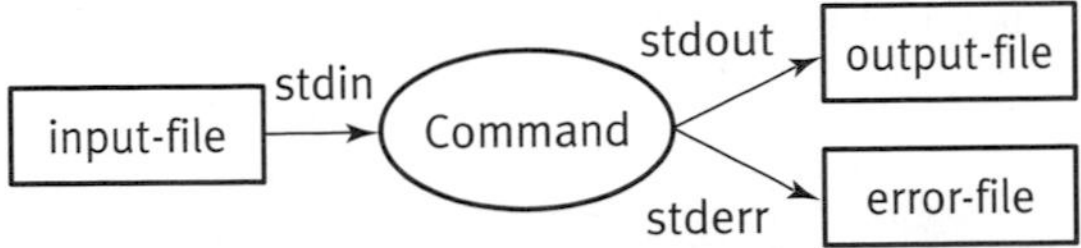


**Figure 12.10** Redirecting stdin, stdout, and stderr in a single command

file sort.error. The reason is that, at the time the shell determines that the students file doesn't exist, the stderr is still attached to the console.

```
$ sort 0< students 1> students.sorted 2> sort.error
$
```

For the following command, the error message goes to the sort.error file if the `sort` command fails because the students file doesn't exist. The reason is that the error redirection is processed by the shell before it determines that the students file is nonexistent.

```
$ sort 2> sort.error 0< students 1> students.sorted
$
```

## 12.10 REDIRECTING WITHOUT OVERWRITING FILE CONTENTS (APPENDING)

By default, output and error redirections overwrite contents of the destination file. To append output or errors generated by a command at the end of a file, replace the > operator with the >> operator. The default file descriptor with >> is 1, but file descriptor 2 can be used to append errors to a file. In the following command the output of `ls -l` is appended to the output.dat file, and the error messages are appended to the error.log file.

```
$ ls -l 1>> output.dat 2>> error.log
$
```

The following command appends contents of the files memo and letter at the end of the file stuff. If the command produces any error message, it goes to the error.log file. If error.log is an existing file, its contents are overwritten with the error message.

```
$ cat memo letter
>> stuff 2> error.log
$
```

If you want to keep the existing contents of error.log and append new error messages to it, use the following command. For this command the previous contents of error.log are appended with any error message produced by the `cat` command.

```
$ cat memo letter >> stuff 2>> error.log
$
```

The Bourne shell, by default, overwrites a file when stdout or stderr of a command is redirected to it, but the Bash, C, Korn, TC, and Z shells have a `noclobber` option that prevents you from overwriting important files accidentally. We discuss this option for the TC shell in Section 12.13, but discuss this option for Bash here.

You can set the `noclobber` option in Bash by using the `set` command with the `-o` option as shown. Of course, if you want to set this option permanently, put the command in your ~/.profile file.

```
$ set -o noclobber
$
```

You can also set the option by using the `set -C` command. When you set the `noclobber` option, you can force overwriting of a file by using the `>|` operator, as in `cat memo letter >| stuff 2>| error.log`. The append operator (>>) is not affected even if the destination file does not exist. You can allow file overwriting by executing the `set +o noclobber` command.

In the following In-Chapter Exercises, you will practice the use of input, output, and error redirection features of LINUX shells (excluding the TC shell) in a command line.

## IN-CHAPTER EXERCISES

**12.3.** Write a command that counts the number of characters, words, and lines in a file called memo in your present working directory and that writes these values into a file called memo.size. If the command fails, the error message should go to a file called error.log. Use I/O and error redirections.

## IN-CHAPTER EXERCISES

**12.4.** Write a shell command to send the contents of the file greetings to doe1@domain.com by using the `mail` command. If the `mail` command fails, the error message should go to a file called mail.errors. Use input and error redirection.

**12.5.** Repeat Exercise 12.4, but append error messages at the end of 'mail.errors'.

## 12.11 LINUX PIPES

The LINUX system allows stdout of a command to be connected to stdin of another command. You can make it do so by using the pipe character (|) according to the following syntax.

**command1 | command2 | command3 | ... | commandN**

**Purpose:** Standard output of 'command1' is connected to stdin of 'command2', stdout of 'command2' is connected to stdin of 'command3',..., and stdout of 'commandN-1' is connected to stdin of 'commandN'

Figure 12.11 illustrates the semantics of this command.

Thus a pipe allows you to send output of a command as input to another command. The commands that are connected via a pipe are called filters. A **filter** belongs to a class of LINUX commands that read input from stdin, process it in some specific fashion, and send it to stdout. Pipes and filters are frequently used in LINUX to perform complicated tasks that cannot be performed with a single command. Some commonly used filters are `cat`, `compress`, `crypt`, `grep`, `gzip`, `lp`, `pr`, `sort`, `tr`, `uniq`, and `wc`.

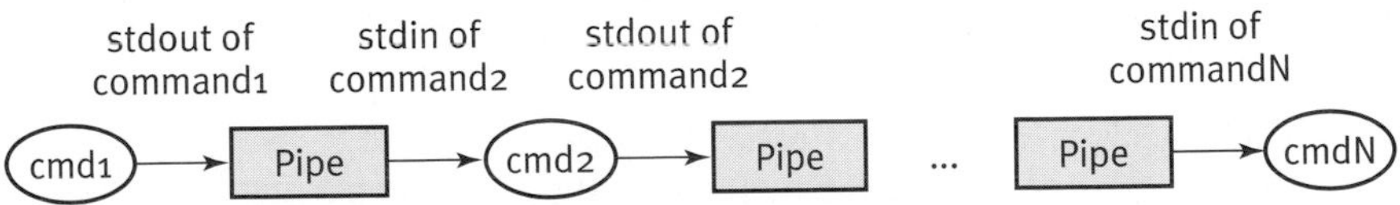


**Figure 12.11** The semantics of a pipeline with *N* commands

For example, in `ls -l | more`, the **more** command takes output of `ls -l` as its input. The net effect of this command is that the output of `ls -l` is displayed one screen at a time. The pipe really acts like a water pipe, taking output of `ls -l` and giving it to `more` as its input, as shown in Figure 12.12.

This command does not use disk to connect standard output of `ls -l` to standard input of `more` because the pipe is implemented in the main memory. In terms of the I/O redirection operators, the command is equivalent to the following sequence of commands.

```
$ ls -l > temp
$ more < temp (or more temp)
[contents of temp]
$ rm temp
$
```

Not only do you need three commands to accomplish the same task, the command sequence is also extremely slow because file read and write operations are involved. Recall that files are stored on a secondary storage device, usually a disk. On a typical contemporary computer system, disk operations are about 1 million times slower than main memory (RAM) operations! The actual performance gain in favor of pipes, however, is much smaller owing to efficient caching of file blocks by the LINUX kernel.

You can use the `sort` utility discussed in Chapter 10 to sort lines in a file. Suppose that you have a file called student_records, which you want to sort, but which may have some repeated lines that you want to appear only once in the sorted file. The `sort -u student_records` command can accomplish this task. As we discussed in Chapter 9, the `uniq` command can also do the task if it is given the sorted version of student_records with repeated lines in it. One way to do the task is to use the following commands. The `more` command is used to show the contents of student_records.

```
$ more student_records
John    Doe     ECE   3.54
Pam     Meyer   CS    3.61
Jim     Davis   CS    2.71
John    Doe     ECE   3.54
```

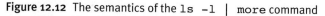

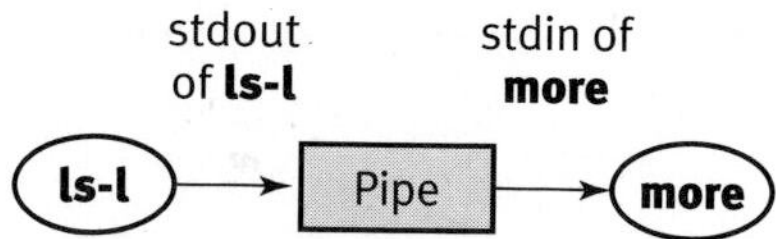


**Figure 12.12** The semantics of the `ls -l | more` command

```
Jason   Kim     ECE   3.97
Amy     Nash    ECE   2.38
$ sort student_records > student_records_sorted
$ uniq student_records_sorted
Amy     Nash    ECE   2.38
Jason   Kim     ECE   3.97
Jim     Davis   CS    2.71
John    Doe     ECE   3.54
Pam     Meyer   CS    3.61
$
```

The same task can be accomplished in one command line by using a pipe, as in

```
$ sort student_records | uniq
Amy     Nash    ECE   2.38
Jason   Kim     ECE   3.97
Jim     Davis   CS    2.71
John    Doe     ECE   3.54
Pam     Meyer   CS    3.61
$
```

The `sort student_records | uniq -u` command can be used to display norepeated lines in sorted order. At times you may need to connect several commands. The following command line demonstrates the use of multiple pipes, forming a pipeline of commands. In this command line, we have used the **grep** and **sort** filters.

```
$ who | sort | grep "John" | mail -S "John's Terminal" doe@coldmail.com
$
```

This command sorts the output of `who`, and sends the lines containing the string John (if any exist) as an e-mail message to doe@coldmail.com, with the subject line John's Terminal. In terms of input and output redirection, this command line is equivalent to the following command sequence.

```
$ who > temp1
$ sort < temp1 > temp2
$ grep "John" temp2 > temp3
$ mail -S "John's Terminal" doe@coldmail.com < temp3
```

```
$ rm temp1 temp2 temp3
$
```

The command with pipes doesn't use any disk files, but the preceding command sequence needs three temporary disk files and six disk I/O (read and write) operations. The number of I/O operations may be a lot more, depending on the size of these files, the system load in terms of number of users currently using the system, and the run-time behavior of other processes running on the system.

A pipe therefore is a LINUX feature that allows two LINUX commands (processes) to communicate with each other. Hence a pipe is also known as an interprocess communication (IPC) mechanism. More specifically, it allows two related processes on the same system to talk to each other. Typically, processes have a parent–child relationship, and communication between processes is one-way only. For example, in `ls | more`, the output of `ls` is read by `more` as input. Thus the one-way communication is from `ls` to `more`. For a two-way communication between processes, at least two pipes must be used. This cannot be accomplished at the command shell level, but it can be done in C/C++ by using the pipe( ) system call. Further discussion of this topic is beyond the scope of this book, but you can refer to any book on LINUX interprocess communication for more information.

I/O redirection and pipes can be used in a single command, as follows.

```
$ grep "John" < Students | lpr -Pspr
$
```

Here, the `grep` command searches the Students file for lines that contain the string John and sends those lines to the `lpr` command to be printed on a printer named spr. Figure 12.13 illustrates the semantics of this command.

In the following command, `egrep` takes its input from ee446.grades and sends its output (lines ending with the character A) to the `sort` utility, which sorts these lines and stores them in the file ee446.As.sorted. The end result is that the names, scores, and grades of all the students who have A grades in ECE446 are stored in the ee446.As.sorted file. Figure 12.14 illustrates the semantics of this command.

```
$ egrep 'A$' < ee446.grades | sort > ee446.As.sorted
$
```

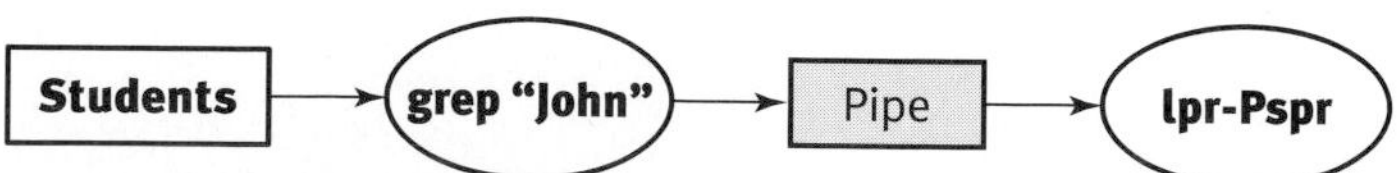


**Figure 12.13** The semantics of the `grep "John" < Students | lpr -Pspr` command

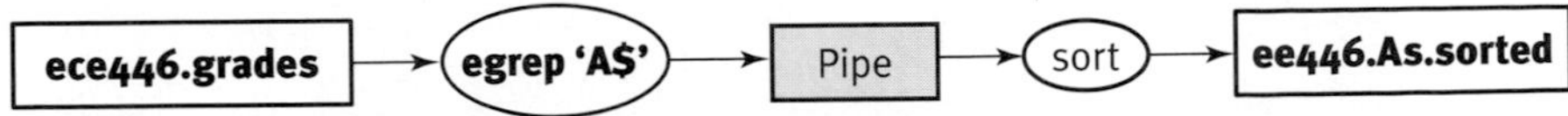


**Figure 12.14** The semantics of `egrep 'A$' < ee446.grades | sort > ee446.As.sorted`

Suppose that, before running the **`rsh server sort < datafile`** command in Section 12.3, you want to be sure that datafile on your local system is consistent with the updated copy on the server, called datafile.server. You can copy datafile.server and compare it with your local copy, datafile. But then you will have three copies, and if you aren't careful you may remove the wrong copy. In this case, you can run the following command to see the differences between your local copy and the copy on server without copying datafile.server to your (local) computer.

```
$ rsh server cat ~/research/pvm/datafile.server | diff datafile -
$
```

In this case, the `cat` command runs on the server, and its output is fed as input to the `diff` command executed on the local machine. The output of the `diff` command also goes to the display screen on the local machine. Figure 12.15 illustrates the semantics of this command.

## 12.12 REDIRECTION AND PIPING COMBINED

You can't use the redirection operators and pipes alone to redirect stdout of a command to a file and connect it to stdin of another command in a single command. However, you can use the `tee` utility to do so. You can use this utility to tell the command shell to send stdout of a command to one or more files, as well as to another command. The following is the syntax of the `tee` utility.

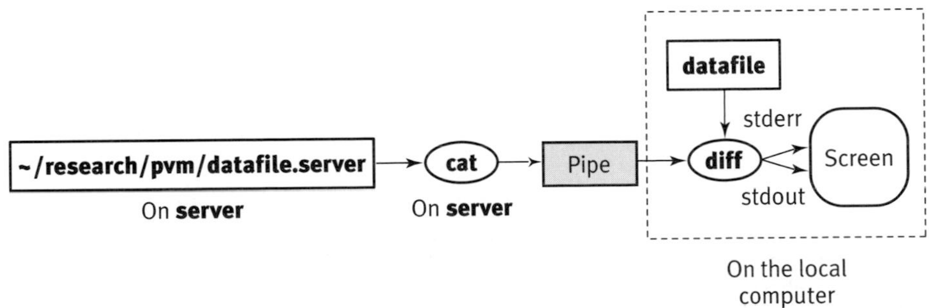


**Figure 12.15** The semantics of `rsh server cat ~/research/pvm/datafile.server | diff datafile -` command

Syntax:

**tee [options] file-list**

**Purpose:** Read standard input and send it to both standard output and to the files in file-list.

**Commonly used options/features:**

| | |
|---|---|
| `-a` | Append to files in file-list and not overwrite them |
| `-i` | Ignore interrupts (See Chapters 13 and 16) |

In the following example, the `tee` utility reads keyboard input and sends it to the display screen and to files file1 and file2. The contents of file1 and file2 are displayed by using the `cat` command.

```
$ tee file1 file2
This is a test of the tee command. This text will be displayed
This is a test of the tee command. This text will be displayed
on the screen as well as put into files file1 and file2.
on the screen as well as put into files file1 and file2.
<Ctrl-D>
$ cat file1
This is a test of the tee command. This text will be displayed
on the screen as well as put into files file1 and file2.
$ cat file2
This is a test of the tee command. This text will be displayed
on the screen as well as put into files file1 and file2.
$
```

The `tee` utility is commonly used to read output of another command via a pipe, instead of reading keyboard input. Also, the command output is saved in files in 'file-list' and redirected to another command instead of displaying it on the screen. Thus the following is the commonly used syntax of this utility.

Syntax: **command1 | tee file1 ... fileN | command2**

**Purpose:** Standard output of command1 is connected to stdin of `tee`, and `tee` sends its input to files file1 through fileN and as stdin of command2

The semantics of this command syntax are that command1 is executed and that its output is stored in files file1 through fileN and sent to command2 as its input. One use of the `tee` utility is given in the following command.

```
$ cat names students | grep "John Doe" | tee file1 file2 | wc -l
$
```

This command extracts the lines from the names and students files that contain the string John Doe, pipes these lines to the `tee` utility, which puts copies of these lines in file1 and file2, and sends them to `wc -l`, which sends its output to the display screen. Thus the lines in the names and students files that contain the string John Doe are saved in file1 and file2, and the line count of such lines is displayed on the monitor screen. Figure 12.16 illustrates the semantics of this command line. Such commands are useful in a shell script where different operations have to be performed on file1 and file2 later in the script.

## 12.13 ERROR REDIRECTION IN THE TC SHELL

The input, output, and append operators (<, >, >>) work in the TC shell as they do in other shells, as previously discussed. However, file descriptors cannot be used with these operators in the TC shell. Also, error redirection works differently in the TC shell than it does in other shells. In the TC shell, the operator for error redirection is `>&`. This operator can also be used in Bash.

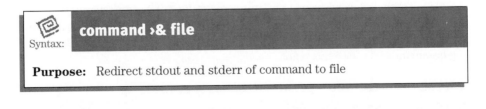

Syntax: **command >& file**

**Purpose:** Redirect stdout and stderr of command to file

For example, the following command redirects output and errors of the `ls -l foo` command to the error.log file. The standard input of the command is still

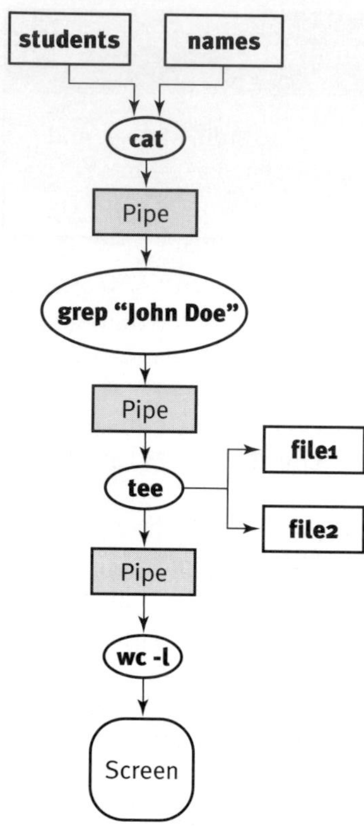


**Figure 12.16** The semantics of the `cat names students | grep "John Doe" | tee file1 file2 | wc -l` command

attached to the keyboard. (We have used the % sign as the shell prompt, which is the default for the TC shell.)

```
% ls -l foo >& error.log
%
```

The TC shell doesn't have an operator for redirecting stderr alone. However, stdout and stderr of a command may be attached to different files if the command is executed in a subshell (by enclosing the command in parentheses). The following commands illustrate this point.

```
% find ~ -name foo -print >& output.error.log
% (find ~ -name foo -print > foo.paths) >& error.log
%
```

All external shell commands are executed by the children of your current shell, also known as subshells (see Chapter 13). When the first command executes, the output and errors of the **find** command go to the output.error.log file. Because the subshell isn't created until the whole command line has been processed (interpreted), the stdout and stderr of the parent shell are redirected to the error.log file because of the **>&** operator. Therefore, the subshell also has its stdout and stderr redirected to the error.log file.

In the second command line, the **find** command is executed under a subshell and inherits the standard files of the parent shell. When the **find** command in parentheses executes, it redirects stdout of the command to the foo.paths file; the stderr of the command remains attached to error.log. Thus the output of the **find** command goes to the foo.paths file, and the errors generated by the command go to the error.log file. Figure 12.17 illustrates the semantics of the second **find** command. This feature is also available in Bash.

You can use the **>>&** operator to redirect and append stdout and stderr to a file. For example, **ls -l foo >>& output.error.log** redirects stdout and stderr of the **ls** command and appends them to the error.log file.

The TC shell also allows stdout and stderr of a command to be attached to the stdin of another command with the **|&** operator. The following is a brief description of this operator.

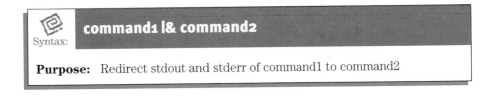

Syntax: **command1 |& command2**

**Purpose:** Redirect stdout and stderr of command1 to command2

In the following command, the stdout and stderr of the **cat** command are attached to the stdin of the **grep** command. Thus the output of the **cat** command, or any error produced by it (e.g., owing to no read permission for file1 or file2), is fed as input to the **grep** command.

```
% cat file1 file2 |& grep "John Doe"
%
```

The I/O redirection and piping operators (| and |&) can be used in a single command. This command is an extension of the previous command in which the stdout of the **grep** command is attached to the stdin of the **sort** command. Furthermore, the stdout and stderr of the **sort** command are attached to the stdin of the **wc -l** command. The command output is the number of lines in file1 and file2 that contain the string "John Doe".

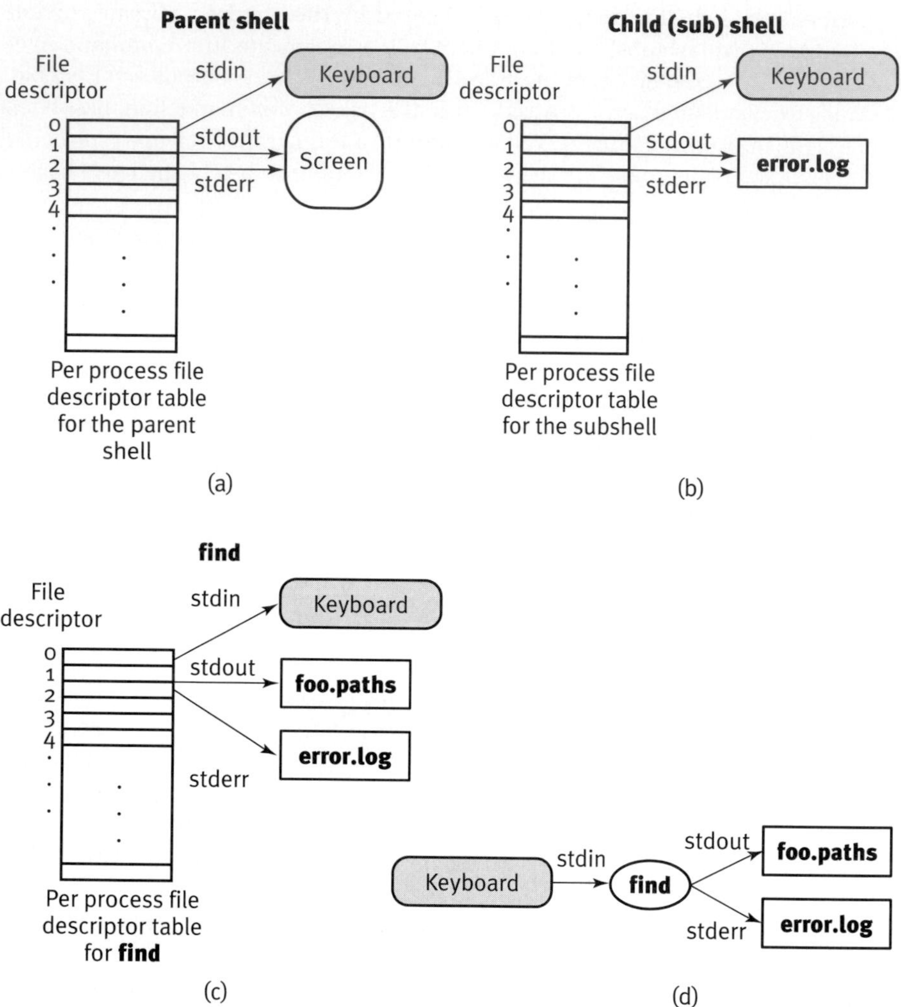


**Figure 12.17** Step-by-step semantics of the `(find ~ -name foo -print > foo.paths) >& error.log` command

```
% cat file1 file2 |& grep "John Doe" | sort |& wc -l
%
```

In the following In-Chapter Exercises, you will practice the use of LINUX pipes, the **tee** command, and the error redirection feature of TC shell.

The TC shell has a special built-in variable that allows you to protect your files from being overwritten with output redirection. This variable is called *noclobber* and, when set, prevents overwriting of existing files with output redi-

**IN-CHAPTER EXERCISES**

**12.6.** Write a shell command that sorts a file students.records and stores the lines containing Davis in a file called Davis.record. Use piping and I/O redirection.

**12.7.** Write a command to copy a file Scores to Scores.bak and send a sorted version of Scores to professor@university.edu via the `mail` command.

**12.8.** Write a TC shell command for copying a file Phones in your home directory to a file called Phones.bak (also in your home directory) by using the `cat` command and the `>&` operator.

rection. You can set the variable by using the `set` command and unset it by using the `unset` command.

```
% set noclobber
[your interactive session]
...
% unset noclobber
%
```

If the *`noclobber`* variable is set, the command `cat file1 > file2` generates an error message if file2 already exists. If file2 doesn't exist, it is created and file1 data are copied into it. The command `cat file1 >> file2` works fine if file2 exists and *`noclobber`* is set, but an error message is generated if file2 doesn't exist. You can use the `>!`, `>>!`, and `>>&!` operators to override the effect of the *`noclobber`* variable if it is set. Therefore, even if the *`noclobber`* variable is set and file2 exists, the command `cat file1 >! file2` copies data from file1 to file2. For the `cat file1 >>! file2` command, if the *`noclobber`* variable is set and file2 doesn't exist, file2 is created and file1 data are copied into it. The `>>&!` operator works in a manner similar to the `>>!` operator. The `cat file1 >> file2` command generates an error message if file2 does not exist.

## 12.14 RECAP OF I/O AND ERROR REDIRECTION

Table 12.1 summarizes the input, output, and error redirection operators in the Bash and TC shells. We did not discuss some of these operators in this chapter; we discuss them in detail in Chapters 15–19 under shell programming. We included these operators in this table because it seems to be the most appropriate place to show all of them together.

**Table 12.1** Redirection Operators and Their Meaning in Bash and TC Shells

| Operator | Bash Shell | TC Shell |
|---|---|---|
| < file | Input redirection from file | Input redirection |
| > file | Output redirection to file | Output redirection |
| >> file | Append standard output to file; create file if it does not exist | Append standard output |
| 0< file | Input redirection from file | |
| 1> file | Output redirection to file | |
| 2> file | Error redirection to file | |
| 1>> file | Append standard output to file | |
| 2>> file | Append standard error to file | |
| `<&m` | Attach standard input to file descriptor m | |
| `>&m` | Attach standard output to file with descriptor m | |
| `m>&n` | Attach file descriptor m to file descriptor n | |
| `<&-` | Close standard input | |
| `>&-` | Close standard output | |
| `m<&-` or `m>&-` | Close file descriptor m | |
| `>&` file | Output and error redirection to file | Output and error redirection to file |
| >\| file | Ignore *noclobber* and assign standard output to file | |
| `>!` file | | Ignore *noclobber* and assign standard output to file |
| `>>!` file | | Ignore *noclobber* and append standard output to file; if file does not exist, create it |
| n>\| file | Ignore *noclobber* and force output from file descriptor n to file | |
| <> file | Assign standard input and standard output to file | |

**Table 12.1** *(continued)*

| Operator | Bash Shell | TC Shell |
|---|---|---|
| n< file | Set file as file descriptor n | |
| n> file | Direct file descriptor n to file | |
| >>&! file | | Ignore `noclobber` and append standard output and standard error to file; create file if it does not exist |
| cmd1 \| cmd2 | Connect standard output of command 'cmd1' to standard input of command 'cmd2' | Connect standard output of command 'cmd1' to standard input of command 'cmd2' |
| cmd1 \|& cmd2 | | Connect standard output and standard error of command 'cmd1' to standard input of command 'cmd2' |
| (cmd > `file1`) >& file2 | | Redirect standard output of the 'cmd' command to file1 and standard error to file2 |

## SUMMARY

LINUX automatically opens three files for every command for it to read input from and send its output and error messages to. These files are called standard input (stdin), standard output (stdout), and standard error (stderr). By default, these files are attached to the terminal on which the command is executed. Thus the shell makes the command input come from the keyboard, and its output and error messages to go to the monitor screen. These default files can be changed to other files by using redirection operators: < for input redirection, and > for output, and error redirection.

The stdin, stdout, and stderr can be referred to by using the integers 0, 1, and 2, called file descriptors for the three standard files, respectively. All open files in LINUX are referred to by similar integers that are used by the kernel to perform operations on these files. In the Bash and POSIX shells the greater-than symbol (>) is used in conjunction with descriptors 1 and 2 to redirect standard output and standard error, respectively.

The standard output of a command can be connected to the standard input of another command via a LINUX pipe. Pipes are created in the main memory and are used to take output of a command and give it to another command without creating a disk file, effectively making two commands talk to each other. For this reason, a pipe is called an interprocess communication (IPC) mechanism, which allows related commands on the same machine to communicate with each other at the shell and application levels.

The I/O and error redirection features and pipes can be used together to implement powerful command lines. However, redirection operators and pipes alone cannot be used to redirect standard output of a command to a file, as well as connect it to standard input of another command. The `tee` utility can be used to accomplish this task, sending standard output of a command to one or more files and to another command.

The TC shell does not support I/O and error redirection with file descriptors. Also, redirecting standard output and standard error of a command to different files is specified differently in the TC shell than it is in the other shells.

## PROBLEMS

1. What are standard files? Name them and state their purpose.
2. Briefly describe input, output, and error redirection. Write two commands of each to show simple and combined use of the redirection operators.
3. What are file descriptors in LINUX? What are the file descriptors of standard file? How can the I/O and error redirection operators be combined with the file descriptors of standard files to perform redirection in the Bash and POSIX shells?
4. Sort a file data1 and put the sorted file in a file called data1.sorted. Give the command that uses both input and output redirection.
5. Give the command to accomplish the task in Problem 4 by using a pipe and output redirection.
6. Give a set of commands, equivalent to the command `ls -l | grep "sarwar" > output.p3`, that use I/O redirection operators only. How does the performance of the given command compare with your command sequence? Explain.
7. What is the purpose of the `tee` command? Give a command equivalent to the command in Problem 6 that uses the `tee` command.
8. Write LINUX shell commands to carry out the following tasks.
   a. Count the number of characters, words, and lines in the file called data1 and display the output on the display screen.
   b. Count the number of characters, words, and lines in the output of the `ls -l` command and display the output on the display screen.
   c. Repeat part (b), but redirect the output to a file called data1.stats.
9. Give the command for searching a file datafile for the string Internet, sending the output of the command to a file called Internet.freq and any error message to a file error.log. Draw a diagram for the command, similar to the ones shown in the chapter, to illustrate its semantics.

10. Give a command for accomplishing the task in Problem 9, sending both the output of the command and any error message to a file called datafile.

11. Give a command to search for lines in /etc/passwd that contain the string sarwar. Store the output of the command in a file called passwd.sarwar in your current directory. If the command fails, the error message must also go to the same file.

12. What is the LINUX pipe? How is pipe different from output redirection? Give an example to illustrate your answer.

13. What do the following commands do under Bash?
    a. `cat 1> letter 2> save 0< memo`
    b. `cat 2> save 0< memo 1> letter`
    c. `cat 1> letter 0< memo 2>&1`
    d. `cat 0< memo | sort 1> letter 2> /dev/null`
    e. `cat 2> save 0< memo | sort 1> letter 2> /dev/null`

14. Consider the following commands under the Bourne shell.
    i. `cat memo letter 2> communication 1>&2`
    ii. `cat memo letter 1>&2 2> communication`

    Where do output and error messages of the **`cat`** command go in each case if
    a. both files (memo and letter) exist in the present working directory, and
    b. one of the two files doesn't exist in the present working directory?

15. Send an e-mail message to doe@domain.com, using the **`mail`** command. Assume that the message is in a file called greetings. Give one command that uses input redirection and one that uses a pipe. Any error message should be appended to a file mail.error.

16. What happens when the following commands are executed on your LINUX system? Why do these commands produce the results that they do?
    a. `cat letter >> letter`
    b. `cat letter > letter`

17. By using output redirection, send a greeting message "Hello, World!" to a friend's terminal.

18. Give a command for displaying the number of users currently logged onto a system.

19. Give a command for displaying the login name of the user who was the first to log on to a system.

20. What is the difference between the following commands?
    a. `grep "John Doe" Students > /dev/null 2>&1`
    b. `grep "John Doe" Students 2>&1 > dev/null`

21. Give a command for displaying the contents of (the files names in) the current directory, three files per line.

22. Give a command that reads its input from a file called Phones, removes unnecessary spaces from the file, sorts the file, and removes duplicate lines from it.
23. Repeat Problem 22 for a version of the file that has unnecessary spaces removed from the file but still has duplicate lines in it.
24. What do the following commands do under the Bash and TC shells?
    a. `uptime | cat - who.log >> system.log`
    b. `zcat secret_memo.Z | head -5`
    c. `ls -l foo >| foobar 2>&1`
25. Give a command that performs the task of the following command except that the `diff` command runs on the machine called 'server'.
    `rsh server cat ~/research/pvm/datafile.server | diff datafile -`
26. Give a command for displaying the lines in a file called employees that are not repeated. What is the command for displaying repeated lines only?
27. Give a command that displays a long list for the most recently created directory.

CHAPTER

# 13

# Processes

**OBJECTIVES**

- To describe the concept of a process and execution of multiple processes on a computer system with a single CPU
- To explain how a shell executes commands
- To discuss process attributes
- To explain the concept of foreground and background processes and explain what a daemon is
- To describe sequential and parallel execution of commands
- To discuss process and job control in LINUX: foreground and background processes, sequential and parallel processes, suspending processes, moving foreground processes into background and vice versa, and terminating processes
- To describe the LINUX process hierarchy
- To cover the commands and primitives `<Ctrl-C>`, `<Ctrl-D>`, `<Ctrl-Z>`, `<Ctrl-\>`, `;`, `&`, `( )`, `bg`, `fg`, `jobs`, `kill`, `limit`, `nice`, `nohup`, `ps`, `pstree`, `sleep`, `suspend`, `top`, `ulimit`

## 13.1 INTRODUCTION

As we have mentioned before, a process is a program in execution. The LINUX system creates a process every time you run an external command, and the process is removed from the system when the command finishes its execution. Process creation and termination are the only mechanisms used by the LINUX system to execute external commands. In a typical time-sharing system such as LINUX, which allows multiple users to use a computer system and run multiple processes simultaneously, hundreds and thousands of processes are created and terminated every day. Remember that the CPU in the computer executes processes and that a typical system has only one CPU. The question is: How does a system with a single CPU execute multiple processes simultaneously? A detailed discussion of this topic is beyond the scope of this textbook, but we briefly address it in Section 13.2. Later in the chapter, we discuss foreground and background processes, daemons, jobs, process and job attributes, and process and job control.

## 13.2 RUNNING MULTIPLE PROCESSES SIMULTANEOUSLY

On a typical computer system that contains a single CPU and runs a time-sharing operating system, multiple processes are simultaneously executed by quickly switching the CPU from one process to the next. That is, one process is executed for a short period of time, and then the CPU is taken away from it and given to another process. The new process executes for a short period of time and then the CPU is given to the next process. This procedure continues until the first process in the sequence gets to use the CPU again. The time a process is "in" the CPU burst before it is switched "out" of the CPU is called a **quantum**. The quantum is usually very short: 100 msec for a typical LINUX system. When the CPU is free (not used by any process), the kernel uses an algorithm to decide which process gets to use the CPU next. The technique used to choose the process that gets to use the CPU is called **CPU scheduling**.

In a time-sharing system, a priority value is assigned to every process, and the process that has the highest priority gets to use the CPU next. Several methods can be used to assign a priority value to a process. One simple method is based on the time that it enters the system. In this scheme, typically, the process that enters the system first is assigned the highest priority; the result is called a **first-come, first-serve (FCFS) scheduling algorithm**. Another scheme is to assign a priority value based on the amount of time a process has used the CPU. Thus a newly arriving process, or a process that spends most of its time performing input and/or output (I/O) operations, gets the highest priority. Processes that spend most of their time performing I/O are known as **I/O-bound processes**. An example of an I/O-bound process is a text editor such as `vi`. Another method, in which a process gets to use the CPU for one quantum and then the CPU is given to another process, is known as the **round robin (RR) scheduling algorithm**. This algorithm is a natural choice for time-sharing systems, wherein all users like to see progress by their processes. If you're interested in the other CPU scheduling algorithms, we encourage you to read a book on operating system principles and concepts. The operating system code that implements the CPU scheduling algorithm is known as the **processor scheduler**. The scheduler for most operating systems, including LINUX, is in the kernel.

The LINUX scheduling algorithm is a blend of all of the algorithms mentioned. It uses a simple formula to assign a priority to every process in the system that is ready to run. The priority for every process in the system is recalculated periodically. When it is time for scheduling, the CPU is given to the process with the *highest* priority. If multiple processes have the same priority, the decision is made on the FCFS basis. LINUX favors processes that have used less CPU time in the recent past. A text editor such as `vi` gets higher priority than a process that computes the value of pi ($\pi$) because `vi` spends most of the time doing I/O (reading keyboard input and displaying it on the screen), and the process that computes $\pi$ spends most of its time doing calculations (using the CPU). Recalculating priority values of all the processes periodically causes process priorities to change dynamically (up and down).

## 13.3 LINUX PROCESS STATES

A LINUX process can be in one of many **states**, as it moves from one state to another, eventually finishing its execution (normally or abnormally) and getting out of the system. A process terminates normally when it finishes its work and exits the system gracefully. A process terminates abnormally when it exits the system because of an exception (error) condition or intervention by its owner or the superuser. The owner of the process can intervene by using a command or a particular keystroke to terminate the process. We discuss these commands and keystrokes later in the chapter. The primary states that a process can be in are shown in the state diagram in Figure 13.1.

The waiting state encompasses several states; we used the term here to keep the diagram simple. Some of the states belonging to the waiting state are listed under the oval representing the state. Table 13.1 gives a brief description of these LINUX process states. The other states that a LINUX process can be in aren't included in this discussion for brevity, as well as the level of coverage of this textbook.

## 13.4 EXECUTION OF SHELL COMMANDS

A shell command can be internal or external. An **internal (built-in) command** is one whose code is part of the shell process. Some of the internal commands

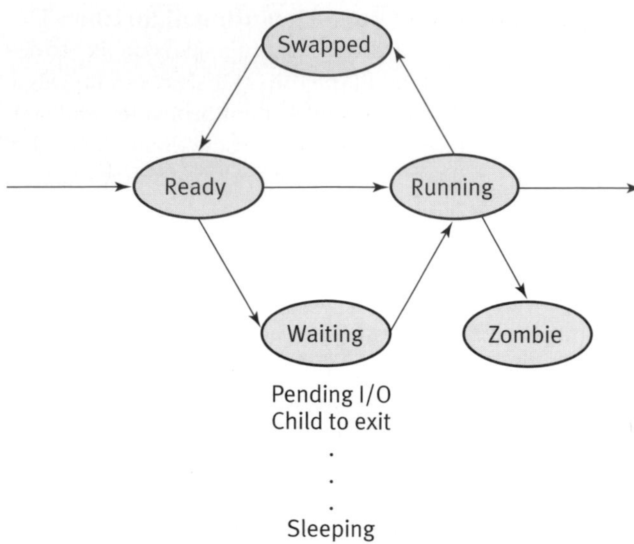


**Figure 13.1** LINUX process state diagram

common in LINUX shells are **.** (dot command), **alias**, **bg**, **cd**, **continue**, **echo**, **exec**, **exit**, **fg**, **jobs**, **pwd**, **set**, **shift**, **test**, **time**, **umask**, **unset**, and **wait**. An **external command** is one whose code is in a file; contents of the file can be binary code or a shell script. Some of the commonly used external commands are **grep**, **more**, **cat**, **mkdir**, **rmdir**, **ls**, **sort**, **ftp**, **telnet**, **lp**, and **ps**. A shell creates a new process to execute a command. While the command process executes, the shell waits for it to finish. In this section we describe how a shell (or any process) creates another process and how external commands are executed by the shell.

A LINUX process can create another process by using the fork system call, which creates an exact main memory copy of the original process. Both processes continue execution, starting with the statement that follows 'fork'. The forking process is known as the **parent process**, and the created (forked) process is called the **child process**, as shown in Figure 13.2. Here, we show a Bash shell that has created a child process (another Bash shell).

For executing an external binary command, a mechanism is needed that allows the child process to become the command to be executed. The LINUX system call exec can be used to do exactly that, allowing a process to overwrite itself with the executable code for another command. A shell uses the fork and exec calls in tandem to execute an external binary command. The sequence of events for the execution of an external command **sort** (whose code is in a binary file) are given in Figure 13.3.

**Table 13.1** A Brief Description of the LINUX Process States

| State | Description |
|---|---|
| Ready | The process is ready to run but doesn't have the CPU. Based on the scheduling algorithm, the scheduler decided to give the CPU to another process. Several processes can be in this state, but on a machine with a single CPU, only one can be executing (using the CPU). |
| Running | The process is actually running (using the CPU). |
| Waiting | The process is waiting for an event. Possible events are an I/O (e.g., disk/terminal read or write) is completed, a child process exits (parent waits for one or more of its children to exit), or the sleep period expires for the process. |
| Swapped | The process is ready to run, but it has been temporarily put on the disk (on the swap space); perhaps it needs more memory and there isn't enough available at this time. |
| Zombie | When the parent of a process terminates before it executes the exit call, it becomes a zombie process. The process finishes and finds that the parent isn't waiting. The zombie processes are finished for all practical purposes and don't reside in the memory, but they still have some kernel resources allocated to them and can't be taken out of the system. All zombies (and their live children) are eventually adopted by the granddaddy, the init process, which removes them from the system. In general, any dying process is said to be in the zombie state. |

The execution of a shell script (a series of shell commands in a file; see Chapters 15–18) is slightly different from the execution of a binary file. In the case of a shell script, the current shell creates a child shell and lets the child shell execute commands in the shell script, one by one. Each command in the script file is executed in the same way that commands from the keyboard are—that is, the child shell creates a child for every command that it executes. While the child shell is executing commands in the script file, the parent shell waits for the child to terminate. When the child shell hits the eof marker in the script file, it terminates.

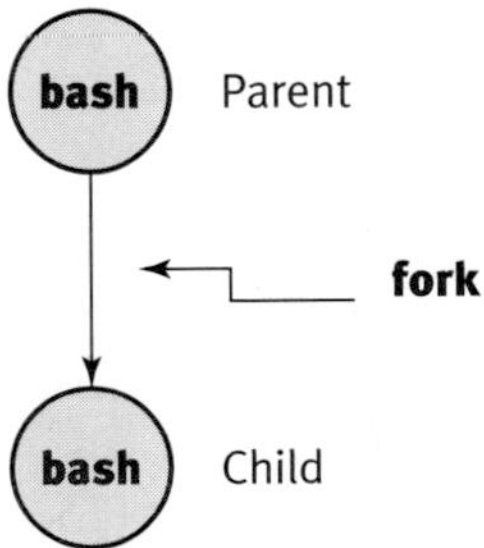


**Figure 13.2** Process creation via the fork system call

**Step 1:** Shell uses **fork** to create a child

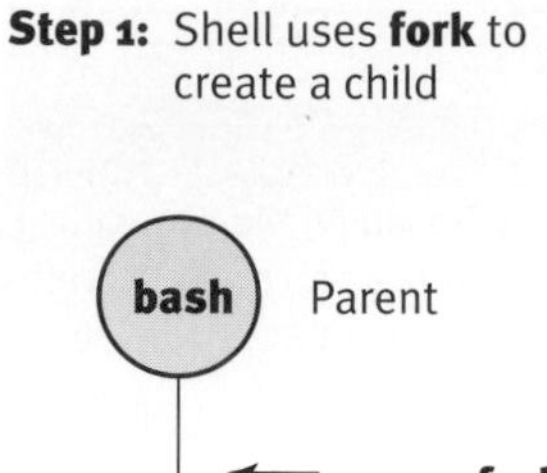


**Step 2:** Child uses **exec** to overwrite itself with the executable file corresponding to the **sort** command.

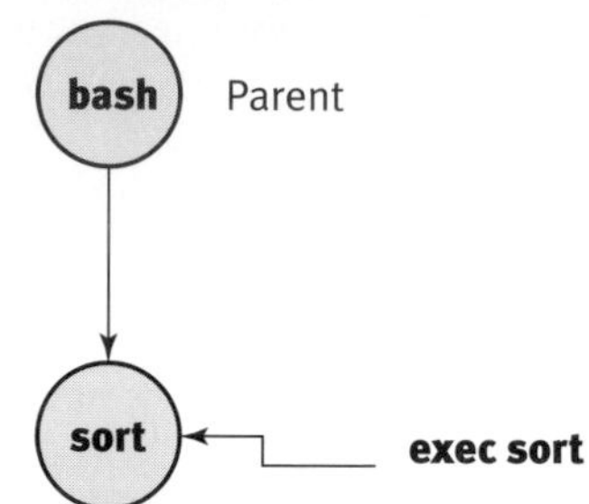

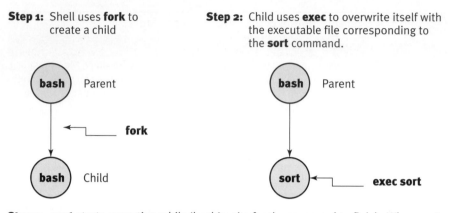

**Step 3:** **sort** starts execution while 'bash' waits for the command to finish. When **sort** finishes, the child process terminates and 'bash' starts execution again, waiting for the user to give it another command to execute.

**Figure 13.3** Steps for execution of a binary program `sort` by a LINUX shell

The only purpose of the child shell (like any other shell) is to execute commands, and eof means no more commands. When the child shell terminates, the parent shell comes out of the waiting state and resumes execution. This sequence of events is shown in Figure 13.4, which also shows the execution of a `find` command in the script file.

Unless otherwise specified in the file containing the shell script, the child shell has the type of the parent shell. That is, if the parent is a Bash, the child is also a Bash. Thus by default the shell script is executed by a "copy" of the parent shell. However, shell script written for any shell (Bash, TC, Z, etc.) can be executed regardless of the type of the current shell. To do so, simply specify the type of the child shell (under which the script should be executed) in the first line of the file containing the shell script as `#!full-pathname-of-the-shell`. For example, the following line dictates that the child shell is TC shell, so the script following this line is executed under the TC shell.

```
#!/bin/tcsh
```

Also, you can execute commands in another shell by running that shell as a child of the current shell, executing commands under it, and terminating the shell. A child shell is also called a **subshell**. Recall that the commands to run

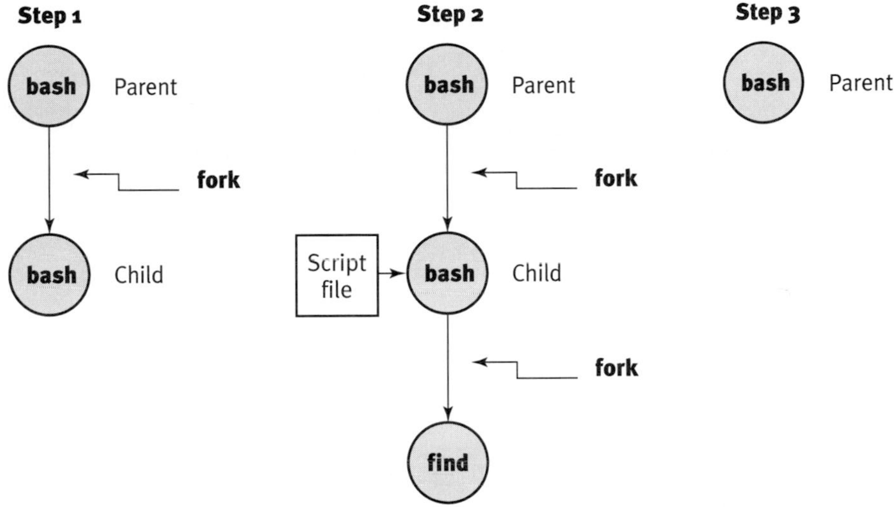


**Figure 13.4** Steps for execution of a shell script by a LINUX shell

various shells are `bash` for the Bourne Again shell, `tcsh` for the TC shell, and `zsh` for the Z shell. To start a new shell process, simply run the command corresponding to the shell you want to run. In the following session, the current shell is the TC shell and the Bash shell runs as its child. The `echo` command is executed under the Bash shell. Then a Z shell is started, and the `echo` command is executed under it. The `ps` command shows the three shells running. Finally, both the Z and Bash shells are terminated when <Ctrl-D> is pressed in succession, and control goes back to the original shell, the TC shell. The first <Ctrl-D> terminates the Z shell, giving control back to the Bash shell. Figure 13.5 illustrates all the steps involved, showing the parent–child relationship between processes.

```
% ps
  PID TTY          TIME CMD
12675 pts/0    00:00:00 tcsh
12695 pts/0    00:00:00 ps
% bash
$ echo This is Bourne Again shell
This is Bourne Again shell
$ zsh
[~]-% echo This is Z shell
```

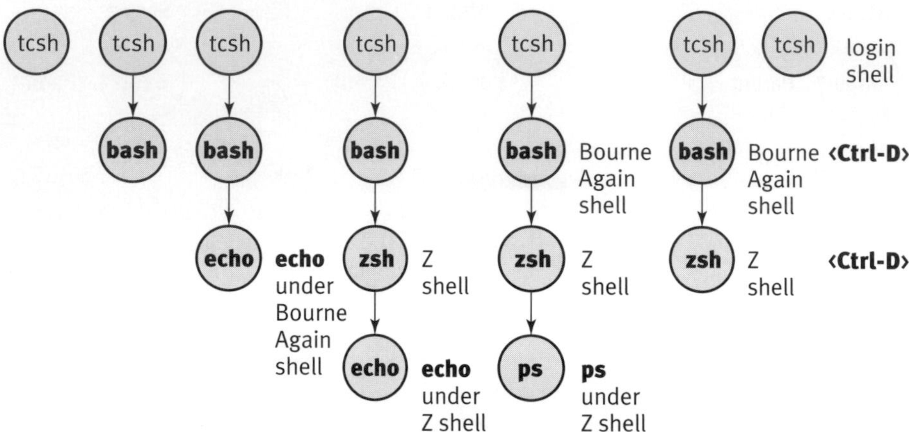


**Figure 13.5** Execution of commands under the child shells (also called subshells)

```
This is Z shell
[~]-% ps
  PID TTY          TIME CMD
12675 pts/0    00:00:00 tcsh
12696 pts/0    00:00:00 bash
12697 pts/0    00:00:00 zsh
12704 pts/0    00:00:00 ps
[~]-% <Ctrl-D>
$ <Ctrl-D>
%
```

## 13.5 PROCESS ATTRIBUTES

Every LINUX process has several attributes, including owner's ID, process name, process ID (PID), process state, PID of the parent process, and length of time the process has been running. From the user's point of view, one of the most useful of these attributes is the PID, which is used as a parameter in several process control commands (discussed later in this chapter). The `ps` command can be used to view the attributes of processes running on a system.

The LINUX `ps` command accepts options for the System V, BSD, and GNU versions of the `ps` command. The System V options may be grouped and must be preceded by a dash; the BSD options may also be grouped and must not be preceded by a dash; and the GNU options are preceded by two dashes. The options of different types may be mixed. The following is a brief description of the **ps** command. We do not discuss the GNU options, but the interested user can use the **man ps** command to see the GNU options.

Syntax:

**ps [options]**

**Purpose:** Report process status
**Output:** Attributes of process running on the system

**Commonly used options/features:**

*System V Options*

| | |
|---|---|
| `-N` | Negate selection |
| `-a` | Display information about all the processes executing on the terminal, including those of other users |
| `-e/-A` | Display information about all the processes running on the system |
| `-j` | Display information in job control format (include parent PID, group ID, session ID, etc.) |
| `-l` | Display long list of the status report |
| `-p` | Display information by process ID |
| `-u ulist` | Display information about processes belonging to the users with the UIDs or user names in ulist (UIDs or user names separated by commas) |
| `-t tlist` | Select processes on teminals is tlist; without the tlist argument, output of the ps command without argument is displayed |

*BSD Options*

| | |
|---|---|
| `U ulist` | Display information about processes belonging to the users with the UIDs or user names in ulist (UIDs or user names separated by commas) |
| `a` | Display information about all the processes executing on the terminal, including those of other users |
| `e` | Display information about all the processes running on the system |
| `f` | Display process hierarchy in ASCII-art form |
| `j` | Display information in job control format (include parent PID, group ID, session ID, etc.) |
| `l` | Display long list of the status report |
| `p` | Display information by process ID |
| `t tlist` | Select processes on teminals in tlist; without the tlist argument, output of the **ps** command without argument is displayed |
| `x` | Select processes without controlling TTYs |

The following sessions demonstrate use of the **ps** command with and without options. The output of the **ps** command shows four fields when executed without options. The output shows that five processes are attached to the terminal: pts/2: tcsh (a TC shell), bash (a Bourne Again shell), pine (e-mail software), banner, and ps, belonging to the user who ran the command. The PIDs of tcsh, bash, pine, banner, and ps are 7628, 7666, 7828, 7829, and 7830, respectively. The tcsh process, the first one in the list and the one with the smallest PID, is called the **session leader** process (i.e., your login shell process); all other processes created in this session are its children or grandchildren. Under LINUX, the execution of a shell process starts a **session** and the processes that execute under it are the components of this session. Each session is assigned a session identifier (SID) and the processes in a session have the same SID. Furthermore, **banner** has run for 33 seconds.

```
$ ps
  PID TTY          TIME CMD
 7628 pts/2    00:00:00 tcsh
 7666 pts/2    00:00:00 bash
 7828 pts/2    00:00:00 pine
 7829 pts/2    00:00:33 banner
 7830 pts/2    00:00:00 ps
$
```

You can use the **a** (or **–a**) option to display all the processes associated with your terminal. The following output of the **ps a** command shows an additional process, the login process, which is executed whenever you log on; your login shell (**tcsh**) is a child of this process. The session leader process is tagged with a dash (**-**) in front of it (**–tcsh** in the following example). Furthermore, the output of the command has an additional column that shows the execution status of each process. The possible status values and their meaning are shown in Table 13.2. In the following example, the first three processes are sleeping, the **pine** process has stopped, and the **banner** and **ps a** processes are runnable (on a computer with a single CPU, one of them is actually running and the other is waiting for the CPU to be assigned to it).

```
$ ps a
  PID TTY      STAT   TIME COMMAND
 7627 pts/2    S      0:00 login -- sarwar
 7628 pts/2    S      0:00 -tcsh
 7666 pts/2    S      0:00 bash
 7828 pts/2    T      0:00 pine
```

**Table 13.2** Some Process States and Their Meaning

| Process State | Meaning |
|---|---|
| D | Uninterruptible sleep (usually doing I/O or waiting for it) |
| N | Low-priority process (a process that has been niced) |
| R | Runnable process: waiting to be scheduled to use CPU |
| S | Sleeping |
| T | Traced or stopped |
| Z | A zombie (defunct) process |
| W | A process that is completely swapped on the disk (no resident pages) |

```
 7829 pts/2  R      0:41 banner
 7831 pts/2  R      0:00 ps a
$
```

You can use the **-r** option to display information about the processes that are currently in the runnable state, as follows:

```
$ ps -r
  PID TTY     STAT  TIME COMMAND
 7829 pts/2  R      1:53 banner
 7832 pts/2  R      0:00 ps -r
$
```

You can use the **-u** option to display the status of all the processes belonging to the users with user IDs in ulist specified after the option, as follows. In this case all the processes belonging to the user with UID 127 are displayed.

```
$ ps -u 127
  PID TTY          TIME CMD
 7505 pts/0    00:00:00 csh
 7539 pts/0    00:00:01 pine
$
```

You can use the **-e**, **-A**, or **e** option to select all the processes on the system. In the following example, we use the **-e** option to perform this task. Note that the init process has the PID 1, the smallest of all the processes on the system. This is the first user process created on a LINUX system when the system is booted and is the granddaddy of all user processes. The ? character under the TTY field means that the process is not associated with any terminal.

```
$ ps -e | more
  PID TTY    TIME     CMD
    1 ?      00:00:03 init
    2 ?      00:00:00 kflushd
    3 ?      00:00:00 kupdate
    4 ?      00:00:00 kpiod
    5 ?      00:00:00 kswapd
  250 ?      00:00:00 portmap
 ...
 7626 ?      00:00:00 in.telnetd
 7627 pts/2 00:00:00 login
 7628 pts/2 00:00:00 tcsh
 7666 pts/2 00:00:00 bash
 7828 pts/2 00:00:00 pine
 7829 pts/2 00:02:36 banner
 7833 pts/2 00:00:00 ps
 7834 pts/2 00:00:00 more
$
```

You can use the `-j` (or `j`) option to display job control–related information about the processes on your system. In the following session, the `ps -j` command is used to display such information about your processes under the current session. PGID is the group ID of a process (same as PID) and SID is the session ID (whenever you log on, LINUX assigns you a new and unique session ID that remains the same until you log out). Additional information about processes, including parent process IDs and process states, can be displayed by using the `j` option (instead of the `-j` option). The second command is used to display information about kent's processes in job control format.

```
$ ps -j
  PID PGID  SID TTY          TIME CMD
 7628 7628 7627 pts/2   00:00:00 tcsh
 7666 7666 7627 pts/2   00:00:00 bash
 7828 7828 7627 pts/2   00:00:00 pine
 7829 7829 7627 pts/2   00:05:08 banner
 7842 7842 7627 pts/2   00:00:00 ps
```

```
$ ps j U kent
 PPID PID  PGID SID  TTY   TPGID STAT  UID TIME COMMAND
 5679 5680 5680 5679 pts/0  5680 S     102 0:00 -tcsh
$
```

You can display a tree of processes, showing the parent-child and sibling relationships between processes, by using the `f` option. The first command in the following session shows the process hierarchy for the processes associated with your current session. The second command displays the process hierarchy for all the processes on the system.

```
$ ps f
  PID TTY    STAT TIME COMMAND
 7628 pts/2 S    0:00 -tcsh
 7666 pts/2 S    0:00 bash
 7828 pts/2 T    0:00  \_ pine
 7829 pts/2 R    6:15  \_ banner
 7843 pts/2 R    0:00  \_ ps f
$ ps -e f | more
  PID TTY  STAT TIME COMMAND
    1 ?     S    0:03 init [3]
    2 ?     SW   0:00 [kflushd]
...
  402 ? S        0:00 inetd
 7503 ? S        0:00  \_ telnetd: lhotse.up.edu [ansi]
 7504 pts/0 S    0:00  |    \_ login -- murty
 7505 pts/0 S    0:00  |        \_ -csh
 7539 pts/0 S    0:01  |            \_ pine
 7544 ?     S    0:00  \_ telnetd: upsun26.egr.up.edu [xterm]
 7545 pts/1 S    0:00  |    \_ login -- vegdahl
 7546 pts/1 S    0:00  |        \_ -csh
 7626 ?     S    0:00  \_ telnetd: upppp18.egr.up.edu [ansi]
 7627 pts/2 S    0:00       \_ login -- sarwar
 7628 pts/2 S    0:00           \_ -tcsh
 7666 pts/2 S    0:00               \_ bash
 7828 pts/2 T    0:00                   \_ pine
 7829 pts/2 R    7:13                   \_ banner
```

```
 7846 pts/2 R     0:00                         \_ ps -e f
 7847 pts/2 S     0:00                         \_ more
  417 ?     S     0:00 named
 ...
$
```

In the following session, we use the `-U` and `-u` options to display the status of processes belonging to the user kent. You can use the `-N` option to negate the effect of any option that has been specified in a command until this option. The second command is used to display the status of all nonroot processes (i.e., processes not owned by root) by using the following command.

```
$ ps j -U kent -u kent
  PID PGID SID TTY      TIME CMD
  672  664 664 ?    00:00:00 qmgr
 7825  664 664 ?    00:00:00 pickup
$ ps -U root -u root -N
  PID TTY          TIME CMD
  250 ?        00:00:00 portmap
  672 ?        00:00:00 qmgr
  711 ?        00:00:00 postmaster
  748 ?        00:00:00 xfs
  803 ?        00:00:00 innd
  805 ?        00:00:00 actived
 1234 ?        00:00:00 httpd
 1235 ?        00:00:00 httpd
 1236 ?        00:00:00 httpd
 1237 ?        00:00:00 httpd
 1238 ?        00:00:00 httpd
 1239 ?        00:00:00 httpd
 1240 ?        00:00:00 httpd
 1241 ?        00:00:00 httpd
 1242 ?        00:00:00 httpd
 1243 ?        00:00:00 httpd
 7505 pts/0    00:00:00 csh
 7539 pts/0    00:00:01 pine
 7546 pts/1    00:00:00 csh
```

```
 7628 pts/2   00:00:00 csh
 7666 pts/2   00:00:00 bash
 7828 pts/2   00:00:00 pine
 7829 pts/2   00:14:18 banner
 7853 pts/2   00:00:00 ps
 7854 pts/2   00:00:00 more
$
```

A frequently used group of options is **aux**, which displays detailed information about all processes with user names. The following is a sample run of the **ps aux** command. The state value SW for some of the processes means that these processes are sleeping; they have been swapped out on the disk completely and have no page in the main memory (this is done for processes that do not awake often). The percentage CPU use is computed by the expression cputime/realtime. For the following example, it is highest for the banner process. The pine process for the user murty is using the most amount of space of all the process that are currently running. The remaining fields are defined in Table 13.3 on page 371. The `ps axf | more` command is used to display all process hierarchies on the system.

```
$ ps aux | more
USER      PID  %CPU %MEM   VSZ   RSS TTY     STAT START  TIME COMMAND
root        1   0.0  0.1  1140   384 ?       S    Dec18  0:03 init [3]
root        2   0.0  0.0     0     0 ?       SW   Dec18  0:00 [kflushd]
root        3   0.0  0.0     0     0 ?       SW   Dec18  0:00 [kupdate]
root        4   0.0  0.0     0     0 ?       SW   Dec18  0:00 [kpiod]
root        5   0.0  0.0     0     0 ?       SW   Dec18  0:00 [kswapd]
bin       250   0.0  0.2  1144   460 ?       S    Dec18  0:00 portmap
root      266   0.0  0.2  1296   524 ?       S    Dec18  0:00 ypbind (master)
root      271   0.0  0.2  1324   584 ?       S    Dec18  0:00 ypbind (slave)
...
root     7503   0.0  0.3  1716   876 ?       S    09:44  0:00 telnetd: lhotse.u up.edu [ansi]
root     7504   0.0  0.6  2240  1360 pts/0   S    09:44  0:00 login -- murty
murty    7505   0.0  0.5  2148  1240 pts/0   S    09:44  0:00 -csh
murty    7539   0.0  1.0  4540  2292 pts/0   S    09:44  0:01 pine
root     7544   0.0  0.3  1716   880 ?       S    09:54  0:00 telnetd: upsun26. egr.up.edu [xterm]
root     7545   0.0  0.6  2240  1360 pts/1   S    09:54  0:00 login -- vegdahl
vegdahl  7546   0.0  0.5  2216  1312 pts/1   S    09:54  0:00 -csh
root     7626   0.0  0.3  1716   880 ?       S    10:01  0:00 telnetd: upppp18. egr.up.edu [ansi]
```

```
root     7627   0.0  0.6  2240  1360  pts/2  S    10:01  0:00 login -- sarwar
sarwar   7628   0.0  0.5  2136  1228  pts/2  S    10:01  0:00 -tcsh
sarwar   7666   0.0  0.5  2056  1208  pts/2  S    10:13  0:00 bash
sarwar   7828   0.0  0.5  4044  1192  pts/2  T    11:04  0:00 pine
sarwar   7829  99.7  0.1  1104   292  pts/2  R    11:04 22:12 banner
sarwar   7857   0.0  0.4  2744  1036  pts/2  R    11:27  0:00 ps aux
sarwar   7858   0.0  0.1  1164  440   pts/2  S    11:27  0:00 more
$ ps axf | more
...
  383 ?      S    0:00 crond
  402 ?      S    0:00 inetd
 7503 ?      S    0:00  \_ telnetd: lhotse.up.edu [ansi]
 7504 pts/0  S    0:00  | \_ login -- murty
 7505 pts/0  S    0:00  |     \_ -csh
 7539 pts/0  S    0:01  |         \_ pine
 7544 ?      S    0:00  \_ telnetd: upsun26.egr.up.edu [xterm]
 7545 pts/1  S    0:00  | \_ login -- vegdahl
 7546 pts/1  S    0:00  |     \_ -csh
 7626 ?      S    0:00  \_ telnetd: uppppl8.egr.up.edu [ansi]
 7627 pts/2  S    0:00      \_ login -- sarwar
 7628 pts/2  S    0:00          \_ -tcsh
 7666 pts/2  S    0:00              \_ bash
 7828 pts/2  T    0:00                  \_ pine
 7829 pts/2  R   23:17                  \_ banner
 7859 pts/2  R    0:00                  \_ ps axf
 7860 pts/2  S    0:00                  \_ more
  417 ?      S    0:00 named
...
$
```

The **ps l** command shows the long listing of processes on the system. Although relatively new users of LINUX do not need to use this option, we describe the details of the output of this option for the sake of completeness, as well as to explain some important concepts related to LINUX process scheduling. Table 13.3 briefly describes the meanings of various fields in the output of the command. Depending on the particular implementation of LINUX that you are using, the output (and its order) may be a little different, but the output will contain almost the same fields.

**Table 13.3** Various Fields of the Output of the `ps 1` command

| Field | Meaning |
|---|---|
| F | Flags: Flags associated with the process. It indicates things like whether the process is a user or kernel process, and why the process stopped or went to sleep. |
| UID | User ID: Process owner's user ID |
| PID | Process ID: Process ID of the process |
| PPID | Parent PID: PID of the parent process |
| PRI | Priority: Priority number of a process that dictates when the process is scheduled. |
| NI | Nice value: The nice value of a process; another parameter used in the computation of a process's priority number. |
| VSZ | Virtual size: The number in this field is the size of the memory image of a process (code+data+stack) in blocks. |
| RSS | Resident set size: The amount of physical memory in kilobytes; it does not include space taken by the page table and kernel task structure for the process. |
| WCHAN | Wait channel: Null for running processes, or processes that are ready to run and are waiting for the CPU to be given to them. For a waiting or sleeping process, this field lists the event the process is waiting for—the kernel function where the process resides. |
| STAT | Process state: See Tables 13.1 and 13.2. |
| TTY | Terminal: The terminal name a process is attached to |
| TIME | Time: The time (in minutes and seconds) a process has currently been running for, or previously ran for before sleeping or stopping. |
| COMMAND | Command: Lists the command line that was used to start this process. The **-f** option is needed to see the full command line; otherwise only the last component of the pathname is displayed. |

```
$ ps l
  F UID   PID  PPID PRI NI  VSZ  RSS WCHAN  STAT TTY     TIME COMMAND
100 121 7628 7627   0  0 2136 1228 rt_sig S    pts/2   0:00 -tcsh
000 121 7666 7628  10  0 2060 1244 wait4  S    pts/2   0:00 bash
000 121 7828 7666   0  0 4044 1192 do_sig T    pts/2   0:00 pine
000 121 7829 7666  18  0 1104  292 -      R    pts/2  49:22 banner
000 121 8007 7666  17  0 2740 1012 -      R    pts/2   0:00 ps l
$
```

The preceding example shows a sample run of the `ps l` command.

If you want to monitor the CPU activity in real time, you can use the `top` command. It displays the status of the most CPU-intensive tasks on the system and allows you to manipulate processes interactively. It can sort the tasks by CPU usage, memory usage, and runtime. Most features can either be selected by an interactive command or by specifying the feature in the personal or systemwide configuration file.

```
$ top
12:02pm up 3 days, 9:04, 2 users, load average: 2.03, 1.84, 1.53
69 processes: 65 sleeping, 3 running, 0 zombie, 1 stopped
CPU states: 97.4% user, 2.5% system, 0.0% nice, 0.0% idle
Mem:  225312K av, 222464K used,  2848K free, 59308K shrd,  4584K buff
Swap: 529184K av,     16K used, 529168K free              192048K cached

  PID USER     PRI NI SIZE  RSS SHARE STAT LIB %CPU %MEM  TIME COMMAND
 7829 sarwar    14  0  292  292   232 R      0 98.0  0.1 56:25 banner
 8084 sarwar     3  0 1204 1204   972 R      0  1.3  0.5  0:00 top
 7993 vegdahl    0  0  772  772   644 D      0  0.3  0.3  0:02 tar
  303 root       0  0    0    0     0 SW     0  0.1  0.0  0:04 rpciod
    1 root       0  0  392  384   332 S      0  0.0  0.1  0:03 init
    2 root       0  0    0    0     0 SW     0  0.0  0.0  0:00 kflushd
    3 root       0  0    0    0     0 SW     0  0.0  0.0  0:00 kupdate
    4 root       0  0    0    0     0 SW     0  0.0  0.0  0:00 kpiod
    5 root       0  0    0    0     0 SW     0  0.0  0.0  0:00 kswapd
  250 bin        0  0  460  460   384 S      0  0.0  0.2  0:00 portmap
...
<Ctrl-C>
$ kill 8597
$ nice –10 banner
$ top banner
12:12pm up 3 days, 9:14, 2 users, load average: 1.00, 1.16, 1.32
68 processes: 64 sleeping, 3 running, 0 zombie, 1 stopped
CPU states: 0.5% user, 1.3% system, 98.0% nice, 0.0% idle
Mem:  225312K av, 219484K used,  5828K free, 58504K shrd,  4584K buff
Swap: 529184K av,    172K used, 529012K free              189488K cached

  PID USER     PRI NI SIZE  RSS SHARE STAT LIB %CPU %MEM TIME COMMAND
```

```
8111 sarwar  20 19  292  292   232 R N    0 98.0  0.1 8:29 banner
8261 sarwar   2  0 1204 1204   972 R      0  1.3  0.5 0:00 top
...
<Crtl-C>
$
```

You can interact with `top` as it runs by using various commands. When you use an interactive command, `top` prompts you with one or more questions related to the chore that you want it to perform. For example, if you press <n>, `top` prompts you for the number of processes to display. You enter the number and hit the <Enter> key for `top` to start displaying the number of processes that you entered. Similarly, if you want to terminate a process, press <k> and `top` prompts you for the PID of the process to be terminated. You enter the PID of the process to be terminated and hit <Enter> for `top` to terminate the process.

In the following In-Chapter Exercises you will use the `ps` command with and without options to appreciate the command output.

**IN-CHAPTER EXERCISES**

**13.1.** Use the `ps` command to display the status of processes that are running in your current session. Can you identify your login shell? What is it?

**13.2.** Run the command to display the status of all the processes running on your system. What command did you run? What are their PIDs? What are the PIDs of the parents of all the processes?

**13.3.** Try the session for the `top` command on your system.

## 13.6 PROCESS AND JOB CONTROL

LINUX is responsible for several activities related to process and job management, including process creation, process termination, running processes in the foreground and background, suspending processes, and switching processes from foreground to background and vice versa. As a LINUX user you can request these process and job control tasks by using the shell commands discussed in this section.

### 13.6.1 Foreground and Background Processes and Related Commands

When you type a command and hit <Enter>, the shell executes the command and returns by displaying the shell prompt. While your command executes, you do not have access to your shell and therefore cannot execute any commands until the current command finishes and the shell returns. When commands execute in this manner, we say that they execute in the **foreground**. More technically, when a command executes in the foreground, it keeps control of the keyboard and the display screen.

At times you will need to run a LINUX command (or any program) that takes a long time to finish and—while the command executes—you will want to do other work. You cannot do so if the command runs in the foreground because the shell doesn't return until the command completes. LINUX allows you to run a command so that—while the command executes—you get the shell prompt back and can do other work. This capability is called running the command in the **background**. You can run a command in the background by ending the command with an ampersand (`&`).

Background processes run with a larger nice value and hence a lower priority. Thus they get to use the CPU only when no higher priority process needs it. When a background process generates output that is sent to the display screen, the screen looks garbled, but if you're using some application, your work isn't altered in any way. You can get out of the application and then get back in to obtain a cleaner screen. Some applications, such as `vi`, allow you to redraw the screen without quitting it. In `vi` (see Chapter 5) pressing <Ctrl-L> in the command mode allows you to do so.

The syntaxes for executing a command in the foreground and background are as follows. Note that no space is needed between the command and `&` but that you can use space for clarity.

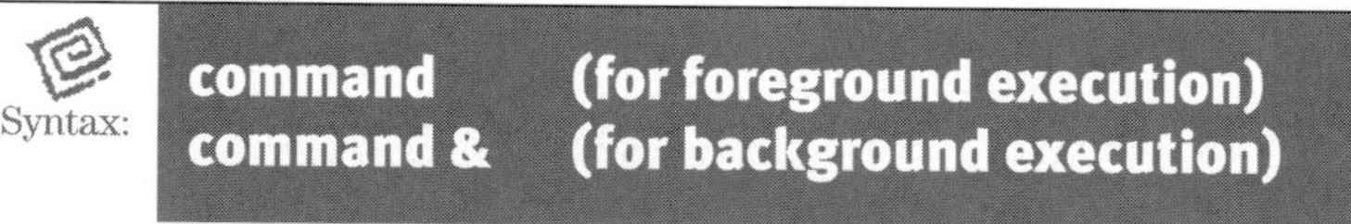

Syntax:
command (for foreground execution)
command & (for background execution)


Let's consider the following command. It searches the whole file structure for a file called foo and stores the pathnames of the directories that contain this file in the file foo.paths; error messages are sent to the file /dev/null, which is the LINUX black hole: Whatever goes in never comes out. (Note that, for the TC shell, you should use the `(find / -name foo -print > foo.paths) >& /dev/null` command.) This command may take several minutes, perhaps hours, depending on the size of the file structure, system load in terms of the number of users logged on, and the number of processes running on the system. So, if you want to do some other work on the system while the command executes, you cannot do so because the command executes in the foreground.

```
$ find / -name foo -print > foo.paths 2> /dev/null
...
$
```

The **find** command is a perfect candidate for background execution because, while it runs, you have access to the shell and can do other work. Thus the preceding command should be executed as follows.

```
$ find / -name foo -print > foo.paths 2> /dev/null &
[1] 23467
$
```

The number shown in brackets is returned by the shell and is the **job number** for the process; the other number is the PID of the process. Here, the job number for this `find` command is 1, and the PID is 23467. A **job** is a process that isn't running in the foreground and is accessible only at the terminal with which it is associated. Such processes are typically executed as background or suspended processes.

The commands that perform tasks that don't involve user intervention and take a long time to finish are good candidates for background execution. Some examples are sorting large files (`sort` command), compiling (`cc` or `make` command), and searching a large file structure for one or more files (`find` command). Commands that do terminal I/O, such as the `vi` editor, aren't good candidates for background execution. The reason is that when such a command executes in the background, it stops as it reads input from the keyboard. The command needs to be brought back to the foreground before it can start running again. The `fg` command allows you to bring a background process to the foreground. Following is a brief description of the syntax for this command.

Syntax:

**fg [%jobid]**

**Purpose:** Resume execution of the process with job number jobid in the foreground or move background processes to the foreground

**Commonly used values for %jobid:**

| | |
|---|---|
| `%` or `%+` | Current job |
| `%-` | Previous job |
| `%N` | Job number *N* |
| `%Name` | Job beginning with Name |
| `%?Name` | Command containing Name |

When the `fg` command is executed without a jobid, it brings the current job into the foreground. The job using the CPU at any particular time is called the **current job**. In the following session, three `find` commands are executed in the background. When the `fg` command is executed it brings the `find / -name foobar`

`-print > foobar.paths 2> /dev/null` command into the foreground. The `fg` command can be executed with a job number as its argument to bring a particular job into the foreground. Thus, in the following session, the `fg %2` command brings job number 2 into the foreground. A string that uniquely identifies a job can also be used in place of a job number. The string is enclosed in double quotes if it has spaces in it. The third `fg` command illustrates this convention. Using `find` alone won't work because more than one command starts with this string.

```
$ find / -inum 23456 -print > pathnames 2> /dev/null &
[1] 13590
$ find / -name foo -print > foo.paths 2> /dev/null &
[2] 13591
$ find / -name foobar -print > foobar.paths 2> /dev/null &
[3] 13596
$ ps
  PID   TTY       TIME CMD
13495 pts/0  00:00:03 bash
13583 pts/0  00:00:11 find
13586 pts/0  00:00:05 find
13587 pts/0  00:00:03 find
$ fg
find / -name foobar -print > foobar.paths 2> /dev/null
<Ctrl-C>
$ fg %2
find / -name foo -print > foo.paths 2> /dev/null
<Ctrl-Z>
$ fg %"find / -inum"
find / -inum 23456 -print > pathnames 2> /dev/null
```

While running a command in the foreground, you may need to suspend it in order to go back to the shell, do something under the shell, and then return to the suspended process. For example, say that you are in the middle of editing a C program file with `vi` and need to compile the program to determine whether some errors have been corrected. You can save changes to the file, suspend `vi`, compile the program to view the results of the compilation, and return to `vi`. You can suspend a foreground process by pressing `<Ctrl-Z>`. You can put a suspended process in the foreground by using the `fg` command and in the background by using the `bg` command (described later in this section). So you can suspend `vi` by pressing `<Ctrl-Z>`, compile the program to identify any further errors, and resume the suspended `vi` session by using the `fg` command. This sequence of events is shown in the following session.

```
$ ps
  PID    TTY       TIME CMD
19984  pts/3  00:00:00 bash
20996  pts/3  00:00:02 ps
$
$ vi lab8.c
#include <stdio.h>
#define SIZE 100

main (int argc, char *argv[])
{
...
~
~
~
<Ctrl-Z>
[1]+ Stopped vi lab8.c
$ ps
  PID  TTY         TIME CMD
19984  pts/3  00:00:02 bash
20988  pts/3  00:00:00 vi
20999  pts/3  00:00:00 ps
$ gcc -o lab8 lab8.c
$ fg %1
#include <stdio.h>
#define SIZE 100

main (int argc, char *argv[])
{
...
~
~
~
:q!
$
```

In the preceding session, the `gcc -o lab8 lab8.c` command is used to compile the C program in the lab8.c file and put the executable in a file called lab8. Understanding what compilation means is not the point here, so don't worry if you don't understand the semantics of the `gcc` command (see Chapter 20). Here, we are merely emphasizing that processes that take a long time to start or those that have executed for a considerable amount of time, are usually suspended; the example of suspending the `vi` command is presented only as an illustration.

You can move the foreground and suspended processes to the background by using the `bg` command. The syntax of this command is exactly like that of the `fg` command.

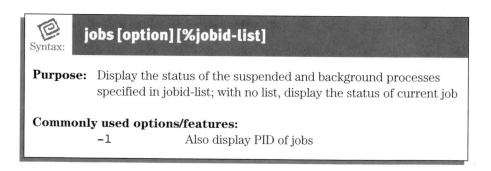

Syntax:

**bg [%jobid-list]**

**Purpose:** Resume execution of suspended processes/jobs with job numbers in jobid-list in the background

**Commonly used values for %jobid:**

| | |
|---|---|
| `%` or `%+` | Current job |
| `%-` | Previous job |
| `%N` | Job number *N* |
| `%Name` | Job beginning with Name |
| `%?Name` | Command containing Name |

If there are multiple suspended processes, the `fg` command without an argument brings the current process into the foreground, and the `bg` command without an argument resumes execution of the current process in the background. You can use the `jobs` command to determine the job numbers of all suspended (stopped) and background processes and which is the current process. The current process is identified by a + and the previous process by a − in the output of the `jobs` command. The following is a brief description of the command.

Syntax:

**jobs [option] [%jobid-list]**

**Purpose:** Display the status of the suspended and background processes specified in jobid-list; with no list, display the status of current job

**Commonly used options/features:**

| | |
|---|---|
| `-l` | Also display PID of jobs |

The optional argument 'jobid-list' can be a list of job numbers starting with % and separated by spaces. The following session shows the command usage with and without the only option and arguments. The **jobs** command reports the status of all jobs without their PIDs. The command with the **-l** option also displays PIDs of the jobs. The following session shows the outputs of the **jobs**, **jobs -l**, **bg%1**, and **bg** commands. Again, in the output of the **jobs** command, the current job is marked with the + sign and the previous job is marked with the − sign. Furthermore, processes executing in the background are in the running state and the suspended processes are in the stopped state. The stopped process state indicates that job numbers 1 and 4 received the stop signal (discussed in Section 16.5), which means that the user pressed <Ctrl-Z> when each job was running in the foreground. The **bg%1** command puts job number 1 in the background, as indicated by the output of the command (note the & at the end of the command). The immediately following **jobs** command indicates that the job moved into the background is in the running state. The **bg** command moves the current job (the `vi` process) into the background. Moreover, the immediately following **jobs** command shows that `vi` is still the current job but it cannot do terminal input. That is, as long as `vi` is in the background, it cannot read keyboard input. So the `vi` process is still in the stopped state.

```
$ find / -inum 23456 -print 2> /dev/null 1>&2
[1]+ Stopped find / -inum 23456 -print 2>/dev/null 1>&2
$ find / -name foo > foo.paths 2> /dev/null &
[2] 13586
$ find / -name foobar > foobar.paths 2> /dev/null &
[3] 13587
$ vi chapter13
~
~
~
~
~
...
~
"chapter13" [New File]
<Ctrl-Z>
[4]+ Stopped vi chapter13
$
```

```
$ jobs
[1] - Stopped              find / -inum 23456 -print 2> /dev/null 1>&2
[2]   Running              find / -name foo > foo.paths 2> /dev/null&
[3]   Running              find / -name foobar > foobar.paths 2> /dev/null&
[4] + Stopped              vi chapter13
$ jobs -l
[1] - 13583 Stopped          find / -inum 23456 -print 2> /dev/null 1>&2
[2]   13586 Running          find / -name foo > foo.paths 2> /dev/null&
[3]   13587 Running          find / -name foobar > foobar.paths 2> /dev/null&
[4] + 13589 Stopped          vi chapter13
$ bg %1
[1] find / -inum 23456 -print&
$ jobs
[1] - Running              find / -inum 23456 -print 2> /dev/null 1>&2
[2]   Running              find / -name foo > foo.paths 2> /dev/null&
[3]   Running              find / -name foobar > foobar.paths 2> /dev/null&
[4] + Stopped              vi chapter13
$ bg
[4] vi chapter13&
$ jobs
[1] - Running              find / -inum 23456 -print 2> /dev/null 1>&2
[2]   Running              find / -name foo > foo.paths 2> /dev/null&
[3]   Running              find / -name foobar > foobar.paths 2> /dev/null&
[4] + Stopped              vi chapter13
$
```

As indicated in the command description, the **bg** command can be passed a list of job numbers for moving multiple suspended jobs into background. Thus the **bg %1 %3** command can be used to move jobs 1 and 3 into the foreground.

The **suspend** command can be used to suspend the current shell process. The **fg** command can be used to return to the last suspended shell. The following session shows the use of the **suspend** command under the Bash and TC shells. The first **suspend** command is used to suspend (stop) the TC shell process and takes you to its parent process, a Bash process. This is confirmed by using the **ps a** command, which shows the TC shell process to be stopped (in T state). The **fg** command is used to bring back the TC shell process. Then a Bash process is started under the current TC shell process and the second **suspend** command is used to suspend the Bash process. The last **fg** command is used to bring back the suspended Bash process. Note that the messages displayed by the command in TC and Bourne Again shells are different.

```
% suspend

[1]+ Stopped tcsh
$ ps a
  PID TTY    STAT TIME COMMAND
20932 pts/0 S    0:00 login -- sarwar
20967 pts/0 S    0:00 bash
21071 pts/0 T    0:00 -csh
21101 pts/0 R    0:00 ps a
$ fg
tcsh
% bash
$ suspend

Suspended (signal)
% fg
bash
$
```

In the following In-Chapter Exercise, you will practice creation and management of foreground and background processes by using the `bg`, `fg`, and `jobs` commands.

**IN-CHAPTER EXERCISE**

**13.4.** Run the sessions presented in this section on your system to practice foreground and background process creation and switching processes from the foreground to the background (the `bg` command) and vice versa (the `fg` command). Use the `jobs` command to display job IDs of the active and suspended processes.

### 13.6.2 LINUX Daemons

Although any process running in the background can be called a daemon, in LINUX jargon a **daemon** is a system process running in the background. Daemons are frequently used in LINUX to offer various types of services to users and to handle system administration tasks. For example, the print, e-mail, and finger services are provided via daemons. The printing services are provided by the printer daemon, lpd. The finger service (see Chapter 14) is handled by the finger daemon, fingerd. The e-mail service (see Chapter 6) is provided by the smtpd daemon, and the Web-browsing service is handled by the httpd daemon. The inetd, commonly known as the LINUX superserver, handles various Internet related services by spawning several daemons at system boot time. Access the /etc/inetd.conf file to view the services offered by this daemon on your system. This file has one line for every service that inetd offers.

### 13.6.3 Sequential and Parallel Execution of Commands

You can type multiple commands on one command line for sequential and/or parallel execution. The following is a brief description of the syntax for **sequential execution** of commands specified in one command line.

Syntax: **cmd1; cmd2; ...; cmdN**

**Purpose:** Execute the 'cmd1', 'cmd2', ..., 'cmdN' commands sequentially

Note that the semicolon is used as a command separator (delimiter) and doesn't follow the last command. No spaces are needed before and after a semicolon, but you can use spaces for clarity. These commands execute one after the other, as though each were typed on a separate line. In the following session, the `date` and `echo` commands execute sequentially as separate processes.

```
$ date; echo Hello, World!
Fri Jun 18 23:43:39 PDT 1999
Hello, World!
$
```

You can specify **parallel execution** of commands in a command line by ending each command with an ampersand (`&`). The commands that terminate with `&` also execute in the background. No spaces are required before or after an `&`, but you can use spaces for clarity. The following is a brief description of the syntax for parallel execution of shell commands specified in one command line.

Syntax: **cmd1& cmd2& ... cmdN&**

**Purpose:** Execute commands 'cmd1', 'cmd2', ..., 'cmdN' in parallel as separate processes

In the following session, the **date** and **echo** commands execute in parallel, followed by the sequential execution of the **uname** and **who** commands. The job and process IDs of the **date** command are 1 and 15575, and those of the **echo** command are 2 and 15576. The **date** and **echo** commands execute in the background, and the **uname** and **who** commands execute in the foreground.

```
$ date & echo Hello, World! & uname; who
[1] 15575
[2] 15576
Sat Dec 23 23:22:37 PST 2000
Hello, World!
Linux
[1]- Done                date
[2]+ Done                echo Hello, World!
sarwar   pts/0   Dec 23 21:14
$
```

In a command line, the last **&** puts all the commands after the previous **&** in one process. In the following command line, therefore, the **date** command executes as one process and all the commands in **who; whoami; uname; echo Hello, World!&** as another process. The process IDs are 15586 and 15587. Because the first process (the **date** command) finishes very quickly (before the second command even starts), the job ID for both is 1 (there is no other job by the time the second process starts).

```
$ date & who; whoami; uname; echo Hello, World! &
[1] 15586
Sat Dec 23 23:26:26 PST 2000
sarwar pts/0 Dec 23 21:14
[1]+ Done                date
sarwar
Linux
[1] 15587
$ Hello, World!
<Enter>
[1]+ Done                echo Hello, World!
$
```

LINUX allows you to group commands and execute them in a child of the current shell as one process by separating commands with semicolons and enclosing them in parentheses. This is called **command grouping**. Because all the commands in a command group execute as a single process, they are executed by the same subshell. However, all the commands execute sequentially. The following is a brief description of the syntax for command grouping.

Syntax:

**(cmd1; cmd2; ...; cmdN)**

**Purpose:** Execute commands 'cmd1', 'cmd2', ..., 'cmdN' sequentially, but as one process

In the following session the `date` and `echo` commands execute sequentially, but as one process.

```
$ (date; echo Hello, World!)
Sat Dec 16 09:27:38 PST 2000
Hello, World!
$
```

You can combine command grouping with sequential execution by separating command groups with other commands or command groups. In the following session, the `date` and `echo` commands execute as one process, followed by the execution of the `who` command as a separate process.

```
$ ( date; echo Hello, World! ); who
Sat Jan 12 15:00:36 PST 2001
Hello, World!
deborahs pts/1   Jan 12 08:05
kittyt   pts/0   Jan 12 07:19
kent     pts/3   Jan 12 11:24
sarwar   pts/2   Jan 12 09:03
$
```

Command groups can be nested. Hence `((date; echo Hello, World!); who)` and `((date; echo Hello, World!); (who; uname))` are valid commands and produce the expected results. Command grouping makes more sense when groups are executed as separate processes, as shown in the following session. In the second group of commands, **(date; echo Hello, World)** and **(who; uname)** execute in the background and the **whoami** command executes in the foreground; all three commands execute in parallel.

Note that the output of the second command is different for the three executions. This is because the output depends on how multiple processes in the command are scheduled. In the first case, the processes are scheduled as they are listed in the command. Thus the commands in the group **( date; echo Hello, World! )** are executed first, followed by the commands in the group **(who; uname)**, and finally the **whoami** command. For the second execution of the command, as can be seen by observing the output, the **whoami** command gets executed before the **uname** command. The third execution of the command results in the execution of the last command (**whoami**) first and the first command last.

```
$ ( date; echo Hello, World! )&
[2] 7149
$ Mon Dec 18 13:27:46 PST 2000
Hello, World!
<Enter>
[2]- Done                   ( date; echo Hello, World! )
$
$ ( date; echo Hello, World! ) & (who; uname) & whoami
[1] 14971
[2] 14972
Sun Jan 14 00:08:30 PST 2001
Hello, World!
deborahs pts/1  Jan 12 08:05
kittyt   pts/0  Jan 12 07:19
kent     pts/3  Jan 12 11:24
sarwar   pts/2  Jan 12 09:03
Linux
sarwar
[1]- Done                   ( date; echo Hello, World! )
[2]+ Done                   ( who; uname )
$
```

```
$ ( date; echo Hello, World! ) & (who; uname) & whoami
[1] 15015
[2] 15016
Sun Jan 14 00:08:41 PST 2001
Hello, World!
deborahs pts/1 Jan 12 08:05
kittyt   pts/0 Jan 12 07:19
kent     pts/3 Jan 12 11:24
sarwar   pts/2 Jan 12 09:03
sarwar
[1]- Done                          ( date; echo Hello, World! )
$ Linux
<Enter>
[2]+ Done                          ( who; uname )
$
$ ( date; echo Hello, World! ) & (who; uname) & whoami
[1] 15027
[2] 15028
sarwar
$ deborahs pts/1 Jan 12 08:05
kittyt  pts/0 Jan 12 07:19
kent    pts/3 Jan 12 11:24
sarwar  pts/2 Jan 12 09:03
Sun Jan 14 00:09:53 PST 2001
Hello, World!
Linux
<Enter>
[1]- Done                          ( date; echo Hello, World! )
[2]+ Done                          ( who; uname )
$
```

It is important to note that the commands in parentheses are executed under a subshell of the current shell. The following session illustrates this point. The **find** command executes under a child of Bash (with PID 16944) and the **ps f** command executes under the current Bash (with PID 16918).

```
$ ( find / -inum 23456 -print > /dev/null 2>&1 ; ls ) &
$ ps f
  PID TTY   STAT TIME COMMAND
16877 pts/0 S    0:00 -tcsh
16918 pts/0 S    0:00 bash
16944 pts/0 S    0:00 \_ bash
16945 pts/0 R    0:15 | \_ find / -inum 23456 -print
16948 pts/0 R    0:00 \_ ps f
$
```

In the following In-Chapter Exercises, you will practice sequential and parallel execution of LINUX commands.

**IN-CHAPTER EXERCISES**

**13.5.** Run the sessions presented in this section on your system to practice sequential and parallel execution of shell commands.

**13.6.** Which of the following commands run sequentially and which run in parallel? How many of the processes run in parallel?

```
(who; date) & (cat temp; uname & whoami)
```

### 13.6.4 Abnormal Termination of Commands and Processes

When you run a command it normally terminates after successfully completing its task. However, a command (process) can terminate prematurely because of a bad argument that you passed to it, such as a directory argument to the `cp` command. At times you may also need to terminate a process abnormally. The need for abnormal termination occurs when you run a process with a wrong argument (e.g., a wrong file name to a `find` command) or when a command is taking too long to finish. We address abnormal termination in relation to both foreground and background processes.

You can terminate a foreground process by pressing `<Ctrl-C>`. You can terminate a background process in one of two ways: (1) by using the `kill` command, or (2) by first bringing the process into the foreground using the `fg` command and then pressing `<Ctrl-C>`. The primary purpose of the `kill` command is to send a **signal** (also known as a **software interrupt**) to a process. The LINUX operating system uses a signal to get the attention of a process. Any one of more than 60 signal types (in Red Hat 7.2; 30 in Mandrake 6.1) can be sent to a LINUX process. A process can take one of three actions upon receiving a signal:

1. accept the default action as determined by the LINUX kernel,
2. ignore the signal, or
3. intercept the signal and take a user-defined action.

For most signals the default action, in addition to some other events, always results in termination of the process. Ignoring a signal doesn't have any impact on the process. A user-defined action is specified in the process as a program statement, and it can take control of the process at a specific piece of code in the process. In a shell script, these actions can be specified by using the `trap` command in the Bourne Again shell. The TC shell provides a limited handling of signals via the `onintr` instruction. In a TC program, these actions are specified by using the signal system call. We discuss the `trap` and `onintr` commands in detail in Chapters 16 and 18, respectively. The description of the signal system call is beyond the scope of this textbook, but you can consult a book on LINUX systems programming to learn how this call is used. Or, for a quick look, view its manual page by using the `man -S2 signal` (or `man -2 signal`) command.

Signals can be generated for various reasons. Some of these reasons are caused by the process itself, whereas others are external to the process. A signal caused by an event internal to a process is known as an **internal signal**, or a **trap** (don't confuse it with the `trap` command). A signal caused by an event external to a process is called an **external signal**. For example, an internal signal is generated for a process when the process tries to execute a nonexisting instruction or to access memory that it isn't allowed to access (e.g., memory belonging to some other process or memory belonging to the LINUX kernel). An external signal can be generated by pressing `<Ctrl-C>`, by you logging out, or by using the `kill` command. The `kill` command can be used to send any type of signal to a process. The following is a brief description of the `kill` command.

Syntax: **kill [-signal_number] proc-list**
**kill -l**

**Purpose:** Send the signal for 'signal_number' to processes whose PIDs or jobIDs are specified in 'proc-list'; jobIDs must start with `%`. The command `kill -l` returns a list of all signal numbers and their names

**Commonly used signal_numbers:**

| | |
|---|---|
| 1 | Hangup (log out or hang up the phone line while using a system via a modem) |
| 2 | Interrupt (`<Ctrl-C>`) |
| 3 | Quit (`<Ctrl-\>`) |
| 9 | Sure kill |
| 15 | Software signal (default signal number) |

The hangup signal is generated when you log out, the interrupt signal is generated when you press <Ctrl-C>, and the quit signal is generated when you press <Ctrl-\>. The `kill` command sends signal number `15` to the process whose PID is specified as an argument. The default action for this signal is termination of the process that receives it. This signal can be intercepted and ignored by a process, as can most of the other signals. In order to terminate a process that ignores signal `15` or other signals, signal number `9`, known as **sure kill**, has to be sent to it. The `kill` command terminates all the processes whose PIDs are given in the PID-list, provided that these processes belong to the user using `kill`. The following session presents some instances of how the `kill` command can be used.

```
$ ps
  PID TTY         TIME CMD
 1322 pts/0 00:00:00 bash
 1831 pts/0 00:34:17 sort
 1837 pts/0 00:12:42 a.out
 1850 pts/0 00:00:10 find
 1851 pts/0 00:00:03 find
 1852 pts/0 00:00:02 find
 1853 pts/0 00:00:00 ps
$ kill 1850
$ kill -2 1851
[1] Terminated     find / -inum 23456 -print >inumpaths 2>/dev/null
$ kill -9 1837
[2]- Interrupt     find / -name foo -print >foopaths 2>/dev/null
$ <Enter>
[3]+ Killed           a.out
$
```

In the first case, signal number `15` is sent to a process with PID 1850. In the second case, signal number `2` (<Ctrl-C>) is sent to a process with PID 1851. In both cases, if the specified signal numbers are not intercepted, the processes are terminated. In the third case, the a.out process ignores signal numbers `2` (<Ctrl-C>) and `15` (software signal) and therefore cannot be terminated unless signal number `9` (sure kill) is sent to it. The `kill` command can be used to terminate a number of processes with one command line. For example, the command `kill -9 1831 1852` terminates processes with PIDs 1831 and

1852. Process ID 0 can be used to refer to all the processes created during the current login. Thus the `kill -9 0` command terminates *all* processes resulting from the current login (i.e., all the processes in your current session) and logs you out.

The **kill** command also works with job numbers. Hence the following command can be used to terminate a process with job number 1. Multiple processes can be terminated by specifying their job numbers in the command line. For example, `kill -9 %1 %3` can be used to terminate processes with job numbers 1 and 3.

```
$ kill -9 %1
$ <Enter>
[1] + Killed    find / -name foo -print > foopaths 2> /dev/null
$
```

Under old shells such as the Bourne shell, when you log out, all the processes running in your session get a hangup signal (signal number `1`) and are terminated per the default action. If you want processes to continue to run even after you have logged out, you need to execute them so that they ignore the hangup signal when they receive it. You can use the LINUX command `nohup` to accomplish this task under the Bourne and C shells. The following is a brief description of the syntax for this command.

Syntax:

**nohup command [args]**

**Purpose:** Run 'command' and ignore the hangup signal

You need to use the `nohup` command for processes that take a long time to finish, such as a program sorting a large file containing hundreds of thousands of customer records. Obviously, you would run such a program in the background so that it runs at a lower priority. The following is a simple illustration of the use of the `nohup` command. Here, the `find` command runs in the background and isn't terminated when you log out or send it signal number `1` (hangup) via the `kill` command. If output of the command is not redirected, it is appended to the nohup.out file by default.

```
$ nohup find / -name foo -print 1> foo.paths 2> /dev/null &
[1] 15928
$
```

You can run multiple commands with **nohup** if they are separated by semicolons. In the following session, GenData generates some data and puts it in a file called employees, and the **sort** command sorts the file and stores the sorted version in the employees.sorted file.

```
$ nohup GenData > employees ; sort employees > employees.sorted &
[2] 15931
$
```

Most modern shells, including the Bash and TC shells, preserve the background processes when you log out. This means that when a shell terminates, all its children processes keep running. Thus you don't need to use the **nohup** command if you want any process to continue to run after you log out. The orphaned processes are adopted by the granddaddy process init. The following session illustrates this point. The output of the **ps f** command shows that the **find** command is run as a child of the tcsh process and has PID 2061. The output of the first **ps -p 2061 -l** command shows that the process ID of the parent of find is 2037 (the tcsh process). <Ctrl-D> is used to terminate the TC shell process. The second **ps f** command shows that the **find** command is still running. The output of the last **ps -p 2061 -l** command shows that the **find** command has been adopted by the init process (PID 1).

```
% find / -name foo -print > & /dev/null &
[1] 2061
% ps f
  PID TTY    STAT TIME COMMAND
 1964 pts/0 S    0:00 bash
 2037 pts/0 S    0:00  \_ tcsh
 2061 pts/0 R    0:03      \_ find / -name foo -print
 2062 pts/0 R    0:00      \_ ps f
% ps -p 2061 -l
  F S UID  PID PPID  C PRI NI ADDR  SZ WCHAN TTY        TIME CMD
000 D 121 2061 2037 13  70  0    - 306 end   pts/0 00:00:04 find
% <Ctrl-D>
$ ps f
  PID TTY    STAT TIME COMMAND
 1964 pts/0 S    0:00 bash
 2063 pts/0 R    0:00  \_ ps f
 2061 pts/0 D    0:03 find / -name foo -print
$ ps -p 2061 -l
```

```
  F S UID   PID PPID C PRI NI ADDR  SZ WCHAN TTY         TIME CMD
000 D 121 2061    1 9  70  0    - 306 end   pts/0  00:00:04 find
$
```

In the following In-Chapter Exercises, you will use the **kill** command to practice abnormal termination of processes, and the **nohup** and **ps -a** commands to appreciate how you can run processes that do not terminate when you log out.

## IN-CHAPTER EXERCISES

**13.7.** Give a command for terminating processes with PID 10974 and jobID 3.

**13.8.** Run the first of the **nohup** commands presented, use **ps** to verify that the command is executing, log out, log in again, and use the **ps -a** command to determine whether the **find** command is running.

**13.9.** Run the **find** command in Exercise 13.8 without the **nohup** command. Log out, log in, and run the **ps -a** command to verify that the **find** command is running.

### 13.6.5 Conditional Command Execution

You can use the logical AND operator **&&** and logical OR operator **||** for conditional execution of commands. The following briefly explains the command syntaxes for these operators.

Syntax: **command1 && command2**
**command1 || command2**

**Purpose:** First Syntax: Execute 'command2' if 'command1' succeeds
Second Syntax: Execute 'command2' if 'command1' fails

In the following session, the **wc first.c** command executes because the string Hello is found in the first.c file. Because the string TryThis is not found in the first.c file, the **wc first.c** command is not executed. Because the string Hi is not found in the first.c file, the **echo** command in the fourth command line is executed. The **echo** command in the last command line is not executed because the **grep** command to the left of **||** is successful.

```
$ cat first.c
#include <stdio.h>
main()
{
        printf("Hello, World!\n");
}
$ grep "Hello" first.c > /dev/null && wc first.c
     5         7       57 first.c
$ grep "TryThis" first.c > /dev/null && wc first.c
$ grep "Hi" first.c > /dev/null || echo " first.c: Hi not found"
first.c: Mucha not found
$ grep "Hello" x.c > /dev/null || echo "x.c: Hi not found"
$
```

## 13.7 PROCESS HIERARCHY IN LINUX

When you turn on your LINUX system, LILO (LInux LOader) locates the LINUX kernel and loads it into memory. It initializes various hardware components such as the disk controller. The process then switches to protected mode, loads the operating system, and executes the code that initializes the various kernel data structures such as the inode and file tables. This process has PID 0. It now starts the **init process** (PID 1) that carries out the rest of the bootup process. The init process starts the daemons kflushd, kupdate, kpiod, and kswapd, with PIDs 2, 3, 4, and 5, respectively. The init process then initializes the file systems and mounts the root file system. It then attempts to execute the /sbin/init program, which runs the mingetty process (usually called the **getty process**) on every active terminal line. The getty process sets the terminal attributes, such as baud rate, as specified in the /etc/termcap file. It then displays the login: prompt, inviting you to log onto the system.

At the `login:` prompt, when you type your login name and press <Enter>, the getty process forks a child. The child execs to become a login process with your login name as its parameter. The **login process** prompts you for your password and checks the validity of your login name and password. If it finds that both are correct, the login process forks a child that execs to become your login shell. If the login process doesn't find your login name in the /etc/passwd file or finds that the password that you entered doesn't match the one in the /etc/passwd (or /etc/shadow) file, it displays an error message and terminates. Control goes back to the getty process, which redisplays the `login:` prompt. Once in your login shell, you can do your work and terminate the shell by pressing <Ctrl-D>. When you do so, the shell process terminates and control goes back to the getty process, which displays the `login:` prompt, and life goes on.

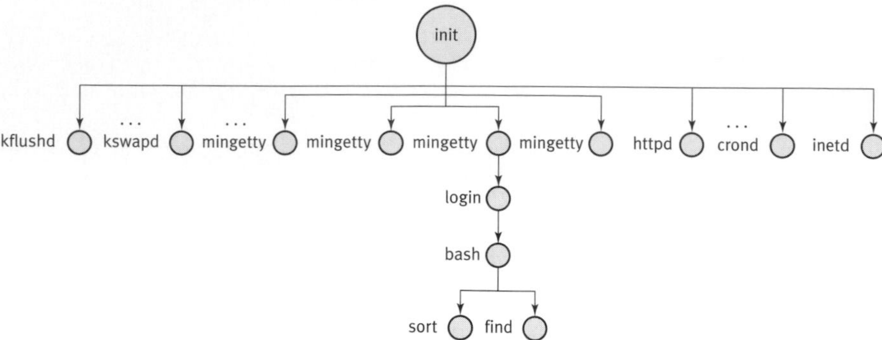


**Figure 13.6** LINUX process hierarchy

Figure 13.6 shows the process hierarchy of a LINUX system schematically. This process diagram shows a system with one user running two processes, **`sort`** and **`find`**, with the Bash shell as the user's login shell.

Thus, when you log on to a LINUX system, the system creates the first process for you, called the login process, which then creates your login shell. In Chapters 2 and 7, we explained how you determine the type of your login shell (Bash, TC, Z, etc.). The login shell interprets/executes your commands by creating processes for all the commands that you execute (see Section 13.3 for details of command execution).

Two LINUX processes exist throughout the lifetime of a system: the swapper and init processes. The getty process, which monitors a terminal line, lives for as long as the terminal is attached to the system. Your login and login shell processes live for as long as you are logged on. All other processes are usually short lived and stay for as long as a command or utility executes.

The **`ps -e f`** (discussed earlier) or **`pstree`** command can be used to display the process tree of currently running processes on the system in a graphical form, showing the parent-child relationship. The **`pstree`** command displays a more compact diagram than the **`ps -e f`** command. The following session shows some sample runs of the **`pstree`** command. The process name preceded by a **+**, sign is the current background process and the process preceded by a **-** sign is the next background process. The output of the **`pstree`** command shows the current process in bold (highlighted) when it is executed with the **`-h`** option, as shown on the opposite page. (The highlighted part does not appear this way when you are using the system via a telnet session.) When used with the **`-a`** option, the **`pstree`** command shows the command with parameters. The last **`pstree`** command is used to display the process hierarchy for process with PID 402: the inetd process (we know the PID of this process from one of the sessions for the **`ps`** command above). The 10*[httpd] notation means that 10 http daemons are running.

```
$ pstree
init-+-actived
     |-amd
     |-atd
     |-automount
     |-crond
     |-gpm
     |-httpd---10*[httpd]
     |-inetd-+-in.telnetd---login---csh---bash---pstree
     |       `-in.telnetd---login---csh---tcsh---man---sh---less
     |-innd
     |-kflushd
     |-klogd
      ...
      ...
$ pstree -h
init-+-actived
     |-amd
     |-atd
     |-automount
     |-crond
     |-gpm
     |-httpd---10*[httpd]
     |-inetd-+-in.telnetd---login---tcsh---bash---pstree
     |       `-in.telnetd---login---csh---tcsh---man---sh---less
     |-innd
     |-kflushd
      ...
$ pstree -a | more
init
  |-actived
  |-amd -a /.automount -l syslog -c 1000 /net /etc/amd.conf
  |-atd
  |-automount –timeout 60 /misc file /etc/auto.misc
  |-crond
  |-gpm -t ps/2
  |-httpd
```

```
 |   |-httpd
 |   |-httpd
 |   |-httpd
 |   |-httpd
 |   |-httpd
 |   |-httpd
 |   |-httpd
 |   |-httpd
 |   |-httpd
 |   `-httpd
 |-inetd
 |   `-in.telnetd
 |       `-login
 |           `-tcsh
 |               `-bash
 |                   |-banner
 |                   |-bash
 |                   |-pine
 |                   `-pstree -a
 |-innd -p4
 |-(kflushd)
...
$ pstree 402 -a
inetd
 |-in.telnetd
 |   `-login
 |       `-csh
 |           `-pine
 |-in.telnetd
 |   `-login
 |       `-csh
 `-in.telnetd
     `-login
         `-tcsh
             `-bash
                 `-pstree 402 -a
$
```

The `ulimit` command can be used under the Bash shell to display the maximum number of processes a user can run simultaneously. The same task can be performed under the TC shell by using the `limit` command. Both commands can be used to display limits on a number of hardware and operating system resources. You can use the `help ulimt` command under Bash to find out more details about the command. The following session shows the use of these commands to determine the process limit under Mandrake 6.1. The process limit on Red Hat 7.2 is 2048.

```
$ ulimit -u
256
$ tcsh
% limit maxproc
maxproc 256
%
```

## SUMMARY

A process is a program in execution. Because it is a time-sharing system, LINUX allows execution of multiple processes simultaneously. On a computer system with one CPU, processes are executed concurrently by scheduling the CPU time and giving it to each process for a short time, called a quantum. Each process is assigned a priority by the LINUX system, and when the CPU is available, it is given to the process with the highest priority.

The shell executes commands by creating child processes using the fork and exec system calls. When a process uses the fork system call, the LINUX kernel creates an exact main memory image of the process. An internal command is executed by the shell itself. An external binary command is executed by the child shell overwriting itself by the code of the command via an exec call. For an external command comprising a shell script, the child shell executes the commands in the script file one by one.

Every LINUX process has several attributes, including process ID (PID), process ID of the parent (PPID), process name, process state (running, suspended, swapped, zombie, etc.), the terminal the process was executed on, the length of time the process has run, and process priority. The `ps` command can be used to display these attributes. The `pstree` command can be used to display process hierarchies.

LINUX processes can be run in the background or the foreground. A foreground process controls the terminal until it finishes, so the shell can't be used for anything else for as long as a foreground process runs. When a process runs in the background, it returns the shell prompt so that the user can do other work as the process executes. Because a background process runs at a lower priority, a command that takes a long time is a good candidate for background execution. A set of commands can be run in a group as separate processes or as one process. Multiple commands can be run from one command line as separate processes by using a semicolon (`;`) as the command separator; enclosed in parentheses these commands can be executed as one process. Commands can be executed concurrently by using ampersand (`&`) as the command separator. Background processes are created by terminating command lines with `&`. System processes (which are executed to provide a service such as printing) executed in background are called daemons.

Suspending processes, moving them from the foreground to the background and vice versa, displaying their status, interrupting them via signals, and terminating them are known as job control, and LINUX has a set of commands that allow these actions. Foreground processes can be moved to the background by suspending them by pressing `<Ctrl-Z>`, followed by executing the `bg` command. Background processes can be moved to the foreground by using the `fg` command. Commands that are suspended or run in the background are also known as jobs. The `jobs` command can be used to view the status of all your jobs. A foreground process can be terminated by pressing `<Ctrl-C>`. The `suspend` command can be used to suspend the current shell process.

The `kill` command can terminate a process with its PID or job ID. The command can be used to send various types of signals, or software interrupts, to processes. Upon receipt of any signal except one, a process can take the default (kernel-defined) action, take a user-defined action, or ignore it. No process can ignore the sure kill, which has been put in place by the LINUX designers to make sure that every process running on a system could be terminated. Commands executed with the `nohup` command keep running even after a user logs out. This command is available for Bourne and C shell compatibility; Bash and TC shells preserve the background processes when you log out.

## PROBLEMS

1. What is a process? How is it known inside the LINUX system?
2. What is CPU scheduling? How does a time-sharing system run multiple processes on a computer system with a single CPU? Be brief but precise.
3. Name three well-known CPU scheduling algorithms. Which are parts of the LINUX scheduling algorithm?
4. What are the main states that a process can be in? What does each state indicate about the status of the process?

5. What is the difference between built-in (internal) and external shell commands? How does a LINUX shell execute built-in and external commands? Explain your answer with an example.
6. Name three process attributes.
7. What is the purpose of the `nice` command in LINUX? (Hint: Read the manual page of the `nice` command).
8. What are foreground and background processes in LINUX? How do you run shell commands as foreground and background processes? Give an example for each.
9. In LINUX jargon, what is a daemon? Give examples of five daemons.
10. What are signals in LINUX? Give three examples of signals. What are the possible actions that a process can take upon receiving a signal? Write commands for sending these signals to a process with PID 10289.
11. Give the command that displays the status of all running processes on your system.
12. Give the command that returns the total number of processes running on your system.
13. Give the sequence of steps (with commands) for terminating a background process.
14. Create a zombie process on your LINUX system. Use the `ps` command to show the process and its state.
15. Give two commands to run the `date` command after 10 sec. Make use of the `sleep` command; read the manual page for this command to find out how to use it.
16. Run a command that would remind you to leave for lunch after one hour by displaying the message "Time for Lunch!"
17. Give a command line for running the `find` and `sort` commands in parallel.
18. Give an example of a LINUX process that does not terminate with `<Ctrl-C>`.
19. Run the following commands on one command line so that they do not terminate when you log out. What command line did you use?

```
find / -inum 23476 -print > all.links.hard 2> /dev/null
find / -name foo -print > foo.paths 2> /dev/null
```

20. Run the following sequence of commands under your shell. What are the outputs of the three `pwd` commands? Why are the outputs of the last two `pwd` commands different?

```
$ pwd
$ bash
$ cd /usr
$ pwd
```

```
...
$ <Ctrl-D>
$ pwd
...
$
```

21. Use the **pstree** and **ps** commands to find out how many mingetty processes are running on your system. Show your command runs with outputs.

CHAPTER

# 14

# Networking and Internetworking

## OBJECTIVES

- To describe networks and internetworks and explain why they are used
- To discuss briefly the TCP/IP protocol suite, IP addresses, protocol ports, and Internet services and applications
- To explain what the client–server software model is and how it works
- To discuss various network software tools for electronic communication, remote login, file transfer, remote command execution, and status reporting
- To describe briefly the secure shell
- To cover the commands and primitives `finger`, `ftp`, `ifconfig`, `nslookup`, `ping`, `rcp`, `rlogin`, `rsh`, `ruptime`, `rusers`, `rwho`, `talk`, `telnet`, `traceroute`

## 14.1 INTRODUCTION

The history of computer networking and the Internet goes back to the late 1960s when the Advanced Research Projects Agency (ARPA) started funding networking research. This research resulted in a wide area network, called ARPANET, by the late 1970s. In 1982, a prototype Internet that used **Transmission Control Protocol/Internet Protocol (TCP/IP)** became operational, with a few academic institutions, industrial research organizations, and the U.S. military using it. By early 1983, all U.S. military sites connected to ARPANET were on the Internet, and the computers on the Internet numbered 562. By 1986 this number had more than quadrupled to 2,308. From then on the size of the Internet doubled every year for the next 10 years, serving about 9.5 million computers by 1996. The first **Web browser**, called Mosaic, was developed at the National Center for Supercomputer Applications (NCSA) and launched in 1991. As a result, in Web browsing (www) surpassed the **file transfer protocol (FTP)** as the major use of the Internet in 1995. Today, the Internet serves somewhere between 200 and 300 million computers and some 1 million computer networks, and users in most of the countries in the world are directly connected to it. UNIX has a special place in the world of networking in general and internetworking in particular because most of the networking protocols were initially implemented on UNIX platforms. Today, most of the Internet services are provided by the server processes running on LINUX- and UNIX-based computers.

## 14.2 COMPUTER NETWORKS AND INTERNETWORKS

When two or more computer hardware resources (computers, printers, scanners, plotters, etc.) are connected, they form a **computer network**. A hardware resource on a network or an internetwork is usually referred to as a **host**. Figure 14.1(a) shows a schematic diagram of a network with six hosts, H1 through H6.

Computer networks are categorized as local area networks (LANs), metropolitan area networks (MANs), and wide area networks (WANs), based on the maximum distance between two hosts on the network. WANs are also known as the long-haul networks. Networks that connect hosts in a room, building, or buildings of a campus are called LANs. The distance between hosts on a LAN can be anywhere from a few meters to about 1 km. Networks that are used to connect hosts within a city, or between small cities, are known as MANs. The distance between hosts on a MAN is about 1 to 20 km. Networks that are used to connect hosts within a state or country are known as WANs. The distance between the hosts on a WAN is in the range of tens of kilometers to a few thousand kilometers.

An **internetwork** is a network of networks. Internetworks can be used to connect networks within a campus or networks that are thousands of kilometers apart. The networks in an internetwork are connected to each other via specialized computers called **routers** or **gateways**. The Internet is the ubiquitous internetwork of

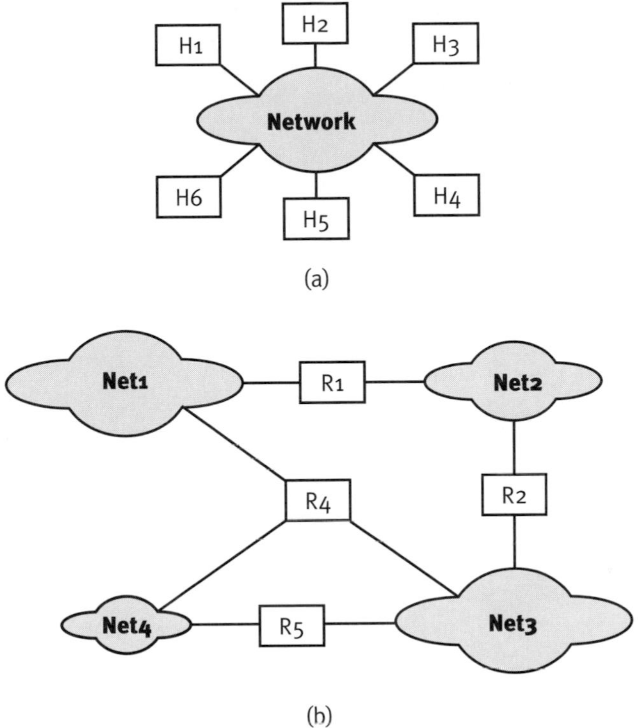


**Figure 14.1** (a) A network of six hosts; (b) An internetwork of four networks

tens of thousands of networks throughout the world. Figure 14.1(b) shows an internetwork of four networks. The four networks, Net1 through Net2, are connected via five routers, R1 through R5. Not all the networks are directly connected and two networks may be connected to each other via multiple **routes**. In Figure 14.1(b), for example, Net2 and Net4 are not directly connected and Net3 and Net4 are connected to each other directly via two routers, R4 and R5. Note that the router R4 also connects directly Net3 and Net1. Routers, such as R4, that can connect more than two networks are known as **multiport** routers.

## 14.3 THE REASONS FOR COMPUTER NETWORKS AND INTERNETWORKS

There are numerous reasons for using networks of computers as opposed to standalone, powerful **minicomputers**, **mainframe computers**, or **supercomputers**. The main reasons include the following.

- Sharing of computing resources: Users of a computer network can share computers, printers, plotters, scanners, files, and application software.

- Network as a communication media: A network is an inexpensive, fast, and reliable communication media between people who live far from each other.
- Cost efficiency: For the same price you get more computing power with a network of workstations than with a minicomputer or mainframe computer.
- Less performance degradation: With a single powerful minicomputer, mainframe computer, or supercomputer, the work comes to a screeching halt if anything goes wrong with the computer, such as a bit in the main memory going bad. With a network of computers, if one computer crashes, the remaining computers on the network are still up and running, allowing continuation of work.

## 14.4 NETWORK MODELS

Various issues are involved in the design and implementation of networks. These issues dictated the design of the two best-known network models.

1. The type of **physical communication medium**, or **communication channel**, used to connect hardware resources. It can be a simple RS-232 cable, telephone lines, coaxial cable, glass fiber, a microwave link, or a satellite link.
2. The **topology** of the network, that is, the physical arrangement of hosts on a network. Some commonly used topologies are bus, ring, mesh, and general graph.
3. The set of rules, called **protocols**, used to allow a host on a network to access the physical medium before initiating data transmission.
4. The protocols used for routing application data (e.g., a Web page) from one host to another in a LAN or from a host in one network to a host in another network in an internetwork.
5. The protocols used for transportation of data from a process on a host to a process on another host in a LAN or from a process on a host in one network to a process on a host in another network in an internetwork.
6. The protocols used by network-based software to provide specific applications such as telnet.

The two best-known network models are the International Standards Organization's Open System Interconnect Reference Model (commonly known as ISO's OSI 7-Layer Reference Model) and the TCP/IP 5-Layer Model. The OSI model was proposed in 1981 and the TCP/IP model in the late 1970s. By 1982, the TCP/IP model was being used by the U.S. military. The TCP/IP model, that has its roots in the Department of Defense Advanced Research Projects Agency (ARPA), is the basis of the Internet and is therefore also known as the Internet Protocol Model. This model consists of five layers, each having a specific purpose and a set of protocols associated with it. The diagram in Figure 14.2 shows the two models, along with an approximate mapping between the two.

| | ISO | Issue | | TCP/IP | Task Handled |
|---|---|---|---|---|---|
| 7 | Application | | | | |
| 6 | Presentation | 6 | 5 | Application | User process: Application details |
| 5 | Session | | | | |
| 4 | Transport | 5 | 4 | Transport | Kernel and hardware: Communications details |
| 3 | Network | 4 | 3 | Network | |
| 2 | Data Link | 3 | 2 | Link | |
| 1 | Physical | 1 and 2 | 1 | Device/Physical | |
| | ISO | | | TCP/IP | |

**Figure 14.2** ISO and TCP/IP layered models, mapping between the two, and the general purpose of a group of layers

Because the TCP/IP model is used in the Internet, we focus only on it. In terms of the six issues previously listed, the first layer in the TCP/IP model deals with the first two issues, the second layer deals with the third issue, the third layer deals with the fourth issue, the fourth layer deals with the fifth issue, and the fifth layer deals with the sixth issue. In terms of their implementation, the first four layers deal with the details of communication between hosts and the fifth layer deals with the details of the Internet services provided by various applications. Most of the first layer is handled by hardware (type of communication medium used, attachments of hosts to the medium, etc.). The rest of the first layer and all of the second layer is handled by the **network interface card (NIC)** in a host. Layers 3 and 4 are fully implemented in the operating system kernel on most existing systems. The first two layers are network hardware specific, whereas the remaining layers work independently of the physical network. On newer systems, the network layer is implemented in hardware.

The following In-Chapter Exercises have been designed for you to appreciate the physical nature of your network environment.

## IN-CHAPTER EXERCISES

**14.1.** Ask your system administrator how many hosts are connected on your LAN. What type of computers are they (PCs or workstations)?

**14.2.** What is the physical media for your network (coaxial cable, twisted pair, or glass fiber)? Ask your instructor or system administrator about the topology of your network (bus, ring, etc.).

**14.3.** The **Ethernet** is the most commonly used link-level protocol for LANs. Does your LAN use Ethernet? If not, what does it use?

## 14.5 THE TCP/IP PROTOCOL SUITE

Several protocols are associated with various layers in the TCP/IP model. These protocols result in what is commonly known as the **TCP/IP suite**, which is illustrated in Figure 14.3. The description of most of the protocols in the suite is beyond the scope of this textbook, but we briefly describe the purpose of those that are most relevant to our discussion. As a user, you see the application layer in the form of applications and utilities that can be executed to invoke various Internet services. Some of the commonly used applications are for electronic mail, Web browsing, file transfer, and remote login. We discuss some of the most useful applications in Section 14.8.

### 14.5.1 TCP AND UDP

The purpose of the transport layer is to transport application data from your machine to a remote machine and vice versa. This delivery service can be a simple, best effort service that does not guarantee reliable delivery of the application data or one that guarantees reliable and in-sequence delivery of the application data. The best effort delivery service is offered by the User Datagram Protocol (UDP), and the completely reliable, in-sequence delivery is offered by the Transmission Control Protocol (TCP). The UDP is a connectionless protocol; that is, it simply sends the application data to the destination without establishing a virtual connection with the destination before transmitting the data. Hence the UDP software on the sender host does not "talk" to the UPD software on the receiver host before sending data. The TCP is a connection-oriented protocol that establishes a virtual connection between the sender and receiver hosts before transmitting application data, leading to reliable, error-free, and in-sequence delivery

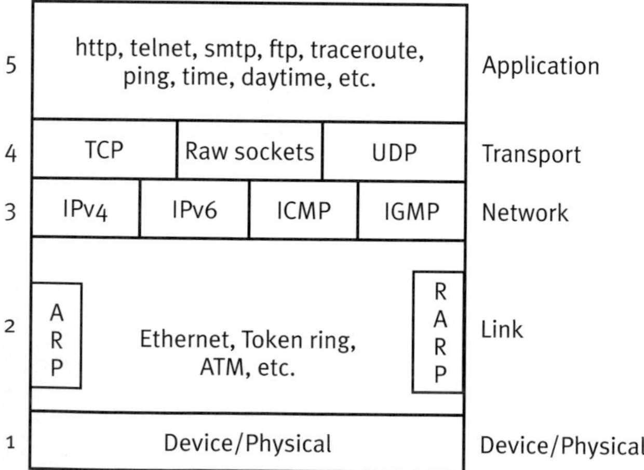


Figure 14.3 The TCP/IP protocol suite

of data. Of course, the overhead for establishing the connection makes TCP more costly than UDP. Thus the UDP is like the U.S. Postal Service handling of first-class mail and the TCP is like the UPS (or FedEx) package delivery service. Most Internet applications such as **telnet** use TCP. In the Internet jargon, a data **packet** transported by TCP is called a *segment* and a data packet transported by UDP is called a *datagram*.

Because multiple client and server processes may be using the TCP and/or UDP at any one time, these protocols identify every process running on a host by 16-bit positive integers from 0 though 65,535, called **port numbers**. Port numbers 0 through 1023 are called *well-known ports* and are controlled by the Internet Assigned Numbers Authority (IANA). Well-known services such as **ftp** are assigned ports that fall in the well-known range (excluding 0). Some of these services allow the use of either TCP or UDP, and IANA tries to assign the same port number to a given service for both TCP and UDP. For example, the ftp service is assigned port number 21, and the http (Web) server is assigned port number 80 for both the TCP and UDP. Most clients can run on any port and are assigned a port by the operating system at the time the client process starts execution. Some clients such as **rlogin** and **rsh** require the use of a reserved port as part of the client–server authentication protocol. These clients are assigned ports in the range 513 through 1023.

### 14.5.2 Routing of Application Data—The Internet Protocol (IP)

As we have mentioned before, the network layer is responsible for routing application data to the destination host. The protocol responsible for this is the Internet Protocol (IP), which transports TCP segments or UDP datagrams containing application data in its own packets called *IP datagrams*. The routing algorithm is connectionless, which means that IP routing is best effort routing and it does not guarantee delivery of TCP packets (segments) or UDP packets (datagrams). Applications that need guaranteed delivery use TCP as their transport level protocol or have it built into themselves. The current version of IP is IPv4, and the new version (not available in most operating systems yet) is IPv6 (commonly known as IPng: Internet Protocol—the Next Generation). In this textbook we primarily discuss IPv4. The discussion on the actual routing algorithms used by IP is beyond our scope here. However, we describe a key component of routing on the Internet—the IP addressing (naming) scheme to identify uniquely a host on the Internet.

The key to routing is the IP assignment of a unique identification to every host on the Internet. It does so by uniquely identifying the network it is on and then uniquely identifying the host on that network. The ID, a 32-bit positive integer in IPv4 and a 128-bit positive integer in IPv6, is known as the host's **IP address**. Every IP datagram has a sender's and a receiver's IP address in it. The sender's IP address allows the receiver host to identify and respond to the sender. Hosts and routers perform routing by examining the destination IP address on an IP datagram.

In IPv4, the IP address is divided into three fields: address class, network ID, and host ID. The address class field identifies the class of the address and dictates the number of bits used in the network ID and host ID fields. This scheme results in five address classes: A, B, C, D, and E, with classes A, B, and C being the most common. Figure 14.4 shows the structures of the five address types. The IP addresses belonging to classes D and E have special use, and their discussion is beyond the scope of this textbook. All IP addresses are assigned by a central authority, the Network Information Center (NIC).

The maximum number of class A, B, and C networks that can be connected to the Internet is given by the expression: $2^7 + 2^{14} + 2^{21}$. Here, 7, 14, and 21 are the number of bits used to specify network IDs in class A, B, and C addresses, respectively. Thus there are $2^7$ class A networks, $2^{14}$ class B networks, and $2^{21}$ class C networks. The sum of these numbers gives a total of 2,113,664 networks! Similarly, the number of bits used to identify host IDs in the three classes of addresses can be used to get the maximum number of hosts that can be connected to the Internet. Thus there are roughly $2^{24}$ hosts per class A network, $2^{16}$ hosts per class B network, and $2^8$ hosts per class C network. The sum of all the hosts on the three types of networks is a total of 3,758,096,400 hosts. The actual number of class A, B, and C networks and hosts are somewhat smaller than the numbers shown, owing to some special addresses (e.g., broadcast and localhost addresses). The broadcast addresses are used to address all hosts on a network. The localhost address is used by a host to send a datagram to itself. Hence an IP datagram with localhost as its destination address is never put on the network.

The number of class A addresses is very small, so these addresses are assigned only to very large organizations and government agencies, such as national laboratories and NASA. The number of class B addresses is relatively large, and these addresses are assigned to large organizations. Hence corporations such as AT&T and

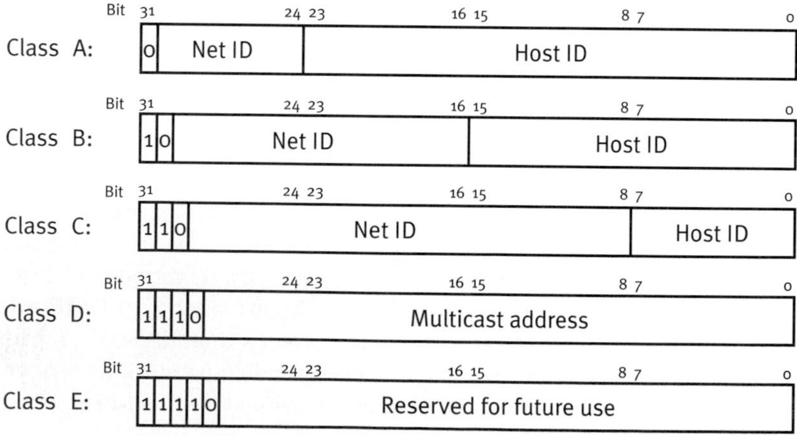


**Figure 14.4** IPv4 address classes

IBM and institutions such as MIT and numerous other national and international universities have been assigned class B addresses. The total number of class C addresses is quite large, so these addresses are assigned to individuals and small- to medium-sized organizations, such as local Internet service providers, small consulting and software companies, community colleges, and universities.

Although the IPv4 addressing scheme can be used to identify a large number of networks and hosts, it will not be able to cope with the rapid growth of the Internet. Among the many advantages of IPv6 is that an extremely large number of hosts can be connected. With the 128-bit address, the maximum number of hosts on the Internet will increase to roughly $2^{128}$, which is greater than $3.4 \times 10^{38}$. This number is roughly $6 \times 2^{28}$ times the present world population. One disadvantage of IPng is that, because the address size is very large, remembering IPv6 addresses becomes very difficult. However, because most users prefer to use symbolic names, remembering IPv6 addresses should not be an issue. Also, some compact notations similar to DDN have been proposed for IPv6 addresses as well.

### 14.5.3 IPv4 Addresses in Dotted Decimal Notation

Although hosts and routers process IPv4 addresses as 32-bit binary numbers, they are difficult for people to remember. For this reason, the IPv4 addresses are given in **dotted decimal notation (DDN)**. In this notation, all four bytes of an IPv4 address are written in their decimal equivalents and are separated by dots. Thus the 32-bit IP address

11000000 01100110 00001010 00010101

is written as

192.102.10.21

in dotted decimal notation. The ranges of valid IP addresses belonging to the five address classes in dotted decimal notation are shown in Table 14.1. Some of the addresses given in the table are special addresses.

**Table 14.1** IPv4 Address Classes and Valid IP Addresses

| Address Class | Range of Valid IP Addresses Lowest | Highest |
|---|---|---|
| A | 0.0.0.0 | 127.255.255.255 |
| B | 128.0.0.0 | 191.255.255.255 |
| C | 192.0.0.0 | 223.255.255.255 |
| D | 224.0.0.0 | 239.255.255.255 |
| E | 240.0.0.0 | 247.255.255.255 |

The internetwork shown in Figure 14.5 connects four networks via four routers, R1 through R4. Net1 is a class A network, Net3 is a class B network, and Net2 and Net4 are class C networks. The way to identify the class of a network is to look at the left-most decimal number in the IP address of a host on the network, in this case, the IP addresses of the routers. Note that the routers are assigned as many IP addresses as the number of networks they connect. Here, for example, router R1, which connects Net1 and Net2, has IP addresses 121.1.1.1 and 192.102.10.1. Similarly, R4 is assigned three IP addresses, as it interconnects three networks Net1, Net2, and Net3.

Of the special addresses, 127.0.0.0 (or 127.x.x.x, where x can be any number between 0 and 255), also known as localhost, is used by a host to send a data packet to itself. It also is commonly used for testing new applications before they are used on the Internet. Another special address, in which the host ID field is all 1s, is the directed broadcast address. This address is used to send a data packet to all hosts on a network, that is, for broadcasting on a local network whose host is using the address as a destination address.

### 14.5.4 Symbolic Names

People prefer to use symbolic names rather than numeric addresses because names are easier to remember, especially with the transition to the 128-bit long numeric addresses in IPv6. Also, symbolic names can remain the same even if numeric addresses change. Like its IP address, the symbolic name of a host on the Internet must be unique. The Internet allows the use of symbolic names by using a hierarchical naming scheme. The symbolic names have the format

hostname.domain_name

where domain_name is the symbolic name referring to the site and is assigned to by the Network Information Center. The host name is assigned and controlled by

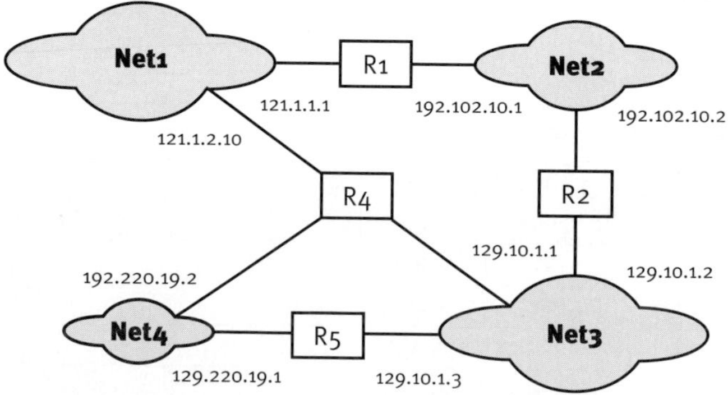


**Figure 14.5** An internetwork of four networks with one class A, one class B, and two class C networks

the site that is allocated the domain_name. The domain_name consists of two (or more) strings separated by a period (.). The right-most string in a domain name is called the *top-level domain*. The string to the left of the right-most period identifies an organization and can be chosen by the organization and assigned to it by the Network Information Center. If the string has already been assigned to another organization under the same top-level domain, another string is assigned in order to keep the domain names unique. There are nine top-level domains: eight for use within the United States and one each for every country, as listed in Table 14.2. The Network Information Center has recently released eight new domains.

For the domain names that consist of more than two strings, the remaining strings are assigned by the organization that owns the domain. Some example domain names are up.edu, intel.com, whitehouse.gov, uu.net, omsi.org, egr.up.edu, cairo.eng.kuniv.edu.kw, ptv.com.pk, www.beavton.k12.or.us, and bbc.co.uk. The strings to the left of a country domain are assigned by authorities in that country. Figure 14.6 illustrates the domain name hierarchy.

Attaching the name of a host to a domain name with a period between them yields the **fully qualified domain name (FQDN)** for the host—for example, egr.up.edu, where egr is the name of a host in the School of Engineering at the University of Portland. However, fully qualified domain names for the hosts on the Internet do not always have three parts. Most organizations allow various groups within the organization to choose the primary names for the hosts that they control and are responsible for. For example, the School of Engineering at the University of

**Table 14.2** Top-Level Internet Domains

| Top-Level Domain | Assigned to |
|---|---|
| ARPA | Now obsolete ARPANET domain |
| COM | Commercial organization |
| EDU | U.S. educational institution |
| GOV | U.S. government agency |
| INT | International organizations |
| MIL | U.S. military |
| NET | Networking organization |
| ORG | Nonprofit organization |
| Country code | AU Australia<br>DE Germany (Deutschland)<br>FI Finland<br>JP Japan<br>PK Pakistan<br>. . .<br>UK United Kingdom<br>US United States of America |

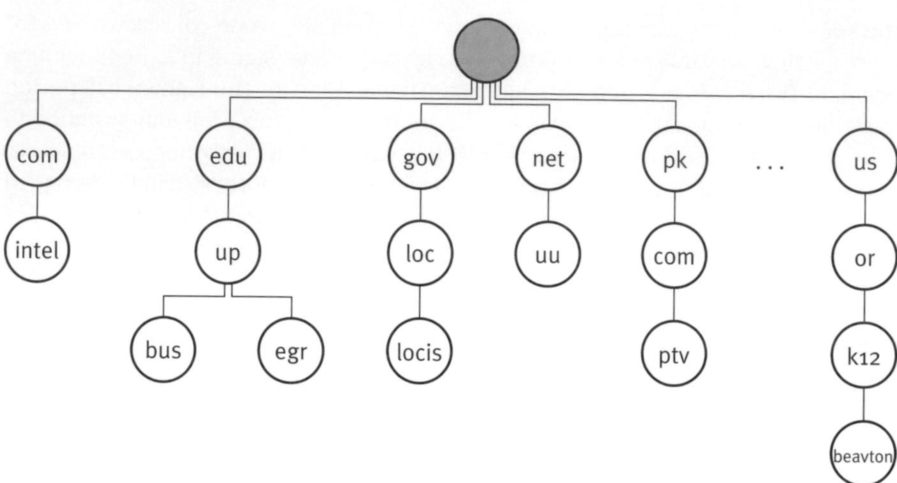


Figure 14.6 A portion of the Internet domain name hierarchy

Portland, which uses the primary name egr.up.edu, uses www.egr.up.edu as the FQDN for its http server. The School of Business Administration, which uses the primary name bus.up.edu, can use the host name www.bus.up.edu for its Web server.

### 14.5.5 Translating Names to IP Addresses—The Domain Name System

Because Internet software deals with IP addresses and people prefer to use symbolic names, application software translates symbolic names to equivalent IP addresses. This translation involves use of a service provided by the Internet known as the **domain name system (DNS)**. The DNS implements a distributed database of name-to-address mappings. A set of dedicated hosts run server processes called **name servers** that take requests from application software (also called the client software; see Section 14.7) and work together to map domain names to the corresponding IP addresses. Every organization runs at least one name server, usually the Berkeley Internet Name Domain (BIND) program. The applications use resolver functions such as `gethostbyname` to invoke the DNS service. The `gethostbyname` resolver function maps a host name (simple or fully qualified) to its IP address, and `gethostbyaddr` maps an IP address to its host name.

An alternative, and old, scheme for using the DNS service is to use a static hosts file, usually /etc/hosts. This file contains the domain names and their IP addresses, one per line. The following command displays a sample /etc/hosts file.

```
$ cat /etc/hosts
#
# Internet host table
#
```

```
127.0.0.1        localhost
139.141.1.3      cairo cairo.eng.kuniv.edu.kw
139.141.1.20     router1
139.141.3.2      london
$
```

There are two problems with this scheme. First, its implementation depends on how the system administrator configures the system. Second, owing to the sheer size of the Internet and its current rate of growth, the static file can be extremely large. If your system provides the NIS Service, you can use the **`ypcat hosts`** command to display domain names and IP addresses of all the hosts on your network.

You can use the **`ifconfig`** command to view the IP address and other information about your host's interface to the network. The following is an example run of the command. The command output shows that the host that you are logged onto has two IP addresses: 127.0.0.1 and 192.102.10.89. The address 127.0.0.1 is the destination address for itself (the localhost), whereas 192.102.10.89 is your host's actual IP address, by which it is known to the outside world. Explanation of the rest of the output is beyond the scope of this textbook

```
$ ifconfig -a
lo0: flags=849<UP,LOOPBACK,RUNNING,MULTICAST> mtu 8232
        inet 127.0.0.1 netmask ff000000
le0: flags=863<UP,BROADCAST,NOTRAILERS,RUNNING,MULTICAST> mtu 1500
        inet 192.102.10.89 netmask ffffff00 broadcast 192.102.10.255
$
```

The `ifconfig` command is normally located in the /sbin directory. So, if you get an error message such as `ifconfig: Command not found`, include the /sbin directory in your search path (see Chapters 4 and 7) and reexecute the command. You can run the `cat /etc/hosts` command to display the domain names and IP addresses of the hosts on your network.

You can use the `nslookup` command to display the IP address of a host whose domain name is passed as a command line argument to it. In the following session, the command is used to find the IP address of the host ibm.com.

```
$ nslookup ibm.com
Server:  guardian.egr.up.edu
Address:  192.102.10.10

Name:    ibm.com
Address:  204.146.80.99

$
```

The **nslookup** command uses the /etc/resolv.conf file to find the host that runs the name server software and passes the request over to it. The name server starts the DNS search to locate the IP address for the host name passed to it. The name server in this case is guardian.egr.up.edu, as shown in the output of the session.

The following In-Chapter Exercises have been designed to enhance your depth of understanding of your own network environment by way of learning the domain names and IP addresses of hosts on your network. You will also use the **nslookup** command to translate domain names to IP addresses.

### IN-CHAPTER EXERCISES

**14.4.** Give the domain names of some hosts on your LAN. Ask your instructor for help if you need any.

**14.5.** List the IP addresses of the hosts identified in Exercise 14.4 in dotted decimal notation. What is the class of your network (A, B, or C)? How did you find out?

**14.6.** Run the **nslookup** utility to confirm the IP addresses of the hosts identified in Exercise 14.4.

## 14.6 INTERNET SERVICES AND PROTOCOLS

Most users do not understand the intricacies of the Internet protocols and its architecture—nor do they need to. They access the Internet by using programs that implement the application-level protocols for various Internet services. Some of the most commonly used services and the corresponding protocols are listed in Table 14.3. The services are listed in alphabetic order and not according to their frequency of use. You can see the /etc/services file on your host to view the Internet services and their well-known port numbers.

The LINUX operating system has some network-related services that aren't necessarily available in other operating systems. They include services for displaying all the users logged onto the hosts in a LAN, remote execution of a command,

**Table 14.3** Popular Internet Services and Corresponding Protocols

| Service | Protocol |
|---|---|
| Electronic mail | SMTP (Simple Mail Transfer Protocol) |
| File transfer | FTP (File Transfer Protocol) |
| Remote login | Telnet |
| Time | Time |
| Web browsing | HTTP (Hyper Text Transfer Protocol) |

real-time chat in a network, and remote copy. We discuss utilities for most of these services in Section 14.8.

## 14.7 THE CLIENT–SERVER SOFTWARE MODEL

Internet services are implemented by using a paradigm in which the software for a service is partitioned into two parts. The part that runs on the host on which the user running the application is logged onto is called the **client software**. The part that usually starts running when a host boots is called the **server software**. On the one hand, the server runs forever, waiting for a client request to come. Upon receipt of a request, it services the client request and waits for another request. On the other hand, a client starts running only when a user runs the program for a service that the client offers. It usually prompts the user for input (command and/or data), transfers the user input to the server, receives the server's response, and forwards the response to the user. Most clients terminate with some sort of quit or exit command.

Most of the applications are connection-oriented client–server models, in which the client sends a connection request to the server and the server either accepts or rejects the request. If the server accepts the request, client and server are said to be connected through a **virtual connection**. From this point on, the client sends user commands to the server as requests. The server services client requests and sends responses to the client, which sends them to the user in a particular format. Communication between client and a server—and the client's interaction with the user—are dictated by the protocol for the service offered by an application. Figure 14.7 shows an overview of the client–server software model.

Thus, when you run a program that allows you to surf the Web, such as Netscape Navigator, an http client process starts running on your host. By default, most clients display the **home page** of the organization that owns the host on which the client runs, although it can be set to any page. When you want to view the Web page of a site, you give the site's **universal resource locator (URL)** to the client process. For displaying a home page, the URL has the format

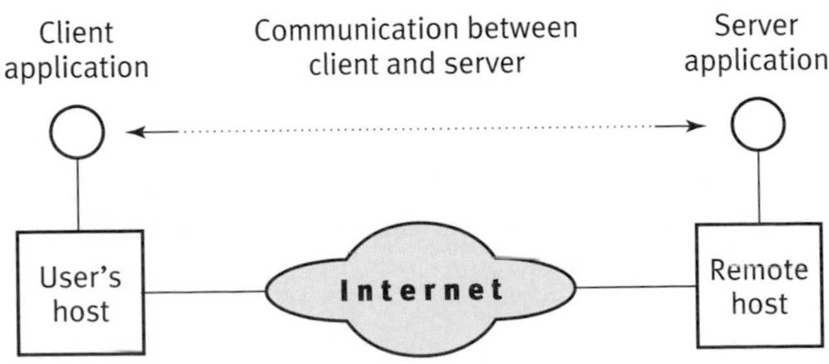


**Figure 14.7** Depiction of the client–server software model

http://host/page

where 'host' can be the fully qualified domain name or IP address (in dotted decimal notation) of the computer that has the home page you want to display and 'page' is the pathname for the file containing the page to be displayed—for example, http://cnn.com, http://192.201.18.91, http://lhotse.up.edu/~koretsky/index.html, and http://www.egr.up.edu/index.html. The client tries to establish a connection with the http server process on the site corresponding to the URL. If the site has the http server running and no security protections such as a password are in place, a connection is established between client and server. The server then sends the Web page to the client, which displays it on the screen, with any audio or video components sent to appropriate devices. Note that 'http' can be replaced with 'ftp' if you want to access an ftp site through your browser, or with 'telnet' if you want to remote logon via the telnet protocol.

You can invoke the client programs for most Internet services by specifying a domain name or IP address, as well as the particular port number, of the host on which a server runs. A client software that has such flexibility built into it is known as a **fully parameterized client**. Such clients are important in terms of the flexibility they offer. They also allow testing of updated server software because server software can be run on a port that is not well known and contacted by the client. A telnet client, discussed in Section 14.8, is a good example of a fully parameterized client.

## 14.8 APPLICATION SOFTWARE

Numerous programs that implement the application-level protocols just discussed are available on networks of LINUX hosts and the Internet. Of the most commonly used applications described here, some are available on LINUX-based systems only, whereas others are available to all the hosts on the Internet.

### 14.8.1 Displaying the Host Name

Network-based applications use the user@host address format to identify a user on a network on the Internet. You can use the `hostname` and `uname` commands (also discussed in Chapter 3) to display the name of the host you are logged on to. On some systems, the host name is shown in the short, simple name format and on others it is displayed in the long, fully qualified domain name format. If you have to identify the host on the network that you are logged onto, you can use the `hostname` command with the `-s` option to display the short format, which is simply the name of the host (the left-most string in the FQDN format). Some systems don't allow you to use this option unless you are the superuser. The following are some examples of the `hostname` and `uname` commands.

```
$ hostname
upibm7.egr.up.edu
```

```
$ hostname -s
upibm7
$ uname -n
upibm7.egr.up.edu
$
```

### 14.8.2 Displaying List of Users Using Hosts on a Network

You can use the **rwho** (remote who) command to display information about the users currently using machines on your network The output of this command is like that of the **who** command. An output line contains the login name of a user, the computer and terminal the user is logged onto, and the date and time the user logged in. The last field is blank if the user is currently typing at the terminal; if a user hasn't typed for one minute or more, **rwho** reports this idle time in minutes and hours. The names of users who haven't typed for one hour or more are omitted from output; entries for such users can be displayed with the **-a** option. The following session shows how the command is used, without and with the **-a** option.

```
$ rwho
bobk     upibm7:ttyC4  Jul 26 12:03   :59
dfrakes  upibm47:ttyp2 Jul 26 11:49   :11
lulay    upsun17:pts/0 Jul 26 10:17   :23
oster    upsun17:pts/2 Jul 26 12:28   :51
sarwar   upibm7:ttyp2  Jul 26 11:15   :34
$ rwho -a
bobk     upibm7:ttyC4      Jul 26 12:03    :59
dfrakes  upibm47:ttyp2     Jul 26 11:49    :11
kent     upibm48:ttyp0     Jul 26 03:41   8:49
kittyt   upibm9:ttyp0      Jul 26 07:36   1:28
kuhn     upsun29:console   Jul 16 13:11  99:59
lulay    upsun17:pts/0     Jul 26 10:17    :23
oster    upsun17:pts/2     Jul 26 12:28    :51
pioster  upsun20:pts/0     Jul 26 09:53   2:41
sarwar   upibm7:ttyp2      Jul 26 11:15    :34
sarwar   upsun29:pts/0     Jul 26 11:24   1:00
$
```

You can use the **rusers** (remote users) command to display the names of the users logged onto the machines on your local network. The login names of the users currently using a machine are displayed in one line per machine format. The following is a brief description of the command.

Syntax:

**rusers [options] [host_list]**

**Purpose:** Display the login names of the users logged on to all the machines on your local network

**Output:** Information about the users logged on to the hosts on your local network in one line per machine format

**Commonly used options/features:**

| | |
|---|---|
| `-a` | Display a host name even if no user is using it |
| `-l` | Display the user information in a long format similar to that displayed by the `who` command |

The `rusers` command broadcasts a query to all the hosts on the network, asking them to reply with user information. It collects all the replies and displays the information in the order received. It waits for one minute to catch late responses. The following is a simple run of the command. Note that host names are displayed in a 16-character field, which is why the edu part of the names is not completely displayed. As shown in the output of the command, the user kent is logged in twice on the upibm8.egr.up.edu host, sarwar is logged onto upsun29.egr.up.edu, and users kittyt and deborahs are logged onto upibm6.egr.up.edu, with kittyt logged on twice.

```
$ rusers
upibm48.egr.up.e kent kent
upsun29.egr.up.e sarwar
upibm6.egr.up.ed kittyt kittyt deborahs
$
```

You can display the names of the users logged on a particular host by specifying the host as an argument to the `rusers` command. The following command displays the login names of the users logged onto the upibm7 host.

```
$ rusers upibm7
upibm7.egr.up.edu  uppp p44 upppp upppp26 kathek khnguyen upppp14 leslie sarwar
sarwar
$
```

As shown in the following session, you can use the **rusers** command with the **-a** option to display host names even if no user is logged onto them. Doing so allows you to find out the names of all the hosts on your network.

```
$ rusers -a
upsun12.egr.up.e
...
upsun27.egr.up.e
upibm48.egr.up.e kent kent
upsun29.egr.up.e sarwar
upsqnt.egr.up.ed
...
upibm3.egr.up.ed
upibm6.egr.up.ed kittyt kittyt deborahs
$
```

Depending on the complexty of your network, the **rusers** command may take several seconds to complete its execution.

### 14.8.3 Displaying the Status of Hosts on a Network

You can use the **ruptime** (remote uptime) command to display the status of all the computers connected to your LAN. Each line of the output has the following format: computer (host) name, system status (up/down), the amount of time the computer has been up (or down; the number before the + sign indicates the number of days), the number of users logged onto each host, and the load factor for each host. You can use the command with the **-u** option to display the status sorted by the number of users. Other useful options are **-l** for sorting by load average and **-t** for sorting by uptime. The following sessions demonstrate use of the **ruptime** command without and with the **-u** option.

```
$ ruptime
upibm0      up   1+09:16,     0 users, load 0.00, 0.00, 0.00
...
upsun29     up  69+23:51,     2 users, load 1.48, 1.35, 1.32
$ ruptime -u
upibm7      up   1+09:25,    10 users, load 0.00, 0.00, 0.00
upibm47   down   5+20:01,
upsun17     up      8:25,     2 users, load 0.00, 0.00, 0.03
```

```
upsun29    up 69+23:57,     1 user,  load 1.30, 1.31, 1.31
...
$
```

Note that upsun29 has been up for almost 70 days and upibm43 down for 5 days.

In the following In-Chapter Exercises, you will use the `ruptime`, `rwho`, and `rusers` commands to appreciate their syntax and output. You will also get a feel for what the Internet is primarily used for.

**IN-CHAPTER EXERCISES**

**14.7.** Use the `ruptime` command on your system to find out how many hosts are connected to your LAN.

**14.8.** Use the `rwho` and `rusers` commands to display information about the users who are currently logged on to the hosts on your network.

**14.9.** Ask your friends and fellow students about the network service they use most often. Which service is it? How many people did you ask?

### 14.8.4 Testing a Network Connection

You can test the status of a network or a particular host on it by using the `ping` command. If the `ping` command doesn't work on your system, use the `whereis` command to find its location, update your search path, and try the command again. It is normally in the /bin directory. The following is a brief description of the command.

Syntax:

**ping [options] hostname**

**Purpose:** Send an IP datagram to 'hostname' to test whether it is on the network (or Internet); if the host is alive, it simply echoes the received datagram

**Output:** Message(s) indicating whether the machine is alive

**Commonly used options/features:**

| | |
|---|---|
| `-c` count | Send and receive 'count' packets |
| `-f` | Send 100 packets per second or as many as can be handled by the network; only the superuser can use this option. |
| `-s` packetsize | Send 'packetsize' packets; the default is 56 bytes (plus an 8-byte header). |

The following session illustrates the use of the **ping** command with and without options. When executed without any argument, the command displays the echoed messages until you hit <Ctrl-C>. Note the difference in the round-trip transmission times due to the physical distance and the quality of the physical communication channel between the host on which we executed the command and the destination hosts (pcc.edu and lums.edu.pk). We used the **-c** option in the following session to send and receive three messages. The **-c** and **-s** options are used in the last command to send and receive two messages 2,048 bytes in size (plus the 8-byte ICMP header).

```
$ ping pcc.edu
PING pcc.edu (192.220.1.109): 56 data bytes
64 bytes from 192.220.1.109: icmp_seq=0 ttl=246 time=13.3 ms
64 bytes from 192.220.1.109: icmp_seq=1 ttl=246 time=13.1 ms
<Ctrl-C>

--- pcc.edu ping statistics ---
2 packets transmitted, 2 packets received, 0% packet loss
round-trip min/avg/max = 13.1/13.2/13.3 ms
$ ping lums.edu.pk
PING lums.edu.pk (203.128.0.2): 56 data bytes
64 bytes from 203.128.0.2: icmp_seq=0 ttl=238 time=1409.7 ms
64 bytes from 203.128.0.2: icmp_seq=1 ttl=238 time=1485.5 ms
64 bytes from 203.128.0.2: icmp_seq=2 ttl=238 time=1641.0 ms
<Ctrl-C>

--- lums.edu.pk ping statistics ---
3 packets transmitted, 3 packets received, 0% packet loss
round-trip min/avg/max = 1409.7/1512.0/1641.0 ms
$ ping -c 3 pcc.edu
PING pcc.edu (192.220.1.109): 56 data bytes
64 bytes from 192.220.1.109: icmp_seq=0 ttl=246 time=19.6 ms
64 bytes from 192.220.1.109: icmp_seq=1 ttl=246 time=13.1 ms
64 bytes from 192.220.1.109: icmp_seq=2 ttl=246 time=33.7 ms

--- pcc.edu ping statistics ---
3 packets transmitted, 3 packets received, 0% packet loss
round-trip min/avg/max = 13.1/22.1/33.7 ms
$ ping -c 2 -s 2048 pcc.edu
```

```
PING pcc.edu (192.220.1.109): 2048 data bytes
2056 bytes from 192.220.1.109: icmp_seq=0 ttl=246 time=80.4 ms
2056 bytes from 192.220.1.109: icmp_seq=1 ttl=246 time=81.7 ms

--- pcc.edu ping statistics ---
2 packets transmitted, 2 packets received, 0% packet loss
round-trip min/avg/max = 80.4/81.0/81.7 ms
$
```

You can use the IP address of a host in place of its host name. For example, you can use `ping 192.220.1.109` instead of `ping pcc.edu`.

### 14.8.5 Displaying Information About Users

You can use the **`finger`** command to display information about users on a local or remote host. The information displayed is extracted from a user's ~/.plan and ~/.project files. The following is a brief description of the command.

Syntax:

**finger [options] [user_list]**

**Purpose:** Display information about the users in 'user_list'; without a 'user_list' the command displays a short status report about all the users currently logged onto the specified hosts

**Output:** User information extracted from the ~/.project and ~/.plan files

**Commonly used options/features:**

| | |
|---|---|
| `-m` | Match 'user_list' to login names only |
| `-s` | For displaying output in a short format |

The following session shows the simplest use of the command in which the information about a single user, Birch Tree, on the host is displayed.

```
$ finger Birch
Login name: btree                   In real life: Birch Tree
Directory: /home/student/tree       Shell: /bin/ksh
On since Jul 30 16:16:02 on pts/0 from upibm7.egr.up.edu
No unread mail
```

```
Project: Hacking LINUX for its sake ...
Plan: To turn from a Windows lizard to a LINUX wizard ...
$
```

You can use the **finger** command with the **-s** option to display the command's output in a short format and the **-m** option to match 'user_list' to login names only. The **finger -m Tree** command displays the same information if the **finger Birch** command if the login name of the user is tree (uppercase and lowercase letters are considered the same by networking commands). However, if the login name of the user is btree and the login name birch doesn't exist in the system, the **finger** command displays a message informing you of this. The following sessions show the use of these options.

```
$ finger -s Birch
Login   Name        TTY  Idle Login  Time   Office  Phone
birch  Birch Tree  /0         Dec 16 10:22  EN29
$ finger -m Birch
finger: Birch: no such user.
$
```

You can use the **finger** command to display information about a user on any host on the Internet, provided that the host offers the finger service and has the finger server (finger daemon: fingerd) running. The following command can be used to display information about a user williams at the iastate.edu domain (site).

```
$ finger williams@iastate.edu
[iastate.edu]
Iowa State University sitewide finger server.
Use `finger "/h"@iastate.edu` for help information.

Login name: williams                 Real name: John J Williams
Address: GE AT
Office Phone: (515)555-9999          Home Phone: (515)555-0000

Plan:
Email:   williams@iastate.edu        FAX: (515)555-0000
Please see my personal web page for my weekly schedule:
         http://volcano.ecpe.iastate.edu/~williams/index.html
```

```
Username TTY    Login at  Idle    Machine     From host
User not logged in.
$
```

The format of the output is generally the same, but it can vary from one site to another. Try the command for some name at mit.edu to see differences in output.

When run without any argument, the **finger** command returns the status of all the users who are currently logged on to your machine. The amount of information displayed varies somewhat, depending on the LINUX system that your host runs. However, every system displays at least the following information. With ***@hostname** as its argument, the command displays the status of all the users who are currently logged on to 'hostname'. Some sites put restrictions on use of the wildcard *. For example, the sites mit.edu and osu.edu require the use of at least two characters in all queries. The following sessions display the status of all the users on the host that you are logged onto and on a remote host, iastate.edu, that allows use of the wildcard *.

```
$ finger
Login    Name             Tty  Idle  Login  Time  Office Office Phone
kathek   Kathe Koretsky    C4    59  Jul 30 13:55
oster    Peter Osterberg  C3    29  Jul 30 16:12
sarwar   Mansoor Sarwar    p0    25  Jul 30 15:21 EN29
upppp    PPP kent          C6 11:02  Jul 30 05:40
upppp44  PPP sarwar        C2  1:22  Jul 30 15:21
$ finger *@iastate.edu
[iastate.edu]
Iowa State University site-wide finger server.
Use `finger "/h"@iastate.edu` for help information.

Login:    Real Name:                     Office:
--------  -----------------------------  -----------------------
aeriksen  Amber Lei Eriksen              Minnesota
bmoorhea  Brian 'SolarCar *IS* my life'  13xb Woode Street
boss      J___ S________                 Rumah
cwright   *&^%???                        here
huypham   Huy Vu Pham                    5509 Belgrade Ave
jarzt     Jennifer M Arzt                731 N. Ireland Ave #2
jbond     *Special Agent 2 Much Soul*
jerry     *unknown*                      nowhere
```

```
kandrese  ****                            ****
kicks     Nicks                           Cardboard Box #
mtnbkr    ********                        It's on my door
rbcarter  **you-know-me**                 **Apt num 3 Czech Republ
$
```

If the DNS can't find a mapping for a domain name, the **finger** command returns an appropriate error message, as in

```
$ finger williams@iastate.com
finger: unknown host: iastate.com
$
```

In the following In-Chapter Exercises, you will use the **ping** and **finger** commands to understand their syntax and various characteristics.

**IN-CHAPTER EXERCISES**

**14.10.** Run the `ping` command to determine whether a remote host that you know about is up.

**14.11.** Give the command for displaying information about yourself on your LINUX host.

**14.12.** Give the command for displaying information about a user on your host, with John as his first or last name.

**14.13.** Give a command for displaying information about all the users who are currently logged on to the site cmu.edu.

## 14.8.6 Remote Login

Most LINUX systems support two commands that allow you to log on to a remote host. One is based on the Internet service for remote log in, telnet, and the other is a LINUX- (and Unix-) only command, **rlogin**. We discuss both commands, but start with the more generic **telnet** command.

### The telnet Command

The telnet protocol is designed to allow you to connect to a remote computer over a network. This protocol allows you to log on to not only LINUX-based computer systems but also any computer system that supports the telnet protocol and has a telnet server process running on it. For example, you can connect a LINUX-based computer system such as a Sun workstation to a Windows-based PC. Although you usually need to have a valid account on the remote system, some remote machines allow you to log on without having an account. After the connection has been established, your host or terminal (or display window in a GUI environment) acts as a terminal connected to the remote host. From this point on, every keystroke on your terminal is sent to the remote host. As we have mentioned before, telnet is implemented as client–server software. In other words, the host to which you want to connect must have a telnet server process running on a well-known port designated for it, and your command execution starts a telnet client process on your host. The well-known port for the telnet server is port number 23. Because the telnet protocol is based on TCP, the telnet client and server processes establish a virtual connection before prompting you for input. Multiple telnet client processes running on the same host or different hosts can communicate with the same telnet server process; that is, multiple users can use a remote host via telnet.

The LINUX command for starting a telnet client process is `telnet`. The following is a brief description of the command.

Syntax:

**telnet [options] [host [port]]**

**Purpose:** To connect to a remote system host via a network; the host can be specified by its name or IP address in dotted decimal notation

**Commonly used options/features:**

| | |
|---|---|
| `-a` | Attempt automatic login |
| `-l` | Specify a user for login |

The telnet client operates in two modes: input mode and command mode. When executed without an argument, the client enters the command mode and displays the `telnet>` prompt. When run with a host argument, the client displays the `login:` prompt to take your login name and password. Once a connection has been established between your client and the server, you interact directly with the telnet client. After establishing the connection, the client enters the input mode. In this mode, the client takes character-at-a-time or line-at-a-time input mode, depending on what the server on the remote host supports; the default mode is character-at-a-time. All input mode data, except `<Ctrl-]>`, known as the telnet *escape character*, are commands for the remote operating system, transferred to it via the telnet server process. The telnet escape character puts telnet in the command mode. Once it is in the command mode, you can use the `?` or `help` command to display a brief summary of the `telnet` commands. Table 14.4 shows some useful `telnet` commands and their purpose.

**Table 14.4** Commonly Used Telnet Commands

| Command | Meaning |
|---|---|
| `?` or `help` | Display a list of telnet commands and their purpose |
| `close` or `quit` | Close the telnet connection |
| `mode` | Try to enter line or character mode |
| `open` host | Make a telnet connection to host |
| `z` | Suspend the telnet session and return to the local host; resume the telnet session with the `fg` command |

The most common use of the **`telnet`** command is without an option. The following session shows the use of **`telnet`** to log on to another host, upsun29, on your network. As shown, after the connection with upsun29 has been established, you are prompted to log in. You must have a valid account on upsun29 to be able to use it via the **`telnet`** command.

```
$ telnet upsun29
Trying 192.102.10.89...
Connected to upsun29.egr.up.edu.
Escape character is '^]'.
LINUX Mandrake release 6.1 (Helios)
Kernel 2.2.13-4mdksmp on an i686

login: sarwar
Password:
Last login: Fri Jul 30 16:16:02 from upibm7.egr.up.ed
Sun Microsystems Inc.  SunOS 5.5.1    Generic May 1996
) SPLAY = (
TERM = (vt100)
$
```

The following session shows how you can use the **`telnet`** command for logging on to a host on a remote site (network). Note that you have to use the FQDN of the host to which you want to telnet. The IP address of the host is 191.220.19.2, so you can execute the **`telnet 191.220.19.2`** command to achieve the same result. The session also shows that you can put telnet into the command mode by pressing `^]` and run various telnet commands before quitting. Some commands, such as **`status`**, return you to the input mode after completing their task. In the following session, we show that you can use the **`z`** command to suspend the telnet client and transfer control to the shell on the local host. The **`ps`** command shows the status of processes on the local machine. The **`fg`** command reverts to the telnet client. The

`<Ctrl-]>` command puts telnet into the command mode, and the **quit** command terminates the telnet session.

```
$ telnet pcc.edu
Trying 192.220.19.2...
Connected to pccaix.sycrci.pcc.edu.
Escape character is '^]'.

HP-UX zeus B.10.20 E 9000/807 (ttyp3)
login: msarwar
msarwar's Password:

Last login: Wed Jul 28 16:57:29 PDT 1999 on /dev/pts/1 from
192.220.11.131

[YOU HAVE NEW MAIL]
$
...
<Ctrl-]>
telnet> z

Suspended
$ ps
 PID TTY STAT TIME COMMAND
 837  p0 S    0:00 bash
 920  p1 S    0:00 /usr/bin/telnet upibm7
1027  p2 T    0:00 /usr/bin/telnet pcc.edu
1028  p2 R    0:00 ps
$ fg
telnet pcc.edu

<Ctrl-]>
telnet> quit
$
```

The following session shows use of the **-a** option to connect automatically to the Ohio State University WHOIS service at osu.edu.

```
$ telnet -a osu.edu
Trying 128.146.225.200...
```

```
Connected to osu.edu.
Escape character is '^]'.

The Ohio State University WHOIS Service - Authorized Use Only

  Usage of the WHOIS service must be consistent with the
  University's instruction, research and service missions.
  Use of this service is not authorized for developing
  mailing lists for the purpose of distributing unsolicited
  advertising, announcements or for mass mailings.

Connected to The Ohio State University WHOIS service, Sat Dec
16 17:52:57 2000.

To display information on an OSU person, enter their name in
one of the following formats:
  lastname
  firstname.lastname
  firstname.middlename.lastname
Abbreviations may be used.
To leave WHOIS enter QUIT.
Whois>
...
Whois> quit
Sat Dec 16 17:58:19 2000

Please direct comments about The Ohio State University WHOIS
service and requests for changes to: 8help@osu.edu

For technical information contact whois@osu.edu

Connection closed by foreign host.C-2000 17:58:19.25
$
```

As shown in the following session, you can use the **telnet** command to connect to a telnet server that isn't running on a well-known port. In this case the server is running on port number 5000. Be sure not to register for anything!

```
$ telnet chess.net 5000
Trying 207.244.122.50...
Connected to chess.net.
```

```
Escape character is '^]'.
...
Welcome to the server! Come in and join the fun!

At the login prompt, enter your handle. If you do not have an account,
enter "guest", and talk to an administrator(*) about registering.

login: guest
You are "guest691". You may use this name to play unrated games.
After logging in, do '/help register' for more info on how to register.

Press return to enter chess.net as "guest691":
<Ctrl-]>
telnet> quit
$
```

You can run the **telnet** command with a well-known port number as an optional parameter to invoke various Internet services such as **smtp**. In the following session, the **telnet** command invokes the daytime service at cs.berkeley.edu. The daytime service is offered at the well-known port 13. Execution of the command causes the daytime server at cs.berkeley.edu to send the current time (including day and date) to your client and close the connection. Your client displays the time and returns to the shell process.

```
$ telnet cs.berkeley.edu 13
Trying 169.229.60.164...
Connected to cs2.CS.Berkeley.EDU.
Escape character is '^]'.
Sat Dec 16 15:15:15 2000
Connection closed by foreign host.
$
```

#### THE rlogin COMMAND

The `rlogin` command allows you to log on to a host on your local network. All the hidden files that are also executed for a regular login are executed for remote login. After logging on, therefore, you are put in your home directory and your login shell is executed. The following is a brief description of the `rlogin` command.

Syntax:

**rlogin [options] host**

**Purpose:** To connect to a remote LINUX or UNIX host via a network; the host can be specified by its name or IP address in the dotted decimal notation

**Commonly used options/features:**

| | |
|---|---|
| `-ec` | Set the escape character to 'c' (the default is ~) |
| `-l user` | Use 'user' as the login name on the remote host |

You can use the **`rlogin`** command to log on to a LINUX host on your network, provided that you have a valid login name and password on the remote host. The following session shows how you can use the command to connect to a LINUX host upsun29 on your network. Note that, unlike the **`telnet`** command, the **`rlogin`** command doesn't prompt you for a login name and password if they are the same on the local and remote hosts. Because the **`rlogin`** command can be used with an IP address in place of the hostname, the **`rlogin 192.102.10.29`** command accomplishes the same task. After using the remote system, you can use the **`logout`** command to log out from the remote system and return to the local system. In the following session we also show that you can use the **`hostname`** and **`whoami`** commands to confirm that you are logged in as the same user (sarwar) and that the machine you log on to is upsun29.

```
$ rlogin upsun29
Last login: Sat Jul 31 18:27:19 from upibm7.egr.up.edu
Sun Microsystems Inc.  SunOS 5.5.1    Generic May 1996
DISPLAY = (pine)
TERM = (vt100)
$
$ hostname
upsun29.egr.up.edu
$ whoami
sarwar
$
...
...
$ logout
Terminal session terminated by sarwar
```

```
rlogin: connection closed.
$ hostname
upibm7.egr.up.edu
$
```

You can use the `-l` option to log on remotely with a login name different from the one you used to log on to the local host. You can use the following command to log on to the remote host upsun with a user name perform. The `rlogin` command

```
$ rlogin upsun -l perform
Password:
Last login: Mon Dec 18 12:08:12 from upsun21.up.edu
SunOS Release 4.1.3 (UPSUN_SERVER) #5: Mon Nov 14 17:31:44 PST 1994
DISPLAY = (upx46:0.0)
TERM = (vt100)
$ whoami
perform
$ hostname
upsun.egr.up.edu
$
```

prompts you for your password, and you must have the password for the user perform for a successful login. If you do not have the right password, `rlogin` lets you try other (or the same) login name(s) a few times.

The following session shows remote login to a LINUX host that is not on your local network. Here, pccaix.sycrci.pcc.edu is the FQDN of a host on the Internet, and the user is msarwar. Of course, you must enter the valid password for msarwar to be able to log in.

```
$ rlogin pccaix.sycrci.pcc.edu -l msarwar
msarwar's Password:
Last login: Sat Jul 31 18:54:26 PDT 1999 on /dev/pts/2 from
upibm7.egr.up.edu
[YOU HAVE NEW MAIL]
$ whoami
msarwar
$ hostname
pccaix
$
```

There is a secure version of **rlogin**, called **slogin**. Whereas **rlogin** communicates with the remote host in clear text, **slogin** does so in encrypted text. The **slogin** command is particularly useful if you do remote login when you are connected to a network through a modem.

In the following In-Chapter Exercises, you will use the **rlogin** and **telnet** commands to understand how they can be used to log on to a remote host on your network or on the Internet.

**IN-CHAPTER EXERCISES**

**14.14.** Use the **rlogin** and **telnet** commands to establish a session on a host on your LAN.

**14.15.** Try to establish a telnet session with the host locis.loc.gov and browse through the library at your own pace.

### 14.8.7 Remote Command Execution

You can use the **rsh** (remote shell) command to execute a command on a remote host on your local network. Remote login is a relatively time-consuming process, but the **rsh** command gives you a faster way to execute commands on remote machines if the purpose of your remote logins is to execute only a few commands. We used this command in Chapter 12 to illustrate the power of I/O redirection in LINUX. Now we discuss it formally. The following is a brief description of the command.

Syntax: **rsh [options] host [command]**

**Purpose:** To execute a command on a remote machine, 'host', on the same network; the **rlogin** command is executed if no 'command' is specified

**Commonly used options/features:**

| | |
|---|---|
| **-l** user | Use 'user' as the login name on the remote host |

When you execute a command on a remote machine, your current directory on the remote machine is set to your home directory and your login shell on the remote machine is used to execute the command. Only the shell environment hidden files (e.g. .bashrc for Bash) are executed before the **rsh** command is executed. The general environment files (.login and .profile) are not executed. The standard files (stdin, stdout, and stderr) for the remote command are attached to

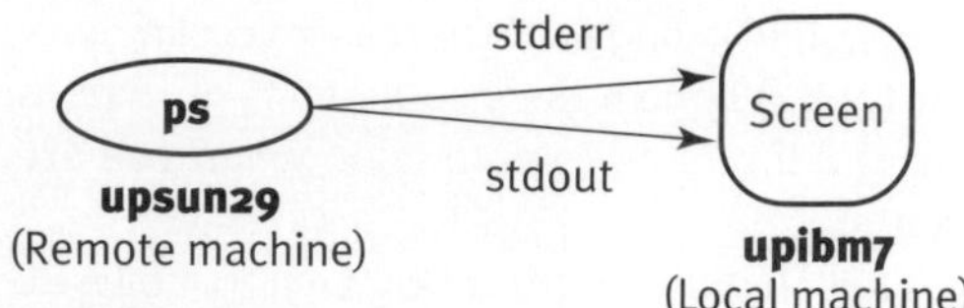

**Figure 14.8** The semantics of the `rsh upsun29 ps` command

the standard files used for your local commands (your terminal by default). Thus, when I/O redirection is used, the redirected files are taken from your local machine unless the command to be executed is enclosed in single quotes. We discuss this concept later in this section, and in all cases we assume that upibm7 is the local machine and that upibm10 is the remote machine.

The following command line executes the **ps** command on the upsun29 host, and its output is sent to the display screen of upibm7 (the local machine). The semantics of the command line are depicted in Figure 14.8.

```
$ rsh upsun29 ps
 PID   TTY     TIME CMD
6525 pts/0     0:02 -ksh
6565 pts/0     0:00 -ksh
6566 pts/0     0:00 sort data | uniq > sorted_data
$
```

The following command line executes the **sort students** command on upsun29, taking input from the students file on upsun29, and sends the results back to the sorted_students file on the local machine, upibm7. If the students file doesn't exist, the error message is also sent back to upibm7. The semantics of the command are illustrated in Figure 14.9.

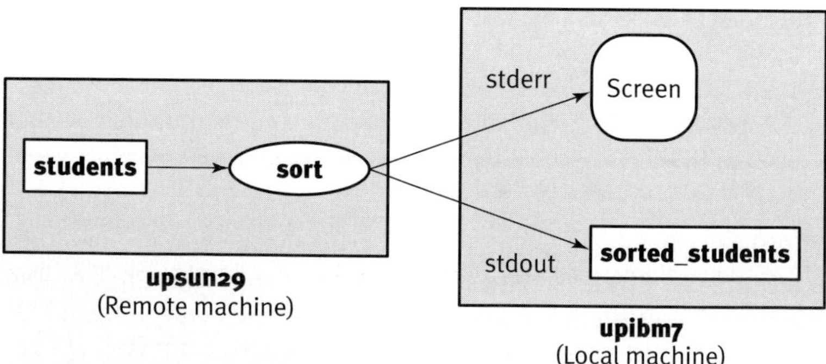

**Figure 14.9** The semantics of the `rsh upsun29 sort students > sorted_students` command

```
$ rsh upsun29 sort students > sorted_students
$
```

In the following command line, however, the **sort** command takes input from the students file on the local machine, upibm7. As with the previous command, the output is sent to the sorted_students file on the local machine.

```
$ rsh upsun29 sort < students > sorted_students
$
```

If you want the **sort** command to take input from a local file students and store the sorted results in a sorted_students file on the remote machine, you must quote the remote command with output redirection, as in

```
$ cat students | rsh upsun29 'sort > sorted_students'
$
```

You can combine the I/O redirection operators with the pipe operator to create powerful command lines that take input from local and remote files, execute commands on local and remote machines, and send the final results to a file on the local or remote machine. We discussed a few such command lines in Chapter 12, which you should revisit at this time.

When used without an argument (which is optional), the **rsh** command reverts to the **rlogin** command. All the rules for the **rlogin** command apply in this case and all the hidden files that are executed during a normal login are executed. The following session shows the use of the **rsh** command without an argument. In the first example, the command is used to log on to upsun29 on the same network. In the second example, the **rsh** command is used to log on to a host on a different network on the Internet.

```
$ rsh upsun29
Last login: Sat Jul 31 18:31:17 from upibm7.egr.up.ed
Sun Microsystems Inc.  SunOS 5.5.1    Generic May 1996
DISPLAY = (pine)
TERM = (vt100)
$
$ rsh pccaix.sycrci.pcc.edu -l msarwar
msarwar's Password:
Last login: Sat Jul 31 18:56:07 PDT 1999 on /dev/pts/2 from
upibm7.egr.up.edu

[YOU HAVE NEW MAIL]
$
```

There is a secure version of **rsh**, called **ssh** (secure shell). Whereas **rsh** communicates with the remote host in cleartxt, **ssh** uses strong cryptography for transmitting data, including commands, password, and files. **ssh** has become a de-facto standard for secure terminal connections within a network or the Internet.

### 14.8.8 File Transfer

You can use the **ftp** (file transfer protocol) command to transfer files to and from a remote machine on the same network or another network. This command is commonly used to transfer files to and from a remote host on the Internet. The following is a brief description of the command.

Syntax: **ftp [options] [host]**

**Purpose:** To transfer files from or to a remote 'host'

**Commonly used options/features:**

| | |
|---|---|
| `-d` | Enable debugging |
| `-i` | Disable prompting during transfers of multiple files |
| `-v` | Show all remote responses |

As we mentioned earlier in the chapter, the file transfer protocol is a client–server protocol based on TCP. When you run the **ftp** command, an FTP client process starts running on your host and attempts to establish a connection with the FTP server process running on the remote host. If the FTP server process is not running on the remote host before the client initiates a connection request, the connection is not made and an **Unknown host** error message is displayed by the **ftp** command. Once an FTP connection has been established with the remote FTP site (a site running an FTP server process is called an *FTP site*), you can run several **ftp** commands for effective use of this utility. However, you must have appropriate access permission to be able to transfer files to the remote site. Most FTP sites allow you to transfer files into your system but not vice versa. Table 14.5 presents some useful **ftp** commands.

Most FTP sites require that you have a valid login name and password on that site to be able to transfer files to or from that site. A number of sites allow you to establish FTP sessions with them by using 'anonymous' as the login name and 'guest' or your full e-mail address as the password. Such sites are said to allow anonymous FTP.

The following session illustrates the use of the **ftp** utility to do an anonymous FTP with the site ftp.uu.net and transfer some files. In the process, we demon-

**Table 14.5** A Summary of Useful FTP Commands

| Command | Meaning |
|---|---|
| `!` [cmd] | Runs 'cmd' on the local machine |
| `!` [cmd] or Help [cmd] | Displays a summary of 'cmd'; without the 'cmd' argument, displays a summary of all FTP commands |
| `ascii` | Puts the FTP channel into ASCII mode; used for transferring ASCII-type files such as text files |
| `binary` | Puts the FTP channel into binary mode; used for transferring non-ASCII files such as files containing executable codes or pictures |
| `cd` | Changes directory; similar to the LINUX `cd` command |
| `close` | Closes the FTP connection with the remote host, but stays inside |
| `dir` remotedir localfile | Saves the listing of 'remotedir' into 'localfile' on the local host; useful for long directory listings, because pipes cannot be used with the FTP commands |
| `get` remotefile [localfile] | Transfer 'remotefile' to 'localfile' in the present working directory on the local machine; if 'localfile' not specified, 'remotefile' used as the name of the local file |
| `ls` [dname] | Shows contents of the designated directory; 'dname', current directory if none specified |
| `mget` remotefiles | Transfers multiple files from the remote host to the local host |
| `mput` localfiles | Transfers multiple files from the local host to the remote host |
| `open` [hostname] | Attempts to open a connection with the remote host; prompts if hostname not specified as parameter |
| `put` localfile [remotefile] | Transfers 'localfile' to 'remotefile' on the remote host; if 'remotefile' not specified, use 'localfile' as name of remote file |
| `quit` | Terminates the FTP session |
| `user` [login_name] | If unable to log on, log on as a user on the remote host by specifying the 'user_name' as the command argument; prompt appears if 'user_name' not specified |

strate the use of FTP commands `cd`, `ls`, `get`, and `mget`. We also demonstrate execution of the `ls` command on the local host. Finally, we terminate the FTP session. This site requires use of the user's e-mail address as the password for anonymous FTP. If you're interested in their contents, uncompress the files that you transfer in the following session and "untar" them (see Chapter 19) to see what they contain.

```
$ ftp ftp.uu.net
Connected to ftp.uu.net.
220 ftp.uu.net FTP server (UUNET ftp server Sun Apr 29 13:59:26 EDT 2001) ready.
Name (ftp.uu.net:sarwar): anonymous
331 Guest login ok, send your complete e-mail address as password.
Password:
230-
230-            Welcome to the UUNET archive.
230-  A service of UUNET Technologies Inc, Falls Church, Virginia
230-  For information about UUNET, call +1 703 206 5600, or see the
230-  files in /uunet-info
...
...
230 Guest login ok, access restrictions apply.
Remote system type is LINUX.
Using binary mode to transfer files.
ftp> cd pub/shells/tcsh
250 CWD command successful.
ftp> ls
200 PORT command successful.
150 Opening ASCII mode data connection for /bin/ls.
total 1330
drwxrwsr-x  7 34      21           512 Feb 27 01:25 .
drwxrwsr-x  7 34      21           512 Mar  1 19:17 ..
...
-rw-rw-r--  1 34      21        524469 May 13 1995 tcsh-6.06.tar.gz
-rw-rw-r--  1 34      21         75767 May 13 1995 tcsh.man.Z
226 Transfer complete.
ftp> get tcsh-6.06.tar.gz
local: tcsh-6.06.tar.gz remote: tcsh-6.06.tar.gz
200 PORT command successful.
150 Opening BINARY mode data connection for tcsh-6.06.tar.gz (524469 bytes).
226 Transfer complete.
524469 bytes received in 100 secs (5.1 Kbytes/sec)
ftp> !ls -l tcsh-6.06.tar.gz
```

```
-rw-------   1 sarwar   faculty   524469 Aug  1 16:50 tcsh-6.06.tar.gz
ftp>
ftp> mget tcsh*
mget tcsh-6.06.tar.gz? n
mget tcsh.man.Z? y
200 PORT command successful.
150 Opening BINARY mode data connection for tcsh.man.Z (75767 bytes).
226 Transfer complete.
75767 bytes received in 15.9 secs (4.6 Kbytes/sec)
ftp> quit
221 Goodbye.
$
```

Once you have established an FTP connection, most sites put you in binary mode so that you can transfer non-ASCII files such as files containing audio and video clips. You can explicitly put the FTP session into binary mode by using the **binary** command, which ensures proper file transfer. You can revert to the ASCII mode by using the **ascii** command.

In the following In-Chapter Exercise, you will use the **ftp** command to transfer a file from a remote host on the Internet.

## IN-CHAPTER EXERCISES

**14.16.** Establish an anonymous FTP session with the host ftp.uu.net and transfer the tcsh-6.06.tar.gz file to your system.

### 14.8.9 Remote Copy

You can use the **ftp** command to transfer files to and from a remote host on another network, but doing so requires that you log on to the remote host. You can use the **rcp** (remote copy) command to copy files to and from a remote machine on the same LAN, without logging on to the remote host. This command isn't needed in a local area environment if you are using a network-based file system such as the **Network File System (NFS)**. In this case, the storage of your files is completely transparent to you, and you can access them from any host on your network, without specifying the name of the host that contains them. The following is a brief description of the command.

Syntax:

**rcp [options] [host:]sfile [host:]dfile**
**rcp [options] [host:]sfile [host:]dir**

**Purpose:** To copy 'sfile' to 'dfile'

**Commonly used options/features:**

| | |
|---|---|
| `-p` | Attempt to preserve file modify and access times; without this option, the command uses the current value of umask to create file permissions. |
| `-r` | Recursively copy files at 'sfile' to 'dir' |

As is obvious from the syntax, you can transfer files from your host to a remote host or from one remote host to another. The `rcp` command fails if the remote host does not "trust" your local host. The name of your local host must be in the /etc/hosts.equiv file on the remote machine for it to be a **trusted host** and for you to be able to use the `rcp`, `rsh`, and `rlogin` commands. You must also have a valid username and password to transfer files to and from the remote host. The format of a line in the file is

hostname [username]

A '−' character can precede both a host name and a username to deny access. A '+' character can be used in place of hostname or username to match any host or user. The following are a few such entries.

| | |
|---|---|
| `uphpux sarwar` | Allows access to the user sarwar on the host uphpux |
| `+ sarwar` | Allows the user sarwar access from any host |
| `upaix - sarwar` | Denies access to the user sarwar on the host upaix |
| `-pc1` | Denies access to all users on the host pc1 |
| `pccvm` | Allows access to all users on the host pccvm |

If the host you are using isn't a trusted host (i.e., it isn't listed in the /etc/hosts.equiv file), you need to create an entry in a file called .rhosts in your home directory on the remote host that contains the name of your host (from which you would use the `rcp` command) and your login name on this host. Thus, if the remote host is upsun29 and you want to use the `rcp` command on a host called upibm7, the entry in the ~/.rhosts file on upsun29 will be the following (assuming that your login name on upibm7 is sarwar).

upibm7 sarwar

This entry informs the networking software, which is in the LINUX kernel, that sarwar is a trusted user on the host upibm7.

The following **rcp** command copies all the files with an html extension from your ~/myweb directory to the ~/webmirror directory on upsun29.

```
$ rcp ~/myweb/*.html upsun29:webmirror
$
```

The following **rcp** command copies the files Chapter[1-9].doc from the ~/linuxbook directory on your system to the ~/linuxbook.backup directory on upsun29.

```
$ rcp ~/linuxbook/Chapter[1-9].doc upsun29:linuxbook.backup
$
```

The following **rcp** command copies all C and C++ source files from your ~/ece446/projects directory on upsun29 to your ~/swprojects.backup directory on your machine.

```
$ rcp upsun29:ece446/projects/*.[c,C] ~/swprojects.backup
$
```

As we have mentioned before, you can also use the **rcp** command to copy files from one remote host to another remote host. The following **rcp** command is used to copy the whole home directory from the www1 host to the www2 host. Note use of the **-r** option to copy subdirectories recursively and use of the **-p** option to preserve existing modification times and access permissions.

```
$ rcp -rp www1:* www2:
$
```

Like **slogin** and **ssh**, the secure version of **rcp**, called **scp**, is also available on some systems.

The following In-Chapter Exercise gives you practice using the **rcp** command in your environment.

## IN-CHAPTER EXERCISE

**14.17.** Use an **rcp** command to copy a file from your machine to another machine on your network. What command did you use? What did it do?

### 14.8.10 Interactive Chat

You can use the **talk** command for an interactive chat with a user on your host or on a remote host over a network. The following is a brief description of the command.

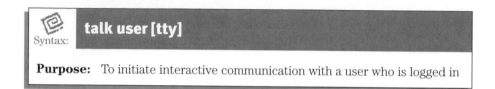

Syntax: **talk user [tty]**

**Purpose:** To initiate interactive communication with a user who is logged in

The user parameter is the login name of the person if he or she is on your host. If the person you want to talk to is on another host, use login_name@host for user. The tty parameter is needed if the person is logged on the same host more than once.

When you use the **talk** command to initiate a communication request, the other user is interrupted with a message on his or her screen informing that person of the request. The other user needs to execute the **talk** command to respond to you. That establishes a communication channel, and both users' display screens are divided in half. The upper half contains the text that you type, and the lower half contains the other user's responses. Both you and the other user can type simultaneously. The **talk** command simply copies the characters that you type at your keyboard on the screen of the other user. The chat session can be terminated when either of you presses <Ctrl-C>. If you are using the vi editor and your screen is corrupted during the communication, your can use <Ctrl-L> to redraw the screen.

Suppose that a user sarwar wants to talk to another user, bob, and that both are logged onto the same host. The following command from sarwar initiates a talk request to bob.

```
$ talk bob
```

As soon as sarwar hits <Enter>, the following message is displayed at the top of bob's screen.

```
[Waiting for your party to respond]

Message from Talk_Daemon@upibm7.egr.up.edu at 13:36 ...
talk: connection requested by sarwar@upibm7.egr.up.edu.
talk: respond with:  talk sarwar@upibm7.egr.up.edu
```

When bob runs the `talk sarwar` command, both bob's and sarwar's screens are divided in half, with the upper halves containing the message `[Connection established]` and the cursor moved to the top of both screens. Both bob and sarwar are ready to talk now. If bob wants to ignore sarwar's request while using a shell, he can simply press <Enter>.

If bob is logged in on another host—say, upsun29—sarwar needs to run the following command to initiate the talk request.

```
$ talk bob@upsun29
```

If sarwar is logged in once on upibm7 and bob wants to communicate with sarwar, his response to the preceding request should be `talk sarwar@upibm7`.

If bob is logged in on upsun29 multiple times, the following command from sarwar initiates a talk request on terminal ttyp2 (one of the terminals bob is logged onto).

```
$ talk bob@upsun29 ttyp2
```

If you want to block all `talk` requests because users keep bothering you with too many requests, execute

```
$ mesg n
$
```

This command works only for your current session. If you want to block all `talk` and `write` requests whenever you log on, put this command in your system or shell startup file (e.g., ~/.profile or ~/.bashrc). Doing so simply takes away the write permission on your terminal file in the /dev directory for group and others. Without any argument, the `mesg` command displays the current status.

In the following In-Chapter Exercise, you will use the `talk` command to establish a chat session with a friend on your network and appreciate the various characteristics of the command.

**IN-CHAPTER EXERCISE**

**14.18.** Establish a talk session with a friend who is currently logged on.

### 14.8.11 Tracing the Route from One Site to Another Site

You can use the `traceroute` command to display the route (the names of the routers in the path) that your e-mail messages, telnet commands, and downloaded files from an FTP site may take from your host to the remote host and vice versa.

It also gives you a feel for the speed of the route. Because this command poses some security threats, many system administrators disable its execution. The security threat stems from the fact that, by displaying a route to a host on the Internet, someone can figure out the internal structure of the network to which the host is connected and the IP addresses of some machines on the network. We show a simple execution of the command to show its output and demonstrate the inner workings of the Internet a bit more. The following command shows the route from the host upibmf.egr.up.edu to locis.loc.edu.

```
$ traceroute locis.loc.gov
traceroute to locis.loc.gov (140.147.254.3), 30 hops max, 38 byte packets
 1 up (192.102.10.9) 0.761 ms 0.703 ms 0.653 ms
 2 192.220.208-11.up.edu (192.220.208.11) 1.333 ms 1.292 ms 1.268 ms
 3 204.245.199.237 (204.245.199.237) 3.202 ms 3.569 ms 3.512 ms
 4 d4-1-1.a02.ptldor01.us.ra.verio.net (157.238.28.249) 7.009 ms 5.042 ms 5.772 ms
 5 ge-1-0-0.r02.ptldor01.us.bb.verio.net (129.250.31.222) 5.502 ms 4.928 ms 7.010 ms
 6 p4-0-1-0.r01.scrmca01.us.bb.verio.net (129.250.2.34) 21.256 ms 19.476 ms 21.223 ms
 7 p4-1-1-0.r00.scrmca01.us.bb.verio.net (129.250.3.17) 21.332 ms 20.880 ms 21.213 ms
 8 uunet.r00.scrmca01.us.bb.verio.net (129.250.9.98) 21.330 ms 19.875 ms 21.239 ms
 9 174.at-5-0-0.XR2.SAC1.ALTER.NET (152.63.52.94) 21.234 ms 20.358 ms 21.224 ms
10 184.at-1-0-0.TR2.SAC1.ALTER.NET (152.63.50.138) 21.253 ms 20.661 ms 21.287 ms
11 127.at-6-1-0.TR2.DCA6.ALTER.NET (152.63.2.253) 97.934 ms 99.035 ms 111.984 ms
12 0.so-3-0-0.XR2.DCA6.ALTER.NET (152.63.11.90) 133.160 ms 107.250 ms 97.514 ms
13 184.ATM7-0.GW3.DCA6.ALTER.NET (152.63.33.9) 99.421 ms 100.569 ms 101.173 ms
14 loc-gw.customer.alter.net (157.130.44.206) 102.946 ms !X * 101.288 ms !X
$
```

Note that the first three routers are on class C networks with network IP addresses 192.102.10, 192.220, and 204.245.199, and all of the remaining routers are on class B networks with network IP addresses 157.238, 129.250, 152.63, and 157.130. The IP address of the destination host (locis.loc.gov) is 140.147.254.3, as shown in the first output line. A line in the trace also contains times taken by the three packets sent by `traceroute` as they go from one router to the next. In this instance, one-way travel time for data is about 0.5 sec from upibmf.egr.up.edu (in Portland, Oregon) to locis.loc.gov (in Washington, D.C.). The explanation of **`!X`** and **`*`** on the last output line is beyond the scope of this textbook, because it requires in-depth understanding of the IP protocol.

## SUMMARY

Computer networking began more than 30 years ago with the development of ARPANET in the late 1960s. Today, computing without networking is unthinkable because of the ubiquitous Internet. Web browsing, file transfer, interactive chat, electronic mail, and remote login are some of the well-known services commonly used by today's computer users. The e-commerce phenomenon has started to change the way people do everyday chores and conduct business. LINUX has a special place in the world of networking in general and internetworking in particular because most of the networking protocols were initially implemented on UNIX platforms. Today, most of the Internet services are provided by server processes running on LINUX and UNIX-based computers.

The core of internetworking software is based on the TCP/IP protocol suite. This suite includes, among several other protocols, the well-known TCP and IP protocols for transportation and routing of application data. The key to routing in the Internet are 32-bit IP addresses (in IPv4). The most heavily used Internet services are for Web browsing (and all the services that it offers, such as e-commerce), electronic mail, file transfer, and remote login. Not only do LINUX systems support all the Internet services, but they also have additional utilities to support local network activities.

The topics discussed in this chapter include the general structure of a network and an internetwork, networking models, the TCP/IP protocol suite, IP addresses, the domain name system (DNS), Internet protocols and services, and LINUX utilities for performing networking- and internetworking-related tasks. These utilities are implemented by using the client–server software model. The utilities discussed in this chapter are `finger` (to find information about users on a host), `FTP` (for file transfer), `ifconfig` and `nslookup` (to translate domain names to IP addresses), `ping` (to find the status of a host), `rcp` (to remote copy on a LINUX host), `rlogin` (to remote login on a LINUX host), `rsh` (to log on to a remote host on a network), `ruptime` (to display information about LINUX hosts on a LAN), `rwho` (to display users who are currently logged onto LINUX hosts in a LAN), `talk` (to initiate interactive chat), `telnet` (for remote login), and `traceroute` (to trace the route of data from the user's host to a destination host).

## PROBLEMS

1. What are computer networks and why are they important?
2. What is an internetwork? What is the Internet?
3. What are the key protocols that form the backbone of the Internet? Where were they developed?
4. What is an IPv4 address? What is its size in bits and bytes? What is dotted decimal notation? What is the size of an IPv6 address in bits and bytes?

5. What are the classes of IPv4 addresses? Given an IPv4 address in binary, how can you tell which class the address belongs to? How can you tell the class of the address when it is expressed in the dotted decimal notation?
6. What is DNS? Name the LINUX command that can be used to translate a host name to its IP address.
7. List two domain names each for sites that are in the following top-level domains: edu, com, gov, int, mil, net, org, au, de, ir, kw, pk, and uk. How did you find them? Don't use examples given in this textbook.
8. How would you find the IP address of the host that runs the name server process, used by **nslookup** to map a domain name to its IP adress? What command did you use to determine your answer?
9. Read the FTP://FTP.isi.edu/in-notes/iana/assignments/port-numbers file to identify port numbers for the following well-known services: FTP, http, time, daytime, echo, ping, and quote-of-the-day.
10. Use the **ruptime** command to display the number of hosts on your network. The output of your command should display this number only.
11. What is the timeout period for the finger protocol? How did you get your answer?
12. How many users have Johnston as part of their name at the osu.edu domain? How did you find out? Write down your command.
13. Give a command that accomplishes the following task.
    ```
    rsh upsun29 sort < students > sorted_students
    ```
14. Show the semantics of the following command by drawing a diagram similar to the ones shown in Figures 14.8 and 14.9. Assume that the name of the local machine is upibm7.
    ```
    cat students | rsh upsun29 sort | rsh upsun21 uniq >
    sorted_uniq_students
    ```
15. Display the /etc/services file on your system and list port numbers for well-known ports for the following services: daytime, time, quote-of-the-day (qotd), echo, smtp, and finger. Did you find all of them? Do the port numbers match with those found in Problem 9?
16. Use the **telnet** command to get the current time via the daytime service at mit.edu. Write down your command line.
17. Fetch the files history.netcount and history.hosts from the directory nsfnet/statistics using anonymous FTP from the host nic.merit.edu. These files contain the number of domestic and foreign networks and hosts on the NSFNET infrastructure. What is the size of Internet in terms of the number of networks and hosts according to the statistics in these files? Although the statistics are somewhat dated, what is your prediction of its size a year from now? Why? Show your work.

18. You create the following entries in your ~/.rhosts file on a host on your network.

```
host1    john.doe
host2    mike.brich
```

What are the consequences if john.doe and mike.birch are users on hosts host1 and host2 in your network? Both users belong to your user group.

19. Give a command for displaying simple names of all the hosts on your network.

20. Use the `traceroute` command to determine the route from your host to locis.loc.gov. What is the approximate travel time for data from your host to locis.loc.gov?

21. Find a host that offers the quote-of-the-day (qotd) service. What is the quote of the day today?

22. How many hosts are (or can be) connected to your network? Write down the command you used to get this information.

CHAPTER

# 15

# Introductory Bash Programming

## OBJECTIVES

- To introduce the concept of shell programming
- To discuss how shell programs are executed
- To describe the concept and use of shell variables
- To discuss how command line arguments are passed to shell programs
- To explain the concept of command substitution
- To describe some basic coding principles
- To write and discuss some shell scripts
- To cover the commands and primitives *, =, ", ', `, &, <, >, ;, |, \, /, [ ], :, `break`, `case`, `continue`, `declare`, `exit`, `export`, `env`, `for`, `if`, `let`, `local`, `ls`, `read`, `readonly`, `set`, `sh`, `shift`, `test`, `typeset`, `while`, `until`, and `unset`

## 15.1 INTRODUCTION

Bash is more than a command interpreter. It has a programming language of its own that can be used to write shell programs for performing various tasks that cannot be performed by any existing command. A shell program, commonly known as a **shell script**, consists of shell commands to be executed by a shell and is stored in an ordinary LINUX file. The shell allows use of a read/write storage place, known as a **shell variable**, for users and programmers to use as a scratch pad for completing a task. The shell also contains **program control flow commands** (also called **statements**) that allow nonsequential execution of the commands in a shell script and repeated execution of a block of commands.

## 15.2 RUNNING A BASH SCRIPT

There are three ways to run a Bash script. The first method is to make the script file executable by adding the execute permission to the existing access permissions for the file. You can do so by running the following command, where script_file is the name of the file containing the shell script. Clearly, in this case you make the script executable for yourself only. However, you can set appropriate access permissions for the file if you also want other users to be able to execute.

```
$ chmod u+x script_file
$
```

Now, you can type `script_name` as a command to execute the shell script. As we described in Chapter 13, the script is executed by a child of the current shell. Note that, with this method, the script executes properly if you are using Bash but not if you are using any other shell. In this case, execute the `/bin/bash` command to run Bash.

The second method of executing a shell script is to run the `/bin/bash` command with the script file as its parameter. Thus the following command executes the script in script_file. If your search path (the *PATH* variable) includes the /bin directory, you can simply use the `sh` command.

```
$ /bin/bash script_file
$
```

The third method, which is also the most commonly used, is to force the current shell to execute a script in Bash, regardless of your current shell. You can do so by beginning a shell script with

```
#!/bin/bash
```

All you need to do is set execute permission for the script file and run the file as a command. When your current shell encounters the string #!, it takes the rest of the line as the absolute pathname for the shell to be executed under which the script in the file is executed. If your current shell is the TC shell, you can replace this line with a colon (**:**), which is known as the **null command** in Bash. When the TC shell reads **:** as the first character, it runs a Bash process that executes the commands in the script. The **:** command returns true. We discuss the return values of commands later in the chapter.

## 15.3 SHELL VARIABLES AND RELATED COMMANDS

A **variable** is a main memory location that is given a name. That allows you to reference the memory location by using its name instead of its address (see Chapter 3). The name of a shell variable can be composed of digits, letters, and underscore, with the first character being a letter or underscore. The case of letters is important and there is no limit on the length of a name. Because the main memory is read/write storage, you can read a variable's value or assign it a new value. For Bash, the value of a variable is always a string of characters, even if you store a number in it. There is no theoretical limit on the length of a variable's value.

Shell variables can be one of two types: **shell environment variables** and **user-defined variables**. Environment variables are used to customize the environment in which your shell runs and for proper execution of shell commands. A copy of these variables is passed to every command that executes in the shell as its child. Most of these variables are initialized when the /etc/profile file executes as you log on. This file is written by your system administrator to set up a common environment for all users of the system. You can customize your environment by assigning different values to some or all of these variables in your ~/.profile start-up file, which also executes when you log on, or the ~/.bashrc, ~/bash_login, and ~/.bash_profile files when Bash starts execution. Table 15.1 lists most of the environment variables whose values you can change. We have described some of these variables in the previous chapters.

These shell environment variables are writable, and you can assign any values to them. Other shell environment variables are read-only, which means that you can use (read) the values of these variables but cannot change them. These variables are most useful for processing **command line arguments** (also known as **positional arguments**), or parameters passed to a shell script at the command line. Examples of command line arguments are the source and destination files in the **cp** command. Some other read-only shell variables are used to keep track of the process ID of the current process, the process ID of the most recent background process, and the exit status of the last command. Some important read-only shell environment variables are listed in Table 15.2.

User-defined variables are used within shell scripts as temporary storage places whose values can be changed when the program executes. These variables can be made read-only as well as passed to the commands that execute in the shell

**Table 15.1** Some Important Writable Bash Environment Variables

| Environment Variable | Purpose of the Variable |
|---|---|
| *BASH* | Full pathname for `bash` |
| *CDPATH* | Contains directory names that are searched, one by one, by the `cd` command to find the directory passed to it as a parameter; the `cd` command searches the current directory if this variable is not set. |
| *EDITOR* | Default editor used in programs such as the e-mail program |
| *ENV* | Path along which LINUX looks to find configuration files |
| *HISTFILE* | Pathname of the history file |
| *HOME* | Name of home directory, when user first logs on |
| *IFS* | The value used by Bash to separate words in a command line |
| *MAIL* | Name of user's system mailbox file |
| *MAILCHECK* | How often (in seconds) the shell should check user's mailbox for new mail and inform user accordingly |
| *PATH* | Variable that contains user's search path—the directories that a shell searches to find an external command or program |
| *PPID* | Process ID of the parent process |
| *PS1* | Primary shell prompt that appears on the command line, which usually set to $ but can be changed to any value, including special values as discussed later in this section |
| *PS2* | Secondary shell prompt displayed on second line of a command if shell thinks that the command is not finished, typically when the command terminates with a backslash (\), the escape character |
| *PWD* | Name of the current working directory |
| *TERM* | Type of user's console terminal |

**Table 15.2** Some Important Read-Only Bash Environment Variables

| Environment Variable | Purpose of the Variable |
|---|---|
| *$0* | Name of program |
| *$1 - $9* | Values of command line arguments 1 through 9 |
| *$** | Values of all command line arguments |
| *$@* | Values of all command line arguments; each argument individually quoted if `$@` is enclosed in quotes, as in "`$@`" |
| *$#* | Total number of command line arguments |
| *$$* | Process ID (PID) of current process |
| *$?* | Exit status of most recent command |
| *$!* | PID of most recent background process |

script in which they are defined. Unlike most other programming languages, in Bash programming language you don't have to declare and initialize shell variables. An uninitialized shell variable is initialized to a **null string** by default. You can initialize variables by using the built-in commands `declare`, `local`, `set`, and `typeset`. We discuss the `declare`, `set`, and `typeset` commands in detail later in this chapter and the `local` command in Chapter 16.

You can display the values of all shell variables (including user-defined variables) and their current values by using the `set` command without any parameters. The `local` command without any argument displays the local variables within a function. As described later in this chapter, the `set` command can also be used to change the values of some of the read-only shell environment variables. The following is a sample run of the `set` command. We show a partial list here to keep you focused and save space.

```
$ set
BASH=/bin/bash
BASH_VERSINFO=([0]="2" [1]="03" [2]="16" [3]="1" [4]="release"
[5]="i586-mandrak
e-linux-gnu")
BASH_VERSION='2.03.16(1)-release'
COLUMNS=80
DIRSTACK=()
DISPLAY=pine
EDITOR=vi
EUID=121
EXINIT='set redraw'
GROUP=faculty
GROUPS=()
HISTFILE=/usr1.d/sarwar/.bash_history
HISTFILESIZE=500
HISTSIZE=500
HOME=/usr1.d/sarwar
HOST=upibmf.egr.up.edu
HOSTNAME=upibmf.egr.up.edu
HOSTTYPE=i586
IFS='
'
KDEDIR=/usr
LANG=C
```

```
LD_LIBRARY_PATH=/usr/X11/lib:/usr/lib:/usr/local/lib
LINES=24
LOGNAME=sarwar
LS_COLORS='no=00:fi=00:di=01;34:ln=01;36:pi=40;33:so=01;35:bd=40;33;01:c
d=40;33;01:or=01;05;37;41:mi=01;05;37;41:ex=01;32:*.cmd=01;32:*.exe=01;3
2:*.com=01;32:*.btm=01;32:*.bat=01;32:*.tar=01;31:*.tgz=01;31:*.tbz2=01;
31:*.arc=01;31:*.arj=01;31:*.taz=01;31:*.lzh=01;31:*.lha=01;31:*.zip=01;
31:*.z=01;31:*.Z=01;31:*.gz=01;31:*.bz2=01;31:*.bz=01;31:*.tz=01;31:*.rp
m=01;31:*.jpg=01;35:*.jpeg=01;35:*.gif=01;35:*.bmp=01;35:*.xbm=01;35:*.x
pm=01;35:*.png=01;35:*.tif=01;35:*.tiff=01;35:'
MACHTYPE=i586-mandrake-linux-gnu
MAIL=/var/spool/mail/sarwar
MAILCHECK=60
MAILER='comp -e vi'
MANPATH=/usr/X11/man:/usr/local/man:/usr/man
NNTPSERVER=news.egr.up.edu
OPTERR=1
OPTIND=1
OSTYPE=linux-gnu
PATH=/usr/sbin:/usr/X11/include/X11:.:/usr1.d/sarwar/bin:/usr/ucb:/bin:/
usr/bin:/usr/include:/usr/X11/lib:/usr/lib:/etc:/usr/etc:/usr/local/bin:
/usr/local/lib:/usr/local/games:/usr/X11/bin
PIPESTATUS=([0]="0" [1]="0")
PPID=29245
PS1='\s-\v\$ '
PS2='> '
PS4='+ '
PWD=/usr1.d/sarwar
REMOTEHOST=upppp18.egr.up.edu
SHELL=/bin/csh
SHELLOPTS=braceexpand:hashall:histexpand:monitor:history:interactive-
comments:emacs
SHLVL=2
SIGNATURE=sarwar@egr.up.edu
TERM=vt100
UID=121
```

```
USER=sarwar
VENDOR=intel
VISUAL=pico
WWW_HOME=http://www.egr.up.edu/
XKEYSYMDB=/usr/lib/X11/XKeysymDB
_=
inbox=/usr1.d/sarwar/Mail/inbox
$
```

The **declare** or **typeset** command shows the same list of shell variables. You can use either the **env** or **printenv** command to display environment variables and their values, but the list won't be as complete as the one displayed by the **declare** or **typeset** command. In particular, the output won't include any function definitions and user-defined variables. The following is a sample output of the **env** command under Mandrake 6.1 (a similar list is displayed under Red Hat 7.0).

You can also use the **env** and **printenv** commands to display environment variables and their values, but the list won't be as complete as the one displayed by the **set** command. In particular, the output doesn't include any function definitions (see Chapter 16) and user-defined variables. The following is a sample output of the **env** command on the same LINUX-based computer that we ran the **set** command on.

```
$ env
PWD=/home/faculty/sarwar
VENDOR=intel
REMOTEHOST=upppp18.egr.up.edu
HOSTNAME=upibmf.egr.up.edu
SIGNATURE=sarwar@egr.up.edu
LD_LIBRARY_PATH=/usr/X11/lib:/usr/lib:/usr/local/lib
inbox=/home/faculty/sarwar/Mail/inbox
MANPATH=/usr/X11/man:/usr/local/man:/usr/man
KDEDIR=/usr
NNTPSERVER=news.egr.up.edu
VISUAL=pico
USER=sarwar
LS_COLORS=no=00:fi=00:di=01;34:ln=01;36:pi=40;33:so=01;35:bd=40;33;01:cd
=40;33;01:or=01;05;37;41:mi=01;05;37;41:ex=01;32:*.cmd=01;32:*.exe=01;32
:*.com=01;32:*.btm=01;32:*.bat=01;32:*.tar=01;31:*.tgz=01;31:*.tbz2=01;3
1:*.arc=01;31:*.arj=01;31:*.taz=01;31:*.lzh=01;31:*.lha=01;31:*.zip=01;3
1:*.z=01;31:*.Z=01;31:*.gz=01;31:*.bz2=01;31:*.bz=01;31:*.tz=01;31:*.rpm
```

```
=01;31:*.jpg=01;35:*.jpeg=01;35:*.gif=01;35:*.bmp=01;35:*.xbm=01;35:*.xp
m=01;35:*.png=01;35:*.tif=01;35:*.tiff=01;35:
MACHTYPE=i586-mandrake-linux-gnu
XKEYSYMDB=/usr/lib/X11/XKeysymDB
MAILER=comp -e vi
MAIL=/var/spool/mail/sarwar
EDITOR=vi
LANG=C
HOST=upibmf.egr.up.edu
DISPLAY=pine
LOGNAME=sarwar
SHLVL=2
GROUP=faculty
WWW_HOME=http://www.egr.up.edu/
SHELL=/bin/csh
HOSTTYPE=i586
OSTYPE=linux-gnu
TERM=vt100
HOME=/home/faculty/sarwar
PATH=/usr/sbin:/usr/X11/include/X11:.:/home/faculty/sarwar/bin:/usr/ucb:
/bin:/usr/bin:/usr/include:/usr/X11/lib:/usr/lib:/etc:/usr/etc:/usr/loca
l/bin:/usr/local/lib:/usr/local/games:/usr/X11/bin
EXINIT=set redraw
_=/usr/bin/env
$
```

In the following In-Chapter Exercises, you will create a simple shell script and make it executable. Also, you will use the **set** and **env** commands to display the names and values of shell variables in your environment.

## IN-CHAPTER EXERCISES

**15.1.** Display the names and values of all the shell variables on your LINUX machine. What command(s) did you use?

**15.2.** Create a file that contains a shell script comprising the **date** and **who** commands, one on each line. Make the file executable and run the shell script. List all the steps for completing this task.

### 15.3.1 Controlling The Prompt

Bash allows you to control your prompt in an easy manner. You can assign one or more of several special characters to your prompt variables (PS1, PS2, etc.) to display several prompts. Some of the commonly used special characters are described in Table 15.3.

In the following session, we show how various special characters change the primary prompt for your shell. Note that you can combine several special characters and assign them to your prompt variable.

```
$ PS1='\w$ '
~/linuxbook/examples/Bash$ date
Thu Feb 15 22:04:43 PST 2001
~/linuxbook/examples/Bash$ PS1='\d$ '
Thu Feb 15$ PS1='\H$ '
upibmg.egr.up.edu$ PS1='\h$ '
upibmg$ PS1='\t$ '
22:15:09$ PS1='\s-\v$ '
bash-2.03$
```

### 15.3.2 Variable Declaration

Bash does not require you to declare variables but you can use the **declare** and **typeset** commands to declare variables, initialize them, and set their attributes. The attributes of a variable dictate the type of values that can be assigned to it and its scope (i.e., where it is accessible). A Bash variable is a string variable by default but you can define a variable to be an integer variable. You can also declare functions and arrays (see Chapter 16) by using these commands. You can mark a

**Table 15.3** Some Useful Prompt Characters and their Descriptions

| Special Character | Description |
|---|---|
| \H | Fully qualified domain name of the host, such as upsun20.egr.up.edu |
| \T | Time in the 12-hour hh:mm:ss format |
| \d | The date in "weekday month date" format |
| \h | Hostname of the computer up to the first dot, such as upsun20 |
| \s | The name of your shell |
| \t | Time in the 24-hour hh:mm:ss format |
| \u | User name of the current user |
| \v | Version of Bash such as 2.03 |
| \w | Current working directory |

variable read-only and make a variable's value available to a child process. The following is a brief description of these commands.

Syntax:

**declare [±options] [name [=value]]**
**typeset [±options] [name [=value]]**

**Purpose:** Declare variables, initialize them, and set their attributes. Inside functions, new copies of the variables are created. Using + instead of - turns attributes off.

**Output:** Without names and options, display names of all shell variables and their values. With options, display names of variables with the given attributes and their values.

**Commonly used options/features:**

| | |
|---|---|
| `-a` | each 'name' is an array |
| `-f` | each 'name' is a function |
| `-i` | 'name' is an integer |
| `-r` | mark each 'name' read-only (cannot be turned off by using +x) |
| `-x` | mark each 'name' exported |

Bash does not require you to declare variables or initialize them. An undeclared and uninitialized variable has an initial value of a null string. Bash also does not require you to specify a variable's attributes at the time of their declaration. You can initialize a variable and set the attributes of a variable at a later time by using the `declare` or `typeset` commands with the options described in the syntax box or by using other commands for setting specific attribues. Declaring an existing variable does not change its current value. In the following session, we demonstrate the use of the `declare` command (you can replace the `declare` command with the `typeset` command).

```
$ declare -i age=42
$ declare -rx OS=LINUX

$ echo $age
42
$ echo $OS
LINUX
```

```
$ declare OS
$ declare age
$ echo $OS
LINUX
$ echo $age
42
$
```

When you use the **declare** and **typeset** commands without arguments, they display the names of all the shell variables in your environment and their values. You can use these commands to view the values of variables with particular attributes. The following session shows some examples. We have shown partial outputs to save space. Note that the **declare -ir** command displays all integer and read-only variables in your environment.

```
$ declare -i
declare -ir EUID="501"
declare -ir PPID="31765"
declare -ir UID="501"
declare -i age="42"
$ declare -x
declare -x BASH_ENV="/home/faculty/sarwar/.bashrc"
declare -x DISPLAY="pine"
declare -x HISTSIZE="1000"
declare -x HOME="/home/faculty/sarwar"
...
$ declare -ir
declare -ar BASH_VERSINFO='([0]="2" [1]="04" [2]="11" [3]="1"
[4]="release" [5]= "i386-redhat-linux-gnu")'
declare -ir EUID="501"
declare -rx OS="LINUX"
declare -ir PPID="31765"
declare -r
SHELLOPTS="braceexpand:hashall:histexpand:monitor:history:interactive
-comments:emacs"
declare -ir UID="501"
```

```
declare -i age="42"
$ declare
BASH=/bin/bash
BASH_ENV=/home/faculty/sarwar/.bashrc
BASH_VERSINFO=([0]="2" [1]="04" [2]="11" [3]="1" [4]="release"
[5]="i386-redhat-linux-gnu")
BASH_VERSION='2.04.11(1)-release'
...
$
```

You can change the value of a variable by using the **name=value** syntax (discussed in detail in section 15.3.3). You can use the syntax to declare generic variables that can be assigned a string value. An integer variable cannot be assigned a noninteger value; doing so results in the variable getting a value of zero. Noninteger variables can be assigned any value because every value is stored as a string. The following session shows some examples. Since ***age*** is declared to be an integer variable, assigning it a value "Forty" results in 0 being assigned to it. On the other hand, since ***name*** and ***place*** are generic variables, they can be assigned any type of value (integer or string).

```
$ declare -i age=42
$ echo $age
42
$ age="Forty"
$ echo $age
0
$ name=John
$ declare place=Mars
$ echo $name $place
John Mars
$ name=2001 place=007
$ echo $name $place
2001 007
$
```

### 15.3.3 Reading and Writing Shell Variables

You can use the following syntax to assign a value to (write) one or more shell variables. The command syntax **variable=value** comprises what is commonly known as the **assignment statement**, and its purpose is to assign `value` to `variable`. The following is the general syntax of the assignment statement in Bash.

Syntax:

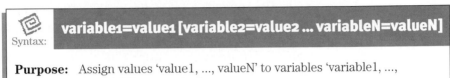

**variable1=value1 [variable2=value2 ... variableN=valueN]**

**Purpose:** Assign values 'value1, ..., valueN' to variables 'variable1, ..., variableN', respectively

Note that there is no space before and after the equals sign (=) in the syntax. If a value contains spaces, you must enclose the value in quotes. Single and double quotes work differently, as discussed later in this section. You can refer to (read) the current value of a variable by inserting a dollar sign (`$`) before the name of a variable, as in `$variable`. You can use the `echo` command to display the values of shell variables. Several other syntaxes and operators can also be used to reference the value of a shell variable. The various syntaxes and operators are described in Table 15.4.

**Table 15.4** Variable Substitution Operators and Their Descriptions

| Operator | Purpose | Description |
|---|---|---|
| `$variable` | To get the value of a variable or null if it is not initialized | Return the value of 'variable' or null if it is not initialized |
| `${variable}` | To get the value of a variable or null if it is not initialized; used when something else is to be appended to the value | Return the value of 'variable' or null if it is not initialized |
| `${variable:-string}` | To get the value of a variable or a known value if it is undefined | If 'variable' exists and is not null, return its value; otherwise return 'string' |
| `${variable:=string}` | To set a variable to a known value if it is undefined and return that value | If 'variable' exists and is not null, return its value; otherwise assign 'string' to 'variable' and return it |
| `${variable:?string}` | To display a message if a variable is undefined | If 'variable' exists and is not null, return its value; otherwise, display 'variable:' followed by 'message' |
| `${variable:+string}` | To test for the existence of a variable | If 'variable' exists and is not null, return 'string'; otherwise return null |

In the following session, we show how shell variables can be read (interpreted) and written (created). The first **echo** command displays a blank line for an uninitialized variable called *name*. Then the *name* variable is initialized to David and the subsequent *echo* command is used to display the value of *name*, which now contains the value David. The output of the **echo ${name:-John} ${place:-Portland}** command is David Portland because *name* has the value David and *place* is uninitialized. The **echo ${place:?"Not defined."}** command displays the message **bash: place: Not defined.** because the variable *place* is not defined. The **echo ${name:+"Defined"}** command displays **Defined** because the *name* variable has been initialized to a nonnull value and the **echo ${place:+"Not defined"}** command displays the null string because the *place* variable has not been defined and is therefore null. The **echo ${place:="San Francisco"}** command assigns the value San Francisco to the *place* variable and displays the same value because the *place* variable is undefined.

```
$ echo $name

$ name=David
$ echo $name
David
$ echo $place

$ echo ${name:-John} ${place:-Portland}
David Portland
$ echo ${place:?"Not defined."}
bash: place: Not defined.
$ echo ${name:+"Defined"}
Defined
$ echo ${place:+"Not defined"}
$ echo ${place:="San Francisco"}
San Francisco
$ echo ${name:-John} ${place:-Portland}
David San Francisco
$
```

In the following session, we show the use of single and double quotes, *, and \ in an assignment statement.

```
$ name=John
$ echo $name
```

```
John
$ name=John Doe
bash: Doe: command not found
$ name="John Doe"
$ echo $name
John Doe
$ name=John*
$ echo $name
John.Bates.letter John.Johnsen.memo John.email
$ echo "$name"
John*
$ echo "The name $name sounds familiar! "
The name John* sounds familiar!
$ echo \$name
$name
$ echo '$name'
$name
$
```

If values that include spaces aren't enclosed in quotes, the shell tries to execute the second word in the value as a command and displays an error message if the word doesn't correspond to a valid command. Also, after the **name=John*** statement has been executed and *$name* is not quoted in the **echo** command, the shell lists the file names in your present working directory that match **John***, with * considered as the shell metacharacter. The variable *$name* must be enclosed in quotes to refer to **John***, as in **echo "$name"**.

Thus the use of double quotes allows variable substitution by special processing of the dollar sign (**$**), but most other shell metacharacters, including the * character, are processed literally. As a result, running the **echo *** command would display the names of all the files in your current directory in one line. The preceding session also shows that you can use single quotes to process the whole string literally. The backslash character can be used to escape the special meaning of any single character, including **$**, and treat it literally.

A command consisting of **$variable** only results in the value of *variable* executed as a shell command. If the value of *variable* comprises a valid command, the expected results are produced. If *variable* doesn't contain a valid command, the shell, as expected, displays an appropriate error message. The following session makes this point with some examples. The variable used in the session is *command*.

```
$ command=pwd
$ $command
/home/faculty/sarwar/linuxbook/examples
$ command=hello
$ $command
bash: hello: command not found
$
```

### 15.3.4 Command Substitution

When a command is enclosed in parentheses and preceded by `$`, as in `$(command)`, or enclosed in backquotes (also known as *grave accents*), the shell substitutes it with the output of the command. The new syntax for \`command\` is `$(command)`. We use both syntaxes in this book. This process is referred to as **command substitution**. The following is a brief description of command substitution.

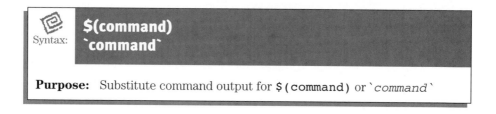

**$(command)**
**\`command\`**

**Purpose:** Substitute command output for `$(command)` or \`*command*\`

The following session illustrates the concept. In the first assignment statement, the variable *command* is assigned a value pwd. In the second assignment statement, the output of the pwd command is assigned to the *command* variable.

```
$ command=pwd
$ echo "The value of command is: $command."
The value of command is: pwd.
$ command=$(pwd)
$ echo "The value of command is: $command."
The value of command is: /home/faculty/sarwar/linuxbook/examples.
$
```

Command substitution can be specified in any command. For example, in the following session, the output of the `date` command is substituted for `$(date)` before the `echo` command is executed.

```
$ echo "The date and time is $(date)."
The date and time is Wed Jan 31 22:51:25 PST 2001.
$
```

We demonstrate the real-world use of command substitution in various ways throughout this chapter and Chapter 16.

The following In-Chapter Exercises have been designed to reinforce the creation and use of shell variables and the concept of command substitution.

**IN-CHAPTER EXERCISES**

**15.3.** Assign your full name to a shell variable called *myname* and echo its value. How did you accomplish the task? Show your work.

**15.4.** Assign the output of `echo "Hello, world! "` command to the *myname* variable and then display the value of *myname*. List the commands that you executed to complete your work.

## 15.3.5 Exporting Environment

When a variable is created, it is not automatically known to children processes. The **export**, **declare -x**, **or typeset -x** command passes the *value* of a variable to children processes. Thus when a shell script is called and executed in another shell script, it doesn't get automatic access to the variables defined in the original (caller) script unless they are explicitly made available to it. These commands can be used to pass the value of one or more variables to any subsequent script. All read/write shell environment variables are available to every command, script, and subshell, so they are exported at the time they are initialized. The following is a brief description of the three commands.

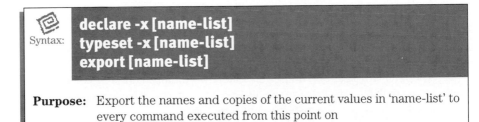

Syntax: **declare -x [name-list]**
**typeset -x [name-list]**
**export [name-list]**

**Purpose:** Export the names and copies of the current values in 'name-list' to every command executed from this point on

The following session presents a simple use of the **declare -x** command. The *name* variable is initialized to John Doe and is marked to be exported to subsequent commands executed under the current shell and any subshells that run under the current shell.

```
$ declare -x name="John Doe"
$
```

We now illustrate the concept of exporting shell variables via some simple shell scripts. Consider the following session.

```
$ cat display_name
echo $name
exit 0
$
$ name="John Doe"
$ display_name

$
```

Note that the shell script in the display_name file displays a null string even though we initialized the *name* variable just before executing this script. The reason is that the *name* variable is not exported before running the script, and the *name* variable used in the script is *local* to the script. Because this local variable *name* is uninitialized, the `echo` command displays the null string—the default value of every uninitialized variable.

You can use the `exit` command to transfer control to the calling process—the current shell process in the preceding session. The only argument of the `exit` command is an optional integer number, which is returned to the calling process as the **exit status** of the terminating process. All LINUX commands return an exit status of 0 upon success (if they successfully perform their tasks) and nonzero upon failure. The return status value of a command is stored in the read-only environment variable `$?` and can be checked by the calling process. In shell scripts, the status of a command is commonly checked and subsequent action taken. We show the use of `$?` in some shell scripts later in the chapter. When the `exit` command is executed without an argument, the LINUX kernel sets the return status value for the script.

In the following session, the *name* variable is initialized and marked to be exported, thus making it available to the display_name script. The session also shows that the return status of the display_name script is 0.

```
$ declare -x name="John Doe"
$ display_name
John Doe
```

```
$ echo $?
0
$
```

We now show that a *copy* of an exported variable's *value* is passed to any subsequent command. In other words, a command has access to the value of the exported variable only; it cannot assign a new value to the variable. Consider the script in the export_demo file.

```
$ cat export_demo
#!/bin/bash
declare -x name="John Doe"
display_change_name
display_name
exit 0
$ cat display_change_name
#!/bin/bash
echo $name
name="Plain Jane"
echo $name
exit 0
$ export_demo
John Doe
Plain Jane
John Doe
$
```

When the export_demo script is invoked, the *name* variable is set to John Doe and marked to be exported so that it becomes part of the environment of all the commands that execute under export_demo as its children. The first **echo** command in the display_change_name script displays the value of the exported variable, *name*. It then initializes a local variable, *name*, to Plain Jane. The second **echo** command therefore echoes the current value of the local variable *name* and displays Plain Jane. When the display_change_name script has finished, the display_name script executes and displays the value of the exported (nonlocal) *name*, thus displaying John Doe.

## 15.3.6 Resetting Variables

A variable retains its value so long as the script in which it is initialized executes. You can reset the value of a variable to null (the default initial value of all variables) by either explicitly initializing it to null or by using the **unset** command. The following is a brief description of this command.

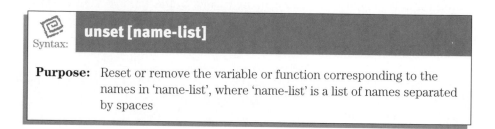

Syntax:

**unset [name-list]**

**Purpose:** Reset or remove the variable or function corresponding to the names in 'name-list', where 'name-list' is a list of names separated by spaces

We discuss functions in Bash in Chapter 16, so we limit the discussion of the **unset** command here to variables only. The following session shows a simple use of the command. The variables *name* and *place* are set to John and Corvallis, respectively, and the **echo** command displays the values of these variables. The **unset** command resets *name* to null. Thus the **echo "$name"** command displays a null string (a blank line).

```
$ declare name=John place=Corvallis
$ echo "$name $place"
John Corvallis
$ unset name
$ echo "$name"

$ echo "$place"
Corvallis
$
```

The following command removes the variables *name* and *place*.

```
$ unset name place
$
```

Another way to reset a variable is to assign it explicitly a null value by assigning it no value and simply hitting <Enter> after the = sign, as in

```
$ country=
$ echo "$country"

$
```

### 15.3.7 Creating Read-Only User-Defined Variables

When programming, you need to use constants at times. You can use **literal constants**, but using **symbolic constants** is good programming practice, primarily because it makes your code more readable. Another reason for using symbolic names is that a constant used at various places in code may need to be changed. With a symbolic constant, the change is made at one place only, but a literal constant must be changed every place it was used. A symbolic constant can be created in Bash by initializing a variable with the desired value and making it read-only by using the `readonly`, `declare -r`, or `typeset -r` command. The following is a brief description of these commands.

Syntax:

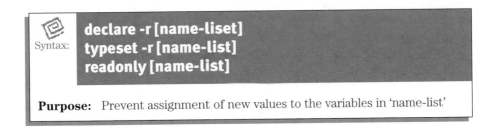

**declare -r [name-liset]**
**typeset -r [name-list]**
**readonly [name-list]**

**Purpose:** Prevent assignment of new values to the variables in 'name-list'

In the following session, the *name* and *place* variables are made read-only after initializing them with Jim and Ames, respectively. Once they have become read-only, assignment to either variable fails.

```
$ declare -r name=Jim place=Ames
$ echo $name $place
Jim Ames
$ name=Art place="Ann Arbor"
bash: name: readonly variable
bash: place: readonly variable
$
```

When the `readonly`, `declare -r`, or `typeset -r` command is executed without arguments, it displays all read-only variables and their values. The following session shows the execution of this command on our system. *BASH_VERSINFO*, *EUID*, *PPID*, and *SHELLOPTS* are environment variables. The variables *name* and *place* are user-defined read-only variables created in the preceding session.

```
$ readonly
declare -ar BASH_VERSINFO='([0]="2" [1]="04" [2]="11" [3]="1" [4]="release" [5]=
"i386-redhat-linux-gnu")'
declare -ir EUID="501"
declare -ir PPID="7658"
declare -r SHELLOPTS="braceexpand:hashall:histexpand:monitor:history:interactive
-comments:emacs"
declare -ir UID="501"
declare -r name="Jim"
declare -r place="Ames"
$
```

You cannot reset the value of a read-only variable. The following session gives an example.

```
$ unset name
bash: unset: name: cannot unset: readonly variable
$
```

### 15.3.8 Reading from Standard Input

So far we have shown how you can assign values to shell variables statically at the command line level or by using the assignment statement in your programs. If you want to write an interactive shell script that prompts the user for keyboard input, you need to use the **read** command to store the user input in a shell variable. This command allows you to read one line of standard input. The following is a brief description of the command.

Syntax:

**read [options] [variable-list]**

**Purpose:** Read one line from standard input and assign words in the line to variables in 'variable-list'

**Commonly used options/features:**

| | |
|---|---|
| `-a name` | Read words into the 'name' array |
| `-e` | Read the whole line into the first variable; the rest of the variables are null |
| `-p prompt` | Display 'prompt' if reading from a terminal |

A line is read in the form of words separated by white spaces (<space> or <Tab> characters, depending on the value of the shell environment variable *IFS*). The words are assigned to the variables in the order of their occurrence, from left to right. If the number of words in the line is greater than the number of variables in 'variable-list', the last variable is assigned the extra words. If the number of words in a line is less than the number of variables, the remaining variables are reset to null.

We illustrate the semantics of the **read** command by way of the following script in the read_demo file.

```
$ cat read_demo
#!/bin/bash
echo -n "Enter input: "
read line
echo "You entered: $line"
echo -n "Enter another line: "
read word1 word2 word3
echo "The first word is: $word1"
echo "The second word is: $word2"
echo "The rest of the line is: $word3"
exit 0
$
```

We now show how the input that you enter from the keyboard is read by the **read** command in that script. In the following run, you enter the same input: **LINUX rules the network computing world!** (you can never overemphasize the power of LINUX!). The first **read** command takes the whole input and puts it in the shell variable *line* without the newline character. In the second **read** command, the first word of your input is assigned to the variable *word1*, the second word is assigned to the variable *word2*, and the rest of the line (without the newline character) is assigned to the variable *word3*. The outputs of the **echo** commands for displaying the values of these variables confirm this point.

```
$ read_demo
Enter input: LINUX rules the network computing world!
You entered: LINUX rules the network computing world!
Enter another line: LINUX rules the network computing world!
The first word is:    LINUX
```

```
The second word is: rules
The rest of the line is: the network computing world!
$
```

The **-n** option in the two **echo** commands that prompt your input is used to force the cursor to stay at the same line after you hit <Enter>. If you don't use this option, the cursor moves to the next line, which is what you like to see happen while displaying information and error messages. However, when you prompt the user for keyboard input, you should keep the cursor in front of the prompt for a more user-friendly interface.

The lines

```
echo -n "Enter input: "
read line
```

can be replaced with **read -p "Enter input: "** to prompt the user for input and store a line of input in the shell variable line.

In the following In-Chapter Exercises, you will use the **read** and **declare** commands to practice reading from stdin in shell scripts and exporting variables to children processes.

**IN-CHAPTER EXERCISES**

**15.5.** Give commands for reading a value into the *myname* variable from the keyboard and exporting it so that commands executed in any child shell have access to the variable.

**15.6.** Copy the value of the *myname* variable to another variable, *anyname*. Make the *anyname* variable readonly and **unset** both the *myname* and *anyname* variables. What happened? Show all your work.

## 15.4 PASSING ARGUMENTS TO SHELL SCRIPTS

In this section we describe how command line arguments can be passed to shell scripts and manipulated by them. As we discussed earlier, you can pass command line arguments, or positional parameters, to a shell script. The values of up to the first nine of these arguments are stored in variables *$1* through *$9*, respectively. You can use the names of these variables to refer to the values of these arguments. If the positional argument that you refer to isn't passed an argument, it has a value of null. The environment variable *$#* contains the total number of arguments passed in an execution of a script. The variables *$** and *$@* both contain the values of all of the arguments, but *$@* has each individual argument in quotes if it is used as *"$@"*. The variable name *$0* contains the name of the script file (the command name). The shell script in the cmdargs_demo file shows how you can use these variables.

```
$ cat cmdargs_demo
#!/bin/bash
echo "The command name is: $0."
echo "The number of command line arguments passed as parameters are $#."
echo "The values of the command line arguments are: $1 $2 $3 $4 $5 $6 $7 $8 $9."
echo "Another way to display values of all of the arguments: $@."
echo "Yet another way is: $*."
exit 0
$ cmdargs_demo a b c d e f g h i
The command name is: cmdargs_demo.
The number of command line arguments passed as parameters are 9.
The values of the command line arguments are: a b c d e f g h i.
Another way to display values of all of the arguments: a b c d e f g h i.
Yet another way is: a b c d e f g h i.
$ cmdargs_demo One Two 3 Four 5 6
The command name is: cmdargs_demo.
The number of command line arguments passed as parameters are 6.
The values of the command line arguments are: One Two 3 Four 5 6   .
Another way to display values of all of the arguments: One Two 3 Four 5 6.
Yet another way is: One Two 3 Four 5 6.
$L
```

Although the shell maintains as many as nine command line arguments at a time, you can write scripts that take more than nine arguments. To do so, use the `shift` command. By default, the command shifts the command line arguments to the left by one position, making *$2* become *$1*, *$3* become *$2*, and so on. The first argument, *$1*, is shifted out. Once shifted, the arguments cannot be restored to their original values. The number of positions to be shifted can be more than one and specified as an argument to the command. The following is a brief description of the command.

**shift [N]**

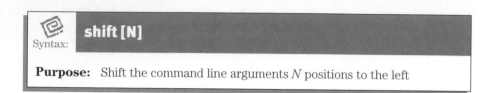

**Purpose:** Shift the command line arguments *N* positions to the left

The script in the shift_demo file shows the semantics of the **shift** command. The first **shift** command shifts the first argument out and the remaining arguments to the left by one position. The second **shift** command shifts the current arguments to the left by three positions. The three **echo** commands are used to display the current value of the program name (*$0*), the values of all positional parameters (*$@*), and the values of the first three positional parameters, respectively. The results of execution of the script are obvious.

```
$ cat shift_demo
#!/bin/bash
echo "The program name is $0."
echo "The arguments are: $@"
echo "The first three arguments are: $1 $2 $3"
shift
echo "The program name is $0."
echo "The arguments are: $@"
echo "The first three arguments are: $1 $2 $3"
shift 3
echo "The program name is $0."
echo "The arguments are: $@"
echo "The first three arguments are: $1 $2 $3"
exit 0
$ shift_demo 1 2 3 4 5 6 7 8 9 10 11 12
The program name is shift_demo.
The arguments are: 1 2 3 4 5 6 7 8 9 10 11 12
The first three arguments are: 1 2 3
The program name is shift_demo.
The arguments are: 2 3 4 5 6 7 8 9 10 11 12
```

```
The first three arguments are: 2 3 4
The program name is shift_demo.
The arguments are: 5 6 7 8 9 10 11 12
The first three arguments are: 5 6 7
$
```

The values of positional arguments can be altered by using the **set** command. The most effective use of this command is in conjunction with command substitution. The following is a brief description of the command.

Syntax: **set [options] [argument-list]**

**Purpose:** To set flags, options, and positional arguments; with no options, display names and values of all shell variables (environment and user-defined); and set positional arguments to the words in 'argument-list'

**Commonly used options/features:**

| | |
|---|---|
| `--` | Do not consider words starting with a '-' as options |
| `-C` | Set noclobber to on and force >\| to overwrite existing files |
| `-a` | Automatically export variables upon assignment |
| `-o [option]` | Set options; display current settings without options. Some of the options are |
|     `hash` | Save command locations in an internal hash table (default setting; can be set by using the -h option) |
|     `history` | Enable history |
|     `noclobber` | Don't allow overwriting of existing files by output redirection (same as -C) |
| `-v` | Verbose mode: display input lines as they are displayed |

The **set** command has a variety of features. Here, we discuss its feature for setting command line arguments.

The following session involves a simple interactive use of the **set** command. The **date** command is executed to show that the output has six fields. The **set $(date)** command sets the positional parameters to the output of the **date** command. In particular, *$1* is set to Thu, *$2* to Feb, *$3* to 1, *$4* to 21:33:09, *$5* to

PST, and *$6* to 2001. The **echo "$@"** command displays the values of all positional arguments. The third echo command displays the date in a commonly used form.

```
$ date
Thu Feb 1 21:32:46 PST 2001
$ set $(date)
$ echo "$@"
Thu Feb 1 21:33:09 PST 2001
$ echo "$2 $3, $6"
Feb 1, 2001
$
```

An option commonly used with the **set** command is **--**. It is used to inform the **set** command that, if the first argument starts with a **-**, it should not be considered an option for the **set** command. The script in set_demo shows another use of the command. When the script is run with a file argument, it generates a line that contains the file name, the file's inode number, and the file size (in bytes). The **set** command is used to assign the output of the **ls -il** command as the new values of the positional arguments *$1* through *$9*. If you don't remember the format of the output of the **ls -il** command, we suggest you run this command on a file before studying the code.

```
$ cat set_demo
#!/bin/bash
filename="$1"
set $(ls -il $filename)
inode="$1"
size="$6"
echo "Name  Inode   Size"
echo
echo "$filename $inode $size"
exit 0
$ set_demo lab3
Name  Inode   Size

lab3  856110  591
$
```

In the following In-Chapter Exercises, you will use the **set** and **shift** commands to reinforce the use of command line arguments and their processing.

**IN-CHAPTER EXERCISES**

**15.7.** Write a Bash script that displays all command line arguments, shifts them to the left by two positions, and redisplays them. Show the script along with a few sample runs.

**15.8.** Update the shell script in Exercise 15.7 so that, after accomplishing the original task, it sets the positional arguments to the output of the `who | head -1` command and displays the positional arguments again.

## 15.5 COMMENTS AND PROGRAM HEADERS

You should develop the habit of putting **comments** in your programs to describe the purpose of a particular series of commands. At times, you should even briefly describe the purpose of a variable or assignment statement. Also, you should use a **program header** for every shell script that you write. These are simply good software engineering practices. Program headers and comments help a programmer who has been assigned the task of modifying or enhancing your code to understand it quickly. They also help you understand your own code, in particular if you reread it after some period of time. Programs written long ago, when putting comments in the program code or creating separate documentation for programs wasn't a common practice, are very difficult to understand and enhance. Such programs are commonly known as **legacy code**.

A good program header must contain at least the following items. In addition, you can insert any other items that you believe to be important or are commonly used in your organization or group as part of its **coding rules**.

1. Name of the file containing the script
2. Name of the author
3. Date written
4. Date last modified
5. Purpose of the script (in one or two lines)
6. A brief description of the algorithm used to implement the solution to the problem at hand

A comment line (including every line in the program header) must start with the number sign (`#`), as in

```
# This is a comment line.
```

However, a comment doesn't have to start at a new line; it can follow a command, as in

```
set -- $(ls -l lab1) # Assign new values to positional parameters and
                     # if the first argument starts with a -, do not
                     # consider it an option for the set command.
                     # This is to handle the output of the ls -l
                     # command if lab1 is an ordinary file.
```

The following is a sample header for the set_demo script.

```
# File Name:            ~/Bash/examples/set_demo
# Author:               Syed Mansoor Sarwar
# Date Written:         February 1, 2001
# Date Last Modified:   February 1, 2001
# Purpose:              To illustrate how the set command works
# Brief Description:    The script runs with a filename as the only command
#                       line argument, saves the filename, runs the set
#                       command to assign output of ls -il command to
#                       positional arguments ($1 through $9), and displays
#                       file name, its inode number, and its size in bytes.
```

We do not show the program headers for all the sample scripts in this textbook for the sake of saving space.

## 15.6 PROGRAM CONTROL FLOW COMMANDS

The program control flow commands/statements are used to determine the sequence in which statements in a shell script execute. There are three basic types of statements for controlling the flow of a script: two-way branching, multiway branching, and repetitive execution of one or more commands. The Bash statement for two-way branching is the `if` statement, the statements for multiway branching are the `if` and `case` statements, and the statements for repetitive execution of some code are the `for`, `while`, and `until` statements.

### 15.6.1 THE `if-then-elif-else-fi` STATEMENT

The most basic form of the `if` statement is used for two-way branching, but the statement can also be used for multiway branching. The following is a brief description of the statement. The words in monospace type are called keywords and must be used as shown in the syntax. Everything in brackets is optional. All the command lists are designed to enable you to accomplish the task at hand.

Syntax:

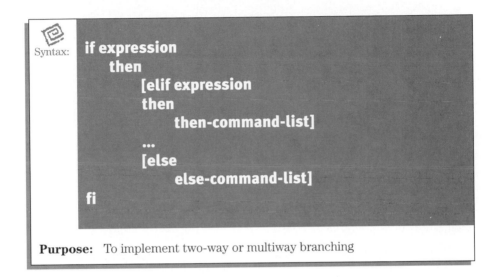

```
if expression
    then
        [elif expression
        then
            then-command-list]
        ...
        [else
            else-command-list]
fi
```

**Purpose:** To implement two-way or multiway branching

Here, an 'expression' is a list of commands. The execution of commands in 'expression' returns a status of true (success) or false (failure). We discuss three versions of the `if` statement that together comprise the statement's complete syntax and semantics. The first version of the `if` statement is without any optional features, which results in the syntax for the statement that is commonly used for two-way branching.

Syntax:

```
if expression
    then
        then-commands
fi
```

**Purpose:** To implement two-way branching

If 'expression' is true, the 'then-commands' are executed; otherwise, the command after `fi` is executed. The semantics of the statement are illustrated in Figure 15.1.

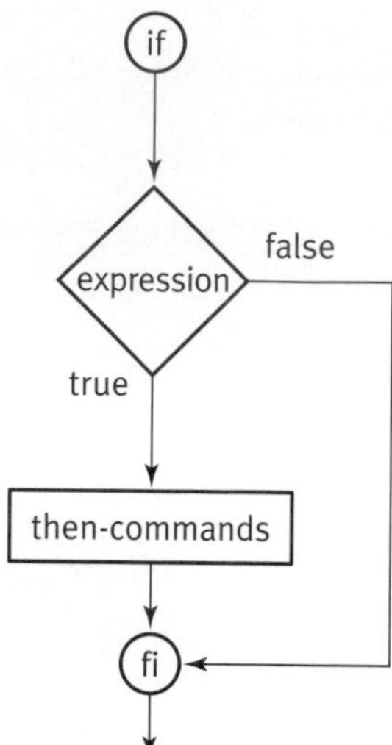


**Figure 15.1** Semantics of the `if-then-fi` statement

The 'expression' can be evaluated with the **`test`** command. It evaluates an expression and returns true or false. The command has two syntaxes: One uses the keyword **`test`** and the other uses brackets. The following is a brief description of the command.

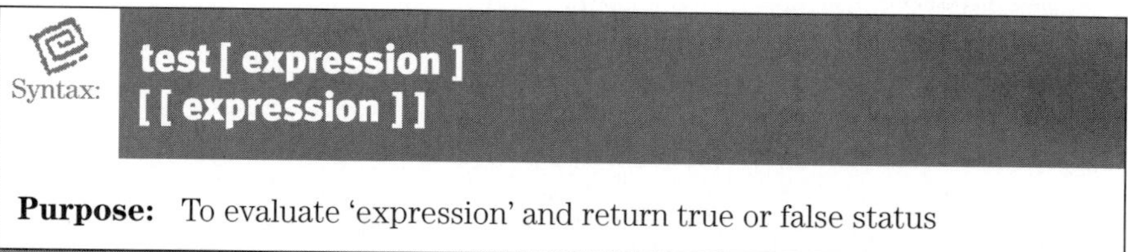

Syntax:

**test [ expression ]**
**[ [ expression ] ]**

**Purpose:** To evaluate 'expression' and return true or false status

An important point about this second syntax is that inner brackets indicate an optional expression and that outer brackets are required because they comprise the **`test`** statement. Also, at least one space is required before and after an operator, a paren, a bracket, or an operand. If you need to continue a test expression to the next line, you must use a backslash (\) before hitting <Enter> so that the shell doesn't treat the next line as a separate command. (Recall that \ is a shell metacharacter.) We demonstrate use of the **`test`** command in the first session but then use the simpler syntax of `[ ]`.

The **`test`** command supports many operators for testing files and integers, testing and comparing strings, and logically connecting two or more expressions to form complex expressions. Table 15.5 describes the meanings of the operators supported by the **`test`** command on most LINUX systems.

**Table 15.5** Some Useful Operators for the `test` Command

| File Testing | | Integer Testing | | String Testing | |
|---|---|---|---|---|---|
| **Expression** | **Return Value** | **Expression** | **Return Value** | **Expression** | **Return Value** |
| `-d` file | True if 'file' is a directory | int1 `-eq` int2 | True if 'int1' and 'int2'are equal | str | True if 'str' is not an empty string |
| `-f` file | True if 'file' is an ordinary file | int1 `-ge` int2 | True if 'int1' is greater than or equal to 'int2' | str1 = str2 | True if 'str1' and 'str2' are the same |
| `-r` file | True if 'file' is readable | int1 `-gt` int2 | True if 'int1' is greater than 'int2' | str1 != str2 | True if 'str1' and 'str2' are not the same |
| `-s` file | True if length of 'file' is nonzero | int1 `-le` int2 | True if 'int1' is less than or equal to 'int2' | `-n` str | True if the length of 'str' is greater than zero |
| `-t` [filedes] | True if file descriptor 'filedes' is associated with the terminal | int1 `-lt` int2 | True if 'int1' is less than 'int2' | `-z` str | True if the length of 'str' is zero |
| `-w` file | True if 'file' is writable | int1 `-ne` int2 | True if 'int1' is not equal to 'int2' | | |
| `-x` file | True if 'file' is executable | | | | |
| `-b` file | True if 'file is a block special file | | | | |
| `-c` file | True if 'file' is a character special file | | | | |
| `-e` file | True if 'file' exists | | | | |
| `-L` file | True if 'file' exists and is a symbolic link | | | | |

| Operators for Forming Complex Expressions | | | |
|---|---|---|---|
| `!` | Logical NOT operator: true if the following expression is false | ( 'expression' ) | Parentheses for grouping expressions; at least one space before and one after each paren |
| `-a` | Logical AND operator: true if the previous (left) and next (right) expressions are true | `-o` | Logical OR operator: true if the previous (left) or next (right) expression is true |

We use the **if** statement to modify the script in the set_demo file so that it takes one command line argument only and checks on whether the argument is a file or a directory. The script returns an error message if the script is run with no or more than one command line argument or if the command line argument is not an ordinary file. The name of the script file is if_demo1.

```
$ cat if_demo1
#!/bin/bash
if test $# -ne 1
   then
      echo "Usage: $0 ordinary_file"
      exit 1
fi
if test -f "$1"
   then
      filename="$1"
      set $(ls -il $filename)
      inode="$1"
      size="$6"
      echo "Name  Inode  Size"
      echo
      echo "$filename  $inode  $size"
      exit 0
fi
echo "$0: argument must be an ordinary file"
exit 1
$ if_demo1
Usage: if_demo1 ordinary_file
$ if_demo1 lab3 lab4
Usage: if_demo1 ordinary_file
$ if_demo1 dir1
if_demo1: argument must be an ordinary file
$ if_demo1 lab3
Name Inode  Size

lab3 856110 591
$
```

In the preceding script, the first `if` statement displays an error message and exits the program if you don't run the script with one command line argument. The second `if` statement is executed if the condition for the first is false—that is, if you run the script with one argument only. This `if` statement produces the desired results if the command line argument is an ordinary file. If the passed argument is not an ordinary file, the condition for the second `if` statement is false and the error message `if_demo1: argument must be an ordinary file` is displayed. Note that the exit status of the script is 1 when it exits because of an erroneous condition and 0 when the script executes successfully and produces the desired results.

An important practice in script writing is to indent properly the commands/statements in it. Proper indentation of programs enhances their readability and makes them easier to understand and upgrade. Note the indentation style used in our sample scripts and follow it when you write your own scripts.

We now discuss the second version of the `if` statement, which also allows two-way branching. The following is a brief description of the statement.

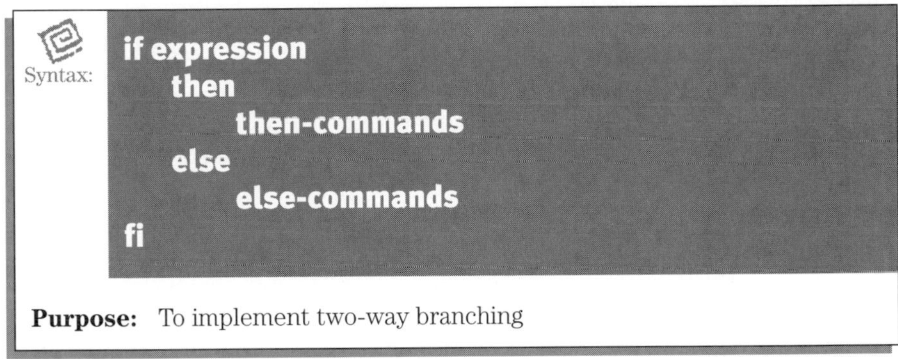

Syntax:

```
if expression
    then
        then-commands
    else
        else-commands
fi
```

**Purpose:** To implement two-way branching

If 'expression' is true, the commands in 'then-commands' are executed; otherwise, the commands in 'else-commands' are executed, followed by the execution of the command after `fi`. The semantics of the statement are depicted in Figure 15.2.

Next, we rewrite the if_demo1 program, using the `if-then-else-fi` statement, and use the alternative syntax for the `test` command. The resulting script is in the if_demo2 file, as shown in the following session. Note that the program looks cleaner and more readable.

```
$ cat if_demo2
#!/bin/bash
if [ $# -ne 1 ]
   then
```

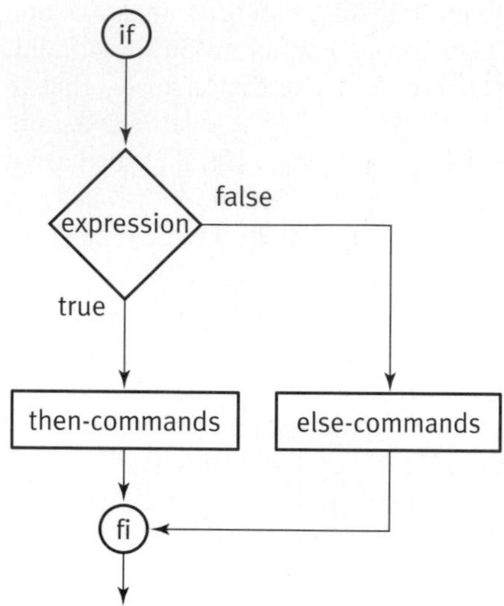


**Figure 15.2** Semantics of the `if-then-else-fi` statement

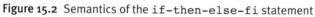

```
        echo "Usage: $0 ordinary_file"
        exit 1
fi
if [ -f "$1" ]
    then
        filename="$1"
        set $(ls -il $filename)
        inode="$1"
        size="$6"
        echo "Name  Inode  Size"
        echo
        echo "$filename  $inode  $size"
        exit 0
    else
        echo "$0: argument must be an ordinary file"
        exit 1
fi
$
```

Finally, we discuss the third version of the `if` statement, which is used to implement multiway branching. The following is a brief description of the statement.

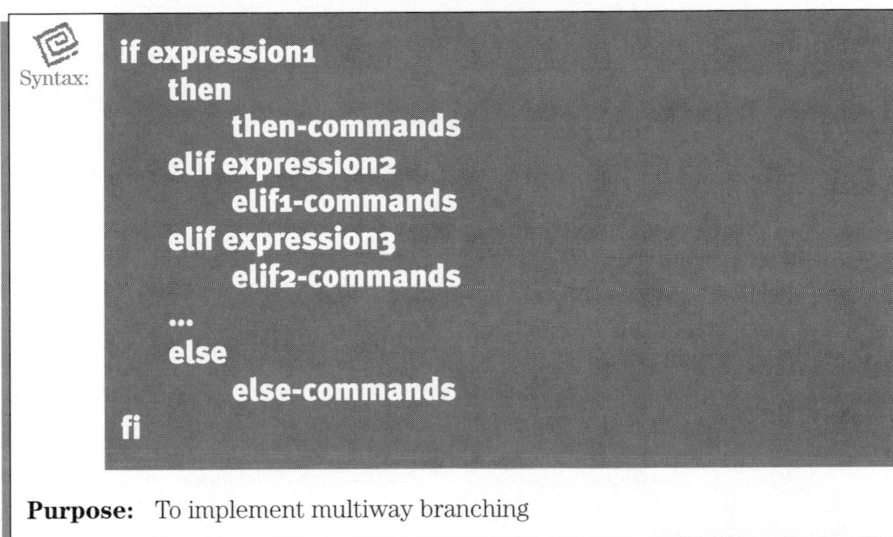

If 'expression1' is true, the commands in 'then-commands' are executed. If 'expression1' is false, 'expression2' is evaluated, and if it is true, the commands in 'elif1-commands' are executed. If 'expression2' is false, 'expression3' is evaluated. If 'expression3' is true, 'elif2-commands' are executed. If 'expression3' is also false, the remaining `elif` expressions are evaluated one by one. If all of the expressions are false, the commands in 'else-commands' are executed. The execution of any command list is followed by the execution of the command after `fi`. You can use any number of `elif`s in an `if` statement to implement multiway branching. The semantics of the statement are depicted in Figure 15.3.

We modify the script in the if_demo2 file so that, if the command line argument is a directory, the program displays the number of files and subdirectories in the directory, excluding hidden files. In addition, the program ensures that the command line argument is an existing file or directory in the current directory before processing it. We also uses the `if-then-elif-else-fi` statement in the implementation. The resulting script is in the if_demo3 file, as shown in the following session.

```
$ cat if_demo3
#!/bin/bash
if [ $# -ne 1 ]
   then
      echo "Usage: $0 file"
      exit 1
   else
   ls "$1" 2> /dev/null 1>&2
```

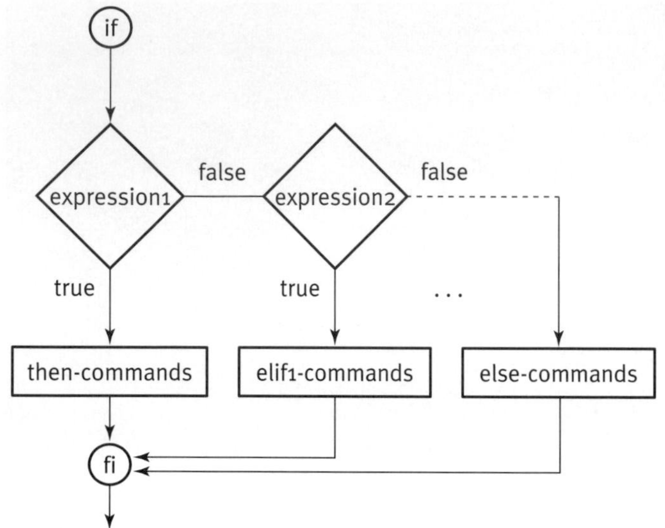


**Figure 15.3** Semantics of the `if-then-elif-else-fi` statement

```
if [ $? -ne 0 ]
   then
     echo "$1: not found"
     exit 1
fi
if [ -f "$1" ]
   then
     filename="$1"
     set (ls -il $filename)
     inode="$1"
     size="$6"
     echo "Name  Inode  Size"
     echo
     echo "$filename  $inode  $size"
     exit 0
  elif [ -d "$1" ]
     then
       nfiles=$(ls "$1" | wc -w)
       echo "The number of files in the directory is $nfiles."
       exit 0
```

```
      else
            echo "$0: argument must be an ordinary file or directory"
            exit 1
   fi
fi
$ if_demo3 file1
file1: not found
$ if_demo3 dir1
The number of files in the directory is 4.
$ if_demo3 lab3
Name  Inode   Size

lab3  856110  591
$L
```

The command `ls "$1" 2> /dev/null 1>&2` is executed to check on whether the file passed as the command line argument exists. The standard error is redirected to /dev/null (the LINUX black hole), and standard output is redirected to standard error by using `1>&2`. Thus the command does not produce any output or error messages; its only purpose is to set the command's return status value in *$?*. If the command line argument exists in the current directory, the **ls** command is successful and *$?* contains `0`; otherwise, it contains a nonzero value. If the command line argument is an ordinary file, the required file-related data are displayed. If the argument is a directory, the number of files in it (including directories) is saved in the *nfiles* variable and displayed using the **echo** command. Note the use of command substitution in the assignment statement. If the passed argument is neither an ordinary file nor a directory, an error message is displayed to inform you accordingly.

In the following In-Chapter Exercises, you will practice the use of the **if** statement, command substitution, and manipulation of positional parameters.

## IN-CHAPTER EXERCISES

**15.9.** Create the if_demo2 script file and run it with no argument, more than one argument, and one argument only. While running the script with one argument, use a directory as the argument. What happens? Does the output make sense?

**15.10.** Write a shell script whose single command line argument is a file. If you run the program with an ordinary file, the program displays the owner's name and last update time for the file. If the program is run with more than one argument, it generates meaningful error messages.

## 15.6.2 The `for` Statement

The `for` statement is the first of three statements that are available in Bash for repetitive execution of a block of commands in a shell script. These statements are commonly known as **loops**. The following is a brief description of the statement.

Syntax:

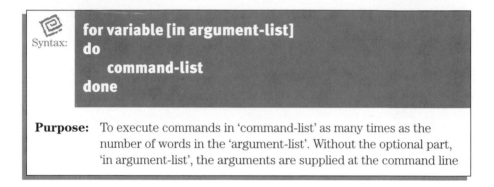

**for variable [in argument-list]**
**do**
**command-list**
**done**

**Purpose:** To execute commands in 'command-list' as many times as the number of words in the 'argument-list'. Without the optional part, 'in argument-list', the arguments are supplied at the command line

The words in 'argument-list' are assigned to 'variable' one by one, and the commands in 'command-list', also known as the body of the loop, are executed for every assignment. This process allows the execution of commands in 'command-list' as many times as the number of words in 'argument-list'. Figure 15.4 illustrates the semantics of the `for` command.

The following script in the for_demo1 file shows use of the `for` command with optional arguments. The variable *`people`* is assigned the words in 'argument-list' one by one, and each time the value of the variable is echoed, until no word remains in the list. At that time, control comes out of the `for` statement and the command following `done` is executed. Then, the code following the `for` statement (the `exit` statement only in this case) is executed.

```
$ cat for_demo1
#!/bin/bash
for people in Debbie Jamie John Kitty Kuhn Shah
do
   echo "$people"
done
exit 0
$ for_demo1
Debbie
Jamie
```

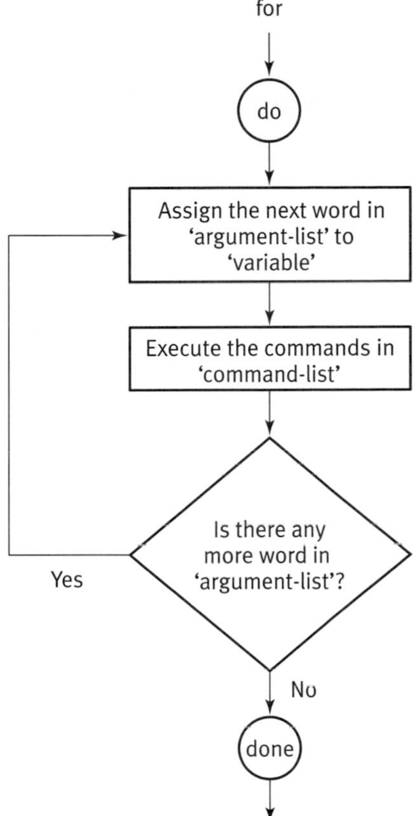
for
do
Assign the next word in 'argument-list' to 'variable'
Execute the commands in 'command-list'
Is there any more word in 'argument-list'?
Yes
No
done

**Figure 15.4** Semantics of the `for` statement

```
John
Kitty
Kuhn
Shah
$
```

The following script in the user_info file takes a list of existing (valid) login names as command line arguments and displays each login name and the full name of the user who owns the login name, one per login. In the sample run, the first value of the *`user`* variable is dheckman. The **`echo`** command displays dheckman: followed by a <Tab>, and the cursor stays at the current line. The **`grep`** command searches the /etc/passwd file for dheckman and pipes it to the **`cut`** command, which displays the fifth field in the /etc/passwd line for dheckman (his full name).

The process is repeated for the remaining two login names (ghacker and msarwar). No user is left in the list passed at the command line, so control comes out of the `for` statement and the `exit 0` command is executed to transfer control back to shell. The command substitution `$(echo $user)` in the `grep` command can be replaced by `"$user"`.

```
$ cat user_info
#!/bin/bash
for user
do
   echo -n "$user: "
   grep $(echo $user) /etc/passwd | cut -f5 -d':'
done
exit 0
$ user_info dheckman ghacker msarwar
dheckman:     Dennis R. Heckman
ghacker:      George Hacker
msarwar:      Mansoor Sarwar
$
```

### 15.6.3 The `while` Statement

The `while` statement, also known as the `while` loop, allows repeated execution of a block of code based on the condition of an expression. The following is a brief description of the statement.

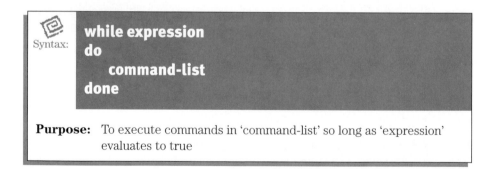

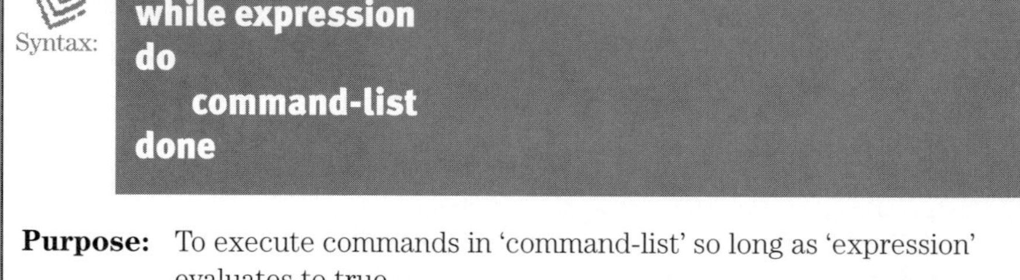

Syntax:
while expression
do
command-list
done
Purpose: To execute commands in 'command-list' so long as 'expression' evaluates to true


The 'expression' is evaluated and, if the result of this evaluation is true, the commands in 'command-list' are executed and 'expression' is evaluated again. This sequence of expression evaluation and execution of 'command-list', known as one

**iteration**, is repeated until the 'expression' evaluates to false. At that time control comes out of the `while` statement and the statement following `done` is executed. Figure 15.5 depicts the semantics of the `while` statement.

The variables and/or conditions in the expression, that result in a true value, must be properly manipulated in the commands in 'command-list' for well-behaved loops—that is, loops that eventually terminate and allow execution of the rest of the code in a script. Loops in which the expression always evaluates to true are known as **nonterminating**, or **infinite**, **loops**. Infinite loops, usually a result of poor design and/or programming, are bad because they continuously use the CPU time without accomplishing any useful task. However, some applications do require infinite loops. For example, all the servers for Internet services such as ftp are programs that run indefinitely, waiting for client requests. Once a server has received a client request, it processes it, sends a response to the client, and waits for another client request. The only way to terminate a process with an infinite loop is to kill it by using the `kill` command. Or, if the process is running in the foreground, pressing `<Ctrl-C>` would also do the trick, unless the process is designed to ignore `<Ctrl-C>`. In that case, you need to put the

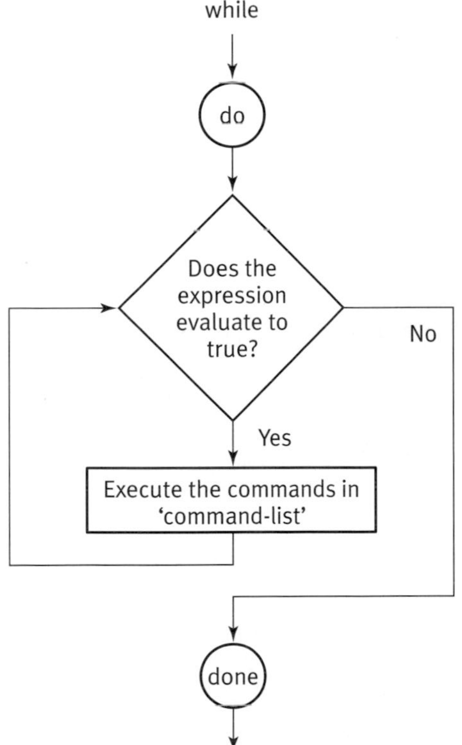
while
do
Does the expression evaluate to true?
No
Yes
Execute the commands in 'command-list'
done

**Figure 15.5** Semantics of the `while` statement

process in the background by pressing <Ctrl-Z> and using the `kill -9` command to terminate it.

The script in the while_demo file shows a simple use of the `while` loop. When you run this script, the *secretcode* variable is initialized to agent007 and you are prompted to make a guess. Your guess is stored in a local variable *yourguess*. If your guess isn't agent007, the condition for the `while` loop is true and the commands between **do** and **done** are executed. This program displays a message tactfully informing you of your failure and prompts you for another guess. Your guess is again stored in the *yourguess* variable, and the condition for the loop is tested. This process continues until you enter agent007 as your guess. This time the condition for the loop becomes false and the control comes out of the `while` statement. The **echo** command following **done** executes, congratulating you for being part of a great gene pool!

```
$ cat while_demo
#!/bin/bash
secretcode=agent007
echo "Guess the code!"
echo -n "Enter your guess: "
read yourguess
while [ "$secretcode" != "$yourguess" ]
do
   echo "Good guess but wrong. Try again!"
   echo -n "Enter your guess: "
   read yourguess
done
echo "Wow! You are a genius!!"
exit 0
$ while_demo
Guess the code!
Enter your guess: star wars
Good guess but wrong. Try again!
Enter your guess: columbo
Good guess but wrong. Try again!
Enter your guess: agent007
Wow! You are a genius!!
$
```

## 15.6.4 The `until` Statement

The syntax of the `until` statement is similar to that of the `while` statement, but its semantics are different. Whereas in the `while` statement the loop body executes so long as the expression evaluates to true, in the `until` statement the loop body executes so long as the expression evaluates to false. The following is a brief description of the statement.

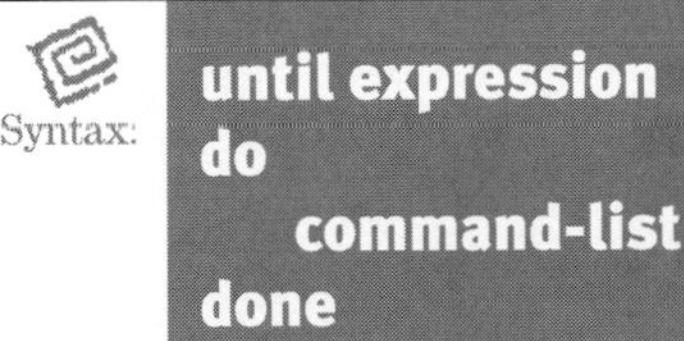

Syntax:

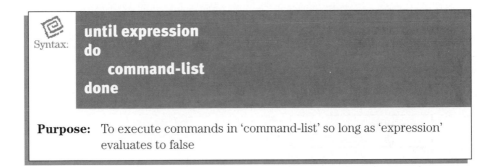

**until expression**
**do**
**command-list**
**done**

**Purpose:** To execute commands in 'command-list' so long as 'expression' evaluates to false

Figure 15.6 illustrates the semantics of the `until` statement.

The code in the until_demo file performs the same task that the script in the while_demo file does (see Section 15.6.3), but it uses the `until` statement instead of the `while` statement. Thus the code between `do` and `done` (the loop body) is executed for as long as your guess is not agent007.

```
$ cat until_demo
#!/bin/bash
secretcode=agent007
echo "Guess the code!"
echo -n "Enter your guess: "
read yourguess
until [ "$secretcode" = "$yourguess" ]
do
   echo  "Good guess but wrong. Try again!"
   echo -n "Enter your guess: "
   read yourguess
done
echo "Wow! You are a genius!!"
exit 0
```

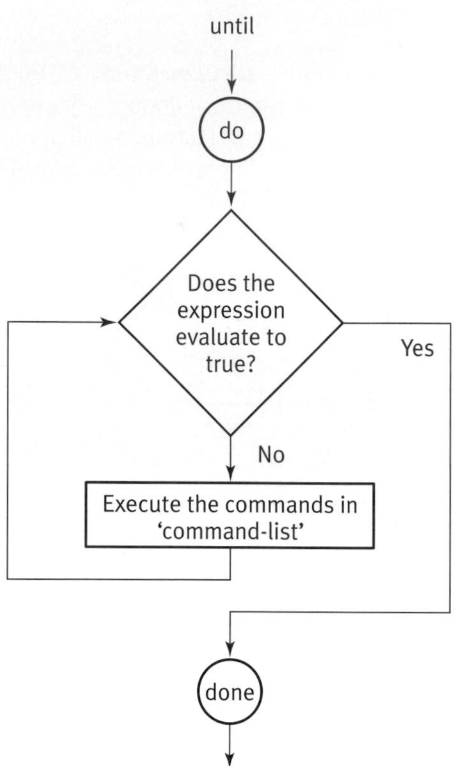


**Figure 15.6** Semantics of the `until` statement

```
$ until_demo
Guess the code!
Enter your guess: Inspector Gadget
Good guess but wrong. Try again!
Enter your guess: Peter Sellers
Good guess but wrong. Try again!
Enter your guess: agent007
Wow! You are a genius!!
$
```

### 15.6.5 The `break` and `continue` Commands

The `break` and `continue` commands can be used to interrupt the sequential execution of the loop body. The `break` command transfers control to the command following `done`, thus terminating the loop prematurely. The `continue` command transfers control to `done`, which results in the evaluation of the condition again and hence continuation of the loop. In both cases the commands in the loop body following these statements are not executed. Thus they are typically part of a conditional statement such as an `if` statement. Figure 15.7 illustrates the semantics of these commands.

In the following In-Chapter Exercises, you will write shell scripts with loops by using the `for`, `while`, and `until` statements.

**IN-CHAPTER EXERCISES**

**15.11.** Write a shell script that takes a list of host names on your network as command line arguments and displays whether the hosts are up or down. Use the `ping` command to display the status of a host and the `for` statement to process all host names.

**15.12.** Rewrite the script in Exercise 15.11, using the `while` statement. Rewrite it again, using the `until` statement.

### 15.6.6 THE case STATEMENT

The `case` statement provides a mechanism for multiway branching similar to a nested `if` statement. However, the structure provided by the `case` statement is more readable. You should use the `case` statement whenever nesting of an `if` statement becomes deeper than three levels (i.e., you are using three `elif`s). The following is a brief description of the statement.

Syntax:

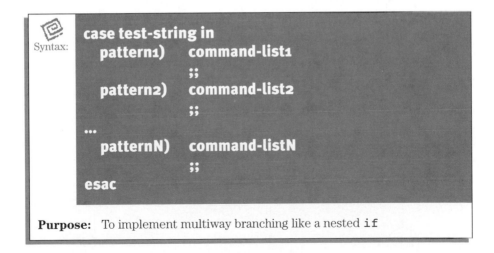

```
case test-string in
   pattern1)   command-list1
               ;;
   pattern2)   command-list2
               ;;
...
   patternN)   command-listN
               ;;
esac
```

**Purpose:** To implement multiway branching like a nested `if`

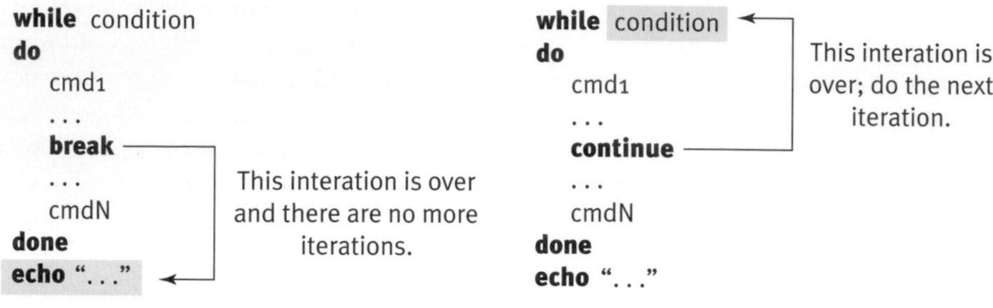


**Figure 15.7** Semantics of the `break` and `continue` commands

The `case` statement compares the value in 'test-string' with the values of all the patterns one by one until either a match is found or no more patterns with which to match 'test-string' remain. If a match is found, the commands in the corresponding 'command-list' are executed and control goes out of the `case` statement. If no match is found, control goes out of `case`. However, in a typical use of the `case` statement, a wildcard pattern matches any value of 'test-string'. Also known as the *default case*, it allows execution of a set of commands to handle an exception (error) condition for situations in which the value in 'test-string' doesn't match any pattern. Back-to-back semicolons (`;;`) are used to delimit a 'command-list'. Without `;;` the first command in the command-list for the next pattern is executed, resulting in unexpected behavior by the program. Figure 15.8 depicts the semantics of the `case` statement.

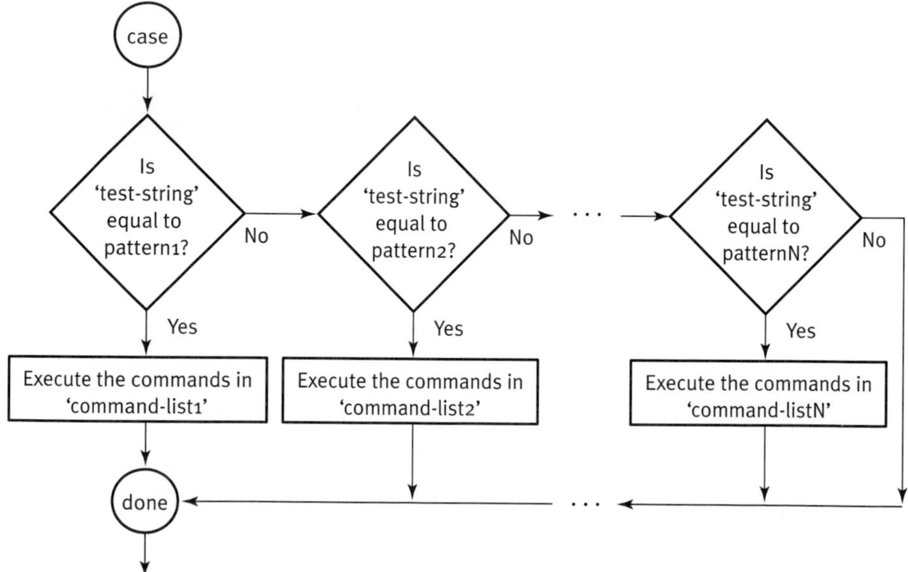


**Figure 15.8** Semantics of the `case` statement

The following script in the case_demo file shows a simple but representative use of the **case** statement. It is a menu-driven program that displays a menu of options and prompts you to enter an option. Your option is read into a variable called *option*. The **case** statement then matches your option with one of the four available patterns (single characters in this case) one by one, and when a match is found, the corresponding 'command-list' (a single command in this case) is executed. Thus at the prompt if you type **d** and hit <Enter>, the **date** command is executed and control goes out of **case**. Then, the program exits after the **exit 0** command executes. A few sample runs of the script follow the code in this session.

```
$ cat case_demo
#!/bin/bash
echo "Use one of the following options:"
echo "   d:    To display today's date and present time"
echo "   l:    To see the listing of files in your present working directory"
echo "   w:    To see who's logged in"
echo "   q:    To quit this program"
echo -n "Enter your option and hit <Enter>: "
read option
case "$option" in
        d)    date
              ;;
        l)    ls
              ;;
        w)    who
              ;;
        q)    exit 0
              ;;
esac
exit 0
$ case_demo
Use one of the following options:
        d:    To display today's date and present time
        l:    To see the listing of files in your present working directory
        w:    To see who is logged in
        q:    To quit this program
```

```
Enter your option and hit <Enter>: d
Tue Apr 14 17:05:55 PDT 2001
$ case_demo
Use one of the following options:
        d: To display today's date and present time
        l: To see the listing of files in your present working directory
        w: To see who is logged in
        q: To quit this program
Enter your option and hit <Enter>: w
kuhn     console    Apr 14 10:18
sarwar   pts/0      Apr 14 16:57
$ case_demo
Use one of the following options:
        d: To display today's date and present time
        l: To see the listing of files in your present working directory
        w: To see who is logged in
        q: To quit this program
Enter your option and hit <Enter>: a
$
```

Note that, when you enter a valid option, the expected output is displayed. However, when you enter input that isn't a valid option (**a** in the preceding session), the program doesn't give you any feedback. The reason is that the **case** statement matches your input with all the patterns, one by one, and exits when there is no match. We need to modify the script slightly so that when you enter an invalid option, it tells you about it and then terminates. To do so we add the following code.

```
    *)      echo "Invalid option; try running the program again."
            exit 1
            ;;
```

We also enhance the script so that uppercase and lowercase inputs are considered to be the same. We use the pipe symbol ( | ) in the patterns to specify a logical OR operation. The enhanced code and some sample runs are shown in the following session.

```
$ cat case_demo
#!/bin/bash
echo "Use one of the following options:"
echo "  d or D: To display today's date and present time"
echo "  l or L: To see the listing of files in your present working directory"
echo "  w or W: To see who's logged in"
echo "  q or Q: To quit this program"
echo -n "Enter your option and hit <Enter>: "
read option
case "$option" in
        d|D)    date
                ;;
        l|L)    ls
                ;;
        w|W)    who
                ;;
        q|Q)    exit 0
                ;;
        *)      echo "Invalid option; try running the program again."
                exit 1
                ;;
esac
exit 0
$ case_demo
Use one of the following options:
        d or D: To display today's date and present time
        l or L: To see the listing of files in your present working directory
        w or W: To see who is logged in
        q or Q: To quit this program
Enter your option and hit <Enter>: D
Thu Apr 16 18:14:22 PDT 2001
$ case_demo
```

```
Use one of the following options:
d or D: To display today's date and present time
        l or L: To see the listing of files in your present working directory
        w or W: To see who is logged in
        q or Q: To quit this program
Enter your option and hit <Enter>: a
Invalid option; try running the program again.
$
```

## SUMMARY

Every LINUX shell has a programming language that allows you to write programs for performing tasks that cannot be performed by existing commands. These programs are commonly known as shell scripts. In its simplest form, a shell script consists of a list of shell commands that are executed by a shell one by one, sequentially. More advanced scripts contain program control flow statements for implementing multiway branching and repetitive execution of a block of commands in a script. The shell programs that consist of Bash commands, statements, and features are called Bash scripts.

The shell variables are the main memory locations that are given names and can be read from and written to. There are two types of shell variables: environment variables and user-defined variables. The environment variables are initialized by the shell at the time of user login and are maintained by the shell to provide a nice work environment. The user-defined variables are used as scratch pads in a script to accomplish the task at hand. Some environment variables such as the positional parameters are read-only in the sense that you cannot change their values without using the `set` command. User-defined variables can also be made read-only by using the `readonly`, `declare`, or `typeset` commands.

Bash commands for processing shell variables are = (for assigning a value to a variable), `set` (for setting values of positional parameters and displaying values of all environment variables), `env` (for displaying values of all shell variables), `export` (for allowing subsequent commands to access shell variables), `read` (for assigning values to variables from the keyboard), `readonly` (for making user-defined variables read-only), `shift` (for shifting command lines arguments to the left by one or more positions), `unset` (to reset the value of a read/write variable to null), `test` (to evaluate an expression and return true or false), and `declare` (for declaring variables, initializing them, and setting/resetting their attributes—marking them as read-only and exported).

The program control flow statements `if` and `case` allow the user to implement multiway branching, the `for`, `until`, and `while` statements allow the user to implement loops, and `break` and `continue` statements allow the user to interrupt sequential execution of a loop in a script. I/O redirection can be used with control flow statements as with other shell commands (see Chapter 16).

## PROBLEMS

1. What is a shell script? Describe three ways of executing a shell script.
2. What is a shell variable? What is a read-only variable? How can you make a user-defined variable read-only? Give an example to illustrate your answer.
3. Which shell environment variable is used to store your search path? Change your search path interactively to include the directories ~/bin and (.). What would this change allow you to do? Why? If you want to make it a permanent change, what would you do? (See Chapter 4 if you have forgotton how to change your search path.)
4. What will be the output if the shell script read_demo in Section 15.3.8 is executed and you give * as input each time you are prompted? Explain your answer.
5. Write a Bash script that takes an ordinary file as an argument and removes the file if its size is zero. Otherwise, the script displays file's name, size, number of hard links, owner, and modify date (in this order) on one line. Your script must do appropriate error checking.
6. Write a Bash script that takes a directory as a required argument and displays the name of all zero length files in it. Do appropriate error checking.
7. Write a Bash script that removes all zero-length ordinary files from the current directory. Do appropriate error checking.
8. Modify the script in Problem 6 so that it removes all zero-length ordinary files in the directory passed as an optional argument. If you don't specify the directory argument, the script uses the present working directory as the default argument. Do appropriate error checking.
9. Run the script in if_demo2 in Section 15.6.1 with if_demo2 as its argument. Does the output make sense to you? Why or why not?
10. Write a Bash script that takes a list of login names on your computer system as command line arguments and displays these login names and full names of the users who own these logins (as contained in the /etc/passwd file), one per line. If a login name is invalid (not found in the /etc/passwd file), display the login name but nothing for full name. The format of the output line is
    login name:    user name
11. What happens when you run a standalone command enclosed in parentheses and preceded by `$`, such as `$(date)`, or backquotes (grave accents), such as `` `date` ``? Why?
12. What happens when you type the following sequence of shell commands?
    a. `name=date`
    b. `$name`
    c. `` `$name` ``
    d. `$($name)`

13. Look at your ~/.profile, ~/.bashrc, ~/.bash_profile, ~/.bash_login, and /etc/profile files and list the environment variables that are exported along with their values. What is the purpose of each variable? What command did you use to list the exported variables?
14. Write a Bash script that takes a list of login names as its arguments and displays the number of terminals that each user is logged onto in a LAN environment.
15. Write a Bash script domain2ip that takes a list of domain names as command line arguments and displays their IP addresses. Use the `nslookup` command. The following is a sample run of this program.

```
$ domain2ip up.edu redhat.com
Name:     up.edu
Address:  192.220.208.9

Name:     redhat.com
Address:  207.175.42.154

$
```

16. Modify the script in the case_demo file in Section 15.6.6 so that it allows you to try any number of options and quits only when you use the `q` option.
17. Write a Bash script that displays the following menu and prompts you for one-character input to invoke a menu option, as follows.
    a. List all files in the present working directory.
    b. Display today's date and time.
    c. Invoke shellscript for Problem 13.
    d. Display whether a file is a "simple" file of a "directory".
    e. Create a backup for a file.
    f. Start a telnet session.
    g. Start an ftp session.
    x. Exit.

    Option (c) requires that you ask for a list of login names and for options (d) and (e) insert a prompt for file names before invoking a shell command/program. For options (f) and (g) insert a prompt for a domain name (or IP address) before initiating a telnet or ftp session. The program should allow you to try any option any number of times and should quit only when you give s option x as input. A good programming practice for you to adopt is to build code incrementally—that is, write code for one option, test it, and then go to the next option.

CHAPTER

# 16 Advanced Bash Programming

## OBJECTIVES

- To discuss numeric data processing
- To explain array processing in Bash
- To describe how standard input of a command in a shell script can be redirected from data within the script
- To explain the signal/interrupt processing capability of Bash
- To describe how file I/O can be performed by using file descriptors and how standard files can be redirected from within a shell script
- To explain functions in Bash
- To discuss debugging of Bash scripts
- To cover the commands and primitives |, <, >, >>, ·, `$((expression))`, `${array_name[subscript]}`, `clear`, `declare`, `exec`, `expr`, `grep`, `kill`, `let`, `local`, `more`, `read`, `readonly`, `sort`, `source`, `stty`, `trap`

## 16.1 INTRODUCTION

We discuss several important, advanced features of Bash in this chapter. They include processing of numeric data, array processing, the here document, signals and signal processing, and redirection of standard files from within a shell script. We also discuss Bash's support of functions that allow the programmer to write general purpose and modular code. Finally, we describe how Bash scripts can be debugged.

## 16.2 NUMERIC DATA PROCESSING

The values of all Bash variables are stored as character strings. Although this feature makes symbolic data processing fun and easy, it does make numeric data processing a bit challenging. The reason is that integer data are actually stored in the form of character strings. In order to perform arithmetic and logic operations on them, you need to convert them to integers and convert the result back to a character string for its proper storage in a shell variable.

Fortunately, there are three ways to perform arithmetic on numeric data in Bash:

1. by using the `let` command
2. by using the shell expansion `$(( expression ))`
3. by using the `expr` command

The expression evaluation is performed in long integers and no overflow check is made. When shell variables are used in an expression, they are expanded (i.e., their values are substituted in the expression) and coerced to (i.e., their data type is treated as) a long before the expression is evaluated. The arithmetic, logic, and relational operators supported by Bash are listed in Table 16.1 in decreasing order of precedence. The operators that are grouped together have equal precedence. The order of evaluation can be altered by enclosing expressions in parentheses. Contants with a leading 0 are treated as octal numbers; those with a leading 0x or 0X are treated as hexadecimal numbers. Otherwise, numbers are treated as decimal numbers. The built-in Bash command `let` allows you to evaluate arithmetic expressions by specifying them as its arguments. If an expression contains spaces or other special characters, it must be enclosed in double quotes. The following is a brief description of the command.

**Table 16.1** Arithmetic Operations Supported by Bash

<table>
<tr><th>Operator</th><th>Meaning</th></tr>
<tr><td>- +</td><td>Unary minus</td></tr>
<tr><td>! ~</td><td>Logical NOT; 1's complement</td></tr>
<tr><td>**</td><td>Exponentiation</td></tr>
<tr><td>* / %</td><td>Multiplication; division; remainder</td></tr>
<tr><td>+ -</td><td>Addition; subtraction</td></tr>
<tr><td><< >></td><td>Bitwise shift left; bitwise shift right</td></tr>
<tr><td><= >= <></td><td>Less than or equal; greater than or equal; not equal</td></tr>
<tr><td>== !=</td><td>equal; not equal</td></tr>
<tr><td>&</td><td>Bitwise AND</td></tr>
<tr><td>^</td><td>Bitwise exclusive-OR (XOR)</td></tr>
<tr><td>|</td><td>Bitwise OR</td></tr>
<tr><td>&&</td><td>Logical AND</td></tr>
<tr><td>||</td><td>Logical OR</td></tr>
<tr><td>= += -= *= /= %= &= ^= |= <<= >>=</td><td>Assignment statement: simple; after addition; after subtraction; after multiplication; after division; after remainder; after bitwise AND; after bitwise XOR; after bitwise OR; after bitwise shift left; after bitwise shift right</td></tr>
</table>

Syntax:

**let expression-list**

**Purpose:** Evaluate arithmetic expressions in the 'expression-list'

If the last expression evaluates to 0, `let` returns 1; otherwise it returns 0. The following session shows an interactive use of the `let` command. Note that `$` is not needed to refer to the value of a shell variable and that quotes are used in the first `let` command because the expressions used in it contain spaces. These examples show variable declaration and arithmetic expression evaluation with the `let` command. The expression `b**x` in the last `let` command means *b* to the power *x*.

```
$ let "a = 8" "b = 13"
$ let c=a+b
$ echo "The value of c is $c."
The value of c is 21.
$ let "a *= b"
$ echo "The new value of a is $a; the product of a and b."
The new value of a is 104; the product of a and b.
$ b=2 x=10 y=20 z=30
$ let K=b**x M=b**y G=b**z
$ echo "In computer jargon 1K is $K, 1M is $M, and 1G is $G."
In computer jargon 1K is 1024, 1M is 1048576, and 1G is 1073741824.
$
```

The following Bash expansion syntax can also be used to evaluate an arithmetic expression. The 'expression' is evaluated and the result is returned.

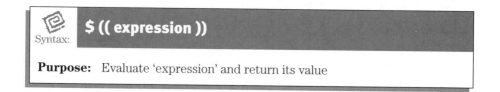

Syntax: **$ (( expression ))**

**Purpose:** Evaluate 'expression' and return its value

Like the `let` command, the `$` sign is not needed to refer to the value of a shell variable. The following session replicates the first two commands in the previous session by using this syntax.

```
$ a=8 b=13
$ echo "The new value of c is $((a+b))."
The new value of c is 21.
$ echo "The new value of a is $(( a *= b )); the product
of a and b."
The new value of a is 104; the product of a and b.
$
```

The following is a brief description of the `expr` command.

Syntax:

**expr args**

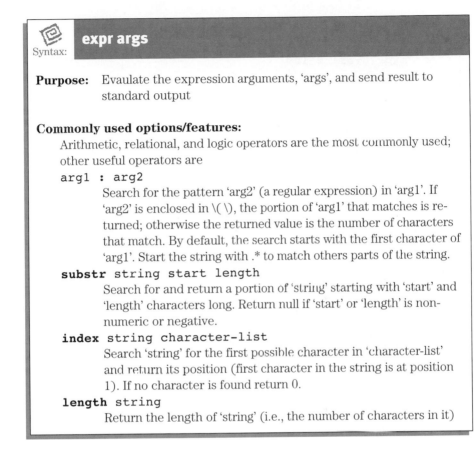

**Purpose:** Evaulate the expression arguments, 'args', and send result to standard output

**Commonly used options/features:**

Arithmetic, relational, and logic operators are the most commonly used; other useful operators are

`arg1 : arg2`
: Search for the pattern 'arg2' (a regular expression) in 'arg1'. If 'arg2' is enclosed in \( \), the portion of 'arg1' that matches is returned; otherwise the returned value is the number of characters that match. By default, the search starts with the first character of 'arg1'. Start the string with .* to match others parts of the string.

**`substr`** `string start length`
: Search for and return a portion of 'string' starting with 'start' and 'length' characters long. Return null if 'start' or 'length' is non-numeric or negative.

**`index`** `string character-list`
: Search 'string' for the first possible character in 'character-list' and return its position (first character in the string is at position 1). If no character is found return 0.

**`length`** `string`
: Return the length of 'string' (i.e., the number of characters in it)

The shell metacharacters such as * must be escaped in an expression so that they are treated literally and not as shell metacharacters. In the following session the first **expr** command increments the value of the shell variable *var1* by 1. The second **expr** command computes the square of *var1*. The last two **echo** commands show the use of the **expr** command to perform integer division and integer remainder operations on *var1*.

```
$ var1=10
$ var1=`expr $var1 + 1`
$ echo $var1
11
$ var1=`expr $var1 \* $var1`
$ echo $var1
121
```

```
$ echo `expr $var1 / 10`
12
$ echo `expr $var1 % 10`
1
$
```

The following examples demonstrate the use of the **expr** command for string processing. The first command displays the index of the location (the value 10 ) for the charater 'r' in the string "Hello, World." The second command displays 0, indicating that no character in the given set of characters ('i' and 'p') is found in the string. The third command is used to display the length of the string and the fourth to display a substring of the string "Hello, World." starting with the character at position 8 and having a length 5. The fifth and sixth **expr** commands show that a string variable can be used in place of an actual string. The variable expansion must be enclosed in double quotes as shown; otherwise, an exception is caused.

```
$ expr index "Hello, World." arp
10
$ expr index "Hello, World." ip
0
$ expr length "Hello, World."
13
$ expr substr "Hello, World." 8 5
World
$ greeting="Hello, World."
$ expr length "$greeting"
13
$ expr substr "$greeting" 8 5
World
$
```

The following countup script takes an integer as a command line argument and displays the range of numbers from 1 to the given number. In the script we use a simple `while` loop to display the current number (starting with 1) and then compute the next numbers, until the current number becomes greater than the target number (which is passed as the command line argument).

```
$ cat countup
#!/bin/bash
if [ $# != 1 ]
     then
          echo "Usage: $0 integer-argument"
          exit 1
fi
target="$1"
current=1

# Loop until 'current' becomes greater than 'target'
while [ $current -le $target ]
do
     echo -n "$current "
     current=$(( current+1 ))
done
echo
exit 0
$

$ countup 5
1 2 3 4 5
$
```

The following script, addall, takes a list of integers as command line arguments and displays their sum. The `while` loop adds the next number in the argument list to the running sum (which is initialized to 0), updates the count of numbers that have been added, and shifts the command line arguments left by one position. The loop then repeats until all command line arguments have been added. The sample run following the code takes the list of the first seven perfect squares and returns their sum.

```
$ cat addall
#!/bin/bash
# File Name:     ~/linuxbook/examples/Bash/addall
# Author:        Syed Mansoor Sarwar
# Written:       August 18, 1999
# Modified:      Feburary 3, 2001
```

```
# Purpose:          To demonstate use of the expr command in processing numeric
#                   data
# Brief Description: Maintain running sum of numbers in a numeric variable
#                    called sum, starting with 0. Read the next integer and
#                    add it to sum. When all elements have been read, stop
#                    and display the answer.
# If run with no arguments, inform the user of command syntax
if [  $# = 0 ]
    then
        echo "Usage: $0 number-list"
        exit 1
fi
sum=0              # Running sum initialized to 0
count=0            # Count the count of numbers passed as arguments
while [ $# != 0 ]
do
    sum=`expr $sum + $1` # Add the next number to the running sum
    if [  $? != 0 ]     # If the expr command failed because of non-integer
        then            # argument, exit here
            exit 1
    fi
    count=$((count+1))  # Update count of numbers added so far
    shift                 # Shift the counted number out
done

# Display final sum
echo "The sum of the given $count numbers is $sum."
exit 0
$
$ addall
Usage: addall number-list
$ addall 1 4 9 16 25 36 49
The sum of the given 7 numbers is 140.
$
```

Although this example neatly explains numeric data processing, it is nothing more than an integer adding machine. We now present a more useful example that uses the LINUX file system. The fs (for files' size) file contains a script that takes a directory as an optional argument and returns the size (in bytes) of all nondirectory files in it.

When you run the program without a command line argument, the script treats your current directory as the argument. If you specify more than one argument, the script displays an error message and terminates. When you execute it with one nondirectory argument only, again the program displays an error message and exits.

The gist of this script is the following code.

```
ls $directory | more |
while read file
do
    ...
done
```

This code generates a list of files in *directory* (with the `ls` command), converts the list into one file name per line list (with the **more** command), and reads each file name in the list (with the **read** command) until no file remains in the list. The **read** command returns true if it reads a line and false when it reads the eof marker. The body of the loop (the code between **do** and **done**) adds the file size to the running total if the file is an ordinary file. When no name is left in the directory list, the program displays the total space (in bytes) occupied by all nondirectory files in the directory and terminates.

If the value of the ***file*** variable is not an existing file, the `[ -d "$file" ]` expression returns false and the error message **Usage: fs [directory name]**, as shown in the following sample run where foo is a nonexisting directory. The `file="$directory"/"$file"` statement is used to construct the relative path name of a file with respect to the directory specified as the command line argument. Without this, the **set -- `ls -l "$file"`** command will be successful only if the directory contains the name of the current directory.

```
$ more fs
#!/bin/bash

# File Name:      ~/linuxbook/examples/Bash/fs
# Author:         Syed Mansoor Sarwar
# Written:        August 18, 1999
# Modified:       February 10, 2001
# Purpose:        To add the sizes of all the files in a directory passed as
#                 command line argument
```

```
# Brief Description: Maintain running sum of file sizes in a variable called sum,
#           initialized to 0. Read all the file names by using the pipeline of
#           ls, more, and while commands. Get the size of next file and add it to
#           the running sum. Stop when all file names have been processed and
#           display the answer.

if [  $# = 0 ]
     then
         directory="."
     elif [ $# != 1 ]
     then
         echo "Usage: $0 [directory name]"
         exit 1
     elif [ ! -d "$1" ]
then
         echo "Usage: $0 [directory name]"
         exit 1
     else
         directory="$1"
fi
sum=0    # Running sum initialized to 0. It is a local variable whose
         # copy is passed to the while loop. If the directory is empty
         # 0 sum is returned.
# Get file count in the given directory; for empty directory, display a
# message and quit.
file_count=`ls $directory | wc -w`
if [ $file_count -eq 0 ]
     then
         echo "$directory: Empty directory."
         exit 0
fi

# for each file in the directory, add the file size to the running total
# The more command is used to output file names one per line so read
# command can be used to read file names.
```

```
ls "$directory" | more |
while read file
do
     file="$directory"/"$file"    # Set pathname for each file
     if [ -f "$file" ]            # If it is an ordinary file
         then                     # then
            set -- `ls -l $file`  # Set command line arguments
            sum=`expr $sum + $5`  # Add size of the next file to
                                  # the running sum
     fi

     # Code to decrement the file_count variable and display the final sum if the
     # last file has been processed. The final sum must be displayed here (inside
     # the while loop) because the loop is executed as a separate process and the
     # current value of 'sum' is not visible outside the loop.

     if [  "$file_count" -gt 1 ]
         then
            file_count=`expr $file_count - 1`
         else
            # Spell out the current directory
            if [  "$directory" = "." ]
                 then
                     directory="your current directory"
            fi
            echo "The size of all ordinary files in $directory is $sum bytes."
     fi
done
exit 0
$ fs dir1 dir2
Usage: ./fs [directory name]
$ fs foo
Usage: ./fs [directory name]
$ fs
The size of all ordinary files in your current directory is 41794 bytes.
```

```
$ fs .
The size of all ordinary files in your current directory is 41794 bytes.
$ fs ..
The size of all ordinary files in .. is 0 bytes.
$ fs ../Bash
The size of all ordinary files in ../Bash is 41794 bytes.
$ fs ~/linuxbook
The size of all ordinary files in /home/faculty/sarwar/linuxbook is 767427 bytes.
$
```

In the following In-Chapter Exercise you will create a Bash script that processes numeric data by using the `expr` command and Bash expansion syntax.

**IN-CHAPTER EXERCISES**

**16.1.** Create the addall script in your directory and run it with the first 10 numbers in the Fibonacci series. What is the result? Does the program produce the correct result? If you aren't familiar with the Fibonacci series, see Section 16.3.

**16.2.** Create the fs script in your directory and try it with sample runs given in the above session.

**16.3.** Try all of the shell sessions in the above session related to the `let` command, expansion syntax, and the `expr` command.

## 16.3 ARRAY PROCESSING

Bash supports one-dimensional arrays. An **array** is a named collection of items of the same type stored in contiguous memory locations. Array items are numbered, with the first item being 0. There is no limit on the size of an array, and array elements (members) are not required to be assigned contiguously. This means that once you have an array variable, you can assign a value to any array slot (see the following example). You can use any of the following syntaxes to declare array variables.

Syntax:

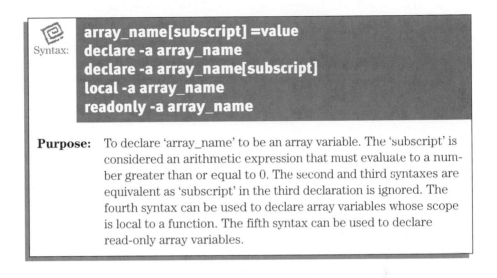

**array_name[subscript] =value**
**declare -a array_name**
**declare -a array_name[subscript]**
**local -a array_name**
**readonly -a array_name**

**Purpose:** To declare 'array_name' to be an array variable. The 'subscript' is considered an arithmetic expression that must evaluate to a number greater than or equal to 0. The second and third syntaxes are equivalent as 'subscript' in the third declaration is ignored. The fourth syntax can be used to declare array variables whose scope is local to a function. The fifth syntax can be used to declare read-only array variables.

Array variables can be initialized at the time of their declaration by using the syntax

```
name=(value1 ... valueN)
```

where, 'value1' is of the form [[subscript]=]string. Note that the subscript is optional but, if supplied, the corresponding value is assigned to the given array slot; otherwise, the slot number in the array the value is assigned to is the last slot assigned plus one. You can reference an array item by using the `${name[subscript]}` syntax. This process is known as **array indexing.** If the 'subscript' is @ or *, all array elements are referenced. The difference between @ and * is that `"${name[*]}"` expands to a single word comprising all elements of the array 'name' and `"${name[@]}"` expands each element of the array 'name' to a separate word.

In the following example, the array variable ***movies*** is assigned three values; the first two values are assigned to locations 0 and 1, and the third is assigned to slot number 65. The **echo** commands are used to display the values of the three variables.

```
$ movies=("Silence of the Lambs" "Malcolm X" [65]="The Birds")
$ echo ${movies[0]}
Silence of the Lambs

$ echo ${movies[1]}
Malcolm X
$ echo ${movies[2]}
$ echo ${movies[65]}
```

```
The Birds
$ echo ${movies[*]}
Silence of the Lambs Malcolm X The Birds
$ echo ${movies[@]}
Silence of the Lambs Malcolm X The Birds
$
```

The `readonly` command with the `-a` option can be used to declare read-only array variables. In the following session, the ***presidents*** array is initialized to four items. The **echo** command is used to display the third element of this array. Since the ***presidents*** array is read-only, the assignment statement for storing a new element, "Gore", in slot number 3 fails. The command for declaring the ***Fibonacci*** array fails as the **local** command can only be used to declare variables within the scope of a function.

```
$ readonly -a presidents=("Reagan" "Bush" "Clinton")
$ echo ${presidents[2]}
Clinton
$ presidents[3]="Gore"
bash: presidents: readonly variable
$ local -a Fibonacci=(0 1 1 2 3 5 8 13 21 34)
bash: local: can only be used in a function
$
```

The size (in bytes) of an array item can be displayed by using the `${#name[subscript]}` syntax. If no subscript is used, the size of the first array element is displayed. If * is used as the subscript, the number of array elements is displayed. In the following session, we display the sizes of items in the ***movies*** array. The first of the two assignment statements is used to insert a new item ("Forest Gump") in the array at slot 16, and the second assignment statement is used to replace the current value ("The Birds") in slot 65 with a new value ("Finding Forester"). Figure 16.1 shows the ***movies*** array before and after making these changes.

```
$ echo ${#movies}
19
$ echo ${#movies[65]}
9
$ echo ${#movies[*]}
3
$ movies[16]="Forest Gump"
```

```
$ movies[65]="Finding Forester"
$ echo ${#movies[*]}
4
$ echo ${movies[0]}; echo ${movies[1]}; echo
${movies[16]}; echo ${movies[65]}
Silence of the Lambs
Malcolm X
Forest Gump
Finding Forester
$
```

It should be obvious by now that any shell variable that is assigned multiple values by using the assignment statement becomes an array variable. Thus, when a variable is assigned a multiword output of a command as a value, it becomes an array variable and contains each field of the output in a separate array slot. In the following example, ***files*** is an array variable whose elements are names of all the files in the current directory. The ***numfiles*** variable contains the number of files in the current directory. The number of files can also be displayed by using the **echo ${#files[*]}** command, as shown. The **echo ${files[*]}** command displays the names of all the files in the current directory, and the **echo ${files[3]}** command displays the third array element.

```
$ files=(`ls`) numfiles=`ls | wc -w`
$ echo ${files[*]}
cmdargs_demo foreach_demo1 if_demo1 if_demo2 keyin_demo
$ echo $numfiles
5
$ echo ${#files[*]}
5
```

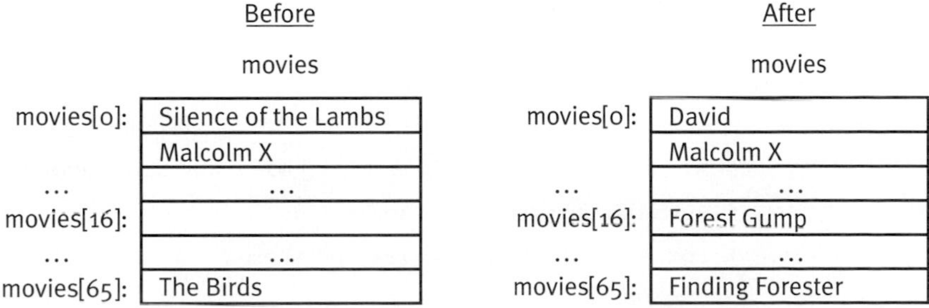


**Figure 16.1** The *movies* array before and after changing its contents

```
$ echo $files[3]
if_demo1
$
```

In the following example, the num_array_demo file contains a script that uses an array of integers, called ***Fibonacci***, computes the sum of integers in the array, and displays the sum on the screen. The ***Fibonacci*** array in this example contains the first 10 numbers of the Fibonacci series. For those who are not familiar with the Fibonacci series, the first two numbers in the series are 0 and 1, and the next Fibonacci number is calculated by adding the previous two numbers. Thus, the first 10 numbers in the Fibonacci series are 0, 1, 1, 2, 3, 5, 8, 13, 21, and 34.

```
F1 = 0
F2 = 1
Fn = Fn-1 + Fn-2   for n >= 3
```

The script in the num_array_demo file is well documented and fairly easy to understand. It displays the sum of first 10 Fibonacci numbers. A sample run of the script follows the code.

```
# File Name:               ~/linuxbook/examples/Bash/num_array_demo
# Author:                  Syed Mansoor Sarwar
# Written:                 August 16, 1999
# Last Modified:           February 12, 2001
# Purpose:                 To demonstrate working with numeric arrays in Bash
# Brief Description:       Maintain running sum of numbers in a numeric
#       variable called sum, starting with 0. Read the next array
#       value and add it to sum. When all elements have been read,
#       stop and display the answer.
#!/bin/bash -xv
# Initialize Fibonacci array to any number of Fibonacci numbers - first ten
# in this case
declare -a Fibonacci=( 0 1 1 2 3 5 8 13 21 34 )
size=${#Fibonacci[*]} # Size of the Fibonacci array as string
index=1          # Array index initialized to point to the second element
sum=0            # Running sum initialized to 0
next=0           # For storing the next array item
while [ $index -le $size ]
do
```

```
    next=$(( ${Fibonacci[$index]}  # Store the next value as integer
    sum=$((sum + next))  # Update the running sum
    index=$((index + 1)) # Increment array index by 1
done
echo "The sum of the given ${#Fibonacci[*]} numbers is $((sum))."
exit 0
$ num_array_demo
The sum of the given 10 numbers is 88.
$
```

In the following In-Chapter Exercise, you will write a Bash script that uses the numeric data processing commands for manipulating numeric arrays.

**IN-CHAPTER EXERCISES**

**16.4.** Write a Bash script that contains two numeric arrays, array1 and array2, initialized to values in the sets {1,2,3,4,5} and {1,4,9,16,25}, respectively. The script should produce and display an array whose elements are the sum of the corresponding elements in the two arrays. Thus the first element of the resultant array is 1+1 = 2, the second element is 2+2 = 4, and so on.

**16.5.** Try all Bash sessions and scripts discussed in this section on your system.

## 16.4 THE HERE DOCUMENT

The **here document** feature of Bash allows you to redirect standard input of a command in a script and attach it to data in the script. Obviously, this feature works with commands that take input from standard input. The feature is used mainly to display menus, although there are some other important uses of this feature. The following is a brief description of the here document.

Syntax:

**command << [-] input_marker**
**... input data ...**
**input_marker**

**Purpose:** To execute 'command' with its input coming from the here document—data between the input start and end markers 'input_marker'

The 'input_marker' is a word that you choose to wrap the input data in for 'command'. The closing marker must be on a line by itself and cannot be surrounded by any spaces. The command and variable substitutions are performed before the here document data are directed to the stdin of the command. Quotes can be used to prevent these substitutions or to enclose any quotes in the here document. The 'input_marker' can be enclosed in quotes to prevent any substitutions in the entire document, as in

```
command <<'Marker'
...
'Marker'
```

A hyphen (`-`) after `<<` can be used to remove leading tabs (not spaces) from the lines in the here document and the input ending marker. This feature allows the here document and the delimiting marker to conform to the indentation of the script. The following session illustrates this point.

```
while [ ... ]
do
    grep ... <<- DIRECTORY
              John Doe ...
              ...
              Art Pohm ...
        DIRECTORY
    ...
done
```

One last, but very important point: Output and error redirections of the command that uses the here document must be specified in the command line, not following the here document ending marker. The same is true of connecting the standard output of the command with other commands via a pipeline, as shown in the following session. Note that the `grep ... <<- DIRECTORY 2> errorfile | sort` command line can be replaced by `(grep ... 2> errorfile | sort) <<- DIRECTORY`.

```
while [ ... ]
do
    grep ... <<- DIRECTORY 2> errorfile | sort
              John Doe ...
              ...
              Art Pohm ...
```

```
            DIRECTORY
        ...
done
```

We can illustrate the use of the here document feature with a simple instance of redirecting stdin of the **cat** command from the here document. The script in the heredoc_demo file is used to display a message for the user and then send a message to the person whose e-mail address is passed as a command line argument. In the following session we use two here documents: One begins with `<< DataTag` and ends with `DataTag`; and the other begins with `<< WRAPPER` and ends with `WRAPPER`.

```
$ cat heredoc_demo
#!/bin/bash

cat << DataTag
This is a simple use of the here document. These data are the
input to the cat command.
DataTag

# Second example
mail -s "Weekly Meeting Reminder" $1 << WRAPPER
Hello,

This is a reminder for the weekly meeting tomorrow.

Mansoor

WRAPPER
echo "Sending mail to $1 ... done."
exit 0
$ heredoc_demo eecsfaculty
This is a simple use of the here document. These data are the
input to the cat command.
Sending mail to eecsfaculty ... done.
$
```

The following script is more useful and makes a better use of the here document feature. The dext (for directory expert) script maintains a directory of names, phone numbers, and e-mail addresses. The script is run with a name as a command line argument and uses the **grep** command to display the directory entry corresponding to the name. The **-i** option is used with the **grep** command in order to ignore the case of letters.

```
$ more dext
#!/bin/bash

if [ $# = 0 ]
    then
        echo "Usage: $0 name"
        exit 1
fi

user_input="$1"
grep -i "$user_input" << DIRECTORY
    John Doe     555.232.0000    johnd@somedomain.com
    Jenny Great 444.6565.1111   jg@new.somecollege.edu
    David Nice   999.111.3333    david_nice@xyz.org
    Don Carr     555.111.3333    dcarr@old.hoggie.edu
    Masood Shah 666.010.9820    shah@Garments.com.pk
    Jim Davis    777.000.9999    davis@great.advisor.edu
    Art Pohm     333.000.8888    art.pohm@great.professor.edu
    David Carr   777.999.2222    dcarr@net.net.gov
DIRECTORY

exit 0
$ dext
Usage: ./dext name
$ dext Pohm
    Art Pohm     333.000.8888    art.pohm@great.professor.edu
$
```

The advantage of maintaining the directory within the script is that it eliminates extra file operations, such as open and read, that would be required if the directory data were maintained in a separate file. The result is a much faster program.

If there are multiple entries for a name, the `grep` command displays all the entries. You can display the entries in sorted order by piping the output of the `grep` command to the `sort` command and enclosing them in parentheses, as in `(grep -i "$user_input" | sort)`. We enhance the dext script in Section 16.7 to include this feature, as well as take multiple names from the command line.

The following In-Chapter Exercise has been designed to reinforce your understanding of the here document feature of Bash.

**IN-CHAPTER EXERCISE**

**16.6.** Create the dext script on your system and run it. Try it with as many different inputs as you can think of. Does the script work correctly?

## 16.5 INTERRUPT (SIGNAL) PROCESSING

We discussed the basic concept of signals in Chapter 13 where we defined them as software interrupts that can be sent to a process. We also stated that there are three possible actions that the process receiving a signal can take:

1. Accept the default action as determined by the LINUX kernel.
2. Ignore the signal.
3. Take a programmer-defined action.

In LINUX several types of signals can be sent to a running program. Some of these signals can be sent via hardware devices such as the keyboard, but all can be sent via the `kill` command, as discussed in Chapter 13. The most common event that causes a hardware interrupt (and a signal) is generated when you press `<Ctrl-C>` and is known as the **keyboard interrupt**. This event causes the foreground process to terminate (the default action). Other events that cause a process to receive a signal include termination of a child process, a process accessing a main memory location that is not part of its **address space** (the main memory area that the process owns and is allowed to access), and a software termination signal caused by execution of the `kill` command without any signal number. Table 16.2 presents a list of some important signals, their numbers (which can be used to generate those signals with the `kill` command), and their purpose.

The interrupt processing feature of Bash allows you to write programs that can ignore signals or execute a particular sequence of commands when particular types of signals are sent to them. This feature is much more powerful than that of the TC shell, which allows programs to ignore a keyboard interrupt (`<Ctrl-C>`) only (see Chapter 18). The `trap` command can be used to intercept signals. The following is a brief description of the command.

Syntax: **trap ['command-list'] [signal-list]**

**Purpose:** To intercept signals specified in 'signal-list' and take default kernel-defined action, ignore the signals, or execute the commands in 'command-list'; note that quotes around 'command-list' are required

**Table 16.2** Some Important Signals, Their Numbers, and Their Purposes

| Signal Name | Signal # | Purpose |
|---|---|---|
| SIGHUP (hang up) | 1 | Informs the process when the user who ran the process logs out, and the process terminates |
| SIGINT (keyboard interrupt) | 2 | Informs the process when the user presses <Ctrl-C> and the process terminates |
| SIGQUIT (quit signal) | 3 | Informs the process when the user presses <Ctrl-\|> or <Ctrl-\> and the process terminates |
| SIGKILL (sure kill) | 9 | Definitely terminates the process when the user sends this signal to it with the `kill -9` command |
| SIGSEGV (segmentation violation) | 11 | Terminates the process upon memory fault when a process tries to access memory space that doesn't belong to it |
| SIGTERM (software termination) | 15 | Terminates the process when the `kill` command is used without any signal number |
| SIGCHLD (child finishes execution) | 17 | Informs the process of termination of one of its children |
| SIGTSTP (suspend/stop signal) | 20 | Suspends the process, usually <Ctrl-Z> |

When you use the **trap** command in a script without any argument (no 'command-list' and no 'signal-list'), the default actions are taken when signals are received by the script. Thus using the **trap** command without any argument is redundant. When the **trap** command is used without any commands in single quotes, the signals in 'signal-list' are ignored by the process. When both a 'command-list' and a 'signal-list' are specified, the commands in 'command-list' execute when a signal in 'signal-list' is received by the script.

Next, we enhance the script in the while_demo file in Chapter 15 so that you cannot terminate execution of this program with `<Ctrl-C>` (signal number 2), the **kill** command without any argument (signal number 15), or the **kill -1** command (to generate the SIGHUP signal). The enhanced version is in the trap_demo file, as shown in the following session. Note that the **trap** command is used to ignore signals 1, 2, 3, 15, and 20. A sample run illustrates this point.

```
$ more trap_demo
#!/bin/bash

# Intercept signals and ignore them
trap '' 1 2 3 15 20
```

```
# Set the secret code
secretcode=agent007

# Get user input
echo "Guess the code!"
echo -n "Enter your guess: "
read yourguess

# As long as the user input is the secret code (agent007 in this case),
# loop here: display a message and take user input gain. When the user
# input matches the secret code, terminate the loop and execute the
# following echo command.
while [ "$secretcode" != "$yourguess" ]
do
    echo "Good guess but wrong. Try again!"
    echo -n "Enter your guess: "
    read yourguess
done
echo "Wow! You are a genius!"
exit 0
$ trap_demo
Guess the code!
Enter your guess: codecracker
Good guess but wrong. Try again!
Enter your guess: agent007
Wow! You are a genius!
$
```

To terminate programs that ignore terminal interrupts, you have to use the `kill` command. You can do so by suspending the process by pressing `<Ctrl-Z>`, using the `ps` command to get the PID of the process, and terminating it with the `kill` command.

You can modify the script in the trap_demo file so that it ignores signals 1, 2, 3, 15, and 20, clears the display screen, and turns off the echo. Whatever input you enter from the keyboard, then, is not displayed. Next, it prompts you for the code word twice. If you don't enter the same code word both times, it reminds you of your bad short-term memory and quits. If you enter the same code word, it clears the display screen and prompts you to guess the code word again. If you don't enter the original code word, the display screen is cleared and you are prompted to guess again. The program doesn't terminate until you have entered the original code word. When you do enter it, the display screen is cleared, a message is displayed at the top left of the screen, and echo is turned on. Because the terminal interrupt is ignored, you can't terminate the program by pressing **<Ctrl-C>**. The **stty -echo** command turns off the echo. Thus, when you type the original code word (or any guesses), it isn't displayed on the screen. The **clear** command clears the display screen and positions the cursor at the top-left corner. The **stty echo** command turns on the echo. The resulting script is in the canleave file, as shown in the following session.

```
$ more canleave
#!/bin/bash

# Ignore signals 1, 2, 3, 15, and 20
trap '' 1 2 3 15 20

# Clear the screen, locate the cursor at the top-left corner,
# and turn off echo
clear
stty -echo

# Set the secret code
echo -n "Enter your code word:
read secretcode
echo

# To make sure that the user remembers the code word
echo -n "Enter your code word again:
read same
echo
if [ $secretcode != $same ]
    then
        echo "Work on your short-term memory before using this code!"
        exit 1
fi

# Get user guess
clear
```

```
echo -n "Enter the code word:
read yourguess
echo

# As long as the user input is not the original code word, loop here: display
# a message and take user input gain. When the user input matches the secret
# code word, terminate the loop and execute the following echo command.
while [ "$secretcode" != "$yourguess" ]
do
    clear
    echo -n "Enter the code word:
    read yourguess
done

# Set terminal to echo mode
clear
echo "Back again!"
stty echo
exit 0
$
```

You can use this script to lock your terminal before you leave it to pick up a printout or get a can of soda, hence the name canleave (can leave). Using it saves you the time otherwise required for the logout and login procedures.

The following In-Chapter Exercise has been designed to reinforce your understanding of the signal handling feature of Bash.

**IN-CHAPTER EXERCISE**

**16.7.** Test the scripts in the trap_demo and canleave files on your LINUX system. Do they work as expected? Be sure that you understand them.

## 16.6 THE exec COMMAND AND FILE I/O

The **exec** command is the command-level version of the LINUX loader. Although it is normally used to execute a command instead of the current shell without creating a new process (it overwrites the current shell with the code of the command to be executed), the **exec** command is used for two distinct purposes:

1. to execute a command/program instead of the current process (under which **exec** is executed, usually a shell), and
2. to open and close file descriptors.

When the **exec** command is used in conjunction with the redirection operators, it allows commands and shell scripts to read/write any type of files, including devices. In this section we describe both uses of this command but focus primarily on the second use.

### 16.6.1 Execution of a Command Without Creating a New Process

The **exec** command can be used to run a command instead of the process (usually a shell) that executes this command. It works with all shells. The following is a brief description of the command.

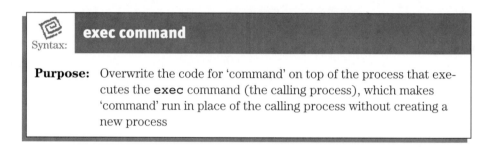

Syntax:

**exec command**

**Purpose:** Overwrite the code for 'command' on top of the process that executes the **exec** command (the calling process), which makes 'command' run in place of the calling process without creating a new process

You can't return to the calling process; once the command has finished, control goes back to the parent of the calling process. If the calling process is your login shell, control goes back to the mingetty process when the **exec** command finishes execution, as in

```
$ exec date
Thu Feb 10 23:08:29 PST 2001
login:
```

When **exec date** finishes, control does not go back to the shell process but to the mingetty process (the parent of the login shell). The semantics of this command execution are shown in Figure 16.2.

If the command is run under a subshell of the login shell, control goes back to the login shell, as clarified in the following session. Here, a TC shell is run as a child of the login shell (a Bash shell) and **exec date** is run under the TC shell. When the **exec date** command finishes, control goes back to the login Bash shell. The sequence shown in Figure 16.3 depicts the semantics of these steps.

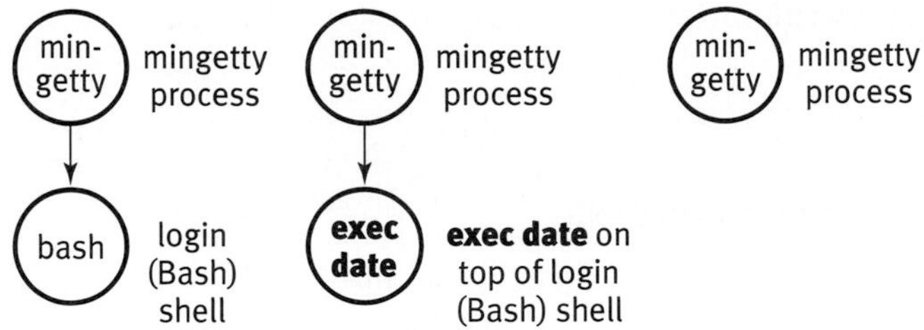


**Figure 16.2** Execution of the `exec date` command under the login shell

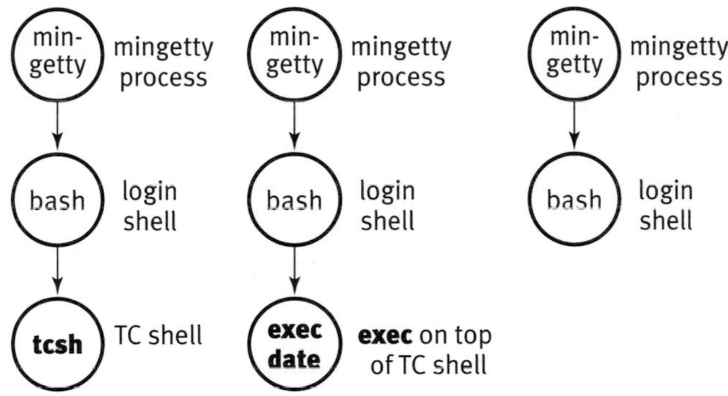


**Figure 16.3** Execution of the `exec date` command under a subshell of the login shell

```
$ ps
  PID TTY          TIME CMD
30680 pts/2    00:00:00 bash
30835 pts/2    00:00:00 ps
$ tcsh
% ps
  PID TTY          TIME CMD
30680 pts/2    00:00:00 bash
30836 pts/2    00:00:00 tcsh
30856 pts/2    00:00:00 ps
% exec date
Sat Feb 10 21:06:10 PST 2001
$ ps
  PID TTY          TIME CMD
```

```
30680 pts/2    00:00:00 bash
30857 pts/2    00:00:00 ps
$
```

### 16.6.2 File I/O via the exec Command

The Bash shell allows you to work with as many as ten file descriptors at a time. Three of these descriptors are set aside for standard input (0), standard output (1), and standard error (2). All 10 descriptors can be used for I/O by using the redirection operators with the **exec** command. Table 16.3 describes the syntax of the **exec** command for file I/O.

When executed from the command line, the **exec < sample** command causes each line in the sample file to be treated as a command and executed by the current shell. That happens because the **exec** command is executed by the shell process whose only purpose is to read commands from stdin and execute them; because the file sample is attached to the stdin, the shell reads its commands from this file. The shell terminates after executing the last line in sample. When executed from within a shell script, this command causes the stdin of the remainder of the script to be attached to sample. The following session illustrates the working of this command when it is executed from the command line. As

**Table 16.3** Syntax of the exec Command for File I/O

| Syntax | Meaning |
|---|---|
| exec < file | Opens 'file' for reading and attaches standard input of the process to 'file' |
| exec > file | Opens 'file' for writing and attaches standard output of the process to 'file' |
| exec >> file | Opens 'file' for writing, attaches standard output of the process to 'file', and appends standard output to 'file' |
| exec n< file | Opens 'file' for reading and assigns it the file descriptor 'n' |
| exec n> file | Opens 'file' for writing and assigns it the file descriptor 'n' |
| exec n<< tag<br>...<br>tag | Opens a here document (data between << 'tag' and 'tag') for reading; the opened file is assigned a descriptor 'n' |
| exec n>> file | Opens 'file' for writing, assigns it file descriptor 'n', and appends data to the end of 'file' |
| exec n>&m | Duplicates 'm' into 'n'; whatever goes into 'file' with file descriptor 'n' will also go into 'file' with file descriptor 'm' |
| exec <&- | Closes standard input |
| exec >&- | Closes standard output |
| exec n<&- | Closes 'file' with descriptor 'n' attached to stdin |
| exec n >&- | Closes 'file' with descriptor 'n' attached to stdout |

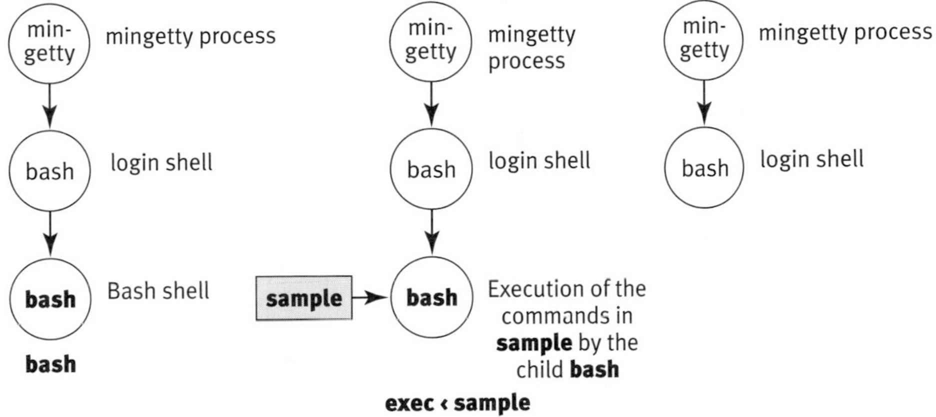


**Figure 16.4** Execution of the `bash` and `exec < sample` commands under the login shell

shown, the sample file contains two commands: **date** and **echo**. A Bash process is run under the login shell (which is also Bash) via the **bash** command. When the **exec < sample** command is executed, the commands in the sample file are executed, the child Bash terminates after finishing execution of the last command in sample (the output of the third **ps** command shows that only the login shell runs after the **exec < sample** command is done), and control returns to the login shell.

So, effectively, when the **exec < sample** command is executed from the command line, it attaches stdin of the current shell to the sample file. When this command is executed from a shell script, it attaches stdin of the shell script to the sample file. In either case, the **exec < /dev/tty** command must be executed to reattach stdin to the terminal. Here, /dev/tty is the pseudo terminal that represents the terminal on which the shell is executed. The following session illustrates use of this command from the command line. The semantics of these steps are shown in Figure 16.4.

```
$ cat sample
date
echo Hello, World!
$ ps
  PID TTY          TIME CMD
30680 pts/2    00:00:00 bash
30886 pts/2    00:00:00 ps
$ bash
```

```
$ ps
  PID TTY          TIME CMD
30680 pts/2    00:00:00 bash
30887 pts/2    00:00:00 bash
30888 pts/2    00:00:00 ps
$ exec < sample
$ date
Sat Feb 10 21:12:29 PST 2001
$ echo Hello, World!
Hello, World!
$ exit
$ ps
  PID TTY          TIME CMD
30680 pts/2    00:00:00 bash
30970 pts/2    00:00:00 ps
$
```

Similarly, when the **exec > data** command is executed from the command line, it causes outputs of all subsequent commands executed under the shell (that normally go to the monitor screen) to go to the data file. Thus you don't see the output of any command on the screen. In order to see the output on the screen again, you need to execute the **exec > /dev/tty** command. After doing so, you can view the contents of the data file to see the outputs of all the commands executed prior to this command. When the **exec > data** command is executed from a shell script, it causes the outputs of all subsequent commands (that normally go to the monitor screen) to go to the data file until the **exec > /dev/tty** command is executed from within the shell script.

Thus, effectively, when the **exec > data** command is executed from the command line, it attaches stdout of the current shell to the data file. When this command is executed from a shell script, it attaches stdout of the shell script to the data file. In either case, the **exec > /dev/tty** command needs to be executed to reattach stdout to the terminal. The following session illustrates use of this command from the command line. Note that, after the **exec > data** command has executed, the outputs of all subsequent commands (**date**, **echo**, and **more**) go to the data file. In order to redirect the output of commands to the screen, the **exec > /dev/tty** command must be executed, as shown in the following session.

```
$ exec > data
$ date
$ echo Hello, World!
```

```
$ uname -mnrs
$ exec > /dev/tty
$ date
Sat Feb 10 21:18:09 PST 2001
$ cat data
Sat Feb 10 21:17:47 PST 2001
Hello, World!
Linux upibmg.egr.up.edu 2.2.13-4mdksmp i686
$
```

Similarly, you can redirect standard output and standard error for a segment of a shell script by using the command.

```
exec > outfile 2> errorfile
```

In this case, output and error messages from the shell script following this line are directed to outfile and errorfile, respectively. (Obviously, file descriptor 1 can be used with > to redirect output.) If output needs to be reattached to the terminal, you can do so by using

```
exec > /dev/tty
```

Once this command has executed, all subsequent output goes to the monitor screen. Similarly, you can use the **exec 2> /dev/tty** command to send errors back to the display screen.

Consider the following shell session. When exec.demo1 is executed, 'file1' gets the line containing Hello, world!, 'file3' gets the contents of 'file2', and 'file4' gets the line `This is great!`. The shell script between the commands **exec < file2** and **exec < /dev/tty** takes its input from 'file2'. Therefore the command `cat > file3` is really `cat < file2 > file3`. The `cat > file4` command takes input from the keyboard as it is executed after the **exec < /dev/tty** command has been executed (which reattaches the stdin of the script to the keyboard). Figure 16.5 illustrates the semantics of the three `cat` commands in the shell script.

```
$ cat exec.demo1
cat > file1
exec < file2
cat > file3
exec < /dev/tty
```

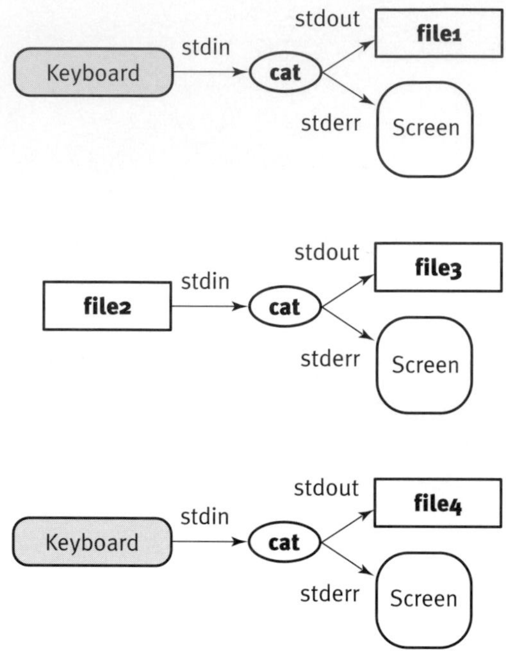


**Figure 16.5** Detachment and reattachment of stdin and stdout inside a shell script

```
cat > file4
$ chmod 755 exec.demo1
$ exec.demo1
Hello, world!
<ctrl-D>
This is great!
<ctrl-D>
$
```

Now, we develop a shell script, diff2, that uses file I/O features of Bash. It takes two files as command line arguments and compares them line by line. If the files are the same, it displays a message that says so and the program terminates. If one file is smaller than the other, it displays a message informing you of that and exits. As soon as the program finds the lines at which the two files differ, it displays an error message informing you of the lines from both files that are different and terminates. The following is the script and a few sample runs.

```
$ cat diff2
#!/bin/bash
```

```
# File Name:  ~/linuxbook/examples/Bash/diff2
# Author:     Syed Mansoor Sarwar
# Written:    February 3, 2001
# Modified:   February 3, 2001
# Purpose:    To see if the two files passed as command line arguments
#             are same or different
# Brief Description:  Read a line from each file and compare them. If
#                     the lines are the same, continue. If they are
#                     different, display the two lines and exit. If one
#                     of the files finishes before the other, display a
#                     message and exit. Otherwise, the files are the
#                     same; display an appropriate message and exit

if [ $# != 2 ]
    then
        echo "Usage: $0 file1 file2"
        exit 1
    elif [ ! -f "$1" ]
    then
        echo "$1 is not an ordinary file"
        exit 1
    elif [ ! -f "$2" ]
    then
        echo "$2 is not an ordinary file"
        exit 1
    else
        :
fi

file1="$1"
file2="$2"

# Open files for reading and assign them file descriptors 3 and 4

exec 3< "$file1"
exec 4< "$file2"

# Read a line each from both files and compare. If both reach EOF, then files
# are the same. Otherwise they are different. 0<&3 is used to attach standard
```

```
# input of the read line1 command to file descriptor 3, 0<&4 is used to attach
# standard input of the read line2 command to file descriptor 4.

while read line1 0<&3
do
    if read line2 0<&4
        then
            # if lines are different, the two files are not the same
            if [ "$line1" != "$line2" ]
                then
                    echo "$1 and $2 are different."
                    echo "      $1: $line1"
                    echo "      $2: $line2"
                    exit 1
            fi
        else
            # if EOF for file2 reached, file1 is bigger than file2
            echo "$1 and $2 are different and $1 is bigger than $2."
            exit 1
    fi
done

# if EOF for file1 reached, file2 is bigger than file1. Otherwise, the two
# files are the same. 0<&4 is used to attach standard input of read to file
# descriptor 4
if read line2 0<&4
    then
        echo "$1 and $2 are different and $2 is bigger than $1."
        exit 1
    else
        echo "$1 and $2 are the same!"
        exit 0
fi

# Close files corresponding to descriptors 3 and 4
exec 3<&-
exec 4<&-
```

```
$ diff2
Usage: ./diff2 file1 file2
$ diff2 test1
Usage: ./diff2 file1 file2
$ diff2 test1 test2 test3
Usage: ./diff2 file1 file2
$ diff2 test1 test2
test1 and test2 are different and test1 is bigger than test2.
$ diff2 test1 test1
test1 and test1 are the same!
$ diff2 test1 test3
test1 and test3 are different.
        test1: Not the same!
        test3: Not the same.
$ cat test1
Hello, world!
Not the same!
Another line.
$ cat test2
Hello, world!
$ cat test3
Hello, world!
Not the same.
$
```

The **exec** command is used to open and close files. The **exec 3< "$file1"** and **exec 4< "$file2"** commands open the files passed as command line arguments for reading and assigns them file descriptors 3 and 4. From this point on, you can read the two files by using these descriptors. The commands `read line1 0<&3` and `read line2 0<&4` read the next lines from the files with files descriptors 3 (for 'file1') and 4 (for 'file2'), respectively. The commands `exec 3<&-` and `exec 4<&-` close the two files. The **:** in the `else` part of the first `if` statement is a null statement that simply returns true.

In the following In-Chapter Exercises, you will use the **exec** command to redirect I/O of your shell to ordinary files. The concept of I/O redirection from within a shell script and file I/O by using file descriptors is also reinforced.

**IN-CHAPTER EXERCISES**

**16.8.** Write command lines for changing stdin of your shell to a file called data and stdout to a file called out, both in your present working directory. If the data file contains the following lines, what happens after the commands are executed?

```
echo -n "The time now is: "
date
echo -n "The users presently logged on are: "
who
```

**16.9.** After finishing the steps in Exercise 16.6, what happens when you type commands at the shell prompt? Does the result make sense to you? Write the command needed to bring your environment back to normal.

**16.10.** Create a file that contains the diff2 script and try it with different inputs.

## 16.7 FUNCTIONS IN BASH

Bash allows you to write functions. **Functions** consist of a series of commands, called the **function body**, that are given a name. You can invoke the commands in the function body by using the function name.

### 16.7.1 The Reasons for Functions

Functions are normally used if a piece of code is repeated at various places in a script. By making a function of this code, you save typing time. Thus, if a block of code is used at say 10 different places in a script, you can create a function of it and invoke it where it is to be inserted by using the name of the function. The trade-off is that the mechanism of transferring control to the function code and returning it to the calling code (from where the function is invoked/called) takes time, which increases slightly the running time of the script.

Another way of saving typing time is to create another script file for the block of code and invoke this code by calling the script as a command. The disadvantage of using this technique is that, because the script file is on the disk, invocation of the script requires loading the script from the disk into the main memory—an expensive operation. Whether they are located in a startup file ( ~/.profile, ~/.bash_profile, or ~/.bashrc), defined interactively in a shell, or defined in the script, the function definitions are always in the main memory. Thus invocation of functions is several times faster than invoking shell scripts (which are on the disk).

## 16.7.2 Function Definition

Before you can use a function, you have to define it. For often-used functions, you should put their definitions in one of your start-up files. This way, the shell records them in its environment when you log on and allows you to invoke them while you use the system. You must execute the start-up file with the **.** (dot) or **source** command after defining a function in it and before using it without logging off and logging on. You can also define functions while interactively using the shell. These definitions are valid for as long as you remain in the session that you were in when you defined the functions.

The definitions for functions that are specific to a script are usually put in the file that contains the script. However, some of general-purpose functions are still placed in a start-up file. Functions can be exported (by using the **export** command) to make them available to all the child processes of the process that contains these functions. If the process containing the function definitions is a shell process, the functions can be invoked by any process that executes under the shell.

The format of function definition is

```
function_name ( )
{
   command-list
}
```

The 'function_name' is the name of the function that you choose, and the commands in 'command-list' comprise the function body. The opening brace ({) and the function name can be on the same line. To define a function interactively, type the function name and parentheses at the shell prompt, followed by a { on a line, one command per line (function grouping can be used), and a } on the last line.

## 16.7.3 Function Invocation/Call

The commands in a function body aren't executed until the function is invoked (called). You can invoke a function by using its name as a command. When you call a function, its body is executed and control comes back to the command following the function call. If you invoke a function at the command line, control returns to the shell after the function finishes its execution.

## 16.7.4 Examples of Functions

The following is a simple example of a function, called **machines**, defined interactively in a shell and invoked. This function returns the names of all the computers on your local network.

```
$ machines ()
> {
> date
> echo "These are the machines on the network:"
> ruptime | cut -f1 -d' ' | more
> }
$ machines
Sun Feb 11 00:34:49 PST 2001
These are the machines on the network:
upibm0
...
upsun1
...
upsun29
$
```

You can use the **set** command to view all the function definitions in your current environment. The following is a sample run of the command. For the sake of brevity, we show only one function definition as part of the output.

```
$ set
...
machines()
{
    dates
    echo "These are the machines on the network:";
    ruptime | cut -f1 - d' ' | more
}
$
```

We now enhance the dext script described in Section 16.4 so that it can take multiple names at the command line. The enhanced version also uses a function `OutputData` to display one or more output records (lines in the directory) for every name passed as the command line argument. In the case of multiple lines for a name, this function displays them in sorted order. A few sample runs are shown following the script.

```
$ cat dext
#!/bin/bash
```

```
if [ $# = 0 ]
    then
        echo "Usage: $0 name"
        exit 1
fi

OutputData()
{
    echo "Info about $user_input"
    (grep -i "$user_input" | sort) << DIRECTORY
    John Doe       555.232.0000    johnd@somedomain.com
    Jenny Great    444.6565.1111   jg@new.somecollege.edu
    David Nice     999.111.3333    david_nice@xyz.org
    Don Carr       555.111.3333    dcarr@old.hoggie.edu
    Masood Shah    666.010.9820    shah@Garments.com.pk
    Jim Davis      777.000.9999    davis@great.advisor.edu
    Art Pohm       333.000.8888    art.pohm@great.professor.edu
    David Carr     777.999.2222    dcarr@net.net.gov
DIRECTORY
    echo                # A blank line between two records
}

# As long as there is at least one command line argument (name), take the
# first name, call the OutputData function to search the DIRECTORY and
# display the line(s) containing the name, shift this name left by one
# position, and repeat the process.

while [ $# != 0 ]
do
    user_input="$1"     # Get the next command line argument (name)
    OutputData          # Display info about the next name
    shift               # Get the following name
done
exit 0
$ dext
Usage: ./dext name
$ dext john
Info about john
```

```
    John Doe      555.232.0000    johnd@somedomain.com

$ dext john masood carr
Info about john
    John Doe      555.232.0000    johnd@somedomain.com

Info about masood
    Masood Shah   666.010.9820    shah@Garments.com.pk

Info about carr
    David Carr    777.999.2222    dcarr@net.net.gov
    Don Carr      555.111.3333    dcarr@old.hoggie.edu
$
```

In the following In-Chapter Exercise, you will write a simple function and a Bash script that uses it.

**IN-CHAPTER EXERCISE**

**16.11.** Write a Bash function called `menu` that displays the following menu. Then write a shell script that uses this function.

```
Select an item from the following menu:
   d.   to display today's date and current time,
   f.   to start an ftp session,
   t.   to start a telnet session, and
   q.   to quit.
```

## 16.8 DEBUGGING SHELL PROGRAMS

You can debug your Bash scripts by using the `-x` (echo) option of the `bash` command. This option displays each line of the script after variable substitution but before its execution. You can combine the `-x` option with the `-v` (verbose) option to display each line of the script (as it appears in the script file) before execution. You can also invoke the `bash` command from the command line to run the script, or you can make it part of the script, as in `#!/bin/bash -xv`. In the latter case, remove the `-xv` options after debugging is complete.

In the following session we show how a shell script can be debugged. The script in the debug_demo file prompts you for a digit. If you enter a value between 1 and 9, it displays `Good input!` and quits. If you enter any other value, it simply exits. When the script is executed and you enter `4`, it displays the message

```
./debug_demo: [4: command not found.

$ cat debug_demo
#!/bin/bash

echo -n "Enter a digit:"
read var1
if ["$var1" -ge 1 -a "$var1" -le 9 ]
    then
        echo "Good input!"
fi
exit 0
$ debug_demo
Enter a digit: 4
./debug_demo: [4: command not found
$
```

We debug the program by using the `bash -xv debug_demo` command. The shaded portion of the run-time trace shows the problem area. In this case, the error is generated because of a problem in the condition for the `if` statement. A closer examination of the shaded area reveals that missing space between [ and 4 is the problem. After we take care of this problem, the script works properly.

```
$ bash -xv debug_demo
#!/bin/bash

echo -n "Enter a digit: "
+ echo -n Enter a digit:
Enter a digit: read var1
+ read var1
4
if ["$var1" -ge 1 -a "$var1" -le 9 ]
    then
        echo "Good input!"
fi
+ `[4' -ge 1 -a 4 -le 9 `]'
debug_demo: [4:command not found
```

```
exit 0
+ exit 0
$
```

The following In-Chapter Exercise has been designed to enhance your understanding of interrupt processing and debugging features of Bash.

**IN-CHAPTER EXERCISE**

**16.12.** Test the scripts in the trap_demo and canleave files on your LINUX system. Do they work as expected? Make sure you understand them. If your versions do not work properly, use the **bash -xv** command to debug them.

## SUMMARY

Bash doesn't have the built-in capability for numeric integer data processing in terms of arithmetic, logic, and shift operations. In order to perform arithmetic and logic operations on integer data, the **expr** command must be used.

The here document feature of Bash allows standard input of a command in a script to be attached to data within the script. The use of this feature results in more efficient programs because no extra file-related operations, such as file open and read, are needed as the data are within the script file and have probably been loaded into the main memory when the script was loaded.

Bash also allows the user to write programs that ignore signals such as keyboard interrupt (<Ctrl-C>). This useful feature can be used, among other things, to disable program termination when it is in the middle of updating a file. The **trap** command can be used to invoke this feature.

Bash has powerful I/O features that allow explicit processing of files. The **exec** command can be used to open a file for reading or writing and to associate a small integer, called a file descriptor, with it. The command line **exec n< file** opens file for reading and assigns it a file descriptor n. The command line **exec n> file** opens file for writing and assigns it a file descriptor n. This feature allows writing scripts for processing files. The command line **exec n<&-** can be used to close a file with descriptor n. The **exec** command provides various other file-related features, including opening a here document and assigning it a file descriptor, which allows the use of a here document anywhere in the script.

Bash programs can be debugged by using the **-x** and **-v** options of the **bash** command. This technique allows viewing the commands in the user's script after variable substitution but before execution.

## PROBLEMS

1. Why are the `expr` and `let` commands needed?
2. What is the here document? Why is it useful?
3. Write a Bash script cv that takes the side of a cube as a command line argument and displays the volume of the cube.
4. Modify the countup script in Section 16.2 so that it takes two integer command line arguments. The script displays the numbers between the two integers (including the two numbers) in ascending order if the first number is smaller than the second, and in descending order if the first number is greater than the second. Name the script count_up_down.
5. Write a Bash script that prompts you for a user ID and displays your login name, your name, and your home directory.
6. Write a Bash script that takes a list of integers as the command line argument and displays a list of their squares and the sum of the numbers in the list of squares.
7. Write a Bash script that takes a machine name as an argument and displays a message informing you whether the host is on the local network.
8. What are signals in LINUX? What types of signals can be intercepted in the Bash scripts?
9. Write a Bash script that takes a file name and a directory name as command line arguments and removes the file if it is found under the given directory and is a simple file. If the file (the first argument) is a directory, it is removed (including all the files and subdirectories under it).
10. Write a Bash script that takes a directory as an argument and removes all the ordinary files under it that have .o, .ps, and .jpg extensions. If no argument is specified, the current directory should be used.
11. Enhance the diff2 script in Section 16.6 so that it displays the line numbers where the two files differ.
12. Enhance the diff2 script of Problem 11 so that, if only one file is passed to it as a parameter, it uses standard input as the second file.
13. Write a Bash script for Problem 16 in Chapter 15, but use functions to implement the service code for various options.

CHAPTER

# 17

# Introductory TC Shell Programming

## OBJECTIVES

- To introduce the concept of shell programming
- To describe how shell programs can be executed
- To explain the concept and use of shell variables
- To discuss how command line arguments are passed to shell programs
- To discuss the concept of command substitution
- To describe some basic coding principles
- To write and discuss some shell scripts
- To cover the commands and primitives *, =, ", ', `, &, <, >, ;, |, \, /, [ ], ( ), `continue`, `csh`, `exit`, `env`, `foreach`, `goto`, `head`, `if`, `ls`, `set`, `setenv`, `shift`, `switch`, `while`, `unset`, `ensetenv`

## 17.1 INTRODUCTION

The TC shell is more than a command interpreter: It has a programming language of its own that can be used to write shell programs for performing various tasks that cannot be performed by any existing command. Shell programs, commonly known as shell scripts, in the TC shell consist of shell commands to be executed by a shell and are stored in ordinary LINUX files. The shell allows use of read/write storage places called shell variables to provide a comfortable work environment for users of the system and for programmers to use as scratch pads for completing a task. The TC shell also has program control flow commands/statements that allow the user to implement multiway branching and repeated execution of a block of commands.

## 17.2 RUNNING A TC SHELL SCRIPT

You can run a TC shell script in one of three ways. The first method is to make the script file executable by adding the execute permission to the existing access permissions for the file. To do so, run the following command, where `script_file` is the name of the file containing the shell script. In this case you make the script executable for yourself (the owner) only. However, you can set appropriate access permissions for the file if you also want to allow other users to execute it.

```
% chmod u+x script_file
%
```

Now, you can type `script_file` as a command to execute the shell script. As described in Chapter 13, the script is executed by a child of the current shell; the script executes properly if you are using the TC shell. It doesn't work properly if you're using any other shell, such as Bash, because you would be trying to run a TC shell script under a non-TC shell process. In this case, execute the `/bin/tcsh` command to run the TC shell.

The second method of executing a shell script is to run the `/bin/tcsh` command with the script file as its parameter. Thus the following command executes the script in `script_file`. If your search path (the *`path`* variable) includes the /bin directory, you can simply use the `tcsh` command.

```
% /bin/tcsh script_file
%
```

The third method, which is also the most commonly used, is to force execution of a script in the TC shell, regardless of your current shell. You can do so by beginning a shell script with

```
#!/bin/tcsh
```

All you need to do is set execute permission for the script file and run the file as a command. When your current shell reads the string **#!**, it takes the rest of the line as the absolute pathname of the shell to be executed, under which the script in the file is executed.

## 17.3 SHELL VARIABLES AND RELATED COMMANDS

A variable is a main memory location that is given a name. That allows you to reference the memory location by using its name instead of its address (see Chapter 3). The name of a shell variable can be composed of digits, letters, and underscore, with the first character being a letter or underscore. A variable name can be up to 20 characters long. Because the main memory is read/write storage, you can read a variable's value or assign it a new value. Like Bash, the value of a variable can be a string of characters or a numeric value. There is no theoretical limit to the length of a variable's value stored as a string.

Shell variables can be of two types: shell environment variables and user-defined variables. You can use environment variables to customize the environment in which your shell runs and for proper execution of shell commands. A copy of these variables is passed to every command that executes in the shell as its child. Most of these variables are initialized when you log on, according to the environment set by your system administrator. You can customize your environment by assigning appropriate values to some or all of these variables in your ~/.login and ~/.cshrc start-up files, which also execute when you log on. (See Chapter 4 for a discussion of start-up files.) Table 17.1 lists most of the environment variables whose values you can change.

The shell environment variables listed in Table 17.1 are writable, and you can assign them any values to make your shell environment meet your needs. Other shell environment variables are read-only. That is, you can use (read) the values of these variables, but you can't change them directly. These variables are most useful for processing command line arguments (also known as positional arguments), the parameters passed to a shell script at the command line. Examples of command line arguments are the source and destination files in the **cp** command. Some other read-only shell variables are used to keep track of the process ID of the current process, the process ID of the most recent background process, and the exit status of the last command. Some important read-only shell environment variables are listed in Table 17.2.

User-defined variables are used within shell scripts as temporary storage places whose values can be changed when the program executes. These variables can be made global and passed to the commands that execute in the shell script in which they are defined. As with most programming languages, you have to declare TC shell variables before using them. A reference to an uninitialized TC shell variable results in an error.

**Table 17.1** Some Important Writable TC Shell Environment Variables

| Environment Variable | Purpose of the Variable |
|---|---|
| *cdpath* | Directory names that are searched, one by one, by the `cd` command to find the directory passed to it as a parameter; the `cd` command searches the current directory if this variable is not set |
| *home* | Name of your home directory, when you first log on |
| *mail* | Name of your system mailbox file |
| *path* | Variable that contains your search path—the directories that a shell searches to find an external command or program |
| *prompt* | Primary shell prompt that appears on the command line, usually set to `%` |
| *prompt2* | Secondary shell prompt displayed on the second line of a command if the shell thinks that the command is not finished, typically when the command line terminates with a backslash (\), the escape character |
| *cwd* | Name of the current working directory |
| *term* | Type of user's console terminal |

**Table 17.2** Some Important Read-Only TC Shell Environment Variables

| Environment Variable | Purpose of the Variable |
|---|---|
| `$0` | Name of the program |
| *$argv[1] - $argv[9]* | Values of command line arguments 1 through 9; use only when they are initialized; reference to uninitialized arguments results in an error message. |
| *$1 - $9* or *${1} - ${9}* | Values of command line arguments 1 through 9 |
| *$argv[*]* or *$** | Values of all of the command line arguments |
| *$argv[m-n]* | Values of command line arguments m through n (for m and n> 1); missing m implies 1 and missing n implies remaining arguments; `$argv[1-]` is equivalent to `$argv[*]` |
| *$#argv* or *$#* | Total number of command line arguments |
| *$$* | Process ID (PID) of the current process; typically used as a file name extension to create (most probably) unique file names |
| *$!* | PID of the most recent background process |

You can display the values of all shell variables (environment and user-defined) and their current values by using the **set** command without any argument. The following is a sample run of the **set** command on a PC running Red Hat 7.0; output on Mandrake 6.2 is similar. We show a partial list here to keep you focused and to save space.

```
% set
COLORS  /etc/DIR_COLORS
_ set
addsuffix
argv    ()
cwd     /home/faculty/sarwar/linuxbook/examples/Tcsh
dirstack        /home/faculty/sarwar/linuxbook/examples/Tcsh
echo_style      both
edit
file    /home/faculty/sarwar/.i18n
gid     501
group   sarwar
history 100
home    /home/faculty/sarwar
owd
path    (/usr/kerberos/bin /usr/kerberos/bin /usr/local/bin /bin
/usr/bin /usr/X11R6/bin . /home/faculty/sarwar/bin)
prompt  [%n@%m %c]$
prompt2 %R?
prompt3 CORRECT>%R (y|n|e|a)?
shell   /bin/tcsh
shlvl   2
sourced 1
status  0
tcsh    6.09.00
term    xterm
tty     pts/0
uid     501
user    sarwar
version tcsh 6.09.00 (Astron) 1999-08-16 (i386-intel-linux) options
8b,nls,dl,al,kan,rh,color,dspm
%
```

You can use the **env** and **printenv** commands to display both the environment variables and their values. The following is a sample output of the **env** command on the same LINUX system that we ran the **set** command on.

```
% env
PWD=/home/faculty/sarwar/linuxbook/examples/Tcsh
REMOTEHOST=upsun25.egr.up.edu
HOSTNAME=upibm44.egr.up.edu
PVM_RSH=/usr/bin/rsh
QTDIR=/usr/lib/qt-2.2.0
LESSOPEN=|/usr/bin/lesspipe.sh %s
XPVM_ROOT=/usr/share/pvm3/xpvm
KDEDIR=/usr
USER=sarwar
LS_COLORS=no=00:fi=00:di=01;34:ln=01;36:pi=40;33:so=01;35:bd=40;33;01:cd
=40;33;01:or=01;05;37;41:mi=01;05;37;41:ex=01;32:*.cmd=01;32:*.exe=01;32
:*.com=01;32:*.btm=01;32:*.bat=01;32:*.sh=01;32:*.csh=01;32:*.tar=01;31:
*.tgz=01;31:*.arj=01;31:*.taz=01;31:*.lzh=01;31:*.zip=01;31:*.z=01;31:*.
Z=01;31:*.gz=01;31:*.bz2=01;31:*.bz=01;31:*.tz=01;31:*.rpm=01;31:*.cpio=
01;31:*.jpg=01;35:*.gif=01;35:*.bmp=01;35:*.xbm=01;35:*.xpm=01;35:*.png=
01;35:*.tif=01;35:
MACHTYPE=i386
MAIL=/var/spool/mail/sarwar
OLDPWD=/home/faculty/sarwar
INPUTRC=/etc/inputrc
BASH_ENV=/home/faculty/sarwar/.bashrc
LANG=en_US
DISPLAY=upx25:0.0
LOGNAME=sarwar
SHLVL=2
SHELL=/bin/bash
USERNAME=
HOSTTYPE=i386-linux
OSTYPE=linux
HISTSIZE=1000
PVM_ROOT=/usr/share/pvm3
TERM=xterm
HOME=/home/faculty/sarwar
```

```
PATH=/usr/kerberos/bin:/usr/kerberos/bin:/usr/local/bin:/bin:/usr/bin:/u
sr/X11R6/bin:.:/home/faculty/sarwar/bin
_=/bin/tcsh
VENDOR=intel
GROUP=sarwar
HOST=upibm44.egr.up.edu
%
```

In the following In-Chapter Exercises, you will create a simple shell script and make it executable. Also, you will use the **set** and **env** commands to display the names and values of shell variables in your environment.

**IN-CHAPTER EXERCISES**

**17.1.** Display the names and values of all shell variables on your LINUX machine. What command(s) did you use?

**17.2.** Create a file that contains a TC shell script comprising the `date` and `who` commands, one on each line. Make the file executable and run the shell script. List all the steps for completing this task.

### 17.3.1 Reading and Writing Shell Variables

You can use any of three commands to assign a value to (write) one or more shell variables (environment or user-defined): `@`, `set`, and `setenv`. The `set` and `setenv` commands are used to assign a string to a variable. The difference is that the `setenv` command declares and initializes a **global variable** (equivalent to an assignment statement followed by execution of the `export` command in Bash), whereas the `set` command declares and initializes a **local variable**. You can use the `@` command to assign a numeric value to a local variable. The following are brief descriptions of the `@` and `set` commands. We describe the `setenv` command in Section 17.3.3.

Syntax:

**set [variable1 [= strval1] variable2 [= strval2] ... variableN [= strvalN]]**
**@ [variable1 = numval1] [variable2 [= numval2] ... [variableN = numvalN]**

**Purpose:** Assign values 'strval1', ... 'strvalN' or 'numval1', ... 'numvalN' to variables 'variable1, ..., variableN', respectively, where a value can be 'strval' for a string value and 'numval' for a numeric value

No space is required before or after the = sign for the `@` and **set** commands, but spaces can be used for clarity. If a value contains spaces, you must enclose the value in parentheses. The **set** command with only the name of a variable declares the variable and assigns it a null value. Unlike Bash, where every variable is automatically initialized, in the TC shell you must declare a variable in order to initialize and use it. Without any arguments, the **set** and `@` commands display all shell variables and their values. (We discuss the `@` command in detail in Chapter 18.) You can refer to (read) the current value of a variable by inserting a dollar sign ($) before the name of a variable, as in `$variable`. You can use `${variable}` in place of `$variable` in order to insulate 'variable' from the characers that follow it. You can use `${?variable}` to check whether 'variable' is set or not; it returns 1 if 'variable' is set and 0 if it is not. You can use the **echo** command to display values of shell variables.

In the following session, we show how shell variables can be read and written. We also show the use of single and double quotes, *, and \ in an assignment statement.

```
% echo $name
name: Undefined variable.
% set name
% echo $name
% set name = John
% echo $name
John
% set name = John Doe II
% echo $name
John
% echo $Doe $II
% set name = (John Doe)
% echo $name
John Doe
% set name = John*
% echo $name
John.Bates.letter   John.Johnsen.memo   John.email
% echo "$name"
John*
% echo "The name $name sounds familiar\!"
The name John* sounds familiar!
% echo \$name
$name
% echo '$name'
```

```
$name
%
```

The preceding session shows that, if values that include spaces are not enclosed in quotes or parentheses, the shell assigns the first word to the variable and the remaining as null-initialized variables. In other words, the command `set name = John Doe II` initializes the *name* variable to John, and declares *Doe* and *II* as string variables. Also, after the `set name=John*` command has been executed and `$name` is not enclosed in quotes in the `echo` command, the shell lists the file names in your present working directory that match `John*`, with `*` considered as the shell metacharacter. Thus running the `echo *` command would display the names of all the files in your current directory in one line. The preceding session also shows that single quotes can be used to process the value of the *name* variable literally. In fact, you can use single quotes to process the whole string literally. The backslash character can be used to escape the special meaning of any single character, including `$`, and treat it literally.

A command line consisting of `$variable` alone results in the value of *variable* being executed as a shell command. If the value of *variable* comprises a valid command, the expected results are produced. If *variable* doesn't contain a valid command, the shell, as expected, displays an appropriate error message. The following session illustrates this point with some samples. The variable used in this session is *command*.

```
% set command = pwd
% $command
/home/faculty/sarwar/linuxbook/examples
% set command = hello
% $command
hello: Command not found.
%
```

### 17.3.2 Command Substitution

When a command is enclosed in backquotes (also known as **grave accents**), the shell executes the command and substitutes the output of the command for the command (including backquotes). This process is referred to as **command substitution**. The following is a brief description of command substitution.

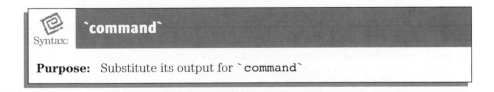

Syntax: **`command`**

**Purpose:** Substitute its output for `command`

The following session illustrates the concept. In the first assignment statement, the variable called *command* is assigned the value pwd. In the second assignment statement, the output of the pwd command is assigned to the *command* variable.

```
% set command = pwd
% echo "The value of command is: $command."
The value of command is: pwd
% set command = `pwd`
% echo "The value of command is: $command."
The value of command is: /home/faculty/sarwar/linuxbook/examples
%
```

Command substitution can be specified in any command. For example, in the following command line, the output of the date command is substituted for `` `date` `` before the echo command is executed.

```
% echo "The date and time is `date`."
The date and time is Fri Mar 2 23:40:08 PST 2001.
%
```

The following In-Chapter Exercises have been designed to reinforce the creation and use of shell variables and the concept of command substitution.

**IN-CHAPTER EXERCISES**

**17.3.** Assign your full name to a shell variable *myname* and echo its value. How did you accomplish the task? Show your work.

**17.4.** Assign the output of echo "Hello, world!" command to the *myname* variable and then display the value of *myname*. List the commands that you executed to complete this task.

### 17.3.3 Exporting Environment

When a variable is created, it is not automatically known to subsequent shells. The setenv command passes the value of a variable to subsequent shells. Thus, when a shell script is called and executed in another shell script, it does not get automatic access to the variables defined in the original (caller) script unless they are explicitly made available to it. You can use the setenv command to assign a value to a string variable and pass the value of the variable to subsequent commands that execute as children of the script. Because all read/write shell environment variables are available to every command, script, and subshell, they are initialized by the `setenv` command. The following is a brief description of the `setenv` command.

Syntax:

**setenv [variable [strval]]**

**Purpose:** Assigns to 'variable' a string value 'strval' and exports 'variable' and a copy of its value so that it is available to every command executed from this point on

The following command line shows a simple use of the command. The *name* variable is initialized to John Doe and is exported to subsequent commands executed under the current shell and any subshell that runs under the current shell. Note that unlike the `set` command, the `setenv` command requires that you enclose multiword values in double quotes, not in parentheses.

```
% setenv name "John Doe"
%
```

In the following session we illustrate the concept of exporting shell variables via some simple shell scripts.

```
% cat display_name
#!/bin/tcsh
echo $name
exit 0
%
% set name=(John Doe)
% display_name
name: Undefined variable.
%
```

Note that the script in the display_name script file displays an undefined variable error message, even though we initialized the *name* variable just before executing this script. The reason is that the *name* variable declared interactively is not exported before running the script, and the *name* variable used in the script is local to the script. As this local variable *name* is uninitialized, the `echo` command displays the error message. As stated before, unlike Bash, the TC shell requires declaration of a variable before its use.

You can use the **exit** command to transfer control out of the executing program and pass it to the calling process, the current shell process in the preceding session. The only argument of the **exit** command is an optional integer number that is returned to the calling process as the exit status of the terminating process. All LINUX commands return an exit status of 0 upon success (if they successfully perform their task) and nonzero upon failure. The return status value of a command is stored in the read-only environment variable ***$?*** and can be checked by the calling process. In shell scripts, the status of a command is checked and then subsequent action is taken. We show the use of the read-only environment variable ***$?*** in some shell scripts later in the chapter. When the **exit** command is executed without an argument, the LINUX kernel sets the return status value for the script.

In the following session, the ***name*** variable is exported after it has been initialized, thus making it available to the display_name script. The session also shows that the return status of the display_name script is 0.

```
% setenv name "John Doe"
% display_name
John Doe
% echo $?
0
%
```

We now show that a copy of an exported variable's value is passed to any subsequent command. That is, a command has access only to the value of an exported variable; it cannot assign a new value to the variable. Consider the following script in the export_demo file.

```
% cat export_demo
#!/bin/tcsh
setenv name "John Doe"
display_change_name
echo "$name"
exit 0
% cat display_change_name
#!/bin/tcsh
echo "$name"
set name = (Plain Jane)
echo "$name"
exit 0
```

```
% export_demo
John Doe
Plain Jane
John Doe
%
```

When the export_demo script is invoked, the *name* variable is set to John Doe and exported so that it becomes part of the environment of the commands that execute under export_demo as its children. The first `echo` command in the display_change_name script displays the value of the exported variable *name*. It then initializes a local variable called *name* to Plain Jane. The second `echo` command therefore echoes the current value of the local variable *name* and displays Plain Jane. When the display_change_name script finishes, the display_name script executes the `echo` command and displays the value of the exported *name* variable, thus displaying John Doe.

### 17.3.4 Resetting Variables

A variable retains its value for as long as the script in which it is initialized executes. You can remove a variable from the environment by using the `unset` and `unsetenv` commands. The following are brief descriptions of the commands.

Syntax:

**unset variable-list**
**unsetenv variable**

**Purpose:** Remove the specified variables from the environment. The variables in 'variable-list' are separated by spaces. The `unset` command is used for the variables declared by using the `set` or `@` commands. The `unsetenv` command is used for variables declared by using the `setenv` command

The following session shows a simple use of the `unset` command. The variables *name* and *place* are set to John and Corvallis, respectively, and the `echo` command displays the values of these variables. The `unset` command resets *name* to null. Thus the `echo "$name"` command displays a null string (a blank line).

```
% set name=John place=Corvallis
% echo "$name $place"
John Corvallis
```

```
% unset name
% echo "$name"
name: Undefined variable.
% echo "$place"
Corvallis
%
```

The following command removes the variables *name* and *place* from the environment.

```
% unset name place
%
```

To reset a variable, explicitly assign it a null value by using the `set` command with the variable name only. Or assign the variable no value and simply hit <Enter> after the = sign, as in

```
% set country=
% echo "$country"
% set place
% echo $place
%
```

Here, the `set` command is used to reset the *country* and *place* variables to null.

### 17.3.5 Creating Read-Only User-Defined Variables

When programming, you need to use constants at times. You can use literal contants, but using symbolic constants is good programming practice, primarily because it makes your code more readable. Another reason for using symbolic names is that a constant used at various places in code may need to be changed. With a symbolic constant, the change is made at one place only, but a literal constant must be changed every place it was used. A symbolic constant can be created in a TC shell by using the `set -r` command. The following is a brief description of the command.

Syntax: **set -r [name[=value]]**

**Purpose:** Display read-only variables or set specified variables to read-only

In the following session, the ***name*** and ***place*** variables are read-only. Both variables are made read-only at the time their creation. Once they have become read-only, assignment to either variable fails.

```
% set -r name=Jim place=Ames
% echo $name $place
Jim Ames
% set name=Art
set: $name is read-only.
% set place=(Ann Arbor)
set: $place is read-only.
%
```

When the `set -r` command is executed without arguments, it displays all user-defined read-only variables and their values, as shown in the following session.

```
% set -r
name Jim
place Ames
%
```

The environment variables cannot be made read-only.

### 17.3.6 Reading from Standard Input

So far we have shown how you can assign values to shell variables statically at the command line or by using the assignment statement. If you want to write an interactive shell script that prompts the user for keyboard input, you need to use the **set** command in order to store the user input in a shell variable, according to the following syntax.

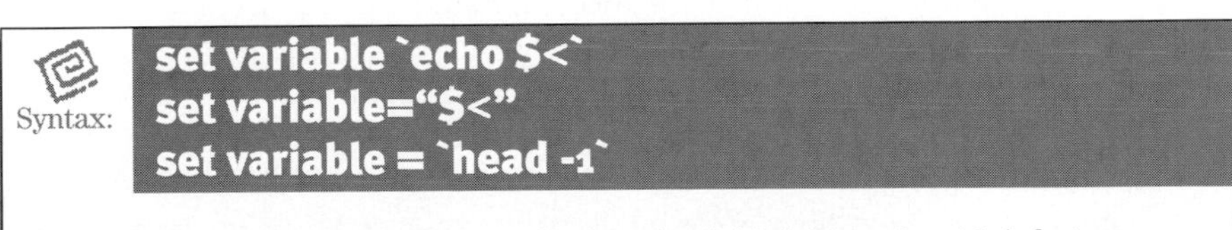

Syntax: **set variable \`echo $<\`**
**set variable="$<"**
**set variable = \`head -1\`**

**Purpose:** Read one line from stdin into 'variable'; `` `head -1` `` is between back quotes

These commands allow you to read one line of keyboard input into 'variable'. If **$<** is not quoted, only the first word in the input line is assigned to 'variable.' You can use the syntax for the second command to assign the first line of keyboard input to 'variable'. Unlike that of Bash, the keyboard input feature of the TC shell doesn't allow assignment of words in a line to multiple variables. However, the words in a line are stored in the form of an array if you use the first or third syntax, and you can access them by using the name of the variable (we discuss arrays in Chapter 18). When you use the second syntax, the whole input line goes into the first array slot.

We illustrate the semantics of the third **set** command with a script in the keyin_demo file, as follows.

```
% cat keyin_demo
#!/bin/tcsh
echo -n "Enter input: "
set line = `head -1`
echo "You entered: $line"
exit 0
%
```

The `set line = `head -1`` command can be replaced by the `set line = "$<"` or `set line = `echo $<`` command.

In the following run, enter **LINUX rules the network computing world!** (you can never overemphasize the power of LINUX!). The `set` command takes the whole input and puts it in the shell variable *line* without the newline character. The output of the `echo` command displays the contents of the shell variable *line*.

```
% keyin_demo
Enter input: LINUX rules the network computing world!
You entered: LINUX rules the network computing world!
%
```

The `-n` option is used with the `echo` command to keep the cursor on the same line. If you don't use this option, the cursor moves to the next line, which is what you want to see happen while displaying information and error messages. However, when you prompt the user for keyboard input, you should keep the cursor in front of the prompt for a more user-friendly interface. The `-n` option in the `echo` command that prompts you for input can be replaced by \c at the end of the command, as in `echo "Enter input: \c"`. The \c character, known as a **special character**, forces the cursor to stay at the same line after displaying Enter input: . The TC shell `echo` command supports many other special characters. These characters, along with their meanings, are listed in Table 17.3. Standard ASCII control sequences can be used to display other special characters, such as ^H for backspace and ^G for bell.

**Table 17.3** Special Characters for the echo Command

| Character | Description |
|---|---|
| \b | Backspace |
| \c | Keep cursor on the same line |
| \f | Form feed |
| \n | Newline (move cursor to next line) |
| \r | Carriage return |
| \t | Horizontal tab |
| \v | Vertical tab |
| \\ | Backslash (escape special meaning of backslash) |
| \0N | Character whose ASCII number is N |

In the following In-Chapter Exercise, you will use the `set` command to practice reading from stdin in shell scripts.

**IN-CHAPTER EXERCISE**

**17.5.** Write commands for reading a value into the *myname* variable from the keyboard and exporting it so that the commands executed in any child shell have access to the variable.

**17.6.** Try the shell sessions involving the `set -r` command on your system.

## 17.4 PASSING ARGUMENTS TO SHELL SCRIPTS

In this section we describe how command line arguments can be passed to shell scripts and manipulated by them. As we discussed in Section 17.3, you can pass command line arguments, also called positional parameters, to a shell script. In TC shell, the values of up to the first nine of these arguments can be referenced by using the names *$argv[1]* through *$argv[9]* (the names *$1* through *$9* can also be used) for the first through nine arguments, respectively. If a positional argument referenced in your script isn't passed an argument, it has a value of null. You can use the names *$#argv* or *$#* to refer to the total number of arguments passed in an execution of the script. The names *$argv[*]*, *argv*, or *$** refer to the values of all of the arguments. The variable name *$0* contains the name of the script file (the command name). If a positional parameter n (n = 1 through 9) is not passed as an argument, a reference to it as *$argv[n]* results in an error message `argv: Subscript out of range`. For this reason, we use *$1* through *$9* (which are initialized to null by default) to refer to positional parameters. In the following session we use the shell script in the cmdargs_demo file to show how you can use these variables.

```
% cat cmdargs_demo
#!/bin/tcsh
echo "The command name is: $0."
echo "The number of command line arguments are $#argv."
echo -n "The values of the command line arguments are: "
echo "$1 $2 $3 $4 $5 $6 $7 $8 $9."
echo "Another way to display values of all of the arguments: $argv[*]."
exit 0
% cmdargs_demo a b c d e f g h i
The command name is: cmdargs_demo.
The number of command line arguments are 9.
The values of the command line arguments are: a b c d e f g h i.
Another way to display values of all of the arguments: a b c d e f g h i.
% cmdargs_demo One Two 3 Four 5 6
The command name is: cmdargs_demo.
The number of command line arguments are 6.
The values of the command line arguments are: One Two 3 Four 5 6   .
Another way to display values of all of the arguments: One Two 3 Four 5 6.
%
```

Although the shell maintains as many as nine command line arguments at a time, you can write scripts that take more than nine arguments. To do so, use the `shift` command. By default, this command shifts the command line arguments to the left by one position, making *$2* become *$1*, *$3* become *$2*, and so on. The first argument, *$1*, is shifted out. Once shifted, the arguments cannot be restored to their original values. More than one position can be shifted if specified as an argument to the command. The following is a brief description of the command.

Syntax:

**shift [variable]**

**Purpose:** Shift the words in 'variable' one position to the left; if no variable name is specified, the command line arguments are assumed

The script in the shift_demo file shows the semantics of the **shift** command with the implicit 'variable', the command line arguments. The **shift** command shifts the first argument out and the remaining arguments to the left by one position. The three **echo** commands are used to display the current values of program names, all positional arguments (*$argv[*]*), and the values of the first three positional parameters, respectively. The results of execution of the script are obvious.

```
% cat shift_demo
#!/bin/tcsh
echo "The name of the program is $0."
echo "The arguments are: $argv[*]."
echo "The first three arguments are: $1 $2 $3."
shift
echo "The name of the program is $0."
echo "The arguments are: $argv[*]."
echo "The first three arguments are: $1 $2 $3."
exit 0
% shift_demo 1 2 3 4 5 6 7 8 9 10 11 12
The program name is shift_demo.
The arguments are: 1 2 3 4 5 6 7 8 9 10 11 12.
The first three arguments are: 1 2 3.
The program name is shift_demo.
The arguments are: 2 3 4 5 6 7 8 9 10 11 12.
The first three arguments are: 2 3 4.
%
```

The values of positional arguments can be altered by using the **set** command with *argv* as its variable argument. The most effective use of this command is in conjunction with command substitution. The following is a brief description of the command.

Syntax: **set argv = [argument-list]**

**Purpose:** Set values of the positional arguments to the arguments in 'argument-list'

The following is a simple interactive use of the command. The **date** command is executed to show that the output has six fields. The **set argv = `date`** command sets the positional parameters to the output of the **date** command. In particular, *$argv[1]* is set to Sat, *$argv[2]* to Mar, *$argv[3]* to 3, *$argv[4]* to 17:12:37, *$argv[5]* to PST, and *$argv[6]* to 2001. The **echo $argv[*]** command displays the values of all positional arguments. The third **echo** command displays the date in a commonly used form.

```
% date
Sat Mar 3 17:12:37 PST 2001
% set argv = `date`
% echo $argv[*]
Sat Mar 3 17:12:59 PST 2001
% echo "$argv[2] $argv[3], $argv[6]"
Mar 3 2001
%
```

The script in set_demo shows another use of the command. When the script is run with a file argument, it generates a line that contains the file name, the file's inode number, and the file size (in bytes). The **set** command is used to assign the output of **ls -il** command as the new values of the positional arguments *$argv[1]* through *$argv[9]*. We show the output of the **ls -il** command in case you don't remember the format of the output of this command.

```
% cat set_demo
#!/bin/tcsh
set filename = $argv[1]
set argv = `ls -il $filename`
echo "The command line arguments are: echo $argv[*]"
set inode = $argv[1]
set size = $argv[5]
echo "Name\tInode\tSize"
echo
echo "$filename\t$inode\t$size"
exit 0
% set_demo lab3
The command line arguments are: 856162 -rwx------ 1 sarwar 668 Aug 13 20:24 lab3
Name  Inode   Size
lab3  856162  668
%
```

In the following In-Chapter Exercises, you will use the `set` and `shift` commands in order to reinforce the use and processing of command line arguments.

**IN-CHAPTER EXERCISES**

**17.7.** Write a shell script that displays all command line arguments, shifts them to the left by two positions, and redisplays them. Show the script along with a few sample runs.

**17.8.** Update the shell script in Exercise 17.1 so that, after accomplishing that task, it sets the positional arguments to the output of the `who | head -1` command and displays the positional arguments again.

## 17.5 COMMENTS AND PROGRAM HEADERS

You should develop the habit of putting comments in your programs describing the purpose of a particular series of commands. At times, you may even want to describe briefly the purpose of a variable or assignment statement. Also, you should use a program header for every shell script that you write. Program headers and comments help a programmer who has been assigned the task of modifying or enhancing your code to understand it quickly. They also help you understand your own code, in particular if you reread it after some period of time. Programs written long ago, when putting comments in the program code or creating separate documentation for programs was not a common practice, are difficult to understand and enhance. Such programs are commonly known as legacy code.

A good program header must contain at least the following items. In addition, you can insert any other items that you feel are important or are commonly used in your organization/group as part of its coding rules.

1. Name of the file containing the script
2. Name of the author
3. Date written
4. Date last modified
5. Purpose of the script (in one or two lines)
6. A brief description of the algorithm used to implement the solution to the problem at hand

A comment line (including every line in the program header) must start with the number sign (`#`), as in

```
# This is a comment line.
```

However, a comment doesn't have to start at a new line; it can follow a command, as in

```
set Var1=a Var2 Var3=b  # Assign "a" to Var1, "b" to Var3, and declare
                        # a variable Var2 with an initial value of null.
```

The following is a sample header for the set_demo script.

```
# File Name:            ~/Tcsh/examples/set_demo
# Author:               Syed Mansoor Sarwar
# Date Written:         March 3, 2001
# Date Last Modified:   March 3, 2001
# Purpose:              To illustrate how the set command works
# Brief Description:    The script runs with a filename as the only
#                       command line argument, saves the filename, runs
#                       the set command to assign output of ls -il
#                       command to positional arguments ($1 through
#                       $9), and displays file name, its inode number,
#                       and its size in bytes.
```

We do not show the program headers for all of the sample scripts in this textbook in order to save space.

## 17.6 PROGRAM CONTROL FLOW COMMANDS

The program control flow commands/statements are used to determine the sequence in which statements in a shell script execute. The three basic types of statements for controlling the flow of a script are two-way branching, multiway branching, and repetitive execution of one or more commands. The TC shell statement for two-way branching is the `if` statement, the statements for multiway branching are the `if` and `switch` statements, and the statements for repetitive execution of some code are the `foreach` and `while` statements. In addition, the TC shell has a `goto` statement that allows you to jump to any command in a program.

### 17.6.1 THE `if-then-else-endif` STATEMENT

The most basic form of the `if` statement is used for two-way branching, but the statement can also be used for multiway branching. The following is a brief description of the statement. The words in monospace type are keywords and must be used as shown in the syntax. Everything in brackets is optional. All the command lists are designed to help you accomplish the task at hand.

Syntax:

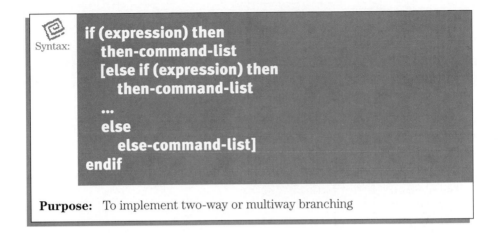

```
if (expression) then
    then-command-list
    [else if (expression) then
        then-command-list
    ...
    else
        else-command-list]
endif
```

**Purpose:** To implement two-way or multiway branching

Here, an 'expression' is a list of commands. The execution of commands in 'expression' returns a status of true (success) or false (failure). The word `then` must appear on the same line as the word `if`; otherwise, you get the error message `if: Empty if`. We discuss the complete syntax and semantics of the `if` statement by presenting three versions of it. The most basic use of the `if` statement is without any optional features and results in the following syntax for the statement, which is commonly used for two-way branching.

Syntax:

```
if (expression) then
    then-commands
endif
```

**Purpose:** To implement two-way branching

If 'expression' is true, the 'then-commands' are executed; otherwise the command after `endif` is executed. The semantics of the statement are shown in Figure 17.1.

You can form an expression by using many operators for testing files, testing and comparing integers and strings, and logically connecting two or more expressions to form complex expressions. Table 17.4 describes the operators that can be used to form expressions, along with their meanings. Operators not related to files are listed in the order of their precedence (from high to low): parentheses, unary, arithmetic, shift, relational, bitwise, and logical. The `==`, `!=`, `=~`, and `!~` operators compare their arguments as strings; all others operate on numbers.

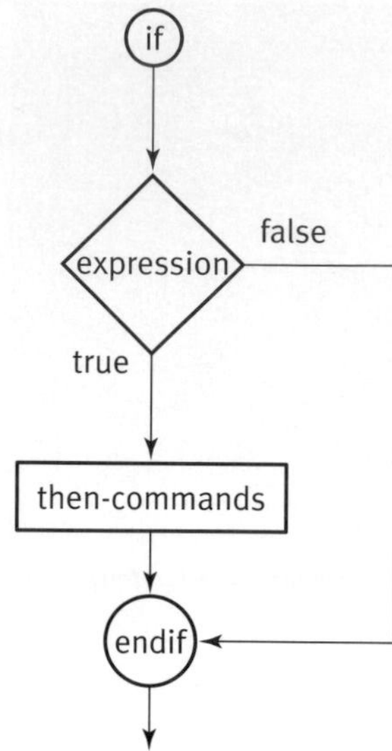


**Figure 17.1** Semantics of the `if-then-endif` statement

We use the preceding syntax of the **if** command to modify the script in the set_demo file so that it takes one command line argument only and checks on whether the argument is a file or a directory. The script returns an error message if the script is run with none or more than one command line argument or if the command line argument is not an ordinary file. The name of the script file is if_demo1.

```
% cat if_demo1
#!/bin/tcsh
if ( ($#argv == 0) || ($#argv > 1) ) then
    echo "Usage: $0 ordinary_file"
    exit 1
endif
if ( -f $argv[1] ) then
    set filename = $argv[1]
    set fileinfo = `ls -il $filename`
    set inode = $fileinfo[1]
    set size = $fileinfo[5]
    echo "Name\tInode\tSize"
    echo "$filename\t$inode\t$size"
    exit 0
endif
```

**Table 17.4** TC Shell Operators for Forming Expressions

<table>
<tr><th>Operator</th><th>Function</th><th>Operator</th><th>Function</th></tr>
<tr><td>Parentheses</td><td></td><td>Relational operators</td><td></td></tr>
<tr><td>( )</td><td>To change the order of evaluation</td><td>></td><td>Greater than</td></tr>
<tr><td></td><td></td><td><</td><td>Less than</td></tr>
<tr><td></td><td></td><td>>=</td><td>Greater than or equal to</td></tr>
<tr><td></td><td></td><td><=</td><td>Less than or equal to</td></tr>
<tr><td></td><td></td><td>!=</td><td>Not equal to (for string comparison)</td></tr>
<tr><td></td><td></td><td>==</td><td>Equal to (for string comparison)</td></tr>
<tr><td>Unary operators</td><td></td><td>Bitwise operators</td><td></td></tr>
<tr><td>-</td><td>Unary minus</td><td>&</td><td>AND</td></tr>
<tr><td>~</td><td>One's complement</td><td>^</td><td>XOR (exclusive OR)</td></tr>
<tr><td>!</td><td>Logical negation (NOT)</td><td>|</td><td>OR</td></tr>
<tr><td>Arithmetic operators</td><td></td><td>Logical operators</td><td></td></tr>
<tr><td>%</td><td>Remainder</td><td>&&</td><td>AND</td></tr>
<tr><td>/</td><td>Divide</td><td>||</td><td>OR</td></tr>
<tr><td>*</td><td>Multiply</td><td></td><td></td></tr>
<tr><td>-</td><td>Subtract</td><td></td><td></td></tr>
<tr><td>+</td><td>Add</td><td></td><td></td></tr>
<tr><td>Shift operators</td><td></td><td></td><td></td></tr>
<tr><td>>></td><td>Shift right</td><td></td><td></td></tr>
<tr><td><<</td><td>Shift left</td><td></td><td></td></tr>
</table>

**File- and String-Related Operators**

| Operator | Function | Operator | Function | Operator | Function |
|---|---|---|---|---|---|
| -b file | True if 'file' is a block special file | -c file | True if 'file' is a character special file | -d file | True if 'file' is a directory |
| -e file | True if 'file' exists | -f file | True if 'file' is ordinary file | -l file | True if 'file' is a symbolic link |
| -o file | True if user owns 'file' | -r file | True if 'file' is readable | -u file | True if 'file' has SUID bit set |
| -w file | True if 'file' is writable | -x file | True if 'file' is executable | -z file | True if length of 'file' is zero bytes |

```
echo "$0: argument must be an ordinary file"
exit 1
% if_demo1
Usage: if_demo1 ordinary_file
% if_demo1 lab3 lab4
Usage: if_demo1 ordinary_file
% if_demo1 dir1
if_demo1: argument must be an ordinary file
% if_demo1 lab3
Name  Inode   Size
lab3  856110  591
%
```

In the preceding script, the first version of the `if` statement contains a compound expression that displays an error message and exits the program if you run the script without a command line argument or with more than one argument. The second `if` statement is executed if the condition for the first `if` is false, that is, if you run the script with one command line argument only. This `if` statement produces the desired results if the command line argument is an ordinary file. If the passed argument isn't an ordinary file, the condition for the second `if` statement is false and the error message `if_demo1: argument must be an ordinary file` is displayed. Note that the exit status of the script is 1 when it exits because of an erroneous condition, and 0 when the script executes successfully and produces the desired results.

An important practice in script writing is to indent properly the commands/statements in it. Proper indentation of programs enhances their readability, making them easier to understand and upgrade. Note the indentation style used in the sample scripts presented in this textbook and follow it when you write scripts.

The second version of the `if` statement syntax also allows two-way branching. The following is a brief description of the statement.

Syntax:

```
if (expression) then
    then-commands
else
    else-commands
endif
```

**Purpose:** To implement two-way branching

If 'expression' is true, the commands in 'then-commands' are executed; otherwise the commands in 'else-commands' are executed, followed by the execution of the command after **endif**. The semantics of the statement are shown in Figure 17.2.

We rewrite the if_demo1 program by using the **if-then-else-endif** statement. The resulting script is in the if_demo2 file, as shown in the following session. Note that the program looks cleaner and more readable.

```
% cat if_demo2
#!/bin/tcsh
if ( ($#argv == 0) || ($#argv > 1) ) then
    echo "Usage: $0 ordinary_file"
    exit 1
endif
if ( -f $argv[1] ) then
    set filename = $argv[1]
    set fileinfo = `ls -il $filename`
    set inode = $fileinfo[1]
    set size = $fileinfo[5]
    echo "Name\tInode\tSize"
    echo
    echo "$filename\t$inode\t$size"
```

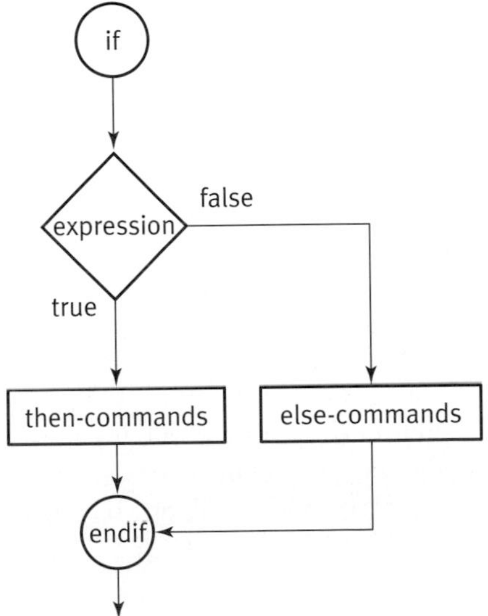


**Figure 17.2** Semantics of the `if-then-else-endif` statement

```
    exit 0
else
    echo "$0 : argument must be an ordinary file"
    exit 1
endif
%
```

The third version of the if statement is used to implement multiway branching. The following is a brief description of the statement.

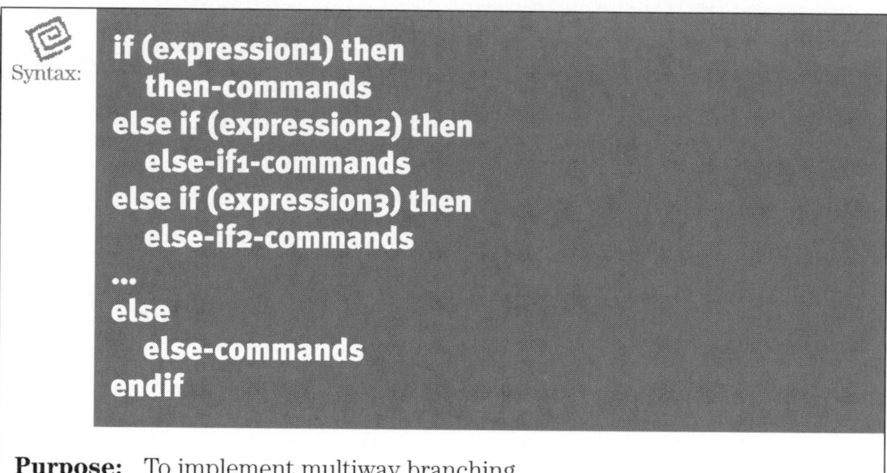

Syntax:

```
if (expression1) then
   then-commands
else if (expression2) then
   else-if1-commands
else if (expression3) then
   else-if2-commands
...
else
   else-commands
endif
```

**Purpose:** To implement multiway branching

If 'expression1' is true, the commands in 'then-commands' are executed. If 'expression1' is false, 'expression2' is evaluated, and if it is true, the commands in 'else-if1-commands' are executed. If 'expression2' is false, 'expression3' is evaluated. If 'expression3' is true, 'else-if2-commands' are executed. If 'expression3' and all subsequent expressions are also false, the commands in 'else-commands' are executed. The execution of any command list is followed by the execution of the command after `endif`. You can use any number of `else-if`s in an `if` statement to implement multiway branching. The semantics of the statement are illustrated in Figure 17.3.

We enhance the script in the if_demo2 script so that if the command line argument is a directory, the program displays the number of files and subdirectories in the directory, excluding hidden files. Implementation also involves use of the `if-then-else-endif` statement. The resulting script is in the if_demo3 file, as shown in the following session.

```
% cat if_demo3
#!/bin/tcsh
```

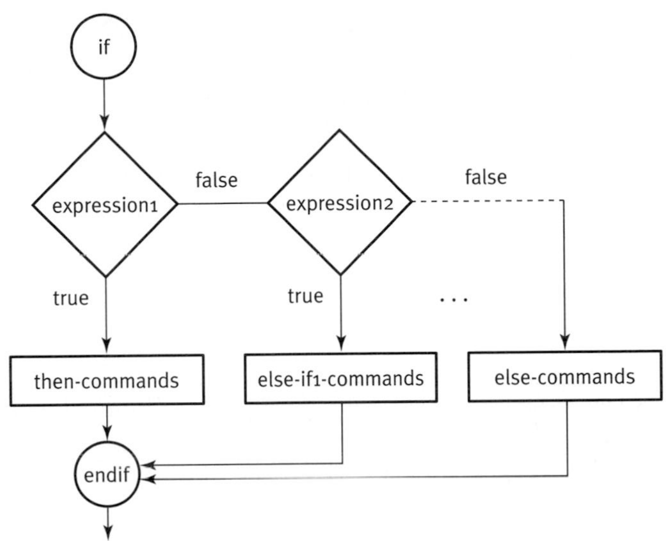


**Figure 17.3** Semantics of the `if-then-else-if-else-endif` statement

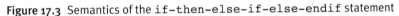

```
if  ( $#argv != 1 ) then
    echo "Usage: $0 file"
    exit 1
else
    if ( -f $argv[1] ) then
        set filename = $argv[1]
        set fileinfo = `ls -il $filename`
        set inode = $fileinfo[1]
        set size = $fileinfo[5]
        echo "Name\tInode\tSize"
        echo
        echo "$filename\t$inode\t$size"
    else if ( -d $argv[1] ) then
            set nfiles = `ls $argv[1] | wc -w`
            echo "The number of files in the directory is: $nfiles."
    else
            echo "$0 : argument must be an existing file or directory"
            exit 1
        endif
    endif
```

```
endif
exit 0
% if_demo3
Usage: if_demo3 file
% if_demo3 foo
if_demo3 : argument must be an existing file or directory
% if_demo3 foo foobar
Usage: if_demo3 file
% if_demo3 if_demo3
Name        Inode    Size
if_demo3    1005892  658
% if_demo3 ../main.h
Name        Inode    Size
../main.h   825745   121
% if_demo3 .
The number of files in the directory is: 3.
% if_demo3 ~/linuxbook/chapters
The number of files in the directory is: 21.
%
```

If the command line argument is an existing file, the required file-related data are displayed. If the argument is a directory, the number of files in it (including directories and hidden files) is saved in the nfiles variable and displayed. If the argument is a non-existing file or directory, the error message `if_demo3: argument must be an existing file or directory` is displayed. The sample runs of the script given above show these cases. The same runs also show the expected outputs when the script is run without an argument and more than one argument.

In the following In-Chapter Exercises, you will practice the use of `if` statement, command substitution, and manipulation of positional parameters.

## IN-CHAPTER EXERCISES

**17.9.** Create the if_demo2 script file and run it with no argument, more than one argument, and one argument only. While running the script with one argument, use a directory as the argument. What happens? Does the output of the script make sense?

**17.10.** Write a shell script whose single command line argument is a file. If you run the program with an ordinary file, the program displays the owner's name and last update time for the file. If the program is run with more than one argument, it generates meaningful error messages.

### 17.6.2 The **foreach** Statement

The **foreach** statement is the first of two statements available in the TC shell for repetitive execution of a block of commands in a shell script. These statements are commonly known as loops. The following is a brief description of the statement.

Syntax:

**foreach variable (argument-list)**
    **command-list**
**end**

**Purpose:** To execute commands in 'command-list' as many times as the number of words in 'command-list'. If 'argument-list' is **$argv**, the arguments are taken from the command line arguments

The words in 'argument-list' are assigned to 'variable' one by one, and the commands in 'command-list', also known as the body of the loop, are executed for every assignment. This process allows execution of the commands in 'command-list' as many times as the number of words in 'argument-list'. Figure 17.4 depicts the semantics of the **foreach** command.

The following script in the foreach_demo1 file shows use of the **foreach** command with optional arguments. The variable ***people*** is assigned the words in 'argument-list' one by one each time the value of the variable is echoed, until no words remain in the list. At this time, control comes out of the **foreach** statement, and the command following **end** is executed. Then, the code following the **foreach** statement (the **exit** statement only in this case) is executed.

```
% cat foreach_demo1
#!/bin/tcsh
foreach people ( Debbie Jamie Tom Kitty Kuhn Larry )
    echo "$people"
end
exit 0
% foreach_demo1
Debbie
Jamie
Tom
Kitty
Kuhn
```

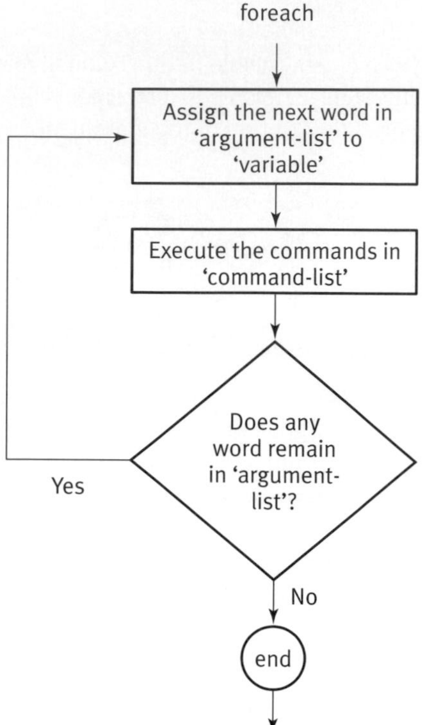


**Figure 17.4** Semantics of the `foreach` statement

```
Larry
%
```

The following script in the user_info file takes a list of existing (valid) login names as command line arguments and displays each login name and the full name of the user who owns the login name, one per login. In the sample run, the first value of the *user* variable is dfrakes. The **echo** command displays dfrakes: followed by a <Tab>, and the cursor stays at the current line. The **grep** command searches the /etc/passwd file for dfrakes and pipes it to the **cut** command, which displays the fifth field in the /etc/passwd line for dfrakes (his full name). The process is repeated for the remaining two login names (dheckman and ghacker). As no user is left in the list passed at the command line, control comes out of the **foreach** statement and the **exit 0** command is executed to transfer control back to shell.

```
% cat user_info
#!/bin/tcsh
foreach user ( $argv )
```

```
    echo -n "$user\t:\t"
    grep `echo $user` /etc/passwd | cut -f5 -d':'
    if ( $? != 0 ) then
         echo " "
    endif
end
exit 0
% user_info dfrakes dheckman ghacker
dfrakes :        Dale Frakes
dheckman:        Dennis R. Heckman
ghacker :        George Hacker
%
```

### 17.6.3 The `while` Statement

The `while` statement, also known as the *while* loop, allows repeated execution of a block of code based on the condition of an expression. The following is a brief description of the statement. Figure 17.5 illustrates the semantics of the `while` statement.

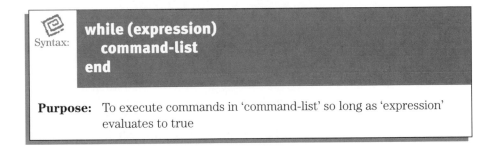

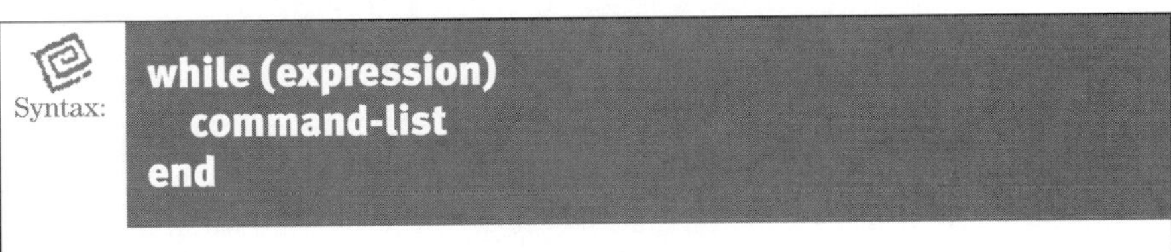

The 'expression' is evaluated and, if the result of this evaluation is true, the commands in 'command-list' are executed and 'expression' is evaluated again. This sequence of expression evaluation and execution of 'command-list', known as one iteration, is repeated until the 'expression' evaluates to false. At that time control comes out of the `while` statement and the statement following `end` is executed.

The variables and/or conditions in the expression that result in a true value must be properly manipulated in the commands in 'command-list' for well-behaved loops, that is, loops that eventually terminate and allow execution of the rest of the code in a script. Loops in which the expression always evaluates to true are known as nonterminating, or infinite, loops. Infinite loops, usually a result of poor design and/or programming, are bad because they continuously use CPU time without accomplishing any useful task. However, some applications require infinite loops. For example, all the servers for Internet services, such as ftp, are

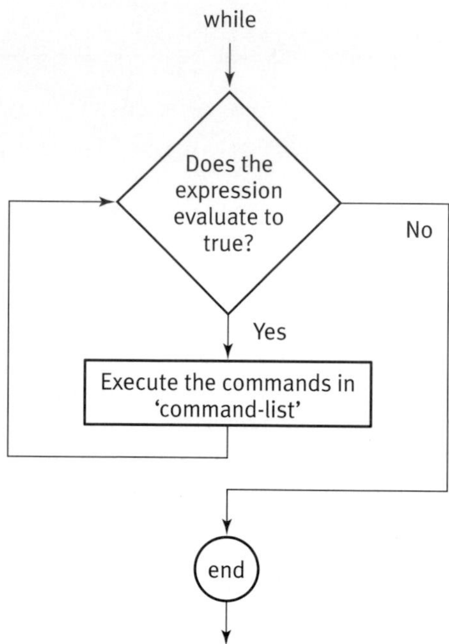


**Figure 17.5** Semantics of the `while` statement

programs that run indefinitely, waiting for client requests. Once a server has received a client request, it processes it, sends a response to the client, and waits for another client request. The only way to terminate a process with an infinite loop is to kill it by using the **`kill`** command. Or, if the process is running in the foreground, pressing <Ctrl-C> would do the trick, unless the process is designed to ignore <Ctrl-C>. In that case, you need to put the process in the background by pressing <Ctrl-Z> and using the **`kill -9`** command to terminate it.

The following script in the while_demo file shows a simple use of the **`while`** loop. When you run this script, the ***`secretcode`*** variable is initialized to agent007, and you are prompted to make a guess. Your guess is stored in the local variable ***`yourguess`***. If your guess is not agent007, the condition for the **`while`** loop is true and the commands between **`while`** and **`end`** are executed. This program displays a tactful message informing you of your failure and prompts you for another guess. Your guess is again stored in the ***`yourguess`*** variable and the condition for the loop is tested. This process continues until you enter agent007 as your guess. This time the condition for the loop becomes false, and control comes out of the **`while`** statement. The **`echo`** command following **`done`** executes, congratulating you for being part of a great gene pool!

```
% cat while_demo
#!/bin/tcsh
```

```
set secretcode = agent007
echo "Guess the code!"
echo -n "Enter your guess: "
set yourguess = `head -1`
while ("$secretcode" != "$yourguess")
     echo "Good guess but wrong. Try again!"
     echo -n "Enter your guess: "
     set yourguess = `head -1`
end
echo "Wow! You are a genius!"
exit 0
% while_demo
Guess the code!
Enter your guess: star wars
Good guess but wrong. Try again!
Enter your guess: columbo
Good guess but wrong. Try again!
Enter your guess: agent007
Wow! You are a genius!
%
```

### 17.6.4 The break, continue, and goto Commands

The `break` and `continue` commands can be used to interrupt the sequential execution of the loop body. The `break` command transfers control to the command following `end`, thus terminating the loop prematurely. A good programming use of the `break` command is to transfer control out of a loop in a nested loop. The `continue` command transfers control to `end`, which results in the evaluation of the loop condition again, hence continuation of the loop. In both cases the commands in the loop body following these statements are not executed. Thus, they are typically part of a conditional statement such as an `if` statement. The `goto` command can be used to transfer control to any command in the script. The following is a brief description of the command.

Syntax: **goto label**

**Purpose:** To execute the command at the 'label'

The **goto** command transfers control to the command at label:, a tag for the command. The use of **goto** is considered a bad programming practice because it makes debugging of programs a daunting task. For this reason, we do not recommend its use, with the exception perhaps of transferring control out of a nested loop (all loops and not just the one that has the **goto** command in it). Figure 17.6 illustrates the semantics of these commands.

In the following In-Chapter Exercises, you will write the TC shell scripts with loops by using the **foreach** and **while** statements.

## IN-CHAPTER EXERCISES

**17.11.** Write a shell script that takes a list of host names on your network as command line arguments and displays whether the hosts are up or down. Use the **ping** command to display the status of a host and the **foreach** statement to process all host names.

**17.12.** Rewrite the script in Exercise 17.11 by using the **while** statement.

### 17.6.5 The switch Statement

The **switch** statement provides a mechanism for multiway branching similar to a nested **if** statement. However, the structure provided by the **switch** statement

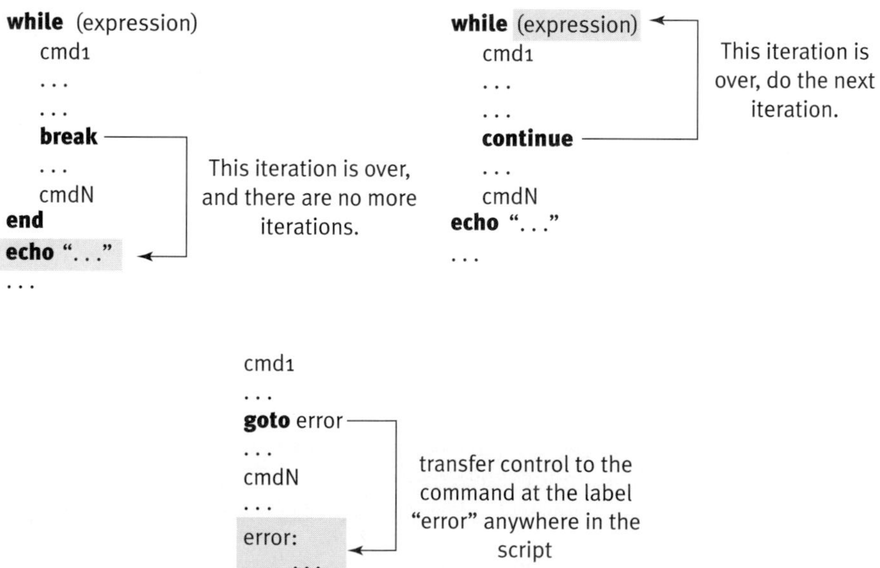


**Figure 17.6** Semantics of the break, continue, and goto commands

is more readable. You should use the **switch** statement whenever the nesting level of an **if** statement becomes deeper than three levels (i.e., you are using three **else-if**s). The following is a brief description of the statement.

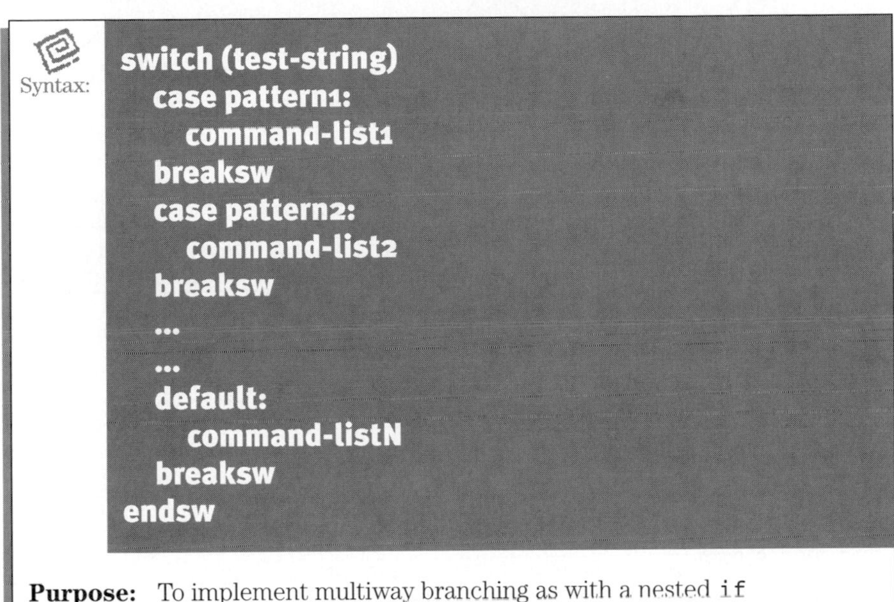

Syntax:

```
switch (test-string)
   case pattern1:
      command-list1
   breaksw
   case pattern2:
      command-list2
   breaksw
   ...
   ...
   default:
      command-listN
   breaksw
endsw
```

**Purpose:** To implement multiway branching as with a nested `if`

The **switch** statement compares the value in 'test-string' with the values of all the patterns one by one until either a match is found or there are no more patterns to match 'test-string' with. If a match is found, the commands in the corresponding 'command-list' are executed and control goes out of the **switch** statement. If no match is found, control goes to commands in 'command-listN'. Figure 17.7 illustrates the semantics of the **switch** statement.

The following script in the switch_demo file shows a simple but representative use of the **switch** statement. It is a menu-driven program that displays a menu of options and prompts you to enter an option. Your input is read into a variable called *option*. The **switch** statement then matches your option with one of the four available patterns (single characters in this case) one by one, and when a match is found, the corresponding 'command-list' (a single command in this case) is executed. Thus, if you type <d> and hit <Enter> at the prompt, the **date** command is executed and control goes out of **switch**. The **exit 0** command is then executed for normal program termination. Note that items enclosed in brackets are logically **OR**'ed. Thus, here, uppercase and lowercase letters are treated the same. A few sample runs of the script follow the code.

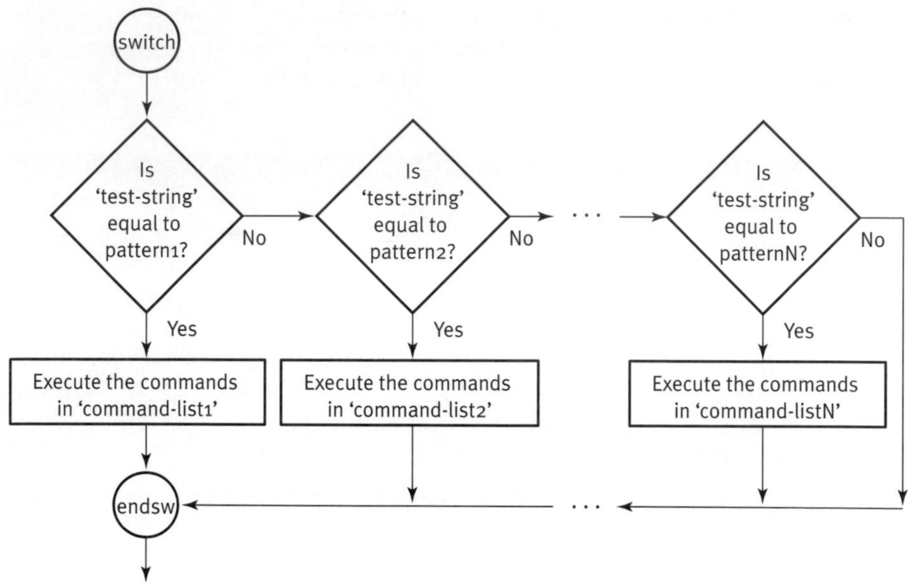


**Figure 17.7** Semantics of the `switch` statement

```
% cat switch_demo
#!/bin/tcsh
echo "Use one of the following options:"
echo " d or D: To display today's date and present time"
echo " l or L: To see the listing of files in your present working directory"
echo " w or W: To see who is logged in"
echo " q or Q: To quit this program"
echo -n "Enter your option and hit <Enter>: "
set option = `head -1`
switch ("$option")
        case [dD]:
                date
        breaksw
        case [lL]:
                ls
        breaksw
        case [wW]:
                who
        breaksw
```

```
        case [qQ]:
                exit 0
        breaksw
        default:
                echo "Invalid option; try running the program again."
                exit 1
        breaksw
endsw
exit 0
% switch_demo
Use one of the following options:
        d or D: To display today's date and present time
        l or L: To see the listing of files in your present working directory
        w or W: To see who is logged in
        q or Q: To quit this program
Enter your option and hit <Enter>: d
Sun Mar 4 12:32:13 PST 2001
% switch_demo
Use one of the following options:
d or D: To display today's date and present time
        l or L: To see the listing of files in your present working directory
        w or W: To see who is logged in
        q or Q: To quit this program
Enter your option and hit <Enter>: W
dfrakes  tty1     Feb 21 08:53
sarwar   pts/0    Mar 4 10:48
% switch_demo
Use one of the following options:
d or D: To display today's date and present time
        l or L: To see the listing of files in your present working directory
        w or W: To see who is logged in
        q or Q: To quit this program
Enter your option and hit <Enter>: a
Invalid option; try running the program again.
%
```

## SUMMARY

Every LINUX shell has a programming language that allows you to write programs for performing tasks that cannot be performed by using the existing commands. These programs are commonly known as shell scripts. In its simplest form, a shell script consists of a list of shell commands that are executed by a shell sequentially, one by one. More advanced scripts use program control flow statements for implementing multiway branching and repetitive execution of a block of commands in the script. The shell programs that consist of TC shell commands, statements, and features are called TC shell scripts.

The shell variables are the main memory locations that are given names and can be read from and written to. There are two types of shell variables: environment variables and user-defined variables. Environment variables, initialized by the shell at the time the user logs on, are maintained by the shell to provide a user-friendly work environment. User-defined variables are used as scratch pads in a script to accomplish the task at hand. Some environment variables such as the positional parameters are read-only in the sense that the user cannot change their values without using the `set` command.

The TC shell commands for processing shell variables are `set` and `setenv` (for setting values of positional parameters and displaying values of all environment variables), `env` (for displaying values of all shell variables), `unset` and `unsetenv` (for removing shell variables from the environment), `set` with "`<&`", `` `echo $<` ``, or `` `head -1` `` (for assigning keyboard input as values of variables), and `shift` (for shifting command line arguments to the left by one or more positions).

The program control flow statements `if` and `switch` allow the user to implement multiway branching, and the `foreach` and `while` statements can be used to implement loops. The `continue`, `break`, and `goto` commands can be used to interrupt the sequential execution of a shell program and transfer control to a statement that (usually) is not the next statement in the program layout.

## PROBLEMS

1. What is a shell script? Describe three ways of executing a shell script.
2. What is a shell variable? What is a read-only variable? How can you make a user-defined variable read-only? Give an example to illustrate your answer.
3. Which shell environment variable is used to store your search path? Change your search path interactively to include the directories ~/bin and (.). What would this change allow you to do? Why? If you want to make it a permanent change, what would you do? (See Chapter 4 if you have forgotton how to change your search path.)
4. What will be the output if the shell script keyin_demo in Section 17.3.6 is executed and you give * as input each time you are prompted?

5. Write a TC shell script that takes an ordinary file as an argument and removes the file if its size is zero. Otherwise, the script displays the file's name, size, number of hard links, owner, and modify date (in this order) on one line. Your script must do appropriate error checking.
6. Write a TC shell script that takes a directory as a required argument and displays the name of all zero-length files in it. Do appropriate error checking.
7. Write a TC shell script that removes all zero-length ordinary files in the current directory. Do appropriate error checking.
8. Modify the script in Problem 6 so that it removes all zero-length ordinary files in the directory passed as an optional argument. If you don't specify the directory argument, the script uses the present working directory as the default argument. Do appropriate error checking.
9. Run the script in if_demo2 in Section 17.6 with if_demo2 as its argument. Does the output make sense to you? Why?
10. Write a TC shell script that takes a list of login names on your computer system as command line arguments, and displays these login names and full names of the users who own these logins (as contained in the /etc/passwd file), one per line. If a login name is invalid (not found in the /etc/passwd file), display the login name but nothing for full name. The format of the output line is the following.
    login name:    user name
11. What happens when you run a standalone command enclosed in backquotes (grave accents), such as **`` `date` ``**? Why?
12. What happens when you execute the following sequence of shell commands?
    a. `set name=date`
    b. `$name`
    c. `` `$name` ``
13. Take a look at your /etc/csh.cshrc, /etc/csh.login, ~/.tcshrc, ~/.cshrc, and ~/.login files and list the environment variables that are exported, along with their values. What is the purpose of each variable? List the names and values of read-only variables.
14. Write a TC shell script that takes a list of login names as its arguments and displays the number of terminals that each user is logged onto in a LAN environment.
15. Write a TC shell script domain2ip that takes a list of domain names as command line arguments and displays their IP addresses. Use the **nslookup** command. The following is a sample run of this program.

```
% domain2ip up.edu redhat.com
Name: up.edu
Address: 192.220.208.9
```

```
Name: redhat.com
Address: 207.175.42.154

$
```

16. Modify the script in the switch_demo file in Section 17.6.5 so that it allows you to try any number of options and quits only when you use the `q` option.
17. Write a TC shell script that displays the following menu and prompts for one-character input to invoke a menu option, as shown.
    a. List all files in the present working directory
    b. Display today's date and time
    c. Invoke the shell script for Problem 13
    d. Display whether a file is a "simple" file of a "directory"
    e. Create a backup for a file
    f. Start a telnet session
    g. Start an ftp session
    h. Exit

    Option (c) requires that you ask the user for a list of login names. For options (d) and (e), prompt the user for file names before invoking a shell command/program. For options (f) and (g), prompt the user for a domain name (or PI address) before initiating a tenet or ftp session. The program should allow the user to try any option any number of times and should quit only when the user gives option h as input.

    A good programming practice is to build code incrementally—that is, write code for one option, test it, and then go to the next option.

CHAPTER

# 18

# Advanced TC Shell Programming

**OBJECTIVES**

- To discuss numeric data processing
- To describe array processing
- To discuss how standard input of a command in a shell script can be redirected to data within the script
- To explain signal/interrupt processing capability of the TC shell
- To cover the commands and primitives =, +=, -=, *=, /=, %=, <, >, |, &, ( ), <<, @, <Ctrl-Z>, `clear`, `onintr`, `set`, `stty`

## 18.1 INTRODUCTION

We did not discuss four features of TC shell programming in Chapter 17: processing of numeric data, array processing, the here document feature, and interrupt processing. In this chapter we discuss these features and give some example scripts that use them. We also describe how TC shell scripts can be debugged.

## 18.2 NUMERIC DATA PROCESSING

The TC shell has a built-in capability for processing numeric data. It allows you to perform arithmetic and logic operations on numeric integer data without explicitly converting string data to numeric data and vice versa. You can use the `@` command to declare numeric variables, the variables that contain integer data. This command allows declaration of local variables only. When used without arguments, the `@` command displays names and values of all shell variables (just like the **set** command). The following is a brief description of the command.

Syntax:

**@ [variable1 operator expression1] [variable2 operator expression2] ...**

**Purpose:** To declare 'variable1' to be a numeric variable, evaluate the arithmetic 'expression1', apply the operator specified in 'operator' on the current value of 'variable1' and the value of 'expression1', and assign the result to 'variable1'; 'variable2' and subsequent variables are assigned numeric values similarly

Expressions are formed by using the arithmetic and logic operators summarized previously in Table 17.4. Although octal numbers can be used in expressions by starting them with 0, the final value of an arithmetic expression is always expressed in decimal numbers. The elements of an expression must be separated by one or more spaces unless the elements are `(`, `)`, `&`, `|`, <, and >. Table 18.1 describes the assignment operators that can be used as 'operator'.

In the following interactive session, the numeric variables ***value1*** and ***value2*** are initialized to 10 and 15, respectively. The **echo** command is used to show that the assignments work properly.

```
% @ value1 = 10
% @ value2 = 15
% echo "$value1 $value2"
```

**Table 18.1** Assignment Operators for the @ Command

| Operator | Meaning |
|---|---|
| = | Assigns the value of the expression on the right-hand side of = to the variable preceding it |
| += | Adds the value of the expression on the right-hand side of = to the current value of the variable preceding it and assigns the result to the variable |
| -= | Subtracts the value of the expression on the right-hand side of = from the current value of the variable preceding it and assigns the result to the variable |
| *= | Multiplies the value of the expression on the right-hand side of = with the current value of the variable preceding it and assigns the result to the variable |
| /= | Divides the value of the variable preceding = by the value of the expression on the right-hand side of = and assigns the result (quotient) to the variable |
| %= | Divides the value of the variable preceding = by the value of the expression on the right-hand side of = and assigns the remainder to the variable |

```
10 15
%
```

In the following session, the `@` command declares two variables, ***difference*** and ***sum***, and initializes them to the values of the expressions. These actions result in the variables ***difference*** and ***sum*** taking the values –5 and 25, respectively.

```
% @ difference = ($value1 - $value2) sum = ($value1 + $value2)
% echo $difference $sum
-5 25
%
```

You can use the ++ and `--` operators to increment or decrement a variable's value by 1. For example, the following three commands are equivalent, all incrementing the value of the ***results*** variable by 1.

```
% @ results++
% @ results += 1
% @ results = ( $results + 1 )
%
```

You can also use the variables declared by using the `set` command to store numeric data. Thus, in the following session, the variables `side`, `area`, and `volume` are declared by using the `set` command and are assigned numeric values by using the `@` command.

```
% set side = 10 area volume
% @ area = $side * $side
% @ volume = $side * $side * $side
% echo $side $area $volume
10 100 1000
%
```

In the following In-Chapter Exercise, you will perform numeric data processing by using the `set` and `@` commands.

**IN-CHAPTER EXERCISE**

**18.1.** Declare two numeric variables *var1* and *var2* initialized to 10 and 30, respectively. Give two versions of a command that will produce and display their sum and product.

## 18.3 ARRAY PROCESSING

An **array** is a named collection of items of the same type stored in contiguous memory locations. Array items are numbered, with the first item being 1. You can access an array item by using the name of the array followed by the item number in brackets. Thus you can use *people[k]* to refer to the *k*th element in the array called *people*. This process is known as **array indexing**. You can declare arrays for strings and integers by using the `set` and `@` commands in the following manner.

Syntax: **set array_name = ( array elements )**
**@ array_name = (array elements)**

**Purpose:** To declare 'array_name' to be an array variable containing 'array elements' in parentheses; with the `@` command 'array elements' are treated as integers and with the `set` command they are treated as strings

You can access the contents of the whole array by using the array name preceded by the dollar sign ($), such as $name. You can access the total number of elements in an array by using the array name preceded by $#, as in $#name. The $?name is 1 if the 'name' array has been initialized and 0 if it hasn't been initialized. You can access *k*th element of the 'name' array by using the **`$name[k]`** syntax and a range of elements m through n by using the `$name[m-n]` syntax. A missing m implies 1 and a missing n implies the remaining array elements.

In the following session, we define a string array of six items, called students, initialized to the words enclosed in parentheses. The contents of the whole array can be accessed by using *`$students`*, as shown in the first `echo` command. Thus, `echo $#students` command displays 6 (the size of the students array), and the `echo $?students` command displays 1, informing you that the array has been initialized.

```
% set students = (David James Jeremy Brian Art Charlie)
% echo $students
David James Jeremy Brian Art Charlie
% echo $#students
6
% echo $?students
1
%
```

In the following session we show how elements of the *`students`* array can be accessed and changed. You can access the *i*th element in the *`students`* array by indexing it as *`$students[i]`* and elements m through n by using *`$students[m-n]`*. Thus, the first `echo` command displays the second item in the *`students`* array. The `set` command changes the value of the second element from James to Mansoor Sarwar. Figure 18.1 depicts the original and modified *`students`* arrays.

```
% echo $students[2]
James
% set students[2] = "Mansoor Sarwar"
```

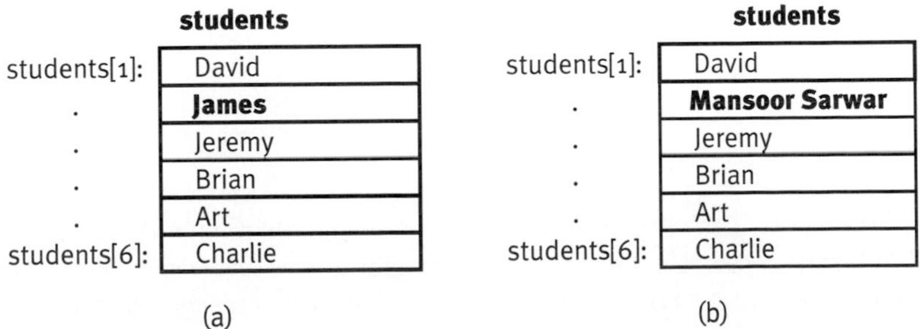


**Figure 18.1** The *`students`* array (a) before and (b) after changing the contents of the second slot

```
% echo $students
David Mansoor Sarwar Jeremy Brian Art Charlie
% echo $students[2]
Mansoor Sarwar
% echo $students[3-5]
Jeremy Brian Art
%
```

Like other variables, an array variable can be removed from the environment by using the **unset** command. In the following session the **unset** command is used to deallocate the ***students*** array. The **echo** command is used to confirm that the array has actually been deallocated.

```
% unset students
% echo $students
students: Undefined variable.
%
```

Therefore any shell variable assigned multiple values with the **set** command becomes an array variable. Thus, when a variable is assigned a multiword output of a command as a value, it becomes an array variable and contains each field of the output in a separate array slot. In the following session, ***files*** is an array variable whose elements are the names of all the files in the present working directory. The ***numfiles*** variable contains the number of files in the current directory. The echo $files[3] command displays the third array element.

```
% set files = `ls` numfiles = `ls | wc -w`
% echo $files
cmdargs_demo foreach_demo1 if_demo1 if_demo2 keyin_demo
% echo $numfiles
5
% echo $files[3]
if_demo1
%
```

You can also use an array declared with the **set** command to contain numeric data. In the following session, the num_array_demo file contains a script that uses an array of integers, called ***Fibonacci***, computes the sum of integers in the array, and displays the sum on the screen. The ***Fibonacci*** array contains the first 10 numbers of the Fibonacci series. If you're not familiar with the Fibonacci series, the first two numbers in the series are 0 and 1 and the next Fibonacci number is calculated by adding the preceding two numbers. Therefore the first 10 numbers in the Fibonacci series are 0, 1, 1, 2, 3, 5, 8, 13, 21, and 34. The Fibonacci series may be expressed mathematically as

$$F_1 = 0,\ F_2 = 1, \text{ and } F_n = F_{n-1} + F_{n-2} \quad (\text{for } n \geq 3).$$

The following script in the num_array_demo file is well documented and fairly easy to understand. It displays the sum of the first 10 Fibonacci numbers. A sample run of the script follows the code.

```
% cat num_array_demo
# File Name:            ~/linuxbook/examples/Tcsh/num_array_demo
# Author:               Syed Mansoor Sarwar
# Written:              August 16, 1999
# Last Modified:        March 4, 2001
# Purpose:              To demonstrate working with numeric arrays
# Brief Description:    Maintain running sum of numbers in a numeric variable called
#                       sum, starting with 0. Read the next array value and add it to
#                       sum. When all elements have been read, stop and display the
#                       answer.
#!/bin/tcsh

# Initialize Fibonacci array to any number of Fibonacci numbers - first ten in this case
set Fibonacci = ( 0 1 1 2 3 5 8 13 21 34 )
@ size = $#Fibonacci    # Size of the Fibonacci array
@ index = 1             # Array index initialized to point to the first element
@ sum = 0               # Running sum initialized to 0

while ( $index <= $size )
        @ sum = $sum + $Fibonacci[$index]    # Update the running sum
        @ index++                            # Increment array index by 1
end
echo "The sum of the given $#Fibonacci numbers is $sum."
exit 0
% num_array_demo
The sum of the given 10 numbers is 88.
%
```

Although this example clearly explains numeric array processing, it isn't of any practical use. We now present a more useful example, wherein the fs file contains a script that takes a directory as an optional argument and returns the size (in bytes) of all ordinary files in it. If no directory name is given at the command line, the script uses the current directory.

When you run the program without a command line argument, it treats your current directory as the argument. If you specify more than one argument, the script displays an error message and terminates. When executed with one nondirectory argument only, the program again displays an error message and exits. When executed with one argument only and the argument is a directory, the program initializes the string array variable ***files*** to the names of all the files in the specified directory (or current directory if none is specified) by using command substitution, or `` `ls $directory` ``. A numeric variable ***nfiles*** is initialized to the number of files in the current directory by using the `@ nfiles = $#files` command. Then, the size of every ordinary file in the ***files*** array is added to the numeric variable ***sum*** (which is initialized to *0*). When no more names are left in the ***files*** array, the program displays the total space (in bytes) used by all ordinary files in the directory and terminates.

```
% cat fs
# File Name:        ~/linuxbook/examples/Tcsh/fs
# Author:           Syed Mansoor Sarwar
# Written:          Mar 4, 2001
# Modified:         August 16, 1999; May 11, 2000; March 4, 2001
# Purpose:          To add the sizes of all the files in a directory passed as
#                   command line argument
# Brief Description:  Maintain running sum of file sizes in a numeric variable
#                     called sum, initialized to 0. Read all the file names
#                     in a string array called files. Get the size of a file
#                     and add it to the running total in sum. Stop when all file
#                     names have been processed and display the answer.
#!/bin/tcsh

if ( $#argv == 0 ) then
    set directory = "."
else if ( $#argv > 1 ) then
    echo "Usage: $0 [directory name]"
    exit 0
else if ( ! -d $argv[1] ) then
    echo "Usage: $0 [directory name]"
```

```
exit 0
else
     set directory = $argv[1]
endif

# Initialize files array to file names in the specified directory
set files = `ls $directory`
@ nfiles = $#files     # Number of files in the specified directory into nfiles
@ index = 1            # Array index initialized to point to the first file name
@ sum = 0              # Running sum initialized to 0

while ( $index <= $nfiles )       # For as long as a file name is left in files
     set thisfile = "$directory"/"$files[$index]"
     if ( -f $thisfile ) then            # If the next file is an ordinary file
         set argv = `ls -l $thisfile`    # Set command line arguments
         @ sum = $sum + $argv[5]         # Add file size to the running sum
         @ index++                       # Add file size to the current total
     else
         @ index++
     endif
end

# Spell out the current directory
if ( "$directory" == "." ) then
     set directory = "your current directory"
endif
echo "The size of all nondirectory files in $directory is $sum bytes."
exit 0
% fs fs
Usage: fs [directory name]
% fs dir1 dir2
Usage: fs [directory name]
% fs dir1
Usage: fs [directory name]
% fs
The size of all nondirectory files in your current directory is 3090 bytes.
```

```
% fs ..
The size of all nondirectory files in .. is 6875330 bytes.
% fs $home
The size of all nondirectory files in /home/faculty/sarwar is 14665746 bytes.
%
```

In the following In-Chapter Exercise, you will write a TC shell script that uses the numeric data processing commands for manipulating numeric arrays.

**IN-CHAPTER EXERCISE**

**18.2.** Write a TC shell script that contains two numeric arrays, ***array1*** and ***array2***, initialized to values in the sets {1,2,3,4,5} and {1,4,9,16,25}, respectively. The script should produce and display an array whose elements are the sum of the corresponding elements in the two arrays. Thus the first element of the resultant array is 1 + 1 = 2, the second element is 2 + 4 = 6, and so on.

## 18.4 THE HERE DOCUMENT

The here document feature of the TC shell allows you to redirect standard input of a command in a script and attach it to data within the script. Obviously then, this feature works with commands that take input from standard input. The feature is used mainly to display menus, although it also is useful in other ways. The following is a brief description of the here document.

Syntax:

**command << input_marker**
**... input data ...**
**input_marker**

**Purpose:** To execute 'command' with its input coming from the here document—data between the input start and end markers 'input_marker'

The 'input_marker' is a word that you choose to wrap the input data in for 'command'. The closing marker must be on a line by itself and cannot be surrounded by any spaces. We explain the use of the here document with a simple redirection of standard input of the **cat** command from the document. The following script in the heredoc_demo file displays a message for the user and then sends a mail message to the person whose e-mail address is passed as a command line argument.

```
% cat heredoc_demo
#!/bin/tcsh

# First example
cat << DataTag
This is a simple use of the here document. These data are the
input to the cat command.
DataTag

# Second example
mail $argv[1] << WRAPPER
Hello,

This is a reminder for the weekly meeting tomorrow.

Mansoor
WRAPPER

echo "Sending mail to $argv[1] ... done"
exit 0
% heredoc_demo eecsfaculty
This is a simple use of the here document. These data are the
input to the cat command.
Sending mail to eecsfaculty ... done
%
```

The following script is a better use of the here document feature. This script, `dext` (for directory expert), maintains a directory of names, phone numbers, and e-mail addresses. The script is run with a name as a command line argument and uses the `grep` command to display the directory entry corresponding to the name. The `-i` option is used with the `grep` command in order to ignore the case of letters. The backslashes are used to continue the `grep` command and visually segregate the directory data from it.

```
% more dext
#!/bin/tcsh

if ( $#argv == 0 ) then
    echo "Usage: $0 name"
```

```
    exit 1
else
    set user_input = "$argv[1]"
    grep -i "$user_input" \
\
<< Directory_Data
John Doe       555.232.0000    johnd@somedomain.edu
Jenny Great    444.656.1111   jg@new.somecollege.edu
David Nice     999.111.3333    david_nice@xyz.org
Jim Davis      777.000.9999    davis@great.advisor.edu
Art Pohm       333.000.8888    art.pohm@great.professor.edu
Directory_Data

endif
exit 0
%
```

The advantage of maintaining the directory within the script is that it eliminates some extra file operations such as open and read that would be required if the directory data were maintained in a separate file. The result is a much faster program.

Completing the following In-Chapter Exercise will enhance your understanding of the here document feature of TC shell.

**IN-CHAPTER EXERCISE**

**18.3.** Create the dext script on your system and run it. Try it with as many different inputs as you can think of. Does the script work correctly?

## 18.5 INTERRUPT (SIGNAL) PROCESSING

We discussed the basic concept of signals in Chapter 13, where we defined them as software interrupts that can be sent to a process. We also stated that the process receiving a signal can take any one of three possible actions:

1. Accept the default action as determined by the LINUX kernel
2. Ignore the signal
3. Take a programmer-defined action

In LINUX several types of signals can be sent to a process. Some of these signals can be sent via the hardware devices such as the keyboard, but all can be sent via the `kill` command, as discussed in Chapter 13. The most common event that causes a hardware interrupt (and a signal) is generated when you press <Ctrl-C> and is known as the keyboard interrupt. This event causes the foreground process to terminate (the default action). Other events that cause a process to receive a signal include termination of a child process, a process accessing a main memory location that is not part of its address space (the main memory area that the program owns and is allowed to access), and a software termination signal caused by execution of the `kill` command without any signal number. Table 18.2 presents a list of some important signals, their numbers (which can be used to generate those signals with the `kill` command), and their purpose.

The signal processing feature of TC shell allows you to write programs that cannot be terminated by a terminal interrupt (<Ctrl-C>). In contrast to Bash support for signal processing, this feature is very limited. The command used to intercept and ignore <Ctrl-C> is `onintr`. The following is a brief description of the command.

Syntax:

**onintr [options]**

**Purpose:** To ignore terminal interrupt (<Ctrl-C>) or intercept it and transfer control to any command

**Options:**

| | |
|---|---|
| `-` | To ignore the terminal interrupt |
| `label:` | To transfer control to the command at 'label' |

When you use the `onintr` command without any option, the default action of process termination takes place when you press <Ctrl-C> while the process is running. Thus using the `onintr` command without any option is redundant. Here, we enhance the script in the while_demo file in Chapter 17 so that you cannot terminate execution of this program with <Ctrl-C>. The enhanced version is in the onintr_demo file, as shown in the following session. Note that the `onintr` command is used to transfer control to the command at the `interrupt_label:` label when you press <Ctrl-C> while executing this program. The code at this label is a `goto` command that transfers control to the `onintr interrupt` command to reset the interrupt handling capability of the code, effectively ignoring <Ctrl-C>. A sample run illustrates this point.

```
% cat onintr_demo
#!/bin/tcsh
# Intercept <Ctrl-C> and transfer control to the command at interrupt_label:
```

**Table 18.2** Some Important Signals, Their Numbers, and Their Purposes

| Signal Name | Signal # | Purpose |
|---|---|---|
| SIGHUP (hang up) | 1 | Informs the process when the user who ran the process logs out and terminates the process |
| SIGINT (keyboard interrupt) | 2 | Informs the process when the user presses <Ctrl-C> and terminates the process |
| SIGQUIT (quit signal) | 3 | Informs the process when the user presses <Ctrl-\|> or <Ctrl-\> and terminates the process |
| SIGKILL (sure kill) | 9 | Definitely terminates the process when the user sends this signal to it with the `kill -9` command |
| SIGSEGV (segmentation violation) | 11 | Terminates the process upon memory fault when a process tries to access memory space that doesn't belong to it |
| SIGTERM (software termination) | 15 | Terminates the process when the `kill` command is used without any signal number |
| SIGCHLD (child finished execution) | 17 | Informs the process of termination of one of its children |
| SIGTSTP (suspend/stop signal) | 20 | Suspends the process, usually <Ctrl-Z> |

```
backagain:
        onintr interrupt

# Set the secret code
set secretcode = agent007

# Get user input
echo "Guess the code!"
echo -n "Enter your guess: "
set yourguess = `head -1`

# As long as the user input is the secret code (agent007 in this case),
    # loop here: display a message and take user input gain. When the user
    # input matches the secret code, terminate the loop and execute the
    # following echo command.
while ( "$secretcode" != "$yourguess" )
    echo "Good guess but wrong. Try again!"
```

```
    echo -n "Enter your guess: "
    set yourguess = `head -1`
end
echo "Wow! You are a genius!"
exit 0
# Code executed when you press <Ctrl-C>
interrupt:
        echo "Nice try -- you cannot terminate me by <Ctrl-C>!"
        goto backagain
```

```
% onintr_demo
Guess the code!
Enter your guess: codecracker
Good guess but wrong. Try again!
Enter your guess: <Ctrl-C>
Nice try -- you cannot terminate me by <Ctrl-C>!
Guess the code!
Enter your guess: agent007
Wow! You are a genius!
%
```

The net effect of using the **onintr** command in the preceding script is to ignore keyboard interrupt. You can achieve the same effect by using the command with the - option. Thus the whole interrupt handling code in the onintr_demo program can be replaced by the `onintr -` command; no code is needed at any label, but then the code doesn't display any message for you when you press <Ctrl-C>.

To terminate programs that ignore terminal interrupts, you have to use the `kill` command. You can do so by suspending the process by pressing <Ctrl-Z>, using the `ps` command to get the PID of the process, and terminating it with the `kill` command.

You can modify the script in the onintr_demo file so that it ignores the keyboard interrupt, clears the display screen, and turns off the echo. Whatever you enter at the keyboard, then, is not displayed. Next, it prompts you for the code word twice. If you don't enter the same code word both times, it reminds you of your bad short-term memory and quits. If you enter the same code word, it clears the display screen and prompts you to guess the code word again. If you don't enter the original code word, the screen is cleared and you are prompted to guess again. The program doesn't terminate until you have entered the original code word. When you do enter it, the display screen is cleared, a message is displayed at the top left of the screen, and echo is turned on. Because the terminal interrupt is ignored, you can't terminate the program by pressing <Ctrl-C>. The `stty`

**-echo** command turns off the echo. Thus, when you type the original code word (or any guesses), it isn't displayed on the screen. The **clear** command clears the display screen and locates the cursor at the top left corner. The **stty echo** command turns on the echo. The resulting script is in the **canleave** file shown in the following session.

```
% more canleave
#!/bin/tcsh

# Ignore terminal interrupt
onintr -

# Clear the screen, locate the cursor at the top-left corner,
# and turn off echo
clear
stty -echo

# Set the secret code
echo -n "Enter your code word: "
set secretcode = `head -1`
echo " "

# To make sure that the user remembers the code word
echo -n "Enter your code word again: "
set same = `head -1`
echo " "
if ( $secretcode != $same ) then
    echo "Work on your short-term memory before using this code!"
    exit 1
endif

# Get user guess
clear
echo -n "Enter the code word: "
set yourguess = `head -1`
echo " "

# As long as the user input is not the original code word, loop here: display
    # a message and take user input again. When the user input matches the secret
    # code word, terminate the loop and execute the following echo command.
```

```
while ( "$secretcode" != "$yourguess" )
    clear
    echo -n "Enter the code word: "
    set yourguess = `head -1`
end

# Set terminal to echo mode
clear
echo "Back again!"
stty echo
exit 0
%
```

You can use this script to lock your terminal before you leave it to pick up a printout or get a can of soda; hence the name canleave (can leave). Using it saves you the time otherwise required for the logout and login procedures.

## 18.6 DEBUGGING SHELL PROGRAMS

You can debug your TC shell scripts by using the `-x` (echo) option of the `tcsh` command. This option displays each line of the script after variable substitution but before execution. You can combine the `-x` option with the `-v` (verbose) option to display each line of the script (as it appears in the script file) before execution. You can also invoke the `tcsh` command from the command line to run the script, or you can make it part of the script, as in `#!/bin/tcsh -xv`.

In the following session we show how a shell script can be debugged. The script in the debug_demo file prompts you for a digit. If you enter a value between 1 and 9, it displays `Good input!` and quits. If you enter any other value, it simply exits. When the script is executed, enter `4`, and it displays the message `Directory stack not that deep`.

```
% cat debug_demo
#!/bin/tcsh

echo -n "Enter a digit: "
set var1 = `head -1`
if (("$var1" >= 1) && ("$var1" <=9)) then
        echo "Good input!"
else
        echo "Bad input:("
endif
```

```
exit 0
% debug_demo
Enter a digit: 4
Directory stack not that deep.
%
```

We debug the program by using the `tcsh -xv debug_demo` command. The line before the error message of the runtime trace shows the problem area, which is the first line of the `if` command. The error message is cryptic and does not point to any particular part of the command that is causing the problem. A careful look at this line reveals that a space is needed between the = sign and the number 9 because "$var1" is being compared with =9 (and not 9 as intended). After this problem is taken care of, the script works properly.

```
% tcsh -xv debug_demo

echo -n "Enter a digit: "
echo -n Enter a digit:
Enter a digit: set var1 = `head -1`
set var1 = `head -1`
head -1
4
if ( ( "$var1" > = 1 ) && ( "$var1" < =9 ) ) then
if ( ( 4 > = 1 ) && ( 4 < =9 ) ) then
Directory stack not that deep.
%
```

The following In-Chapter Exercise has been designed to enhance your understanding of the interrupt processing and debugging features of TC shell.

## IN-CHAPTER EXERCISE

**18.4.** Test the scripts in the onintr_demo and canleave files on your LINUX system. Do they work as expected? Be sure that you understand them. If your versions do not work properly, use the `tcsh -xv` command to debug them.

## SUMMARY

The TC shell has the built-in capability for numeric integer data processing in terms of arithmetic, logic, and shift operations. Combined with the array processing feature of the language, this allows the programmer to write useful programs for processing large data sets with relative ease. The numeric variables can be declared and processed by using the `@` and `set` commands.

The here document feature of the TC shell allows standard input of a command in a script to be attached to data within the script. The use of this feature results in more efficient programs. The reason is that no extra file-related operations, such as file open and read, are needed as the data are within the script file and have probably been loaded into the main memory when the script was loaded.

The TC shell also allows the user to write programs that ignore signals such as terminal interrupt (<Ctrl-C>). This feature can be used, among other things, to disable program termination when it is in the middle of updating a file. The `onintr` command can be used to invoke this feature.

The TC shell programs can be debugged by using the `-x` and `-v` options of the `tcsh` command. This technique allows viewing the commands in the user's script after variable substitution but before execution.

## PROBLEMS

1. Is the `expr` command needed in the TC shell?
2. What is the here document? Why is it useful?
3. Modify the num_array_demo script in Section 18.3 so that it takes the numbers to be added as the command line arguments. Use the `while` control structure and integer arrays.
4. The dext script in Section 18.4 takes a single name as a command line argument. Modify this script so that it takes a list of names as command line arguments. Use the `foreach` control structure to implement your solution.
5. The script in the canleave file discussed in Section 18.5 is designed to ignore keyboard interrupt. How can this program be terminated? Be precise.
6. Write a TC shell script that takes integer numbers as command line arguments and displays their sum on the screen.
7. Write a TC shell script that takes an integer number from the keyboard and displays the Fibonacci numbers equal to the number entered from the keyboard. Thus, if the user enters 7, the script displays the first seven Fibonacci numbers.
8. What are signals in LINUX? What types of signals can be intercepted in TC shell scripts?
9. Enhance the code of Problem 7 so that it cannot be terminated by pressing <Ctrl-C>. When the user presses <Ctrl-C>, your script gives a message to the user and continues.
10. Modify the script in Problem 6 so that it reads integers to be added as a here document.

CHAPTER

# 19

# File System Backup

## OBJECTIVES

- To describe how files and directories can be archived and restored in LINUX
- To explain recovery of a subset of archived files
- To cover the commands and primitives |, >, `afio`, `amanda`, `backup`, `cd`, `compress`, `dump`, `file`, KBackup, `lbu`, `ls`, `pwd`, `tar`, `tbackup`, `tob`, `uncompress`

## 19.1 INTRODUCTION

The LINUX operating system has several utilities that allow you to archive your files and directories in a single file. System administrators normally use a tape as the storage media for archiving complete file system structures as backups so that, when a system crashes for some reason, files can be recovered. LINUX-based computer systems normally crash for reasons beyond the operating system's control, such as a disk head crash because of a power surge. LINUX rarely causes a system to crash because it is a well-designed, coded, and tested operating system. In a typical installation, backup is done every day during off hours (late night or early morning) when the system is not normally in use.

As a normal LINUX user, you can also archive your work if you want to. You normally would archive files related to a project so that you can transfer them to someone via e-mail, FTP, or a secondary storage media (tape, floppy, or CD-ROM). The primary reason for making an archive is the convenience of dealing with (sending or receiving) a single file instead of a complete directory hierarchy. Without an archive, the sender may have to send several files and directories (a file structure) that the receiver would have to restore in the correct order. Without an archiving facility, depending on the size of the file structure, the task of sending, receiving, and reconstructing the file structure can be very time-consuming.

LINUX has several utilities that can be used for archiving files. These utilities, also known as the low-level backup programs, include `tar`, `cpio`, `afio` (an enhanced version of `cpio`), and `dump`. There are shell scripts (see Chapters 15–18) that allow you to carry out complete and incremental backups (backup of new files and files that were changed since the last backup) on different types of storage media known as high-level backup programs. Some of these programs are `amanda`, `backup`, `KBackup`, `tbackup`, `lbu` (LINUX Backup Utility), and `tob`. We discuss the `tar` utility as it is one of the easiest and most widely used. Discussion on most of the other utilities can be found in a good book on LINUX system administration. Many software packages are distributed in the `tar` format. We discuss the GNU version of the `tar` utility (available on the LINUX systems).

## 19.2 ARCHIVING AND RESTORING FILES VIA tar

In Chapter 10, we discussed file compression by using the `compress` and `gzip` commands, and pointed out that compression saves disk space and transmission time. However, compressing small files normally doesn't result in much compression. Moreover, compressing files of one **cluster** in size (the minimum unit of disk storage; one or more sectors) or less doesn't help save disk space even if compression does result in smaller files, because the system ends up using one cluster to save the compressed file anyway. But if compression does result in a smaller file, you save time in transmitting the compressed version. If the disk block size is 512 bytes and a cluster consists of more than two blocks, you can use the **tar** command to pack files together in one file, with a 512-byte tar header at the beginning of each file, as shown in Figure 19.1.

The **tar** (tape archive) utility was originally designed to save file systems on tape as a backup so that files could be recovered in the event of a system crash. It is still used for that purpose, but it is also commonly used these days to pack a directory hierarchy as an ordinary disk file. Doing so saves disk space and transmission time while a directory hierarchy is being transmitted electronically. The saving in disk space results primarily from the fact that empty space within a cluster is not wasted. A brief description of the **tar** utility is found on page 612.

## 19.2.1 ARCHIVING FILES

You can use the **tar** command for archiving (also known as packing) a list of files and/or directories by using the **c** or **r** option. The **c** option creates a new archive, whereas the **r** option appends files at the end of the current archive. The most common use of the **tar** command is with the **c** option.

In the examples presented in this chapter, we use the directory structure shown in Figure 19.2.

The following session shows that there are two directories under the linuxbook directory, called current and final. In addition, each of these directories contains six files (see Figure 19.2), displayed by the **ls -l** commands.

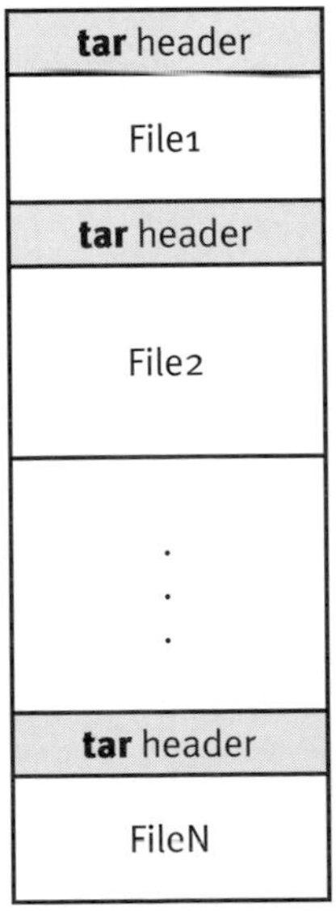

| **tar** header |
|---|
| File1 |
| **tar** header |
| File2 |
| . . . |
| **tar** header |
| FileN |

**Figure 19.1** Format of a tar file

Syntax:

## tar [options] [files]
## The use of - in front of an option is not mandatory

**Purpose:** Archive (copy in a particular format) files to or restore files from tape (which can be an ordinary file); directories are archived and restored recursively.

**Commonly used options/features:**

| | |
|---|---|
| Option Format: | Function_letter [Modifier] |
| Function_letter: | |
| `c` | Create a new tape and record archive files on it |
| `r` | Record files at the end of tape (append operation) |
| `t` | List tape's contents (names of files archived on it) in a format such as **`ls -l`** |
| `u` | Update tape by adding files on it if not on or if modified since last written to tape |
| `x` | Extract (restore) files from tape; entire tape if none specified |
| Modifier: | |
| `b` N | Use N as the blocking factor (1 default; 20 maximum) |
| `f` Arch | Use Arch as the archive for archiving or restoring files; default is /dev/mto. If Arch is `-`, standard input is read (for extracting files), or standard output is written (for creating an archive)—a feature used when tar is used in a pipeline. |
| `h` | Follow symbolic links |
| `l` | Display error message if links aren't found |
| `o` | Change ownership (user ID and group ID) to the user running tar |
| `v` | Use verbose mode: Display function letter x for extraction or for an archive |
| `z` | Compress/decompress an archive |

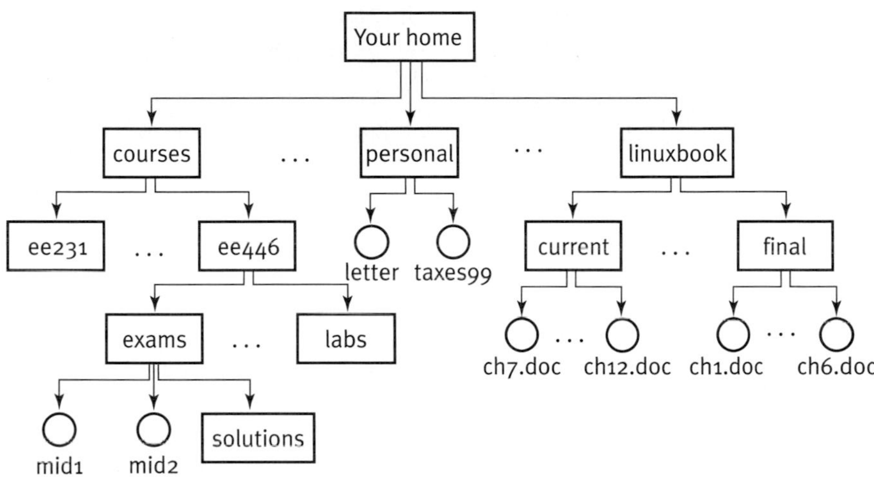


**Figure 19.2** A sample file structure

```
$ cd linuxbook
$ pwd
/home/faculty/sarwar/linuxbook
% ls -l
drwx------   2 sarwar faculty       512 Jul 22 13:21 current
drwx------   2 sarwar faculty       512 Jul 22 13:21 final
$ cd current
$ ls -l
-rw-------   1 sarwar faculty    204288 Jul 19 13:06 ch07.doc
-rw-------   1 sarwar faculty     87552 Jul 19 13:06 ch08.doc
-rw-------   1 sarwar faculty     86016 Jul 19 13:06 ch09.doc
-rw-------   1 sarwar faculty    121344 Jul 19 13:06 ch10.doc
-rw-------   1 sarwar faculty    152576 Jul 19 13:06 ch11.doc
-rw-------   1 sarwar faculty    347648 Jul 19 13:06 ch12.doc
$ cd ..
$ cd final
$ ls -l
-rw-------   1 sarwar faculty     41984 Jul 19 13:06 ch1.doc
-rw-------   1 sarwar faculty     54272 Jul 19 13:06 ch2.doc
```

```
-rw-------    1 sarwar faculty    142848 Jul 19 13:06 ch3.doc
-rw-------    1 sarwar faculty     86528 Jul 19 13:06 ch4.doc
-rw-------    1 sarwar faculty    396288 Jul 19 13:06 ch5.doc
-rw-------    1 sarwar faculty    334848 Jul 19 13:06 ch6.doc
$
```

If you want to create an archive of the linuxbook directory on a tape drive /dev/rmt0 (the name may be different on your system), you can use the following command after changing "directory" to linuxbook. The **v** (verbose) option is used to view the files and directories that are being archived. Unless you are the system administrator, in all likelihood you don't have access permission to use (read or write) the tape drive. Thus the shell will give you the following error message. If you do have proper access permissions for the tape drive, an archive of the linuxbook directory is created on the tape. Not only do you need access privileges to /dev/rmt0 but you also need to mount it first.

```
$ tar cvf /dev/rmt0 .

tar: /dev/rmt0: Permission denied

tar: Error is not recoverable: exiting now

$
```

You can create an archive on a disk file—in a directory that you have the write permission for—by using the following command. Here, we made ~/linuxbook our current directory and created a tar archive of this directory in a file called linuxbook.tar. Note that .tar is not an extension required by the `tar` utility. We have used this extension because it allows us to identify tar archives by looking at the file name. With no such extension, we have to use the `file` command to identify our tar archive files, as shown in the last command line in the session (in case you have forgotten what the `file` command does).

```
$ cd ~/linuxbook
$ tar cvf linuxbook.tar .
./
tar: ./linuxbook.tar is the archive; not dumped
./.lastlogin
./current/
./current/ch7.doc
```

```
./current/ch8.doc
./current/ch9.doc
./current/ch10.doc
./current/ch11.doc
./current/ch12.doc
./final/
./final/ch1.doc
./final/ch2.doc
./final/ch3.doc
./final/ch4.doc
./final/ch5.doc
./final/ch6.doc
$ ls -l
total 3010
drwx------    2 sarwar faculty      512 Jan 9 00:02 current
drwx------    2 sarwar faculty      512 Jan 9 00:03 final
-rw-------    1 sarwar faculty  2064896 Jan 9 13:48 linuxbook.tar
$ file linuxbook.tar
linuxbook.tar: GNU tar archive
$
```

You can also create the tar archive of the current directory by using the following command line. The - argument informs **tar** that the archive is to be sent to standard output, which is redirected to the linuxbook.tar file. As we discussed in Chapter 15, the back quotes (grave accents) are used for command substitution, that is, to execute the **find** command and substitute its output for the command, including the grave accents. The output of the **find . -print** command (the names of all the files and directories in the current directory) are passed to the **tar** command as its parameters. These file and directory names are taken as the list of files to be archived by the **tar** command. Thus the net effect of the command line is that a tar archive of the current directory is created in linuxbook.tar.

```
$ tar cvf - `find . -print` > linuxbook.tar
./
tar: ./linuxbook.tar same as archive; not dumped
```

```
./current/
./current/ch1.doc
...
$
```

In the following In-Chapter Exercise, you'll use the **tar** command with the **c** option to create an archive of a directory.

**IN-CHAPTER EXERCISE**

**19.1.** Create a tar archive of the labs directory hierarchy in your home directory. What command line(s) did you use? What is the name of your archive file?

### 19.2.2 Restoring Archived Files

You can restore (unpack) an archive by using the function option **x** of the **tar** command. To restore the archive created in Section 19.2.1, and place it in a directory called ~/backups, you can run the following command sequence. The **cp** command copies the archive file, assumed to be in your home directory, to the directory (~/backups) where the archived files are to be restored. The **cd** command is used to make the destination directory the current directory. Finally, the **tar** command is used to do the restoration. Note that the destination directory is the current directory.

```
$ cp linuxbook.tar ~/backups
$ cd ~/backups
$ tar xvf linuxbook.tar
./
./.lastlogin
./current/
./current/ch7.doc
./current/ch8.doc
./current/ch9.doc
./current/ch10.doc
./current/ch11.doc
./current/ch12.doc
```

```
./final/
./final/ch1.doc
./final/ch2.doc
./final/ch3.doc
./final/ch4.doc
./final/ch5.doc
./final/ch6.doc
$ ls -l
total 3010
drwx------    2 sarwar faculty      512 Jan 9 00:02 current
drwx------    2 sarwar faculty      512 Jan 9 00:03 final
-rw-------    1 sarwar faculty  2064896 Jan 9 12:38 linuxbook.tar
$
```

Note that the linuxbook.tar file remains intact after it has been unpacked. This result makes sense considering that the primary purpose of the tar archive is to back up files, and it should remain intact after restoration in case the system crashes after restoration but before it is archived again. After restoration of the linuxbook.tar file, your directory structure looks like that shown in Figure 19.3.

At times, you may need to restore a subset of files in a tar archive. System administrators often do this after a system crashes (usually caused by a disk head crash resulting from a power surge) and destroys some user files. In such cases, system administrators restore only those files from the tape archive that reside on the damaged portion of the disk. Selective restoration is possible with the function option **x** so long as the pathname(s) of the file(s) to be restored are known. If you don't remember the pathnames of the files to be restored, you can use the function option `t` to display the pathnames of files and directories on the archive file. The output of the `tar` command with the `t` option is in a format similar to the output of the `ls -l` command, as shown in the following session. As marked in the sample, the first field specifies file type and access permissions, the second field specifies login_name/group_name of the owner of the file, the third field shows the file size in bytes, the next several fields show the time and date that the file was last modified, and the last field shows the pathname of the file as stored in the archive.

If an archive contains a large number of files, you can pipe the output of the `tar t` command to the **more** command for page-by-page view. If you know the name of the file but not its pathname, you can pipe output of the `tar` command with the `t` option to the **grep** command. Files can also be restored, or their pathnames viewed, selectively. The following session illustrates these points.

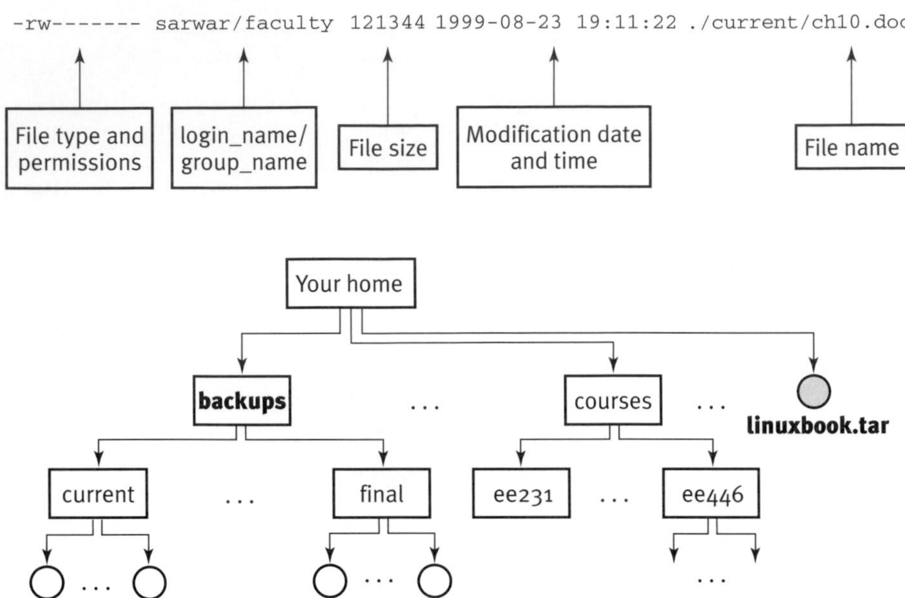


**Figure 19.3** Restoring linuxbook.tar in ~/backups

```
$ tar tvf unixbook.tar
drwx------ sarwar/faculty      0 2001-01-09 00:14:56 ./
-rw------- sarwar/faculty      0 1999-08-23 19:42:22 ./.lastlogin
drwx------ sarwar/faculty      0 2001-01-09 00:02:12 ./current/
-rwxrw---- sarwar/faculty 204288 1999-08-23 19:11:22 ./current/ch7.doc
-rwxrw---- sarwar/faculty  87552 1999-08-23 16:49:31 ./current/ch8.doc
-rwxrw---- sarwar/faculty  86016 1999-08-23 17:11:42 ./current/ch9.doc
-rwxrw---- sarwar/faculty 121344 1999-08-23 19:11:22 ./current/ch10.doc
-rwxrw---- sarwar/faculty 152576 1999-08-23 16:49:31 ./current/ch11.doc
-rwxrw---- sarwar/faculty 347648 1999-08-23 17:11:42 ./current/ch12.doc
drwx------ sarwar/faculty      0 2001-01-09 00:03:13 ./final/
-rwxrw---- sarwar/faculty  41984 1999-08-23 19:01:04 ./final/ch1.doc
-rwxrw---- sarwar/faculty  54272 1999-08-23 15:54:57 ./final/ch2.doc
-rwxrw---- sarwar/faculty 142848 1999-08-23 15:11:26 ./final/ch3.doc
-rw------- sarwar/faculty  86528 1999-08-23 19:45:32 ./final/ch4.doc
-rwxrw---- sarwar/faculty 396288 1999-08-23 09:24:01 ./final/ch5.doc
```

```
-rwxrw---- sarwar/faculty 334848 1999-08-23 09:24:15 ./final/ch6.doc
$
```

If you want to restore the file ch10.doc in the ~/linuxbook/current directory, you can use the following command sequence. Be sure that you give the pathname of the file to be restored, not just its name.

```
$ cd ~/linuxbook
$ tar -xvf ~/backups/linuxbook.tar ./current/ch10.doc
./current/ch10.doc
$
```

The output of this `tar` command shows that the file ch10.doc has been restored in the ~/backups/current directory. You can confirm this result by using the `ls -l ~/backups/current` command.

The following command can be used to perform the task of copying the whole directory hierarchy in your current directory to the ~/linuxbook/backups directory. The `tar` command to the left of the pipe creates the archive of the current directory and passes it as input to the `tar` command on the right side of the pipe. Recall that the commands in parentheses (on the right) are executed under a subshell.

```
$ tar -cf - . | ( cd ~/linuxbook/backups; tar -xvf - )
./
./ch1.doc
./ch2.doc
./ch3.doc
./ch4.doc
./ch5.doc
./ch6.doc
./ch7.doc
./ch8.doc
./ch9.doc
./ch10.doc
./ch11.doc
./ch12.doc
./ch13.doc
```

```
./ch11.doc
./ch14.doc
./ch15.doc
./ch16.doc
./ch17.doc
./ch18.doc
./ch19.doc
./ch20.doc
./ch21.doc
$
```

In the following In-Chapter Exercises, you will use the `tar` command with `t` and `x` options to appreciate how attributes of the archived files can be viewed and how archived files can be restored.

**IN-CHAPTER EXERCISES**

**19.2.** List the attributes of the files in the archive that you created in Exercise 19.1 and identify the sizes of all the files in it. What command did you use?

**19.3.** Copy the archive file that you created in Exercise 19.1 to a file called mytar. Unarchive mytar in a directory called dir.backup in your home directory. Show the commands that you used for this task.

### 19.2.3 Copying Directory Hierarchies

You can use the `tar` command to copy one directory to another directory. You can also use the `cp -r` command to do so, but the disadvantage of using this command is that the file access permissions and file modification times aren't preserved. The access permissions of the copied files and directories are determined by the value of umask, and the modification time is set to current time. Also, the `-r` option is not available on all LINUX systems.

More commonly, the `tar` command is used to archive the source directory, create the destination directory, and untar (unpack) the archived directory in this latter directory. The entire task can be performed with one command by using command grouping and piping. In the following session the ~/linuxbook/examples directory is copied to the ~/linuxbook/examples.bak directory. The `tar` command to the left of pipe sends the archive to stdout, and the `tar` command to the right of pipe unpacks the archive it receives at its stdin. The `ls -l` command is used to confirm the semantics of the command. (Note: Don't hit `<Enter>` after `cd`;

the line wraps around due to line length and the length of the pathname for the examples.bak file.)

```
$ ( cd ~/linuxbook/examples; tar -cvf - . ) | ( cd
~/linuxbook/examples.bak; tar -xvf - )
./
./.lastlogin
./Cshell/
./Cshell/if_demo1
./Cshell/if_demo2
...
./Bshell/copy
./Bshell/fileinfo
./Bshell/diff2
./Bshell/fileinfo
./Bshell/testdriver
./Bshell/timeit
$ ls -l examples examples.bak
examples:
total 3
drwx------ 3 sarwar faculty 1536 Dec 10 11:39 Bshell
drwx------ 3 sarwar faculty 1024 Aug 21 1999 Cshell

examples.bak:
total 3
drwx------ 3 sarwar faculty 1536 Dec 10 11:39 Bshell
drwx------ 3 sarwar faculty 1024 Aug 21 1999 Cshell
$
```

The advantages of using this command line are that both the `cd` and `tar` commands are available on all LINUX systems and that the copied files have the access permissions and file modification times for the source files.

You can also use the `tar` command to copy directories to a remote machine on a network. In the following command line, the ~/linuxbook/examples directory is copied to the ~/linuxbook/examples.bak directory on a remote machine called upsun21. The `rsh` command (see Chapter 14) is used to execute the quoted command group on upsun21. Because the `tar` command isn't run in verbose mode, it runs silently and you don't see any output on the display screen.

```
$ (cd ~/Linuxbook/examples; tar cf - .) | rsh upsun21 "cd
  ~/Linuxbook/example.bak; tar xf -"
$
```

## 19.3 SOFTWARE DISTRIBUTIONS IN THE tar FORMAT

Companies often use the `tar` command to distribute their software because it results in a single file that the customer needs to copy and a savings in disk space compared to the unarchived directory hierarchies that may contain the software to be distributed. Also, most companies keep their distribution packs (in the tar format) on their Internet sites, which their customers can download via the `ftp` command. Thus the tar format also results in less copying time and reduced work by the customer, who uses only one `get` (or `mget`) command (an FTP command) versus several sequences of commands if directory hierarchies have to be downloaded.

Because the sizes of software packages are increasing, owing to their graphical interfaces and multimedia formats, archives are compressed before they are put on FTP sites. The users of the software need to uncompress the downloaded files before restoring them.

Let's consider a file, tcsh-6.06.tar.Z, that we downloaded from an FTP site. In order to restore this file, we have to uncompress and untar it, as shown in the following command sequence.

```
$ uncompress tcsh-6.06.tar.Z
$ tar xvf tcsh-6.06.tar
[command output]
$
```

If a software pack is distributed on a secondary storage media (floppy, tape, or CD-ROM), you need to copy appropriate files to the appropriate directory and repeat these commands.

If you want to distribute some software that is stored in a directory hierarchy, you first need to make an archive for it by using the `tar` command and then compress it by using the `compress` command (or some other similar utility). These steps create a tar archive in a compressed file that can be placed in an ftp repository or on a Web page or sent as an e-mail attachment.

Disk file backups are also commonly used to pack large inactive or less frequently used files to save disk space.

The `-z` option of the GNU version of the `tar` utility can be used to generate the compressed version of the tar archive. This option can also be used to restore the compressed version of the tar archive. The use of this option eliminates use of the `gzip` (or `gunzip`) utility to compress or uncompress an archive and then the `tar` command; the two-step process can be performed by the `tar` command alone. In the following session, the first command generates a compressed tar archive of the current directory in the ~/linuxbook/backups/lb.tar.gz file and the second command restores the compressed tar archive from the same file into the current directory.

```
$ tar -zcf ~/linuxbook/backups/lb.tar.gz .
$ tar -zxvf ~/linuxbook/backups/lb.tar.gz
$
```

## SUMMARY

LINUX has several utilities, also known as low-level backup programs, for creating archive (backup) copies of your files and directories, including `afio`, `cpio`, `dump`, and `tar`. There are also several shell scripts, commonly known as high-level backup programs, including `amanda`, `backup`, `KBackup`, `tbackup`, `lbu`, and `tob`, that allow you to carry out complete or incremental backups. The `tar` command is the most commonly used. The backups can be in the form of tape or disk files. For tape backups, not only does a user need access privileges to the tape device file, the file needs to be mounted first. Disk file backups are commonly used for software distribution but can also be used to pack large inactive files to save disk space. In a network of LINUX machines, users can create archives of their files and directories on remote machines by using command groups that use the `tar` and `rsh` commands.

## PROBLEMS

1. What is the meaning of the term *archive*?
2. What is the `tar` command used for? Give all its uses.
3. What are the names of the device files for the tapes drives on your system? What are the access permissions for these files?
4. Give a command line for creating a tar archive of your current directory. Give commands for compressing and keeping the archive in the backups directory in your home directory.
5. Give commands for restoring the backup file in Problem 4 in the ~/backups directory.
6. Give a command line for copying your home directory to a directory called home.back so that access privileges and file modify time are preserved.
7. Why is the `tar` command preferred over the `cp -r` command for creating backup copies of directory hierarchies?
8. Suppose that you download a file, linuxbook.tar.gz, from an FTP site. As the file name indicates, it is a tar archive file in compressed form. Give the sequence of commands for restoring this archive and installing it in your ~/linuxbook directory.
9. Carry out the task outlined in Problem 8, using a single command line.

CHAPTER

# 20

# LINUX Tools for Software Development

## OBJECTIVES

- To summarize computer programming languages at different levels
- To discuss interpreted and compiled languages and the compilation process
- To briefly describe the software engineering life cycle
- To discuss LINUX program generation tools for C to perform the following tasks: editing, indenting, compiling, handling module-based software, creating libraries, source code management, and revision control
- To describe LINUX tools for static analysis of C programs: verifying code for portability and profiling
- To discuss LINUX tools for dynamic analysis of C programs: debugging, tracing, and monitoring performance
- To cover the commands and primitives `admin`, `ar`, `gcc`, `ci`, `co`, `cvs`, `delta`, `emacs`, `gdb`, `get`, `grep`, `help`, `ident`, `indent`, `make`, `rcsmerge`, `nm`, `rcs`, `ranlib`, `rlog`, `strip`, `time`

## 20.1 INTRODUCTION

A typical LINUX system has support for several high-level languages, both interpreted and compiled. These languages include C, C++, Pascal, Java, LISP, and FORTRAN. However, most of the application software for the LINUX platforms is developed in the C language, the language in which the LINUX operating system is written. Thus a range of software engineering tools are available for use in developing software in this language. Many of these tools can also be used for developing software in other programming languages, C++ in particular.

The LINUX operating system has a wealth of software engineering tools for program generation and static and dynamic analysis of programs. They include tools for editing source code, indenting source code, compiling and linking, handling module-based software, creating libraries, profiling, verifying source code for portability, source code management, debugging, tracing, and performance monitoring. In this chapter, we describe some of the commonly used tools in the development of C-based software. The extent of discussion of these tools varies from brief to detailed, depending on their usefulness and how often they are used in practice. Before discussing these tools, however, we briefly describe various types of languages that can be used to write computer software. In doing so, we also discuss both interpreted and compiled languages.

## 20.2 COMPUTER PROGRAMMING LANGUAGES

Computer programs can be written in a wide variety of programming languages. The native language of a computer is known as its **machine language**, the language comprising the instruction set of the CPU inside the computer. Recall that the instruction set of a CPU consists of instructions that the CPU understands. These instructions enable the performance of various types of operations on data, such as arithmetic, logic, shift, and I/O operations. Today's CPUs are made of **bistate devices** (devices that operate in on or off states), so CPU instructions are in the form of 0s and 1s (0 for the off state and 1 for the on state). The total number of instructions for a CPU and the maximum length (in bytes) of an instruction is CPU dependent. Whereas reduced instruction set computers (RISC) based CPUs have several hundred simple instructions, complex instruction set computers (CISC) based CPUs have tens of complex instructions. Programs written in a CPU's machine language are called **machine programs**, commonly known as **machine codes**. The machine language programs are the most efficient because they are written in a CPU's native language. However, they are the most difficult to write because the machine language is very different from any spoken language; the programmer has to write these programs in 1s and 0s, and a change in one bit can cause major problems. Debugging machine language programs is a very challenging and time-consuming task as well. For these reasons, programs are rarely written in machine languages today.

In assembly language programming, machine instructions are written in English-like words, called *mnemonics*. Because programs written in assembly language are closer to the English language, they are relatively easier to write and debug. However, these programs must be translated into the machine language of the CPU used in your computer before you can execute them. This process of translation is carried out by a program called an **assembler**. You have to execute a command to run an assembler, with the file containing an assembly language program as its argument. Although assembly languages are becoming less popular, they are still used to write time-critical programs for controlling real-time systems (e.g., the controllers in drilling machines for oil wells) that have limited amounts of main storage.

In an effort to bring programming languages closer to the English language—and make programming and debugging task easier—high-level languages (HLLs) were developed. Commonly used high-level languages are Ada, C, C++, Java, Javascript, BASIC, FORTRAN, LISP, Pascal, and Prolog. Some of these languages are interpreted (e.g., Javascript and LISP), whereas others are compiled (e.g., C, C++, and Java). On the one hand, programs written in an interpreted language are executed one instruction at a time by a program called an **interpreter**, without translating them into the machine code for the CPU used in the computer. On the other hand, programs written in compiled languages must be translated into the machine code for the underlying CPU before they are executed. This translation is carried out by a program called a **compiler**, which generates the assembly version of the high-level language program. The assembly version has to go through further translation before the executable code is generated. The compiled languages run many times faster than the interpreted languages because compiled languages are directly executed by the CPU, whereas the interpreted languages are executed by a piece of software (an interpreter).

However, the Java language is not compiled in the traditional sense. Java programs are translated into a form known as the Java Bytecode, which is then interpreted by an interpreter, called the Java Virtual Machine (JVM) or the Java Interpreter (JIT).

To simplify the task of writing computer programs further, languages at a higher level even than the HLLs were developed. They include scripting and visual languages such as LINUX shell programming, Perl, visual BASIC, and visual C++. Some of these languages are interpreted; others are compiled. Figure 20.1 shows the proximity of various types of programming languages to the hardware, ease of their use, and relative speed at which programs are executed.

As the level of programming languages increases, the task of writing programs becomes easier and programs become more readable. The trade-off is that programs written in HLLs take longer to run. For interpreted programs, the increase in program running time is due to the fact that another program (the interpreter) runs the program. For compiled languages, the compilation process takes longer and the resulting machine code is usually much bigger than it would be if written in assembly language by hand. However, time saved because of ease of programming in HLLs far outweighs the increase in code size. Figure 20.1 also shows some language statement examples to demonstrate the increased readability of programs as the level of programming languages increases.

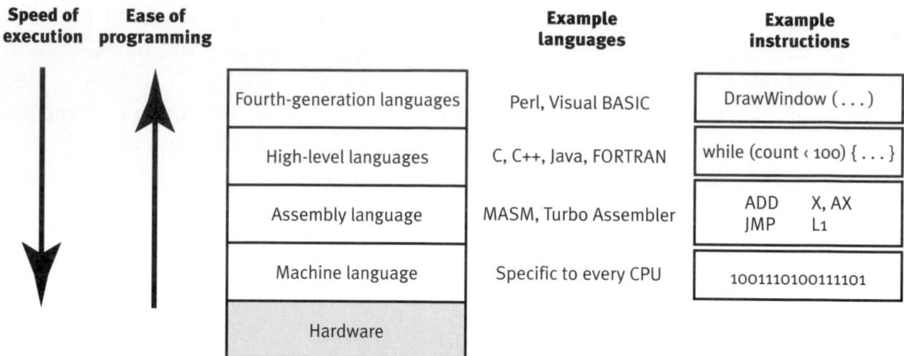


**Figure 20.1** Levels of programming languages, with examples, ease of programming, and speed of execution

## 20.3 THE COMPILATION PROCESS

Because our focus in this chapter is on LINUX tools—primarily for the C programming language (a compiled language)—we need to describe briefly the compilation process before moving on. As we stated in Section 20.2, computer programs written in compiled languages must be translated to the machine code of the CPU used in the computer system on which they are to execute. This translation is usually a three-step process consisting of compilation, assembly, and linking. The compilation process translates the source code (e.g., a C program) to the corresponding assembly code for the CPU used in the computer system. The assembly code is then translated to the corresponding machine code, known as object code. Finally, the object code is translated to the executable code. Figure 20.2 outlines the translation process.

The object code consists of machine instructions, but it isn't executable because the source program may have used some library functions that the assembler can't resolve references to because the code for these functions isn't in the source file(s). The linker performs the task of linking (connecting) the object code for a program and the object code in a library and generates the executable binary code.

The translation of C programs goes through a preprocessing stage before it is compiled. The **C preprocessor** translates program statements that start with the # sign. Figure 20.3 outlines the compilation process for C programs. The entire translation process is carried out by a single compiler command. We discuss various LINUX compilers later in this chapter.

## 20.4 THE SOFTWARE ENGINEERING LIFE CYCLE

A software product is developed in a sequence of phases, collectively known as the **software life cycle**. Several life-cycle models are available in the literature and used in practice. The life cycle used for a specific product depends on its size, the nature of the software to be developed (scientific, business, etc.), and the design methodol-

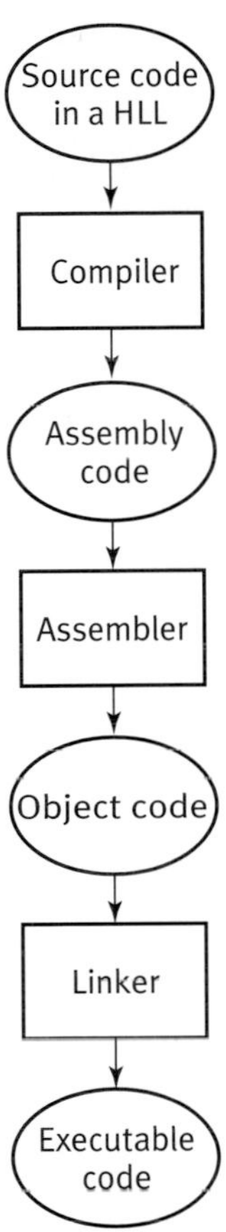


**Figure 20.2** The process of translating a high-level language program to executable code

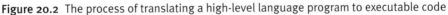

ogy used (object-oriented or classical). Some of the commonly used life-cycle models are build-and-fix, water-fall, and spiral. The common phases in most life-cycle models are requirement analysis, specifications, planning, design, coding, testing, installation, and maintenance. A full discussion of life-cycle models and their phases is outside the scope of this textbook, but we discuss the coding phase in detail—in particular, the LINUX program development tools that can be used in this phase.

The program development process consists of three steps: program generation, static analysis of the source code, and dynamic analysis of the executable code. The purpose of the **program generation phase** is to create source code and generate the executable code for the source code. Hence it involves tools for editing text files, indenting the source code properly, compiling the source code, handling module-based software, creating libraries, managing the source code, and controlling revisions. The **static analysis phase** consists of verifying the source code for portability and measuring metrics related to the source code (e.g., the number of calls to a function and the time taken by each function). The **dynamic**

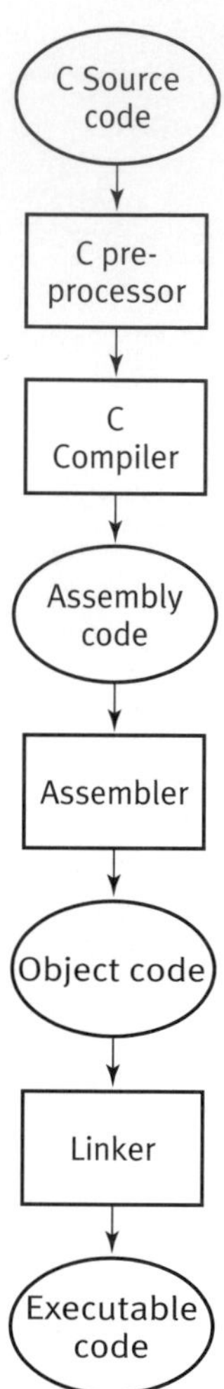


**Figure 20.3** The process of translating C programs to executable code

**analysis phase** comprises debugging, tracing, and monitoring the performance of the software, including testing it against product requirements. In the rest of this chapter we describe LINUX tools for all three steps. The depth of discussion on each tool depends on its usefulness, the frequency of its use, and how widely it is available on various LINUX platforms.

## 20.5 PROGRAM GENERATION TOOLS

The program generation phase consists of creating source code and generating the executable code for it. Hence, it involves tools for editing text files, indenting the source code properly, compiling the source code, handling module-based software, creating libraries, managing the source code, and controlling revisions. In this section we discuss the LINUX tools for supporting these tasks.

### 20.5.1 Generating C Source Files

Any text editor can be used to generate C program source files. We discussed the most frequently used LINUX editors (`pico`, `vi`, `emacs`, and `xemacs`) in Chapter 5.

### 20.5.2 Indenting C Source Code

Proper indentation of source code is an important part of good coding practice, primarily because it enhances the readability of the code. The best known indentation style for C was proposed by Brian Kernighan and Dennis Ritchie in *The C Programming Language,* the first book on the C language. This style is commonly known as the K&R (for *K*ernighan and *R*itchie) indentation style. Most programmers who do not work in C aren't familiar with this style. The LINUX `indent` command can be used to properly indent a C program. The following is a brief description of this command.

Syntax:

**indent [options] [input-files]**
**indent [options] [single-input-file] [-o output-file]**

**Purpose:** This command reads a syntactically correct program specified in 'input-file', indents it according to some commonly accepted C program structure by inserting or deleting spaces, and saves the formatted program in 'input-file' if it is specified in the command line. If the output file is not specified, the formatted version replaces the original version after saving the original version in a file that has the same name as 'input-file' and extension BAK.

**Commonly used options / features:**

`/**INDENT OFF**/`
`/**INDENT ON**/`

The source code between these two comments is not formatted by `indent`. Note that `*INDENT OFF*` and `*INDENT ON*` are strings without spaces; you can use spaces before and after these strings.

| | |
|---|---|
| `-bad` | Force blank lines after declarations |
| `-bap` | Force blank lines after function bodies |
| `-bl` | Format according to Pascal syntax |
| `-bls` | Put braces on the line after struct declaration lines |
| `-kr` | Format according to the Kernighan & Ritchie coding style |
| `-orig` | Format according to the original Berkeley coding style |
| `-st` | Send formatted program to standard output |

If no input files are specified in the command line or '-' is specified as input file, the **indent** command reads input from standard input. By default, the **indent** command formats a program according to the GNU style indentation. By default, it preserves all user newlines. In the following session, the C program code in the second.c file is indented by using various options. The **indent second.c** command saves the original file in second.c~ file and puts the indented version in the second.c file. The default indentation style is shown as the output of the **more second.c** command. The **more second.c~** command is used to display the backup of the original file. Some implementations of the indent command use the .BAK extension in place of ~.

```
$ more second.c
main()
{
int i,j;
for (i=0,j=10; i < j; i++)
{
printf("LINUX Rules the Networking World!\n");
}
}
$ indent second.c
$ ls
second.c second.c~
$ more second.c
main ()
{
  int i, j;
  for (i = 0, j = 10; i < j; i++)
    {
      printf ("LINUX Rules the Networking World!\n");
    }
}
$ more second.c~
main()
{
int i,j;
for (i=0,j=10; i<j; i++)
{
```

```
printf("LINUX Rules the Networking World!\n");
}
}
$
```

You can send the indented program to standard output by using the **-st** option. The following session demonstrates the use of these options. In the first command, the program is formatted by using the default (GNU) indentation style and displayed on the screen. You can save the formatted version of the program in a file called second.output by using the `indent -st second.c > second.output` command, as shown. You can perform the same task by using the `indent second.c -o second.out` or `cat second.c | indent -o second.out` command.

```
$ indent -st second.c
main ()
{
  int i, j;
  for (i = 0, j = 10; i < j; i++)
    {
      printf ("LINUX Rules the Networking World!\n");
    }
}
$ indent -st second.c > second.output
$
```

The following session shows how the C program can be formatted according to the popular K&R (the **-kr** option) and Berkeley coding (the **-orig** option) styles. The **-bad** option is used in the second command to insert a blank line after variable declarations.

```
$ indent -kr -st second.c
main()
{
    int i, j;
    for (i = 0, j = 10; i < j; i++) {
        printf("LINUX Rules the Networking World!\n");
    }
}
```

```
$ indent -bad -kr -st second.c
main()
{
    int i, j;

    for (i = 0, j = 10; i < j; i++) {
        printf("LINUX Rules the Networking World!\n");
    }
}
$ indent -orig -st second.c
main()
{
    int             i,
                    j;
    for (i = 0, j = 10; i < j; i++) {
        printf("LINUX Rules the Networking World!\n");
    }
}
$
```

The indentation can also be turned off and on by using the C++ comment style, `//*INDENT OFF*` and `//*INDENT ON*`. When the C style is used for turning formatting off or on, the indent program does not look for the closing */. You can, therefore, use `/**INDENT OFF*` or `/**INDENT ON*` control strings to turn indendation off or on, respectively.

**IN-CHAPTER EXERCISES**

**20.1.** Create the second.c file shown in this section and indent it according to the K&R and original Berkeley styles by using the `indent` commands.

### 20.5.3 Compiling C Programs

The most commonly used C compiler for LINUX is `gcc` (GNU C/C++ compiler). This compiler is written for ANSI C, the most recent standard for C language. The `gcc` command on LINUX systems is a symbolic link to `gcc`. All C++ compilers, such as `g++` (GNU compiler for C++), can also be used to compile C programs. The `g++` compiler invokes gcc with options necessary to make it recognize C++

source code. We primarily discuss the **gcc** compiler because it is the most widely used C compiler on LINUX platforms. The following is a brief description of the **gcc** command.

Syntax:

**gcc [options] file-list**

**Purpose:** This command can be used to invoke the C compilation system. When executed, it preprocesses, compiles, assembles, and links to generate executable code. The executable code is placed in the a.out file by default. The command accepts several types of files and processes them according to the options specified in the command line. The files can be archive files (.a extension), C source files (.c extension), C source files (.C, .cc, or .cxx extension), assembler files (.s extension), preprocessed files (.i extenstion), or object files (.o extension). When a file extension is not recognizable, the command assumes the file to be an object or library/archive file. The files are specified in 'file-list'.

**Commonly used options / features:**

| | |
|---|---|
| `-ansi` | Enforce full ANSI conformance |
| `-c` | Suppress the linking phase and keep object files (with .o extension) |
| `-g` | Create symbol table, profiling, and debugging information for use with the gdb (GNU DeBugger) |
| `-llib` | Link to the library |
| `-mconfig` | Optimize code for 'config' CPU ('config' can specify a wide variety of CPUs, including Intel 80386, 80486, Motorola 68K series, RS6000, AMD 29K series, and MIPS processors) |
| `-o file` | Create executable in 'file', instead of the default file a.out |
| `-O[level]` | Optimize. You can specify 0-3 as 'level'; generally, higher the number for 'level', the higher the level of optimization. No optimization is done if 'level' is 0. |
| `-pg` | Provide profile information to be used with the profiling tool `gprof` |
| `-S` | Do not assemble or link the .c files, and leave assembly versions in corresponding files file .s extension |
| `-v` | Verbose mode: Display commands as they are invoked |
| `-w` | Suppress warnings |
| `-W` | Give extra and more verbose warnings |

The **gcc** command can be used with and without options. We describe some basic options here and some in later sections of this chapter. One of the commonly used options, even by the beginners, is **-o**. You can use this option to inform **gcc** that it should store the executable code in a particular file in stead of the default a.out file. In the following session, we show compilation of the C program in the first.c file, with and without the **-o** option. The `gcc first.c` command produces the executable code in the a.out file and the `gcc -o slogan first.c` command produces the executable code in the slogan file. The **ls** command is used to show the names of the executable files generated by the two `gcc` commands.

```
$ cat first.c
main ()
{
      printf("LINUX Rules the Networking World!\n");
}
$ ls
first.c   second.c
$ gcc first.c
$ ls
a.out      first.c second.c
$ a.out
LINUX Rules the Networking World!
$ gcc -o slogan first.c
$ ls
a.out      first.c second.c slogan
$ slogan
LINUX Rules the Networking World!
$
```

#### DEALING WITH MULTIPLE SOURCE FILES

You can use the **gcc** command to compile and link multiple C source files and create an executable file, all in a single command line. For example, you can use the following command line to create the executable file called polish for the C source files driver.c, stack.c, and misc.c.

```
$ gcc driver.c stack.c misc.c -o polish
$
```

If one of the three source files is modified, you need to retype the entire command line, which creates two problems. First, all three files are compiled into their object modules, although only one needs recompilation, which results in longer compilation time, particularly if the files are large. Second, retyping the entire line may not be a big problem when you're dealing with three files (as here), but you certainly won't like having to do it with a much larger number of files. To avoid these problems, you should create object modules for all source files and then recompile only those modules that are updated. All the object modules are then linked together to create a single executable file.

You can use the **gcc** command with the **-c** option to create object modules for the C source files. When you compile a program with the **-c** option, the compiler leaves an object file in your current directory. The object file has the name of the source file and an .o extension. You can link multiple object files by using another **gcc** command. In the following session, we compile three source modules, driver.c, stack.c, and misc.c, separately to create their object files, and then use another **gcc** command to link them and create a single executable file, polish.

```
$ gcc -c driver.c
$ gcc -c stack.c
$ gcc -c misc.c
$ gcc misc.o stack.o driver.o -o polish
$ polish
[output of the program]
$
```

You can also compile multiple files with the **-c** option. In the first of the following command lines we compile all three source files with a single command to generate the object files. The compiler shows the names of the files as it compiles them. The order in which files are listed in the command line isn't important. The second command line links the three object files and generates one executable file, polish.

```
$ gcc -c driver.c stack.c misc.c
$ gcc misc.o stack.o driver.o -o polish
$
```

Now, if you update one of the source files, you need to generate only the object file for that source file by using the `gcc -c` command. Then you link all the ob ject files again (using the second of the **gcc** command lines) to generate the executable.

### Linking Libraries

The C compilers on LINUX systems link appropriate libraries with your program when you compile it. Sometimes, however, you have to tell the compiler explicitly to link the needed libraries. You can do so by using the **gcc** command with the **-l** option, immediately followed by the letters in the library name that follow the string lib and before the extension. Most libraries are in the /lib directory. You have to use a separate **-l** option for each library that you need to link. In the following session, we link the math library (/lib/libm.a) to the object code for the program in the power.c file. We used the first **gcc** command line to show the error message generated by the compiler if the math library is not linked. The message says that the symbol pow is not found in the file power.o (the file in which it is used). The name of the math library is libm.a, so we use the letter m (that follows the string lib and precedes the extension) with the **-l** option.

```
$ cat power.c
#include <math.h>

main()
{
        float   x,y;

        printf ("The program takes x and y from stdin and displays x^y.\n");
        printf ("Enter integer x: ");
        scanf ("%f", &x);
        printf ("Enter integer y: ");
        scanf ("%f", &y);
        printf ("x^y is: %6.3f\n", pow((double)x,(double)y));
}
$ gcc power.c -o power
/tmp/ccj67RX0.o: In function `main':
/tmp/ccj67RX0.o(.text+0x62): undefined reference to `pow'
collect2: ld returned 1 exit status
$ gcc power.c -lm -o power
$ power
The program takes x and y from stdin and displays x^y.
Enter integer x: 9.82
Enter integer y: 2.3
```

```
x^y is: 191.362
$
```

In the following In-Chapter Exercise, you will use the **gcc** compiler to create an executable for a C source file.

**IN-CHAPTER EXERCISE**

**20.2.** Create executable code for the C program in the power.c file and place it in a file called XpowerY. What command(s) line did you use? Run XpowerY to confirm that the program works properly.

### 20.5.4 Handling Module-Based C Software

Most useful C software is divided into multiple source (.c and .h) files. This software structure has several advantages over a monolithic program stored in a single file. First, it leads to more modular software, which results in smaller program files that are less time-consuming to edit, compile, test, and debug. It also allows recompilation of only those source files that are modified, rather than the entire software system. Furthermore, the multimodule structure supports **information hiding**, the key feature of object-oriented (OO) design and programming.

However, the multimodule implementation also has its disadvantages. First, you must know the files that comprise the entire system, the interdependencies of these files, and the files that have been modified since you created the last executable system. Also, when you're dealing with multimodule C software, compiling multiple files to create an executable sometimes becomes a nuisance because two long command lines have to be typed: one to create object files for all C source files, and the other to link the object files to create one executable file. An easy way out of this inconvenience is to create a simple shell script that does this work. The disadvantage of this technique is that, even if a single source file (or a header file) is modified, all object files are re-created, most of them unnecessarily.

LINUX has a much more powerful tool, called **make**, that allows you to manage compilation of multiple modules into an executable. It provides you a robust and flexible mechanism for building large-scale projects. The **make** utility reads a specification file, called makefile, that describes how the modules of a software system depend on each other. The **make** utility uses this dependency specification in the makefile and the times when various components were modified, in order to minimize the amount of recompilation. This utility is very useful when your software system consists of tens of files and several executable programs. In such a system remembering and keeping track of all header, source, object, and executable files can be a nightmare. The following is a brief description of the make utility.

Syntax:

**make [options] [targets] [macro definitions]**

**Purpose:** This utility updates a file based on the dependency relationship stored in a file, called makefile or Makefile. 'Options', 'targets', and 'macro definitions' can be specified in any order.

**Commonly used options/features:**

| | |
|---|---|
| `-d` | Display debugging information |
| `-f file` | This option allows you to instruct the `make` utility to read interdependency specification from 'file'; without this option, the file name is treated as makefile or Makefile. A file name '-' implies standard input. |
| `-h` | Display a brief description of all options |
| `-n` | Do not run any makefile commands; just display them |
| `-s` | Run in silent mode, without displaying any messages |

The make utility is based on interdependencies of files, target files that need to be built (e.g., executable or object file(s)), and commands that are to be executed to build the target files. These interdependencies, targets, and commands are specified in the makefile as **make rules**. The following is the syntax of a make rule.

Syntax:

**target-list: dependency-list**
**<Tab> command-list**

**Purpose:** The syntax of a make rule

Here, 'target-list' is a list of target files separated by one or more spaces, 'dependency-list' is a list of files separated by one or more spaces that the target files depend on, and 'command-list' is a list of commands, separated by the newline character, that have to be executed to create the target files. Each command in the 'command-list' starts with the <Tab> character. The comment lines start with the # character. An alternative syntax for a make rule is `target-list: dependency-list; command-list` where 'command-list' is a series of commands separated by semicolons. No tabs should precede targets.

The makefile consists of a list of make rules that describe the dependency relationships between files that are used to create an executable file. The **make** utility uses the rules in the makefile to determine which of the files that comprise your program need to be recompiled and relinked to re-create the executable. Thus, for example, if you modify a header (.h) file, the **make** utility recompiles all those files that include this header file. The files that contain this header file must be specified in the corresponding makefile. The directory that contains the source files and the makefile is commonly called the build directory.

The following makefile can be used for the power program discussed in Section 20.5.3.

```
$ cat makefile
#  Sample makefile for the power program
#  Remember: each command line starts with a TAB

power: power.c
       gcc power.c -o power -lm
$
```

If the executable file power exists and the source file power.c hasn't been modified since the executable file was created, running **make** will give the message that the executable file is up to date for power.c. Therefore **make** has no need to recompile and relink power.c. At times you will need to force remaking of an executable because (for example) one of the system header files included in your source has changed. In order to force re-creation of the executable, you will need to change the last update time. One commonly used method for doing so is to use the **touch** command and rerun **make**. The following session illustrates these points.

```
$ make
make: 'power' is up to date.
$ touch power.c
$ make
gcc power.c -o power -lm
$
```

When you use the **touch** command with one or more existing files as its arguments, it sets their last update time to the current time. When used with a nonexistent file as an argument, it creates a zero length file (empty file) with that name.

In the following In-Chapter Exercise, you will use the **make** command to create an executable for a single source file.

**IN-CHAPTER EXERCISE**

**20.3.** Create the executable code for the C program in the power.c file and place it in a file called XpowerY. Use the **make** utility to perform this task, by using the makefile given above. Run XpowerY to confirm that the program works properly.

In order to show a next level use of the **make** utility, we partition the C program in the power.c file into two files: power.c and compute.c. The following session shows the contents of these files. The compute.c file contains the **compute** function, which is called from the **main** function in power.c. To generate the executable in the power file, we need to compile the two source files independently and then link them, as shown in the two **gcc** command lines at the end of the session.

```
$ cat power.c
double compute(double x, double y);
main()
{
        float   x,y;

        printf ("The program takes x and y from stdin and displays x^y.\n");
        printf ("Enter integer x: ");
        scanf ("%f", &x);
        printf ("Enter integer y: ");
        scanf ("%f", &y);
        printf ("x^y is: %6.3f\n", compute(x,y));
}
$ cat compute.c
#include <math.h>
double compute (double x, double y)
{
        return (pow ((double) x, (double) y));
}
$ gcc -c compute.c power.c
```

```
$ gcc compute.o power.o -o power -lm
$
```

The dependency relationship of the two source files is quite simple in this case. To create the executable file power, we need two object modules: power.o and compute.o. If either of the two files power.c or compute.c is updated, the executable needs to be re-created. Figure 20.4 shows this first cut on the dependency relationship.

The make rule corresponding to this dependency relationship is therefore the following. Note that the math library has to be linked because the **compute** function in the compute.c file uses the **pow** function in this library.

```
power: power.o compute.o
       gcc power.o compute.o -o power -lm
```

We also know that the object file power.o is built from the source file power.c and that the object file compute.o is built from the source file compute.c. Figure 20.5 shows the second cut on the dependency relationship.

Thus the make rules for creating the two object files are as follows.

```
power.o: power.c
         gcc -c power.c
compute.o: compute.c
         gcc -c compute.c
```

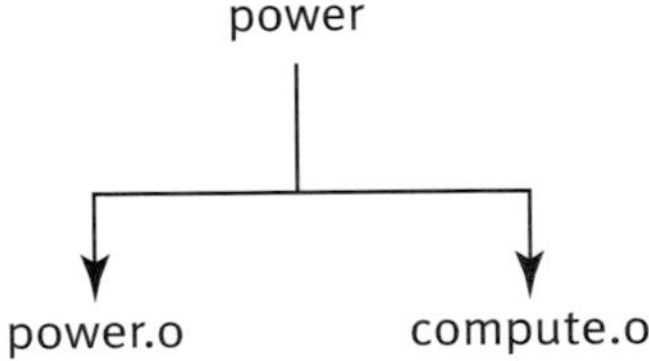


**Figure 20.4** First cut on the make dependency tree

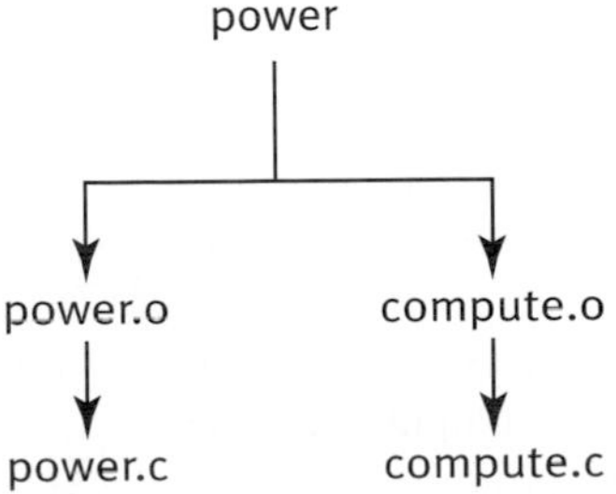


**Figure 20.5** Second cut on the make dependency tree

The final makefile is shown in the following session. Note that the rules are separated by one blank line for clarity; the **make** utility doesn't require a blank line between make rules.

```
$ cat makefile
power: power.o compute.o
        gcc power.o compute.o -o power -lm

power.o: power.c
        gcc -c power.c

compute.o: compute.c
        gcc -c compute.c
$
```

The following is an execution of the **make** utility with the preceding makefile. Note the order in which the commands for the three make rules execute. The command for generating the executable file, as expected, runs at the end.

```
$ make
gcc -c power.c
gcc -c compute.c
gcc power.o compute.o -o power -lm
$
```

In the following In-Chapter Exercise, you will use the **make** utility to create the executable code for a C source code that is partitioned into two files.

## IN-CHAPTER EXERCISE

**20.4.** Create the two source files power.c and compute.c and follow the steps just discussed to create the executable file power by using the **make** utility.

We now change the structure of our software and divide it into six files called main.c, compute.c, input.c, compute.h, input.h, and main.h. The contents of these files are shown in the following session. Note that the compute.h and input.h files contain declarations (prototypes) of the **compute** and **input** functions but not their definitions; the definitions are in the compute.c and input.c files. The main.h file contains two prompts to be displayed to the user.

```
$ cat compute.h
/* Declaration/Prototype of the "compute" function */
double compute(double, double);
$ cat input.h
/* Declaration/Prototype of the "input" function */
double input (char *);
$ cat main.h
/* Declaration of prompts to users */
#define PROMPT1 "Enter the value of x: "
#define PROMPT2 "Enter the value of y: "
$ cat compute.c
#include <math.h>
#include "compute.h"
double compute (double x, double y)
{
        return (pow ((double) x, (double) y));
}
$ cat input.c
#include "input.h"

double input(char *s)
{
        float x;

        printf ("%s", s);
        scanf ("%f", &x);
        return (x);
}
$ cat main.c
#include "main.h"
#include "compute.h"
#include "input.h"

main()
{
        double x, y;
```

```
        printf ("The program takes x and y from stdin and displays x^y.\n");
        x = input(PROMPT1);
        y = input(PROMPT2);
        printf ("x^y is: %6.3f\n", compute(x,y));
}
$
```

To generate the executable for the software, you need to generate the object files for the three source files and link them into a single executable. The following commands are needed to accomplish this task. Note that, as before, you need to link the math library while linking the compute.o file to generate the executable in the power file.

```
$ gcc -c main.c input.c compute.c
$ gcc main.o input.o compute.o -o power -lm
$
```

Figure 20.6 shows the dependency relationship between these files.

The makefile corresponding to this dependency relationship is

```
$ cat  makefile
power: main.o input.o compute.o
        gcc main.o input.o compute.o -o power -lm

main.o: main.c main.h input.h compute.h
        gcc -c main.c

input.o: input.c input.h
        gcc -c input.c
```

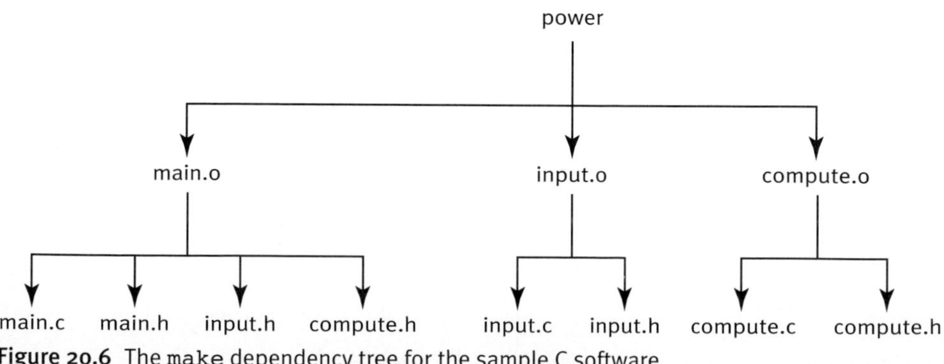


**Figure 20.6** The make dependency tree for the sample C software

```
compute.o: compute.c compute.h
        gcc -c compute.c
$
```

Execution of the **make** command results in the execution of the rules associated with all targets in the makefile.

```
$ make
gcc -c main.c
gcc -c input.c
gcc -c compute.c
gcc main.o input.o compute.o -o power -lm
$
```

In the following In-Chapter Exercise, you will use the **make** utility to create an executable for a multimodule C source.

## IN-CHAPTER EXERCISE

**20.5.** Create the three source and header files just discussed and then use the **make** command to create the executable in the file power. Use the preceding makefile to perform your task.

If the make rules are in a file other than makefile (or Makefile), you need to run the **make** command with the **-f** option, as in **make -f my.makefile**.

The make rules as shown in the preceding makefile contain some redundant commands that can be removed. The **make** utility has a predefined rule that invokes the **gcc -c xxx.c -o xxx.o** command for every rule, as in

```
xxx.o: xxx.c zzz.h
       gcc -c xxx.c
```

Furthermore, the **make** utility recognizes that the name of an object file is usually the name of the source file. This capability is known as a standard dependency, and because of it you can leave xxx.c from the dependency list corresponding to the target xxx.o. The following makefile therefore works as well as the one given previously.

```
$ cat makefile
power: main.o input.o compute.o
         gcc main.o input.o compute.o -o power -lm
```

```
main.o: main.h input.h compute.h
input.o: input.h
compute.o: compute.h
$
```

Running the **make** command with this makefile produces the following result.

```
$ make
gcc    -c main.c -o main.o
gcc    -c input.c -o input.o
gcc    -c compute.c -o compute.o
gcc main.o input.o compute.o -o power -lm
$
```

The **make** utility supports simple macros that allow simple text substitution. You must define the macros before using them; they are usually placed at the top of the makefile. A macro definition can have one of the following two forms.

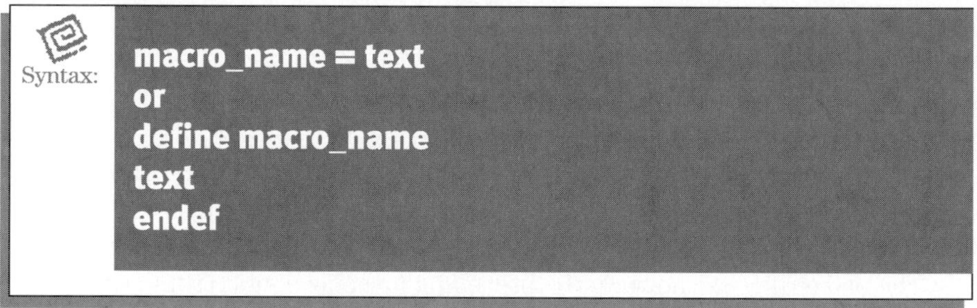

Syntax:
macro_name = text
or
define macro_name
text
endef


With this rule in place, 'text' is substituted for every occurrence of $('macro_name') in the rest of the makefile. In addition, the **make** utility has some built-in macros, such as *CFLAGS*, that are set to default values and are used by the built-in rules, such as execution of the `gcc $(CFLAGS) -c xxx.c -o xxx.o` command for a predefined rule, as previously described. The default value of the *CFLAGS* macro is usually *-O* (for optimization), but it can be changed to any other flag(s) for the **gcc** compiler. On our system *CFLAGS* is set to null; no options. The **make** utility uses several built-in macros for the built-in rules.

The following makefile shows the use of **user-defined macros** and some useful make rules that can be invoked at the command line. It also shows that the commands for make rules are not always compiler or linker commands; they can be any shell commands.

```
$ cat makefile
CC = gcc
OPTIONS = -03 -o
OBJECTS = main.o input.o compute.o
SOURCES = main.c input.c compute.c
HEADERS = main.h input.h compute.h

power: $(OBJECTS)
        $(CC) $(OPTIONS) power $(OBJECTS) -lm

main.o: main.h input.h compute.h

input.o: input.h

compute.o: compute.h

all.tar: $(SOURCES) $(HEADERS) makefile
        tar -cvf - $(SOURCES) $(HEADERS) makefile > all.tar

clean:
        rm *.o
$
```

When the **make** command is executed, the commands for the last two targets (all.tar and clean) are not executed, because these targets do not depend on anything and nothing depends on them. You can invoke the commands associated with these targets by passing the targets as parameters to the **make** command. The advantage of putting these rules in the makefile is that you don't have to remember which files to archive (by using the **tar** command in this case) and which to remove once the final executable has been created. The **make clean** command invokes the `rm *.o` command to remove all object files that are created in the process of creating the executable for the software. The following session shows the output of **make** when executed with two targets as command line arguments. The tar archive is placed in the all.tar file.

```
$ make all.tar clean
tar -cvf - main.c input.c compute.c main.h input.h compute.h makefile > all.tar
main.c
input.c
compute.c
```

```
main.h
input.h
compute.h
makefile
rm *.o
$
```

The **make** utility has several built-in (internal) macros that you can use for brevity. Some of the commonly used internal macros and what they stand for are described in Table 20.1.

We update our makefile to incorporate the use of some of these internal macros. The updated makefile and some sample runs of the **make** command are shown in the following session. Note that when a command in the command list for a target is preceded by @, it is not echoed when the **make** utility is executing (i.e., building the target). Of course, you can display these (and other makefile commands) by executing the **make -n** command. We have also used an alternative syntax for the definition of the CC macro. The command for the clean target has been changed to force the removal of the executable file power, any core file, and all object files.

```
$ more makefile
# Updated makefile that uses some built-in macros and
# @-preceded commands

define CC
    gcc
endef
OPTIONS = -O3 -o
```

**Table 20.1** Some Commonly Used Internal Macros for the make Utility

| Internal Macro | Meaning |
|---|---|
| $@ | The name of the current target. When used in make rules for making libraries, it stands for the library name |
| $? | The list of dependencies (i.e., the files that a target depends on) that have changed more recently than the current target |
| $< | The name of the current dependency that has been modified more recently than the current target |
| $^ | A space-separated list of all dependencies without duplications |

```
OBJECTS = main.o input.o compute.o
SOURCES = main.c input.c compute.c
HEADERS = main.h input.h compute.h

complete: power
        @echo "Build complete"
power: $(OBJECTS)
        $(CC) $(OPTIONS) $@ $^ -lm
        @echo "The executable is in the 'power' file."
main.o: main.h input.h compute.h
compute.o: compute.h
input.o: input.h
all.tar: $(SOURCES) $(HEADERS) makefile
        tar -cvf - $^ > all.tar
clean:
        rm -f *.o core power
$ make
gcc    -c main.c -o main.o
gcc    -c input.c -o input.o
gcc    -c compute.c -o compute.o
gcc -O3 -o power main.o input.o compute.o -lm
The executable is in the 'power' file.
Build complete
$ make all.tar clean
tar -cvf - main.c input.c compute.c main.h input.h
compute.h makefile > all.tar
main.c
input.c
compute.c
main.h
input.h
compute.h
makefile
rm -f *.o core power
$
```

You can invoke the command for cleaning without any problem if the current directory does not have a file called clean. If a file called clean did exist in your current directory, invocation of the command results in the message **make: 'clean' is up to date.**, as shown.

```
$ touch clean
$ make clean
make: 'clean' is up to date.
$
```

You can use a special target file, called .PHONY, to overcome this problem. The dependency for .PHONY is clean and there is no command list. The updated lines that take care of the problem follow, along with the invocation of the rule for cleaning.

```
$ more makefile
...
.PHONY: clean
clean:
        rm -f *.o core power
$ touch clean
$ make clean
rm -f *.o core power
$
```

In the following In-Chapter Exercise, you will run the preceding makefile sessions on your system to further enhance your understanding of the `make` utility.

**IN-CHAPTER EXERCISE**

**20.6.** Use the preceding makefile to create the executable in the file power. Go through all the sessions discussed in this section.

### 20.5.5 Creating, Modifying, and Extracting from Libraries/Archives

The LINUX operating system allows you to archive (bundle) object files into a single library file. In other words, it allows you to use the name of one file instead of a number of object files in a makefile and allows function-level software reuse of C programs. The `ar` tool, also called a **librarian**, allows you to perform this task. The following is a brief description of this utility.

Syntax:

**ar key archive-name [file-list]**

**Purpose:** This utility allows creation and manipulation of archives. For example, it can be used to create an archive of the object files in 'file-list' and store it in the file called 'archive-file'

**Commonly used options/features:**

| | |
|---|---|
| `d` | Delete a file from an archive |
| `q` | Append a file to an existing archive |
| `r` | Create a new archive or overwrite an existing archive |
| `t` | Display the table of contents of an archive |
| `s` | Force generation of the archive symbol table |
| `x` | Extract one or more files from an archive and store them in the current working directory |
| `v` | Generate a verbose output |

The 'archive-name' must end with the .a extension. Once an archive file has been created for a set of object modules, these modules can be accessed by the C compiler and the LINUX loader (`ld`) by specifying the archive file as an argument. (The `ld` command can be used to explicitly link object files and libraries.) The compiler or the loader automatically links the object modules needed from the archive.

A key is like an option for a command. However, unlike with most LINUX commands, you don't have to insert a hyphen (`-`) before a key for the `ar` command, but you can use it if you want to. In the following examples of the `ar` command, we do not insert a hyphen before a key.

#### Creating an Archive

You can create an archive by using the `ar` command with the `r` key. The following command line creates an archive of the input.o and compute.o files in mathlib.a. Note that we have not used `-r`, although we could have.

```
$ ar r mathlib.a input.o compute.o
$
```

If mathlib.a exists, the command line overwrites it with the new archive. Once the archive has been created in your current directory, you can link it to the main.c file by using the compiler command

```
$ gcc main.c mathlib.a -o power -lm
$
```

You can use the q key to append the object modules at the end of an existing archive. Thus, in the following example, the object modules input.o and compute.o are appended at the end of the existing archive mathlib.a. If the mathlib.a archive doesn't exist, it is created.

```
$ ar q mathlib.a input.o compute.o
$
```

Once you have created an archive of some object modules, you can remove the original modules, as in

```
$ rm compute.o input.o
$
```

If you want to archive all of the object files in your current directory in the newlib.a archive, you can use the following command.

```
$ ar r newlib.a `ls *.o`
$
```

The command sbustitution is used to generate names of all the object files in the current directory.

#### Displaying the Table of Contents

You can display the table of contents of an archive by using the `ar` command with the `t` key. The following command displays the table of contents of the mathlib.a archive.

```
$ ar t mathlib.a
input.o
compute.o
$
```

#### Deleting Object Modules from an Archive

You can delete one or more object modules from an archive by using the `ar` command with the `d` key. In the following session, the first `ar` command deletes the object module input.o from the mathlib.a archive, and the second displays the new table of contents (confirming the removal of input.o object module from the archive).

```
$ ar d mathlib.a input.o
$ ar t mathlib.a
compute.o
$
```

### Extracting Object Modules from an Archive

You can extract one or more object modules from an archive by using the **ar** command with the **x** key. The following command line can be used to extract the object module compute.o from the mathlib.a archive and put it in your current directory.

```
$ ar x mathlib.a compute.o
$
```

Although we have shown the use of the **ar** command from the command line, you can also run the command as part of a makefile so that an archive of the object files of a software product is created after the executable file has been created. Doing so allows future use of any general-purpose object modules (one or more functions in these modules) created as part of the software. It can be done by putting an archiving command in the command list for the last target, such as 'power' in our makefile.

We enhance our makefile so that the compute.o and input.o object modules are appended to the mathlib.a library after the final executable has been created. The following session shows the resultant makefile and a sample run of the make command.

```
$ more makefile
# Updated makefile that uses some built-in macros and
# @-preceded commands. It also archives some of the
# newly generated object modules in a library.

CC = gcc
OPTIONS = -O3 -o
OBJECTS = main.o input.o compute.o
SOURCES = main.c input.c compute.c
HEADERS = main.h input.h compute.h
ARCHIVE = compute.o input.o
LIBRARY = mathlib.a
AR_KEYS = qv

complete: power
	@echo "The build is complete"
```

```
power: $(OBJECTS)
        $(CC) $(OPTIONS) $@ $^ -lm
        @echo "The executable is in the 'power' file."
        @echo
        @echo "Archiving object modules ..."
        ar $(AR_KEYS) $(LIBRARY) $(ARCHIVE)
        @echo
        @echo "Archiving is complete."
        @echo
main.o: main.h input.h compute.h
compute.o: compute.h
input.o: input.h
all.tar: $(SOURCES) $(HEADERS) makefile
        tar -cvf - $^ > all.tar
.PHONY: clean
clean:
        rm -f *.o core power
$ make
gcc    -c main.c -o main.o
gcc    -c input.c -o input.o
gcc    -c compute.c -o compute.o
gcc -O3 -o power main.o input.o compute.o -lm
The executable is in the 'power' file.

Archiving object modules ...
ar qv mathlib.a compute.o input.o
a - compute.o
a - input.o

Archiving is complete.

The build is complete
$
```

In the following In-Chapter Exercise, you will use the `ar` command with various options to appreciate its various characteristics in dealing with libraries of object files.

## IN-CHAPTER EXERCISE

**20.7.** Use the commands just discussed to create an archive, delete an object file from the archive, display the table of contents for an archive, and extract an object file from the archive. Show your work.

### ORDERING ARCHIVES

Object files aren't maintained in any particular order in an archive file created by the `ar` command; the order is dependent on the order in which the modules were inserted in the archive. The `ranlib` command can be used to add a table of contents to one or more archives that are passed as its parameters. This utility performs the same task as the `ar` command with the `s` key. An archive with such a table of contents speeds up the linking phase and allows functions in the archive to call each other, regardless of their location in the archive. The following is a brief description of the `ranlib` command.

Syntax:

**ranlib [-vV] archive-list**

**Purpose:** This utility generates and adds a table of contents (an index) to each archive in 'archive-list'

The following `ranlib` command adds a table of contents to the mathlib.a archive. The `ar s mathlib.a` command can also be used to perform the same task.

```
$ ranlib mathlib.a
$
```

The `ranlib -v` command displays the version number of `ranlib`.

### DISPLAYING LIBRARY INFORMATION

The `nm` utility can be used to display the symbol table (names, types, sizes, entry points, etc.) of library and object files. The command displays one line for each object (function and global variable) in a library or object file. The output informs you about the functions available in a library and the functions that these library functions depend on. The information displayed by the `nm` utility is useful for debugging libraries. The following is a brief description of the utility.

**nm [options] [objectfile-list]**

**Purpose:** Display the symbol table of the object and library files in 'objectfile-list'; if no object file is given, use the a.out file

**Commonly used options / features:**

| | |
|---|---|
| `-D` | Display dynamic symbols only (useful when working with dynamic libraries) |
| `-V` | Display the version number of **nm** on standard error |
| `-f format` | Display output in 'format', which can be bsd, sysv, or posix; default is bsd |
| `-g` | Display external symbols only |
| `-l` | For each symbol, find and display the filename and line number. |
| `-n, -v` | Sort external symbols by address |
| `-u` | Display only the undefined symbols, those external to each object module |

In the following session, the **nm -V** command is used to display the version of the **nm** command, and the **nm mathlib.a** command is used to display the information about the mathlib.a library that we created earlier in this section. The **-n** option is used to display external symbols by address, that is, according to their order in the object files in the mathlib.a library. The output of the **nm -n mathlib.a** command shows, for example, that the printf call is made before the scanf call in the input.o object module.

```
$ nm -V
GNU nm 2.9.1
Copyright 1997 Free Software Foundation, Inc.
This program is free software; you may redistribute it under the terms of
the GNU General Public License. This program has absolutely no warranty.
$ nm mathlib.a

compute.o:
00000000 T compute
00000000 t gcc2_compiled.
         U pow
```

```
input.o:
00000000 t gcc2_compiled.
00000000 T input
         U printf
         U scanf

$ nm -n mathlib.a

compute.o:
         U pow
00000000 T compute
00000000 t gcc2_compiled.

input.o:
         U printf
         U scanf
00000000 t gcc2_compiled.
00000000 T input
$

$ nm -l /usr/lib/libc.a
...
ctype.o:
         U __ctype_b          (null):0
         U __ctype_tolower    (null):0
         U __ctype_toupper    (null):0
00000000 t gcc2_compiled.
00000000 T isalnum
00000018 T isalpha
00000034 T iscntrl
0000004c T isdigit
00000084 T isgraph
00000068 T islower
000000a0 T isprint
000000bc T ispunct
000000d4 T isspace
000000f0 T isupper
```

```
0000010c T isxdigit
0000010c T isxdigit
00000128 T tolower
00000148 T toupper
...
$
```

In the following example, we use the `-f` and `-l` options to display the symbol table for the bugged.o file with line numbers in the System V format. The output shows the absolute pathname of the C source file and line number where a symbol occurs. The line numbers are listed after the file names, such as, get_input on line 31 in the bugged.c file. The class U means that it is an undefined symbol, usually an external variable, a library function, or a function in another object module.

```
$ nm -f sysv -l bugged.o

Symbols from bugged.o:
Name                  Value    Class        Type         Size   Line   Section
get_input           |000000b0|   T  |                    |      |      |
/home/faculty/sarwar/linuxbook/chapters/ch20/bugged.c:31
getchar             |        |   U  |                    |      |      |
/home/faculty/sarwar/linuxbook/chapters/ch20/bugged.c:37
main                |00000010|   T  |                    |      |      |
/home/faculty/sarwar/linuxbook/chapters/ch20/bugged.c:13
malloc              |        |   U  |                    |      |      |
/home/faculty/sarwar/linuxbook/chapters/ch20/bugged.c:34
mcount              |        |   U  |                    |      |      |
/home/faculty/sarwar/linuxbook/chapters/ch20/bugged.c:13
null_function1      |00000070|   T  |                    |      |      |
/home/faculty/sarwar/linuxbook/chapters/ch20/bugged.c:25
null_function2      |00000090|   T  |                    |      |      |
/home/faculty/sarwar/linuxbook/chapters/ch20/bugged.c:28
printf              |        |   U  |                    |      |      |
/home/faculty/sarwar/linuxbook/chapters/ch20/bugged.c:19
$
```

### 20.5.6 Version Control

Studies have shown that about two-thirds of the cost of a software product is spent on maintenance. As we have mentioned before, the maintenance of a software product comprises corrective maintenance and enhancement. In corrective maintenance, the errors and bugs found after installation are fixed. In enhancement, the product is enhanced to include more features, such as an improved user interface. Regardless of its type, maintenance means changing and/or revising the source code for the product and generating new executables. As you revise source code, you may need to undo changes made to it and go back to an earlier version of the software. Moreover, if a team of programmers is working on a piece of software, each team member should be able to check out and check in editable (modifiable) versions of the software. In the remainder of the chapter, we discuss the LINUX tools that support such features. We use the terms *revision*, *version*, *release*, and *delta* interchangeably.

**Version control** is the task of managing revisions to a software product. Typical software for version control allows you to

- lock out other users from changing a file while one user is altering it (provide a check-out and check-in system of file access);
- create different versions of a file;
- help identify revisions to a file;
- store and retrieve different versions of a file;
- merge multiple versions of the same file to create a new "final" file;
- maintain a history of all versions of every file related to a product;
- access earlier versions of all the files of a product; and
- limit access to a file to a subset of users on the system.

Several LINUX tools allow you to control versions of your files and almost all of them use the Revision Control System (RCS) as their engine. We discuss RCS and CVS (Concurrent Version System).

### The Revision Control System (RCS)

The **Revision Control System (RCS)** was designed to perform all of the version control tasks. In RCS, the version numbers start with 1.1. When you request a particular version of a file, RCS starts with the latest version and makes changes in it to re-create the requested version. The RCS way of creating a version is usually faster because most people work forward and create a newer version based on the current version, rather than on an older version. The version numbers in RCS are maintained in the format release.level.branch.sequence.

RCS maintains several versions of a file in a special "rcs-format." You can't edit this file by using normal LINUX editors such as `vi`. But, once this file has been created, you can access a version of your original file by using RCS-specific commands to create a new version (check-out and check-in procedures), view the current editing activity on an RCS file, or view revisions made to the file. We describe the commands for performing the most common tasks. All the RCS utilities are in the /usr/bin directory. Add this directory to your search path (in the shell variable ***PATH*** or `path`) if it isn't already there.

*Working with RCS* The first step to using RCS is to create a directory called RCS in the directory that contains the files you want to manage with RCS. This directory contains the revision control information on your files, including the latest version of each file, along with the information that can be used by RCS to create previous versions. An access list is maintained for every RCS file that contains the login names of the users who can access the file. Login names can be added to or deleted from the list.

*Creating an RCS History File* The **`ci`** command is used to create and manage RCS history files. The following is a brief description of the utility.

Syntax:

**ci [options] filename**

**Purpose:** This utility allows creating and administering RCS history files; names of history files have ',v' postfix

**Commonly used options/features:**

| | |
|---|---|
| `-f [rev]` | Check in a revision even if it is not different from the preceding one. |
| `-l [rev]` | Check in a revision and immediately check out again and lock it. |
| `-r`ver | Check in the modified file as version number 'ver' |
| `-u` | Check in a file but keep a read-only version and remove any lock. |

Along with the access list, an RCS file contains multiple revisions of the text, a change log, descriptive text, and some control attributes such as file lock. In order for you to access a file, you must be its owner or the super user, or your login name must be on the access list.

Once you have created an RCS history file, you can remove the original. From now on you will access the source file by using the RCS-specific commands, and these files work with RCS history files only. In the following session, we use the **`ci`** command to create (check in) an RCS history file called RCS/input.c,v. After depositing a new revision, **`ci`** prompts you for a log message that you can enter to summarize the change. This message must be terminated with a `<Ctrl-D>` or period (.) on a new line.

```
$ ci input.c
RCS/input.c,v <-- input.c
enter description, terminated with single '.' or end of file:
NOTE: This is NOT the log message!
>> Initial version of the input.c file created by Syed Mansoor Sarwar
>> .
initial version: 1.1
done
$
```

After creating the RCS/input.c,v file, the `ci` command removes the original file, input.c. You can use the `-u` option to check in a file and keep a read-only copy of the original in the current directory. In the following example, we check in the input.c file but keep a read-only, as shown by the output of the `ls -l input.c` command. The `ci` command did not prompt for a log message because the file was not changed. If the file is updated the check in command prompts you for a log message, as shown later.

```
$ ci -u input.c
RCS/input.c,v  <--  input.c
ci: RCS/input.c,v: no lock set by sarwar
$ ls -l input.c
-r--------    1 sarwar  faculty       137 Mar 15 14:31 input.c
$
```

In the following In-Chapter Exercise, you will use the `ci` command to create an RCS history file.

**IN-CHAPTER EXERCISE**

**20.8.** Create the RCS history file for input.c. What command(s) did you use? What is the pathname of the history file?

*Checking Out an RCS File* The `co` utility is used to check out a file and store it in the corresponding working file. The following is a brief description of the utility.

Syntax:

## co [options] file-list

**Purpose:** This utility allows checking out of files in 'file-list' from the corresponding RCS history file, and storing them in the corresponding working files.

**Commonly used options/features:**

| | |
|---|---|
| `-l` | Check out a file for editing in locked mode |
| `-rver` | Check out 'ver' version of the specified file |
| `-u[ver]` | Check out an unreserved (read-only) version of the specified file |
| `-v` | Display version number of RCS |

Without any option, the **co** command checks out a read-only copy of the file. The **-l** option is used to check out a file for editing. The use of this option locks the file so that only one user can check it out for editing. You can use the following command to check out input.c for editing.

```
$ co -l input.c
RCS/input.c,v --> input.c
revision 1.1 (locked)
done
$
```

After you have finished editing input.c, you can check in its new version by using the **ci** command. In the following session, we check in a new version of input.c and keep a read-only copy of it in the current directory.

```
$ ci -u input.c
RCS/input.c,v <-- input.c
new release: 1.2; previous revision: 1.1
enter log message, terminated with single '.' or end of file
>> Added a comment header to the file.
>> .
done
$
```

Note that the new version of input.c in RCS has the same release number (1) as the locked version but a new level number (2).

If a particular revision of a file has been checked out for editing, execution of a command for checking out the same version of the file results in an exception message that gives the user the opportunity to remove the checked-out version or exit. The following command line illustrates this point. We checked out version 1.1 of the input.c file before issuing the **co** command. The command prompts the user to remove the already checked-out version or abort check out. In this case we just hit <Enter> at the prompt to abort check out.

```
$ co -l input.c
RCS/input.c,v  -->  input.c
revision 1.1 (locked)
writable input.c exists; remove it? [ny](n):<Enter>
co checkout aborted
$
```

In the following In-Chapter Exercise, you use the **co** and **ci** commands to practice check-in and check-out procedures under RCS.

**IN-CHAPTER EXERCISE**

**20.9.** Check out an editable copy of input.c, make changes to it, and check in the new version. Write the sequence of commands that you used to perform this task.

*Creating a New Version of a File* If you want to retrieve a new version of a file, you must first create it. You can create a new version of a file by using the **ci** command with the **-r** option. In the following session, version 2.1 of the input.c file is created and stored in the RCS directory. Note that we use **-r2** as a shortcut for **-r2.1**.

```
$ ci -r2 input.c
RCS/input.c,v <-- input.c
new revision: 2.1; previous revision 1.2
enter log message, terminated with single '.' or end of file
>> Just showing how a new version of a file can be created.
>> .
```

```
done
$
```

*Checking Out Copies of Specific Versions* In RCS, you can check out an existing version of a file by using the `co` command with the `-r` option. If the checked-out version has the highest revision number, the new version generated at check-in time has the same release number with the level number (or sequence number if the file is a branch of a particular release) automatically incremented by 1. If the checked-out version isn't the latest, a branch of the file is generated.

In the following session, we check out version 1 of the input.c file for editing. By default, the `co` command always checks out the highest version of a release, or version 1.2 here. Note that we used the `ci -r` command in the previous section to create a new release (release 2) of this file. A higher release exists for the input.c file, so the `ci` command created a new branch at the checked-out level, resulting in version number 1.2.1.1.

```
$ co -l -r1 input.c
RCS/input.c,v --> input.c
revision 1.2 (locked)
done
$ vi input.c
... editing session ...
$ ci input.c
RCS/input.c,v <-- input.c
new revision: 1.2.1.1; previous revision 1.2
enter log message, terminated with single '.' or end of file
>> Just showing how a branch of a file can be created.
>> .
done
$
```

To create a branch of an RCS file explicitly, we specify a version number with the branch number of the version in the `ci` command. In the following example, we create branch 1 of revision number 2.1 of input.c, resulting in the creation of version 2.1.1.1 of the file.

```
$ co -l input.c
RCS/input.c,v --> input.c
```

```
revision 2.1 (locked)
done
$ vi input.c
... editing session ...
$ ci -r2.1.1 input.c
RCS/input.c,v <-- input.c
new revision: 2.1.1.1; previous revision 2.1
enter log message, terminated with single '.' or end of file
>> Just showing how a branch of a file can be created explicitly.
>> .
done
$
```

Figure 20.7 illustrates how revision numbers of the input.c file are related. The first (left-most) digit is the release number, the second digit is the level number, the third digit is the branch number, and the fourth (right-most) digit is the sequence number.

In the following In-Chapter Exercise, you will use the **co** and **ci** commands to create specific versions of a file.

## IN-CHAPTER EXERCISE

**20.10.** Create versions 1.2 and 2.1 of the input.c file. What command lines did you use?

*Abandoning Changes* If you've made changes to a file that didn't work out, you can undo the changes and uncheck out the file by using the **rcs** utility. The following is a brief description of the **rcs** utility.

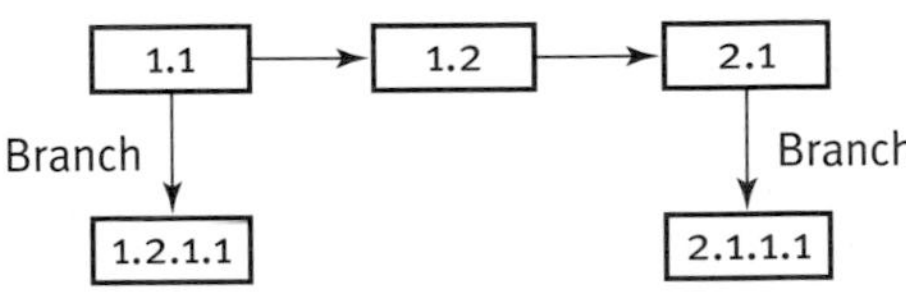


**Figure 20.7** The version tree for input.c

Syntax:

## rcs [options] file-list

**Purpose:** This utility allows control of RCS files, that is, it allows their attributes to be changed

**Commonly used options / features:**

| | |
|---|---|
| `-alogins` | Add the login names in the comma-separated list 'logins' to the access list (i.e., allow the users in 'logins' to check out editable versions of the files specified 'file-list' and check them back in) |
| `-e[logins]` | Remove the login names in the comma-separated list 'logins' from the access list (i.e., disallow the users in 'login' to check out editable versions of files in 'file-list') |
| `-l[rev]` | Check out revision 'rev' of a file without overwriting it, i.e., lock revision 'rev'; use the latest revision of 'rev' is not specified |
| `-orange` | Remove versions of a file given 'range'; the range rev1:rev2 means revisions from 'rev1' to 'rev2'; :rev means from the beginning of the branch containing 'rev' up to (and including) 'rev'; rev: means revision from revision 'rev' to the end of the branch containing 'rev' |
| `-u[rev]` | Unlock revision 'rev': abandon changes made to the file and uncheck out the file |

When you check out a file with the `co -l` command, it is locked and you can edit it and install changes made to the file by using the `ci` command. If the file is unlocked, the `ci` command does not install the changes made to the file. You can use the `rcs -u` command to unlock a file checked out for editing. Although a copy of the checked out file remains in your directory, any changes made to it before and after unlocking it cannot be installed in the RCS file. In order for you to be able to install changes made to the file, you must relock it or check it out again, overwriting the existing (unlocked) version. In the following session, we check out the input.c file by using the `co -l` command, save a backup copy of the file in input.c.bak, make changes to the checked out file, and unlock it with the `rcs -u input.c` command. We then use the `ci` command to install changes made to the file. Although the `ci` command does not tell us so, the changes made to the file are not installed. We confirm this by checking out the input.c file again and comparing it with the previously saved file input.c.bak.

```
$ co -l input.c
RCS/input.c,v  -->  input.c
revision 2.1 (locked)
done
$ cp input.c input.c.bak
$ vi input.c
...
$ rcs -u input.c
RCS file: RCS/input.c,v
2.1 unlocked
done
$ ci input.c
RCS/input.c,v  <--  input.c
ci: RCS/input.c,v: no lock set by sarwar
$ co -l input.c
RCS/input.c,v  -->  input.c
revision 2.1 (locked)
writable input.c exists; remove it? [ny](n): y
done
$ diff input.c input.c.bak
$
```

*Locking a File Without Overwriting (Taking Care of a Mistake)* When you execute the `ci -u input.c` command, a read-only copy of input.c is left in your current directory. A word of caution: If you change permissions for input.c to make it writable and make changes to it, these changes can be problematic because they cannot be installed in the RCS/filename,v file in the RCS database because you didn't properly check out an editable version of the file by using the `co -l input.c` command.

You can overcome this problem by locking input.c with the `rcs -l` command without checking it out from the RCS directory and overwriting the existing file (that you updated by mistake). This command followed by the `ci -u input.c` command installs the changes in the RCS/input.c,v file and leaves a read-only copy in the current directory. This command creates a new version. The following session illustrates these points.

```
$ co -u input.c
RCS/input.c,v  -->  input.c
revision 1.2 (unlocked)
done
$ chmod 700 input.c
$ vi input.c
...
$ ci input.c
RCS/input.c,v  <--  input.c
ci no lock set by sarwar
$ rcs -l input.c
RCS file: RCS/input.c,v
1.2 locked
done
$ ci -u input.c
RCS/input.c,v  <--  input.c
new revision: 1.3; previous revision: 1.2
enter log message, terminated with single '.' or end of file
>> Demonstrated file locking.
>> .
done
$
```

*Removing a Version* RCS allows you to remove any (including nonleaf) version of a file by using the `rcs` command with the `-o` option. If the removed version is an intermediate version, the remaining versions are not renumbered. In the following session, we remove version 1.1 of input.c.

```
$ rcs -o1.1 input.c
RCS file: RCS/input.c,v
deleting revision 1.1
done
$
```

A range of versions can be deleted by specifying the range after the **-o** option. For example, the **rcs -o2.1:3.2 input.c** command deletes versions 2.1 through 3.2 of the input.c file. Similarly, the **rcs -o:2.2 input.c** command deletes versions 1.1 through 2.2 (including 2.2) of the input.c file and **rcs -o4.1: input.c** command deletes versions 4.1 on of the input.c file (including 4.1).

The following In-Chapter Exercise has been designed to enhance your understanding of the versions of a file in RCS. The exercise particularly asks you to use the **rcs -o** command to delete a version of a file.

## IN-CHAPTER EXERCISE

**20.11.** Remove version 1.2 of the input.c file just discussed in RCS: Give the command line for performing this task.

*Working in Groups* Working in groups is quite straightforward. All you need do is place the RCS subdirectory (or subdirectories) in a shared directory. You then run all RCS utilities by specifying the complete pathnames for the RCS files and editing files in your local directories. An alternative to creating a common shared directory is to maintain all RCS directories in one user's directory and create symbolic links (see Chapter 11) to this directory in the directories of the remaining members of the group. Of course, appropriate access privileges must be set for all components in the pathname for the RCS directory.

In the following session, we check out an editable version of the input.c file, assuming that the only RCS directory is in the /home/shared directory.

```
$ co -l /home/shared/RCS/input.c,v
RCS/input.c,v --> input.c
revision 2.1.1.1 (locked)
done
$
```

After making changes to the input.c file, we can check it back in by using the following command. The **-u** option is used to keep a read-only copy in the current directory.

```
$ ci -u /home/shared/input.c
/home/shared/RCS/input.c,v <-- input.c
new revision: 2.1.1.2; previous revision 2.1.1.1
```

```
enter log message, terminated with single '.' or end of file
>> Illustrated working in groups.
>> .
done
$
```

The preceding command lines need long pathnames, so the users in the group may want to create one-line scripts to handle check-in and check-out procedures. The following are Bash scripts for the procedures checkin and checkout.

```
$ cat checkin
#!/bin/bash
# Check in command line; keep a read-only copy in the current directory
ci -u /home/shared/RCS/$1,v
$ cat checkout
#!/bin/bash
# Check out command line; check out an editable copy of the file
co -l /home/shared/RCS/$1,v
$
```

After creating these scripts, you need to make them executable for yourself by using the **chmod u+x** command, as in

```
$ chmod u+x checkin checkout
$
```

Now you can use the **checkin input.c** command to check in the input.c file in the /home/shared/RCS directory and the **checkin input.c** command to check out an editable version of the input.c file from the /home/shared/RCS directory.

An alternative to creating script files checkin and checkout is for users in the group to create a symbolic link, called RCS, to the /home/shared/RCS directory and use short names (simple file names).

*Displaying the History of RCS Files* You can use the **rlog** command to display the history of RCS files. The following is a brief description of the command.

Syntax:

**rlog [options] file-list**

**Purpose:** Display history (log messages and other information) of RCS files in 'file-list'

**Commonly used options / features:**

| | |
|---|---|
| `-L` | Display history of files that have been checked out for editing (i.e., files that have been locked) |
| `-R` | Display file names only |
| `-l[users]` | Display information about files locked by users whose login names are given in 'users', a comma-separated list of login names |
| `-r[revs]` | Display information about revisions given in 'revs', a comma-separated list of revisions; rev1:rev2, :rev2, or rev1: can be used to specify a range of revisions |

Without any option the `rlog` command displays the history of all the revisions that have been made to the files in 'file-list'. The following command displays the history of input.c file.

```
$ rlog input.c
RCS file: RCS/input.c,v
Working file: input.c
head: 2.1
branch:
locks: strict
access list:
symbolic names:
keyword substitution: kv
total revisions: 6;     selected revisions: 6
description:
The first version of the input.c file
----------------------------
revision 2.1
date: 2001/03/16 01:18:55;  author: sarwar; state: Exp; lines: +1 -0
```

```
branches: 2.1.1; 2.1.2;
Just showing how a new version of a file can be created.
----------------------------
revision 1.2
date: 2001/03/16 01:12:25;  author: sarwar; state: Exp; lines: +2 -0
branches: 1.2.1;
Added a comment header to the file.
----------------------------
revision 1.1
date: 2001/03/16 01:11:37;  author: sarwar; state: Exp;
Initial revision
----------------------------
revision 1.2.1.1
date: 2001/03/16 01:20:57;  author: sarwar; state: Exp; lines: +1 -0
Just showing how a branch of a file can be created.
----------------------------
revision 2.1.2.1
date: 2001/03/16 01:35:54;  author: sarwar; state: Exp; lines: +1 -0
*** empty log message ***
----------------------------
revision 2.1.1.1
date: 2001/03/16 01:33:46;  author: sarwar; state: Exp; lines: +2 -14
*** empty log message ***
=============================================================================
$
```

The following command line displays files that have been checked out by the user jonathan for editing. The files checked out for read-only are not included in this list.

```
$ rlog -L -R -ljonathan RCS/*
RCS/compute.c,v
RCS/input.c,v
$
```

In the following In-Chapter Exercise, you will display the check-in check-out history of an RCS file by using the `rlog` command.

**IN-CHAPTER EXERCISE**

**20.12.** Execute the `rlog input.c` command on your system. What did it display? Does the output make sense?

*Breaking Locks* If you must update a file (perhaps to fix a bug in it) that has been checked out by another user in your group for editing, you can use the **rcs -u** command to uncheck out this file. Then check out an editable copy of the same file without overwriting the existing file, make appropriate changes to it, and check it back in. We show this sequence of events in the following session. The first **co** command checks out input.c. The second **co** command displays the message generated when the command is used to check out a file that has already been checked out. The `rcs -u input.c` command unchecks out the input.c file. The `rlog` command shows that input.c is no longer checked out. Once the file has been unlocked (unchecked out), the last three commands check out the input.c file, edit it, and check it back in (retaining a read-only version in the current directory).

```
$ co -l input.c
RCS/input.c,v  -->  input.c
revision 1.2 (locked)
done
$ co -l input.c
RCS/input.c,v  -->  input.c
revision 1.2 (locked)
writable input.c exists; remove it? [ny](n): n
co checkout aborted
$ rcs -u input.c
RCS file: RCS/input.c,v
1.3 unlocked
done
$ rlog -L -R -lsarwar input.c
$ co -l input.c
...
$ vi input.c
...
$ ci -u input.c
...
$
```

*Displaying Differences Between Versions* You can use the **rcsdiff** command to display differences between different versions of a file. Without any argument, it displays differences between the current and the last checked-in versions. The **rcsdiff** command calls the **diff** command to produce the difference output. You can use this utility to find differences between two or more revisions of a file before merging them. The following is a brief description of the utility.

Syntax:

**rcsdiff [options] filename**

**Purpose:** This utility allows comparison of different versions of the same file and displays the differences between them

**Commonly used options/features:**

| | |
|---|---|
| -rver | Used to specify version number 'ver' for the file to be compared with the working file (checked out for editing) |

The following **rcsdiff** command line displays the differences between the latest revision and the last checked-out version of the input.c file. This command is useful for determining what changes have been made to input.c since the last check in.

```
$ rcsdiff input.c
===================================================================
RCS file: RCS/input.c,v
retrieving version 2.1
diff -r2.1 input.c
[output of the above diff command]
$
```

You can explicitly name the two versions to be compared by using the **-r** option. The following command line displays the difference output between versions 1.2 and 2.1 of input.c.

```
$ rcsdiff -r1.2 -r2.1 input.c
RCS file: RCS/input.c,v
retrieving revision 1.2
retrieving revision 2.1
```

```
diff -r1.2 -r2.1
1,2d0
< /* Just a test */
[remaining output of the above diff command]
$
```

*Merging Versions* The **rcsmerge** command can be used to merge the differences between two versions of a file into the working file. These versions are the current version and a version specified in the command line, or the two versions specified in the command line. The following is a brief description of the utility.

Syntax:

**rcsmerge [options] filename**

**Purpose:** This utility merges two revisions of an RCS file into the working file

**Commonly used options/features:**

| | |
|---|---|
| `-r`ver | Used to specify the version number 'ver' for the file |
| `-p` | Output changes to standard output rather than the current version |

If the currently checked-out version of input.c is 1.4 and you want to merge the changes made on version 1.1.1.2 into this file, you can run the following command. By default, the **rcsmerge** command overwrites the existing file with the merged file. You can use the **-p** option to redirect the merged version to stdout, which can then be redirected to another file. The use of **-p** option is highly recommended because the command sometimes doesn't work as you expect it to. If you don't use this option, the current version is changed and there is nothing to fall back on. In the following **rcsmerge** command we combine the currently checked-out version (1.4) and version 1.1.1.2 of the input.c file and store it in merged_input.c. With the **-p** option, you can remove the merged_input.c file and go back to input.c.

```
$ rcsmerge -r1.1.1.2 -p input.c > merged_input.c
RCS file: RCS/input.c,v
retrieving revision 1.1.1.2
retrieving revision 1.4
Merging differences between 1.1.1.1 and 1.4 into input.c; result to stdout
$
```

You can merge any two versions of an RCS file by specifying them in the command line. For example, the following **rcsmerge** command merges versions 1.2 and 3.2 of input.c and stores the merged version in the merged_input.c file.

```
$ rcsmerge -r1.2 -r3.2 -p input.c > merged_input.c
RCS file: RCS/input.c,v
retrieving revision 1.2
retrieving revision 3.2
Merging differences between 1.2 and 3.2 into input.c;
result to stdout
$
```

You can use the following command to undo changes between revisions 1.2 and 2.1 in your currently checked out version of input.c. Note the order of revisions (later revision first).

```
$ rcsmerge -r2.1 -r1.2 input.c
RCS file: RCS/input.c,v
retrieving revision 2.1
retrieving revision 1.2
Merging differences between 2.1 and 1.2 into input.c
$
```

In the following In-Chapter Exercise, you will practice merging various versions of an RCS file.

## IN-CHAPTER EXERCISE

**20.13.** Create a few versions of input.c file and execute the **rcsmerge** command to merge them all into the merged_input.c file.

*Limiting Access Rights to RCS Files* Any user can check out an RCS file, provided that the user has appropriate permissions for the file and has access to the file's pathname. You can protect your RCS files by restricting access to one or more users by using the **-a** and **-e** options of the **rcs** command. As mentioned in the brief description of the **rcs** command, you can use the **-a** option to allow check-out rights on a file to one or more users. All other users are allowed to check out a read-only copy of the file. You can use the **-e** option to remove one or more users from the list. Multiple **-a** and **-e** options can be used in a command line.

In the following session, we demonstrate the use of both options. The first **rcs** command adds users matt, chang, and mona to the list of users allowed to check out an editable version of the input.c file and check it back in; no other user is allowed to perform these tasks. The second **rcs** command adds the user davis to the list of users who can access the file. The last **rcs** command denies chang the access right for editing input.c. The outputs of the **rlog** commands show the current access lists.

```
$ rcs -amatt,chang,mona input.c
RCS file: RCS/input.c,v
done
$ rcs -adavis input.c
RCS file: RCS/input.c,v
done
$ rlog -h RCS/input.c,v
RCS file: RCS/input.c,v
Working file: input.c
head: 2.1
branch:
locks: strict
access list:
        matt
        chang
        mona
        davis
symbolic names:
keyword substitution: kv
total revisions: 6
=============================================================
$ rcs -echang input.c
RCS file: RCS/input.c,v
done
$ rlog -h RCS/input.c,v
...
access list:
        matt
```

```
        mona
        davis
...
================================================================
$
```

You can specify multiple `-e` or `-a` options with an `rcs` command line to allow or deny access to different users. In the following `rcs` command line, users sirini, chris, and kahn are allowed to access an editable version of the input.c file, but users liz and beena aren't.

```
$ rcs -asirini,chris -akahn -eliz -ebeena input.c
$
```

In the following In-Chapter Exercise, you will use the `rcs` command with `-a` and `-e` options to set different access rights for different users on an RCS file.

## IN-CHAPTER EXERCISE

**20.14.** Give a command line that allows users peter and aziz editing rights to the RCS/input.c,v file and takes away the same rights from user mary.

*RCS Special Character Sequences* You can place any of several special character sequences in a comment header of a source file. These character sequences are processed specially by RCS and are expanded to include information from the RCS log for the file. The general format for these special sequences is $string$. This sequence results in the expansion of 'string' by RCS. This expansion takes place when you check a file into the RCS directory and is in place the next time you check out the file. Table 20.2 shows some of these sequences and their expanded values.

**Table 20.2** RCS Special Character Sequences and Their Expanded Values

| Character Sequence | Replaced with |
|---|---|
| $Author$ | Author's login name |
| $Date$ | Current date and time |
| $RCSfile$ | Name of the RCS file |
| $Revision$ | The highest revision number |
| $Source$ | Name of the source file |

The comment header

```
/*
 * Author:     $Author$
 * Date:       $Date$
 * Module:     $RCSfile$
 * Revision:   $Revision$
 * Status:     $Id$
 */
```

in the input.c file expands to

```
/*
 * Author:     $Author: sarwar $
 * Date:       $Date: 2001/03/17 08:21:14 $
 * Module:     $RCSfile: input.c,v $
 * Revision:   $Revision: 2.2 $
 * Status:     $Id: input.c,v 2.2 2001/03/17 08:21:14 sarwar Exp $
 */
```

when the file is checked in.

The most commonly used sequence is $Id$, which is expanded by RCS to include the RCS file name, revision number, date, time, login name of the user making changes, and the RCS state of the file. If you want to put this information in an executable file, you need to include the following C/C++ code in the source file.

```
static char rcsid[] = "$Id$";
```

This code gets compiled into your C/C++ program. The code can be local or global.

You can use the `ident` utility to display the expanded RCS special character sequences in a file. It works on both source and binary files. The following `ident` command displays the expanded forms of the special strings in the input.c file.

```
$ ident input.c
input.c:
     $Author: sarwar $
     $Date: 2001/03/17 08:21:14 $
     $RCSfile: input.c,v $
     $Revision: 2.2 $
     $Id: input.c,v 2.2 2001/03/17 08:21:14 sarwar Exp $
$
```

*Miscellaneous RCS Utilities* There are several other RCS utilities that an advanced user may need to learn. See the man page for the `rcs` command on your LINUX system to learn what commands are available and to learn more about them.

*Using RCS from Within* `emacs` You can check in and check out files and run other RCS utilities from within the `emacs` editor. To do so, you need to run the editor in the vc mode. The `^cvv` command does the next right thing in most cases. For example, if a file is read-only, `^cvv` will check it out for editing. If the file is an editable version, `^cvv` will check the file in. The `^cvu` command unchecks out the current file and reverts to the previous version. The `^cvl` command shows the RCS history (version log) of the file. The `^cvh` command inserts a special character sequence, the RCS Id header, at the current cursor position.

### BEYOND RCS

Several freeware version control systems, mostly built on top of the RCS system, act as front ends to the RCS system. Many have been developed in-house by companies. One of the most popular of these systems is the standard version control system for LINUX, called Concurrent Versions System (CVS). It is optimized to allow you to apply RCS commands to multiple files in various directories and allows concurrent file check outs without locking the file. The latter feature is implemented by using **lazy locking**, which allows multiple users to check out a file for editing that you have already checked out, without having to break your lock.

### CONCURRENT VERSIONS SYSTEM (CVS)

The **Concurrent Versions System** (**CVS**) is a front end for RCS. It is the LINUX tool of choice for version control in a multi-developer, multi-directory environment. It allows you to perform many tasks that cannot be performed or are tedious to perform with RCS. The following are some of the salient features of CVS.

1. It allows you to organize your sources in the form of a directory hierarchy, called a **module,** and check out the whole module for modification.
2. It allows multiple software developers in a team to check out and modify source modules concurrently. Under RCS, file modification operations are serialized by allowing only one developer to check out a file for editing (the file is "locked" by this developer); others can check out this file for read-only. CVS allows multiple developers to modify of a file concurrently and it guarantees **conflict resolution** without loss of any changes to the file.
3. It allows you to tag a software release symbolically and check out this version at any point in time during the development and maintenance phases of the software by using this tag. It also allows you to check out a copy of

any previous software release, regardless of the current state of the software. You can also check out a software release for a particular date.

We describe some of the basic features of CVS in this section.

You need to use the **cvs** utility to interact with CVS. This utility is to be invoked with different commands to perform the various tasks involved in software revision control. Although **cvs** has a wealth of commands that you can use to perform many chores related to version control, we will focus on the basic commands that are commonly used in practice. The following is a brief description of the command.

Syntax: **cvs [cvs-options] command [command-options-and-arguments]**

**Purpose:** This command allows you to invoke features of CVS for performing various tasks related to software version control

**Commonly used options / features:**

| | |
|---|---|
| `-H [cvs-command]` | Display usage information for 'cvs-command'; if 'cvs-command' is not specified, display a brief description of the cvs command |
| `-d CVS-root-dir` | Use 'CVS-root-dir' as the absolute pathname for the source repository; overrides the setting of the environment variable CVSROOT |
| `-e editor` | Use 'editor' to enter revision log information; overrides the settings of the environment variables CVSEDITOR and EDITOR; the default editor, `vi` |
| `-n` | Attempt to execute the given cvs-command but don't make any changes; just issue reports |
| `-t` | Trace program execution and display the sequence of cvs activities that take place for the execution of a cvs-command; useful for understanding the semantics of cvs-commands |

We discuss some of the more commonly used options and commands of the **cvs** command below.

*Displaying CVS Help* You can use the **cvs -H** command to display a brief description of the **cvs** command. The **cvs * -H** command can be used to display the purpose of every **cvs** command. The following session shows sample runs of the two commands.

```
$ cvs -H
Usage: cvs [cvs-options] command [command-options-and-arguments]
  where cvs-options are -q, -n, etc.
    (specify —help-options for a list of options)
  where command is add, admin, etc.
    (specify —help-commands for a list of commands
    or —help-synonyms for a list of command synonyms)
  where command-options-and-arguments depend on the specific command
    (specify -H followed by a command name for command-specific help)
  Specify --help to receive this message

The Concurrent Versions System (CVS) is a tool for version control.
For CVS updates and additional information, see
    Cyclic Software at http://www.cyclic.com/ or
    Pascal Molli's CVS site at http://www.loria.fr/~molli/cvs-index.html
$ cvs * -H
CVS commands are:
        add          Add a new file/directory to the repository
        admin        Administration front end for rcs
        annotate     Show last revision where each line was modified
        checkout     Checkout sources for editing
        commit       Check files into the repository
        diff         Show differences between revisions
        edit         Get ready to edit a watched file
        editors      See who is editing a watched file
        export       Export sources from CVS, similar to checkout
        history      Show repository access history
        import       Import sources into CVS, using vendor branches
        init         Create a CVS repository if it doesn't exist
        log          Print out history information for files
```

```
        login         Prompt for password for authenticating server.
        logout        Removes entry in .cvspass for remote repository.
        rdiff         Create 'patch' format diffs between releases
        release       Indicate that a Module is no longer in use
        remove        Remove an entry from the repository
        rtag          Add a symbolic tag to a module
        status        Display status information on checked out files
        tag           Add a symbolic tag to checked out version of files
        unedit        Undo an edit command
        update        Bring work tree in sync with repository
        watch         Set watches
        watchers      See who is watching a file
(Specify the --help option for a list of other help options)
$
```

You can get help about any CVS command by using the **cvs -H** command with the command name as its argument. In the following session, we display the help information for the add and commit commands.

```
$ cvs -H add
Usage: cvs add [-k rcs-kflag] [-m message] files...
      -k       Use "rcs-kflag" to add the file with the specified kflag.
      -m       Use "message" for the creation log.
(Specify the —help global option for a list of other help options)
$ cvs -H commit
Usage: cvs commit [-nRlf] [-m msg | -F logfile] [-r rev] files...
      -n       Do not run the module program (if any).
      -R       Process directories recursively.
      -l       Local directory only (not recursive).
      -f       Force the file to be committed; disables recursion.
      -F file  Read the log message from file.
      -m msg   Log message.
      -r rev Commit to this branch or trunk revision.
(Specify the --help global option for a list of other help options)
$
```

*Creating a Source Repository* The sources maintained by CVS are kept in a directory called the **source repository.** The source repository contains the RCS history (",v") files for the sources and a directory, called CVSROOT, that contains administrative files. You don't need to access files in the CVSROOT directory while performing simple, routine development tasks. Before you start using CVS, you need to set up the location of your source repository, create it, and move the source modules into it. In order to modify your source modules, you check them out into your work area. After modifying your copies of the source modules, you check their updated versions back in to the source repository.

You can inform CVS of the location of your source repository in one of two ways. You can specify the pathname of the source repository as an argument to the **cvs -d** command or set up the environment variable, ***CVSROOT***, to contain the absolute pathname of the source repository. Since the location of a source repository normally stays the same during the development of a product, setting it up in a system or shell startup file saves a lot of time. You can choose any name for your source repository but cvsroot is commonly used. For the examples in this book, we want to make the ~/cvsroot directory as our source repository and set up the ***CVSROOT*** variable to this pathname in a startup file (.profile or ~/.bashrc for Bash and ~/.chsrc or ~/.tcshrc for TC shell). We also use the ***CVSAREA*** variable (a user-defined variable) to store the location of our CVS work area, where the checked out modules are to be stored for modification. In the following session, we show how to perform this task for Bash.

```
$ cat ~/.bashrc
...
CVSAREA=~/projects
CVSROOT=~/cvsroot
export CVSAREA CVSROOT
$ source ~/.bashrc
$ echo $CVSROOT
/home/faculty/sarwar/cvsroot
$
```

For the TC shell, you will insert the following lines in the ~/.tcshrc file.

```
setenv CVSAREA ~/projects
setenv CVSROOT ~/cvsroot
```

Although we are using a subdirectory in our home directory as the source repository, in an actual development environment you would like it to be outside any team member's home directory such as /home/local/cvsroot.

After setting the environment variable, you need to create the source repository by using the **cvs init** command, as shown below.

```
$ cvs init
$
```

If the pathname in the ***CVSROOT*** variable is incorrect, you don't have the write permissions for the directory that contains the source repository (cvsroot), or you forgot to export the ***CVSROOT*** variable, the **cvs init** command terminates with an error message informing you of the problem. If you have not set up the ***CVSROOT*** variable, you can use the **cvs** command with the **–d** option to inform CVS of the location of the source repository, as shown below.

```
$ cvs –d ~/cvsroot init
$
```

After the **cvs init** command has executed successfully, a directory named CVSROOT is created in the source repository. This directory, created for every source repository, contains a set of administrative files used by CVS for maintaining various logs. The following session shows a snapshot of this directory.

```
$ cd
$ ls -l cvsroot
total 1
drwxrwxr-x 2 sarwar faculty 1024 Apr 18 13:21 CVSROOT
$ cd cvsroot
$ ls CVSROOT
checkoutlist   config         editinfo   loginfo,v notify,v  taginfo,v
checkoutlist,v config,v       editinfo,v modules   rcsinfo   verifymsg
commitinfo     cvswrappers    history    modules,v rcsinfo,v verifymsg,v
commitinfo,v   cvswrappers,v  loginfo    notify    taginfo
$
```

*Importing Sources into the Repository* After creating a repository, you need to import your project source files to it before managing them with CVS. You need to use the **cvs import** command for this purpose. The Syntax box on page 688 gives a brief description of the **cvs import** command.

In the following session, we change directory to project1, the directory that contains the source files that we would like to manage with CVS. We use the **ls** command to ensure that we are importing the correct files into the repository. The

Syntax:

## cvs import [options] repository vendor-tag release-tag

**Purpose:** This command imports new sources into the source repository or updates the repository by incorporating changes to the sources as a vendor branch

**Commonly used options / features:**

| | |
|---|---|
| `-b branch` | Set vendor branch ID to 'branch' |
| `-d` | Use file's modification time as the import time |
| `-m message` | Log the message 'message' we want the history files to show |

`cvs import` command is used to import these sources into the source repository. The **`-m`** option is used to supply a message to CVS that we would like to be displayed with the history files. Without this option, the **`cvs import`** command puts you in an editor for you to enter the message. The name of the editor to be invoked is taken from the environment variable ***CVSEDITOR***. If this variable is not set, then the editor name is taken from the variable ***EDITOR***. If neither variable is set, then the `vi` editor is invoked. The command line argument 'project1' is the name of the directory to contain your source files and the argument 'DemoCVS' is the vendor tag. The last argument must be 'start'.

```
$ cd $CVSAREA/project1
$ ls
compute.c compute.h input.c input.h main.c main.h makefile
$ cvs import -m "Imported Demo Sources" project1 DemoCVS start
N project1/compute.c
N project1/compute.h
N project1/input.c
N project1/input.h
N project1/main.c
N project1/main.h
N project1/makefile
No conflicts created by this import
$
```

After you have imported the source modules into the source repository, you should remove your original source modules so that you don't become confused with two sets of modules.

Having imported the sources into the source repository, you need to set appropriate access permissions for the source repository, the history files in CVSROOT directory in the source repository, and the project1 directory in the source repository. CVS creates all ",v" files as read-only and you should not change permissions of these files as they are to be checked in and out through the **cvs** utility. The subdirectories in the source repository must be writable by all members of your development group who have permission to modify files in these directories. A common way to accomplish this goal is to create a LINUX user group consisting of the members of the development team and to make this group the owner of the source repository. For the sake of examples in this chapter, we set access privileges of the source repository to read/write for every member of our team.

*Checking Out Source Files* After importing sources into the repository and setting appropriate permissions on them, you are ready to check out the source files. You should only modify the checked out modules and not the modules in the source repository. You can check out the source modules by using the **cvs checkout** command. This command allows you to check out any number of source files simultaneously. If you want to check out a module (the complete source tree) for a project, you need to specify the name of the directory in the CVS source repository that contains it. The following Syntax box contains a brief description of the command.

Syntax:

**cvs checkout [options] modules**

**Purpose:** This command checks out source 'modules' for editing

**Commonly used options / features:**

| | |
|---|---|
| `-D date` | Check out versions as of 'date' |
| `-P` | Prune empty directories |
| `-R` | Process directories recursively |
| `-d dir` | Check out module into the directory 'dir' instead of module name(s) |
| `-j ver` | Merge in changes made between the current version and version 'ver' |
| `-r ver` | Check out version 'ver' (a version number or tag) |

In the following session, we check out the project1 module. The **cvs checkout project1** command creates the project1 directory in your current directory (your CVS work area) and populates it with the sources from the project1 directory in the source repository. The project1 directory in your work area also contains a directory called CVS. As shown below, the CVS directory contains three files, called Repository, Entries, and Root. These files contain information that CVS maintains about the checked out files. The CVS directory is used by the CVS system and you should not administer it.

```
$ cd $CVSAREA/projects
$ cvs checkout project1
cvs checkout: Updating project1
U project1/compute.c
U project1/compute.h
U project1/input.h
U project1/main.c
U project1/main.h
U project1/makefile
$ cd project1
$ ls -l
total 8
drwx------    2 sarwar   faculty       512 Apr 21 15:22 CVS
-rw-r--r--    1 sarwar   faculty       128 Apr 21 15:15 compute.c
-rw-r--r--    1 sarwar   faculty        87 Apr 21 15:15 compute.h
-rw-r--r--    1 sarwar   faculty       351 Apr 21 15:15 input.c
-rw-r--r--    1 sarwar   faculty        76 Apr 21 15:15 input.h
-rw-r--r--    1 sarwar   faculty       297 Apr 21 15:15 main.c
-rw-r--r--    1 sarwar   faculty       121 Apr 21 15:15 main.h
-rw-r--r--    1 sarwar   faculty       489 Apr 21 15:15 makefile
$ cd CVS
$ ls -l
total 3
-rw-------    1 sarwar   faculty       313 Apr 21 15:22 Entries
-rw-------    1 sarwar   faculty         9 Apr 21 15:13 Repository
-rw-------    1 sarwar   faculty        47 Apr 21 15:13 Root
$ more Entries
/input.c/1.1.1.1/Sat Apr 21 22:15:58 2001//
/compute.c/1.1.1.1/Sat Apr 21 22:15:58 2001//
/compute.h/1.1.1.1/Sat Apr 21 22:15:58 2001//
```

```
/input.h/1.1.1.1/Sat Apr 21 22:15:59 2001//
/main.c/1.1.1.1/Sat Apr 21 22:15:59 2001//
/main.h/1.1.1.1/Sat Apr 21 22:15:59 2001//
/makefile/1.1.1.1/Sat Apr 21 22:15:59 2001//
$ more Repository
project1
$ more Root
/home/faculty/sarwar/cvsroot
$
```

*Making and Committing Changes to Source Files* You are now ready to make changes to the checked out module (project1 in our case) by using the editor of your choice. After making necessary changes to the source files in your work area, you can apply them to the source repository with the `cvs commit` command. Here is a brief description of the `cvs commit` command.

Syntax:

**cvs commit [options] file-list**

**Purpose:** This command checks in changes in the files in 'file-list' into the source repository

**Commonly used options / features:**

| | |
|---|---|
| `-F file` | Read the log message from 'file' |
| `-R` | Process directories recursively |
| `-f` | Force the files in 'file-list' to be committed; disables recursion |
| `-m message` | Log the message 'message' |
| `-r ver` | Commit to this version |

In the following session, we modify the input.c file with the `vi` editor and apply these changes to the source repository with the `cvs commit` command. As with the `cvs import` command, if you don't use the `-m` option, CVS puts you in an editor to allow you log a message in the history file. The output of the `cvs commit` command shows that CVS produces version 1.2 of the input.c file.

```
$ vi input.c
...
$ cvs commit -m "Enhanced user interface" input.c
Checking in input.c;
```

```
/home/faculty/sarwar/cvsroot/project1/input.c,v <— input.c
new revision: 1.2; previous revision: 1.1
done
$
```

Since CVS allows multiple users to check out the same source files concurrently, conflicts may arise when you commit changes to a file that is being updated by other developers. CVS informs you of such circumstances so you can resolve the conflicts. Suppose that you and some other member of your team have concurrently checked out the above source tree. If you try to install changes to a source file after the other member has already done so, CVS will inform you accordingly. The following session illustrates this point. The error message informs you that the changes that you are trying to install were made to an older version of the input.c file.

```
$ cvs commit -m "Testing concurrent checkout" input.c
cvs commit: Up-to-date check failed for 'input.c'
cvs [commit aborted]: correct above errors first!
$
```

You can solve this problem by updating your working copy of the input.c file with the newer version in the repository, making changes to the updated version, and then committing these changes. The CVS command **update** can be used to deal with concurrent checkouts and to merge a new source file in the CVS repository with an altered source file that you checked out prior to the newly installed changes to this source. If you try to update a source that you have not checked out, this command works like the **checkout** command.

In the following session, we use the **update** command to bring up to date the input.c file. The **update** command could not merge the repository version of input.c (version 1.2) with your version (updated copy of version 1.1) because your changes were made to the same sections of the file that were made to the repository version that was last committed by your team member. In this case, CVS checks out a version of input.c that includes everything it had before (in version 1.1) as well as changes made to it by you and your team member who last installed changes. Your current version of the input.c file (that you could not commit) is saved in the .#input.c.1.1.1.1 file in your current directory, as shown by the **ls -a** command in the following session.

```
$ cvs update input.c
RCS file: /home/faculty/sarwar/cvsroot/project1/input.c,v
retrieving revision 1.1.1.1
retrieving revision 1.2
```

```
Merging differences between 1.1.1.1 and 1.2 into input.c
rcsmerge: warning: conflicts during merge
cvs update: conflicts found in input.c
C input.c
$ ls -a
.                  ..  compute.c input.c main.c makefile
.#input.c.1.1.1.1 CVS compute.h input.h main.h
$
```

The **more** command below shows the version of input.c that has been checked out to you. The section of source between <<<<<<< and ======= is what was in your working input.c file, and the section of source between ======= and >>>>>>> is what was in the source repository. CVS informs you of the situation but leaves the conflict resolution up to you. You can edit this file to make appropriate changes and commit the final version of the file. In this case, we keep both changes and install them, as shown below. Note that a new version (1.3) of the input.c file is created in the source repository.

```
$ more input.c
...
<<<<<<< input.c
#include <string.h>
=======
#include <ctype.h>

>>>> 1.2
#include "input.h"
double input(char *s)
{
...
$ vi input.c
...
#include <string.h>
#include <ctype.h>

...
$ cvs commit -m "Final version" input.c
Checking in input.c;
/home/faculty/sarwar/cvsroot/project1/input.c,v <-- input.c
```

```
new revision: 1.3; previous revision: 1.2
done
$
```

*Adding New Files to a Module in the Repository* You can use the **cvs add** command to add new files to a module in the source repository. Once the new files are in your CVS working directory, running the **cvs add** command marks them for inclusion in the source repository. You need to run the **cvs commit** command in order to make these files available to other users. In the following session, we add the misc.c file to the project1 module in the source repository and make it available to other users. As expected, the file is assigned a version number 1.1.

```
$ cvs add misc.c
cvs add: scheduling file 'misc.c' for addition
cvs add: use 'cvs commit' to add this file permanently
$ cvs commit -m "A new file for the project1 module" misc.c
RCS file: /home/faculty/sarwar/cvsroot/project1/misc.c,v
done
Checking in misc.c;
/home/faculty/sarwar/cvsroot/project1/misc.c,v  <-- misc.c
initial revision: 1.1
done
$
```

*Removing a File from the Source Repository* You can use the **cvs remove** command to remove a file from a module in the source repository. Before marking the file for removal, you must remove it from your working directory with the **rm** command and then run the **cvs remove** command. Finally, you need to run the **cvs commit** command to remove the file from the source repository. In the following session, we remove the misc.c file from the project1 module in the source repository.

```
$ rm misc.c
$ cvs remove misc.c
cvs remove: scheduling 'misc.c' for removal
cvs remove: use 'cvs commit' to remove this file permanently
$ cvs commit -m "Testing file removal" misc.c
Removing misc.c;
/home/faculty/sarwar/cvsroot/project1/misc.c,v  <-- misc.c
new revision: delete; previous revision: 1.1
done
$
```

You can use the -R option with the `cvs remove` command to process directories recursively.

*Freezing and Extracting a Version* You can use the `cvs rtag` command to to tag the files in a module in the source repository. This allows you to *freeze* a release of the product but allows continued development for the next release. You can recreate a tagged release even if it has been changed.

Syntax:

**cvs rtag [options] tag module-list**

**Purpose:** This command adds a symbolic tag to the modules in 'module-list'

**Commonly used options / features:**

| | |
|---|---|
| `-D` | Use existing date as the tag |
| `-F` | Move the tag if it already exists |
| `-R` | Process directories recursively |
| `-b` | Make the tag a "branch" tag to allow concurrent development |
| `-d` | Delete the given tag |
| `-r ver` | Assign 'rev' as the tag |

In the following session, we freeze project1 with a tag Release_0_1.

```
$ cvs rtag Release_0_1 project1
cvs rtag: Tagging project1
$
```

You can extract a frozen version of a module with the `cvs export` command. Here is a brief description of the `cvs export` command.

Syntax:

**cvs export [options] module**

**Purpose:** This command exports sources in 'module' with a particular tag

**Commonly Used Options / Features:**

| | |
|---|---|
| `-D date` | Export version of the 'date' date |
| `-d dir` | Export into the 'dir' directory instead of the module name |
| `-r ver` | Export sources with the 'rev' as tag |

In the following session, we extract the Release_0_1 release of project1.

```
$ cvs export -r Release_0_1 project1
cvs export: Updating project1
U project1/compute.c
...
$
```

You can use the **-d** option to check out the unfrozen release in a directory with a name other than the name of the module being unfrozen. The **cvs export -r Release_0_1 -d prj1R1 project1** command extracts the Release_0_1 release of the project1 module and puts the files in the prj1R1 directory instead of the project1 directory.

*After Work Clean Up* Once you have installed changes to a module, you should release the working directory by using the **release** command. This command removes all the files in your working directory after checking that all your modifications have been committed. If any file was modified but not committed, CVS will inform you accordingly. A file modified but not committed has a marker M in front of it and a file unknown to CVS has a ? character in front of it. A file tagged with a ? character is usually a binary file (executable or core file) that you may have generated as you tested your modifications. The following session shows an example of this command.

```
$ cd ..
$ ls
project1
$ cvs release project1
You have [0] altered files in this repository.
Are you sure you want to release directory 'project1': y
$
```

*Remote Repositories* CVS allows you to maintain your work area and source repositories on different machines. You need to use the following format for accessing a source repository maintained on a remote host.

user-name@remote-host:source-repository

Here 'source-repository' is the absolute pathname of the source repository. If your user name is the same on both hosts, then you can omit 'user-name@'. Suppose that your local machine is willamette.pdx.com and your user name on it is john.

You want to access a module project1 in the source repository /home/share/projects on a remote host columbia.pdx.com. If your user name on the remote machine is also john, then you need to use the following command to check out the project1 module.

```
$ cvs -d columbia.pdx.com:/home/share/projects checkout project1
...
$
```

If your user name on the remote host is dave (not john), then you need to use the following command to check out project2.

```
$ cvs -d dave@columbia.pdx.com:/home/share/projects checkout project1
...
$
```

CVS uses the **rsh** command to perform remote operations, which means that your local host must be a trusted host and/or you must be a trusted user on the remote host. Thus the remote host's /etc/hosts.equiv file must have an entry like the following for you (user name john) to be able to access the remote source repository.

willamette.pdx.com john

If such an entry does not exit in the /etc/hosts.equiv file on the remote host then the remote user's (dave in our case) ~/.rhosts file must contain this entry.

## 20.6 STATIC ANALYSIS TOOLS

**Static analysis** of a program involves analyzing the structure and properties of your program without executing it. Such analyses are usually meant to determine the level of portability of your code for multiple platforms, the number of lines of code (LOC), the number of function calls/points (FPs) in your program, and the percentage of time taken by each function in the code. During the planning phase of a software project, parameters such as LOC and FPs (taken from previously completed similar projects) are commonly used in **software cost models** that are used to estimate the number of person-months needed to complete a software project and hence the software cost.

Static analyses tools allow you to measure those parameters. In the following sections we describe the **gprof** command, which can be used to produce an execution profile of C programs.

## 20.6.1 Profiling C Source Code

At times you may want to know how long a program spends in each function when it is executed. You can use the LINUX tool **`gprof`** to display an execution profile of your program in terms of the functions used and percentage of time taken by each function. The **`gprof`** tool is quite effective in identifying expensive portions of your program because it identifies the functions that are causing bottlenecks in the software. You can use this information to improve the performace of certain portions of a program by optimizing them. A brief description of the tool follows.

Syntax:

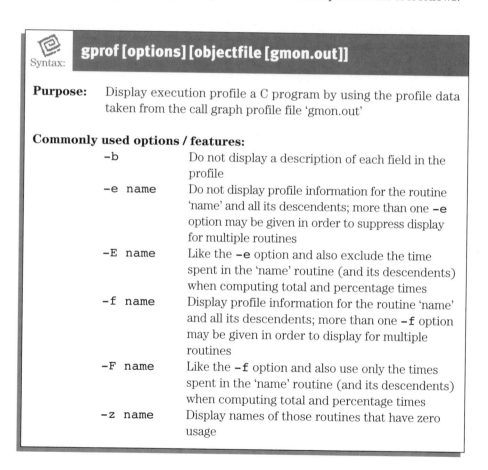

**gprof [options] [objectfile [gmon.out]]**

**Purpose:** Display execution profile a C program by using the profile data taken from the call graph profile file 'gmon.out'

**Commonly used options / features:**

| | |
|---|---|
| `-b` | Do not display a description of each field in the profile |
| `-e name` | Do not display profile information for the routine 'name' and all its descendents; more than one **`-e`** option may be given in order to suppress display for multiple routines |
| `-E name` | Like the **`-e`** option and also exclude the time spent in the 'name' routine (and its descendents) when computing total and percentage times |
| `-f name` | Display profile information for the routine 'name' and all its descendents; more than one **`-f`** option may be given in order to display for multiple routines |
| `-F name` | Like the **`-f`** option and also use only the times spent in the 'name' routine (and its descendents) when computing total and percentage times |
| `-z name` | Display names of those routines that have zero usage |

When you specify an object file as a parameter to the **`gprof`** command, it reads the given object and establishes the relation between its symbol table and the call graph profile in the gmon.out file. The output shows two types of profiles. The first profile shows the functions sorted according to the time they represent, including the times of their call graph descendants. The second profile shows the total execution times, call counts, time in milliseconds a call spent in the routine itself, and time in milliseconds a call spent in the routine itself including its descendants. The string <spontaneous> is displayed in the name field, and all the other fields are blank, if the parent of a function cannot be dertermined. The values displayed and their meanings are shown in Table 20.3.

The first step in using `gprof` is to compile your program with a particular option that asks the compiler to insert appropriate code in the object module for counting the number of times that each function is executed and the time spent in each function. To test your program, use the `gcc` compiler command with the `-p` (or `-pg`) option. A program compiled with this option generates profiling information when executed. This information is stored in a file called gmon.out. You then use the `gprof` command to display the program profile. The sequence of steps needed are shown in the following session. We used the simple program example that we've been using throughout the book in order to keep the profile simple and

**Table 20.2** Fields in the Output of the `gprof` Command and their Meaning

| Field | Meaning |
|---|---|
| | **First Listing** |
| `% time` | Percentage of the total running time used by a function |
| `cumulative seconds` | The number of seconds accounted for by a function and those listed above it. |
| `self seconds` | The number of seconds accounted for by a function only |
| `calls` | Total number of times a function is called; blank for a function that is not profiled |
| `self us/call` | The average number of microseconds spent in a function per call; blank for a function that is not profiled |
| `total us/call` | The average number of microseconds spent in a function and its descendents per call; blank for a function that is not profiled |
| `name` | The name of the function; the index show the location of the function in the gprof listing |
| | **Second Listing** |
| `index` | A unique number given to every element of the table/listing |
| `% time` | The percentage of the total time that was spent in a function and its children |
| `self` | The amount of time spent in a function |
| `children` | The amount of time spent by a function's children; a + followed by a number indicates that recursive calls were made to the function |
| `called` | Total number of times a function is called |
| `name` | Name of the current function |

easy to explain. We've used the **-b** option with the **gprof** command in order to keep the output short. Without this option, every term used in the output is clearly described as part of the output.

```
$ gcc -p input.c compute.c main.c -lm
$ a.out
The program takes x and y from stdin and displays x^y.
Enter the value of x: 4
Enter the value of y: 3
x^y is: 64.000
$ ls -l gmon.out
-rw-------    1 sarwar    faculty       370 Mar 17 12:05 gmon.out
$ gprof -b
Flat profile:
Each sample counts as 0.01 seconds.
no time accumulated

 %   cumulative    self              self      total
time   seconds    seconds   calls   us/call   us/call  name
0.00      0.00       0.00       2      0.00      0.00  input
0.00      0.00       0.00       1      0.00      0.00  compute

                       Call graph

granularity: each sample hit covers 4 byte(s) no time propagated

index % time    self  children    called     name
                0.00    0.00       2/2           main [10]
[1]      0.0    0.00    0.00       2         input [1]
-----------------------------------------------
                0.00    0.00       1/1           main [10]
[2]      0.0    0.00    0.00       1         compute [2]
-----------------------------------------------

Index by function name

   [2] compute                  [1] input
$
```

The first part of the output shows that the input function and the compute function are each called twice. The second part of the output shows that the input and the compute functions are called from the main function. All the times are shown as 0 microsecond because both functions take very short time to execute. The output displays `no time accumulated` at the top.

The following session shows the execution of a program for generating the Huffman tree, Huffman codes, average code length (ACL), and code efficiency against ASCII coding of the letters in a text file, called Data. An obvious observation is that MakeListNode, MakeTreeNode, AddOrderedListNode, and DeleteFirstListNode are some of the most heavily called functions. The call graph shows from where and how often various functions are called. It is easy to conclude that, in order to make it an efficient program, these functions must be made as efficient as possible.

```
$ gcc -p Huffman.c -o Huffman
$ Huffman Data
Char    Freq    Huffman Code
|       21      0001111110000
4       21      0001111110001
q       42      000111111001
&       42      011010100010
X       63      011010100011
...
t       10878   0101
e       12936   0111
        59934   11
ACL Huffman code: 4.560958 ascii: 8 efficiency: 0.570120
$ gprof
Flat profile:
Each sample counts as 0.01 seconds.
  %   cumulative   self              self     total
 time   seconds   seconds   calls   us/call   us/call  name
100.00      0.03      0.03       1  30000.00  30000.00  getstatistics
  0.00      0.03      0.00     241      0.00      0.00  MakeListNode
  0.00      0.03      0.00     239      0.00      0.00  MakeTreeNode
  0.00      0.03      0.00     159      0.00      0.00  AddOrderedListNode
  0.00      0.03      0.00     158      0.00      0.00  DeleteFirstListNode
```

```
  0.00      0.03      0.00        1        0.00        0.00  CopyList
  0.00      0.03      0.00        1        0.00        0.00  HuffmanCode
  0.00      0.03      0.00        1        0.00        0.00  MakeHuffmanTree
  0.00      0.03      0.00        1        0.00        0.00  printresults

                              Call graph

granularity: each sample hit covers 4 byte(s) for 33.33% of 0.03 seconds

index % time    self  children    called     name
                0.03    0.00       1/1           main [2]
[1]    100.0    0.03    0.00       1         getstatistics [1]
                0.00    0.00      80/239         MakeTreeNode [4]
                0.00    0.00      80/159         AddOrderedListNode [5]
-----------------------------------------------
                                                 <spontaneous>
[2]    100.0    0.00    0.03                 main [2]
                0.03    0.00       1/1           getstatistics [1]
                0.00    0.00       2/241         MakeListNode [3]
                0.00    0.00       1/1           CopyList [7]
                0.00    0.00       1/1           MakeHuffmanTree [9]
                0.00    0.00       1/1           HuffmanCode [8]
                0.00    0.00       1/1           printresults [10]
-----------------------------------------------
                0.00    0.00       2/241         main [2]
                0.00    0.00      80/241         CopyList [7]
                0.00    0.00     159/241         AddOrderedListNode [5]
[3]      0.0    0.00    0.00     241         MakeListNode [3]
-----------------------------------------------
                0.00    0.00      79/239         MakeHuffmanTree [9]
                0.00    0.00      80/239         getstatistics [1]
                0.00    0.00      80/239         CopyList [7]
[4]      0.0    0.00    0.00     239         MakeTreeNode [4]
-----------------------------------------------
                0.00    0.00      79/159         MakeHuffmanTree [9]
                0.00    0.00      80/159         getstatistics [1]
```

```
[5]      0.0    0.00    0.00     159        AddOrderedListNode [5]
                0.00    0.00     159/241        MakeListNode [3]
-----------------------------------------------
                0.00    0.00     158/158        MakeHuffmanTree [9]
[6]      0.0    0.00    0.00     158        DeleteFirstListNode [6]
-----------------------------------------------
                0.00    0.00       1/1          main [2]
[7]      0.0    0.00    0.00       1        CopyList [7]
                0.00    0.00      80/239        MakeTreeNode [4]
                0.00    0.00      80/241        MakeListNode [3]
-----------------------------------------------
                                 158            HuffmanCode [8]
                0.00    0.00       1/1          main [2]
                0.00    0.00     158/158        MakeHuffmanTree [9]
[6]      0.0    0.00    0.00     158        DeleteFirstListNode [6]
-----------------------------------------------
                0.00    0.00       1/1          main [2]
[7]      0.0    0.00    0.00       1        CopyList [7]
                0.00    0.00      80/239        MakeTreeNode [4]
                0.00    0.00      80/241        MakeListNode [3]
-----------------------------------------------
                                 158            HuffmanCode [8]
                0.00    0.00       1/1          main [2]
[8]      0.0    0.00    0.00       1+158    HuffmanCode [8]
                                 158            HuffmanCode [8]
-----------------------------------------------
                0.00    0.00       1/1          main [2]
[9]      0.0    0.00    0.00       1        MakeHuffmanTree [9]
                0.00    0.00     158/158        DeleteFirstListNode [6]
                0.00    0.00      79/239        MakeTreeNode [4]
                0.00    0.00      79/159        AddOrderedListNode [5]
-----------------------------------------------
                0.00    0.00       1/1          main [2]
[10]     0.0    0.00    0.00       1        printresults [10]
-----------------------------------------------
```

```
Index by function name

   [5] AddOrderedListNode        [8] HuffmanCode            [4] MakeTreeNode
   [7] CopyList                  [9] MakeHuffmanTree        [1] getstatistics
   [6] DeleteFirstListNode       [3] MakeListNode          [10] printresults
$
```

## 20.7 DYNAMIC ANALYSIS TOOLS

**Dynamic analysis** of a program involves its analysis during run time. As we have mentioned before, this phase comprises debugging, tracing, and performance monitoring of the software, including testing it against product requirements. In this section, we discuss the two useful LINUX tools for tracing the execution of a program and debugging it (`gdb`) and measuring the running time of a program in actual time units (`time`).

### 20.7.1 Source Code Debugging

The task of debugging software is time-consuming and difficult. It consists of monitoring the internal working of your code while it executes, examining values of program variables and values returned by functions, and executing functions with specific input parameters. As we have stated before, most C programmers tend to use the printf calls at various places in their programs to display values of program variables and to find the origin of a bug and then remove it. This technique is simple and works quite well for small programs. However, for large software, where an error may be hidden deep in a function call hierarchy, this technique takes a lot of editing time for adding and removing printf calls in the source file. The proper debugging method under such circumstances is to use a **symbolic debugger**. Typical facilities available in a symbolic debugger include

- running programs,
- setting break points,
- single stepping,
- listing source code,
- editing source code,
- accessing and modifying variables,
- tracing program execution, and
- searching for functions and variables.

The standard debugger on LINUX systems is `gdb` (GNU DeBugger). Although `gdb` can be used for debugging C, C++, and Modula-2 programs, here we discuss its features for debugging C programs only. You can invoke this debugger by using the `gdb` command. Once it starts running, it reads commands from the keyboard to perform various tasks and quits when you give it the **quit** command. The following is a brief description of the **gdb** command.

Syntax:

**gdb [options] [execprog [core|PID]]**

**Purpose:** Allows execution of a program 'execprog' to be traced, to determine what goes on inside it, hence helping you identify the location of a bug in the program. You can also specify a core file or the PID of a running program.

**Commonly used options / features:**

| | |
|---|---|
| `-c core` | Use 'core' as the core file to examine |
| `-h` | List command options with brief explanations |
| `-n` | Do not execute commands in the ~/.gdbinit file after processing all command line options |
| `-q` | Do not display and introductory and copyright message |
| `-s file` | Use symbol table from the 'file' file |

During startup, **gdb** searches for ~/.gdbinit file and executes the commands in it. You can use the **-n** option to ask **gdb** to ignore this file.

### Using gdb

Before debugging a program with **gdb** (or any other debugger), you must compile it with the **-g** compiler option to include the symbol table in the executable. We use the program in the bugged.c file to show various features of **gdb**. The program prompts you for keyboard input, displays the input, and exits. We use several functions to demonstrate the features of **gdb** for displaying the stack trace and setting break points at function boundaries. The following session shows program code, its compilation without the **-g** option, and its execution.

```
$ nl -ba bugged.c
1    /*
2    * Sample C program bugged with a simple, yet nasty error
3    */
4
```

```
#include <stdio.h>

#define PROMPT "Enter a string: "
#define SIZE 255

char *get_input(char *);
void null_function1 ();
void null_function2 ();

int main ()
{
    char *input;

    null_function1 ();
    null_function2 ();
    input = get_input(PROMPT);
    (void) printf("You entered: %s.\n", input);
    (void) printf("The end of buggy code!\n");
    return(0);
}

void null_function1 ()
{ }

void null_function2 ()
{ }

char *get_input(char *prompt)
{
    char *str;

    (void) printf("%s", prompt);
    for (*str = getchar(); *str != '\n'; *str = getchar())
        str++;
    *str = '\0'; /* string terminator */
```

```
        return(str);
   }
$ cc bugged.c -o bugged
$ bugged
Enter a string: Hello, world!
Segmentation fault
$
```

Note that the program prompts you for input and faults without echoing what you enter from the keyboard. That happens frequently in C programming, particularly with programmers who are new to C or aren't careful about initializing pointer variables in their programs and rely on the compiler. It's time to use **gdb**!

*Entering the* **gdb** *Environment* As we've mentioned before, in order to enter the **gdb** environment, you must compile your C program with the **-g** compiler option. This option creates an executable file that contains the symbol table and debugging, relocation, and profiling information for your program. After the code compiles successfully, you can then use the **gdb** command to debug your code, as in the following session. Note that **(gdb)** is the prompt for the **gdb** debugger.

```
$ gcc -g bugged.c -o bugged
$ gdb -q bugged
(gdb)
```

Once you are inside the **gdb** environment, you can run many commands to monitor the execution of your code. You can use the **help** command to get information about the **gdb** commands. Without any argument, the **help** command displays the list of classes of the **gdb** commands. You can get information about the commands in any class by passing the class name as an argument to the **help** command. In the following session, the **help** command shows the names of classes of all **gdb** commands, and the **help running** command displays a brief description of the commands for running the program. The **help tracepoints** command displays a brief description of the commands that can be used for tracing program execution without stopping the program. Finally, the **help trace** command displays a brief description of the trace command.

```
(gdb) help
List of classes of commands:
aliases -- Aliases of other commands
breakpoints -- Making program stop at certain points
data -- Examining data
files -- Specifying and examining files
```

```
internals -- Maintenance commands
obscure -- Obscure features
running -- Running the program
stack -- Examining the stack
status -- Status inquiries
support -- Support facilities
tracepoints -- Tracing of program execution without stopping the program
user-defined -- User-defined commands

Type "help" followed by a class name for a list of commands in that class.
Type "help" followed by command name for full documentation.
Command name abbreviations are allowed if unambiguous.
(gdb) help running
Running the program.

List of commands:

attach -- Attach to a process or file outside of GDB
continue -- Continue program being debugged
detach -- Detach a process or file previously attached
finish -- Execute until selected stack frame returns
go -- Usage: go <location>
handle -- Specify how to handle a signal
info handle -- What debugger does when program gets various signals
jump -- Continue program being debugged at specified line or address
kill -- Kill execution of program being debugged
next -- Step program
nexti -- Step one instruction
run -- Start debugged program
set args -- Set argument list to give program being debugged when it is started
set environment -- Set environment variable value to give the program
set follow-fork-mode -- Set debugger response to a program call of fork or vfork
set scheduler-locking -- Set mode for locking scheduler during execution
show args -- Show argument list to give program being debugged when it is started
show follow-fork-mode -- Show debugger response to a program call of fork or vfork
show scheduler-locking -- Show mode for locking scheduler during execution
signal -- Continue program giving it signal specified by the argument
```

```
step -- Step program until it reaches a different source line
stepi -- Step one instruction exactly
target -- Connect to a target machine or process
thread -- Use this command to switch between threads
thread apply -- Apply a command to a list of threads
apply all -- Apply a command to all threads
tty -- Set terminal for future runs of program being debugged
unset environment -- Cancel environment variable VAR for the program
until -- Execute until the program reaches a source line greater than the current

Type "help" followed by command name for full documentation.
Command name abbreviations are allowed if unambiguous.
(gdb) help tracepoints
Tracing of program execution without stopping the program.

List of commands:

actions -- Specify the actions to be taken at a tracepoint
collect -- Specify one or more data items to be collected at a tracepoint
delete tracepoints -- Delete specified tracepoints
disable tracepoints -- Disable specified tracepoints
enable tracepoints -- Enable specified tracepoints
end -- Ends a list of commands or actions
passcount -- Set the passcount for a tracepoint
save-tracepoints -- Save current tracepoint definitions as a script
tdump -- Print everything collected at the current tracepoint
tfind -- Select a trace frame;
tfind end -- Synonym for 'none'
tfind line -- Select a trace frame by source line
tfind none -- Deselect any trace frame and resume 'live' debugging
tfind outside -- Select a trace frame whose PC is outside the given range
tfind pc -- Select a trace frame by PC
tfind range -- Select a trace frame whose PC is in the given range
tfind start -- Select the first trace frame in the trace buffer
tfind tracepoint -- Select a trace frame by tracepoint number
trace -- Set a tracepoint at a specified line or function or address
tstart -- Start trace data collection
```

```
tstatus -- Display the status of the current trace data collection
tstop -- Stop trace data collection
while-stepping -- Specify single-stepping behavior at a tracepoint

Type "help" followed by command name for full documentation.
Command name abbreviations are allowed if unambiguous.
(gdb) help trace
Set a tracepoint at a specified line or function or address.
Argument may be a line number, function name, or '*' plus an address.
For a line number or function, trace at the start of its code.
If an address is specified, trace at that exact address.

Do "help tracepoints" for info on other tracepoint commands.
(gdb)
```

In addition to the **gdb**-specific commands, **gdb** also allows you to execute all shell commands.

*Executing a Program* You can run your program inside the **gdb** environment by using the **run** command. The following command executes the bugged program. The program prompts you for input. When you enter the input (**Hello, world!** in this case), and hit <Enter>, the program fails when it tries to execute the statement that uses the C library call getc. The error message is cryptic for beginners and those who aren't familiar with LINUX jargon. All the error message says is that a signal of type SIGSEGV was received by the program when it was executing the statement that uses the C library call getc. The message does not tell us part of the bugged.c program causes this library call. We must step through the program execution to determine where the failure occurs.

```
(gdb) run
Starting program:
/home/faculty/sarwar/linuxbook/chapters/ch20/bugged
Enter a string: Hello, world!

Program received signal SIGSEGV, Segmentation fault.
0x2ab20921 in getc () from /lib/libc.so.6
(gdb)
```

*Tracing Program Execution* To find out what went wrong, we need to narrow down what part of the code may be causing the problem. There are several ways to do this in **gdb**. We do so by first backtracing the program with the **backtrace** command. This command prints the current location within the program and a stack trace that shows how the current location was reached. The following snapshot shows that the program was at location (memory address) 0x2ab20921 in the getc ( ) in the /lib/libc.so.6 library when the program received the SIGSEGV signal.

```
(gdb) backtrace
#0  0x2ab20921 in getc () from /lib/libc.so.6
#1  0x80484a8 in get_input (
    prompt=0x804851c "Enter a string: ") at bugged.c:35
#2  0x804841a in main () at bugged.c:18
(gdb)
```

We know that there is no function called getc ( ) in our program and that this library function was invoked right after **Enter a string:** was displayed on the screen. We also know that the code following the **printf** statement that displays this string is a **for** statement. The only library call in the for statement is getchar ( ). We conclude that the getc ( ) library call results from the getchar ( ) call in our program. Since the getchar ( ) call is used to read keyboard input character-by-character and return it, the getc ( ) is a lower-level library call that performs this task. The assignment statement in our `for` loop is used to store the character returned by getchar ( ) store it in memory location pointed to by the ***str*** variable. The most likely reason for the error is that ***str*** is pointing to a location that does not belong to this program's address space. We examine value of the character pointer 'str' to determine whether that is the case.

*Setting Break Points* Before you can display the value of a variable or examine the execution of a piece of code more closely, you have to execute the program without interruption until control reaches the statement or function that you want to study more closely. The process of stopping a program this way is known as setting **break points.** You can set break points in **gdb** by using the **break** command. In our gdb session, we set break point at the **for** loop and run the program again, as shown.

```
(gdb) break 36
Breakpoint 1 at 0x80484a0: file bugged.c, line 36.
(gdb) run
The program being debugged has been started already.
Start it from the beginning? (y or n) y
Starting program: /home/faculty/sarwar/linuxbook/chapters/ch20/bugged
Enter a string: Hello, world!
Breakpoint 1, get_input (prompt=0x804851c "Enter a string: ")
```

```
at bugged.c:36
36 str++;
(gdb)
```

*Single-Stepping Through Your Program* Always set your break points in a way that allows you to view the execution of all or part of your code statement by statement. The process of tracing program execution statement by statement is known as **single-stepping** through your program. Single-stepping, combined with tracing variables, allows you to study program execution closely. Single-stepping can be done by using the `step` command. This command executes the next source line, stepping into a function if necessary. The `next` command can be used to do this, but it executes a function in its entirety. In the following session, the `step` command is used to single-step through the code after a break point is set at source line 36. It shows the execution of the `for` loop 13 times (equal to the number of characters in the input string Hello, world!). On the last `step` command, the error message appears again. The hexadecimal number to the left of the last line (second line of the error message) contains the memory address (0x2ab20921) of the statement in the getc ( ) function that causes the exception. You can use the `x` command to display the contents of this memory location. The output of the `x` command shows that the problem occurs at the 145th byte in the getc ( ) function. We still don't know the reason for the failure.

```
(gdb) step
35          for (*str = getchar(); *str != '\n'; *str = getchar())
(gdb) step
36              str++;
(gdb) step
35          for (*str = getchar(); *str != '\n'; *str = getchar())
(gdb) step
36              str++;
(gdb) step
...
(gdb) step
35          for (*str = getchar(); *str != '\n'; *str = getchar())
(gdb) step
0x2ab20921 in getc () from /lib/libc.so.6
(gdb) step
Single-stepping until exit from function getc,
which has no line number information.

Program received signal SIGSEGV, Segmentation fault.
```

```
0x2ab20921 in getc () from /lib/libc.so.6
(gdb) x 0x2ab20921
0x2ab20921 <getc+145>: 0x83c310c4
(gdb)
```

*Displaying Value of a Variable or Expression* In order to determine the cause of program failure, we need to examine the value of the only variable, `str`, involved in the `for` loop. You can display the value of a variable or expression by using the `print` command. We need to display the value of the `str` variable to get more clues about the problem. In order to do so, we need to rerun the program so that it stops before the first execution of the `for` loop. Remember that we've already set a break point for this purpose. At the break point, we use the `print` command to display the value of the pointer variable `str` and find out that this variable already points to something, which is not an empty string as we would expect. It seems that `str` is pointing to a region in the memory that does not belong to our program's address space. We use the `x` command to display the value pointed to by `str` and find that it points to something called `_GLOBAL_OFFSET_TABLE_`, which is not part of our program.

```
(gdb) run
The program being debugged has been started already.
Start it from the beginning? (y or n) y

Starting program: /usr1.d/sarwar/linuxbook/chapters/ch20/bugged
Enter a string: Hello, world!

Breakpoint 1, get_input (prompt=0x804851c "Enter a string: ")
    at bugged.c:36
36 str++;
(gdb) print str
$2 = 0x804957c "H\225\004\bP÷«*@Z«*$\t²*ñ²º*\036\203\004\b¼3®*\204\235±*"
(gdb) x 0x804957c
0x804957c <_GLOBAL_OFFSET_TABLE_>:      0x08049548
(gdb)
```

*Listing Program Code* Now that we know that the `str` variable is not initialized properly, we display the program code to see what it is initialized to. We use the `list` command to display all or part of our source code. This command can be used to display a range of lines or functions. In the following session, we use the `help` command to find out how to use the `list` command, then display the get_input function to see initialization of the `str` variable.

```
(gdb) help list
List specified function or line.
With no argument, lists ten more lines after or around previous listing.
"list -" lists the ten lines before a previous ten-line listing.
One argument specifies a line, and ten lines are listed around that line.
Two arguments with comma between specify starting and ending lines to list.
Lines can be specified in these ways:
  LINENUM, to list around that line in current file,
  FILE:LINENUM, to list around that line in that file,
  FUNCTION, to list around beginning of that function,
  FILE:FUNCTION, to distinguish among like-named static functions.
  *ADDRESS, to list around the line containing that address.
With two args if one is empty it stands for ten lines away from the
other arg.
(gdb) list get_input,
        {
            char *str;

            (void) printf("%s", prompt);
            for (*str = getchar(); *str != '\n'; *str = getchar())
                str++;
            *str = '\0'; /* string terminator */
            return(str);
        }
(gdb)
```

*Fixing the Bug* From the listing of the get_input function, we find out that **`str`** is a local variable that is never initialized. Since local variables are allocated space on stack, **`str`** has an initial value that was previously stored in the location that **`str`** represents. This value is 0x804957c (in hexadecimal) and points to some unknown value called `_GLOBAL_OFFSET_TABLE_`. Therefore, our program tries to write to a location that is outside its process address space (i.e., doesn't belong to it). This attempt is a clear violation that results in the program receiving a signal SIGSEGV, causing premature program termination and the error message `Segmentation fault`. Figure 20.8 illustrates the segmentation violation.

To fix the bug, all you need to do is initialize the **`str`** pointer to a memory space that has been allocated to the program. We use the malloc library call for this purpose. The revised get_input function is shown in the following session,

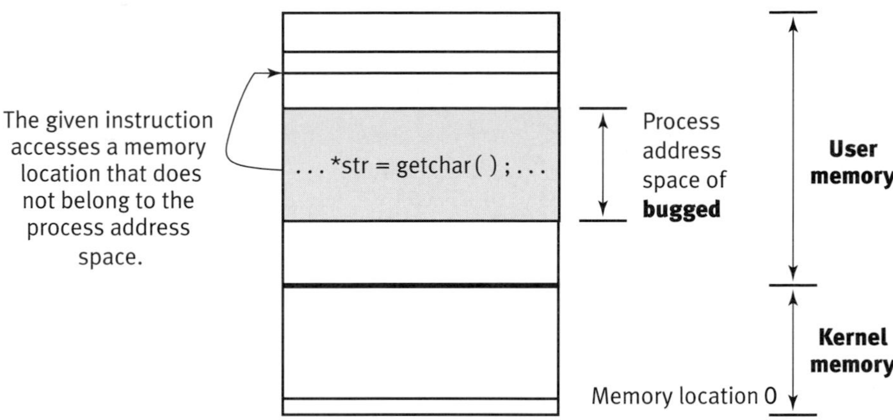
The given instruction accesses a memory location that does not belong to the process address space.
. . . *str = getchar ( ) ; . . .
Process address space of **bugged**
**User memory**
**Kernel memory**
Memory location 0

**Figure 20.8** The memory (segmentation) access violation causing program failure

along with the compilation and proper execution of the program. The changes in the code have been highlighted.

```
$ cat bugged.c
/*
* Sample C program bugged with a simple, yet nasty error
*/

#define PROMPT "Enter a string: "
#define SIZE 255

char *get_input(char *);
void null_function1 ();
void null_function2 ();

int main ()
{
    char *input;
    null_function1 ();
    null_function2 ();
    input = get_input(PROMPT);
    (void) printf("You entered: %s.\n", input);
    (void) printf("The end of buggy code!\n");
    return(0);
}
```

```
str = (char *) malloc (SIZE * (sizeof (char)));
temp = str;
void null_function1 ()
{ }

void null_function2 ()
{ }

char *get_input(char *prompt)
{
    char *str, *temp;
    str = (char *) malloc (SIZE * (sizeof (char)));
    temp = str;
    (void) printf("%s", prompt);
    for (*str = getchar(); *str != '\n'; *str = getchar())
        str++;
    *str = '\0'; /* string terminator */
    return(temp);
}
$
```

*Leaving* `gdb` *and Wrapping Up* You can use the `quit` command to leave `gdb` and return to your shell.

```
(gdb) quit
$
```

Once your code has been debugged, you can decrease the size of the binary file, releasing some disk space, by removing from it the information generated by the `-g` option of the C compiler to be used by debugging and profiling utilities. You can do so by using the `strip` command. The information stripped from the file contains the symbol table and relocation, debugging, and profiling information. In the following session we show the long list for the bugged file before and after execution of the `strip` command. Note that the size of the file has decreased from 7,233 bytes to 3,348 bytes, resulting in more than 50% saving in disk space. Alternatively, you can recompile the source to generate an optimized executable by using various options.

```
$ ls -l bugged
-rwx------    1 sarwar   faculty    7233 Mar 20 16:27 bugged
$ strip bugged
```

```
$ ls -l bugged
-rwx------    1 sarwar   faculty    3348 Mar 20 16:45 bugged
$
```

In the following In-Chapter Exercise, you will make extensive use of **gdb** to understand its various features.

**IN-CHAPTER EXERCISE**

**20.15.** Go through all **gdb** commands discussed in this section to appreciate how **gdb** works. If some of the commands used in this section don't work on your system, use the **help** command to list the **gdb** commands and use those that are available in your version of **gdb**.

### 20.7.2 RUN-TIME PERFORMANCE

The **run-time performance** of a program or any shell command can be measured and displayed by using the **time** command. This command reports three times: elapsed time, system time, and user time in the format hours:minutes.seconds. Elapsed time is the actual time taken by the program to finish running, system time is the time taken by system activities while the program was executing, and user time is the time taken by execution of the program code. Because LINUX is a time-sharing system, elapsed time is not always equal to the sum of system and user time, because many other users' processes may be running while your program executes. The following is a brief description of the command.

Syntax: **time [command]**

**Purpose:** Report the run-time performance of 'command' in terms of its execution time. It reports three times: elapsed time (actual time taken by command execution), system time (time spent on system activities while the command was executing), and user time (time taken by the command code itself)

The **time** command sends its output to stderr. So, if you want to redirect the output of the **time** command to a disk file, you must redirect its stderr (not its stdout) to the file.

There are two versions of the **time** command: the built-in command for the TC shell and the **/usr/bin/time** command. The output of the built-in **time** command is quite cryptic, whereas the output of the `/usr/bin/time` command is very readable. When the TC shell version of the `time` command is executed without a command argument, it reports the length of time the current TC shell has been running. The reported time includes the time taken by all its children, that is, all the commands that have run under the shell. The other version of the command doesn't have this feature.

The following `time` command, executed under the TC shell, reports how long the current shell has been running: 2 hr, 33 min, and 17 sec. In the output, `u` represents user time and `s` represents system time. You can use the TC shell built-in `time` command in a shell script to time it.

```
% time
2.0u 4.0s 2:33:17 0% 0+0k 0+0io 0pf+0w
%
```

The following command reports the time taken by the `find` command. For the sake of brevity, we have not displayed the error messages generated by the `find` command because of improper access privileges for certain directories. Note that the output contains additional information such as the number of page faults and swaps that occur while the `find` command executed. The discussion on this part of the output is beyond the scope of this book.

```
$ /usr/bin/time find /usr -name socket.h -print
0.87user 2.83system 0:03.71elapsed 99%CPU (0avgtext+0avgdata 0maxresident)k
0inputs+0outputs (110major+41minor)pagefaults 0swaps
$
```

As we've mentioned before, the sum of user and system times doesn't always equal elapsed time, especially if a program is idle and doesn't use the CPU for a while due to program I/O. In the example, however, the elapsed time is off by only .01 sec.

Because the `time` command can be used to measure the running time of any program, you can use it with an executable of your own—a binary image or a shell script. The following session shows the running time of the quick_sort program when it is executed to sort numbers in the in_data file. Note that the elapsed time equals the system time plus the user time, as the command was run late at night when the system was not running any other user processes.

```
$ /usr/bin/time quick_sort in_data
44.87user 2.53system 1:49.42elapsed 91%CPU (0avgtext+0avgdata 0maxresident)k
0inputs+0outputs (110major+41minor)pagefaults 0swaps
$
```

There are other ways of measuring the running time of a program that give you better precision, but using the `time` command to perform this task is the easiest way, and we certainly recommend it for beginners.

## SUMMARY

LINUX supports all contemporary high-level languages (both interpreted and compiled), including C, C++, Pascal, Java, Javascript, FORTRAN, BASIC, and LISP. We described the translation process that a program in a compiled language such as C has to go through before it can be executed. We also described briefly a typical software engineering life cycle and discussed in detail the program development process and the tools available in LINUX for this phase of the life cycle. The discussion of tools focused on their use for developing production-quality C software.

The program development process comprises three phases: code generation, static analysis, and dynamic analysis. The LINUX code generation tools include text editors (`emacs`, `xemacs`, `pico`, and `vi`) C language enhancers (`indent`), compilers (`gcc` and `g++`), tools for handling module-based software (`make`), tools for creating libraries (`ar`, `nm`, and `ranlib`), and tools for version control (RCS, CVS, and their related commands).

The purpose of the static analysis phase is to identify features of the software that may be bugs or nonportable, and measure metrics such as lines of code (LOC), function points (FPs), and repetition count for functions. The LINUX tool `gprof` can be used for this purpose.

The purpose of the dynamic analysis phase is to analyze programs during their execution. The tools used during this phase are meant to trace program execution in order to debug them and measure their run-time performance in terms of their execution time. The commonly used LINUX tools for this phase of the software life cycle are debuggers and tracing tools (`gdb`) and tools for measuring running times of programs (`time`).

LINUX has several tools for other phases of a software life cycle, but a discussion on them is outside the scope of this textbook.

## PROBLEMS

1. What are the differences between compiled and interpreted languages? Give three examples of each.
2. Give one application area each for assembly and high-level languages.
3. Write the steps that a compiler performs on a source program in order to produce an executable file. State the purpose of each step. Your answer should be precise.
4. What are the `-o`, `-l`, and `-O` options of the `gcc` command used for? Give an example command line for each and describe what it does.

5. Give the compiler commands used to create an executable called prog from C source files myprog.c and misc.c. Assume that misc.c uses some functions in the math library. What is the purpose of each command?
6. What are the three steps of the program development process? What are the main tasks performed at each step? Write the names of LINUX tools that can be used for these tasks.
7. Give a shell command that can be used to determine the number of lines of code (LOC) in the program stored in the scheduler.c file.
8. Write advantages and disadvantages of automating the recompilation and relinking process by using the **make** command, as opposed to manually doing this task.
9. Consider this makefile and follow the instructions.

```
CC = gcc
OPTIONS = -O3 -o
OBJECTS = main.o stack.o misc.o
SOURCES = main.c stack.c misc.c
HEADERS = main.h stack.h misc.h

polish: main.c $(OBJECTS)
        $(CC) $(OPTIONS) power $(OBJECTS) -lm
main.o: main.c main.h misc.h
stack.o: stack.c stack.h misc.h
misc.o: misc.c misc.h
```

   List the following.
   a. Names of macros
   b. Names of targets
   c. Files that each target is dependent on
   d. Commands for constructing the targets named in part (b)
10. For the makefile in Problem 9, give the dependency tree for the software.
11. What commands are executed for the main.o, stack.o, and misc.o targets? How do you know?
12. For the makefile in Problem 9, what happens if you run the **make** command on your system? Show the output of the command.
13. Use the **nm** command to determine the number of times the strcmp call is used in the libstdc++.a library.
14. Can you remove versions 1.1 and 1.2 from the version tree shown in Figure 20.7? Why or why not?
15. Create version 2.1 of the s.input.c file after creating versions 1.1, 1.2, 1.3, and 1.2.1.1. What command did you use? Show the command with its output.

16. Suppose that the input.c file has versions 1.1 through 1.6 and that you need to delete version 1.3. How can you accomplish this task if the file is managed under
    a. RCS (RCS/input.c,v)?
    b. $CVSROOT/project1/input.c,v
17. Under CVS and RCS, you have checked out the latest version of the input.c file. What would happen if you tried to check out the same file again? Why?
18. Give the command line that restricts access of the RCS log file RCS/input.c,v so that only users dale and kent can edit any version of this file. What is the command line for taking editing rights away from users alumed and tomm?
19. The following code is meant to prompt you for integer input from the keyboard, read your input, and display it on the screen. The program compiles but it doesn't work properly. Use the **gdb** command to find the bugs in the program. What are they? Fix the bugs, recompile the program, and execute it to be sure that the corrected version works. Show the working version of the program.

```
#include <stdio.h>

#define PROMPT  "Enter an integer: "

void get_input(char *, int *);

void main ()
{
        int     *user_input;
        get_input(PROMPT, user_input);
        (void) printf("You entered: %d.\n", user_input);
}

void get_input(char *prompt, int *ival)
{

        (void) printf("%s", prompt);
        scanf ("%d", ival);

}
```

20. What does the `time bash` command line do when executed under the TC shell?
21. Give the command line to redirect the output of the `/usr/bin/time polish` command to a file called polish_output. Assume that you are using Bash.

CHAPTER

# 21

# XFree86 and the LINUX Graphical User Interfaces

**OBJECTIVES**

- To explain the relationship of the components of the predominant graphical user interfaces to LINUX
- To describe the basic concepts and implementation of XFree86
- To give an overview of the GNOME desktop management system
- To give an overview of the KDE desktop management system
- To provide an Internet resource list to supplement the chapter objectives

## 21.1 INTRODUCTION

The fundamental assumption of this chapter is that a graphical user interface (GUI) can be most efficiently used to control the dialog between a single user and an application program running on a standalone or networked computer, using the intermediary of the LINUX operating system. The components of a user's dialog with an application program can be simplified to the software component blocks shown in Figure 21.1.

For example, a user presses a mouse button to signify a graphical pick in an application window shown on-screen. That choice, or event, is recognized by and acted on by the window manager controlling that window. This event is passed along to the desktop manger, which uses the protocols of XFree86, the network protocol component, to pass the request to LINUX. LINUX then passes the request to the application software program for further disposition. This can also work in reverse: An application software program generates a request for a graphical service and passes this request to LINUX, which in turn passes the request to XFree86. XFree86 uses the facilities of the desktop manager and window manager to display the graphical request on the screen of the user's computer.

It is important to note that you can either use the facilities of a nonintegrated GUI system (i.e., one that only uses the functions of a window manager and XFree86 to work within the LINUX environment) or the facilities of an integrated GUI system, which uses the desktop manager (and perhaps a session manager) as an intermediate software link in the chain shown in Figure 21.1. For example, if you install LINUX on your computer, you may wish to install only XFree86 and a default window manager, such as fvwm2. This would constitute a nonintegrated GUI installation. The event-generation chain of interactivity, as

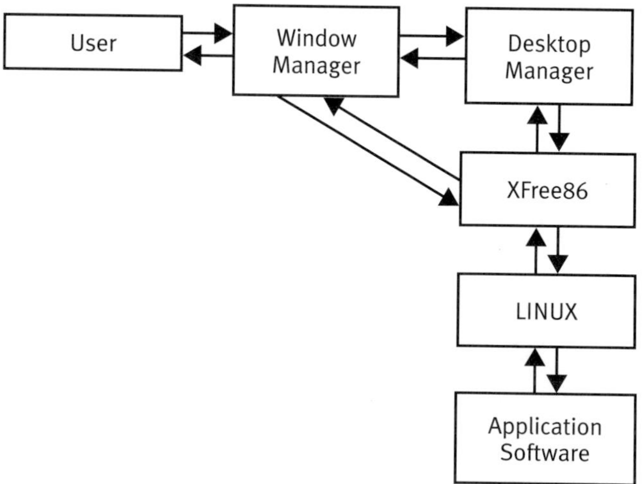


**Figure 21.1** Components of a GUI

seen in Figure 21.1, would start at the user and proceed through the window manager, then jump to XFree86. An integrated approach would involve installing a desktop manager, such as GNOME or KDE. The event-generation chain, as seen in Figure 21.1, would start at the user and proceed through the window manager, then the desktop manager, then XFree86. Most users take the integrated installation approach. Section 21.2 deals exclusively with a nonintegrated installation. Sections 21.3 and 21.4 deal with integrated installations.

Note that if you have done a nonintegrated installation of LINUX and you have not specified that the X Window System start automatically when your computer boots up, you must type **startx** at the LINUX command prompt in order for XFree86 and a default window manager to take control of your display. This assumes that you have a character interface to begin with.

In this chapter, we define XFree86 as a network protocol for graphical interaction between a user and one or more computer systems running LINUX. This means that XFree86 is a software system specifically designed to work over a network to pass user-generated events to the application program and then channel graphical responses, or requests for graphical output, back to the user. The forms of interactivity, via event-driven input and multiwindow display output, are detailed for XFree86 from the user perspective.

Since one of the chief arbiters of the user-computer interactive dialog is the window management system or desktop management system, we define and detail the functionality of these kinds of programs. Specifically, we describe the operations in the GNOME and KDE desktop management systems, the two most important implementations of desktop managers in all releases of LINUX. We also give a functional overview of window managers, particularly fvwm in a nonintegrated installation, and the Sawfish window manager in the GNOME-integrated installation, to expose you to the look and feel of a modern desktop manager and its capabilities. Finally, we list Internet resources that enable you to find more information on all the topics presented in this chapter.

## 21.2 THE BASICS OF XFREE86

### 21.2.1 Comparisons and Advantages

Contemporary user-computer interactivity falls into two basic categories, as mentioned in previous chapters. In one category, where a character user interface (CUI) is implemented, the user types commands on a command line using a keyboard, and components of the operating system handle this input and take appropriate action. In the other category, the user gives input via a graphical user interface (GUI) and components of the operating system take appropriate action. Hybrid styles of interactivity are a mixture of the two categories. Up to this point, you have relied almost entirely on a CUI to activate the functionality of LINUX. This chapter, introduces a LINUX GUI system, known as XFree86.

XFree86 is a derivative of the X Window System, a network protocol developed to provide a GUI to the UNIX operating system. XFree86 is an X Window System "system" itself and contains much of the same source code as the X Window System. (For more information on the X Window System, see Table 21.10). Unlike the X Window System, XFree86 has device drivers for Intel-based PCs, specifically input/output devices and graphics devices. The current release of XFree86 for LINUX is based on the most current release of X Window System. (For more information on XFree86, see Table 21.10).

On the surface XFree86 appears to the user like other popular operating system window managers, such as those found on the Macintosh and in Windows 95/98. There is an important distinction, however, between window system, window manager, and desktop manager. Briefly stated, the **window system** provides the generic functionality of a GUI, a **window manager** simply has particular implementations of the functionality provided by the window system, and the **desktop manager** provides a graphical method of interacting with the operating system. For example, interactive resizing of a window by the user is a generic function of a window system, whereas in a particular window manager sizing is done using icons or slider buttons. The desktop manager provides the user with the graphic means to work with operating system functions, such as file maintenance. A desktop manager might present a picture of folders connected in a treelike structure and allow the user to manipulate files in those folders by dragging and dropping icons. A modern window manager can include some or all of the functional features of a desktop manager. We describe the role that a window manager plays in XFree86 and give examples of window manager functionality in Section 21.2.3.

## IN-CHAPTER EXERCISES

**21.1** What is the name of the window manager in Windows 95/98?

**21.2** What is the name of the window manager on a Macintosh?

What XFree86 does for a user of networked computers is exactly like what an operating system does for the user of a standalone computer. On a standalone computer, the complex details of managing the hardware resources to accomplish tasks is left to the operating system. The user is shielded by the operating system from the complex details of actually accomplishing a task, such as copying a file from one place to another on a fixed disk. On a system of networked computers, XFree86 manages the hardware resources of many computers across the network, to accomplish tasks for an individual user. Also, in a networked, distributed-system environment, where many machines are connected via a communications link, XFree86 serves as a manager of the components of the user's interaction with application programs and system resources transparently; in other words, the user can run an application program on a remote machine and the mechanics of the interaction work exactly as if the application were executing on a standalone machine that was right in front of the user.

The advantage of XFree86 over a traditional LINUX CUI is that it enables you to accomplish predefined tasks quickly and easily by using a GUI under LINUX. For example, dragging icons to delete files is faster than typing commands to do the same thing, particularly if the file names are long and complex. Another, not so obvious, advantage of having a GUI for LINUX is that it makes your style of interaction with the operating system very similar to your style of interaction with applications. For example, modern engineering applications are graphics-based and have a common look and feel; pull-down menus almost always include functions such as cut, copy, and paste. Having a GUI for LINUX makes interaction between an operating system and applications uniform.

### 21.2.2 The Key Components of Interactivity—Events and Requests

When you work with a computer, you provide input in a variety of ways, and the computer, after doing some processing, gives you feedback. For text and graphics feedback, the computer usually responds by displaying information on the screen.

On a modern computer workstation, you are able to use several devices, such as keyboard, mouse buttons, digitizing tablet, trackball, and so on, to provide input to an application program in the form of **interrupt-driven interaction.** The application is processing data or in a wait state until signaled by a particular input device. Interrupts from one or more devices are known as *input events,* which can be ordered in time by forming a list, or queue. With applications written for XFree86, the client application can then process this queue of input events, do the work necessary to form a response to the events, and then output the responses as requests for graphical output to the server. A schematic illustration of this is shown in Figure 21.2.

A key concept of XFree86 that sometimes causes confusion is the difference between *server* and *client.* One possible cause for this confusion is that traditionally, on a computer network, a server is thought of as a machine that transmits files to many other machines, whereas in XFree86, a server is the hardware and/or software

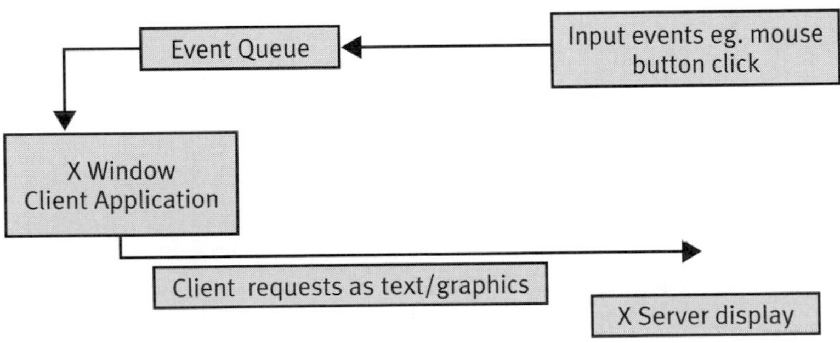

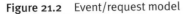

**Figure 21.2** Event/request model

that actually takes input from and displays output to the user. For example, the keyboard, mouse, and display screen in front of you are part of the server; they graphically "serve" information to you. The client is an application program that connects to the server, receives input events from the server, and makes output requests to the server. Sometimes in XFree86 jargon the client is spoken of as a hardware device (e.g., a workstation, or computer). In this text we always use the word *client* to refer to an application, rather than a piece of hardware. In XFree86, a server and client can exist on the same workstation or computer and use interprocess communications (IPC) mechanisms, such as LINUX pipes or sockets, to transfer information between them. A **local client** is an application running on the machine you are sitting in front of. A **remote client** is an application running on a machine connected to your server via a network connection. Whether a client application is local or remote, it still looks and feels exactly the same to the user of XFree86.

Figure 21.3 depicts three client applications—X,Y, and Z—displaying their output on an XFree86 server. Each application is running on a different machine. Remote Client X is running on a machine linked to the XFree86 server via a LAN hookup, an Ethernet. Remote Client Y is running on a machine linked to the XFree86 server via a WAN hookup, the Internet. Local Client Z is running directly on the workstation that is the server, using LINUX sockets to display output requests on the server screen. Not shown in Figure 21.3 is that each of the clients gets input events via this server as well.

Another critical aspect of XFree86 is that the GUI for each client is independent of the GUI of the window manager itself. In other words , each client application can open a window on the server screen and use its own style of GUI buttons, icons, pull-down menus, and so on. The window manager, which is simply another

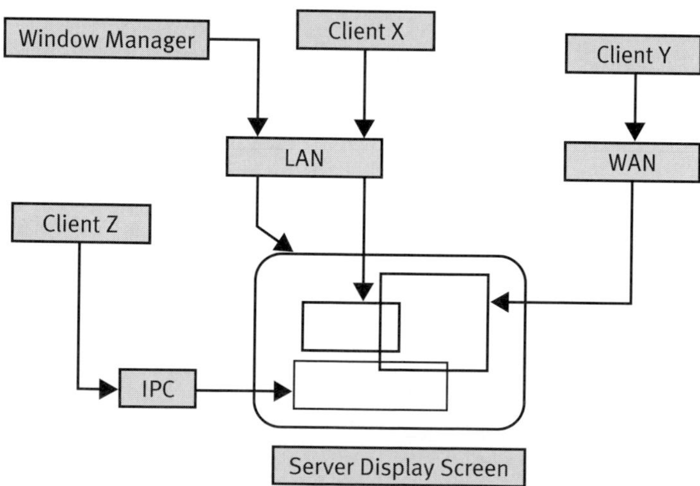


Figure 21.3 Client and server topologies

client application, handles the display of all other client windows. Figure 21.3 illustrates this point.

**IN-CHAPTER EXERCISES**

**21.3** If the client can queue events, would it be advantageous for the server to queue requests? Why or why not?

**21.4** From what you know of network programming in LINUX, is the meaning of client–server the same in network programming as it is in XFree86? If it is not the same, what is the salient difference?

The important aspect of the window manager being just another client of the XFree86 server is that you can use any of the available XFree86 window managers, such as fvwm, mwm, or twm, to suit your particular needs. You can even use your own window manager, if you have the time and resources to write one. It is worth noting that only one window manager can be active on a given server at one time.

### 21.2.3 The Role of a Window Manager in the User Interface and fvwm

As implied in Section 21.2.2, the user interface of XFree86 has two basic parts: the application user interface, which is how each client application presents itself in one or more windows on the server screen display, and the window manager or management interface, which controls the display of and organizes all client windows. The application user interface is built into (i.e., written in a high-level programming language) a client application. It uses either subroutine calls to a library of basic XFree86 protocol operatives, or uses a standard XFree86 toolkit of predefined window elements, such as icons, buttons, and sliders. In this section we concentrate on the general functions that a window manager provides to control the appearance and operability of client application windows. In particular, we examine fvwm, a standard window manager that comes ready to run with XFree86. All window managers in XFree86 are highly customizable, both by the system administrator and by the user. Compare this to other operating system window managers that are built into the operating system but cannot be customized to any real extent. You can modify the appearance and functionality of fvwm, as we show in Section 21.2.3.2.

Note that the fvwm window manager of your LINUX system can be one of either two major classes of fvwm window manager versions: fvwm1 or fvwm2. There is a significant difference in the appearance and customization of these two versions. In the following sections, we use an fvwm1 variant of the basic fvwm window manager, and describe the features and operability of that class of fvwm. Depending on your LINUX installation, you will have an .fvwmrc or .fvwm2rc configuration file in your home directory; looking for these files is a simple way of finding out which version of fvwm you are operating with.

#### 21.2.3.1 Functions and Appearance of the Window Manager Interface

If you have had some experience using Windows 95/98 or a Macintosh, you will recognize many of the general functions, shown in Table 21.1, that a window manager provides. Note that these functions are particular implementations of possibly more than one generic window system service—those provided by the XFree86 protocol.

#### 21.2.3.2 The Appearance and Operation of FVWM

It is worth examining and identifying the components of a typical XFree86 window display. Figure 21.4 illustrates some implementations of the functions listed in Table 21.1, shown in a full-screen display using the fvwm window manager. The background of this screen display (R) is the **root window.** All other windows that open on the screen are children of this parent window. In fact, a single parent window of one client can itself spawn many subwindows, which are all children of that client's parent. An important aspect of this relationship is when parent windows obscure or cover child windows, or when child windows cannot exist outside of the frame defined for the parent window. In the first instance, simply uncovering the child, if possible, allows you to operate in the child window. In the second instance, the parent window may become cluttered, due to the existence of too many uncovered children on top of it. Note that Figure 21.4 shows no covered windows and visually is similar to what is known as a **tiled display.** Also note that,

**Table 21.1** Window Manager General Functions

| Item | Function | Description |
|---|---|---|
| A | (De)Iconify window | Reduces window to a small, representative picture or enlarges to a full-size window |
| B | Create new window | Launches or runs a new client application |
| C | CUI to operating system | Allows the user to open one or more windows and type commands into those windows. |
| D | Desktop management | Maintains graphical files, speed buttons, and special clients like time-of-day clock |
| E | Destroy window | Closes the connection between the server and client |
| F | Event focus | Specifies which client is receiving events from devices such as the mouse or keyboard |
| G | Modify window | Resizes, moves, stacks, and tiles one or more windows |
| H | Virtual screens | Maps more than one screen area onto the physical screen of the server |
| I | Pop-up/pull-down menus | Activates utility menus by holding down mouse buttons to run client applications |

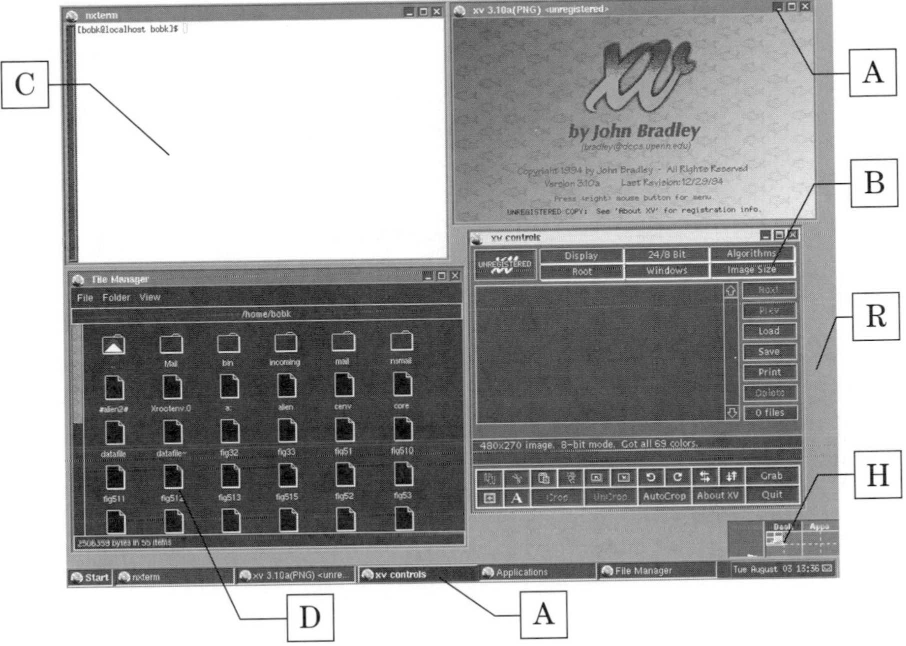


**Figure 21.4** XFree86 fvwm screen display

at the bottom of the screen display, several icons represent miniaturized glyphs of client windows.

When you hold down the left-most, middle, or right-most mouse button with the graphics cursor in the root window, you can use pop-up or cascading pull-down menus (function I in Table 21.1). Typically, these menus fall into three general categories. Depending on how fvwm has been configured at installation, one button may present a cascading pull-down menu of predefined client applications that you can run by making a menu choice. To open a client–server connection and launch the application, you simply make the menu choice. An example of the cascading choices found on a typical pull-down menu of this type is shown in Figure 21.5. A second button may display a list of all open windows and allow you to bring any of them to the top of the stack of windows displayed on the screen, making that window the current window. A third button may display a menu of window modification operations that you can perform by making a menu choice. Typically these modification operations are move, resize or reproportion, raise in the stack to expose the window, lower the window in the stack, (de)iconify the window, (un)maximize the window, and destroy or close the window.

The (de)iconify window function (item A in Table 21.1) is accomplished by use of the button labeled A in the title bar of the frame surrounding a client

| START | | | | |
|---|---|---|---|---|
| Programs | > | PROGRAMS | | |
| System Utilities | | Administration | | |
| Preferences | | Graphics | > | GRAPHICS |
| Window Operations | | Networking | | Viewers |
| Lock Screen/Screen Saver | | Utilities | | The GIMP |
| About fvwm | | | | xpaint |
| Exit Fvwm | | | | Xv |

**Figure 21.5** Pull-down menu to launch client applications

application window in Figure 21.4. This particular client application window is running a graphics file visualization tool known as xv. Clicking the left-most mouse button on this screen button reduces the window to an icon, also labeled A in the figure. An open client application window is labeled B. Each client application window is surrounded by a frame containing several window manager components that allow you to apply the modify window function (item G in Table 21.1).

Another client application window—an xterminal, or xterm for short—labeled C in Figure 21.4, provides a CUI to the operating system of the computer this server is linked to by default. Some window modification components surrounding an xterm window are further described in Figure 21.6. The focus of the server is sometimes known as the *current position* of the graphics cursor in the screen display (function F in Table 21.1). When the focus of the server is in an xterm window and the shell prompt appears at the upper-left corner of the window, you can type in the LINUX commands you have learned in this book to have the operating system of the machine that is running this xterm client take actions.

A typical desktop management tool (function D in Table 21.1), a hierarchic graphical file system display, is labeled D in Figure 21.4. A typical virtual screen menu (function H in Table 21.1) is labeled H. To use this menu of virtual screens, simply position the graphics cursor with the mouse over one of the tiles in the virtual screen menu and click the left-most mouse button. Another portion of the root window is displayed, enabling you to place other client application windows in that tile. The desktop is not limited by the size of the physical screen display, because a virtual screen display consists of the space that is defined by the area of all the tiles in the virtual screen menu.

The fvwm window modification components included in a frame that is placed around an xterm window shown in Figure 21.6 provide functions A, E, and G in Table 21.1. The button labeled A in Figure 21.6 is used to iconify or deiconify the xterm window. When one screen tile becomes too cluttered with windows, you can iconify some of the windows to unclutter the display.

The button labeled E in Figure 21.6 gracefully closes the xterm window, severing the client–server connection cleanly. However, for many client applications, using this button does not gracefully terminate the client–server connection. Usually, within the application user interface provided by the client application, (i.e. inside the window) a pull-down menu choice or other action allows for a graceful exit from the application and a clean disconnect of client from server. There are several dangers inherent in not gracefully exiting an application, foremost of which is that you might lose important data you haven't saved. Also, on networks with software licensing managers, not gracefully leaving an application does not free up its token to other users of the network, which is bad network etiquette.

The button labeled G in Figure 21.6 allows you to modify the size of the window by maximizing the window in the current virtual screen tile. This simply

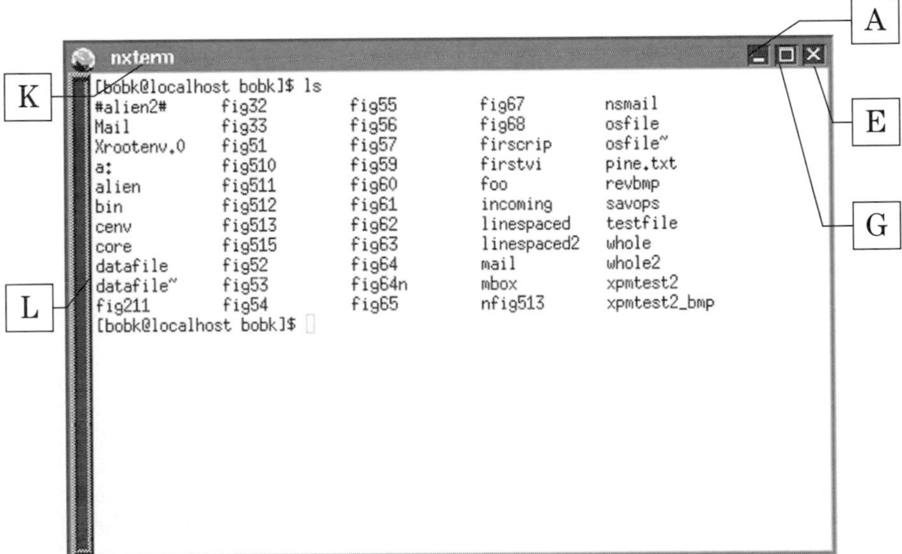


**Figure 21.6** The xterm window and modify components

means that you can quickly enlarge the window frame and its contents to take up the entire area of the current tile. To return the window to its original size, click the maximize button again.

An important functional element not labeled in Figure 21.6 is the resize handle, which is activated by moving the graphics cursor to the extreme edges of the frame. The handle allows you to use the mouse and pointer button on it to resize and reproportion the window interactively.

Two other important components of this typical window frame provide supplemental functions of the window manager. These are the title bar (labeled K), which provides identifying text for this window, and a slider bar (labeled L), which allows you to scroll the contents of the window up and down. Another function of the title bar is to allow you to reposition the entire window and its contents by using the pointing button on the mouse.

### 21.2.4 Customizing XFree86 and fvwm

XFree86 itself, and fvwm in particular, are highly customizable to suit the interactive needs of a wide range of users. It is worth knowing how you can effectively achieve that customization. We examine three approaches to changing the appearance and functionality of the window system and the window manager. The first approach involves changing the characteristics of applications that run under XFree86 by specifying command line options. The second approach involves modifying or creating an initialization file for the window system, then invoking that initialization file, by either restarting the window system or logging off and then logging back in. The third approach involves modifying or creating an initialization file for the window manager, in our case fvwm, and then invoking that initialization file.

A word of caution is necessary at this point: If you do not know what a modification does to the operation of the window manager or system, don't make it! Certainly before making any modifications to the XFree86 environment, you should become familiar with the default operations that have been set up at installation. Then make backup copies of any initialization files you want to change and modify the files; if unexpected behavior results, you can always return to the defaults.

#### 21.2.4.1 Command Line Changes to an XFree86 Application

Once you have seen and worked with the default operations of a particular application, you can run that application with customized display characteristics by typing a command, along with appropriate options and arguments. In this section we modify the display and operating characteristics of the xterm terminal emulator window, using the xterm command and its options. We also run three other applications using command line options and arguments. The following is a brief description of the xterm command.

Syntax:

**xterm [[+][−]toolkitoption ...] [[+][−]option ...]**

**Purpose:** Run a terminal emulation program in its own window to allow you to type LINUX commands. The + adds the option, the − subtracts the option.

**Output:** A window with display characteristics determined by "toolkitoption" and options.

**Commonly used options/features:**

| | |
|---|---|
| `-ah` | Always highlight the text cursor |
| `-e program [ arguments ... ]` | Run 'program' (and 'command line arguments') in the xterm window |
| `-sb` | Scroll some number of lines off the top of the window, save them, and display a scrollbar so that those lines can be viewed |

For example, in order to affect the kind of shell that is run in the xterm window when it starts up, type the command line **`$ xterm -ls &.`** This option indicates that the shell that is started in the xterm window will be a login shell. To start an xterm window with an ordinary subshell running in it, type **`$ xterm +ls &.`** To have the window manager start the xterm window with a scroll bar, which would allow you to scroll backward or forward through the text that has been displayed on screen and retained in a buffer, type **`$ xterm -sb &.`** A more complete listing of toolkitoptions and options for the xterm command is given in the Appendix.

The following session shows how to run other applications using command line options. The three applications which we run, xclock, xbiff, and xv, are sized and positioned with the `-geometry` command line option and its arguments, which are the same for all three applications. The xclock application displays an analog time-of-day clock on the screen as an icon. The xbiff application displays a mailbox and flag on screen; the flag goes up when mail arrives in your system mailbox. The xv application is a graphics file viewing program as shown in Section 21.2.3.2. In order to size and position the application windows on your display screen, you must be aware of the way in which the screen coordinates are derived. The coordinate system for screen locations in XFree86 is as shown in Figure 21.7.

The origin, 0 in X and 0 in Y, is in the upper-left corner of the screen. The direction of increasing X is to the left and increasing Y is down. The screen resolution of your display—how many pixels in X and Y can be addressed—depends on

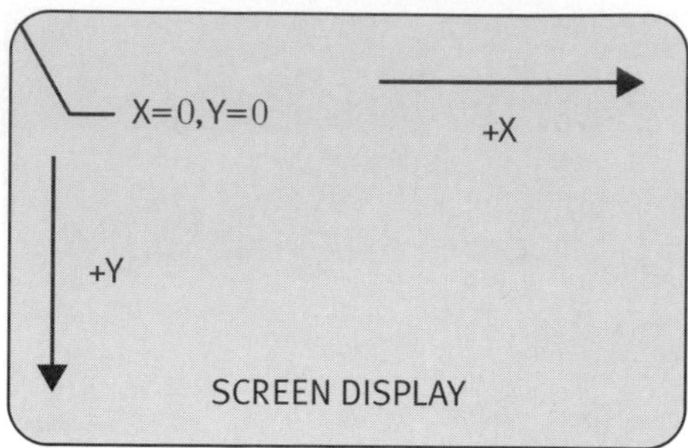


**Figure 21.7** Screen coordinate system

what kind of monitor and graphics card you have and the settings of the XFree86 preferences. To run the applications, in an xterm window type

```
$ xclock -geometry 100x100+10+10 &
$ xbiff -geometry 50x50+120+10 &
$ xv -geometry 200x160+10+120 &
$
```

Figure 21.8 shows the appearance, relative size, and position of each of the applications windows after all three have run. The arguments for the `-geometry` option are X-pixel size of window, Y-pixel size of window, X-position of upper-left corner of window, and Y-position of upper-left corner of window. Thus the command `xclock -geometry 100x100+10+10` sizes the xclock to be 100 × 100 pixels, and positions its upper-left corner at the coordinates X = 10 and Y = 10 relative to (0, 0).

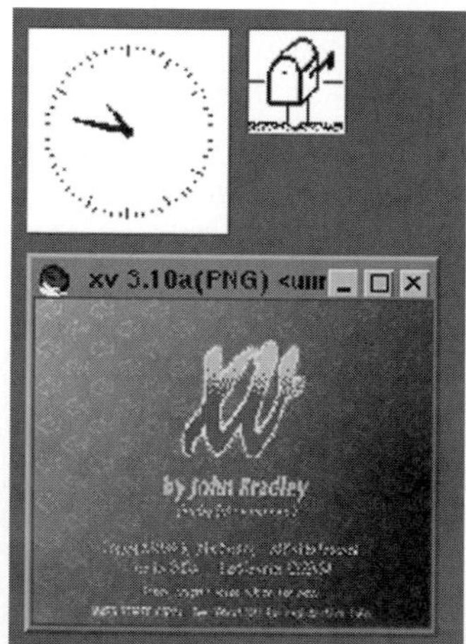


**Figure 21.8** Three applications run with command line options

To close down an XFree86 application gracefully, you can use the client application mechanisms, which might be a pull-down menu choice or a button press. For example, there is a button on the xv controls screen menu that allows you to quit xv. To close xclock or xbiff, you can find the PID of each by using the **`ps`** command, then issue a kill signal for that PID. For example, if xclock had a PID of 904, as shown in the output from **`ps`**, typing the command **`$ kill 904`** in an xterm window would close the xclock application.

To learn more about the options for xclock and xbiff, see the appropriate LINUX manual pages on your system. To find out more about the options for xv, either see the appropriate LINUX manual page on your system or get an Adobe Acrobat or PostScript version of the documentation on xv at ftp://ftp.cis.upenn.edu/pub/xv/docs.

## IN-CHAPTER EXERCISES

**21.5** Run an xclock sized at 75 × 75 located at (200, 200).

**21.6** If you run xv with no arguments, what is the default window size of the display that xv places on screen? How did you find this out?

**21.7** After consulting the manual page for xterm, either on your system or in the Appendix, run an xterm with its background color set to green.

**21.8** Run an xterm with the scroll bars disabled or enabled.

#### 21.2.4.2 Preference Changes in .Xdefaults and .xinitrc Initialization Files

Instead of typing command line options for applications you run on a regular basis or starting specific applications whenever you begin an XFree86 session, you can group these common preference changes in two different initialization files. First, however, we need to discuss some additions and modifications you can make to a file named .Xdefaults, which is your personal copy of the file that sets the systemwide defaults for XFree86. Your personal copy takes precedence over the systemwide default file. Then we discuss other additions that you can make to an initialization file that starts up applications, named .xinitrc.

The following sample .Xdefaults file is a standard default file supplied by our system manager to control the appearance of windows and specify which resources will be used with either all or with specific applications.

```
$ cat .Xdefaults
# Standard .Xdefaults for U of P user accounts (k.t. 4/6/93 rev5.3)
#
    .BorderWidth: 10
    .BitmapIcon: on
    .MakeWindow.Background: white
```

```
      .MakeWindow.Border: grey
      .MakeWindow.BodyFont: cor
      .MakeWindow.Foreground: black
      .MakeWindow.Freeze: on
      .MakeWindow.Mouse: #e6f
      .MakeWindow.MouseMask: black
      .MakeWindow.ClipToScreen:on
      .Menufreeze: on
      .Menubackground: white
      .Panefont: 8x13
      .SelectionFont: 8x13
      .SelectionBorder: black
      .Paneborderwidth: 1
TK*graphics_device: POSTGRAP
TK*text_display: True
AutoCAD-Graph.geometry: 800x650+0+50
AutoCAD-Render.geometry: 700x500+50+100
AutoCAD-Text.geometry: 800x650+20+70
AutoCAD-ToolBar.geometry: 386x242+841+161
```

The first block of lines beginning with period (.) specifies display characteristics of all windows. Another way of doing this is to use the metacharacter asterisk (*) to specify all windows. Such as

```
*Foreground  black
```

would change the foreground color of all unspecified windows to black. To modify only the display attributes of a particular application window, you could type

```
AutoCAD*Background:       green
```

and that line would change the background of the main AutoCAD window to the color green.

The remaining lines in the file set particular resources for specific applications. For example, the line `TK*graphics_device: POSTGRAP` sets the graphics output device, or printer, for the application TK Solver to be a PostScript device. The line `AutoCAD-Render.geometry: 700x500+50+100` sets the size of the AutoCAD Render viewport to be 700 × 500 pixels and places that viewport at the coordinates 50 in X and 100 in Y away from the upper-left corner of the screen.

If you want certain key applications to start automatically whenever you log on, you can create or modify an initialization file named .xinitrc in your home directory with your favorite text editor and place the names of those key applications in that file. These new defaults will not take effect until you log on for the next session after you make the changes. For example, the following .xinitrc file starts key applications and sets a default color for the root window

```
xsetroot          -solid        green
xterm        -geometry     120x80+20+40
netscape     -geometry     166x340+160+10
fvwm &
```

The first line in this file sets the root window color to solid green. The second line opens a terminal emulator window, sized and positioned as indicated, as soon as you log on. The third line runs the Netscape browser at the size and position indicated. The fourth line starts the fvwm window manager.

#### 21.2.4.3 Typical Changes in .fvwmrc to Customize the fvwm Window Manager

To make specific changes in the look and feel of the fvwm window manager, you can create or modify the .fvwmrc file in your home directory. If you do not already have a .fvwmrc file in your home directory, get one from your system administrator. You can edit this file with your favorite text editor, such as vi or emacs, and use the facilities of that editor, such as search and replace, to make modifications efficiently. You can then customize fvwm to your preferences by making changes in the coded directives and commands in this file. The structure and order of coded directives and commands that should be in this file are shown in Table 21.2. In general, this information shows you the extent to which you can customize.

**Table 21.2** The .fvwmrc directives

| Block | Function | What It Does |
|---|---|---|
| A | Colors and fonts | Changes colors and fonts used in window borders and menus |
| B | Activity modes | Places focus and icons |
| C | mwm emulation | Provides compatible Motif window manager operations |
| D | Desktop | Sets the style of the virtual desktop and pager |
| E | Modules | Sets the paths to modules and icons |
| F | Decorations | Sets the window styles and decorations, such as width of borders |
| G | Functions | Defines functions bound to mouse and mouse buttons |
| H | Menus | Defines user menus shown in the root window |

Table 21.3 lists some samples of commands and directives from blocks A through F listed in Table 21.2. Commented lines in the .fvwmrc file begin with the pound sign (#); therefore placing a # before a line in the file turns the directive found on that line into a comment, thus negating its effect. For example, if you don't want all the icons to follow you around the virtual desktop and into every virtual screen, simply add a # in front of the line in block C, which reads StickyIcons. This is where the search and replace or find feature of your text editor comes in handy.

If you want to be able to move into any virtual screen simply by rolling the mouse, find the line in your .fvwmrc file that reads

```
EdgeScroll 100 100
```

and make sure that line is not commented out. The arguments of the EdgeScroll command let you flip through 100% of each virtual screen display as you roll the mouse and change the current position into any of the virtual screen tiles. Otherwise, you would have to use the tiled display found in the lower-right hand corner of Figure 21.4 (labeled H) and click on the appropriate tile to map that virtual tile into the actual screen coordinates.

To build complex functions into the .fvwmrc file, you must remember to forward reference them in the file, which means that you should place them in the file before calling them in any way. The following is an example of a complex function, which should be in directive block G of .fvwmrc (Table 21.2). It moves (changes screen placement) or raises (brings to the top of the window stack) a window using mouse movement and pointer-button clicks.

**Table 21.3** Examples of .fvwmrc Directives

| Block | Example | What It Does |
|---|---|---|
| A | HiForeColor grey90 | Sets selected windows foreground color to grey |
| | Font -adobe-helvetica-medium-r-*-*-14_*-*-*-*-*-*-* | Sets the font used for menus |
| B | ClickToFocus | Focus follows current position |
| | StickyIcons | All icons shown in all vitual windows |
| C | MWMBorders | Uses Motif-style border reliefs for windows |
| D | DeskTopSize 8x2 | Sets the virtual desktop to be 8 × 2 times screen |
| E | ModulePath /usr/lib/X11/fvwm | Sets the path to icon pixel maps |
| F | Style "xclock" NoTitle, NoHandles, Sticky | Decoration of clock on the desktop |

```
Function "Move-or-Raise"
        Move    "Motion"
        Raise   "Motion"
        Raise   "Click"
        RaiseLower   "DoubleClick"
EndFunction
```

The most useful aspect of window manager customization is being able to define your own menus activated by the mouse buttons when the current position is located in a specific place on screen. For example, when the current position is in the root window, the pop-up menus Utilities, Window Ops, and winlist are activated by, or bound to, the mouse buttons. This is accomplished by the following three lines of code in the .fvwmrc file:

```
Mouse 1      R   A   Popup "Utilities"
Mouse 2      R   A   Popup "Window Ops"
Mouse 3      R   A   Module "winlist" FvwmWinlist transient
```

These menus are made up of a collection of menu choices that either run applications or generate other cascading submenu choices. For example, the module "winlist" calls on a resource to display a list of all open windows on screen. The R on each line means that this menu is activated in the root window. The A on each line means that you can use any keystroke modifier in addition to pressing the mouse button.

To help you define your own pop-up menu, we present the following customized pop-up menu definition, which can be bound to the right-most (#3) mouse button.

```
# MORE EE
# A collection of three electrical engineering software tools plus another cascading pop-up menu
Popup "more ee"
      Title  "More EE Programs"
      Exec   "spiceit - SPICE simulator"   exec /usr/local/bin/spiceit &
      Exec   "xschedit - schematic editor" exec /usr/local/bin/xschedit &
      Exec   "xsymed - symbol editor"            exec /usr/local/bin/xsymed &
      Nop    ""
      Popup "EMULATION"                          emulation
EndPopup
```

After the comments explaining the contents of the menu in brief, any menu must begin with a line that contains the Popup command. A title that can be referenced by other menus follows the Popup command; in other words, if later in the .fvwmrc file, you want to call this menu as a submenu, you would refer to it with the name more ee . Next, a title "More EE Programs", which will appear as text at the top of the menu, is placed on its own line. The three programs—spiceit, xschedit, and xsymed—are placed after the Exec command, and the paths to those three programs are listed on each line following the entry that will appear in the pop-up menu for each. A blank line in the menu is achieved with the Nop command. Another cascading submenu, titled EMULATION, is placed on a line after a Popup command. The name of the menu that is activated when this choice is made is emulation, which has been defined in lines of code before the more ee menu definition. Finally, the menu must end with the EndPopup command. Figure 21.9 shows what this menu will look like on screen.

To bind this menu to the right-most mouse button and have it activated when the current position is in the root window, the following lines must appear in .fvwmrc. Note that the previous binding of the winlist module to this mouse button has been commented out of the file.

```
#Mouse 3      R    A    Module "winlist" FvwmWinlist transient
Mouse 3       R    A    Popup "more ee"
```

For a more detailed description of the options available for customizing fvwm, see the fvwm manual page. To gain more familiarity with the features and utilities of a nonintegrated GUI installation, do Problems 1 through 12 at the end of this chapter.

## 21.3 THE GNOME DESKTOP MANAGER

The GNU Network Object Model Environment (GNOME) was developed as an outgrowth of the GNU Project. (For more information on the GNU Project, see Chapter 2. For more information on GNOME, visit http://www.gnome.org.) The GNOME desktop manager is an **integrated system,** in the sense that it provides a consistent and uniform implementation of functions such as an application programmers interface (API), object request broker (ORB), window management, desktop configuration tools, session management, and, most important, application programs. The uniformity of these functions in an integrated system necessarily goes beyond

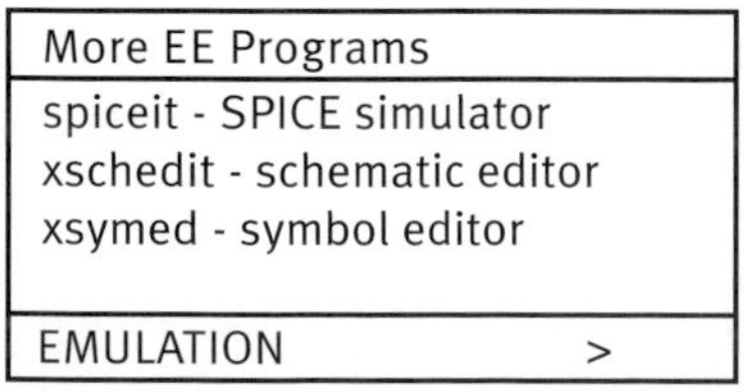

| More EE Programs |
|---|
| spiceit - SPICE simulator<br>xschedit - schematic editor<br>xsymed - symbol editor |
| EMULATION > |

**Figure 21.9** A customized pop-up menu

the rudimentary provisions that XFree86 and the X Window System make for creating and maintaining a graphical interface to LINUX. The drawbacks of these systems are their size and complexity. In the sections that follow, we have assumed that when you installed your version of LINUX, you installed and specified the GNOME desktop manager and/or the KDE desktop manager to start automatically. In this section, we show the appearance of the GNOME desktop running under Red Hat LINUX 7.0.

### 21.3.1 Logging In and Out, and the Appearance of the GNOME Desktop

As your computer boots up, a login window appears on screen. Chapter 3, Section 3.4 showed you how to log on and off using a text-based interface. Depending on which integrated system was designated as the default when you or your system administrator installed LINUX, you will see a login dialog box for either GNOME or KDE. You can now enter your username and password. The login dialog box also allows you to make other important system choices, such as changing the type of session you will have with the computer (generally either a GNOME GUI session or a KDE GUI session), rebooting the operating system, or halting the operating system in preparation for powering down the computer. Most LINUX network users will only log on and off using this dialog box. If you have LINUX running on a standalone computer, you may have to restart or reboot the computer using the other dialog box choices. When halting the system, it is always a good idea to allow LINUX to completely "unload" itself before turning off the power to the computer. After you have successfully logged on a GNOME session, your screen display should look like Figure 21.10.

The GNOME desktop has a very similar look and feel to desktop systems such as Macintosh and Windows 98/2000. One notable difference is that you use a single click of the left mouse button to launch a program in GNOME. In Figure 21.10, notice the pictures in the bar at the bottom of the screen display. This bar, or panel, acts as an information center and launching pad for many of the desktop facilities and application programs. For example, the small Netscape logo is a **launcher button** that launches the Netscape browser. Among the icons arranged along the left side of the screen display is what looks like a garbage can with the word *Trash* beneath it. Objects dragged and dropped onto this icon are deleted from the computer.

There are two open windows in the center of the screen display, GNOME Search Tool and bobk @ localhost.localdomain: /home/bobk. The first is a GNOME application window that allows you to search for files on the computer. The second window is an xterm for LINUX commands, similar to the console you would work in if you did not have a GUI to LINUX. If you click and hold down the right mouse button when the cursor is in the background area of the desktop, a menu appears allowing you to accomplish some common tasks, such as create a new folder on the desktop, or view and edit desktop icon properties. Figure 21.11 shows this menu.

At this point, if you wanted to log out of the current session or take other system actions such as reboot or halt the LINUX operating system, you would make the Program menu choice Log out, as shown in Figure 21.12. In the following sections, we describe the components and important features of the GNOME desktop.

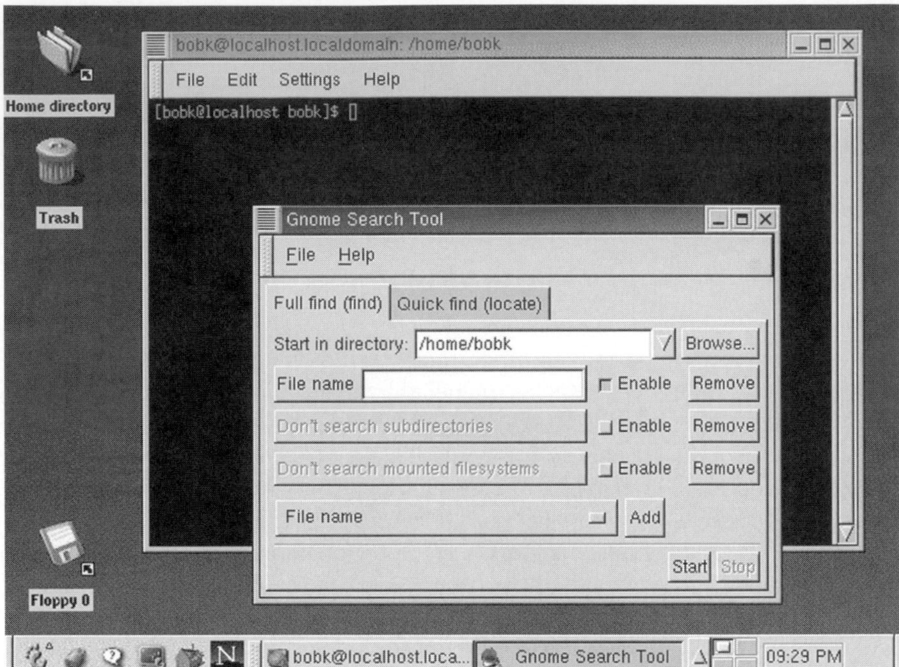


**Figure 21.10** GNOME desktop

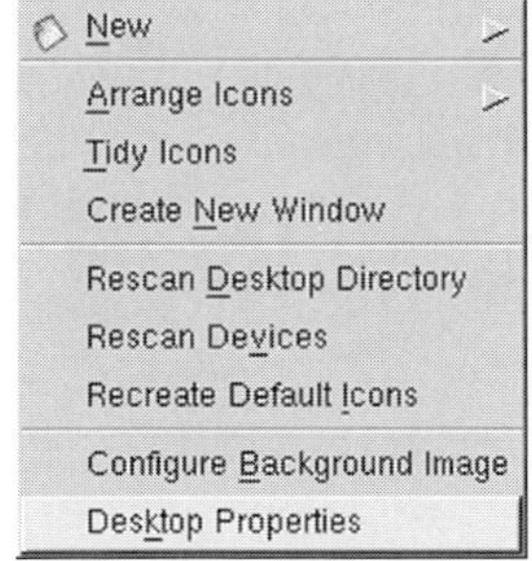


**Figure 21.11** Right-click menu

## 21.3.2 The GNOME Panel

The components of the GNOME panel, which appears across the bottom of the screen, are named and briefly described in Table 21.4, and are shown in Figure 21.13.

The most important component of the panel is the main menu (B). The main menu contains fly-out menus that enable you to launch a preset list of programs, favorite programs, applets (small, GNOME-specific programs), and KDE menus

**Figure 21.12** GNOME main menu

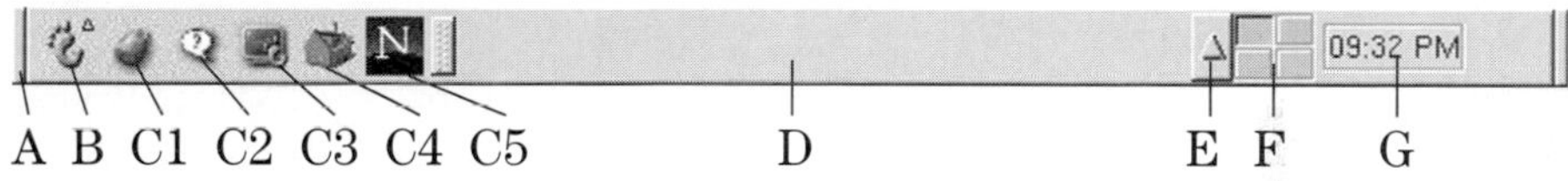


**Figure 21.13** GNOME panel components

(from within GNOME, if you have KDE installed). It also contains the Run button, which allows you to launch additional applications using text-based commands, and a panel configuration tool to add objects to the panel, remove the whole panel, or create new panels. Finally, the Lock screen button allows you to lock the screen with password protection so it cannot be tampered with when you are away from the display and the Log out button ends the session. As shown in Figure 21.14, the Programs fly-out menu lists application programs and utilities that can be launched from this menu. It also contains buttons to launch the file manager and the GNOME help system.

**Table 21.4** GNOME Panel Component Descriptions

| Label | Component Name | Description |
|---|---|---|
| A | Roll-up arrow | Moves the panel out of the way, left and right |
| B | Main menu | Launches applications and desktop utilities, similar to the Windows Start menu |
| C1–5 | Launcher/applet buttons | Launches general applications or GNOME-specific applications or applets |
| D | Pager | Similar to the Windows taskbar, shows open windows (Shown blank in Figure 21.13.) |
| E | Pager button | Lists open windows in a cascading fashion |
| F | Virtual desktop icon | Shows the tiles of a virtual screen display |
| G | Clock | Digital clock |

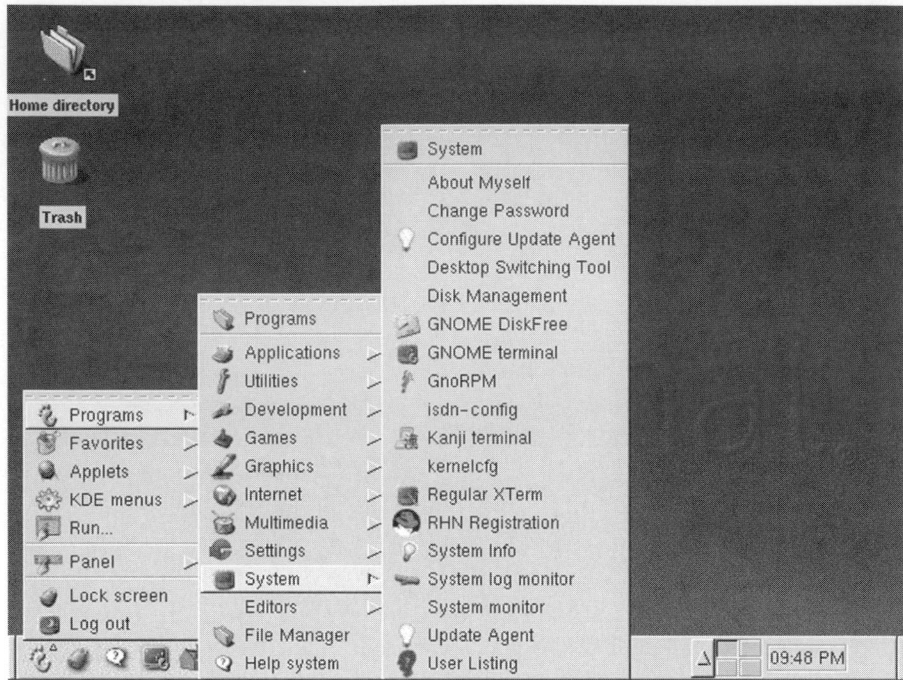


**Figure 21.14** Programs menu with System fly-out menu activated

Right-clicking on any of the objects in the GNOME panel activates a menu that allows you to manipulate that particular object. For example, if you right-click over the Lock screen button (item C1 in Figure 21.13), menu choices allow you to remove that button from the panel, move that button to a new location on the panel, accomplish functions of that button such as locking the screen, and configure preferences for that button. You can also obtain help on that button from this menu. These choices are shown in Figure 21.15.

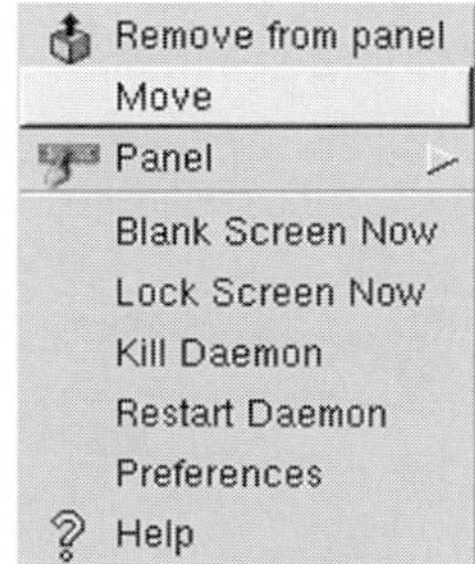


**Figure 21.15** Right-click menu on a panel object

### 21.3.3 Customizing the Panel

One of the most useful aspects of the GNOME desktop manager is the ease with which you can reconfigure almost every component of it. This applies to the panel as well. For example, if you wanted to change the content and structure of the panel menus, you can use the GNOME menu editor. You launch this utility by making the fly-out menu choices Main Menu > Programs > Settings > Menu Editor. Figure 21.16 shows the general appearance of the menu editor. Practice Session 21.1 shows you how to create a new menu choice, assuming you are running GNOME on a LINUX system with the emacs package installed. If emacs has not been installed, skip ahead to Practice Session 21.3, and install emacs following the instruction steps for Xemacs, then return to Practice Session 21.1.

**Practice Session 21.1**

**Step 1:** From the main menu, make the fly-out menu choices Programs > Settings > Menu Editor. A window will open on your screen similar to that shown in Figure 21.16.

**Step 2:** In the left panel, where a menu tree appears, click once on Favorites (user menus). If you have not added anything to this menu before, you should have no entries in this branch of the tree. If you do not have this submenu, use the New Submenu toolbar icon to create it.

**Step 3:** In the toolbar that appears at the top of the GNOME menu editor window, left-click on the New Item icon. A new, untitled branch will appear in the tree. The name bar in the right panel also now contains the name "untitled."

**Step 4:** Press <backspace>. This should erase the name "untitled" from the name bar in the right panel. Then type **`emacs`** into the name bar, **`emacs text editor`** in the comment bar, **`emacs`** in the command bar, and leave the type bar as "Application."

**Step 5:** Left-click in the icon box, and an icon selection window will open on screen, similar to Figure 21.17. Left-click on the emacs icon, then click OK .

**Step 6:** In the GNOME menu editor window, click on the Save button. In the menu tree in the left panel, emacs now appears as a menu choice under the Favorites menu. The GNOME menu editor screen should now look like Figure 21.18

**Step 7:** Quit the GNOME menu editor by making the pull-down menu choice File > Exit.

**Step 8:** From the main menu on the panel, make the fly-out menu choices Favorites > emacs. You should now see a GNU emacs window. Quit emacs.

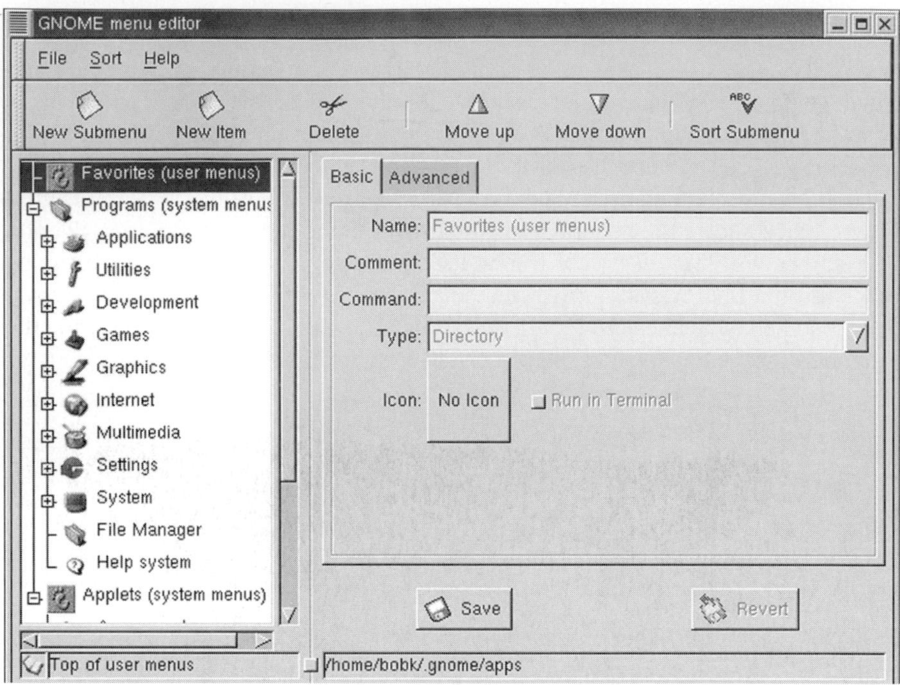


Figure 21.16 GNOME menu editor

Figure 21.17 Icon selection window

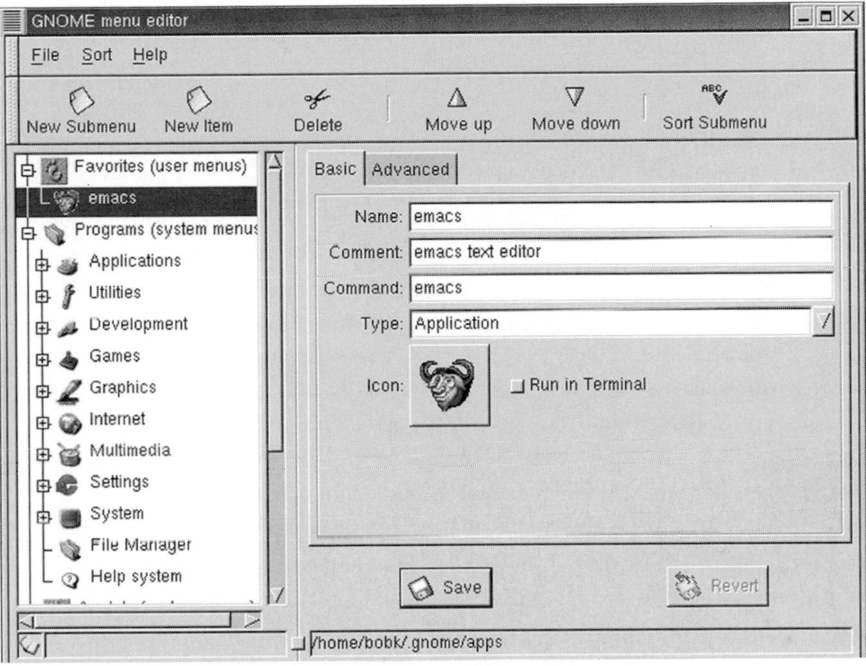


**Figure 21.18** GNOME menu editor window with emacs menu choice

## IN-CHAPTER EXERCISES

**21.9** Create a new folder under Programs with the GNOME menu editor, name that folder Fun Stuff, and add any application menu choices that you like to it, using the methods described in Practice Session 21.1.

**21.10** Using the GNOME menu editor, create application menu choices under Main Menu > Programs > Editors for emacs, vi, vim, and pico, and any other editors of your choice. On our system, Xemacs is already found as a menu choice under Editors. Be aware that only the editors installed with your LINUX system will be available.

In addition to adding menus to the GNOME panel, you can also add several other objects to enhance your graphical interactivity with the desktop. One of these objects is a **drawer,** or list of graphical icons that unfolds from the panel vertically or horizontally. You can store icons in the drawer that accomplish common tasks, similar to the text found as submenu choices in a fly-out menu. Practice Session 21.2 shows you how to add the drawer and icons in Figure 21.20. If these menu choices are not available on your system, you can substitute any other application that is convenient.

## Practice Session 21.2

**Step 1:** Make the GNOME main menu choice Panel > Add to Panel > Drawer. A drawer icon is now added to your panel, similar to the icon shown on the far left of Figure 21.19.

**Step 2:** Right-click over the drawer icon and use the Move menu choice to move the drawer icon to the right of the Netscape icon on the panel, as seen in Figure 21.20.

**Step 3:** Right-click over the Drawer button at the top of the empty drawer space (a down arrow is in this button). Make the fly-out menu choices Panel > Add to Panel > Applet > Amusements > Fifteen. The icon for launching the applet Fifteen is added to the drawer display. You can close the drawer by left-clicking on the down arrow at the top of the drawer display.

**Step 4:** Repeat Step 3 to add the applet Sound Monitor, found under Panel > Add to Panel > Applet > Multimedia > Sound Monitor.

**Step 5:** Right-click the Sound Monitor icon in the drawer and use the Move menu choice to move it above the Fifteen icon.

**Step 6:** Repeat Step 3 again to add the Gnotes applet, found under Panel > Add to Panel > Applet > Utility > Gnotes.

**Step 7:** Right-click over the Gnotes icon in this drawer and use the Move menu choice to move it above the Sound Monitor icon. Your final drawer display should look like Figure 21.20.

**Step 8:** Finally, try out each of these new icons. The game Fifteen can be played right in the drawer. Left-clicking on the Gnotes icon places sticky notes all over your desktop; the Sound Monitor is useful for controlling levels of sound generated in your system's sound card. Please note that in order for sound to work in GNOME, you must have enabled it in the GNOME Control Center. To get help with using this applet, right-click over the Sound Monitor and choose the help menu.

## IN-CHAPTER EXERCISE

**21.11** Add a new drawer to your panel containing some of your most often used applications, such as Xemacs, the pine e-mail program, and the File Manager. To make these additions, you will have to make the menu choices Panel > Add to panel > Launcher... . A dialog box will appear, allowing you to add a launcher button to the drawer, similar to the dialog box in the GNOME menu editor you used in Practice Session 21.1.

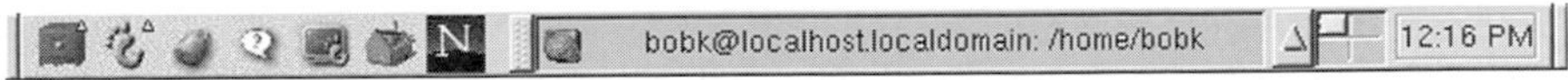


Figure 21.19 New drawer added to the panel

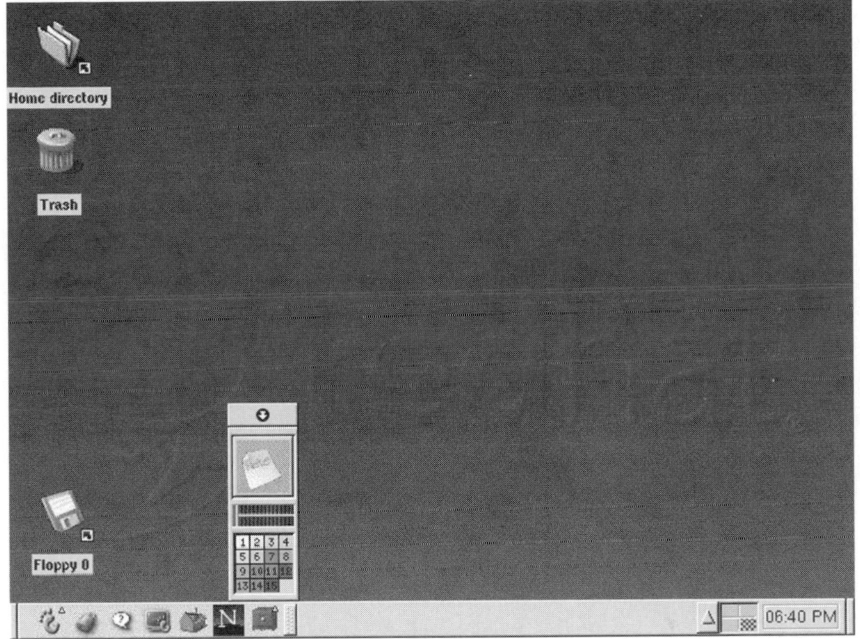


Figure 21.20 Panel with new drawer icons added

## 21.3.4 GnoRPM Installation of New Packages

If you are interested in learning how to install a LINUX system, you should read the Installation Appendix at the end of this book for details of how to do a complete and simple install of the system and application programs. When you or the system admistrator installs your LINUX system, some useful applications, known as **packages,** may not have been installed. This is usually the case when someone wants an expeditious install, without having to individually specify each package to be installed. It is also the case when you do not know the capabilities of a package when you install the system and thus omit it from the installation, but then find out later what the capabilities of a certain package are, and now want to have that package on your system without having to re-install the entire system. The GnoRPM application will allow you to install new packages, as long as they follow the Red Hat package format. The GnoRPM application will also allow you to upgrade, or reinstall on an individual basis or collectively, new and improved versions of packages that have bcome available since your initial LINUX system installation. We do not cover other methods of doing package upgrades here.

You can add and upgrade packages on your system via an Internet connection with GnoPRM, but we do not cover that option here. Also note that if new and improved packages become available, and you download them via the Internet from Red Hat or your LINUX system vendor, you can always move them to your harddrive or onto your system via floppy disk to make them available to the GnoRPM application. You would then simply change the default location where GnoRPM finds new packages.

For a description of the capabilities of the Xemacs text editor, see Chapter 5, Section 5.5. If Xemacs is already installed on your system, you may follow along with the description of GnoRPM and simply use another new package in place of Xemacs. In Practice Session 21.3, we assume you are running Red Hat LINUX 7.0, that your new package is available on a CD, that Xemacs is not initially installed, and that you have access to the Root password. If you did the initial installation yourself from a CD-ROM, you should be able to proceed. Otherwise, contact your system administrator for help installing new or upgraded packages.

## Practice Session 21.3

**Step 1:** To verify that you have the Xemacs package available, insert the Xemacs CD in your CD-ROM drive. A file management window should open on screen, simlar to the one shown in Figure 21.21.

**Step 2:** Find the Xemacs package by scrolling down the right panel of the file management window. If it is not available, insert the CD that contains this package.

**Step 3:** Close the file management window using the pull-down menu choice File > Close window.

**Step 4:** From the main menu, make the fly-out menu choice Programs > System > GnoRPM. An input window will open, asking you for the Root password. Type in the Root password, then left-click the OK button. The GnoRPM window will open, showing a snapshot of your system's installed packages.

**Step 5:** In the file-tree panel on the left side of the GnoRPM window, open Applications > Editors by left-clicking. Your screen should now look like Figure 21.22, with the notable exception that you will probably not have the number of editors shown.

**Step 6:** Left-click the Install button, a floppy disk icon in the upper left of the GnoRPM window. An Install window will open on screen, showing you the packages available on your CD, as shown in Figure 21.23.

**Step 7:** Left-click to open the folders Applications – Editors. Place a check mark by left-clicking in the box to the right of Xemacs.

**Step 8:** Left-click on the Install button at the bottom of the Install window. An Installing progress window will open on screen, showing you the installation progress.

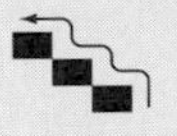

## Practice Session 21.3 (cont.)

**Step 9:** Left-click on the Close button of the Install window.

**Step 10.** Quit the GnoRPM application by making the pull-down menu choice Packages > Quit.

**Step 11:** Add a menu choice to your main menu programs or to a drawer for the new application by using the procedures from Practice Sessions 21.1 or 21.3. Then launch Xemacs using the new menu choice or button.

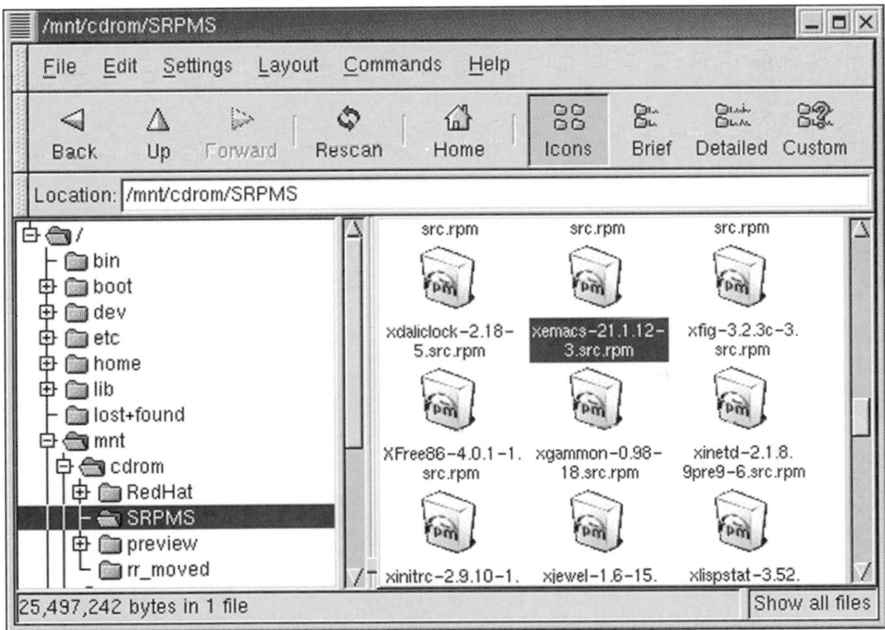


**Figure 21.21** CD-ROM contents showing new Xemacs package

## IN-CHAPTER EXERCISES

**21.12** Use GnoRPM, or a similar graphical front-end package installation program, to install a new package on your LINUX system. Write down the steps you used.

**21.13** Use GnoRPM to upgrade existing packages on your system via an Internet connection. Write down the steps you used.

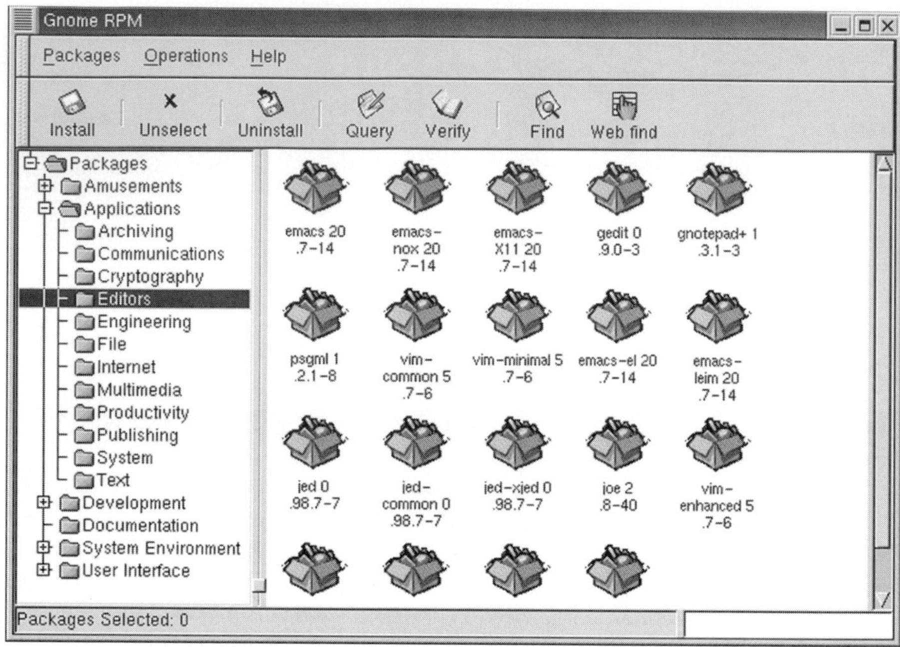


**Figure 21.22.** GnoRPM window showing installed editors

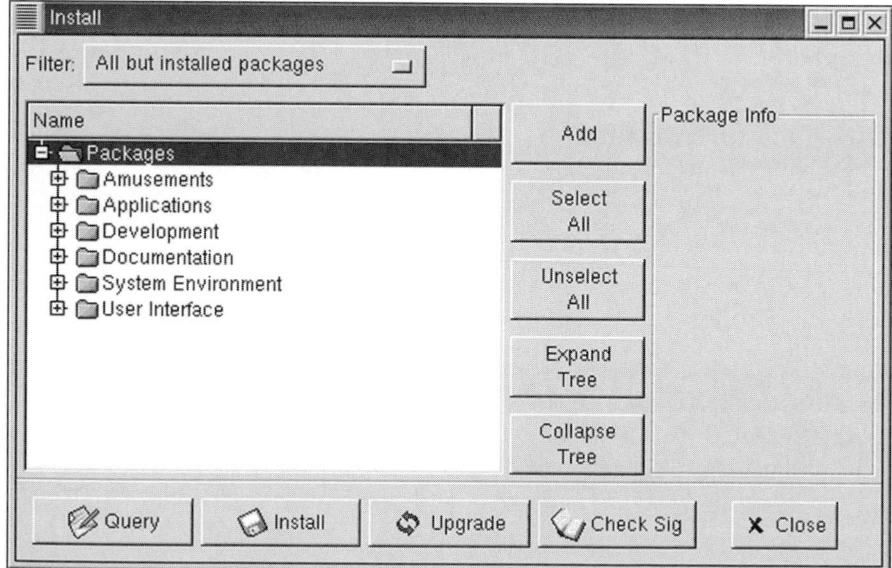


**Figure 21.23** New package groups available on CD

Several other options are available for maintaining packages on your LINUX system with GnoRPM. You can inquire about packages and their dependencies on your system, uninstall packages, verify the correct installation of new and upgraded packages, and upgrade packages on an individual or collective basis. These functions and others, such as obtaining packages via an Internet connection, are available via the toolbar button choices at the top of the GnoRPM window and in the Install window. For help with these features, use the GnoRPM Help pull-down menu that describes the main window, the query window, the install window, the find window, and the Web find window.

### 21.3.5 The Sawfish Window Manager

The program that you work with most directly in the GNOME desktop environment is the window manager. The appearance and interactivity of GNOME windows, from simple terminal windows to application windows, is controlled by the window manager. The most popular window manager for GNOME is called **Sawfish,** a derivative of the Sawmill window manager. Several other window managers are also available, the most popular being IceWM, WindowMaker, Enlightenment, AfterStep, and FVWM2. For more information on these window managers, see Internet Resources 3 through 8 in Table 21.10.

The Sawfish window manager gives a window "dressing", or standard interactive techniques and their related features, to expedite your work within that window. For example, a slider button (item F in Figure 21.24) is provided in an xterminal window to allow you to graphically scroll backward or forward through the text that has been displayed on the xterminal screen. For more examples of these features, see Table 21.5 and the graphical references to Figure 21.24.

**Table 21.5** Window Components of Sawfish

| Item | Name | Description |
|---|---|---|
| A | Attributes menu | Sets attributes for this window, such as frame type and style, history, and depth |
| B | Title bar | Shows current path and allows window movement |
| C | Control buttons | Minimizes, maximizes, and kills window |
| D | Menus | Application-specific menu choices for xterminal |
| E | Body | Xterminal console display |
| F | Scroll bar | Allows user to scroll contents of text in this window |
| G | Border | Resizes window with handles |
| H | Position button | Repositions the menus |

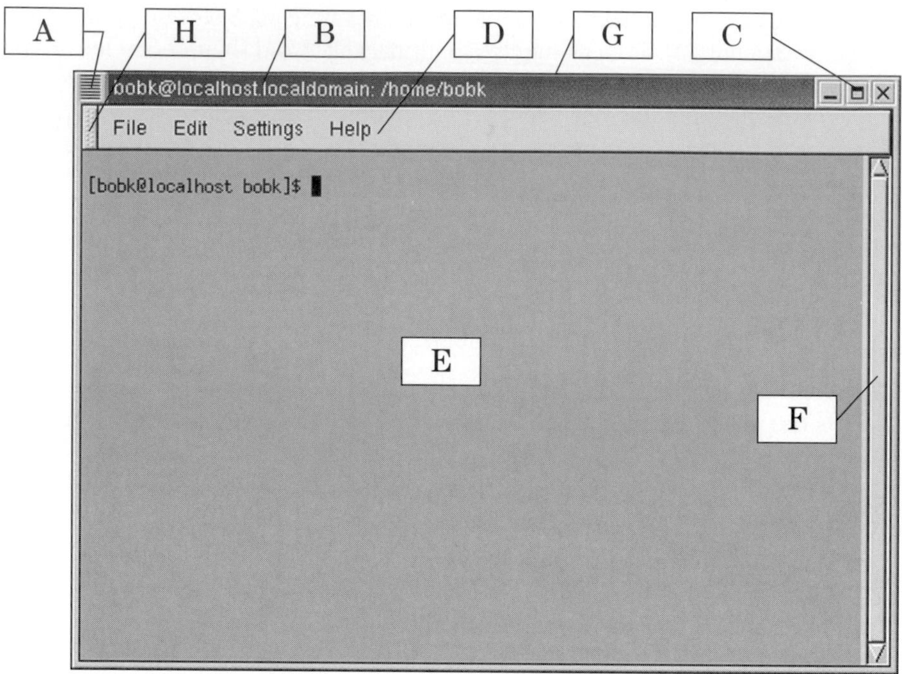


Figure 21.24 Sawfish version of an xterminal window

As previously mentioned, the window manager provides a frame within which the application can display its graphical output, and within which you can interact with the application program through user-generated events. The look (appearance of buttons, style and color, its theme) and feel (how buttons work, how menus are activated) of the window manager is independent of the look and feel of the application running in area E of Figure 21.24. Because of this, you can reconfigure the appearance and interactivity of the Sawfish window manager without affecting the look or interactivity of any application running inside the window manager's border. Practice 21.4 explains the steps necessary to reconfigure the Sawfish window manager so that it has a different look and feel. In Practice Session 21.4, you will change the interaction style known as edge flipping. **Edge flipping** is the ability to move between tiles of the virtual desktop (as seen in the GNOME panel) by moving the cursor to the edge of one of the virtual screen tiles, then the mouse to move it into an adjacent tile. You will also change the appearance of Sawfish to the microGUI theme. We assume that you are using the Sawfish window manager with Cool Clean look as the default.

## Practice Session 21.4

**Step 1:** From the main menu, make the fly-out menu choice Programs > Settings > GNOME Control Center. The GNOME Control Center window will appear.

**Step 2:** In the GNOME Control Center window, in the left panel, highlight the tree choice Desktop > Window Manager, as shown in Figure 21.25. The available window managers for your system appear in the right panel. Note that your screen display may show other window managers, depending on what was installed with your system.

**Step 3:** Highlight Sawfish in the right panel of the GNOME Control Center window by left-clicking on it once if it is not the current window manager.

**Step 4:** Left-click once on the button labeled Run Configuration for Sawfish. The Sawfish configurator window that opens should look like Figure 21.26.

**Step 5:** Left-click on the Workspaces branch of the tree display in the left panel of the Sawfish configurator window, then left-click again on the Edge Flipping branch in the same panel. Your screen display should now look like Figure 21.27.

**Step 6:** Left-click on the Select the next desktop button. If it is already selected, left-click on it to deactivate it.

**Step 7:** Left-click on the Workspaces branch of the tree display in the left panel to close it.

**Step 8:** Left-click on the Appearance branch of the tree display in the left panel. In the middle of the right panel, make the pull-down menu choice microGUI. Your screen display will change, and all windows, including the Sawfish configurator window, will take on the look of the microGUI theme (Figure 21.28). Feel free at this point to experiment with the other themes available until you find one that you like.

**Step 9:** Left-click on the OK button at the bottom right of the Sawfish configurator window. The Sawfish configurator window will close. Left-click on the OK button in the GNOME Control Center window, then make the File > Exit choice in the GNOME Control Center window.

**Step 10:** Now move through your window displays in the different virtual tiles of the desktop using edge flipping, or if you turned edge flipping off, notice how limited your movements are without it. Also notice the difference in appearance between your default desktop theme in Sawfish and the new one you have chosen.

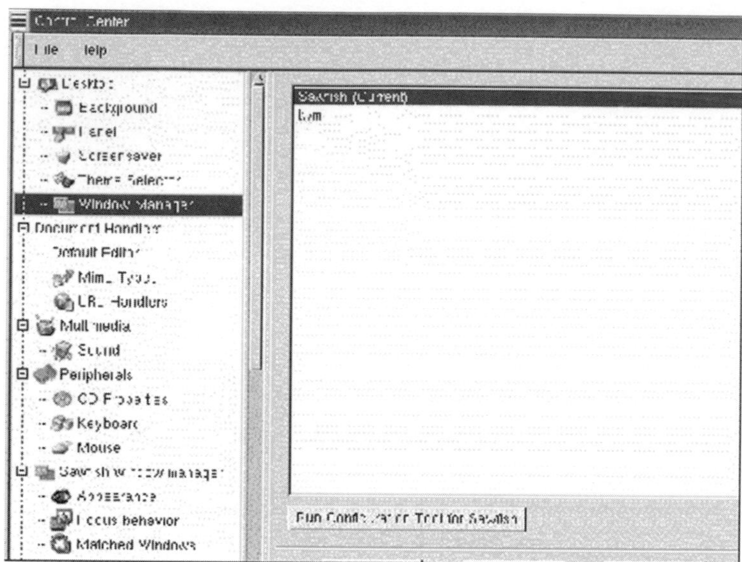


**Figure 21. 25** GNOME Control Center window manager tree choices

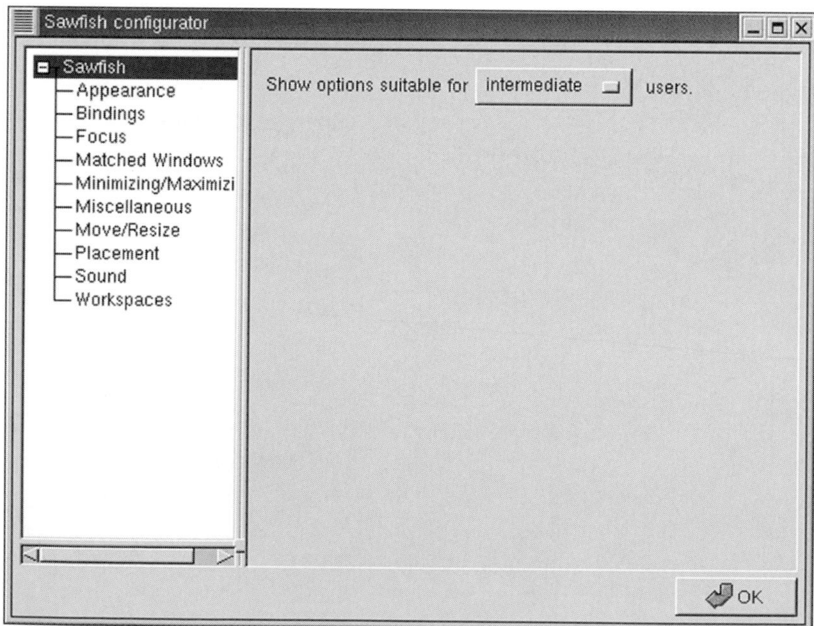


**Figure 21.26** Sawfish configurator window

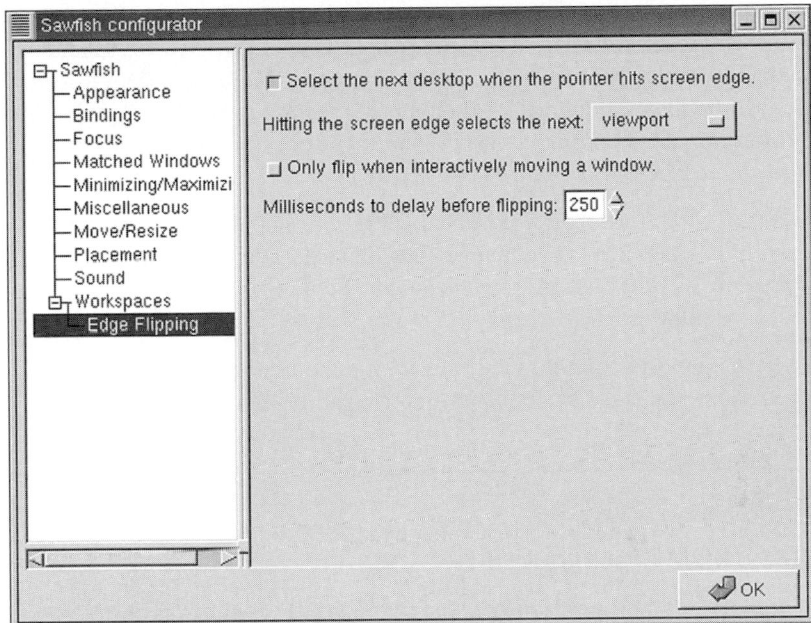


**Figure 21.27** Sawfish Workspaces Edge Flipping configurator

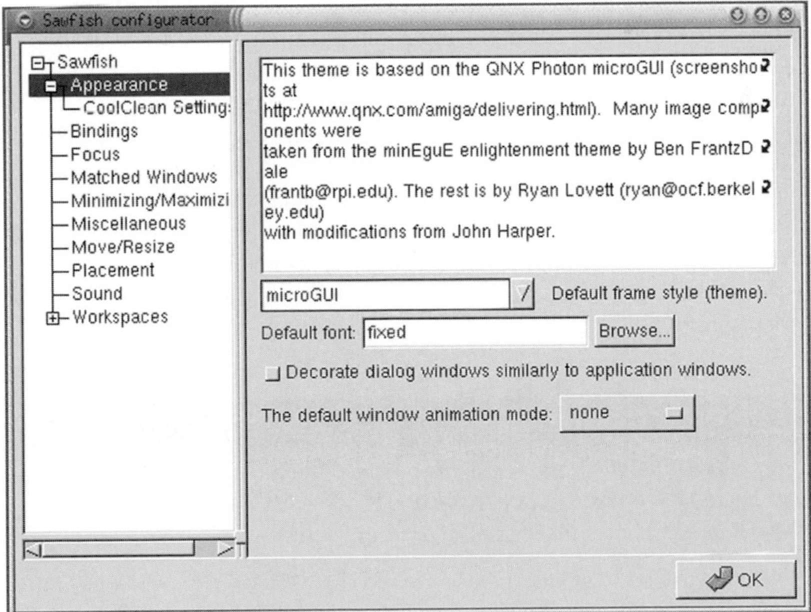


**Figure 21.28** Sawfish configurator microGUI window

**IN-CHAPTER EXERCISES**

**21.14** Launch the GNOME Control Center and use the Sawfish configurator to find the keyboard bindings for the following commands: `GNOME logout`, `cycle windows`, `next workspace`, `previous workspace`, `activate workspace 1`, `activate workspace 2`.

**21.15** Use the Sawfish configurator to change the Focus behavior so that the current position is focused in a window on entry and exit from that window. How is this different from clicking in a window to change the focus to that window?

**21.16** Use the Sawfish configurator to change the method of placement of newly launched windows to be interactive rather than best-fit or any other default method.

## 21.3.6 The GNOME Control Center

The most important configuration tool for the GNOME desktop is the GNOME Control Center. This utility configures your system by using GNOME applications known as **capplets.** These small GNOME programs allow you to make a variety of changes in the performance of the GNOME desktop. For example, as shown in Section 21.3.5, a capplet allowed you to change and customize the window manager. To launch the GNOME Control Center, make the main menu choices Programs > Settings > GNOME Control Center.

Two important areas of the GNOME Control Center window are shown in Figure 21.29. The panel on the left is the menu tree of capplets available to the GNOME Control Center on your system. By clicking on one of the main branches or sub-branches of this tree, you can launch the capplet associated with that particular tree item. For example, when you left-click on the Peripherals main branch after launching the GNOME Control Center, two capplets become available: the Keyboard capplet, and the Mouse capplet. Left-clicking the Keyboard capplet allows you to change various performance parameters of your keyboard, as shown in Figure 21.29.

**IN-CHAPTER EXERCISES**

**21.17** Launch the GNOME Control Center and use the Sawfish window manager branches to undo the changes you made with the Sawfish configurator tool in In-Chapter Exercises 21.15 and 21.16.

**21.18** Which Sawfish window manager branch in the GNOME Control Center allows you to change the number and arrangement of the virtual screen tiles shown in the panel? What is the default number and arrangement of virtual screen tiles in the panel for your system? Change yours to be $2 \times 2$.

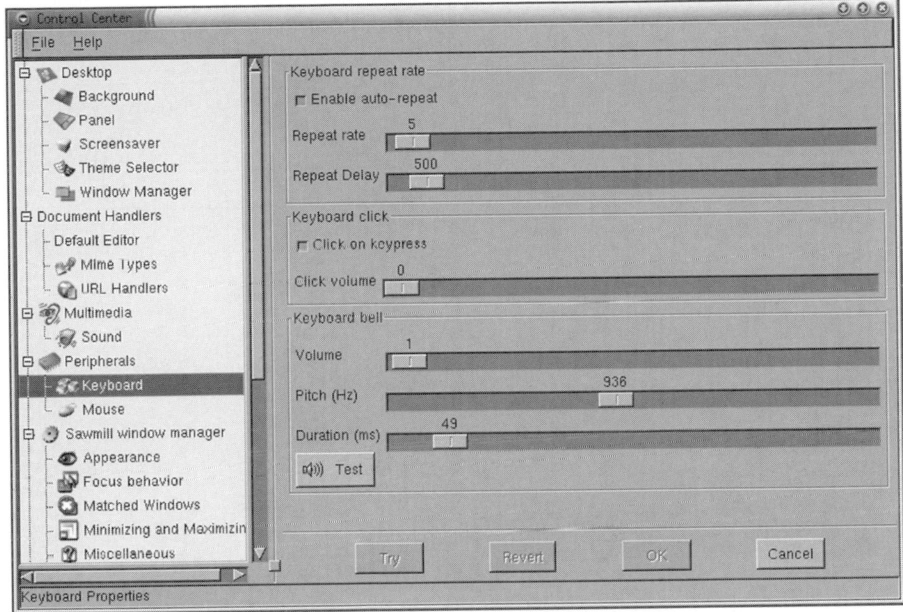


Figure 21.29 GNOME Control Center Keyboard properties capplet

## 21.3.7 File Management with the GNOME File Manager

An extremely useful utility of the GNOME desktop is the file manager, or **GNU Midnite Commander (GMC).** Many users will understandably find this utility an expeditious substitute for many of the LINUX file maintenance commands. The GNOME File Manager offers a graphical way of doing common file maintenance operations. The GNOME File Manager is a graphical front-end version of Midnite Commander, an older system that ran in a terminal window. The GNOME File Manager can be launched by making the main menu choices Programs > File Manager. The GNOME File Manager opens in a window and on our LINUX system by default shows the contents of the current working directory, as shown in Figure 21.30. There are two important areas of this window: the tree view in the left panel, which shows the file structure of your system, and the directory window in the right panel, which shows the folders and files as icons in the currently-selected branch of the directory tree. For example, in Figure 21.30 the home directory of user bobk is highlighted in the directory tree (as well as shown in the title bar of the File Manager window), and the icons representing folders and ordinary files are shown in the directory window. In addition, several icons at the top of the File Manager window allow you to change the appearance of file displays very quickly. For example, the Back button lets you make the previously viewed directory the currently viewed directory. Several file properties and actions on files appear on the pull-down menus at the top of the File Manager window. A list of the important properties and actions is given in Table 21.6.

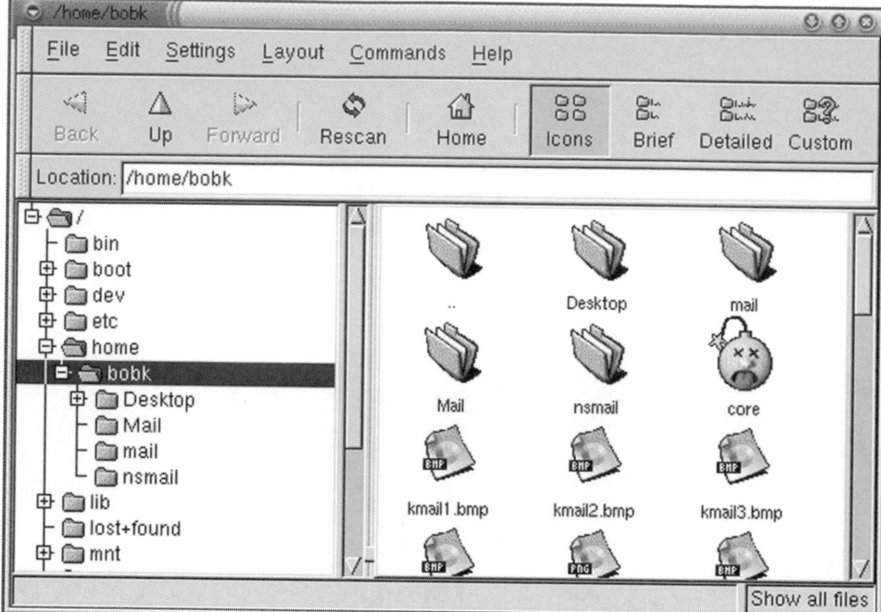


**Figure 21.30** GNOME file manager window

One of the most useful pull-down menu choices is Commands > Find File, which allows you to designate where in the file structure of the system you want to start a search and what file name you want to search for. This utility is very similar to the text-based LINUX `find` command. For example, if you wanted to find all files in your home directory that ended in the file extension .png, you would make the Commands > Find File pull-down menu choice, then supply the infor-

**Table 21.6** Properties and Actions of the File Manager Pull-Down Menus

| Pull-Down Menu Choices | Description |
|---|---|
| File > New > Directory | Creates a new subdirectory or folder |
| File > Open | Views the contents of a file using default program |
| File > Copy | Creates a duplicate of selected file(s) |
| File > Delete | Removes file(s) |
| File > Move | Changes the path location of selected file(s) |
| Layout > Sort by | Sorts display by various attributes, such as name or type |
| Layout > Filter View | Uses file attributes to limit the display of files |
| Commands > Find File | Finds specified file(s) starting at a path location |
| Commands > Run | Executes a shell command |

mation in the proper text bars of the Find File window as shown in Figure 21.31. When you clicked on the OK button, a dialog box would open, show you the names of the found files, and allow you to take further action based on the results, such as change the tree and directory views of the File Manager window to the subdirectory or path location of the files that were found.

**IN-CHAPTER EXERCISES**

**21.19** Use the GNOME File Manager Find File utility to find all files starting at the root directory that end with the file extension .bmp. How many files were found? Use the Change to this directory button to change the file manager display to one of the subdirectories on your system that contain a .bmp file. Use the File Manager pull-down menu choice File > Open to open the found .bmp file. What do you see? What program was used by default on your system to open the .bmp file?

**21.20** Use the GNOME File Manager Find File utility to find all files starting in your home directory that begin with the letter M (uppercase).

To gain familiarity with the features and utilities of GNOME, go on to Problems 13 through 16 at the end of this chapter.

## 21.4 THE KDE DESKTOP MANAGER

The K Desktop Environment (KDE) was developed by a volunteer programmer organization. To learn about the history and mission of the KDE organization, visit http://www.kde.org. Similar to GNOME the KDE is an **integrated system,** in that it provides a consistent and uniform implementation of functions such as an application programmers interface (API), object request broker (ORB), window

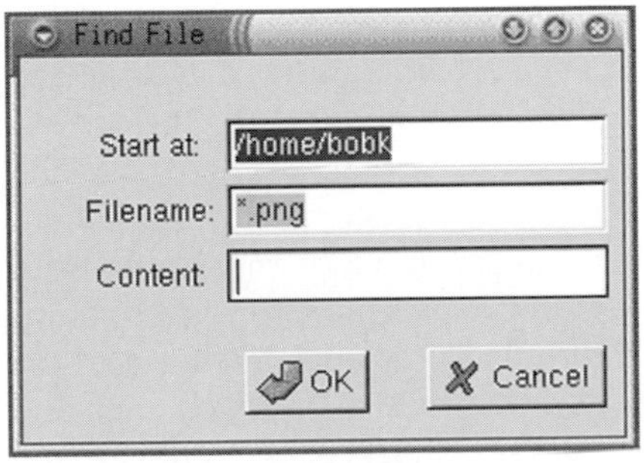

**Figure 21.31** Find File window

management, desktop configuration tools, session management, and, most importantly, application programs. The uniformity of these functions in an integrated system necessarily goes beyond the rudimentary provisions that XFree86 and the X Window System make for creating and maintaining a graphical interface to LINUX. The drawbacks of these systems are their size and complexity. In the sections that follow, we assume that KDE and/or GNOME start automatically in your version of LINUX. We show the appearance of the KDE running under Red Hat LINUX 7.0.

*Note:* If you have not specified that KDE start automatically when your LINUX system boots up, but you have installed KDE as your default GUI, you can always begin a KDE session by typing **startx** at the LINUX shell prompt after you have logged on. We leave installation of KDE as a problem at the end of the chapter.

### 21.4.1 Logging In and Out

As your computer boots up, a login window appears on screen. Chapter 3, Section 3.4 showed you how to log on and off using a text-based interface. Depending on which integrated system was designated as the default when you or your system administrator installed LINUX, you will see a login dialog box for either KDE or GNOME. You can now enter your username and password. The login dialog box also allows you to make other important system choices, such as changing the type of session you will have with the computer (generally either a KDE GUI session or a GNOME GUI session), rebooting the operating system, or halting the operating system in preparation for powering down the computer. Most LINUX network users will only log on and off using this dialog box. If you have LINUX running on a standalone computer, you may have to restart, or reboot the computer using the other dialog box choices. When halting the system, it is always a good idea to allow LINUX to completely "unload" itself before turning off the power to the computer. After you have successfully logged on a KDE session, your screen display should look like Figure 21.32.

The KDE desktop has a very similar look and feel to desktop systems such as Macintosh and Windows 98/2000, as well as the GNOME desktop covered in Section 21.3. One of the most notable differences between KDE and Windows or Mac operations is that you use a single click of the left-most mouse button to launch a program in KDE. In Figure 21.32, notice the pictures in the bar at the bottom of the screen display. This bar or panel acts as an information center and launching pad for many of the desktop's facilities and application programs. Among the icons arranged along the left side of the screen display is what looks like a garbage can with the word *Trash* beneath it. Objects dragged and dropped onto this icon are deleted from the computer.

There are two open windows in the center of the screen display, Mail client and bobk@localhost.localdomain: /home/bobk. The first is a KDE application window, known as Kmail, that allows you to work with e-mail, similar to what is shown in Chapter 6. The second window is an xterm for LINUX commands, similar to the console you would work in if you did not have a GUI to LINUX. If you click and hold down the right mouse button when the cursor is in the background area of the desktop, a menu appears allowing you to accomplish some common tasks,

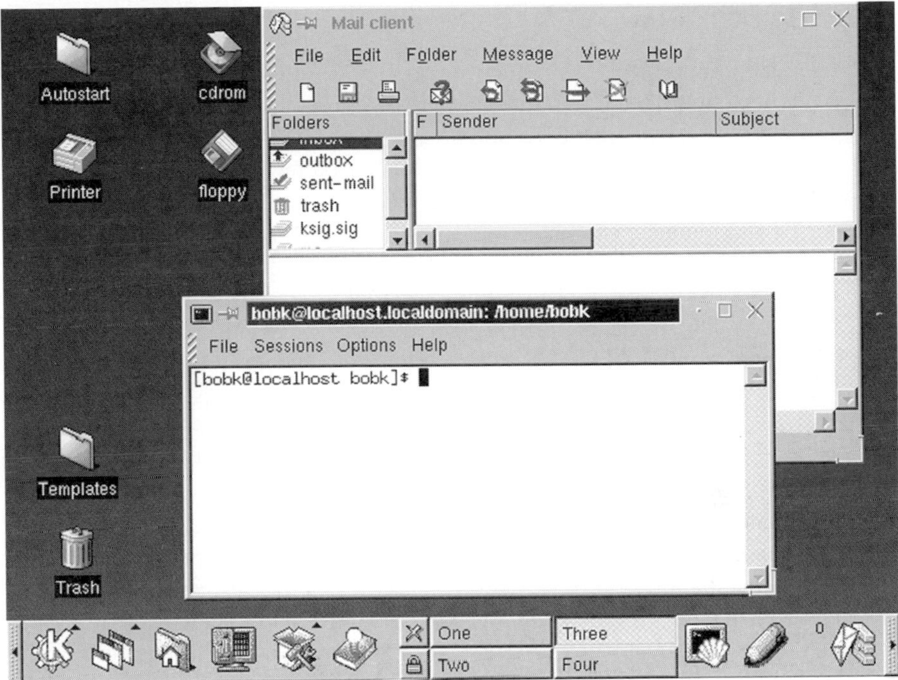


**Figure 21.32** The KDE screen display

such as create a new folder on the desktop, or view and edit desktop icon properties. Figure 21.33 shows this menu.

At this point, if you wanted to log out of the current session, or take other system actions such as reboot or halt the LINUX operating system, you would make the Logout menu choice, as seen in Figure 21.33. In the following sections, we describe the components and important features of KDE.

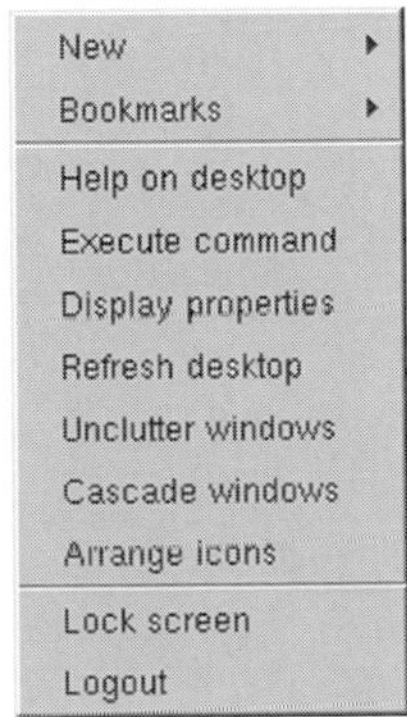


**Figure 21.33** Right-click menu

### 21.4.2 The KDE Panel

By far the most important component on KDE is the KDE panel, which appears across the bottom of the screen display. The components of the panel are named and briefly described in Table 21.7, and are shown in Figure 21.32.

The most important component of the KDE panel is the main menu icon. When you left-click on the icon, the main menu, shown in Figure 21.34, appears. It contains fly-out menus that enable you to launch a preset list of applications and utilities. For example, as shown in Figure 21.35, the utilities fly-out menu of the main menu lists useful utilities, including the kpackage program, which allows you to add new or updated applications to your LINUX system. We discuss the details of using kpackage in Section 21.4.4. A number of other fly-out menus activated from the main menu allow you to launch user applications, graphics applications, Internet tools, multimedia tools, and other systemwide and development applications. The Lock Screen button on the main menu allows you to lock the screen with password protection so it cannot be tampered with when you are away from the display, and the Logout button ends the session.

Right-clicking on any of the objects in the KDE panel activates a menu that allows you to manipulate that particular object. For example, if you right-click over the KDE Control Center icon (item E in Figure 21.36), menu choices allow you to remove that button from the panel, move that button to a new location on the panel, or obtain and change properties of that application, as shown in Figure 21.37. The Move choice, highlighted in Figure 21.37, allows you to move the KDE Contol Center icon left or right in relation to the other icons on the KDE panel.

**Table 21.7** KDE Panel Component Descriptions

| Label | Component Name | Description |
|---|---|---|
| A | Collapse bar | Moves the panel out of the way left and right, and reveals or hides it |
| B | Main menu | Launches applications and desktop utilities, similar to the windows start menu |
| C | Windows list | Lists and manipulates open windows on the desktop |
| D | File manager | Allows file maintenance |
| E | Control center | Allows customization or changes in basic KDE configuration |
| F | Toolbox | Launches system utilities such as Knotes, KOrganizer, text editor, and xterminal |
| G | Help | Launches on-line help |
| H | Pager | Switches between four tiles of a virtual desktop screen |
| I | Terminal | Opens a terminal window that contains a shell prompt |
| J | Editor | Launches kwrite, a simple text editor |
| K | Mail client | Launches Kmail, a fully-functional e-mail system |

**Figure 21.34** KDE main menu

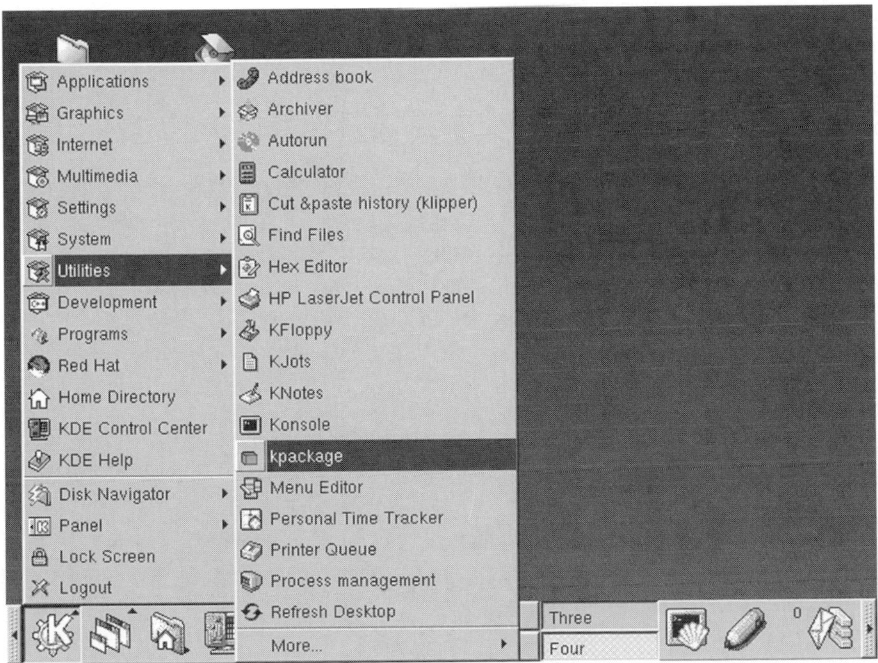


**Figure 21.35** Utilities submenu of the KDE main menu

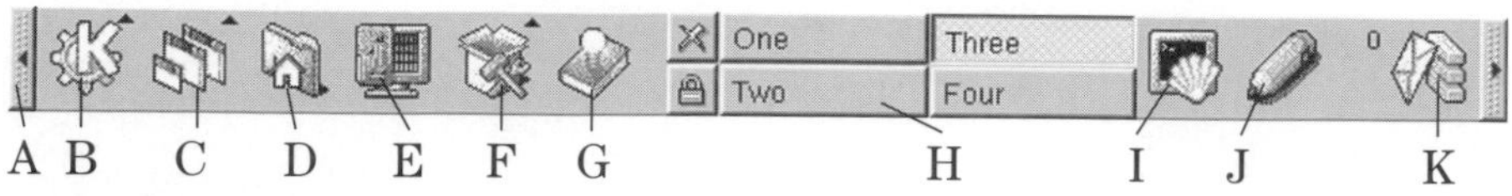


Figure 21.36 KDE panel components

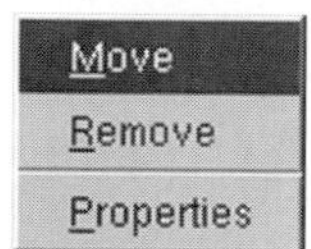


Figure 21.37 Right-click menu on a KDE panel object

One of the most useful aspects of KDE is the ease with which you can reconfigure almost every component of it. This applies to the KDE panel as well. For example, you can use the KDE main editor to change the content and structure of the panel menus. You launch this utility by making the fly-out menu choices Main Menu > Panel > Edit Menus. Figure 21.38 shows the general appearance of the Menu Editor. Practice Session 21.5 shows you how to create a new application

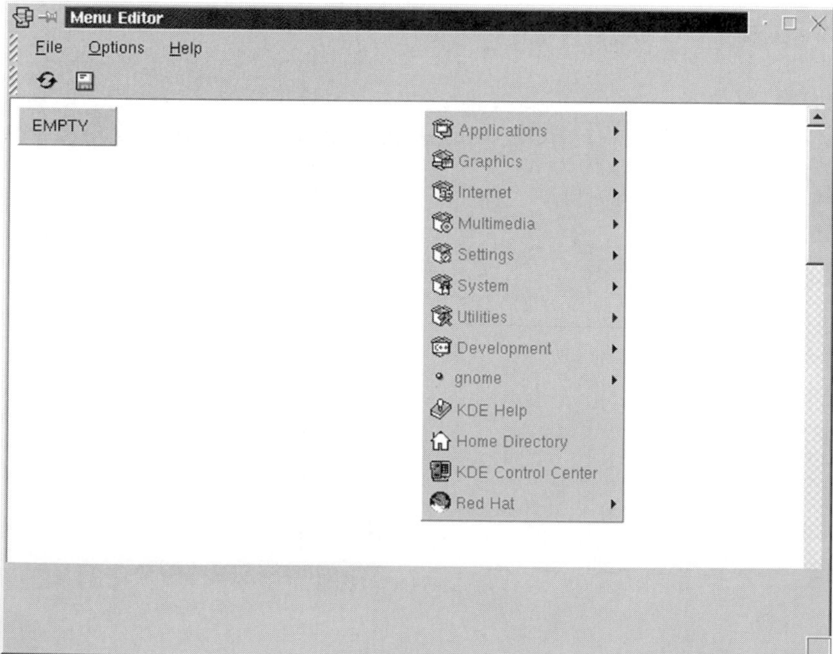


Figure 21.38 KDE menu editor window

menu choice in your personal menus, assuming you are running KDE on your LINUX system with the emacs package installed. If emacs has not been installed, skip ahead to Practice Session 21.6 and install emacs, following the steps for installing of Xemacs, then return to Practice Session 21.5.

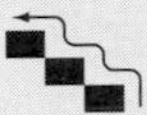

## Practice Session 21.5

**Step 1:** From the main menu, make the fly-out menu choices Programs > Panel > Edit Menus. The Menu Editor window will open on your screen, as shown in Figure 21.38.

**Step 2:** Two menus appear in that window, a personal menu on the left, shown as empty in Figure 21.38, and the default menu on the right.

**Step 3:** From the main KDE Menu, make the fly-out menu choice Programs > File Manager. The kfm file manager window will open.

**Step 4:** Use the location bar in the kfm file manager window to locate the file /usr/bin/emacs. An icon for it should appear in the kfm window when you have found it, similar to Figure 21.39. Don't click on this icon to launch emacs! If you accidently launch the program, make the pull-down menu choice Files > Exit Emacs to terminate the emacs program. Also make sure that you use the resize handles on the sides of both the kfm window and the menu editor window so they are tiled on the screen display, not obscuring each other.

**Step 5:** Hold down the left mouse button, and drag and drop the emacs icon from the kfm file manager window onto the empty menu box in menu editor window. Emacs should now appear as a menu choice in your Personal menu, as shown in Figure 21.40.

**Step 6:** In the KDE menu editor window, make the pull-down menu choice File > Save.

**Step 7:** Quit the KDE menu editor by making the pull-down menu choice File > Quit.

**Step 8:** From the KDE main menu on the panel, make the fly-out menu choices Personal > emacs. You should now see a GNU emacs window. Quit emacs.

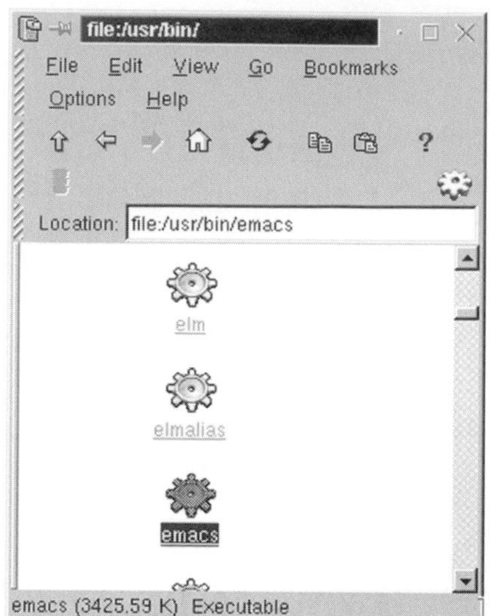


**Figure 21.39** The kfm file manager window

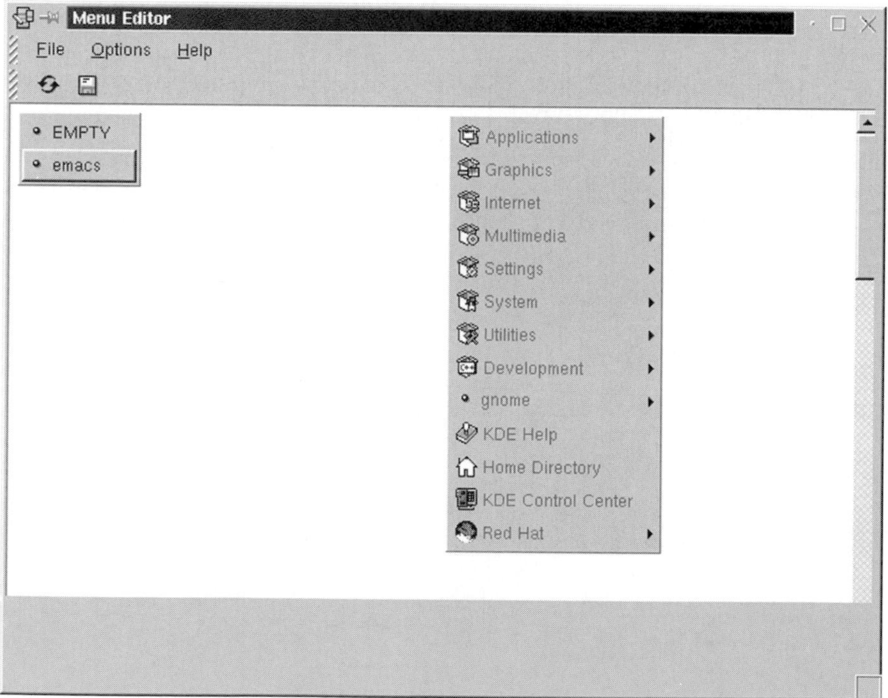


**Figure 21.40** The KDE menu editor window with emacs menu choice

**IN-CHAPTER EXERCISES**

**21.21** Use the KDE menu editor to add any application menu choices you like to your personal menu, using the methods described in Practice Session 21.5.

**21.22** Using the KDE menu editor, create application menu choices under Main Menu > Personal for vi, vim, and pico, and any other editors of your choice. On our system, Xemacs is already found as a menu choice under Editors. Be aware that only the editors installed with your LINUX system will be available.

### 21.4.3 New Packages Installation

If you are interested in learning how to install a LINUX system, you read the Installation Appendix at the end of this book for details of how to do a complete and simple install of the system and application programs. When you or your system administrator installs your LINUX system, some useful applications, or packages, may not have been installed. This is usually the case when someone wants an expeditious install, without having to individually specify each package to be installed. It is also the case when you do not know the capabilities of a package when you install the system and thus omit it from the installation, but then find out later what the capabilities of a certain package are, and now want to have that package on your system without having to re-install the entire system. The **kpackage** application will allow you to install new packages, as long as they follow the Red Hat package format. The kpackage application will also allow you to upgrade or reinstall, on an individual basis or collectively, new and improved versions of packages that have been made available since your initial LINUX system installation. We do not cover other methods of doing package upgrades here.

You can add and upgrade packages on your system via an Internet connection with kpackage, but we do not cover that option here. Also note that if new and improved packages become available, and you download them via the Internet from Red Hat or your LINUX system vendor, you can always move them to your hard-drive or onto your system via floppy disk to make them available to the kpackage application. You would then simply change the default location where kpackage finds new packages.

To prepare for Practice Session 21.6, review Chapter 5, Section 5.5, which describes the capabilities of the Xemacs text editor. If Xemacs is already installed on your system, you may follow along with the description of kpackage and simply use another new package in place of Xemacs. In Practice Session 21.6, we assume that you are running Red Hat LINUX 7.0, that your new package is available on a CD, that Xemacs is not initially installed, and that you have access to the Root password. If you did the initial installation yourself from a CD-ROM, you should be able to proceed. Otherwise, contact your system administrator for help installing new or upgraded packages. If kpackage itself is not available on your KDE system, you can log out and start a GNOME session to use GnoRPM to install kpackage (see Section 21.3.4).

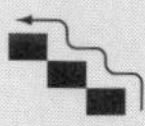

## Practice Session 21.6

**Step 1:** To verify that you have the Xemacs package available, insert the Xemacs CD in your CD-ROM drive. A kfm file manager window should open on screen, simlar to the one shown in Figure 21.41.

**Step 2:** Find the Xemacs package by clicking on the folder SRPMS, or whichever appropriate folder is available for your system. If it is not available, insert the CD that contains this package.

**Step 3:** Close the kfm file manager window using the pull-down menu choice File > Close.

**Step 4:** From the KDE main menu, make the fly-out menu choice Utilities > kpackage. An input window will open, asking you for the Root password. Type in the Root password, then left-click the OK button. After querying the RPM database for installed packages on your system, the kpackage window will open, showing a snapshot of your system's installed packages.

**Step 5:** In the kpackage window, choose File > Open. The Select Document to Open window will appear on screen, similar to that shown in Figure 21.42.

**Step 6:** In the Select Document to Open window, type **/mnt/cdrom/** into the location bar, as shown in Figure 21.42. The folders on your CD will be displayed in the window, as shown in Figure 21.42.

**Step 7:** Double left-click on the folder that contains the xemacs package. On our CD, this was the SRPMS folder. When a list of the packages in that folder appears in the window, scroll left with the scroll bar, then left-click on the xemacs package icon to select it.

**Step 8:** Left-click on the OK button at the bottom of the Select Document to Open window.

**Step 9:** The kpackage window will appear as an Install Package display, as shown in Figure 21.43. Leave the default boxes in this window checked: Upgrade, Replace Packages, and Check Dependencies. If you wanted to test the install procedure, you would check only that box in the Install Package display.

**Step 10:** Left-click on the Install button at the bottom of the Install Package display in the kpackage window. A progress bar will show you the progress of the package install. On our system, this took about three minutes. At the end of installation, the kpackage window will close automatically.

**Step 11:** Add a menu choice to your main menu personal menu for the new application by using the procedures from Practice Session 21.5. Then launch Xemacs using the new menu choice or button.

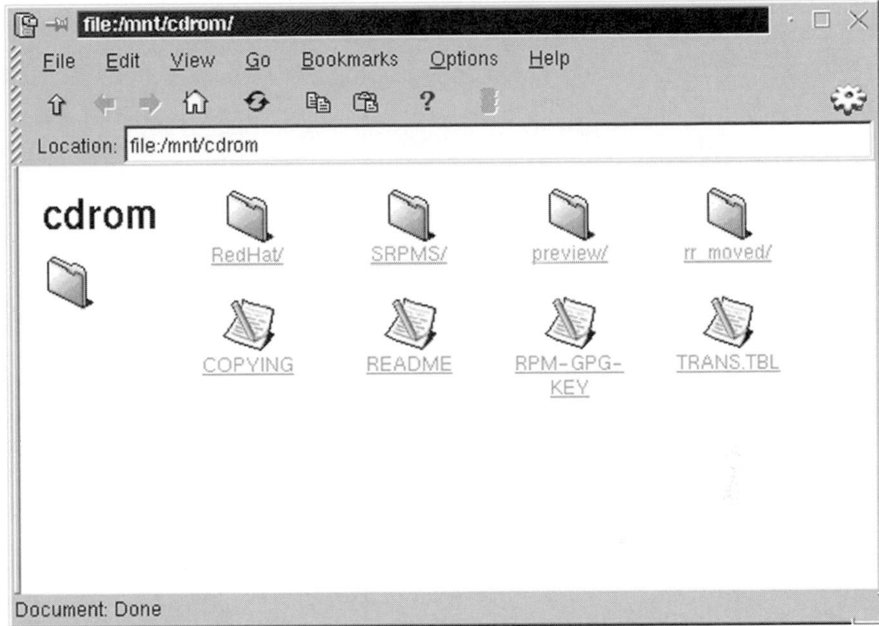


**Figure 21.41** Contents of CD for loading new packages

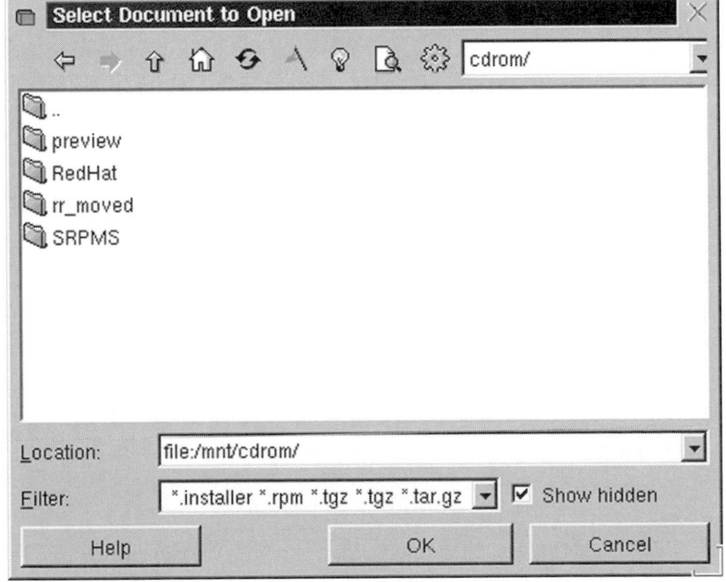


**Figure 21.42** Select Document to Open window

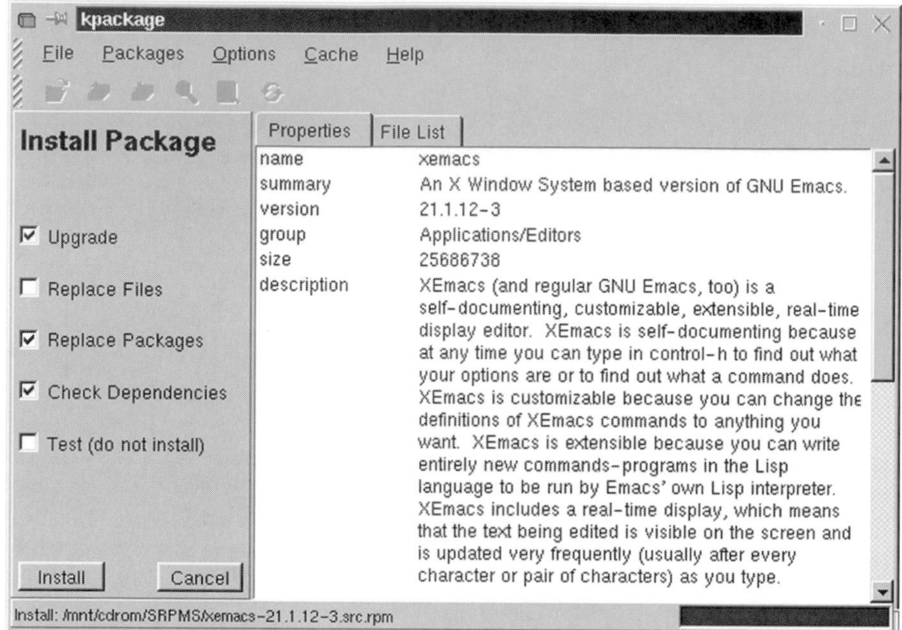


**Figure 21.43** Install Package display in the kpackage window

## IN-CHAPTER EXERCISES

**21.23** Use kpackage, or a similar graphical front-end package installation program, to install a useful new package on your LINUX system. Write down the steps you used.

**21.24** Use kpackage to upgrade existing packages on your system via an Internet connection. Write down the steps you used.

Several other options are available for maintaining packages on your LINUX system with kpackage. You can inquire about packages and their dependencies on your system, uninstall packages, verify the correct installation of new and upgraded packages, and upgrade packages on an individual or collective basis. These functions and others, such as obtaining packages via an Internet connection, are available via the toolbar button choices at the top of the kpackage window and in the Install Package display. For help with these features, use the kpackage help pull-down menu that describes the main window, the query window, the install window, the find window, and the Web find window.

### 21.4.4 The K Window Manager

The program that you work with most directly in the KDE desktop environment is the window manager. The appearance and interactivity of KDE windows, from simple terminal windows to application windows, is controlled by the window manager. The default window manager for KDE is called **KWM.** Several other window managers are available, the most popular being Sawfish, IceWM, WindowMaker, Enlightenment, AfterStep, and FVWM2. For more information on these window managers, see Table 21.10, items 5 through 8.

KWM gives a window "dressing", or standard interactive techniques and their related features, to expedite your work within that window. For example, a scroll bar (item F in Figure 21.44) is provided in an xterminal window to allow you to graphically scroll backward or forward through the text that has been displayed on the xterminal screen. For more examples of these features, see Table 21.8 and the graphical references to Figure 21.44.

As previously mentioned, the window manager provides a frame within which the application can display its graphical output, and within which you can interact with the application program through user-generated events. The look (appearance of buttons, style and color, its theme) and feel (how buttons work, how menus are activated) of the window manager is independent of the look and feel of the application running in area E of Figure 21.44. Because of this, you can reconfigure the appearance and interactivity of KWM without affecting the look or interactivity of any application running inside the window manager's border. In Practice Session 21.7 you will change the interaction style known as edge flipping. Edge flipping is the ability to move between tiles of the virtual

**Table 21.8** Window Components of KWM

| Item | Name | Description |
|---|---|---|
| A | Menu button | Moves, iconifies, resizes, and makes sticky |
| B | Title bar | Shows current path and allows window movement |
| C | Control buttons | Minimizes, maximizes and kills window |
| D | Menus | Application-specific menu choices for xterminal |
| E | Body | Xterminal console display |
| F | Scroll bar | Allows user to scroll contents of text in this window |
| G | Border | Resizes window with handles |
| H | Sticky button | Makes window sticky, or always visible throughout the virtual tiles of the desktop |
| J | Position button | Repositions the application menus |

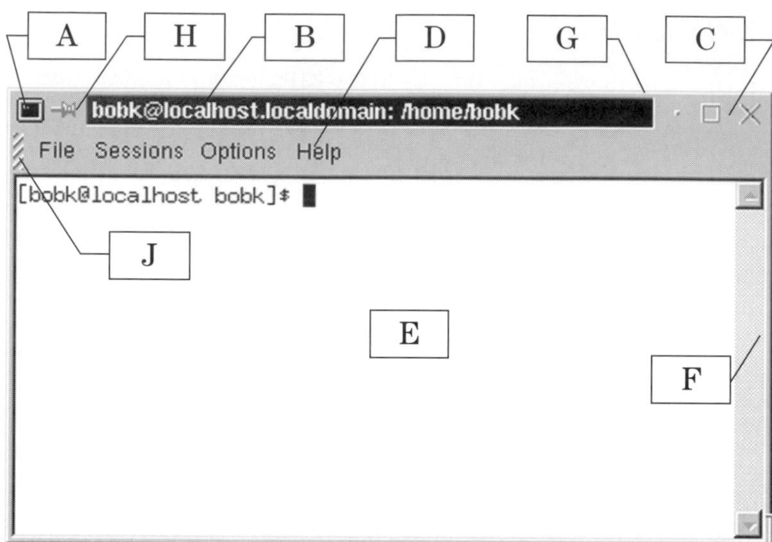


**Figure 21.44** KWM display of xterminal window

desktop (as seen in the KDE pager of the panel) by moving the cursor to the edge of one of the virtual screen tiles, then rolling the mouse to move it into an adjacent tile. You will also change the appearance of KWM to the Wood theme. We assume that you are using KWM and that it has the Default Theme look as the default. We also assume that your virtual desktop tile is 1, as seen in the panel pager.

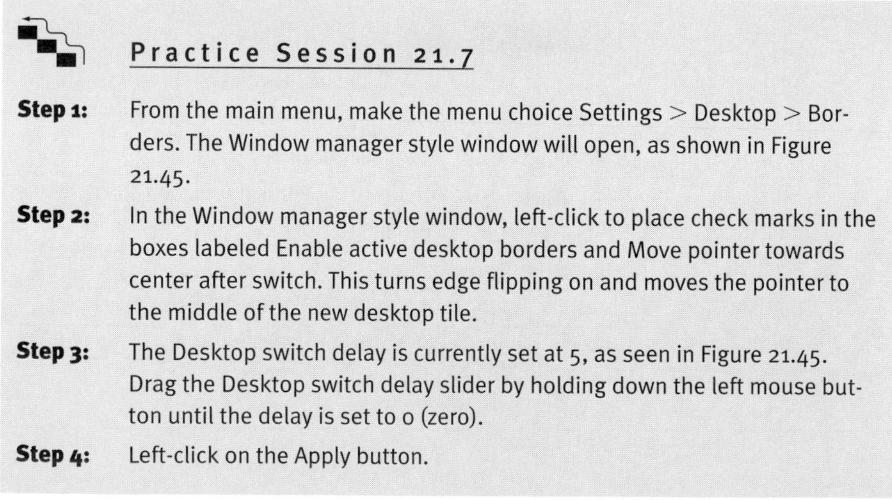

## Practice Session 21.7

**Step 1:** From the main menu, make the menu choice Settings > Desktop > Borders. The Window manager style window will open, as shown in Figure 21.45.

**Step 2:** In the Window manager style window, left-click to place check marks in the boxes labeled Enable active desktop borders and Move pointer towards center after switch. This turns edge flipping on and moves the pointer to the middle of the new desktop tile.

**Step 3:** The Desktop switch delay is currently set at 5, as seen in Figure 21.45. Drag the Desktop switch delay slider by holding down the left mouse button until the delay is set to 0 (zero).

**Step 4:** Left-click on the Apply button.

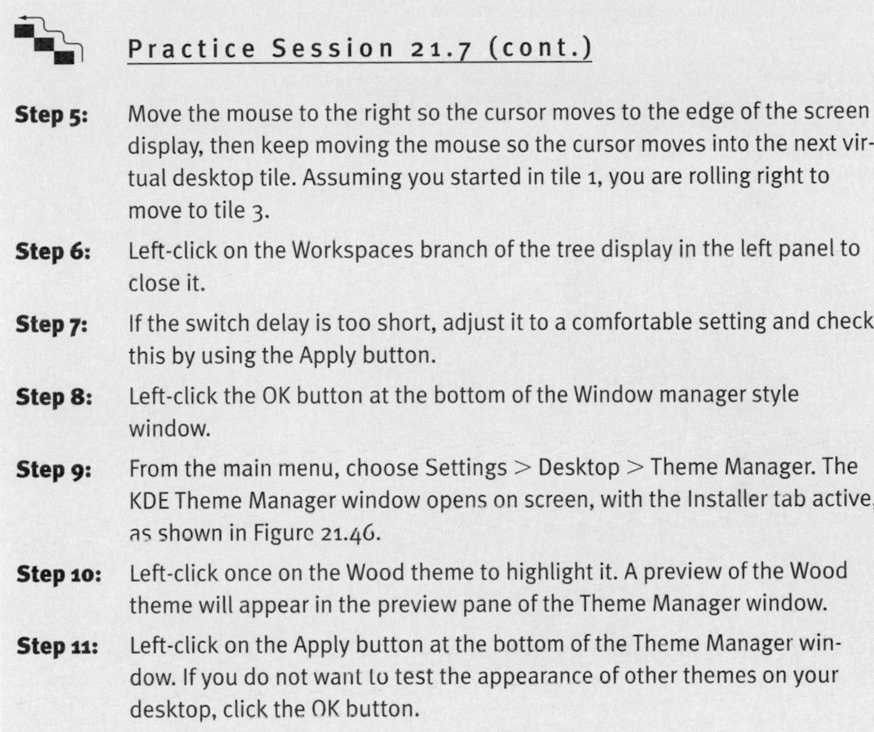

## Practice Session 21.7 (cont.)

**Step 5:** Move the mouse to the right so the cursor moves to the edge of the screen display, then keep moving the mouse so the cursor moves into the next virtual desktop tile. Assuming you started in tile 1, you are rolling right to move to tile 3.

**Step 6:** Left-click on the Workspaces branch of the tree display in the left panel to close it.

**Step 7:** If the switch delay is too short, adjust it to a comfortable setting and check this by using the Apply button.

**Step 8:** Left-click the OK button at the bottom of the Window manager style window.

**Step 9:** From the main menu, choose Settings > Desktop > Theme Manager. The KDE Theme Manager window opens on screen, with the Installer tab active, as shown in Figure 21.46.

**Step 10:** Left-click once on the Wood theme to highlight it. A preview of the Wood theme will appear in the preview pane of the Theme Manager window.

**Step 11:** Left-click on the Apply button at the bottom of the Theme Manager window. If you do not want to test the appearance of other themes on your desktop, click the OK button.

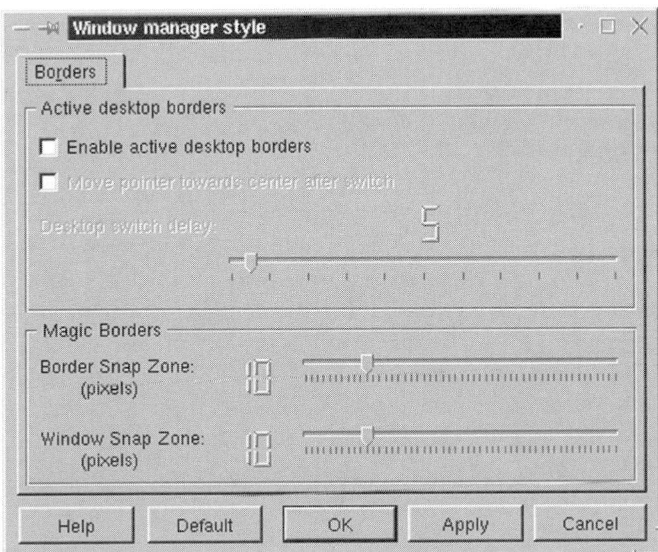


**Figure 21.45** Window manager style window

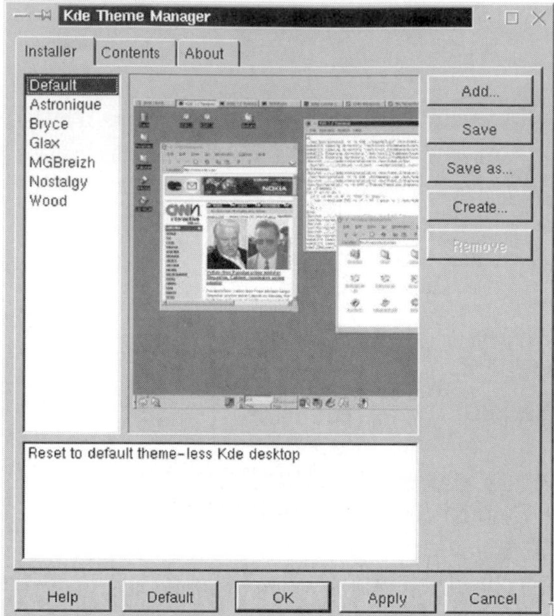


**Figure 21.46** KDE Theme Manager window showing Default theme

## 21.4.5 The KDE Control Center

The most important configuration tool for the KDE is the KDE Control Center. This utility configures single-user attributes, as well as systemwide attributes for all users. A single user with ordinary privileges is allowed to make a variety of changes in the performance of the KDE. For example, as shown in Figure 21.47, you can use a series of on-screen menu choices to change the focus behavior in KDE windows as the mouse rolls the current position screen cursor in them. To launch the KDE Control Center, make the main menu choice KDE Control Center, or use the panel icon KDE Control Center (item E in Figure 21.36). Two important areas of the KDE Control Center window are shown in Figure 21.47. The panel on the left is the menu tree of options that you can modify using the KDE Control Center on your system. Clicking on one of the main branches or subbranches of this tree produces a configuration display in the right panel associated with that particular tree item. For example, when you left-click on the Window Behavior main branch, one of the several subbranch options available is Properties, which allows you to change the focus policy, that is, how windows respond when the current position cursor is dragged into them. If you choose the Focus follows mouse option, as shown in Figure 21.47, when the current position cursor moves between open windows those windows will be made current; that is, you can input text and graphics into them, depending on which window the cursor is in. When you click the Apply button at the bottom of the KDE Control Center window, that attribute or option change will immediately take effect.

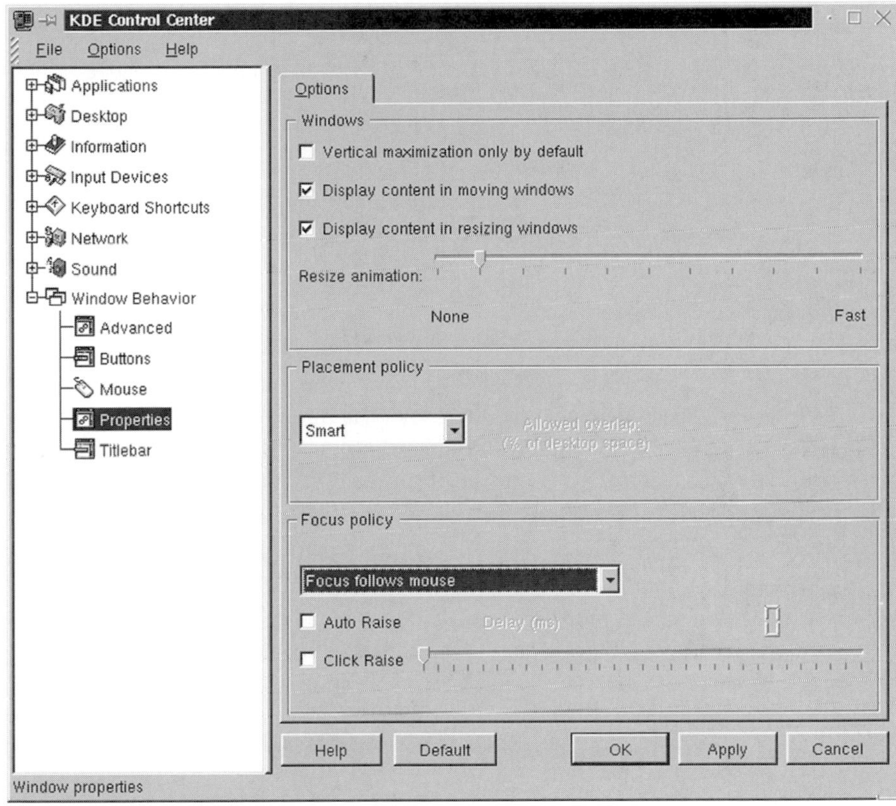


**Figure 21.47** KDE Control Center window

## IN-CHAPTER EXERCISES

**21.25** Use the KDE Control Center to shift the focus policy between the default on your system and all of the other options available, such as Click to focus, Focus follows mouse, Classic focus follows mouse, and Classic sloppy focus. Apply these changes, and note the differences between them. Which do you like best? Which do you like least, and why?

**21.26** Use the KDE Control Center to undo or make modifications similar to those in Practice Session 21.7. Steps 1 through 8 of Practice Session 21.7 are accomplished with the Desktop > Borders subbranches of the KDE Control Center tree. Steps 9 through 12 of Practice Session 21.7 are accomplished with the Desktop > Theme manager subbranches of the KDE Control Center tree.

### 21.4.6 File Management with kfm

The kfm allows you to see and edit not only the files on your LINUX system, particularly the files you have in your home and working directories, but also the directory structure that contains them. You can do this using the LINUX file maintenance commands discussed in this textbook, but using a graphical approach usually saves you time. When you make the KDE main menu choice Programs > File Manager, the kfm window opens on screen, as shown in Figure 21.48.

In Figure 21.48 kfm shows the contents of the current working directory. There are four important areas of this window:

1. The tree view in the left panel shows the file structure of your system.
2. The directory window in the right panel shows the folders and files as icons by default in the currently selected branch of the directory tree. For example, in Figure 21.48, the home directory of user bobk is highlighted in the directory tree (as well as shown in the title bar of the KFM window), and the icons representing folders and ordinary files are shown in the Directory window.
3. Several icons at the top of the kfm window allow you to take actions and change the appearance of file displays very quickly. For example, the Back button allows you to make the previously viewed directory the currently viewed directory.

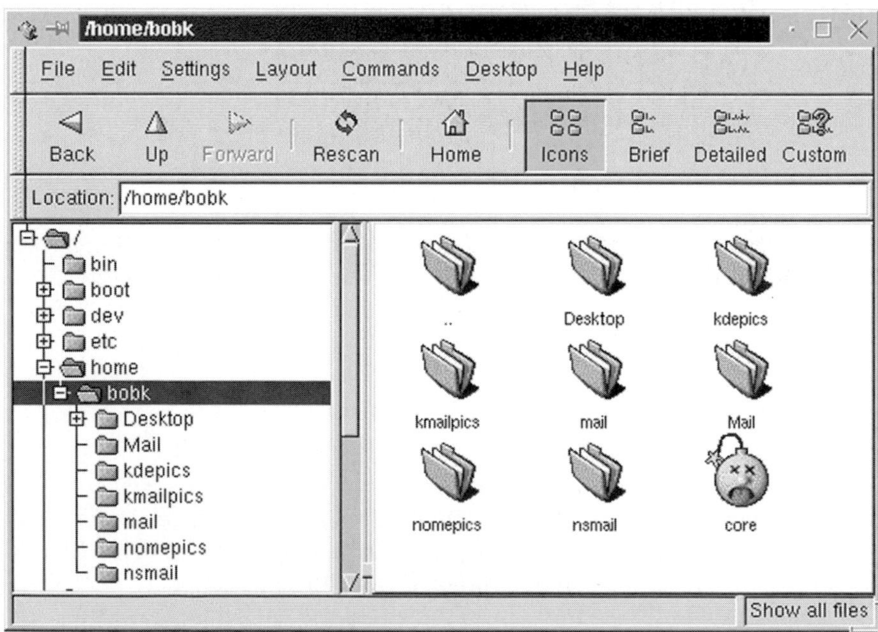


**Figure 21.48** The kfm window

4. Several file properties and actions appear on the pull-down menus at the top of the kfm window. A list of the important properties and actions is given in Table 21.9.

One of the most useful pull-down menu choices is Commands > Find File, which allows you to designate where in the file structure of the system you want to start a search and what file name to search for. This utility is very similar to the text-based LINUX find command. For example, if you wanted to find all files starting at the root directory that ended in the file extension .png, you would make the Commands > Find File pull-down menu choice, then supply the information in the proper text bars of the Find File window, as shown in Figure 21.49. When you clicked on the OK button, a dialog box would open, show you the names of the found files, and allow you to take further action based on the results, such as change the tree and directory views of the kfm window to the subdirectory or path location of the files that were found.

## IN-CHAPTER EXERCISES

**21.27** Use the kfm Find File utility to find all files starting at the root directory that end with the file extension .bmp. How many files were found? Use the Change to this directory button to change the kfm display to one of the subdirectories on your system that contain a .bmp file. Use the kfm pull-down menu choice File > Open to open the found .bmp file. What do you see? What program was used by default on your system to open the .bmp file?

**21.28** Use the kfm Find File utility to find all files starting in your home directory that begin with the letter M (uppercase).

**Table 21.9** Properties and Actions of the kfm Pull-Down Menus

| Pull-Down Menu Choices | Description |
|---|---|
| File > New > Directory | Creates a new subdirectory or folder |
| File > Open | Views the contents of a file using default program |
| File > Copy | Creates a duplicate of selected file(s) |
| File > Delete | Removes file(s) |
| File > Move | Changes the path location of selected file(s) |
| Layout > Sort by | Sorts display by various attributes, such as name and type |
| Layout > Filter View | Uses file attributes to limit the display of files |
| Commands > Find File | Finds specified file(s) starting at a path location |
| Commands > Run Command | Executes a shell command |

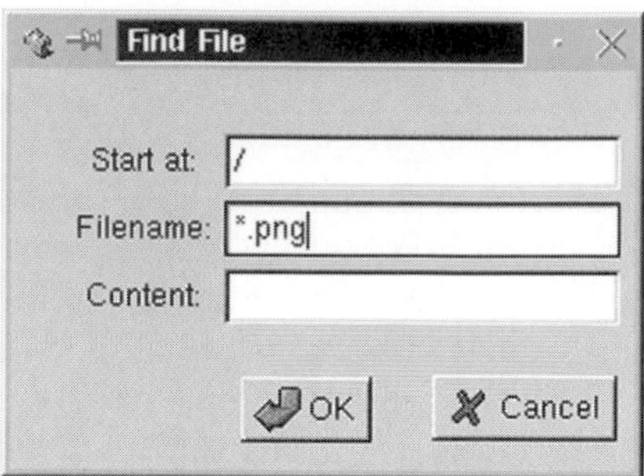


**Figure 21.49** Find File window

To gain familiarity with the features and utilities of the KDE, go on to Problems 17 through 20 at the end of this chapter.

## 21.5 INTERNET RESOURCES

Table 21.10 lists Web pages that you can explore to learn more about the topics covered in this chapter. Many of these sites also include downloadable files that you can use to enhance and extend the GUI capabilities of your LINUX system.

**Table 21.10** Internet Resources

| Text Reference | URL | Description |
|---|---|---|
| 1 | http://www.X.org | X Window System management organization |
| 2 | http://www.xfree86.org | XFree86 management organization |
| 3 | http://sawmill.sourceforge.net/ | Sawfish window manager |
| 4 | http://icewm.sourceforge.net/ | IceWM window manager |
| 5 | http://www.windowmaker.org | WindowMaker window manager |
| 6 | http://www.enlightenment.org | Enlightenment window manager |
| 7 | http://www.afterstep.org | AfterStep window manager |
| 8 | http://www.fvwm.org | FVWM2 window manager |
| 9 | http://www.gnome.org | GNOME management organization |
| 10 | http://www.kde.org | KDE management organization |
| 11 | ftp://ftp.cis.upenn.edu/pub/xv/docs | xv .pdf or PostScript documents |

## SUMMARY

From the user perspective the operability of LINUX is greatly improved by deployment of a graphical user interface (GUI). The current predominant GUI systems are built on a network protocol called the X Window System. These GUI systems can be classified as either integrated or nonintegrated. A nonintegrated system generally utilizes only the functionality of a window manager. An integrated system generally couples the window manager with other higher-level programs that achieve desktop management and session management. Examples of integrated systems are GNOME and KDE.

XFree86 is a system derived from the X Window System that has more device-specific drivers for Intel-based hardware. XFree86 is a protocol for networked graphical interaction between a user and one or more computer systems running LINUX. The user interface has two basic parts: the application user interface, which is how each client application presents itself in one or more windows on the server screen display, and the window manager or management interface, which controls the display of and organizes all client windows. The chief arbiter of the interactive dialog between user and computer system is the window manager. The fvwm window manager offers all of the amenities of other popular window systems, plus it allows you to manage the graphical output from LINUX application programs.

The basic model of interactivity is an event-request loop between application client and graphical server. In XFree86, the client application can process input events, do the work necessary to form a response to the events, and output the responses as requests for graphical output to the server.

XFree86, and fvwm in particular, are highly customizable to suit the interactive needs of a wide range of users. This chapter covered three approaches to changing the appearance and functionality of a nonintegrated window system, as well as the window manager. The first approach involved changing the characteristics of applications that run under XFree86 by specifying command line options. The second approach involved modifying or creating an initialization file for the window system, then invoking that initialization file, either by restarting the window system or by logging off and then logging back on. The third approach involved modifying or creating an initialization file for the window manager, fvwm, then invoking that initialization file.

We also covered the functionality of the two predominant integrated desktop management systems, GNOME and KDE. These systems can be used to expedite work within the LINUX environment, particularly personal productivity and file management operations. We specifically showed the customization possible within both systems to allow a user to work more efficiently.

## PROBLEMS

1. Give definitions, in your own words, for the following terms as they relate to the XFree86: window system, window manager, desktop manager, client, server, focus, iconify, maximize, minimize, xterm, application user interface, management interface.
2. Which XFree86 window manager is used on your computer system? How can you identify and recognize which window manager you are using by default?
3. Examine the window manager configuration file for the window manager you are using on your system (e.g., /usr/lib/X11R6/lib/X11/.fvwmrc). If one is available, examine your home directory and compare your own personal copy of that window manager configuration with the systemwide file. Make the following changes to your personal window manager configuration file if they have not already been made, and note the changes in your style of interaction with the window manager.
    a. Comment out the ClickToFocus directive.
    b. Comment out the StickyIcons directive.
    c. Set DeskTopSize to $2 \times 2$
4. Which command allows another user to have his or her windows displayed on your screen under XFree86? What would be its advantages of doing this? What would be its disadvantages? Explain why this is possible under XFree86.
5. Identify the xterm options that are set on your computer system. What is the default size of an xterm window? What is the default background color for an xterm window? What do you think are the most useful xterm options for you?
6. Which file must you change in order to have the default window manager be mwm? Change your window manager in this file and restart your system or log on, using the new window manager. Note the differences in operation between your new window manager and your initial default window manager. Why would you *not* want to stop execution of the window manager in the middle of a session on your computer system?
7. When you hold down the left-most mouse button with the screen cursor in the root window of your XFree86 display, what appears on your screen? What appears when you hold down the middle mouse button? What appears when you hold down the right-most mouse button? What controls the appearance and content of the menus that are presented to you when you take these actions? If you hold down the right-most mouse button when the screen cursor is over the title bar of a window on your display, what happens? What menu is presented to you?
8. Do all windows launched on your XFree86 display have the same components (i.e., scroll bars, iconify button, title bar, and resize handles)? What facility controls the look and feel of these components? How do these components

compare in function and operation to what you might be familiar with from another GUI—for example, on a Mac or under Windows95/98?

9. Use you favorite Web browser to explore the site http://www.xfree86.org. What are the objectives of this organization?
10. Use the xpaint application to design a bit-mapped image for use as an icon in a pull-down menu. For example, if you were going to design a menu choice for reading from a file, your bit-mapped image might look like a book that is open for reading. Save the image and use an image-viewing application to view the image you designed.
11. After completing Problem 10, find an X-based application on your network that allows you to customize menu items. Design icon images for use with the application using xpaint and install them for use with the application.
12. If your system has a desktop manager, such as GNOME or KDE, compare the file maintenance facilities of that XFree86 desktop manager with the LINUX commands that do file maintenance. What are the advantages of the desktop manager's file facilities? What are the advantages of the LINUX commands that do file maintenance? Can you see the advantage of using both at the same time?
13. What are three major components of the GNOME desktop? Give a brief description of each.
14. How can you create a new panel in GNOME? List the steps and menu choices necessary to accomplish this.
15. How do you add a background image to a GNOME panel?
16. What is a session manager. How is it different from a desktop management system or a window manager?
17. What are the three major components of KDE? Give a brief description of each.
18. How do you change the size and position of the KDE panel?
19. Outline the installation procedure for the KDE system if you obtain the software as packages over the Internet. When would it be necessary for you to do this installation?
20. How can you use kpackage to upgrade KDE itself? What components of KDE would need to be upgraded? Are these components available over the Internet, and if so, from where?
21. Why would someone want to do a nonintegrated installation of LINUX, either without a GUI (a text-based interface) or with only a window manager running?
22. Why are server-class installations of LINUX done without a GUI?

# Appendix A: LINUX Installations

This appendix describes the installation of three popular LINUX systems: Caldera 2.4, Mandrake 7.2, and Red Hat 7.0. There are a few things that you should keep in mind before installing any of the three LINUX systems. First, to prepare the installation/boot disk you must have a computer with Microsoft Windows 95 installed. Second, we recommend that you have a high-speed CD-ROM drive. Our lab tests show that Mandrake LINUX, for instance, does not even start with a 4X CD-ROM drive. Third, make sure that you have the right video driver with you at the time of installation. With the wrong video drivers, you may get unexpected results, such as the installation causing the computer to hang up. Also, you may end up having a text-mode LINUX, rather than a GUI-mode LINUX, even if you specifically check GUI-mode installation. Finally, we emphasize that you install at a minimum of 800 × 600 resolution; parts of GUI-mode LINUX may cause problems at a lower resolution.

## HARDWARE SPECIFICATIONS OF OUR SYSTEM

Intel Celeron 400MHz processor

98 MB SDRAM

8.4 GB hard drive

44X CD-ROM drive

IBM P50 color monitor

3.5" floppy disk drive

PS/2 keyboard and mouse

## BRANDS AND VERSIONS OF LINUX

Caldera Systems OpenLinux eDesktop 2.4

Mandrake LINUX 7.2

Red Hat LINUX 7.0

## CONVENTIONS

We call the computer you are installing LINUX on the **LINUX computer**. We call the floppy disk that you are using to start the LINUX installation process the **install floppy**.

## CALDERA SYSTEMS OPENLINUX eDESKTOP 2.4

You need the following:

One CD-ROM: Caldera Systems OpenLinux eDesktop 2.4

One blank 3.5" floppy disk, to be used to make the install floppy

Access to a computer with Windows95 installed

## PREPARING THE INSTALL FLOPPY FOR CALDERA SYSTEMS OPENLINUX eDESKTOP 2.4

1. Boot up your Windows 95 computer and wait till you are in Windows.
2. Insert the Caldera OpenLinux eDesktop 2.4 CD in the CD-ROM drive.
3. Insert a blank 3.5" floppy in drive a:.
4. Click **Start**.
5. Click **Run**.
6. In the command line, type **`dosprmpt`**.
7. Click **OK**. You will shell out to the DOS prompt (e.g., c:\windows).
8. Assuming your CD-ROM drive is d:, type **d**: and press <Enter>.
9. At d:\> prompt, type **`cd col\tools\rawrite`**.
10. Type **`rawrite2 –f d:\col\launch\floppy\install.144 –d a:`** and press <Enter>.
11. Press <Enter> when prompted with the message `"Please insert a formatted diskette into drive A: and press -ENTER- :"`. Your install floppy will be ready in about a minute.
12. Remove the install floppy and Caldera OpenLinux eDesktop 2.4 CD from the respective drives.
13. Label the floppy disk as "Caldera OpenLinux eDesktop 2.4 install floppy".
14. Keep it with your Caldera OpenLinux eDesktop 2.4 CD.

## STARTING CALDERA OPENLINUX eDESKTOP2.4 INSTALL PROCESS

This install assumes that there is no operating system installed on the computer and the hard drive is not partitioned.

1. Boot up your computer with the install floppy in drive a: and Caldera LINUX CD in the CD-ROM drive. This will start the installation process through Caldera Systems OpenLinux Installation Wizard called Lizard. Wait until Lizard starts.

Note: To navigate, click **Back** to go back a step; click **Next** to move a step forward. Click **Help** to get help on the screen at hand.

2. This is the very first screen that asks for your input in Select Language. The default language selection is English. It shows Lizard Version: 20000223-1 on lower left corner of the screen. Click **Next**.
3. At the **Set Up Mouse:** you can either keep the default mouse (your mouse if auto-detected) or change to a different mouse. You can also test your mouse by clicking **Test mouse here!** with the left, middle, or right mouse button. Click **Next**.
4. The **Select Keyboard Type:** screen shows you an array of keyboard models and layouts. It lets you test your keyboard if you want to do so. Make appropriate changes if you want to or keep the defaults. Click **Next**.
5. At **Select Monitor:** select your monitor if it is on the list. If it is not on the list, click the **+** sign beside **Typical Monitors** and select a resolution your monitor supports. Click **Next**.
6. At **Select Video Mode:** select the resolution that you would like to have while running LINUX. You can also click **Test this Mode** to see whether the resolution you picked works. Click **Next**.

   Note: If you test the mode, your screen may hang. If this happens, restart the installation process and go on with the installation without testing video mode.
7. At **Select Target:** you have four choices:
   - **Entire hard disk**
   - **Free disk space**
   - **Prepared partition(s)**
   - **Custom (Expert only)**

   Select the **Entire hard disk** option. This will partition and format the hard drive for LINUX installation automatically. Click **Next**.
8. At **Select Disk:** the **Next** button is grayed out. Click **Prepare selected disk for Linux**. This partitions and formats the disk for LINUX. When this is done, the **Next** button will turn on and the **Prepare selected disk for Linux** button will gray out. Click **Next**.
9. At **Software Selection:** you have seven choices:
   - **Minimum Installation (220 MB)**
   - **Recommended (750 MB)**
   - **All Packages (1310 MB)**
   - **Business Workstation (610 MB)**
   - **Development Workstation (930 MB)**
   - **Home Computer (730 MB)**
   - **Custom (floppy required)**

Select **Home Computer** to install the software for your daily needs. Click **Next**.

Note: You can always install or uninstall packages using OpenLinux Administration Tools at any time after the installation is complete

10. At **Set Login Name(s):** enter the password for your root account twice. Create at least one user account by entering the following information:

```
Real Name: John Doe
Login Name: jdoe
User Password: XXXXXXXX
Retype: XXXXXXXX
```

where `John Doe` is the name of the user, `jdoe` is the user name, and `XXXXXXXX` stands for an eight-character password that you choose for the user. The actual password that you enter will not be displayed. Click **Add User** and then click **Next**.

Note: Unless you enter all the information, the **Next** button will remain grayed out. It is always a good idea to create at least one user account, because root account is for administration purposes only.

At this point, package installation starts whether you add user information or not.

11. At **Set Up Networking:** you are given the following three options:
    - **No ethernet**
    - **Ethernet configured using DHCP**
    - **Ethernet configured statically**

    Because you are only preparing the computer for home use as a standalone system, select the **No ethernet** option. Click **Next**. At this point, you may want to wait until package installation is complete. You would not get a **Set Up Modem** screen (Step 12) if you had configured TCP/IP; in that case, it would use LAN to get Internet connectivity.

12. For simplicity, skip modem configuration (**Set Up Modem**) until after the installation is complete. Click **Next**. You will be in **Set Up ISP** screen.

    If you do select a modem, you will be asked to enter the following information:
    - **Model**
    - **Device (/dev/ttys0)**
    - **Speed (e.g., 56000)**
    - **Flowcontrol (e.g., Hardware)**
    - **Command**
    - **Initstring (e.g., ATZ)**

If your modem is not in the list, try a **Generic** model that has the same speed as your modem. Then set the device; manually type the device if it is not in the pull down list (e.g., **/dev/ttys0(COM1)**).

Enter the required information and click **Next**.

13. At **Set Up Internet Provider:** select **Use dial-up networking**. In the provider window, look for your ISP (Internet Service Provider). If it is not listed, select **User defined** and click **Details**. Enter the following information:

    - **Name:** (Name of your ISP)
    - **Phone:** (Dial-in phone number of your ISP)
    - **DNS Server:**
    - **Secondary DNS:**

    Select **Speaks PPP natively** if it needs to be selected. When you have entered all the information, click **OK**. Select **Save authentication information** if you do not want to enter your login name and password each time you want to connect to the Internet. Click **Next**.

14. At **Set Up Boot Loader:** the **Write master boot record** entry is not checked by default. We recommend that you leave it that way.

    (Select this option if you want to install LINUX on your second hard drive.) Click **Next**.

15. If **Test Sound:** detects a sound card, you can click **Test digital sound** to see whether the sound works. (On some systems, this is not shown.) Click **Next**.

16. Because you are preparing a home system, you will set up a local printer at **Set Up Printer:** Type a Name for the printer and select the correct model from the drop-down list.

    If your printer is not in the list, select the one that is closest to your printer. Test it by clicking **Test** button. If a page does not print or prints garbage, try another printer. If you have more than one printer driver installed, select the one you will most often print to and click **Use as default**. Select **Port (/dev/lp0(LPT1))**, a parallel port. Select **Paper** (e.g., letter size). Click **Add** and then click **Next**.

17. At **Choose Time Zone:** select your time zone from the pull-down window and click **Next**. You can also choose time zone by selecting a city on the map. **Hardware clock is set to local time** is the default and you may want to keep it that way.

18. The **Entertainment:** game screen runs until the packages are installed. Pac-Man is running. Play the game if you like at this point by clicking **Continue**. Click **Next** when the **Next** button turns on.

19. At **Rescue Disk:** insert a blank floppy disk in the drive and click **Write Disk**. This creates a boot floppy. You will be able to boot LINUX with this

floppy if your boot information is damaged on your hard drive. Click **Finish** when this is done.

20. In a few moments, you will be at the Caldera OpenLinux login screen. The default **Session type** is KDE; your choices are KDE and Failsafe. Remove the floppy disk and CD-ROM from the respective drives. Label the floppy disk "Rescue Disk."
21. Type your login name and password and click **Go!**

Caldera OpenLinux eDesktop 2.4 is now up and running on LINUX computer.

## MANDRAKE LINUX 7.2

You need the following:

Two CD-ROMs: Mandrake LINUX 7.2 Install CD and Mandrake LINUX 7.2 Extension CD

One blank 3.5" floppy disk, to be used to make the install floppy

Access to a computer with Windows95 installed

## PREPARING INSTALL FLOPPY FOR MANDRAKE LINUX 7.2

1. Boot up your Windows95 computer and wait till you are in Windows.
2. Insert the Mandrake LINUX 7.0 Install CD in the CD-ROM drive.
3. Insert a blank 3.5" floppy in drive a:.
4. Click **Start**.
5. Click **Run**.
6. In the command line, type **`dosprmpt`**.
7. Click `OK`. You will shell out to the DOS prompt (e.g., c:\windows).
8. Assuming your CD-ROM drive is d:, type **`d:`** and press <Enter>.
9. At **d:\>** prompt, type **`cd dosutils`** and press <Enter>.
10. Type **`rawrite –f d:\images\cdrom.img –d a:`** and press <Enter> .
11. Press <Enter> when prompted with the message `"Please insert a formatted diskette into drive A: and press -ENTER- :"`. Your install floppy will be ready in about a minute.
12. Remove the install floppy and Mandrake LINUX 7.2 Install CD from the respective drives.
13. Label the floppy disk "Mandrake LINUX 7.2 install floppy".
14. Keep it with your Mandrake LINUX 7.2 CDs.

## STARTING MANDRAKE LINUX 7.2 INSTALL PROCESS

This install assumes that there is no operating system installed on the computer and the hard drive is not partitioned.

1. Boot up your computer with the install floppy in drive a: and Mandrake LINUX Install CD in the CD-ROM drive. This will start the installation process.
2. At **Linux Mandrake:** you can press **<F1>** for more options or <Enter> to install or upgrade a system running Linux-Mandrake. If you do not press any key, installation starts automatically in a few seconds. Let the installation begin without pressing any key.
3. At **Choose your language:** the default is English. This is the language it would use during installation. Click **OK**.
4. From **Screen Description:** on during the installation, click **OK** to go on with your selection; click **Cancel** to cancel your selection or the current screen; click **Help** on the bottom left of the screen to get help on the current screen. All screen titles appear vertically on the left side of screen at all times. There is a star (✪) beside each screen title. The current screen has a gold star (✪); previous screen has a green star (✪); the screen yet to come has a red star (✪). At the very bottom of this column of screen titles, there are four tiny, rectangular buttons. The button on the far left has the default color scheme for the screen. You can click any other button to change the color scheme for the installation screens at any time during installation. Besides your mouse, you can also use <Tab> to navigate the screen.
5. At **Terms of license:** if you click **Refuse**, the installation will stop and the system will halt and wait for you to reboot. Click **Accept** to continue with the installation.
6. At **Select installation class:** you have three choices:
   - **Recommended**
   - **Customized**
   - **Expert**

   The default is **Recommended**, the easiest of the choices. Click **Install** to go ahead with the default selection. Once you click **Install**, you should see **Hard drive detection**, **Configuring mouse**, and **Choose your keyboard** screens in quick succession.
7. At **Setup file systems:**, depending on the partitioning status of your hard drive, you may have up to four choices:
   - **Use existing partition**
   - **Erase entire disk**
   - **Use free space**
   - **Expert mode**

Click **Use free space** or **Erase entire disk**. Depending on your computer model you will have either two choices, **Use free space** and **Expert mode** or three choices, **Use existing partition**, **Erase entire disk**, or **Expert mode**. Click **Use free space** in the first case or **Erase entire disk** partition in the second case. Avoid **Expert mode**, because it is complicated.

8. **Format partitions:** partitions and formats the hard drive. When it is done, it gives you three types of installations to choose from:
   - **Minimum (300 MB)**
   - **Recommended (700 MB)**
   - **Complete (1100 MB)**

   Click **Recommended (700 MB)**, the default selection. During some of our installations, we never got this choice (or the default went by really fast).
9. At **Install system:** installs Linux-Mandrake Operating System and the packages that accompany it. You can cancel the installation process at any point by clicking **Cancel**. This process takes a little while (during our installation, it took 12 minutes). Near the end of this process, it ejects the Install CD and asks for the Extension CD. Remove the Install CD and insert the Extension CD. Also remove the install floppy. Click **OK**.
10. **Configure networking:** gives you the following choices for Internet or LAN connectivity:
    - **Configure a normal modem connection**
    - **Configure an ISDN connection**
    - **Configure a DSL (or ADSL) connection**
    - **Configure a cable connection**
    - **Configure local network**
    - **Disable networking**
    - **Done**

    Click one of the choices, depending on the type of modem or network card you have. You can configure modem or network connectivity at any time from within X Windows Environment after the installation. Click **Done**.
11. At **Configure time zone:** select your time zone and click **OK**.
12. If you have a printer connected to your computer, **Configure printer:** will prompt you to configure it. Otherwise, you will not see this screen. You can configure your printer at any time while in X Windows after the installation.
13. At **Set root password:** type the root password twice and click **OK**.
14. At **Add a user:**, create at least one user account by entering the following information:

```
Real name: John Doe
User name: jdoe
Password: XXXXXXXX
Password (again): XXXXXXXX
```

where `John Doe` is the name of the user, `jdoe` is the user name, and `XXXXXXXX` stands for an eight-character password that you choose for the user (the password that you enter is not displayed). Click **Accept user** and then click **Done**.

Note: You don't always want to use the root account, because this gives you administrative rights on the computer. By always using this account, you may inadvertently make changes to the system configuration that you may regret, so it is always a good idea to log on with a user account for regular use of the computer

15. The screens **Create a bootdisk** and **Install bootloader** do not ask you for any input.
16. At **Configure X:** choose your monitor and display resolution, if needed. When you are done, click **OK**. Note: If your video card does not support at least 800 × 600 resolution, LINUX may not work properly.
17. The next screen will prompt you to enter a default user. If you do enter a default user at this point, it will log on that user by default when you use your LINUX computer after the installation. If you click **Cancel**, you will have a text-based LINUX logon. Without entering the default user, click **OK**. This way, you will have a graphical user interface (GUI) and will get the logon prompt every time you want to use LINUX computer. The default **Window Manager** or **Session Type** is KDE. You can always choose a different session type at the logon prompt. Here is your choice from the drop-down list:

    KDE

    Gnome

    IceWM

    Sawfish

    Default

    Failsafe
18. At **Congratulations, installation is complete:** click **OK**. The Extension CD will eject. Remove the CD and let the computer reboot.
19. **Hardware Discovery Utility 0.68:** is the screen you will see after the computer is rebooted. (On some computers, you may not see this.) Wait 30 seconds for the **Welcome to localhost** logon prompt. The default **Session Type** is KDE. Type your login name and password and click **Go!**

Mandrake LINUX 7.2 is now up and running on LINUX computer.

## RED HAT LINUX 7.0

You need the following:

Two CD-ROMs: Red Hat LINUX 7.0 Disc1 and Red Hat LINUX 7.0 Disc2

One blank 3.5" floppy disk, to be used to make the install floppy

Access to a computer with Windows95 installed

## PREPARING INSTALL FLOPPY FOR RED HAT LINUX 7.0

1. Boot up your Windows95 computer and wait till you are in Windows.
2. Insert Red Hat LINUX 7.0 Disc1 in the CD-ROM drive.
3. Insert a blank 3.5" floppy in drive a:.
4. Click **Start**.
5. Click **Run**.
6. In the command line, type **`dosprmpt`**.
7. Click **OK**. You will shell out to the DOS prompt (e.g.; c:\windows). Assuming your CD-ROM drive is d:.
8. Type **`d`**: and press <Enter>.
9. At d:\> prompt, type **`cd dosutils`** and press <Enter>.
10. Type **`rawrite –f d:\images\boot.img –d a:`** and press <Enter>.
11. Press <Enter> when prompted with the message: "**Please insert a formatted diskette into drive A: and press -ENTER- :**".
12. Your install floppy will be ready in about a minute.
13. Remove the install floppy and Red Hat LINUX 7.0 Disc1 from the respective drives.
14. Label the floppy disk "Red Hat LINUX 7.0 install floppy".
15. Keep it with your Red Hat LINUX 7.0 CDs.

## STARTING RED HAT LINUX 7.0 INSTALL PROCESS

This install assumes that there is no operating system installed on the computer and the hard drive is not partitioned.

1. Boot up the computer with the install floppy in drive a: and Red Hat LINUX 7.0 Disc1 in CD-ROM drive. This will start the installation process.
2. At **Welcome to Red Hat LINUX 7.0!** wait 60 seconds or press <Enter> and let the installation begin.

3. During the installation process, click **Back** to go back a step; click **Next** to move forward a screen; and check **On Line Help** on the left side of the screen to get help on the screen at hand.
4. **Language Selection:** is the first screen that asks for your input. The default selection is English; this is the language the program will use during installation. Click **Next**.
5. At **Keyboard Configuration:** make any changes that you need and click **Next**.
6. At **Mouse Configuration:** if your mouse is the same as default, click **Next**. Otherwise, make necessary changes before you click **Next**.
7. At **Red Hat LINUX 7.0 System Installer Welcome:** click **Next**.
8. At **Install Type:** you have four choices:
   - **Workstation**
   - **Server System**
   - **Custom System**
   - **Upgrade**

   The default is **Workstation**. Click **Next**.
9. At **Automatic Partitioning:** you have three choices:
   - **Automatically partition and REMOVE DATA**
   - **Manually partition with Disk Druid**
   - **Manually partition with fdisk [Expert only]**

   The default is **Automatically partition**. Keep the default and click **Next**.
10. At **Time Zone Selection:** make appropriate changes if needed and click **Next**.
11. At **Account Configuration:** enter the root password twice and create at least one user account by providing the following information:

    ```
    Root Password: YYYYYYYY
    Confirm: YYYYYYYY
    Account Name: jdoe
    Password: XXXXXXXX
    Password (confirm): XXXXXXXX
    Full Name: John Doe
    ```

    where `YYYYYYYY` stands for an eight-character password for the root user, `jdoe` is the user name, `XXXXXXXX` stands for an eight-character password that you choose for the user, and John Doe is the name of the user. Passwords should be at least six characters long. Use <Tab> to navigate the screen. The passwords that you enter are not displayed. Click **Add** and then click **Next**.

    Note: You don't always want to use the root account, because this gives you administrative rights on the computer. By always using this account, you may inadvertently make changes to the system configuration that you may regret, so it is always a good idea to log on with a user account for regular use of the computer.

12. At **Package Group Selection:** you have three choices:
    - **GNOME**
    - **KDE**
    - **Games**

    **GNOME** is the default choice. Keep the default and check **KDE** so that you can complete the work in Chapter 21. Leave **Games** unselected. Click **Next**.
13. At **Monitor Configuration:** select your monitor and click **Next**.

    Select screen resolution during installation. If your video card does not support at least 800 × 600 resolution, LINUX may not work properly.
14. At **X Configuration:** make any changes to your video hardware. This is also where you can give Red Hat LINUX 7.0 a character/text-based user interface or a graphical user interface. The default is text based. Click **Use Graphical Login** to make LINUX run in GUI. Make any other changes and click **Next**.
15. At **About to Install:** click **Next** to begin Red Hat LINUX 7.0 installation; the installation log is saved in /tmp/install.log. Save it for future reference.
16. At **Installing Packages:** formats file systems: /boot file system, swap space, and so on. It installs several hundred packages and takes a while.
17. At **Bootdisk Creation:** Insert a blank 3.5" floppy disk in the drive and click **Next**. This creates a Red Hat LINUX 7.0 boot disk. You can bypass creating a boot disk by clicking **Skip Boot Disk Creation**. Click **Next**.
18. At **Congratulations, Installation is complete:** remove the floppy disk and Click **Exit**. This ejects the CD from the drive and reboots the system. Remove the CD and let the system reboot.
19. Within a minute or so, you will be at the LINUX log on prompt in GUI mode; GNOME will be the default session type.
20. Log on as root or with the user account you created during installation and click **Go**.

Red Hat LINUX Workstation 7.0 is now up and running on LINUX computer.

# Appendix B: Command Dictionary

***Prototype***
***We present information about each command in the following format.***

**command name**—What it does

**Syntax:** `command` [options...] ['option arguments'...] ['command arguments'...]
[Other pertinent forms of command syntax...]

**Purpose:** A short description of the major purpose of the command

**Options and Option Arguments:** A complete list of options and their arguments

**Command Arguments:** A complete list of command arguments

---

**apmd**—Advanced power management (APM) daemon

**Syntax:** `apmd` [ `-c` 'check_seconds' ] [ `-P` 'proxy_cmd' ] [ `-p` 'percent_to_log' ] [ `-qVvW` ]
[ `-w` 'warn_percent' ] [ `-?` ]

**Purpose:** APM monitoring daemon that works in conjunction with the APM BIOS driver in the OS kernal

**Options and Option Arguments:**

- `-c` 'seconds', `--check seconds` Control how many seconds to block on the /dev/apm_bios device
- `-P` 'proxy_cmd', `--apmd_proxy proxy_cmd` Identify the command to invoke when certain APM driver events are reported
- `-p` 'percent_change', `--percentage percent_change` Log information every time the percentage of available power changes (discharge or recharge) by 'percent_change'
- `-V, --version` Print the daemon's version and exit
- `-v, --verbose` Enable verbose mode, wherein each event reported by the APM driver is logged
- `-w` 'warn_percent', `--warn warn_percent` When the battery is not being charged and the percentage of available power drops below 'warn_percent', log a warning at 'Alert' level
- `-q`, `--quiet` Disable the warnings identified by `-W` and `-w`
- `-?`, `--help` Print a usage message and exit

**Command Arguments:** None

---

**apropos**—Search the `whatis` database for strings

**Syntax:** `apropos` 'keyword' ...

**Purpose:** Search a set of database files containing short descriptions of system commands for keywords and display the result on stdout.

**Options and Option Arguments:** None

**Command Arguments:** None

---

**ar**—Create, modify, and extract files from portable archives

**Syntax:** `ar` [-][`dmpqrtx`][`abcfilNoPsSvV`] ['membername'] ['count'] 'archive files'...

**Purpose:** Create, modify, and extract from archives. An archive is a single file holding a collection of other files in a structure that makes it possible to retrieve the original individual files (called members of the archive).

**Options and Option Arguments:**

| | |
|---|---|
| `d` | Delete modules from the archive |
| `m` | Move members in an archive |
| `p` | Print the specified members of the archive to stdout |
| `q` | Quick append; add files to the end of archive without checking for replacement |
| `r` | Insert files into archive (with replacement) |
| `t` | Display a table listing the contents of archive |
| `x` | Extract members (named files) from the archive |

A number of modifiers may immediately follow **`p`** to specify variations on an operation's behavior.

| | |
|---|---|
| `a` | Add new files after an existing member of the archive |
| `b` | Add new files before an existing member of the archive |
| `c` | Create the archive |
| `f` | Truncate names in the archive |
| `i` | Insert new files before an existing member of the archive |
| `l` | This modifier is accepted but not used |
| `N` | Use the count parameter; preserve the original dates of members when extracting them |
| `P` | Use the full pathname when matching names in the archive |
| `s` | Write an object-file index into the archive or update an existing one |
| `S` | Do not generate an archive symbol table |
| | Normally, **`ar r`**... inserts all files listed into the archive |
| `v` | Request the verbose version of an operation |
| `V` | Show version number of **`ar`** |

**Command Arguments:**

| | |
|---|---|
| 'membername' | Name of the files in the archive. |
| 'count' | Position of the files in the archive. |
| 'archive files'... | Name of the archive. |

---

**arch**—Print machine architecture

**Syntax:** `arch`

**Purpose:** On current LINUX systems, prints things such as "i386", "i486", "i586", "alpha", "sparc", "arm", "m68k", "mips", "ppc"

**Options and Option Arguments:** None

**Command Arguments:** None

---

## **arp**—Manipulate the system ARP cache

**Syntax:** `arp` [`-vn`] [`-H` 'type'] [`-i` 'if'] `-a` ['hostname']
`arp` [`-v`] [`-i` if] `-d` 'hostname' ['pub']
`arp` [`-v`] [`-H` 'type'] [`-i` 'if'] `-s` 'hostname' 'hw_addr' ['temp']
`arp` [`-v`] [`-H` 'type'] [`-i` 'if'] `-s` 'hostname' 'hw_addr' ['netmask' 'nm'] 'pub'
`arp` [`-v`] [`-H` 'type'] [`-i` 'if'] `-Ds` 'hostname' ifa ['netmask' 'nm'] 'pub'
`arp` [`-vnD`] [`-H` 'type'] [`-i` 'if'] `-f` ['filename']

**Purpose:** Manipulate the kernel's ARP cache in various ways. The primary options are clearing an address mapping entry and manually setting one up.

**Options and Option Arguments:**

`-v`, `--verbose` Tell the user what is going on by being verbose

`-n`, `--numeric` Show numerical addresses instead of trying to determine symbolic host, port, or user names

`-H` 'type', `--hw-type type` When setting or reading the ARP cache, tell `arp` which class of entries it should check for

`-a` ['hostname'], `--display [hostname]` Show the entries of the specified hosts

`-d` 'hostname', `--delete hostname` Remove any entry for the specified host

`-D`, `--use-device` Use the interface ifa's hardware address

`-i` 'if', `--device` Select an interface

`-s` 'hostname' 'hw_addr', `--set hostname` Manually create an ARP address mapping entry for host 'hostname'

`-f` 'filename', `--file filename` Similar to the `-s` option

**Command Arguments:** None

---

## **as**—Portable GNU assembler

**Syntax:** `as` [`-a`[dhlns][=file]] [`-D`] [`--defsym` 'SYM'='VAL'] [`-f`] [`--gstabs`] [`-I` 'path'] [`-K`] [`-L`] [`-M`|`--mri`] [`-o` 'objfile'] [`-R`] [`--traditional-format`] [`-v`] [`-w`] [`--`|'files'...]

**Purpose:** Assemble the output of the GNU C compiler gcc for use by the linker ld

**Options and Option Arguments:**

`-a` Turn on assembly listings

`-D` Accepted only for script compatibility with calls to other assemblers

`--defsym` 'SYM'='VAL' Define the symbol 'SYM' to be 'VAL' before assembling the input file. Value must be an integer constant. As in C, a leading 0x indicates a hexadecimal value, and a leading 0 indicates an octal value.

`-f` 'fast'–Skip preprocessing (assume source is compiler output)

`-I` 'path' Add path to the search list for .include directives

| | |
|---|---|
| `--gstabs` | Generate stabs debugging information for each assembler line. This may help debugging assembler code, if the debugger can handle it. |
| `-K` | Issue warnings when difference tables altered for long displacements |
| `-L` | Keep (in symbol table) local symbols |
| `-M, --mri` | Assemble in MRI compatibility mode |
| `-o` 'objfile' | Name object-file output from `as` |
| `-R` | Fold data section into text section |
| `--traditional-format` | Use same format as native assembler when possible |
| `-v` | Announce as version |
| `-W, --no-warn` | Suppress warning messages |
| `--fatal-warnings` | Consider warnings to be fatal |
| `--warn` | Just warn on warnings |
| `--`\|'files'... | Source files to assemble, or stdin (--) |
| `-A`var | Specify which variant of the 960 architecture is the target |
| `-b` | Add code to collect statistics about branches taken |
| `-no-relax` | Do not alter compare-and-branch instructions for long displacements; error if necessary |
| `-l` | Shorten references to undefined symbols, from two words to one |
| `-mc68000\|-mc68010\|-mc68020` | Specify what processor in the 68000 family is the target (default 68020) |

**Note:** Options may be in any order and may be before, after, or between filenames. The order of filenames is significant.

**Command Arguments:**

| | |
|---|---|
| 'files' | Object files to assemble, otherwise stdin is used. |

---

**at**—Queue, examine, or delete jobs for later execution

**Syntax:** `at` [`-V`] [`-q` 'queue'] [`-f` 'file'] [`-mldbv`] 'time'

`at -c` 'job' ['job'...]

**Purpose:** Read commands from stdin or a specified file that are to be executed at a later time using /bin/sh.

**Options and Option Arguments:**

| | |
|---|---|
| `-V` | Print the version number to standard error |
| `-q` 'queue' | Use the specified queue |
| `-m` | Send mail to the user when the job has completed even if there was no output |
| `-f` 'file' | Read the job from file rather than standard input |
| `-l` | Alias for a similar command, `atq` |
| `-d` | Alias for `atrm` |
| `-v` | Show the time the job will be executed<br>Times displayed will be in the format "1997-02-20 14:50" unless the environment variable |

| | |
|---|---|
| | *POSIXLY_CORRECT* is set, in which case it will be "Thu Feb 20 14:50:00 1997". |
| `-c` | cats the jobs listed on the command line to standard output |

**Command Arguments:**

| | |
|---|---|
| 'time' | The time the job is to be run, specified as 1, 2, or 4 digits |

---

## banner—Print large banner on printer

**Syntax:** `/usr/games/banner` [ `-w`'n' ] 'message' ...

**Purpose:** Print a large, high-quality banner on the standard output. If the message is omitted, it prompts for and reads one line of its standard input.

**Options and Option Arguments:**

| | |
|---|---|
| `-w`'n' | Width in *n* characters of printout |

**Command Arguments:**

| | |
|---|---|
| 'message'... | The banner message to be printed out |

---

## bash—GNU Bourne-Again Shell

**Syntax:** `bash` [options] ['file']

`sh` [options] ['file']

**Purpose:** Bourne-Again Shell-compatible command language interpreter that executes commands read from the standard input or from a file. Bash also incorporates useful features from the Korn and C shells (ksh and csh).

**Options and Option Arguments:**

| | |
|---|---|
| `-c` 'string' | If the `-c` option is present, commands are read from 'string'. If there are arguments after the string, they are assigned to the positional parameters, starting with $0. |
| `-r` | If the `-r` option is present, the shell becomes restricted. |
| `-i` | If the `-i` option is present, the shell is interactive. |
| `-s` | If the `-s` option is present, or if no arguments remain after option processing, commands are read from the standard input. This option allows the positional parameters to be set when invoking an interactive shell. |
| `-D` | A list of all double-quoted strings preceded by $ is printed on the standard ouput. These are the strings that are subject to language translation when the current locale is not C or POSIX. This implies the `-n` option; no commands will be executed. |
| `--A` | Signals the end of options and disables further option processing. Any arguments after the -- are treated as filenames and arguments. An argument of - is equivalent to --. |

Bash also interprets a number of multicharacter options. These options must appear on the command line before the single-character options in order for them to be recognized.

| | |
|---|---|
| `--dump-po-strings` | Equivalent to `-D`, but the output is in the GNU get_text po (portable object) file format. |
| `--dump-strings` | Equivalent to `-D`. |
| `--help` | Display a usage message on standard output and exit successfully |
| `--login` | Act as if invoked as a login shell |
| `--noediting` | Do not use the GNU readline library to read command lines when the shell is interactive |
| `--noprofile` | Do not read either the systemwide startup file /etc/profile or any of the personal initialization files ~/.bash_profile, ~/.bash_login, or ~/.profile. By default, **`bash`** reads these files when it is invoked as a login shell. |
| `--norc` | Do not read and execute the personal initialization file ~/.bashrc if the shell is interactive. This option is on by default if the shell is invoked as **`sh`**. |
| `--posix` | Change the behavior of bash where the default operation differs from the POSIX 1003.2 standard to match the standard |
| `--rcfile` 'file' | Execute commands from file instead of the standard personal initialization file ~/.bashrc if the shell is interactive |
| `--restricted` | The shell becomes restricted |
| `--rpm-requires` | Produce the list of files that are required for the shell script to run. This implies '`-n`' and is subject to the same limitations as compile-time error checking; Backticks, [] tests, and evals are not parsed, so some dependencies may be missed. |
| `--verbose` | Equivalent to `-v` |
| `--version` | Show version information for this instance of **`bash`** on the standard output and exit successfully. |

**Command Arguments:**

If arguments remain after option processing and neither the `-c` nor the `-s` option has been supplied, the first argument is assumed to be the name of a file containing shell commands. If **`bash`** is invoked in this fashion, **`$0`** is set to the name of the file, and the positional parameters are set to the remaining arguments. Bash reads and executes commands from this file, then exits. Bash's exit status is the exit status of the last command executed in the script. If no commands are executed, the exit status is 0.

---

## bc—Arbitrary precision calculator language

**Syntax:** `bc` [ `-lwsqv` ] [long-options] [ 'file' ... ]

**Purpose:** A language that supports arbitrary precision numbers with interactive execution of statements. There are some similarities in the syntax to the C programming language.

**Options and Option Arguments:**

| | |
|---|---|
| `-l` | Define the standard math library |
| `-w` | Give warnings for extensions to POSIX **`bc`** |
| `-s` | Process exactly the POSIX **`bc`** language |
| `-q` | Do not print the normal GNU **`bc`** welcome |

| | |
|---|---|
| `-v` | Print the version number and copyright, and quit |
| `--mathlib` | Define the standard math library |
| `--warn` | Give warnings for extensions to POSIX `bc` |
| `--standard` | Process exactly the POSIX `bc` language |
| `--quiet` | Do not print the normal GNU `bc` welcome. |
| `--version` | Print the version number and copyright and quit. |

**Command Arguments:**

| | |
|---|---|
| 'file'... | Input for calculator can be taken from file or stdin. |

---

**bison**—GNU project parser generator (yacc replacement)

**Syntax:** `bison` [ `-b` 'file-prefix' ] [ `--file-prefix=`'file-prefix' ] [`-d` ] [ `--defines` ] [ `-k` ] [ `--token-table` ] [ `-l` ] [ `--no-lines` ] [ `-n` ] [ `--no-parser` ] [ `-o` 'outfile' ] [ `--output-file=`'outfile' ] [ `-p` 'prefix' ] [ `--name-prefix=`'prefix' ] [ `-r`][ `--raw`] [ `-t` ][ `--debug` ][ `-v` [ `--verbose` ] [ `-V` ][ `--version` ] [ `-y` ][ `--yacc` ] [ `-h` ] [ `--help` ] [`--fixed-output-files` ] 'file'

**Purpose:** A parser generator in the style of `yacc`

**Options and Option Arguments:**

| | |
|---|---|
| `-b` 'file-prefix' `--file-prefix=`'file-prefix' | Specify a prefix to use for all bison output file names. The names are chosen as if the input file were named file-prefix.c. |
| `-d --defines` | Write an extra output file containing macro definitions for the token type names defined in the grammar and the semantic value type *YYSTYPE,* as well as a few external variable declarations. |
| `-r --raw` | The token numbers in the name.h file are usually the yacc-compatible translations. If this switch is specified, bison token numbers are output instead. |
| `-k --token-table` | Cause the name.tab.c output to include a list of token names in order by their token numbers; this is defined in the array yytname. |
| `-l --no-lines` | Don't put any line preprocessor commands in the parser file |
| `-n --no-parser` | Do not generate the parser code into the output |
| `-o` 'outfile' `--output-file=`'outfile' | Specify the name outfile for the parser file |
| `-p` 'prefix' `--name-prefix=`'prefix' | Rename the external symbols used in the parser so that they start with prefix instead of yy |
| `-t --debug` | Output a definition of the macro *YYDEBUG* into the parser file, so that the debugging facilities are compiled |
| `-v --verbose` | Write an extra output file containing verbose descriptions of the parser states and what is done for each type of look-ahead token in that state |
| `-V --version` | Print the version number of bison and exit |
| `-h --help` | Print a summary of the options to bison and exit |
| `-y --yacc --fixed-output-files` | Imitate yacc's output file name conventions |

**Command Arguments:**

| | |
|---|---|
| 'file' | A file contaning context-free grammar. |

---

## bzip2— A block-sorting file compressor, v1.0

**Syntax:** `bzip2` [ `-cdfkqstvzVL123456789` ] [ 'filenames' ... ]

**Purpose:** Compress files using the Burrows-Wheeler block-sorting text compression algorithm and Huffman coding

**Options and Option Arguments:**

| | |
|---|---|
| `-c --stdout` | Compress or decompress to standard output |
| `-d --decompress` | Force decompression |
| `-z --compress` | The complement to `-d`: forces compression, regardless of the invokation name |
| `-t --test` | Check integrity of the specified file(s), but don't decompress them |
| `-f --force` | Force overwrite of output files |
| `-k --keep` | Keep (don't delete) input files during compression or decompression |
| `-s --small` | Reduce memory usage for compression, decompression, and testing |
| `-q --quiet` | Suppress nonessential warning messages |
| `-v --verbose` | Verbose mode—show the compression ratio for each file processed |
| `-L --license -V --version` | Display the software version, license terms, and conditions |
| `-1` to `-9` | Set the block size to 100 K, 200 K ... 900 K when compressing |
| `--` | Treat all subsequent arguments as file names, even if they start with a dash |

**Command Arguments:**

| | |
|---|---|
| 'filenames'... | Files to compress |

---

## cal—Display a calendar

**Syntax:** `cal` [`-mjy`] ['month' ['year']]

**Purpose:** Display a simple calendar. If arguments are not specified, the current month is displayed.

**Options and Option Arguments:**

| | |
|---|---|
| `-m` | Display Monday as the first day of the week (default is Sunday) |
| `-j` | Display Julian dates (days one-based, numbered from January 1) |
| `-y` | Display a calendar for the current year |

**Command Arguments:** None

---

## cat—Concatenate files and print on the standard output

**Syntax:** `cat` [options] ['File']...

**Purpose:** Concatenate file(s), or standard input, to standard output

**Options and Option Arguments:**

| | |
|---|---|
| `-A`, `--show-all` | Equivalent to `-vET` |
| `-b`, `--number-nonblank` | Number nonblank output lines |
| `-e` | Equivalent to `-vE` |
| `-E`, `--show-ends` | Display $ at end of each line |
| `-n`, `--number` | Number all output lines |
| `-s`, `--squeeze-blank` | Never more than one single blank line |
| `-t` | Equivalent to `-vT` |
| `-T`, `--show-tabs` | Display TAB characters as `^I` |
| `-u` | (ignored) |
| `-v`, `--show-nonprinting` | Use ^ and `M-` notation, except for LFD and TAB |
| `--help` | Display this help and exit |
| `--version` | Output version information and exit |

**Command Arguments:**

| | |
|---|---|
| 'file' | File to be displayed, otherwise stdin to stdout |

---

**cc—See gcc**

---

**cd**—Change working directory

**Syntax:** `cd` ['directory']

**Purpose:** Change the present working directory to 'directory' or return to home directory

**Options and Options Arguments:** None

**Command Arguments:** None

---

**chgrp**—Change file group ownership

**Syntax:** `chgrp [ -fhR ]` 'group' 'file'

**Purpose:** Change the group associated with a file

**Options:**

| | |
|---|---|
| `-f` | Force; do not report errors |
| `-h` | If file is a symbolic link, change group of the symbolic link. Without this option, the group of the file referenced by the symbolic link is changed. |
| `-R` | Recursive; **`chgrp`** descends through the directory and any subdirectories, setting the specified group ID as it proceeds. When a symbolic link is encountered, the group of the target file is changed (unless the `-h` option is specified), but no recursion takes place. |

**Command Arguments:**

| | |
|---|---|
| 'group' | A group name from the group database or a numeric group ID. Either specifies a group ID to be given to each file named by one of the 'file' operands. If a numeric 'group' operand exists in the group database as a group name, the group ID number associated with that group name is used as the group ID. |
| 'file' | A path name of a file whose group ID is to be modified |

---

## chmod—Change mode of a file

**Syntax:** `chmod` [options] 'mode' 'file'...

**Purpose:** Change the file access modes of file(s)

**Options:**

| | |
|---|---|
| `-f` | Force; do not report errors |
| `-R` | Recursive; with directories specified in file(s), `chmod` recursively descends the directory structure and changes specified files access modes. |

**Command Arguments:**

| | |
|---|---|
| 'mode' | Either a symbolic or absolute designation of class and access permission |
| 'file'... | One or more files that the access is applied to |

---

## chown—Change file ownership

**Syntax:** `chown [ -fhR ]` 'owner'[:'group'] 'file'...

**Purpose:** Change the owner of a file or files

**Options:**

| | |
|---|---|
| `-f` | Do not report errors |
| `-h` | If the file is a symbolic link, change the owner of the symbolic link. Without this option, the owner of the file referenced by the symbolic link is changed. |
| `-R` | Recursive. `chown` descends through the directory and any subdirectories, setting the ownership ID as it proceeds. When a symbolic link is encountered, the owner of the target file is changed (unless the `-h` option is specified), but no recursion takes place. |

**Command Arguments:**

| | |
|---|---|
| 'owner'[:'group'] | A user ID and optional group ID to be assigned to 'file.' The 'owner' portion of this operand must be a user name from the user database or a numeric user ID. Either specifies a user ID to be given to each file named by 'file.' If a numeric 'owner' exists in the user database as a user name, the user ID number associated with that user name will be used as the user ID. Similarly, if the 'group' portion of this operand is present, it must be a group name from the group database or a numeric group ID. Either specifies a group ID to be given to each file. If a numeric group operand exists in the group database as a group name, the group ID number associated with that group name will be used as the group ID. |
| 'file' | A path name of a file whose user ID is to be modified |

---

## chpasswd—Update password file in batch

**Syntax:** `chpasswd [-e]`

**Purpose:** Read a file of user name and password pairs from standard input and use this information to update a group of existing users. Each line is of the format user_name:password. The named user must exist. The supplied password will be encrypted as necessary and the password age updated, if present. This command is intended to be used in a large system environment where many accounts are created at a time.

**Options:**

| | |
|---|---|
| `-e` | Without the `-e` switch, the passwords are expected to be cleartext. With the `-e` switch, the passwords are expected to be in encrypted form. |

**Command Arguments:** None

---

## chsh—Change login shell

**Syntax:** `chsh` [ `-s shell` ] [ `-l` ] [ `-u` ] [ `-v` ] [ 'username' ]

**Purpose:** Change login shell. If a shell is not given on the command line, `chsh` prompts for one.

**Options and Option Arguments:**

| | |
|---|---|
| `-s`, `--shell` | Specify login shell |
| `-l`, `--list-shells` | Print the list of shells listed in /etc/shells and exit |
| `-u`, `--help` | Print a usage message and exit |
| `-v, --version` | Print version information and exit |

**Command Arguments:**

| | |
|---|---|
| 'username' | User name to change shell for, if user has the privileges |

---

## cmp—Compare two files

**Syntax:** `cmp` [ `-l` ] [ `-s` ] 'file1' 'file2' [ 'skip1' ] [ 'skip2' ]

**Purpose:** Compare two files and locate where they first differ.

**Options:**

| | |
|---|---|
| `-l` | Write the byte number (decimal) and the differing bytes (octal) for each difference |
| `-s` | Write nothing for differing files; return exit statuses only |

**Command Arguments:**

| | |
|---|---|
| 'file1' | A path name of the first file to be compared. If 'file1' is -, the standard input is used. |
| 'file2' | A path name of the second file to be compared. If 'file2' is -, the standard input is used. |
| 'skip1,' 'skip2' | Initial byte offsets into 'file1' and 'file2' |

---

## col—Filter reverse line feeds from input

**Syntax:** `col` [`-bfpx`] [`-l` 'num']

**Purpose:** Filter out reverse (and half-reverse) line feeds so the output is in the correct order with only forward and half-forward line feeds, and replace white-space characters with tabs where possible. This can be useful in processing the output of nroff(1) and tbl(1). `col` reads from standard input and writes to standard output.

**Options and Option Arguments:**

| | |
|---|---|
| `-b` | Do not output any backspaces, printing only the last character written to each column position |
| `-f` | Forward half-line feeds are permitted (fine mode). Normally characters printed on a half-line boundary are printed on the following line. |
| `-p` | Force unknown control sequences to be passed through unchanged. Normally, **`col`** will filter out any control sequences from the input other than those recognized and interpreted by itself. |
| `-x` | Output multiple spaces instead of tabs |
| `-l` 'num' | Buffer at least 'num' lines in memory. By default, 128 lines are buffered. |

**Command Arguments:** None

---

## **comm**—Select or reject lines common to two files

**Syntax:** `comm [-123]` 'file1' 'file2'

**Purpose:** Show line-by-line comparison of two sorted files

**Options:**

| | |
|---|---|
| `-1` | Suppress the output column of lines unique to 'file1' |
| `-2` | Suppress the output column of lines unique to 'file2' |
| `-3` | Suppress the output column of lines duplicated in 'file1' and 'file2' |

**Command Arguments:**

| | |
|---|---|
| 'file1' | A path name of the first file to be compared. If 'file1' is -, the standard input is used. |
| 'file2' | A path name of the second file to be compared. If 'file2' is -, the standard input is used. |

---

## **cp**—Copy files

**Syntax:** `cp [-fip]` 'source file' 'target file'
`cp [-fip]` 'source file'... 'target'
`cp -r|-R [-fip]` 'source dir'... 'target'

**Purpose:** Copy one or more files in two basic ways: duplicate and to a directory

**Options:**

| | |
|---|---|
| `-f` | Unlink; if a file descriptor for a destination file cannot be obtained, attempt to unlink the destination file and proceed. |
| `-i` | Interactive; **`cp`** will prompt for confirmation whenever the copy would overwrite an existing 'target'. A y answer means that the copy should proceed. Any other answer prevents **`cp`** from overwriting 'target'. |
| `-p` | Preserve; **`cp`** duplicates not only the contents of 'source file' but also preserves the owner and group ID, permissions modes, modification and access time. |

| | |
|---|---|
| `-r` | Recursive; `cp` will copy the directory and all its files, including any subdirectories and their files, to 'target'. |
| `-R` | Same as `-r`, except pipes are replicated, not read from |

**Command Arguments:**

| | |
|---|---|
| 'source file' | Pathname of a regular file to be copied |
| 'source dir' | Pathname of a directory to be copied |
| 'target file' | Pathname of an existing or nonexisting file, used for the output when a single file is copied |
| 'target' | Pathname of a directory to contain the copied files |

---

## **cpio**—Copy file archives in and out

**Syntax:** `cpio -i` [ options ] [ 'pattern' ... ]

`cpio -o` [ options ]

`cpio -p` [ options ] 'directory'

**Purpose:** Copy files in to and out from an archive. The `-i`, `-o`, and `-p` options select the action to be performed. The following modes describe each of the actions:

*Copy In Mode*

`cpio -i` (copy in) extracts files from the standard input, which is assumed to be the product of a previous `cpio -o`. Only files with names that match 'pattern' are selected.

*Copy Out Mode*

`cpio -o` (copy out) reads the standard input to obtain a list of path names and copies those files onto the standard output together with path name and status information.

*Pass Mode*

`cpio -p` (pass) reads the standard input to obtain a list of pathnames of files that are conditionally created and copied into the destination 'directory' tree based on the options.

**Options and Option Arguments:**

| | |
|---|---|
| `-i` | (copy in) `cpio -i`; extract files from the standard input |
| `-o` | (copy out) `cpio -o`; read the standard input to obtain a list of pathnames and copies those files onto the standard output |
| `-p` | (pass) `cpio -p`; read the standard input to obtain a list of pathnames of files |

The following options can be appended in any sequence to the `-o`, `-i`, or `-p` options:

| | |
|---|---|
| `-a` | Reset access times of input files after they have been copied. Access times are not reset for linked files when `cpio -pla` is specified (mutually exclusive with `-m`). |
| `-A` | Append files to an archive. The `-A` option requires the `-O` option. Valid only with archives that are files or that are on floppy diskettes or hard disk partitions |

| | |
|---|---|
| `-b` | Reverse the order of the bytes within each word (use only with the `-i` option) |
| `-B` | Block input/output 5120 bytes to the record |
| `-c` | Read or write header information in ASCII character form for portability |
| `-C` 'bufsize' | Block input/output 'bufsize' bytes to the record, where 'bufsize' is replaced by a positive integer |
| `-d` | Create directories as needed |
| `-E` 'file' | Specify an input file ('file') that contains a list of filenames to be extracted from the archive (one filename per line) |
| `-f` | Copy in all files except those in 'pattern' |
| `-H` 'header' | Read or write header information in 'header' format |
| `-I` 'file' | Read the contents of 'file' as an input archive |
| `-k` | Attempt to skip corrupted file headers and I/O errors that may be encountered |
| `-l` | Whenever possible, link files rather than copying them |
| `-L` | Follow symbolic links; default is not to follow symbolic links |
| `-m` | Retain previous file modification time |
| `-M` 'message' | Define a 'message' to use when switching media |
| `-O` 'file' | Direct the output of `cpio` to 'file' |
| `-r` | Interactively rename files |
| `-R` 'user ID' | Reassign ownership and group information for each file to 'user ID' |
| `-s` | Swap bytes within each half word |
| `-S` | Swap halfwords within each word |
| `-t` | Print a table of contents of the input; no files created |
| `-u` | Copy unconditionally (normally, an older file will not replace a newer file with the same name) |
| `-v` | Verbose; print a list of filenames |
| `-V` | Special verbose; print a dot for each file read or written |

**Command Arguments:**

| | |
|---|---|
| 'directory' | Pathname of an existing directory to be used as the target of `cpio -p`. |
| 'pattern' | Expressions making use of a pattern-matching notation similar to that used by the shell. |

---

## **crontab**—User crontab file

**Syntax:** `crontab` [ 'filename' ]

`crontab` [`-elr`] 'username'

**Purpose:** Arrange jobs to run a specified times

**Options:**

| | |
|---|---|
| `-e` | Edit a copy of the current user's crontab file or create an empty file to edit if crontab does not exist |
| `-l` | List the crontab file for the invoking user |
| `-r` | Remove a user's crontab file from the crontab directory |

**Command Arguments:**

| | |
|---|---|
| 'filename' | Name of a file that contains the crontab commands. You may type commands at stdin and end with <Ctrl-D>. |
| 'username' | Used by superuser to change the crontab file for a user. |

---

## cut—Cut out selected fields of each line of a file

**Syntax:** `cut -b` 'list' [ `-n` ] [ 'file' ... ]
`cut -c` 'list' [ 'file' ... ]
`cut -f` 'list' [ `-d` 'delim' ] [ `-s` ] [ 'file' ... ]

**Purpose:** Select characters or tab fields from an input file and sends to stdout

**Options and Option Arguments:**

| | |
|---|---|
| 'list' | A comma-separated or blank-character-separated list of integer field numbers (in increasing order), with optional – to indicate ranges (e.g., 1,4,7; 1-3,8; -5,10 (short for 1-5,10); or 3- (short for third through last field)) |
| `-b` 'list' | The 'list' following `-b` specifies byte positions. |
| `-c` 'list' | The 'list' following `-c` specifies character positions. |
| `-d` 'delim' | The character following `-d` is the field delimiter (`-f` option only). |
| `-f` 'list' | The 'list' following `-f` is a list of fields assumed to be separated in the file by a delimiter character (see `-d`). |
| `-n` | Do not split characters. When `-b` 'list' and `-n` are used together, 'list' is adjusted so that no multibyte character is split. |
| `-s` | Suppresses lines with no delimiter characters in case of `-f` option. |

**Command Arguments:**

| | |
|---|---|
| 'file' | Pathname of an input file. If no 'file' operands are specified or if a 'file' operand is `-`, the standard input will be used. |

---

## date—Write the date and time to stdout

**Syntax:** `date` [`-u`] [+'format']
`date` [`-a` [`-`]'sss.fff']
`date` [`-u`] [['mmdd']'HHMM' | 'mmddHHMM'['cc']'yy']['.SS']

**Purpose:** Display or set clock time and calender date

**Options and Option Arguments:**

| | |
|---|---|
| -a [–]'sss.fff' | Slowly adjust the time by 'sss.fff' seconds ('fff' represents fractions of a second). This adjustment can be positive or negative. The system's clock will be sped up or slowed down until it has drifted by the number of seconds specified. |
| -u | Display (or set) the date in Greenwich Mean Time (GMT, universal time), bypassing the normal conversion to (or from) local time |

**Command Arguments:**

| | |
|---|---|
| 'mm' | Month number |
| 'dd' | Day number in the month |
| 'HH' | Hour number (24 hour system) |
| 'MM' | Minute number |
| 'SS' | Second number |
| 'cc' | Century minus one |
| 'yy' | Last two digits of the year number |

---

## dd—Convert and copy a file

**Syntax:** `dd` [ 'operand'='value' ... ]

**Purpose:** Copy files between devices

**Options:** None

**Command Arguments:**

| | |
|---|---|
| if='file' | Specify the input path; standard input is the default |
| of='file' | Specify the output path; standard output is the default |
| ibs='n' | Specify the input block size in 'n' bytes (default is 512) |
| obs='n' | Specify the output block size in 'n' bytes (default is 512) |
| bs='n' | Set both input and output block sizes to 'n' bytes, superseding ibs= and obs= |
| cbs='n' | Specify the conversion block size for block and unblock in bytes by 'n' (default is 0) |
| files='n' | Copy and concatenate 'n' input files before terminating (for tapes) |
| skip='n' | Skip 'n' input blocks (using the specified input block size) before starting to copy |
| iseek='n' | Seek 'n' blocks from beginning of input file before copying |
| oseek='n' | Seek 'n' blocks from beginning of output file before copying |
| seek='n' | Skip 'n' blocks (using the specified outputblock size) from beginning of output file before copying |
| count='n' | Copy only 'n' input blocks |
| conv='value'[,'value'...] | Where 'values' are comma-separated symbols from the following list: |

| | |
|---|---|
| ascii | Convert EBCDIC to ASCII |
| ebcdic | Convert ASCII to EBCDIC, if converting fixed-length ASCII records |
| ibm | Slightly different map of ASCII to EBCDIC |
| block | Treat input as a sequence of newline-terminated or eof-terminated variable-length records independent of the input block boundaries |
| unblock | Convert fixed-length records to variable length |
| lcase | Map uppercase characters specified by the LC_CTYPE keyword to the corresponding lower-case character |
| ucase | Map lowercase characters specified by the LC_CTYPE keyword to the corresponding upper-case character. |
| swab | Swap every pair of input bytes |
| noerror | Do not stop processing on an input error |
| notrunc | Do not truncate the output file |

All operands will be processed before any input is read.

---

**df**—Report number of free disk blocks and files

**Syntax:** `df` [ `-F` 'FSType' ][ `-abegklntV` ][ `-o` 'FSType-specific options' ][ 'directory' | 'block device' | 'resource'...]

**Purpose:** Display available disk space

**Options and Option Arguments:**

| | |
|---|---|
| `-a` | Report on all file systems, including ones whose entries have the ignore option set |
| `-b` | Print the total number of kilobytes free |
| `-e` | Print only the number of files free |
| `-F` 'FSType' | Specify the 'FSType' on which to operate |
| `-g` | Print the entire statvfs(2) structure |
| `-k` | Print the allocation in kilobytes |
| `-l` | Report on local file systems only |
| `-n` | Print only the 'FSType' name |
| `-o` 'FSType-specific options' | Specify 'FSType-specific options' |
| `-P` | Same as `-k` except in 512-byte units |
| `-t` | Print full listings with totals |
| `-V` | Echo the complete set of file system specific command lines, but do not execute them |

**Command Arguments:**

| | |
|---|---|
| 'directory' | Represents a valid directory name |
| 'block device' | Represents a block special device (e.g., /dev/dsk/c1d0s7); the corresponding file system need not be mounted |
| 'resource' | Represents an NFS resource name |

**diff**—Display line-by-line differences between pairs of text files

**Syntax:** `diff` [ `-bitw` ] [ `-c` | `-e` | `-f` | `-h` | `-n` ] 'file1' 'file2'

`diff` [ `-bitw` ] [ `-C` 'number' ] 'file1' 'file2'

`diff` [ `-bitw` ] [ `-D` 'string' ] 'file1' 'file2'

`diff` [ `-bitw` ] [ `-c` | `-e` | `-f` | `-h` | `-n` ] [ `-l` ] [ `-r` ] [ `-s` ] [ `-S` 'name' ] 'directory1' 'directory2'

**Purpose:** Display differences on lines of two files

**Options and Option Arguments:**

| | |
|---|---|
| `-b` | Ignore trailing blanks (spaces and <Tabs>)and treat other strings of blanks as equivalent. |
| `-i` | Ignore the case of letters (e.g., 'A' equals 'a') |
| `-t` | Expand <Tab> characters in output lines |
| `-w` | Ignore all blanks |

*The following options are mutually exclusive.*

| | |
|---|---|
| `-c` | Produce a list of differences with three lines of context |
| `-C` 'number' | Produce a list of differences identical to that produced by `-c` with 'number' lines of context |
| `-e` | Produce a script of only `a`, `c`, and `d` commands for the editor ed, which will re-create 'file2' from 'file1' |
| `-f` | Produce a similar script, not useful with ed, in the opposite order |
| `-h` | Expedient |
| `-n` | Produce a script similar to `-e`, but in the opposite order and with a count of changed lines on each insert or delete command |
| `-D` 'string' | Create a merged version of 'file1' and 'file2' with C preprocessor controls included |

*The following options are used for comparing directories.*

| | |
|---|---|
| `-l` | Produce output in long format |
| `-r` | Apply `diff` recursively to common subdirectories encountered |
| `-s` | Report files that are the identical, which would not otherwise be mentioned |
| `-S` 'name' | Start a directory diff in the middle, beginning with the file 'name' |

**Command Arguments:**

| | |
|---|---|
| 'file1' 'file2' | Pathname of a file or directory to be compared. If either 'file1' or 'file2' is `-`, the standard input will be used in its place |
| 'directory1' 'directory2' | Pathname of a directory to be compared |

Note: If only one of 'file1' and 'file2' is a directory, diff will be applied to the nondirectory file and the file contained in the directory file with a filename that is the same as the last component of the nondirectory file.

**du**—Summarize disk usage

**Syntax:** `du [ -ador ] [ 'file'... ]`

**Purpose:** Display information on disk useage of files and directories

**Options:**

| | |
|---|---|
| `-a` | In addition to the default output, report the size of each file not of type directory in the file hierarchy rooted in the specified file |
| `-d` | Do not cross file system boundaries |
| `-o` | Do not add child directories' usage to a parent's total |
| `-r` | Generate messages about directories and files that cannot be read |

**Command Arguments:**

| | |
|---|---|
| 'file' | Pathname of a file whose size is to be written. If no 'file' is specified, the current directory is used. |

---

**dump**—Display the values of all variables in the current or named function

**Syntax:** `dump ['func'] [> 'file']`

**Purpose:** Dump prints the values of variables

**Options and Option Arguments:**

| | |
|---|---|
| 'func' | A named function |

**Command Arguments:**

| | |
|---|---|
| 'file' | Output to named file |

---

**echo**—Echo arguments

**Syntax:** `echo ['string'...]`

**Purpose:** Display a message on stdout

**Options and Option Arguments:** None

**Command Arguments:**

| | |
|---|---|
| 'string' | String to be written to standard output. If any operand is -n, it will be treated as a string, not an option. The following character sequences will be recognized within any of the arguments: |
| \a | Alert character |
| \b | Backspace |
| \c | Print line without newline |
| \f | Formfeed |
| \n | Newline |
| \r | Carriage return |
| \t | Tab |
| \v | Vertical tab |
| \\ | Backslash |
| \0'n' | Where 'n' is the 8-bit character whose ASCII code is the 1-, 2-, or 3-digit octal number representing that character |

## **emacs**—Full-screen text editor

**Syntax:** `emacs` [ command line switches ] [ 'files' ... ]

**Purpose:** Provide a full-screen text editor with word processing and program development capabilities

**Options and Option Arguments:**

| | |
|---|---|
| +'number' | Go to the line specified by 'number' (do not insert a space between the + and the number) |
| `-q` | Do not load an init file |
| `-u` 'user' | Load 'user's init file |
| `-t` 'file' | Use specified 'file' as the terminal instead of using stdin/stdout; must be the first argument specified in the command line |
| `-f` 'function' | Execute the lisp function 'function' |
| `-l` 'file' | Load the lisp code in the file 'file' |
| `-batch` 'commandfile' | Executes `emacs` in batch mode from 'commandfile' |
| `-kill` | Exit `emacs` while in batch mode |

**X Window Options and Option Arguments:**

| | |
|---|---|
| `-rn` 'name' | Specifies the program name that the user should use when looking up defaults in the user's X resources; must be the first option specified in the command line |
| `-name` 'name' | Specifies the name that should be assigned to the `emacs` window |
| `-r` | Display the `emacs` window in reverse video |
| `-i` | Use the "kitchen sink" bitmap icon when iconifying the `emacs` window |
| `-font` 'font' | Set the `emacs` window's font to that specified by font |
| `-b` 'pixels' | Set the `emacs` window's border width to the number of pixels specified by 'pixels' |
| `-ib` 'pixels' | Set the window's internal border width to the number of pixels specified by 'pixels' |
| `-geometry` 'geometry' | Set the `emacs` window's width, height, and position as specified. The geometry specification is in the standard X format. The width and height are specified in characters; the default is 80 × 24 |
| `-fg` 'color' | On color displays, sets the color of the text |
| `-bg` 'color' | On color displays, sets the color of the window's background |
| `-bd` 'color' | On color displays, sets the color of the window's border |
| `-cr` 'color' | On color displays, sets the color of the window's text cursor |
| `-ms` 'color' | On color displays, sets the color of the window's mouse cursor |
| `-d` 'displayname' | Create the `emacs` window on the display specified by 'displayname'; must be the first option specified in the command line |

| | |
|---|---|
| `-nw` | Tells **`emacs`** not to use its special interface to X. If user uses this switch when invoking **`emacs`** from an **`xterm`** window, display is done in that window; must be the first option specified in the command line |

**Command Arguments:**

| | |
|---|---|
| 'files' ... | Files you wish to edit. |

---

## **expr**—Evaluate arguments as an expression

**Syntax:** `expr` 'arguments'

**Purpose:** Take character strings and evaluate as expressions

**Options and Option Arguments:** None

**Command Arguments:**

| | |
|---|---|
| 'arguments' | Terms of the expression, separated by blanks. Characters special to the shell must be escaped. Strings containing blanks or other special characters should be quoted. |

The following list of operators and keywords is in order of increasing precedence, with equal precedence operators grouped within braces, {}.

| | |
|---|---|
| 'expr' \| 'expr' | Returns the first 'expr' if it is neither null nor 0; otherwise returns the second 'expr' |
| 'expr' \& 'expr' | Returns the first 'expr' if neither 'expr' is Null or 0; otherwise returns 0 |
| 'expr' { =, \>, \>=, \<, \<=, != } 'expr' | Returns the result of an integer comparison if both arguments are integers; otherwise returns the result of a lexical comparison |
| 'expr' { +, - } 'expr' | Addition or subtraction of integer-valued arguments |
| 'expr' { *, /, % } 'expr' | Multiplication, division, or remainder of the integer-valued arguments |
| 'expr' : 'expr' | The matching operator; compares the first argument with the second argument, which must be a regular expression |
| ('expr' ) | Pattern symbols; can be used to return a portion of the first argument |
| 'integer' | An argument consisting only of an (optional) unary minus followed by digits |
| 'string' | A string argument that cannot be identified as an 'integer' argument or as one of the expression operator symbols |

---

## **file**—Determine file type

**Syntax:** `file` [ `-h` ] [ `-m` 'mfile' ] [ `-f` 'ffile' ] 'file'

`file` [ `-h` ] [ `-m` 'mfile' ] `-f` 'ffile'

`file -c` [ `-m` 'mfile' ]

**Purpose:** Classify 'file' according to data type content

**Options and Option Arguments:**

| | |
|---|---|
| `-c` | Check magic file for format errors |
| `-h` | Do not follow symbolic links |
| `-f` 'ffile' | 'ffile' contains a list of the files to be examined |
| `-m` 'mfile' | Use 'mfile' as an alternate magic file, instead of /etc/magic |

**Command Arguments:**

| | |
|---|---|
| 'file' | Pathname of a file to be tested |

---

## find—Find files

**Syntax:** `find` 'path'... 'expression'

**Purpose:** Display files along 'path'... that are specified in 'expression'

**Options and Option Arguments:** None

**Command Arguments:**

| | |
|---|---|
| 'path'... | Pathname of a starting point in the directory hierarchy |
| 'expression' | Valid expressions are as follows: |
| -atime 'n' | True if the file was accessed 'n' days ago |
| -cpio 'device' | Always true; write the current file on 'device' |
| -ctime 'n' | True if the file's status was changed 'n' days ago |
| -depth | Always true; causes descent of the directory hierarchy |
| -exec 'command' | True if the executed 'command' returns a zero |
| -follow | Always true; causes symbolic links to be followed |
| -fstype 'type' | True if the file system to which the file belongs is of type 'type' |
| -group 'gname' | True if the file belongs to the group 'gname' |
| -inum 'n' | True if the file has inode number 'n' |
| -links 'n' | True if the file has 'n' links |
| -local | True if the file system type is not a remote file system type |
| -ls | Always true; prints current pathname |
| -mount | Always true; restricts the search to the file system containing the directory specified |
| -mtime 'n' | True if the file's data was modified 'n' days ago |
| -name 'pattern' | True if 'pattern' matches the current file name |
| -ncpio 'device' | Always true; write the current file on 'device' in `cpio -c` format. |
| -newer 'file' | True if the current file has been modified more recently than the argument 'file' |
| -nogroup | True if the file belongs to a group not in the /etc/group file |
| -nouser | True if the file belongs to a user not in the /etc/passwd file |
| -ok 'command' | Like -exec except that the generated command line is printed with a question mark first and is executed only if the user responds by typing **y** |

| | |
|---|---|
| -perm [-]'mode' | The 'mode' argument is used to represent file mode bits. |
| -print | Always true; causes the current pathname to be printed. |
| -prune | Always yields true; Do not examine any directories or files in the directory structure below the 'pattern' just matched |
| -user 'uname' | True if the file belongs to the user 'uname' |
| -xdev | Same as the -mount primary |

---

**finger**—Display information about local or remote users

**Syntax:** `finger` [ `-bfhilmpqsw` ] [ 'username'... ] ['username@hostname']

**Purpose:** Display information about users

**Options:**

| | |
|---|---|
| `-b` | Suppress printing the user's home directory and shell in a long format |
| `-f` | Suppress printing the header that is normally printed in a nonlong format |
| `-h` | Suppress printing of the .project file in a long format |
| `-i` | Force "idle" output format, which is similar to short format |
| `-l` | Force long output format |
| `-m` | Match arguments only on user name (not first or last name) |
| `-p` | Suppress printing of the .plan file in a long format |
| `-q` | Force quick output format, which is similar to short format |
| `-s` | Force short output format |
| `-w` | Suppress printing the full name in a short format |

**Command Arguments:**

| | |
|---|---|
| 'username' | A local user; may be a first or last name, or an account name |
| ['username@hostname'] | Remote user at remote host |

---

**fmt**—Simple text formatter

**Syntax:** `fmt` [ `-c` ] [ `-s` ] [ `-w` 'width' | –'width' ] [ 'inputfile'... ]

**Purpose:** Format text using simple designations

**Options and Option Arguments:**

| | |
|---|---|
| `-c` | Crown margin mode. Preserve the indentation of the first two lines within a paragraph and align the left margin of each subsequent line with that of the second line |
| `-s` | Split lines only. Do not join short lines to form longer ones. |
| `-w` 'width' \| –'width' | Fill output lines to up to 'width' columns |

**Command Arguments:**

| | |
|---|---|
| 'inputfile'... | Input file names; if omitted, the stdin |

---

**ftp**—File transfer program

**Syntax:** `ftp` [ `-dgintv` ] [ 'hostname' ]

**Purpose:** Transfer files over a network.

**Options:**

| | |
|---|---|
| `-d` | Enable debugging |
| `-g` | Disable filename "globbing" |
| `-i` | Turn off interactive prompting during multiple file transfers |
| `-n` | Do not attempt "auto-login" upon initial connection |
| `-t` | Enable packet tracing |
| `-v` | Show all responses from the remote server, as well as report on data transfer statistics |

*Interactive commands at the* ftp> *prompt:*

| | |
|---|---|
| `!` [ 'command' ] | Run 'command' as a shell command on the local machine |
| `$` 'macro-name' [ 'args' ] | Execute the macro 'macro-name' that was defined with the **`macdef`** command. |
| `account` [ 'passwd' ] | Supply a supplemental password required by a remote system for access to resources once a login has been successfully completed |
| `append` 'local-file' [ 'remote-file' ] | Append a local file to a file on the remote machine |
| `ascii` | Set the "representation type" to "network ASCII" |
| `binary` | Set the "representation type" to "image" |
| `bye` | Terminate the FTP session with the remote server and exit ftp |
| `case` | Toggle remote computer file name case mapping during **`mget`** commands |
| `cd` 'remote-directory' | Change the working directory on the remote machine to 'remote-directory' |
| `cdup` | Change the remote machine working directory to the parent of the current remote machine working directory |
| `close` | Terminate the FTP session with the remote server and return to the command interpreter |
| `delete` 'remote-file' | Delete the file 'remote-file' on the remote machine |
| `debug` | Toggle debugging mode |
| `dir` [ 'remote-directory' ] [ 'local-file' ] | Print a listing of the directory contents in the directory, 'remote-directory', and, optionally, place the output in 'local-file' |
| `disconnect` | Same as **`close`** |
| `form` [ 'format-name' ] | Set the carriage control format subtype of the "representation type" to 'format-name' |

`get` 'remote-file' [ 'local-file' ] Retrieve the 'remote-file' and store it on the local machine.

`glob` Toggle filename expansion, or "globbing," for `mdelete`, `mget`, and `mput`

`hash` Toggle hash sign (#) printing for each data block transferred

`help` [ 'command' ] Print an informative message about the meaning of 'command'. If no argument is given, ftp prints a list of the known commands

`lcd` [ 'directory' ] Change the working directory on the local machine

`ls` [ 'remote-directory' | `-al` ] [ 'local-file' ] Print an abbreviated list of the contents of a directory on the remote machine

`macdef` 'macro-name' Define a macro

`mdelete` 'remote-files' Delete the 'remote-files' on the remote machine

`mdir` 'remote-files' 'local-file' Like `dir`, except multiple remote files may be specified

`mget` 'remote-files' Expand the 'remote-files' on the remote machine and do a `get` for each filename thus produced

`mkdir` 'directory-name' Make a directory on the remote machine

`mls` 'remote-files' 'local-file' Like `ls`, except multiple remote files may be specified

`mode` [ 'mode-name' ] Set the "transfer mode" to 'mode-name'

`mput` 'local-files' Expand wild cards in the list of local files given as arguments and do a put for each file in the resulting list

`nmap` [ 'inpattern' 'outpattern' ] Set or unset the filename mapping mechanism

`ntrans` [ 'inchars' [ 'outchars' ] ] Set or unset the filename character translation mechanism

`open` 'host' [ 'port' ] Establish a connection to the specified 'host' FTP server

`prompt` Toggle interactive prompting

`proxy` 'ftp-command' Execute an FTP command on a secondary control connection

`quit` Same as `bye`

`quote` 'arg1' 'arg2' ... Send the arguments specified, verbatim, to the remote server

`recv` 'remote-file' [ 'local-file'] Same as `get`

`remotehelp` [ 'command-name' ] Request help from the remote FTP server

`rename` 'from' 'to' Rename the file 'from' on the remote machine to have the name 'to'

`reset` Clear reply queue

`runique` Toggle storing of files on the local system with unique filenames

`send` 'local-file' [ 'remote-file' ] Same as `put`

`sendport` Toggle the use of PORT commands

`status` Show the current status of ftp

| | |
|---|---|
| `struct` [ 'struct-name' ] | Set the file structure to 'struct-name' |
| `sunique` | Toggle storing of files on remote machine under unique file names |
| `trace` | Toggle packet tracing (unimplemented) |
| `type` [ 'type-name' ] | Set the "representation type" to 'type-name' |
| `user` 'user-name' [ 'password' ] [ 'account' ] | Identify yourself to the remote FTP server |
| `verbose` | Toggle verbose mode. In verbose mode, all responses from the FTP server are displayed to the user |
| ? [ 'command' ] | Same as help |

**Command Arguments:**

| | |
|---|---|
| 'hostname' | Establishes a connection to a remote computer using domain name system |

---

## gcc, g++—GNU project C and C++ Compiler (gcc-2.96)

**Syntax:** `gcc` [ 'option' | 'filename' ]...

`g++` [ 'option' | 'filename' ]...

**Purpose:** The C and C++ compilers are integrated. Both process input files through one or more of four stages: preprocessing, compilation, assembly, and linking. Source filename suffixes identify the source language, but which name is used for the compiler governs default assumptions: The gcc compiler assumes preprocessed (.i) files are C and assumes C style linking; while the g++ compiler assumes preprocessed (.i) files are C++ and assumes C++ style linking.

**Options and Option Arguments:**

Options must be separate. For example, **`-dr`** is quite different from **`-d -r`**. The following options are grouped by type. Explanations appear in the sections that follow.

| | |
|---|---|
| *Overall Options* | `-c`, `-S`, `-E`, `-o` 'file', `-pipe`, `-v`, `-x` 'language' |
| *Language Options* | `-ansi`, `-fcond-mismatch`, `-fdollars-in-identifiers`, `-fexternal-templates`, `-fno-asm`, `-fno-builtin`, `-fhosted`, `-fno-hosted`, `-ffreestanding`, `-fno-freestanding`, `-fno-strict-prototype`, `-fsigned-bitfields`, `-fsigned-char`, `-funsigned-bitfields`, `-funsigned-char`, `-fwritable-strings`, `-traditional`, `-traditional-cpp`, `-trigraphs` |
| *Assembler Option* | `-Wa`,option |
| *Linker Options* | `-llibrary`, `-nostartfiles`, `-nostdlib`, `-static`, `-shared`, `-symbolic`, `-Xlinker`, `-Wl`, `-u` symbol |

***Overall Options***

| | |
|---|---|
| `-x` 'language' | Specify explicitly the language for the following input files (rather than choosing a default based on the file name suffix). Applies to all following input files until the next **`-x`** option. Possible values of language are c, objective-c, c-header, c++, cpp-output, assembler, and assembler-with-cpp. |

`-x none` Turn off any specification of a language, so that subsequent files are handled according to their filename suffixes (as they are if `-x` has not been used at all).

If you want only some of the four stages (preprocess, compile, assemble, link), you can use `-x` (or filename suffixes) to tell gcc where to start, and options `-c`, `-S`, or `-E` to say where gcc is to stop. Note that some combinations (e.g., `-x cpp-output -E`) instruct gcc to do nothing at all.

`-c` Compile or assemble the source files, but do not link. The compiler output is an object file corresponding to each source file. By default, gcc makes the object file name for a source file by replacing the suffix `.c`, `.i`, `.s`, and so on with `.o`. Use `-o` to select another name. gcc ignores any unrecognized input files (those that do not require compilation or assembly) with the `-c` option.

`-S` Stop after the stage of compilation proper; do not assemble. The output is an assembler code file for each nonassembler input file specified. By default, gcc makes the assembler filename for a source file by replacing the suffix `.c`, `.i`, and so on with `.s`. Use `-o` to select another name. gcc ignores any input files that don't require compilation.

`-E` Stop after the preprocessing stage; do not run the compiler proper. The output is preprocessed source code, which is sent to the standard output. gcc ignores input files that don't require preprocessing.

`-o` 'file' Place output in 'file'. This applies regardless to whatever sort of output gcc is producing, whether it be an executable file, an object file, an assembler file, or preprocessed C code. Because only one output file can be specified, it does not make sense to use `-o` when compiling more than one input file, unless you are producing an executable file as output.

If you do not specify `-o`, the default is to put an executable file in a.out, the object file for source.suffix in source.o, its assembler file in source.s, and all preprocessed C source on standard output.

`-v` Print (on standard error output) the commands executed to run the stages of compilation. Also print the version number of the compiler driver program and of the preprocessor and the compiler proper.

`-pipe` Use pipes rather than temporary files for communication between the various stages of compilation. This fails to work on systems where the assembler cannot read from a pipe, but the GNU assembler has no trouble.

### *Language Options*

The following options control the dialect of C that the compiler accepts:

**`-ansi`** Support all ANSI standard C programs. This turns off certain features of GNU C that are incompatible with ANSI C, such as the asm, inline, and typeof keywords, and predefined macros such as *UNIX* and *VAX* that identify the type of system you are using. It also enables the undesirable and rarely used ANSI trigraph feature, and disallows **$** as part of identifiers.

The **`-ansi`** option does not cause non-ANSI programs to be rejected gratuitously. For that, **`-pedantic`** is required in addition to **`-ansi`**.

The preprocessor predefines a macro __STRICT_ANSI__ when you use the **`-ansi`** option. Some header files may notice this macro and refrain from declaring certain functions or defining certain macros that the ANSI standard doesn't call for; this is to avoid interfering with any programs that might use these names for other things.

**`-fno-asm`** Do not recognize asm, inline, or typeof as a keyword. These words may then be used as identifiers. You can use __asm__, __inline__, and __typeof__ instead. **`-ansi`** implies **`-fno-asm`**.

**`-fno-builtin`** Don't recognize built-in functions that do not begin with two leading underscores. Currently, the functions affected include _exit, abort, abs, alloca, cos, exit, fabs, labs, memcmp, memcpy, sin, sqrt, strcmp, strcpy, and strlen. The **`-ansi`** option prevents alloca and _exit from being built-in functions.

**`-fhosted`** Compile for a hosted environment; this implies the **`-fbuiltin`** option and that suspicious declarations of main should be warned about.

**`-ffreestanding`** Compile for a free-standing environment; this implies the **`-fno-builtin`** option and that main has no special requirements.

**`-fno-strict-prototype`** Treat a function declaration with no arguments, such as 'int foo ();', as C would treat it—as saying nothing about the number of arguments or their types (C++ only). Normally, such a declaration in C++ means that the function foo takes no arguments.

**`-trigraphs`** Support ANSI C trigraphs. The **`-ansi`** option implies **`-trigraphs`**.

**`-traditional`** Attempt to support some aspects of traditional C compilers. For details, see the GNU C manual; the duplicate list here has been omitted.

**`-traditional-cpp`** Attempt to support some aspects of traditional C preprocessors. This includes the items that specifically mention the preprocessor, but none of the other effects of **`-traditional`**.

| | |
|---|---|
| `-fdollars-in-identifiers` | Permit the use of **$** in identifiers (C++ only). You can also use **`-fno-dollars-in-identifiers`** to explicitly prohibit use of $. (GNU C++ allows $ by default on some target systems but not others.) |
| `-fexternal-templates` | Produce smaller code for template declarations by generating only a single copy of each template function where it is defined (C++ only). To use this option successfully, you must also mark all files that use templates with either '#pragma implementation' (the definition) or '#pragma interface' (declarations). When the code is compiled with **`-fexternal-templates`**, all template instantiations are external. You must arrange for all necessary instantiations to appear in the implementation file; you can do this with a typedef that references each instantiation needed. Conversely, when you compile using the default option **`-fno-external-templates`**, all template instantiations are explicitly internal. |
| `-fcond-mismatch` | Allow conditional expressions with mismatched types in the second and third arguments. The value of such an expression is void. |
| `-funsigned-char` | Let the type char be unsigned, like unsigned char. Each kind of machine has a default for what char should be. It is either like unsigned char by default or like signed char by default. |
| `-fsigned-char` | Let the type char be signed, like signed char. |
| `-fsigned-bitfields`<br>`-funsigned-bitfields`<br>`-fno-signed-bitfields`<br>`-fno-unsigned-bitfields` | Control whether a bitfield is signed or unsigned, when declared with no explicit 'signed' or 'unsigned' qualifier. By default, such a bit field is signed, because this is consistent: The basic integer types, such as int, are signed types. However, when you specify **`-traditional`**, bitfields are all unsigned no matter what. |
| `-fwritable-strings` | Store string constants in the writable data segment and don't uniquize them. This is for compatibility with old programs that assume they can write into string constants. **`-traditional`** also has this effect. |

***Assembler Option***

| | |
|---|---|
| `-Wa` | Pass option as an option to the assembler. If option contains commas, it is split into multiple options at the commas. |

***Linker Options***

These options come into play when the compiler links object files into an executable output file. They are meaningless if the compiler is not doing a link step.

| | |
|---|---|
| `object-file-name` | A file name that does not end in a special recognized suffix is considered to name an object file or library. (Object files are distinguished from libraries by the linker according to the file contents.) If gcc does a link step, these object files are used as input to the linker. |

| | |
|---|---|
| `-llibrary` | Use the library named library when linking. The linker searches a standard list of directories for the library, which is actually a file named liblibrary.a. The linker then uses this file as if it had been specified precisely by name. The directories searched include several standard system directories plus any that you specify with `-L`.<br>Normally the files found this way are library files—archive files whose members are object files. The linker handles an archive file by scanning through it for members that define symbols that have so far been referenced but not defined. If the linker finds an ordinary object file rather than a library, the object file is linked in the usual fashion. The only difference between using an `-l` option and specifying a file name is that `-l` surrounds library with lib and .a and searches several directories. |
| `-lobjc` | Special case of the `-l` option. |
| `-nostartfiles` | Do not use the standard system start-up files when linking. The standard libraries are used normally. |
| `-nostdlib` | Don't use the standard system libraries and start-up files when linking. Only the files you specify will be passed to the linker. |
| `-static` | On systems that support dynamic linking, this prevents linking with the shared libraries. On other systems, this option has no effect. |
| `-shared` | Produce a shared object that can then be linked with other objects to form an executable. Only a few systems support this option. |
| `-symbolic` | Bind references to global symbols when building a shared object. Warn about any unresolved references (unless overridden by the link editor option `-Xlinker -z -Xlinker` defs). Only a few systems support this option. |
| `-Xlinker option` | Pass option as an option to the linker. You can use this to supply system-specific linker options that GNU CC does not know how to recognize. If you want to pass an option that takes an argument, you must use `-Xlinker` twice, once for the option and once for the argument. For example, to pass `-assert definitions`, you must write `-Xlinker -assert -Xlinker definitions`. Writing `-Xlinker "-assert definitions"` does not work, because this passes the entire string as a single argument, which is not what the linker expects. |
| `-Wl` | Pass option as an option to the linker. If option contains commas, it is split into multiple options at the commas. |

| | |
|---|---|
| `-u` 'symbol' | Pretend the 'symbol' symbol is undefined, to force linking of library modules to define it. You can use `-u` multiple times with different symbols to force loading of additional library modules. |

**Command Arguments:** None

---

## grep—Search a file for a pattern

**Syntax:** `grep` [ `-bchilnsvw` ] 'regular-expression' [ 'filename' ... ]

**Purpose:** Search in file(s) for a pattern that matches a regular expression

**Options :**

| | |
|---|---|
| `-b` | Precede each line by the block number on which it was found |
| `-c` | Print only a count of the lines that contain the pattern |
| `-h` | Prevent the name of the file containing the matching line from being appended to that line |
| `-i` | Ignore upper and lowercase distinction during comparisons |
| `-l` | Print only the names of files with matching lines, separated by newline characters. |
| `-n` | Precede each line by its line number in the file (first line is 1) |
| `-s` | Suppress error messages about nonexistent or unreadable files |
| `-v` | Print all lines except those that contain the pattern |
| `-w` | Search for the expression as a word as if surrounded by \< and \> |

**Command Arguments:**

| | |
|---|---|
| 'filename'... | Pathname of a file to be searched for the patterns. If no 'file' operands are specified, the standard input will be used. |
| 'regular-expression' | Regular expression |

---

## gunzip—Expand files

**Syntax:** `gunzip` [ `-acfhlLnNrtvV` ] [`-S` suffix] [ 'name' ... ]

**Purpose:** Take a list of files on the command line and replace each file whose name ends with .gz, -gz, .z, -z, _z, or .Z and which begins with the correct magic number with an uncompressed file without the original extension. Also recognizes the special extensions .tgz and .taz as shorthand for .tar.gz and .tar.Z, respectively.

**Options and Option Arguments:**

| | |
|---|---|
| `-a --ascii` | ASCII text mode: Convert eol using local conventions. This option is supported only on some nonLINUX systems. For MSDOS, CR LF is converted to LF when compressing, and LF is converted to CR LF when decompressing. |

| | |
|---|---|
| `-c --stdout --to-stdout` | Write output on standard output; keep original files unchanged. If there are several input files, the output consists of a sequence of independently compressed members. To obtain better compression, concatenate all input files before compressing them. |
| `-d --decompress --uncompress` | Decompress |
| `-f --force` | Force compression or decompression even if the file has multiple links or the corresponding file already exists, or if the compressed data is read from or written to a terminal. If the input data is not in a format recognized by **`gzip`**, and if the option **`--stdout`** is also given, copy the input data without change to the standard ouput: Let **`zcat`** behave as **`cat`**. If **`-f`** is not given, and when not running in the background, **`gzip`** prompts to verify whether an existing file should be overwritten. |
| `-h --help` | Display a help screen and quit |
| `-l --list` | For each compressed file, list the following fields:<br>compressed size — Size of the compressed file<br>uncompressed size — Size of the uncompressed file<br>ratio — compression ratio (0.0% if unknown)<br>uncompressed_name — name of the uncompressed file |
| `-L --license` | Display the gzip license and quit |
| `-n --no-name` | When compressing, do not save the original file name and time stamp by default. (The original name is always saved if the name had to be truncated.) When decompressing, do not restore the original filename if present (remove only the gzip suffix from the compressed filename) and do not restore the original time stamp if present (copy it from the compressed file). This option is the default when decompressing. |
| `-N --name` | When compressing, always save the original filename and time stamp; this is the default. When decompressing, restore the original file name and time stamp if present. This option is useful on systems which have a limit on filename length or when the time stamp has been lost after a file transfer. |
| `-q --quiet` | Suppress all warnings |
| `-r --recursive` | Travel the directory structure recursively. If any of the file names specified on the command line are directories, gzip will descend into the directory and compress all the files it finds there (or decompress them in the case of **`gunzip`** ). |
| `-S .suf --suffix .suf` | Use suffix .suf instead of .gz. Any suffix can be given, but suffixes other than .z and .gz should be avoided to avoid confusion when files are transferred to other systems. A null suffix forces |

gunzip to try decompression on all given files regardless of suffix, as in

```
gunzip -S "" * (*.* for MSDOS)
```

Previous versions of gzip used the .z suffix. This was changed to avoid a conflict with pack(1).

| | |
|---|---|
| `-t --test` | Test; check the compressed file integrity |
| `-v --verbose` | Verbose; display the name and percentage reduction for each file compressed or decompressed |
| `-V --version` | Version; display the version number and compilation options; then quit |
| `-# --fast --best` | Regulate the speed of compression using the specified digit #, where `-1` or `--fast` indicates the fastest compression method (less compression) and `-9` or `--best` indicates the slowest compression method (best compression). The default compression level is -6 (that is, biased toward high compression at expense of speed). |

**Command Arguments:**

| | |
|---|---|
| 'name'... | Files to be decompressed. |

## gzip—Compress files

**Syntax:** `gzip [ -acdfhlLnNrtvV19 ] [-S suffix] [ 'name' ... ]`

**Purpose:** Reduce size of named files using Lempel-Ziv coding (LZ77). Whenever possible, each file is replaced by one with the extension .gz, while keeping the same ownership modes, access, and modification times. (The default extension is `-gz` for VMS, z for MSDOS, OS/2 FAT, Windows NT FAT, and Atari.) If no files are specified, or if a file name is -, the standard input is compressed to the standard output. `gzip` will only attempt to compress regular files; it will ignore symbolic links. If the compressed filename is too long for its file system, `gzip` truncates it. `gzip` attempts to truncate only the parts of the file name longer than three characters. (A part is delimited by dots.) If the name consists of small parts only, the longest parts are truncated. For example, if filenames are limited to 14 characters, gzip.msdos.exe is compressed to gzi.msd.exe.gz. Names are not truncated on systems that do not have a limit on filename length. By default, `gzip` keeps the original filename and timestamp in the compressed file. These are used when decompressing the file with the `-N` option. This is useful when the compressed filename was truncated or when the time stamp was not preserved after a file transfer. Compressed files can be restored to their original form using `gzip -d` or `gunzip` or `zcat`. If the original name saved in the compressed file is not suitable for its filesystem, a new name is constructed from the original one to make it legal.

**Options and Option Arguments:**

See `gunzip`

**Command Arguments:**

| | |
|---|---|
| 'name'... | File to be compressed. |

## head—Display first few lines of files

**Syntax:** `head [ '-number' | -n 'number' ] [ 'filename'... ]`

**Purpose:** Display the beginning of a file

**Options and Option Arguments:**

| | |
|---|---|
| `-n` 'number' | The first 'number' lines of each input file will be copied to stdout. The 'number' option argument must be a positive decimal integer. |
| '-number' | The 'number' argument is a positive decimal integer with the same effect as the **`-n`** 'number' option. |

**Command Arguments:**

| | |
|---|---|
| 'filename'... | Pathname of an input file. If no 'file' operands are specified, the stdin will be used. |

---

## kill—Send a signal to a process

**Syntax:** `kill [-signum]` 'pid', 'signum'

**Purpose:** Terminate one or more process IDs

**Options:**

| | |
|---|---|
| `-signum` | Signal number or name of a process preceding pid |

**Command Arguments:**

| | |
|---|---|
| 'pid' | Process ID number of one or more processes to be terminated. |
| 'signum' | Signal number; 9 kill, 15 software terminate, 18 stop are common ones. |

---

## less—Display one screenful of a file at a time

**Syntax:** `less [-[+]aBcCdeEfgGiImMnNqQrsSuUVwX]`
`[-b` 'bufs'] `[-h` 'lines'] `[-j` 'line'] `[-k` 'keyfile']
`[-{oO}` 'logfile'] `[-p` 'pattern'] `[-P` 'prompt'] `[-t` 'tag']
`[-T` 'tagsfile'] `[-x` 'tab'] `[-y` 'lines'] `[-[z]` 'lines'] `[+[+]`'cmd'] `[--]` ['filename']...

**Purpose:** Similar to `more`; allow backward movement in the file as well as forward movement

**Options and Option Arguments:**

| | |
|---|---|
| `-?` | Display a summary of the commands |
| `--help` | Same as **`-?`** |
| `-a` | Cause searches to start after the last line displayed on the screen, thus skipping all lines displayed on the screen |
| `-b` 'n' | Specify the number of buffers that 'n' `less` will use for each file |
| `-B` | Disable the automatic allocation of buffers for pipes |
| `-c` | Cause full screen repaints to be painted from the top line down |
| `-C` | Like **`-c`**, but screen cleared before it is repainted |
| `-d` | Suppress error message normally displayed if terminal is dumb |
| `-e` | Cause '`less`' to exit automatically the second time it reaches eof |
| `-E` | Cause '`less`' to automatically exit the first time it reaches eof |
| `-f` | Force nonregular files to be opened (A nonregular file is a directory or a device special file.) |

| | |
|---|---|
| `-g` | Highlight only the particular string found by the last search command |
| `-G` | Suppress all highlighting of strings found by search commands |
| `-h` 'n' | Specify a maximum number of lines 'n' to scroll backward |
| `-i` | Cause searches to ignore case; that is, uppercase and lowercase are considered identical |
| `-I` | Like `-i`, but searches ignore case even if the pattern contains uppercase letters |
| `-j` 'n' | Specify a line 'n' on the screen where the "target" line is to be positioned |
| `-k` 'filename' | Cause `less` to open and interpret 'filename' as a key file |
| `-m` | Cause `less` to prompt verbosely (like `more`), with the percent into the file. By default, `less` prompts with a colon. |
| `-M` | Cause `less` to prompt even more verbosely than `more` |
| `-n` | Suppress line numbers |
| `-N` | Cause a line number to be displayed at the beginning of each line in the display |
| `-o` 'filename' | Cause `less` to copy its input to named file as it is being viewed |
| `-O` 'filename' | Like `-o`, but will overwrite an existing file without confirmation |
| `-p` 'pattern' | Equivalent to specifying +/'pattern'; that is, it tells `less` to start at the first occurrence of 'pattern' in the file |
| `-P` 'prompt' | Provide a way to tailor the three prompt styles to the user's preference |
| `-q` | Cause "quiet" operation |
| `-Q` | Cause totally "quiet" operation (e.g., the terminal bell is never rung) |
| `-r` | Cause "raw" control characters to be displayed |
| `-s` | Cause consecutive blank lines to be squeezed into a single blank line |
| `-S` | Cause lines longer than the screen width to be chopped rather than folded |
| `-t` 'tag' | Edit the file containing 'tag' |
| `-T` 'tagsfile' | Specify a tags file to be used instead of "tags" |
| `-u` | Cause backspaces and carriage returns to be treated as printable characters |
| `-U` | Cause backspaces, tabs, and carriage returns to be treated as control characters |
| `-V` | Display the version number of `less` |
| `--version` | Same as `-V` |

| | |
|---|---|
| `-w` | Cause blank lines to be used to represent lines past the end of the file. By default, a tilde character (~) is used. |
| `-x` 'n' | Sets tab stops every 'n' positions. The default for 'n' is 8. |
| `-X` | Disable sending the termcap initialization and deinitialization strings |
| `-y`'n' | Specify a maximum number of lines to scroll forward |
| `-[z]`'n' | Change the default scrolling window size to 'n' lines |
| -" | Change the filename quoting character |
| `--` | A command line argument of `--` marks the end of option arguments |
| `+` | If a command line option begins with `+`, the remainder of that option is taken to be an initial command to **`less`** |

**Command Arguments:**

| | |
|---|---|
| ['filename']... | List of files less operates on. If not specified, **`less`** takes input from stdin. |

---

**ln**—Make hard or symbolic links to files

**Syntax:** `ln [-fns]` 'source file' ['target']

`ln [-fns]` 'source file'... 'target'

**Purpose:** Create hard link to a file

**Options:**

| | |
|---|---|
| `-f` | Link files without questioning the user, even if the mode of 'target' forbids writing |
| `-n` | If the link is an existing file, do not overwrite the contents of the file |
| `-s` | Create a symbolic link |

**Command Arguments:**

| | |
|---|---|
| 'source file' | Pathname of file to be linked. This can be either a regular or special file. If the **`s`** option is specified, 'source file' can also be a directory. |
| 'target' | Pathname of the new directory entry to be created, or of an existing directory in which the new directory entries are to be created. |

---

**lpr**—Send a job to the printer

**Syntax:** `lpr [ -P` 'printer' `] [ -#` 'copies' `] [ -C` 'class' `]`

`[ -J` 'job' `] [ -T` 'title' `] [ -i [` 'indent' `] ] [ -w` 'cols' `]`

`[ -m ] [ -h ] [ -s ] [` 'filename' ... `]`

**Purpose:** Send files to the printer

**Options and Option Arguments:**

| | |
|---|---|
| `-P` 'printer' | Send output to the named 'printer' |
| `-#` 'copies' | Produce the number of 'copies' indicated for each named file |

| | |
|---|---|
| `-C` 'class' | Print 'class' as the job classification on the burst page |
| `-J` 'job' | Print 'job' as the job name on the burst page |
| `-T` 'title' | Use 'title' instead of the file name for the title |
| `-I` ['indent'] | Indent output 'indent' <space> characters. Eight <space> characters is the default |
| `-w` 'cols' | Use 'cols' as the page width for `pr` |
| `-m` | Send mail upon completion |
| `-h` | Suppress printing the burst page |
| `-s` | Use full pathnames (not symbolic links) of the files to be printed rather than trying to copy them. |

**Command Arguments:**

| | |
|---|---|
| ['filename'...] | Files to be submitted to print queue and printed. |

---

**ls**—List contents of directory

**Syntax:** `ls` [ `-aAbcCdfFgilLmnopqrRstux1` ] [ 'file'... ]

**Purpose:** For each 'file' that is a directory, list contents of the directory; for each 'file' that is an ordinary file, repeat its name and any other information requested

**Options:**

| | |
|---|---|
| `-a` | List all entries, including those that begin with a dot (.), which are normally not listed. |
| `-A` | List all entries, including those that begin with a dot (.), with the exception of the working directory (.) and the parent directory (..). |
| `-b` | Force printing of nonprintable characters to be in the octal '\ddd' notation |
| `-c` | Use time of last modification of the i-node (file created, mode changed, etc.) for sorting (`-t`) or printing (`-l` or `-n`). |
| `-C` | Multicolumn output with entries sorted down the columns |
| `-d` | If an argument is a directory, list only its name (not its contents) |
| `-f` | Force each argument to be interpreted as a directory; list the name found in each slot |
| `-F` | Put a slash (/) after each filename if the file is a directory, an asterisk (*) if the file is an executable, and an at-sign (@) if the file is a symbolic link |
| `-g` | Same as `-l`, except that the owner is not printed |
| `-i` | For each file, print the i-node number in the first column of the report |
| `-l` | List in long format, giving mode, ACL indication, number of links, owner, group, size in bytes, and time of last modification for each file |
| `-L` | If an argument is a symbolic link, list the file or directory the link references rather than the link itself |
| `-m` | Stream output format; files are listed across the page, separated by commas |

| | |
|---|---|
| `-n` | The same as `-l`, except that the owner's UID and group's GID numbers are printed, rather than the associated character strings |
| `-o` | The same as `-l`, except that group is not printed |
| `-p` | Put a slash (/) after each filename if the file is a directory |
| `-q` | Force printing of nonprintable characters in filenames as the character question mark (?) |
| `-r` | Reverse the order of sort to get reverse alphabetic or oldest first, as appropriate |
| `-R` | Recursively list subdirectories encountered |
| `-s` | Give size in blocks, including indirect blocks, for each entry |
| `-t` | Sort by time stamp (latest first) instead of by name |
| `-u` | Use time of last access instead of last modification for sorting (with the `-t` option) or printing (with the `-l` option) |
| `-x` | Multicolumn output with entries sorted across rather than down the page |
| `-1` | Print one entry per line of output |

**Command Arguments:**

| | |
|---|---|
| 'file' | Pathname of file to be written; if specified file is not found, a diagnostic message will be output stderr. |

---

**mail**—Read mail or send mail to users

**Syntax:** *Sending mail*

`mail` [ `-tw` ] [ `-m` 'message type' ] 'recipient'...

*Reading mail*

`mail` [ `-ehpPqr` ] [ `-f` 'file' ]

**Purpose:** Send or read e-mail to/from other users

**Options and Option Arguments:**

*The following affect sending mail.*

| | |
|---|---|
| `-m` 'message type' | Add a Message-Type: line to the message header with the value of 'message type' |
| `-t` | Add a To: line to the message header for each 'recipient' |
| `-w` | Send a letter to a remote recipient without waiting for the completion of the remote transfer program |

*The following affect reading mail.*

| | |
|---|---|
| `-e` | Do not mail |
| `-h` | Display a window of headers initially, rather than the latest message |
| `-p` | Print all messages without prompting for disposition |
| `-P` | Print all messages with 'all' header lines displayed, rather than the default selective header line display |
| `-q` | Mail terminates after interrupts |

| | |
|---|---|
| `-r` | Print messages in first-in, first-out order |
| `-f` 'file' | Use 'file' (e.g., mbox) instead of the default 'mailfile' |

*For each message, the user is prompted with a ? and a line is read from the standard input. The following commands are available to determine the disposition of the message:*

| | |
|---|---|
| `#` | Print the number of the current message |
| `-` | Print previous message |
| `<new-line>`,`+`, or `n` | Print next message |
| `!command` | Escape to the shell to do 'command' |
| `a` | Print message that arrived during the mail session |
| `d`, or `dp` | Delete current message and print next message |
| `d` 'n' | Delete message number 'n'; do not go on to next message |
| `dq` | Delete message and quit mail |
| `h` | Display a window of headers around current message |
| `h` 'n' | Display a window of headers around message number 'n' |
| `h a` | Display headers of all messages in the user's 'mailfile' |
| `h d` | Display headers of messages scheduled for deletion |
| `m` [ 'persons' ] | Mail (and delete) the current message to the named 'persons' |
| 'n' | Print message number 'n' |
| `p` | Print current message again, overriding any indications of binary (i.e., unprintable) content |
| `P` | Override default brief mode and print current message again, displaying all header lines |
| `q`, or `<Ctrl-D>` | Put undeleted mail back in 'mailfile' and quit `mail` |
| `r` [ 'users' ] | Reply to the sender and other 'users' then delete message |
| `s` [ 'files' ] | Save message in the named 'files' (mbox is default) and delete the message |
| `u` [ 'n' ] | Undelete message number 'n' (default is last read) |
| `w` [ 'files' ] | Save message contents, without any header lines, in named 'files' (mbox is default) and delete message |
| `x` | Put all mail back in 'mailfile' unchanged and exit `mail` |
| `y` [ 'files' ] | Same as `-w` option |
| `?` | Print a command summary |

**Command Arguments:**

| | |
|---|---|
| 'recipient'... | Usually a valid username or Internet e-mail address. When 'recipients' are named, `mail` assumes a message is being sent. It reads from the standard input up to an eof (<Ctrl-D>) or, if reading from a terminal device, until it reads a line consisting of just a period. When either of those indicators is received, `mail` adds the letter to the mailfile for each 'recipient' |

## make—Maintain, update, and regenerate related programs and files

**Syntax:** `make` [ `-d dd D DD e` [`-f` 'makefile' ] ...] [ 'target' ] [ 'macro'='value' ]

**Purpose:** Maintain the most current versions of executable program modules

**Options and Option Arguments:**

| | |
|---|---|
| `-d` | Display the reasons why make chooses to rebuild a target |
| `-dd` | Display the dependency check and processing in vast detail |
| `-D` | Display the text of the 'makefiles' read-in |
| `-DD` | Display the text of the 'makefiles', make.rules file, the statefile, and all hidden-dependency reports |
| `-e` | Environment variables override assignments within 'makefiles' |
| `-f` 'makefile' | Use the description file makefile. A - as the 'makefile' argument denotes stdin. Contents of 'makefile', when present, override the standard set of implicit rules and predefined macros. |

**Command Arguments:**

| | |
|---|---|
| 'target' | Target names, which are the executable modules |
| 'macro'='value' | Macro definition, which overrides any regular definition for the specified macro within the makefile itself, or in the environment. |

---

## man—Find and display reference manual pages

**Syntax:** `man` [ `-` ] [ `-adFlrt` ] [ `-M` 'path' ] [ `-T` 'macro-package' ] [`-s` 'section' ] 'name' ...
`man` [ `-M` 'path' ] `-k` 'keyword' ... `man` [ `-M` 'path' ] `-f` 'file' ...

**Purpose:** Display the LINUX on-line reference manual pages

**Options and Option Arguments:**

| | |
|---|---|
| `-a` | Show all manual pages matching 'name' within the manpath search path |
| `-d` | Debug; display what a section-specifier evaluates to, method used for searching, and paths searched by man |
| `-f` 'file'... | Attempt to locate manual pages related to any of the given 'files' |
| `-F` | Force man to search all directories specified by manpath or the man.cf file, rather than using the windex lookup database |
| `-k` 'keyword' ... | Print out one-line summaries from the windex database (table of contents) that contain any of the given 'keywords' |
| `-l` | List all manual pages found matching 'name' within the search path |
| `-M` 'path' | Specify an alternate search path for manual pages |
| `-r` | Reformat the manual page, but do not display it |
| `-s` 'section' ... | Specify sections of the manual for `man` to search |
| `-t` | Arrange for the specified manual pages to be formatted for a troff display |

| | |
|---|---|
| `-T` 'macro-package' | Format manual pages using 'macro-package' rather than the standard `man` macros |

**Command Arguments:**

| | |
|---|---|
| 'name' | Keyword or the name of a standard utility |

---

## mesg—Permit or deny messages

**Syntax:** `mesg` [`-n` | `-y` | `n` | `y` ]

**Purpose:** Allow other users to send write, talk, or other utility messages to user's console window

**Options:**

| | |
|---|---|
| `-n` \| `n` | Deny permission to other users to send message to the terminal |
| `-y` \| `y` | Grant permission to other users to send messages to the terminal |

**Command Arguments:** None

---

## mkdir—Make directories

**Syntax:** `mkdir` [ `-m` 'mode' ] [ `-p` ] 'dir'...

**Purpose:** Create one or more directories under a parent directory

**Options and Option Arguments:**

| | |
|---|---|
| `-m` 'mode' | Allow users to specify the mode to be used for new directories. Choices for modes can be found in under command `chmod`. |
| `-p` | Create 'dir' by creating all the nonexisting parent directories first. The mode given to intermediate directories will be the difference between 777 and the bits set in the file mode creation mask. The difference, however, must be at least 300 (write and execute permission for the user). |

**Command Arguments:**

| | |
|---|---|
| 'dir' | Pathname of a directory to be created |

---

## more—Browse or page through a text file

**Syntax:** `more` [ `-cdflrsuw` ] [ `-`'lines' ] [ `+`'linenumber' ] [ `+/`'pattern' ] [ 'filename' ... ]

**Purpose:** Display file(s) one screenful at a time on the console window

**Options and Option Arguments:**

| | |
|---|---|
| `-c` | Clear before displaying. Redraws the screen instead of scrolling (for faster displays) |
| `-d` | Display error messages rather than ringing the terminal bell if an unrecognized command is used |
| `-s` | Squeeze; replace multiple blank lines with a single blank line |
| `-f` | Do not fold long lines |
| `-l` | Do not treat formfeed characters (<Ctrl-L>) as page breaks |
| `-r` | Ignore control characters not interpreted in some way |

| | |
|---|---|
| `-u` | Suppress generation of underlining escape sequences |
| `-w` | Normally, **`more`** exits when it comes to the end of its input. With **`-w`**, however, more prompts and waits for any key to be struck before exiting. |
| `-`'lines' | Display the indicated number of 'lines' in each screen, rather than the default (the number of lines in the terminal screen less two). |
| `+`'linenumber' | Start up at 'linenumber' |
| `+/`'pattern' | Start up two lines above the line containing the regular expression 'pattern' |

**Command Arguments:**

| | |
|---|---|
| 'filename' ... | Files to be scrolled through |

---

## mv—Move or rename files

**Syntax:** `mv` [`-fi`] 'source' 'target file'

`mv` [`-fi`] 'source'... 'target dir'

**Purpose:** Move files and directories and rename them

**Options:**

| | |
|---|---|
| `-f` | Move file(s) without prompting even if writing over an existing 'target' |
| `-i` | Prompt for confirmation whenever the move would overwrite an existing 'target'. A **y** answer means that the move should proceed. Any other answer prevents **`mv`** from overwriting the 'target'. |

**Command Arguments:**

| | |
|---|---|
| 'source' | Pathname of a file or directory to be moved |
| 'target file' | New pathname for the file or directory being moved |
| 'target dir' | Pathname of an existing directory into which the input files are being moved. |

---

## nice—Change scheduling priority of a command

**Syntax:** `nice` [ `-`'increment' | `-n` 'increment' ] 'command' [ 'argument' ... ]

**Purpose:** Execute a command line at a lower priority than it ordinarily has

**Options and Option Arguments:**

| | |
|---|---|
| `-`'increment' \| `-n` 'increment' | The 'increment' must be in the range of 1–19; if not specified, an 'increment' of 10 is assumed. An 'increment' greater than 19 is equivalent to 19. |

**Command Arguments:**

| | |
|---|---|
| 'command' | Name of a command that is to be invoked |
| 'argument' | Any string to be supplied as an argument when the command is invoked |

---

## nm—Print name list of an object file

**Syntax:** `nm` [ `-AChlnPprRsuVv` ] [ `-ox` ] [ `-g` | `-u` ] [ `-t` 'format' ] 'file'...

**Purpose:** Display the symbol table of each ELF object file that is specified by 'file'

**Options and Option Arguments:**

| | |
|---|---|
| `-A` | Write the full pathname or library name of an object on each line |
| `-C` | Clarify C++ symbol names before printing them |
| `-g` | Write only external (global) symbol information |
| `-h` | Do not display the output heading data |
| `-l` | Distinguish between weak and global symbols by appending a * to the key letter for weak symbols |
| `-n` | Sort external symbols by name before they are printed |
| `-o` | Print the value and size of a symbol in octal instead of decimal (equivalent to `-t o`) |
| `-p` | Produce easy to parse, terse output. Each symbol name is preceded by its value (blanks if undefined) and one of the following letters: |
| | A — Absolute symbol |
| | B — bss (uninitialized data space) symbol |
| | D — Data object symbol |
| | F — File symbol |
| | N — Symbol has no type. |
| | S — Section symbol |
| | T — Text symbol |
| | U — Undefined |
| `-P` | Write information in a portable output format, as specified in stdout |
| `-r` | Prepend the name of the object file or archive to each output line |
| `-R` | Print the archive name (if present), followed by the object file and symbol name |
| `-s` | Print section name instead of section index |
| `-t` 'format' | Write each numeric value in the specified format. The format is dependent on the single character used as the 'format' option argument: |
| | d — Write offset in decimal (default) |
| | o — Write offset in octal |
| | x — Write offset in hexadecimal |
| `-u` | Print undefined symbols only |
| `-u` | Print long list for each undefined symbol |
| `-v` | Sort external symbols by value before they are printed |
| `-V` | Print the version of the `nm` command executing on the stderr |
| `-x` | Print the value and size of a symbol in hexadecimal instead of decimal |

**Command Arguments:**

| | |
|---|---|
| 'file' | Pathname of an object file, executable file, or object-file library |

**nohup**—Run a command immune to hangups

**Syntax:** `nohup` 'command' [ 'arguments' ]

**Purpose:** Execute the named command and arguments after user has logged out

**Options and Option Arguments:** None

**Command Arguments:**

| | |
|---|---|
| 'command' | Command to be invoked; if the 'command' operand names any special utilities, the results are undefined. |
| 'arguments' | Any string to be supplied as an argument when invoking the 'command' operand |

---

**paste**—Merge corresponding or subsequent lines of files

**Syntax:** `paste` [`-s`] [`-d` 'list'] 'file'...

**Purpose:** Merge corresponding lines of files into vertical columns

**Options and Option Arguments:**

| | |
|---|---|
| `-d` 'list' | Unless a backslash character (\) appears in 'list', each character in 'list' is an element specifying a delimiter character. If a backslash character appears in 'list', the backslash character and one or more characters following it are an element specifying a delimiter character. |
| `-s` | Concatenate all of the lines of each separate input file in command line order. The newline character of every line except the last line in each input file will be replaced with the <Tab> character, unless otherwise specified by the `-d` option. |

**Command Arguments:**

| | |
|---|---|
| 'file' | Pathname of an input file. If - is specified for one or more of the files, the standard input will be used; the standard input will be read one line at a time, circularly, for each instance of -. |

---

**pine**—Program for Internet news and e-mail

**Syntax:** `pine` [ options ] [ 'address'...]

**Purpose:** Provide a full-screen display e-mail system

**Options and Option Arguments:**

| | |
|---|---|
| `-c` 'context-number' | Number corresponding to folder collection to which the `-f` command line argument should be applied. By default the `-f` argument is applied to the first defined folder collection. |
| `-d` 'debug-level' | Output diagnostic information at 'debug-level' (0–9) to the current .pine-debug file. A value of 0 turns debugging off and suppresses the .pine-debug file. |
| `-f` 'folder' | Open 'folder' (in first defined folder collection) instead of Inbox. |
| `-F` 'file' | Open named text file and view with pine browser |
| `-h` | Help: list valid command line options |
| `-i` | Start up in the Folder Index screen |

| | |
|---|---|
| `-I` 'keystrokes' | Initial (comma separated list of) keystrokes that `pine` should execute on startup |
| `-k` | Use function keys for commands |
| `-l` | Expand all collections in Folder List display |
| `-n` 'number' | Start up with current message number set to number |
| `-o` | Open first folder read-only |
| `-p` 'config-file' | Use 'config-file' as the personal configuration file instead of the default .pinerc |
| `-P` 'config-file' | Use 'config-file' as the configuration file instead of default systemwide configuration file pine.conf |
| `-z` | Enable ^Z and sigtstp so `pine` may be suspended. |
| `-conf` | Produce a sample/fresh copy of the systemwide configuration file, pine.conf, on the stdout. This is distinct from the per-user .pinerc file. |
| `-create_lu` 'addrbook' 'sort-order' | Create auxiliarly index (look-up) file for 'addrbook' and sort 'addrbook' in 'sort-order', which may be 'dont-sort', 'nickname', 'fullname', 'nickname-withlists-last', or 'fullname-with-lists-last' |
| `-pinerc` 'file' | Output fresh pinerc configuration to 'file' |
| `-sort` 'order' | Sort Folder Index display in one of the following orders: 'arrival', 'subject', 'from', 'date', 'size', 'ordered-subj' or 'reverse'. Arrival order is the default. |
| '-option'='value' | Assign 'value' to the config option 'option' e.g. (-signature-file=sig1 or -featurelist=signature-at-bottom) |

**Command Arguments:**

| | |
|---|---|
| 'address'... | Send mail to 'address'.... ,which will cause `pine` to go directly into the message composer. |

---

**pr**—Paginate and print files

**Syntax:** `pr` [+'page'] [`-`'column'] [`-adFmrt`] [`-e`['char']['gap']] [`-h` 'header'] [`-i`['char']['gap']] [`-l` 'lines'] [`-n`['char']['width']] [`-o` 'offset'] [`-s`['char']] [`-w` 'width'] [`-fp`] ['file'...]

**Purpose:** Format files in pages, according to options, and display on stdout

**Options and Option Arguments:**

| | |
|---|---|
| +'page' | Begin output at page number page of the formatted input |
| -'column' | Produce multicolumn output arranged in 'column' columns (default is 1) and written down each column in the order in which the text is received from the input file |
| `-a` | Modify the effect of the `-`'column' option so that the columns are filled across the page in a round-robin order |
| `-d` | Produce double-spaced output |
| `-e`['char']['gap'] | Expand each input <Tab> character to the next greater column position specified by the formula 'n' *'gap'+1, where 'n' is an integer > 0. If any nondigit |

| | |
|---|---|
| | character, 'char', is specified, it will be used as the input <Tab> character |
| `-f` | Use a formfeed character for new pages |
| `-h` 'header' | Use the string 'header' to replace the contents of the 'file' operand in the page header. |
| `-l` 'lines' | Override the 66-line default and reset the page length to 'lines' |
| `-m` | Merge files; stdout will be formatted so that `pr` writes one line from each file specified by 'file', side by side into text columns of equal fixed widths, in terms of the number of column positions |
| `-n`['char']['width'] | Provide 'width'-digit line numbering (default for 'width' is 5). If 'char' (any nondigit character) is given, it will be appended to the line number to separate it from whatever follows (default for 'char' is a <Tab> character) |
| `-o` 'offset' | Each line of output will be preceded by 'offset' spaces. |
| `-p` | Pause before beginning each page if the stdout is directed to a terminal |
| `-r` | Write no diagnostic reports on failure to open files |
| `-s`['char'] | Separate text columns by the single character 'char' instead of by the appropriate number of <space> characters (default for 'char' is the <Tab>) |
| `-t` | Write neither the five-line identifying header nor the five-line trailer usually supplied for each page. Quit writing after the last line of each file without spacing to the end of the page. |
| `-w` 'width' | Set the width of the line to 'width' column positions for multiple text-column output only. |
| `-F` | Fold the lines of the input file. When used in multi-column mode (with the `-a` or `-m` options), lines will be folded to fit the current column's width; otherwise, they will be folded to fit the current line width (80 columns). |
| `-i`['char']['gap'] | In output, replace <space> characters with <Tab> characters wherever one or more adjacent <space> characters reach column positions 'gap'+1, 2*'gap'+1, 3*'gap'+1, and so forth. If 'gap' is 0 or is omitted, default <Tab> settings at every eighth column position are assumed. If any nondigit character, 'char', is specified, it will be used as the output <Tab> character. |

**Command Arguments:**

| | |
|---|---|
| 'file' | Pathname of a file to be written. If no 'file' operands are specified, or if a 'file' operand is -, the stdin will be used. |

---

**ps**—Report process status

**Syntax:** ps [ `-aAcdefjl` ] [ `-g` 'grplist' ] [ `-n` 'namelist' ] [[ `-o` 'format' ] ... ] [ `-p` 'proclist' ] [ `-s` 'sidlist' ] [ `-t` 'term' ] [ `-u` 'uidlist' ] [ `-U` 'uidlist' ] [ `-G` 'gidlist' ]

**Purpose:** Display active processes information

**Options and Option Arguments:**

| | |
|---|---|
| `-a` | Print information about all processes most frequently requested |
| `-A` | Write information for all processes |
| `-c` | Print information in a format that reflects scheduler properties |
| `-d` | Print information about all processes except session leaders |
| `-e` | Print information about every process now running |
| `-f` | Generate a full listing |
| `-g` 'grplist' | List only process data whose group leader's ID number(s) appears in 'grplist' (A group leader is a process whose process ID number is identical to its process group ID number.) |
| `-G` 'gidlist' | Write information for processes whose real group ID numbers are given in 'gidlist'. The 'gidlist' must be a single argument in the form of a blank- or comma-separated list. |
| `-j` | Print session ID and process group ID |
| `-l` | Generate a long listing (See below) |
| `-n` 'namelist' | Specify the name of an alternative system namelist file in place of the default. |
| `-o` 'format' | Write information according to the 'format' specification given in 'format' |
| `-p` 'proclist' | List only process data whose process ID numbers are given in 'proclist' |
| `-s` 'sidlist' | List information on all session leaders whose IDs appear in 'sidlist' |
| `-t` 'term' | List only process data associated with 'term' |
| `-u` 'uidlist' | List only process data whose effective user ID number or login name is given in 'uidlist' |
| `-U` 'uidlist' | Write information for processes whose real user ID numbers or login names are given in 'uidlist' |

**Command Arguments:** None

---

**ranlib**—Convert archives to random libraries

**Syntax:** 'ranlib' 'archive'

**Purpose:** 'ranlib' adds a table of contents to archive libraries, which converts each archive to a form that can be linked more rapidly.

**Options and Option Arguments:** None

**Command Arguments:**

| | |
|---|---|
| 'archive' | Archive library. |

---

**rcp** —Remote file copy

**Syntax:** `rcp` [ `-p` ] 'filename1' 'filename2'

`rcp` [ `-pr` ] 'filename'... 'directory'

**Purpose:** Copy files between one or more network-connected machines

**Options:**

| | |
|---|---|
| `-p` | Attempt to give each copy the same modification times, access times, modes, and ACLs if applicable as the original file |
| `-r` | Copy each subdirectory rooted at 'filename'; destination must be a directory. |

**Command Arguments:**

Each 'filename' or 'directory' argument is either a remote file name of the form 'hostname:path' or a local file name (containing no colon (:) characters, or backslash (\) before any colon characters). If a 'filename' is not a full pathname, it is interpreted relative to the home directory on 'hostname'. Hostnames may also take the form 'username@hostname:filename' to use 'username' rather than the current local user name as the user name on the remote host. Internet domain addressing of the remote host takes the form 'username@host.domain:filename', which specifies the username to be used, the hostname, and the domain in which that host resides. File names that are not full pathnames will be interpreted relative to the home directory of the user named 'username', on the remote host.

---

## rlogin—Remote login

**Syntax:** `rlogin` [ `-L` ] [ `-8` ] [ `-e` 'c' ] [ `-l` 'username' ] 'hostname'

**Purpose:** Connect via network connection to a remote host

**Options and Option Arguments:**

| | |
|---|---|
| `-L` | Allow the rlogin session to be run in litout mode |
| `-8` | Pass 8-bit data across the net instead of 7-bit data |
| `-e` 'c' | Specify a different escape character, 'c', for the line used to disconnect from the remote host |
| `-l` 'username' | Specify a different 'username' for the remote login. If this option is not used, the remote user name is the same as the local username. |

**Command Arguments:**

| | |
|---|---|
| 'hostname' | Listed in the 'hosts' database, which may be contained in the /etc/hosts file, the Network Information Service (NIS) hosts map, the Internet domain name server, or a combination of these. Each host has one official name (the first name in the database entry) and optionally one or more nicknames. Either official host names or nicknames may be specified in 'hostname'. |

---

## rm—Remove files (unlink)

**Syntax:** `rm` [ `-fir` ] 'file'...

**Purpose:** Remove the directory entry specified by each 'file' argument

**Options:**

| | |
|---|---|
| `-f` | Remove all files (whether write-protected or not) in a directory without prompting the user. In a write-protected directory, however, files are never removed (whatever their permissions are), but no messages are displayed. If the removal of a write-protected directory is attempted, this option will not suppress an error message. |

| | |
|---|---|
| `-i` | Prompt for confirmation before removing any files. Overrides the `-f` option and remains in effect even if the standard input is not a terminal. |
| `-r` | Recursively remove directories and subdirectories in the argument list. The directory will be emptied of files and removed. The user is normally prompted for removal of any write-protected files which the director contains. The write-protected files are removed without prompting, however, if the `-f` option is used, or if the standard input is not a terminal and the `-i` option is not used. Symbolic links that are encountered with this option will not be traversed. If the removal of a nonempty, write-protected directory is attempted, the command will always fail (even if the `-f` option is used), resulting in an error message. |

**Command Arguments:**

| | |
|---|---|
| 'file' | Pathname of file to be removed |

---

## rmdir—Remove directories

**Syntax:** `rmdir` [`-ps`] 'dirname'...

**Purpose:** Delete the empty directories specified from the parent directory. To delete nonempty directories, see the `rm -r` command.

**Options:**

| | |
|---|---|
| `-p` | Allow users to remove the directory 'dirname' and its parent directories, which become empty. A message is printed on the stderr about whether the whole path is removed or part of the path remains for some reason. |
| `-s` | Suppress the message printed on the stderr when `-p` is in effect. |

**Command Arguments:**

| | |
|---|---|
| 'dirname' | Pathname of an empty directory to be removed |

---

## rpm—Red Hat package manager

**Syntax:** `rpm` ['options']

**Purpose:** Package manager that can be used to build, install, query, verify, update, and uninstall individual software packages. A package consists of an archive of files and package information, including name, version, and description.

One of the following basic modes must be selected: initialize database, rebuild database, build package, recompile package, build package from tarball, query, show query tags, install, freshen, uninstall, verify, signature check, resign, add signature, set owners and groups, and show configuration.

*Database maintenance:*

```
rpm -i [--initdb]
rpm -i [--rebuilddb]
```

*Building:*

```
rpm [-b|t] [package_spec]+
rpm [--rebuild] [sourcerpm]+
rpm [--tarbuild] [tarredsource]+
```

*Querying:*

`rpm [--query] [queryoptions]`

`rpm [--querytags]`

*Maintaining installed packages:*

`rpm [--install] [installoptions] [package_file]+`

`rpm [--freshen|-F] [installoptions] [package_file]+`

`rpm [--uninstall|-e] [uninstalloptions] [package]+`

`rpm [--verify|-V] [verifyoptions] [package]+`

*Signatures:*

`rpm [--verify|-V] [verifyoptions] [package]+`

`rpm [--resign] [package_file]+`

`rpm [--addsign] [package_file]+`

*Miscellaneous:*

`rpm [--showrc]`

`rpm [--setperms] [package]+`

`rpm [--setgids] [package]+`

**General Options:**

These options can be used in all the different modes.

| | |
|---|---|
| **-vv** | Print lots of ugly debugging information. |
| **--quiet** | Print as little as possible; normally only error messages will be displayed |
| **--help** | Print a longer usage message then normal |
| **--version** | Print a single line containing the version number of **rpm** being used |
| **--rcfile** 'filelist' | Each of the files in the colon-separated 'filelist' is read sequentially by **rpm** for configuration information. The default 'filelist' is /usr/lib/rpm/rpmrc:/etc/rpmrc:~/.rpmrc. Only the first file in the list must exist, and tildes (~) will be expanded to the value of $HOME. |
| **--root** 'dir' | Use the system-rooted at 'dir' for all operations. Note that this means the database will be read or modified under 'dir' and any pre- or postscripts are run after a **chroot()** to 'dir'. |
| **--dbpath** 'path' | Use rpm database in 'path'. |
| **--justdb** | Update only the database, not the file system |
| **--ftpproxy** 'host', **--httpproxy** 'host' | Use 'host' as an ftp or http proxy host. |
| **--ftpport** 'port', **--httpport** 'port' | Use 'port' as the FTP or HTTP port on the proxy host. See ftp/http options. |
| **-pipe** 'cmd' | Pipes the output of **rpm** to the 'cmd' command |

**Options for Installation and Upgrading:**

The general form of an **rpm** install command is **rpm -i [install-options]** 'package-file'+. This installs a new package. The general form of an **rpm** upgrade command is **rpm -U [install-options]** 'package-file'+.

This upgrades or installs the package currently installed to the version in the new **rpm**. This is the same as install, except all other versions of the package are removed from the system. **rpm [-F|—freshen] [install-options]** 'package_file' + will upgrade packages, but only if an earlier version currently exists. The 'package_file' may be specified as an ftp or http URL, in which case the package will be downloaded before being installed.

| | |
|---|---|
| `--force` | Same as `--replacepkgs`, `--replacefiles`, and `--oldpackage` |
| `-h`, `--hash` | Print 50 hash marks as the package archive is unpacked. Use with `-v` for a nice display. |
| `--oldpackage` | Allow an upgrade to replace a newer package with an older one |
| `--percent` | Print percentages as files are unpacked from the package archive. This is intended to make `rpm` easy to run from other tools. |
| `--replacefiles` | Install the packages even if they replace files from other, already installed, packages |
| `--replacepkgs` | Install the packages even if some of them are already installed on this system |
| `--allfiles` | Install or upgrade all the missing ok files in the package, whether or not they exist |
| `--nodeps` | Do not do a dependency check before installing or upgrading a package |
| `--noscripts` | Do not execute the preinstall or postinstall scripts |
| `--notriggers` | Do not execute scripts that are triggered by the installation of this package |
| `--ignoresize` | Do not check mount file systems for sufficient disk space before installing this package |
| `--excludepath` 'path' | Do not install file whose name begins with 'path'. |
| `--excludedocs` | Don't install any files marked as documentation (including man pages and texinfo documents) |
| `--includedocs` | Install documentation files. This is the default behavior |
| `--test` | Do not install the package; simply check for and report potential conflicts |
| `--ignorearch` | Allow installation or upgrading even if the architectures of the binary `rpm` and host do not match |
| `--ignoreos` | Allow installation or upgrading even if the operating systems of the binary `rpm` and host do not match |
| `--prefix` 'path' | This sets the installation prefix to 'path' for relocatable packages |
| `--relocate` 'oldpath'='newpath' | For relocatable packages, translate the files that would be put in 'oldpath' to 'newpath'. |
| `--badreloc` | In conjunction with `-relocate`, force the relocation even if the package isn't relocatable |
| `--noorder` | Do not reorder the packages for an install. The list of packages would normally be reordered to satisfy dependencies |

**Command Arguments:** None

## rsh—Remote shell

**Syntax:** `rsh [ -n ] [ -l 'username' ] 'hostname' 'command'` `rsh 'hostname' [ -n ] [ -l 'username' ] 'command'`

**Purpose:** Execute a command on a remote host computer

**Options and Option Arguments:**

| | |
|---|---|
| `-l` 'username' | Use 'username' as the remote username instead of the user's local username. (In the absence of this option, the remote username is the same as the local username.) |
| `-n` | Redirect the input of `rsh` to /dev/null. Needed to avoid conflicts between `rsh` and the shell that invokes it. |

**Command Arguments:**

| | |
|---|---|
| 'username' | The local user's username |
| 'hostname' | Name of the remote host computer the local user wants to execute 'command' on. |
| 'command' | Command the local user wants to execute. |

## ruptime—Show host status of local machines

**Syntax:** `ruptime [ -alrtu ]`

**Purpose:** Give a status line display showing each machine on the local network; these are formed from packets broadcast by each host on the network once a minute.

**Options:**

| | |
|---|---|
| `-a` | Count even those users who have been idle for 1 hour or more |
| `-l` | Sort display by load average |
| `-r` | Reverse sorting order |
| `-t` | Sort display by up time |
| `-u` | Sort display by number of users |

**Command Arguments:** None

## rwho—Who is logged in on local machines

**Syntax:** `rwho [ -a ]`

**Purpose:** Produce output similar to `who`, but for all machines on the network. If no report has been received from a machine for 5 minutes, `rwho` assumes the machine is down and does not report users last known to be logged into that machine.

**Options:**

| | |
|---|---|
| `-a` | Report all users, whether or not they have typed to the system in the past hour |

**Command Arguments:** None

## sed—Stream editor

**Syntax:** `sed [ -n ] [ -e 'script' ] ... [ -f 'script file' ] ... [ 'file' ... ]`

**Purpose:** Read one or more text files and make editing changes according to a script of editing commands. The script is obtained from either the 'script' option argument string, or a combination of the option arguments from the `e` 'script' and `-f` 'script file' options.

**Options and Option Arguments:**

| | |
|---|---|
| `-e` 'script' | The 'script' argument is an edit command for `sed`; if there is just one `-e` option and no `-f` option, the flag `-e` may be omitted. |
| `- f` 'script file' | Take the script from 'script file', which consists of editing commands, one per line |
| `-n` | Suppress the default output |

**Command Arguments:**

| | |
|---|---|
| 'file' | Pathname of a file whose contents will be read and edited. If multiple 'file' operands are specified, the named files will be read in the order specified and the concatenation will be edited. If no 'file' operands are specified, the stdin will be used. |
| 'script' | A string to be used as the script of editing commands. The application must not present a 'script' that violates the restrictions of a text file except that the final character need not be a newline character. |

---

## sleep—Create a process that waits a specified time

**Syntax:** `sleep` 'time'

**Purpose:** Suspend the process that executes sleep for the 'time' specified

**Options:** None

**Command Arguments:**

| | |
|---|---|
| 'time' | Interval specified in seconds |

---

## sort—Sort, merge, or sequence check text files

**Syntax:** `sort` [ `-cmu` ] [ `-o` 'output' ] [ `-T` 'directory' ] [ `-y` [ 'kmem' ]] [ `-dfiMnr` ] [ `-b` ] [ `t` 'char' ] [ `-k` 'keydef' ] [ 'file'...]

**Purpose:** Sort the lines in 'file', usually in alphabetical order. Comparisons are based on one or more sort keys extracted from each line of input. By default, there is one sort key: the entire input line. Lines are ordered according to a collating sequence.

**Options and Option Arguments:**

| | |
|---|---|
| `-c` | Check that the single input file is ordered as specified by the arguments and the collating sequence in effect |
| `-m` | Merge only; the input files are assumed to be already sorted |
| `-u` | Unique; suppress all but one in each set of lines having equal keys |
| `-o` 'output' | Specify the name of an output file to be used instead of stdout |
| `-T` 'directory' | Place temporary files in 'directory' |
| `-y` 'kmem' | Amount of main memory initially used by sort; if 'kmem' is present, sort will start using that number of kilobytes of memory. |

*The following options override the default ordering rules. When ordering options appear independent of any key field specifications, the requested field ordering rules are applied globally to all sort keys. When attached to a specific key, the specified ordering options override all global ordering options for that key.*

| | |
|---|---|
| `-d` | "Dictionary" order: only letters, digits, and blanks (<spaces> and <Tabs>) are significant in comparisons |
| `-f` | Fold lowercase letters into uppercase |
| `-i` | Ignore nonprintable characters |
| `-M` | Compare as months.The first three nonblank characters of the field are folded to uppercase and compared |
| `-n` | Restrict the sort key to an initial numeric string, consisting of optional blank characters, optional minus sign, and zero or more digits with an optional radix character and thousands separators (as defined in the current locale), which will be sorted by arithmetic value |
| `-r` | Reverse the sense of comparisons |

*The treatment of field separators can be altered using the following options.*

| | |
|---|---|
| `-b` | Ignore leading blank characters when determining the starting and ending positions of a restricted sort key. |
| `-t` 'char' | Use 'char' as the field separator character. |

*Sort keys can be specified using the following options.*

| | |
|---|---|
| `-k` 'keydef' | Restricted sort key field definition with format defined as: `-k` 'field start' [ 'type' ] [ 'field end' [ 'type' ] ] |

**Command Arguments:**

| | |
|---|---|
| 'file' | Pathname of a file to be sorted, merged or checked. If no 'file' operands are specified, or if a 'file' operand is -, stdin will be used. |

---

**strip**—Strip symbol table, debugging, and line number information from an object file

**Syntax:** `strip` [`-lVx`] 'file'...

**Purpose:** Strip removes the symbol table, debugging information, and line number information from elf object files

**Options:**

| | |
|---|---|
| `-l` | Strip line number information only; do not strip the symbol table or debugging information |
| `-V` | Print, on stderr, the version number of strip |
| `-x` | Do not strip the symbol table; debugging and line number information may be stripped. |

**Command Arguments:**

| | |
|---|---|
| 'file' | Pathname referring to an executable file |

---

**stty**—Set the options for a terminal

**Syntax:** `stty` [ `-a` ] [ `-g` ] [ 'modes' ]

**Purpose:** Set certain terminal I/O options for the device that is the current stdin, without arguments, report the settings of certain options

**Options:**

| | |
|---|---|
| `-a` | Write to stdout all of the option settings for the terminal |
| `-g` | Report current settings in a form that can be used as an argument to another **`stty`** command. Emits termios-type output if the underlying driver supports it; otherwise, it emits termio-type output. |

**Control Modes:**

| | |
|---|---|
| parenb (-parenb) | Enable (disable) parity generation and detection |
| parext (-parext) | Enable (disable) extended parity generation and detection for mark and space parity |
| parodd (-parodd) | Select odd (even) parity or mark (space) parity if parext is enabled |
| cs5 cs6 cs7 cs8 | Select character size |
| 0 | Hang up line immediately |
| 110 - 460800 | Set terminal baud rate to the number given, if possible (All speeds are not supported by all hardware interfaces.) |
| ispeed 0 - 460800 | Set terminal input baud rate to the number given, if possible |
| ospeed 0 - 460800 | Set terminal output baud rate to the number given, if possible |
| hupcl (-hupcl) | Hang up (do not hang up) connection on last close |
| hup (-hup) | Same as hupcl (-hupcl) |
| cstopb (-cstopb) | Use two (one) stop bits per character |
| cread (-cread) | Enable (disable) the receiver |
| crtscts (-crtscts) | Enable output hardware flow control |
| crtsxoff (-crtsxoff) | Enable input hardware flow control |
| clocal (-clocal) | Assume a line without (with) modem control |
| loblk (-loblk) | Block (do not block) output from a noncurrent layer |
| defeucw | Set the widths of multibyte Extended Unix Code (EUC) characters |

**Input Modes:**

| | |
|---|---|
| ignbrk (-ignbrk) | Ignore (do not ignore) break on input |
| brkint (-brkint) | Signal (do not signal) INTR on break |
| ignpar (-ignpar) | Ignore (do not ignore) parity errors |
| parmrk (-parmrk) | Mark (do not mark) parity errors |
| inpck (-inpck) | Enable (disable) input parity checking |
| istrip (-istrip) | Strip (do not strip) input characters to seven bits |
| inlcr (-inlcr) | Map (do not map) NL to CR on input |
| igncr (-igncr) | Ignore (do not ignore) CR on input |
| icrnl (-icrnl) | Map (do not map) CR to NL on input |
| iuclc (-iuclc) | Map (do not map) uppercase alphabetics to lowercase on input |

| | |
|---|---|
| ixon (-ixon) | Enable (disable) START/STOP output control |
| ixany (-ixany) | Allow any character (only DC1) to restart output |
| ixoff (-ixoff) | Request that the system send (not send) Start/Stop characters when the input queue is nearly empty/full |
| imaxbel (-imaxbel) | Echo (do not echo) BEL when the input line is too long |

**Output Modes:**

| | |
|---|---|
| opost ( - opost) | Postprocess output (do not postprocess output; ignore all other output modes) |
| olcuc (-olcuc) | Map (do not map) lowercase alphabetics to uppercase on output |
| onlcr (-onlcr) | Map (do not map) NL to CR-NL on output |
| ocrnl (-ocrnl) | Map (do not map) CR to NL on output |
| onocr (-onocr) | Do not (do) output CRs at column zero |
| onlret (-onlret) | On the terminal NL performs (does not perform) the CR function |
| ofill (-ofill) | Use fill characters (use timing) for delays |
| ofdel (-ofdel) | Fill characters are DELs (NULs) |
| cr0 cr1 cr2 cr3 | Select style of delay for carriage returns |
| nl0 nl1 | Select style of delay for linefeeds |
| tab0 tab1 tab2 tab3 | Select style of delay for horizontal tabs |
| bs0 bs1 | Select style of delay for backspaces |
| ff0 ff1 | Select style of delay for formfeeds |
| vt0 vt1 | Select style of delay for vertical tabs |

**Local Modes:**

| | |
|---|---|
| isig (-isig) | Enable (disable) the checking of characters against the special control characters INTR, QUIT, SWTCH, and SUSP |
| icanon (-icanon) | Enable (disable) canonical input (ERASE and KILL processing) |
| xcase (- xcase) | Canonical (unprocessed) upper/lowercase presentation |
| echo (-echo) | Echo back (do not echo back) every character typed |
| echoe (-echoe) | Echo (do not echo) ERASE character as a backspace-space-backspace string |
| echok (-echok) | Echo (do not echo) NL after KILL character |
| lfkc (-lfkc) | The same as echok (-echok); obsolete |
| echonl (-echonl) | Echo (do not echo) NL |
| noflsh (- noflsh) | Disable (enable) flush after INTR, QUIT, or SUSP |
| stwrap (-stwrap) | Disable (enable) truncation of lines longer than 79 characters on a synchronous line |
| tostop (-tostop) | Send (do not send) SIGTTOU when background processes write to the terminal |
| echoctl (-echoctl) | Echo (do not echo) control characters as ^'char', delete as ^? |

| | |
|---|---|
| echoprt (-echoprt) | Echo (do not echo) erase character as character is "erased" |
| echoke (-echoke) | BS-SP-BS erase (do not BS-SP-BS erase) entire line on line kill |
| flusho (-flusho) | Output is (is not) being flushed |
| pendin (-pendin) | Retype (do not retype) pending input at next read or input character |
| iexten (-iexten) | Enable (disable) special control characters |
| stflush (-stflush) | Enable (disable) flush on a synchronous line after every write |
| stappl (-stappl) | Use application mode (use line mode) on a synchronous line |

**Hardware Flow Control Modes:**

| | |
|---|---|
| rtsxoff (-rtsxoff) | Enable (disable) RTS hardware flow control on input |
| ctsxon (-ctsxon) | Enable (disable) CTS hardware flow control on output |
| dtrxoff (-dtrxoff) | Enable (disable) DTR hardware flow control on input |
| cdxon (-cdxon) | Enable (disable) CD hardware flow control on output |
| isxoff (-isxoff) | Enable (disable) isochronous hardware flow control on input |

**Clock Modes:**

| | |
|---|---|
| xcibrg | Get transmit clock from internal baud rate generator |
| xctset | Get the transmit clock from transmitter signal element timing (DCE source) lead, CCITT V.24 circuit 114, EIA-232-D pin 15 |
| xcrset | Get transmit clock from receiver signal element timing (DCE source) lead, CCITT V.24 circuit 115, EIA-232-D pin 17 |
| rcibrg | Get receive clock from internal baud rate generator |
| rctset | Get receive clock from transmitter signal element timing (DCE source) lead, CCITT V.24 circuit 114, EIA-232-D pin 15 |
| rcrset | Get receive clock from receiver signal element timing (DCE source) lead, CCITT V.24 circuit 115, EIA-232-D pin 17 |
| tsetcoff | Transmitter signal element timing clock not provided |
| tsetcrbrg | Output receive baud rate generator on transmitter signal element timing (DTE source) lead, CCITT V.24 circuit 113, EIA-232-D pin 24 |
| tsetctbrg | Output transmit baud rate generator on transmitter signal element timing (DTE source) lead, CCITT V.24 circuit 113, EIA-232-D pin 24 |
| tsetctset | Output tranmitter signal element timing (DCE source) on transmitter signal element timing (DTE source) lead, CCITT V.24 circuit 113, EIA-232-D pin 24 |

| | |
|---|---|
| tsetcrset | Output receiver signal element timing (DCE source) on transmitter signal element timing (DTE source) lead, CCITT V.24 circuit 113, EIA-232-D pin 24 |
| rsetcoff | Receiver signal element timing clock not provided |
| rsetcrbrg | Output receive baud rate generator on receiver signal element timing (DTE source) lead, CCITT V.24 circuit 128, no EIA-232-D pin |
| rsetctbrg | Output transmit baud rate generator on receiver signal element timing (DTE source) lead, CCITT V.24 circuit 128, no EIA-232-D pin |
| rsetctset | Output transmitter signal element timing (DCE source) on receiver signal element timing (DTE source) lead, CCITT V.24 circuit 128, no EIA-232-D pin |
| rsetcrset | Output receiver signal element timing (DCE source) on receiver signal element timing (DTE source) lead, CCITT V.24 circuit 128, no EIA-232-D pin |

**Command Arguments:** None

---

## tail—Deliver the last part of a file

**Syntax:** `tail` [ `-f` | `-r` ] [ `-c` 'number' | `-n` 'number' ] [ 'file' ]
`tail` [ + 'number' [ `l` | `b` | `c` ] [ `f` ]] [ 'file' ]
`tail` [ + 'number' [ `l` ] [ `f` | `r` ]] [ 'file' ]

**Purpose:** By default, display the last 10 lines of 'file'. Copying begins at a point in the file indicated by the `c` 'number', `-n` 'number', or +'number' options (if +'number' is specified, begins at distance number from the beginning; if – 'number' is specified, from the end of the input; if 'number' is NULL, the value 10 is assumed). Hence, 'number' is counted in units of lines or bytes according to the `-c` or `-n` options, or lines, blocks, or bytes, according to the appended option `l`, `b`, or `c`. When no units are specified, counting is by lines.

**Options and Option Arguments:**

`-b` Units of blocks

`-c` 'number' The 'number' option argument must be a decimal integer whose sign affects the location in the file, measured in bytes, to begin the copying:

| | |
|---|---|
| + | Copying starts relative to the beginning of the file |
| - | Copying starts relative to the end of the file |
| none | Copying starts relative to the end of the file |

`-c` Units of bytes

`-f` Follow; if the input file is not a pipe, the program will not terminate after the line of the input file has been copied but will enter an endless loop

`-l` Units of lines

`-n` 'number' — Equivalent to `-c` 'number', except the starting location in the file is measured in lines instead of bytes. The origin for counting is 1; that is, `-n +1` represents the first line of the file, `-n -1` the last.

`-r` — Reverse; copy lines from the specified starting point in the file in reverse order. The default for `r` is to print the entire file in reverse order.

**Command Arguments:**

'file' — Pathname of an input file. If no 'file' operands are specified, the standard input will be used.

---

## talk—Talk to another user

**Syntax:** `talk` 'address' [ 'terminal' ]

**Purpose:** Two-way, screen-oriented communication program

**Options:** None

**Command Arguments:**

'address' — The recipient of the talk session; one form of 'address' is the 'username', as returned by `who`. Other address formats and how they are handled are unspecified.

'terminal' — If the recipient is logged in more than once, 'terminal' can be used to indicate the appropriate terminal name. If 'terminal' is not specified, the talk message will be displayed on one or more accessible terminals in use by the recipient. The format of 'terminal' will be the same as that returned by `who`.

---

## tar—Create archives and add or extract files

**Syntax:** `tar c` [`bBefFhiloPvwX` ] [ 'block' ] [ 'tarfile' ] [ 'exclude-file' ]{ `-I` 'include-file' | `-C` 'directory file' | 'file' }...

`tar r` [ `bBefFhilvw` ] [ 'block' ]{ -I 'include-file' | `-C` 'directory file' | 'file' } ...

`tar t` [ `BefFhilvX` ] [ 'tarfile' ][ 'exclude-file' ] { `-I` 'include-file' | 'file' } ...

`tar u` [ `bBefFhilvw` ] [ 'block' ] [ 'tarfile' ] 'file' ...

`tar x` [ `BefFhilmopvwX` ] [ 'tarfile' ] [ 'exclude-file' ] [ 'file' ... ]

**Purpose:** Archive and extract files to and from a single file, called a tarfile. Actions are controlled by the key option and its arguments. The key is a string of characters containing exactly one function letter (`c`, `r`, `t`, `u`, or `x`) and zero or more function modifiers (letters or digits), depending on the function letter used. The key string contains no <space> characters. Function modifier arguments are listed on the command line in the same order as their corresponding function modifiers appear in the key string. Use of a hyphen (-) in front of the key option is not required.

The `-I` 'include-file', `-C` 'directory file', and 'file' command arguments specify which files or directories are to be archived or extracted. In all cases, appearance of a directory name refers to the files and (recursively) subdirectories of that directory. Arguments appearing within braces ({}) indicate that one of the arguments must be specified.

**Options and Option Arguments:**

| | |
|---|---|
| `-I` 'include-file' | Open include file containing a list of files, one per line, and treat as if each file appeared separately on the command line. If a file is specified in both the exclude file and the include file (or on the command line), it will be excluded. |
| `-C` 'directory file' | Perform a **`chdir`** operation on directory and perform the **`c`** (create) or **`r`** (replace) operation on file.This option enables archiving files from multiple directories not related by a close common parent. |

*Key Function Letters.*

| | |
|---|---|
| `c` | Create: Writing begins at the beginning of the tarfile, instead of at the end |
| `r` | Replace; the named 'files' are written at the end of the tarfile |
| `t` | Table of contents; the names of the specified files are listed each time they occur in the tarfile |
| `u` | Update; the named 'files' are written at the end of the tarfile if they are not already in the tarfile, or if they have been modified since last written to that tarfile |
| `x` | Extract or restore; the named 'files' are extracted from the tarfile and written to the directory specified in the tarfile, relative to the current directory. |

*Key Function Modifiers.*

| | |
|---|---|
| `b` | Blocking factor; use when reading or writing to raw archives. The 'block' argument specifies the number of 512-byte blocks to be included in each read or write operation performed on the tarfile. The minimum is 1; the default is 20. |
| `B` | Block; force **`tar`** to perform multiple reads (if necessary) to read exactly enough bytes to fill a block. This function modifier enables **`tar`** to work across the Ethernet, since pipes and sockets return partial blocks even when more data is coming. |
| `e` | Error; exit immediately with a positive exit status if any unexpected errors occur |
| `f` | File; use the 'tarfile' argument as the name of the tarfile |
| `F` | With one **`F`** argument, **`tar`** excludes all directories named SCCS and RCS from the tarfile |
| `h` | Follow symbolic links as if they were normal files or directories. Normally, **`tar`** does not follow symbolic links. |
| `i` | Ignore directory checksum errors |
| `l` | Link; output error message if unable to resolve all links to the files being archived. If `l` is not specified, no error messages are printed. |
| `m` | Modify; the modification time of the file is the time of extraction. This function modifier is valid only with the **`x`** function. |

| | |
|---|---|
| `o` | Ownership; assign to extracted files the user and group identifiers of the user running the program, rather than those on tarfile. This is the default behavior for users other than root. |
| `p` | Restore the named files to their original modes and ACLs if applicable, ignoring the present umask. |
| `P` | Suppress the addition of a trailing "/" on directory entries in the archive |
| `v` | Verbose; output the name of each file preceded by the function letter. With the **`t`** function, **`v`** provides additional information about the tarfile entries. |
| `w` | What; output the action to be taken and the name of the file, then await the user's confirmation. If the first keystroke is **y**, the action is performed; otherwise, the action is not performed. |
| `X` | Exclude; use the 'exclude-file' argument as a file containing a list of relative pathnames for files (or directories) to be excluded from the tarfile when using the functions **`c`**, **`x`**, or **`t`**. |

**Command Arguments:**

| | |
|---|---|
| 'file' | Pathname of a regular file or directory to be archived (when the **`c`**, **`r`** or **`u`** functions are specified), extracted (**`x`**) or listed (**`t`**). When 'file' is the pathname of a directory, the action applies to all of the files and (recursively) subdirectories of that directory. |

---

## **tee**—Duplicate the standard input

**Syntax:** `tee` [`-ai`] ['file'...]

**Purpose:** Duplicate the stdin, one copy to stdout, other copy to a file

**Options and Option Arguments:**

| | |
|---|---|
| `-a` | Append the output to the files rather than overwriting them |
| `-i` | Ignore interrupts |

**Command Arguments:**

| | |
|---|---|
| 'file' | Pathname of an output file |

---

## **telnet**—User interface to a remote system

**Syntax:** `telnet` [ `-8ELcdr` ] [ `-e` 'escape char' ] [ `-l` 'user' ] [ `-n` 'tracefile' ] [ 'host' [ 'port' ] ]

**Purpose:** Allow communication with another host. If telnet is invoked without arguments, it enters command mode, indicated by its prompt telnet>. In this mode, it accepts and executes its associated commands. If it is invoked with arguments, it performs an open command with those arguments.

**Options and Option Arguments:**

| | |
|---|---|
| `-8` | Specifies an 8-bit data path |
| `-E` | Stops any character from being recognized as an escape character |

| | |
|---|---|
| `-L` | Specifies an 8-bit data path on output, which causes the binary option to be negotiated on output. |
| `-c` | Disable the reading of the user's .telnetrc file |
| `-d` | Set the initial value of the debug toggle to true |
| `-e` 'escape char' | Set the initial escape character to 'escape char' |
| `-l` 'user' | When connecting to a remote system that understands the environ option, send 'user' to the remote system as the value for the variable ***user*** |
| `-n` 'tracefile' | Opens 'tracefile' for recording trace information |
| `-r` | Specifies a user interface similar to rlogin |

**Command Arguments:**

| | |
|---|---|
| 'host' | DNS host name of remote computer to connect to |
| 'port' | Standard or nonstandard virtual connection on the telnet server |

---

## test—Evaluate condition(s) or make execution of actions dependent on the evaluation of condition(s)

**Syntax:** `test` [ 'condition' ] [ 'condition' ]

**Purpose:** In a shell script, evaluate the 'condition' and indicate the result of the evaluation by its exit status. An exit status of 0 indicates that the condition evaluated as true and an exit status of 1 indicates that the condition evaluated as false.

**Options and Option Arguments:** None

**Command Arguments:**

| | |
|---|---|
| 'condition' | An expression that contains one or more criteria |

---

## touch—Change file access and modification times

**Syntax:** `touch` [`-acm`] [`-r` 'ref file'] 'file'...

`touch` [`-acm`] [`-t` 'time'] 'file'...

`touch` [`-acm`] ['date time'] 'file'...

**Purpose:** Set the access and modification times of each file, or create 'file' if it does not already exist.

**Options and Option Arguments:**

| | |
|---|---|
| `-a` | Change the access time of 'file'; do not change the modification time unless `-m` is also specified |
| `-c` | Do not create a specified 'file' if it does not exist |
| `-m` | Change the modification time of 'file'; do not change the access time unless `-a` is also specified. |
| `-r` 'ref file' | Use the corresponding times of the file named by 'ref file' instead of the current time |
| `-t` 'time' | Use the specified 'time' instead of the current time. The 'time' will be a decimal number of the form [[CC]YY]MMDDhhmm[.SS], where each two digits represents the following: |

| | |
|---|---|
| 'MM' | The month of the year [01–12] |
| 'DD' | The day of the month [01–31] |

| | |
|---|---|
| 'hh' | The hour of the day [00–23] |
| 'mm' | The minute of the hour [00–59] |
| 'CC' | The first two digits of the year |
| 'YY' | The second two digits of the year |
| 'SS' | The second of the minute [00–60] |

**Command Arguments:**

| | |
|---|---|
| 'file' | Pathname of a file whose times are to be modified |
| 'date time' | Use the specified 'date time' instead of the current time. The 'date time' is a decimal number of the form MMDDhhmm[YY], where each two digits represent the following: |

| | |
|---|---|
| 'MM' | The month of the year [01–12] |
| 'DD' | The day of the month [01–31] |
| 'hh' | The hour of the day [00–23] |
| 'mm' | The minute of the hour [00–59] |
| 'YY' | The second two digits of the year (optional) |

---

## tr—Translate characters

**Syntax:** `tr [-cs]` 'string1' 'string2'

`tr -s|-d [-c]` 'string1'

`tr -ds [-c]` 'string1' 'string2'

**Purpose:** Copy stdin to stdout with substitution or deletion of selected characters. The options specified and the 'string1' and 'string2' command arguments control translations that occur while copying characters and single-character collating elements.

**Options:**

| | |
|---|---|
| `-c` | Complement the set of characters specified by 'string1' |
| `-d` | Delete all occurrences of input characters that are specified by 'string1' |
| `-s` | Replace instances of repeated characters with a single character |

**Command Arguments:**

| | |
|---|---|
| 'string1' 'string2' | Translation control strings. Each string represents a set of characters to be converted into an array of characters used for the translation. |

---

## uniq—Report or filter out repeated lines in a file

**Syntax:** `uniq [-c|-d|-u] [-f` 'fields'] [ `-s` 'char'] ['input file' ['output file']]

`uniq [-c|-d|-u]` [-'n'] [+'m'] ['input' 'file' ['output file']]

**Purpose:** Read an input file comparing adjacent lines, and write one copy of each input line on the output. The second and succeeding copies of repeated adjacent input lines will not be written. Repeated lines in the input will not be detected if they are not adjacent.

**Options and Option Arguments:**

| | |
|---|---|
| `-c` | Precede each output line with a count of the number of times the line occurred in the input |
| `-d` | Suppress the writing of lines that are not repeated in the input |
| `-f` 'fields' | Ignore the first 'fields' fields on each input line when doing comparisons, where 'fields' is a positive decimal integer. A field is the maximal string matched by the basic regular expression [[:blank:]]*[^[:blank:]]* |
| `-s` 'chars' | Ignore the first 'chars' characters when doing comparisons, where 'chars' is a positive decimal integer |
| `-u` | Suppress the writing of lines that are repeated in the input. |
| -'n' | Equivalent to `-f` 'fields' with 'fields' set to 'n' |
| +'m' | Equivalent to `-s` 'chars' with 'chars' set to 'm' |

**Command Arguments:**

| | |
|---|---|
| 'input file' | A path name of the input file. If input file is not specified, or if the input file is `-`, the standard input will be used. |
| 'output file' | A path name of the output file. If output file is not specified, the standard output will be used. The results are unspecified if the file named by 'output file' is the file named by 'input file'. |

---

**W**—Display information about currently logged-in users

**Syntax:** `w` [ `-hlsuw` ] [ 'user' ]

**Purpose:** Display a summary of the current activity on the system, including what each user is doing

**Options:**

| | |
|---|---|
| `-h` | Suppress the heading |
| `-l` | Produce a long form of output, which is the default |
| `-s` | Produce a short form of output. In the short form, the tty is abbreviated, and the login time and CPU times are left off, as are the arguments to commands. |
| `-u` | Produce the heading line that shows the current time, the length of time the system has been up, the number of users logged into the system, and the average number of jobs in the run queue over the last 1, 5, and 15 minutes |
| `-w` | Produce a long form of output, which is also the same as the default |

**Command Arguments:**

| | |
|---|---|
| 'user' | Name of a particular user for whom login information is displayed. If specified, output is restricted to that user. |

---

**wc**—Display a count of lines, words, and characters in a file

**Syntax:** `wc` [ `-c` | `-m` | `-C` ] [ `-lw` ] [ 'file'... ]

**Purpose:** Read one or more input files and, by default, write the number of newline characters, words, and bytes contained in each input file to the standard output

**Options:**

| | |
|---|---|
| `-c` | Count bytes |
| `-m` | Count characters |
| `-C` | Same as `-m` |
| `-l` | Count lines |
| `-w` | Count words delimited by white space characters or newline characters |

If no option is specified the default is `-lwc` (count lines, words, and bytes.)

**Command Arguments:**

| | |
|---|---|
| 'file' | Pathname of an input file. If no 'file' operands are specified, stdin will be used. |

---

**whereis**—Locate the binary, source, and manual page files for a command

**Syntax:** `whereis` [ `-bmsu` ] [ `-BMS` 'directory'... `-f` ] 'filename'...

**Purpose:** Locates source, binary, and manual sections for specified files

**Options:**

| | |
|---|---|
| `-b` | Search only for binaries |
| `-m` | Search only for manual sections |
| `-s` | Search only for sources |
| `-u` | Search for unusual entries. A file is said to be unusual if it does not have one entry of each requested type |
| `-B` | Change or otherwise limit the places where `whereis` searches for binaries |
| `-M` | Change or otherwise limit the places where `whereis` searches for manual sections |
| `-S` | Change or otherwise limit the places where `whereis` searches for sources |
| `-f` | Terminate the last directory list and signals the start of file names, and *must* be used when any of the `B`, `-M`, or `-S` options are used. |

**Command Arguments:**

| | |
|---|---|
| 'filename' | Binary, source, and manual page files. |

---

**which**—Locate a command; display its pathname or alias

**Syntax:** `which` [ 'filename' ] ...

**Purpose:** Take a list of names and look for the files that would be executed if these names were typed as commands. Each argument is expanded if it is aliased and searched for along the user's path. Both aliases and path are taken from the user's shell resource file.

**Options and Option Arguments:** None

**Command Arguments:**

| | |
|---|---|
| 'filename' | A file containing a list of names that are commands |

---

## who—Who is on the system

**Syntax:** `who` [ `-abdHlmpqrstTu` ] [ 'file' ]
`who -q` [ `-n` 'x' ] [ 'file' ]
`who` 'am I'

**Purpose:** List the user's name, terminal line, login time, elapsed time since activity occurred on the line, and the process-ID of the command interpreter (shell) for each current LINUX system user

**Options and Option Arguments:**

| | |
|---|---|
| `-a` | Process /var/adm/utmp or the named 'file' with `-b`, `-d`, `-l`, `-p`, `-r`, `-t`, `-T`, and `-u` options turned on. |
| `-b` | Indicate the time and date of the last reboot |
| `-d` | Display all processes that have expired and not been respawned by `init` |
| `-H` | Output column headings above the regular output |
| `-l` | List only those lines on which the system is waiting for someone to log in |
| `-m` | Output only information about the current terminal |
| `-n` 'x' | Take a numeric argument, 'x', which specifies the number of users to display per line; 'x' must be at least 1. |
| `-p` | List any other process that is currently active and has been previously spawned by `init` |
| `-q` | (Quick `who`) Display only the names and the number of users currently logged on; all other options are ignored |
| `-r` | Indicate the current 'run-level' of the `init` process |
| `-s` | (Default) List only the 'name', 'line', and 'time' fields |
| `-T` | Same as the `-s` option, except that the 'state idle', 'pid', and 'comment' fields are also written |
| `-t` | Indicate the last change to the system clock (via the date command) by root |
| `-u` | List only those users who are currently logged on |

**Command Arguments:**

| | |
|---|---|
| 'am I' | In the "C" locale, limit the output to describing the invoking user, equivalent to the `–m` option. The `am` and `i` or `I` must be separate arguments. |
| 'file' | Specify pathname of a file to substitute for the database of logged-on users that `who` uses by default. |

---

## write—Write to another user

**Syntax:** `write` 'user' [ 'terminal' ]

**Purpose:** Read lines from the user's standard input and write them to the terminal of another user. When first invoked, writes the message

```
Message from 'sender-login-id' [sending-terminal] [date]...
```

to 'user'. When it has successfully completed the connection, the sender's terminal will be alerted twice to indicate that what the sender is typing is being written to the recipient's terminal.

**Options and Option Arguments:** None

**Command Arguments:**

| | |
|---|---|
| 'user' | User (login) name of the person to whom the message will be written. This argument must be of the form returned by `who`. |
| 'terminal' | Terminal identification in the same format provided by `who` |

---

## xterm—Start an xterm terminal emulator window

**Syntax:** `xterm` [toolkit options] [options]

**Purpose:** Open an xterminal terminal emulator window in which LINUX commands can be typed. Usually this window provides VT100/102 or Tektronix display capability.

**Options and Option Arguments (as of X11 Rel 6.3):**

*xtoolkit options.*

| | |
|---|---|
| `-bg` 'color' | Specify 'color' to use for the background of the window. Default is white. |
| `-bd` 'color' | Specify 'color' to use for the border of the window. Default is black. |
| `-bw` 'number' | Specify the width in pixels of the border surrounding the window |
| `-fg` 'color' | Specify the 'color' to use for displaying text. Default is black. |
| `-fn` 'font' | Specify 'font' to be used for displaying normal text. Default is 'fixed'. |
| `-name` 'name' | Specify application 'name' under which resources are to be obtained, rather than the default executable file name; 'name' should not contain . or * characters. |
| `-title` 'string' | Specify the window title 'string', which may be displayed by window managers if the user so chooses. Default title is the command line specified after the `-e` option, if any; otherwise the application name. |
| `-rv` | Indicate that reverse video should be simulated by swapping the foreground and background colors. |
| `-geometry` 'geometry' | Specify the preferred size and position of the window |
| `-display` 'display' | Specify the X server to contact |
| `-xrm` 'resourcestring' | Specify 'resourcestring' to be used. This is especially useful for setting resources that do not have separate command line options. |
| `-iconic` | Indicate that `xterm` should ask the window manager to start it as an icon rather than as the normal window |
| `-dc` | Disable the escape sequence to change the vt100 foreground and background colors, the text cursor color, the mouse cursor foreground and background colors, and the Tektronix emulator foreground and background colors |

| | |
|---|---|
| `+dc` | Enable the escape sequence to change the vt100 foreground and background colors, the text cursor color, the mouse cursor foreground and background colors, and the Tektronix emulator foreground and background |

*Options.*

| | |
|---|---|
| `-help` | Cause **`xterm`** to print out a verbose message describing its options |
| `-132` | Normally, the vt102 deccolm escape sequence that switches between 80 and 132 column mode is ignored. This option causes the deccolm escape sequence to be recognized, and the xterm window will resize appropriately. |
| `-ah` | Indicate that **`xterm`** should always highlight the text cursor. By default, **`xterm`** will display a hollow text cursor whenever the focus is lost or the pointer leaves the window. |
| `+ah` | Indicate that **`xterm`** should do text cursor highlighting based on focus |
| `-ai` | Disable active icon support if that feature was compiled into **`xterm`** |
| `+ai` | Enable active icon support if that feature was compiled into **`xterm`** |
| `-aw` | Indicate that auto-wraparound should be allowed, so cursor automatically wraps to the beginning of the next line when when it is at the rightmost position of a line and text is output |
| `+aw` | Indicate that auto-wraparound should not be allowed |
| **`-b`** 'number' | Specify the size of the inner border (the distance between the outer edge of the characters and the window border) in pixels. The default is 2. |
| `-bdc` | Disable the display of characters with bold attribute as color rather than bold |
| `+bdc` | Enable the display of characters with bold attribute as color rather than bold |
| `-cb` | Set the vt100 resource cutToBeginningOfLine to false |
| `+cb` | Set the vt100 resource cutToBeginningOfLine to true |
| **`-cc`** 'characterclassrange'**:**'value'[,...] | Set classes indicated by the given ranges for use in selecting by words. |
| `-cm` | Disable recognition of ANSI colorchange escape sequences |
| `+cm` | Enable recognition of ANSI colorchange escape sequences |
| `-cn` | Indicate that newlines should not be cut in line-mode selections |
| `+cn` | Indicate that newlines should be cut in line-mode selections |

| | |
|---|---|
| `-cr` 'color' | Specify the color to use for text cursor. The default is to use the same foreground color that is used for text. |
| `-cu` | Indicate that **`xterm`** should work around a bug in the **`more`** program that causes it to incorrectly display lines that are exactly the width of the window and are followed by a line beginning with a <Tab> (the leading tabs are not displayed). |
| `+cu` | Indicate that **`xterm`** should not work around the **`more`** bug |
| `-dc` | Disable recognition of color-change escape sequences |
| `+dc` | Enable recognition of color-change escape sequences |
| `-e` 'program' [ 'arguments' ... ] | Specify the program (and its command line arguments) to be run in the **`xterm`** window. Sets the window title and icon name to be the base name of the program being executed if neither **`-T`** nor **`-n`** are given on the command line. *This must be the last option on the command line.* |
| `-fb` 'font' | Specify 'font' to be used when displaying bold text. This font must be same height and width as the normal font. If only one of the normal or bold fonts is specified, it will be used as the normal font, and bold font will be produced by overstriking this font. The default is to overstrike the normal font. |
| `-fi` | Set the font for active icons if that feature was compiled in to **`xterm`** |
| `-im` | Turn on the **`useInsertMode`** resource |
| `+im` | Turn off the **`useInsertMode`** resource |
| `-j` | Indicate that **`xterm`** should do jump scrolling. Normally, text is scrolled one line at a time; this option allows **`xterm`** to move multiple lines at a time so that it doesn't fall as far behind. Its use is strongly recommended because it makes **`xterm`** much faster when scanning through large amounts of text. The vt100 escape sequences for enabling and disabling smooth scroll as well as the VT Options menu can be used to turn this feature on or off. |
| `+j` | Indicate that **`xterm`** should not do jump scrolling |
| `-ls` | Indicate that the shell that is started in the **`xterm`** window will be a login shell |
| `+ls` | Indicate that the shell that is started should not be a login shell (i.e., it will be a normal subshell) |
| `-mb` | Indicate that **`xterm`** should ring a margin bell when the user types near the right end of a line. This option can be turned on and off from the VT Options menu. |
| `+mb` | Indicate that margin bell should not be rung |

| | |
|---|---|
| `-mc` 'milliseconds' | Specify the maximum time between multiclick selections |
| `-ms` 'color' | Specifies the color to be used for the pointer cursor. The default is to use the foreground color. |
| `-nb` 'number' | Specify the number of characters from the right end of a line at which the margin bell, if enabled, will ring. The default is 10. |
| `-nul` | Enables the display of underlining |
| `+nul` | Disables the display of underlining |
| `-rw` | Indicates that reverse wraparound should be allowed. This allows the cursor to back up from the leftmost column of one line to the rightmost column of the previous line. This is very useful for editing long shell command lines and is encouraged. This option can be turned on and off from the VT Options menu. |
| `+rw` | Indicates that reverse wraparound should not be allowed |
| `-s` | Indicates that **`xterm`** may scroll asynchronously, meaning that the screen does not have to be kept completely up to date while scrolling |
| `+s` | Indicates that **`xterm`** should scroll synchronously |
| `-sb` | Indicates that some number of lines that are scrolled off the top of the window should be saved and that a scrollbar should be displayed so that those lines can be viewed. This option may be turned on and off from the VT Options menu. |
| `+sb` | Indicates that a scrollbar should not be displayed |
| `-sf` | Indicates that Sun Function Key escape codes should be generated for function keys |
| `+sf` | Indicates that the standard escape codes should be generated for function keys |
| `-si` | Indicates that output to a window should not automatically reposition the screen to the bottom of the scrolling region. This option can be turned on and off from the VT Options menu. |
| `+si` | Indicate that output to a window should cause it to scroll to the bottom |
| `-sk` | Indicate that pressing a key while using the scrollbar to review previous lines of text should cause the window to be repositioned automatically in the normal position at the bottom of the scroll region |
| `+sk` | Indicate that pressing a key while using the scrollbar should not cause the window to be repositioned |
| `-sl` 'number' | Specify the number of lines to save that have been scrolled off the top of the screen. The default is 64. |
| `-t` | Indicate that **`xterm`** should start in Tektronix mode, rather than in vt102 mode. Switching between the two windows is done using the Options menus. |

| | |
|---|---|
| `+t` | Indicate that **`xterm`** should start in vt102 mode |
| `-tm` 'string' | Specify a series of terminal setting keywords followed by the characters that should be bound to those functions, similar to the stty program. Allowable keywords include intr, quit, erase, kill, eof, eol, swtch, start, stop, brk, susp, dsusp, rprnt, flush, weras, and lnext. Control characters may be specified as ^char (e.g., ^c or ^u) and ^? may be used to indicate delete. |
| `-tn` 'name' | Specify the name of the terminal type to be set in the ***`term`*** environment variable. |
| `-ulc` | Disable the display of characters with underline attribute as color rather than with underlining |
| `+ulc` | Enable the display of characters with underline attribute as color rather than with underlining |
| `-ut` | Indicate that **`xterm`** should not write a record into the system log file /etc/utmp |
| `+ut` | Indicate that **`xterm`** should write a record into the system log file /etc/utmp |
| `-vb` | Indicate that a visual bell is preferred over an audible one. Instead of ringing the terminal bell whenever a <Ctrl-G> is received, the window will be flashed |
| `+vb` | Indicate that a visual bell should not be used |
| `-wf` | Indicate that **`xterm`** should wait for the window to be mapped the first time before starting the subprocess so that the initial terminal size settings and environment variables are correct. It is the application's responsibility to catch subsequent terminal size changes. |
| `+wf` | Indicate that **`xterm`** show not wait before starting the subprocess |
| `-C` | Indicate that this window should receive console output. This is not supported on all systems. To obtain console output, user must be the owner of the console device and must have read and write permission for it. When running X under **`xdm`** on the console screen user may need to have the session startup and reset programs explicitly change the ownership of the console device in order to get this option to work. |
| `-S`'ccn' | Specify the last two letters of the name of a pseudo-terminal to use in slave mode, plus the number of the inherited file descriptor. The option is parsed **`"%c%c%d"`**. This allows **`xterm`** to be used as an input and output channel for an existing program and is sometimes used in specialized applications. |

**Command Arguments:** None

# Glossary

**Absolute Pathname** A pathname that starts with the root directory.
**Access Permissions** See Access Rights.
**Access Privileges** See Access Rights.
**Access Rights** The type of operations that a user can perform on a file. In LINUX, access rights for a file can be read, write, and execute. The execute permission for a directory means permission to search the directory. The owner of a file dictates who can and cannot access the file for various types of file operations.
**Access Time** The time taken to access a main memory location for reading or writing.
**Address Bus** A set of parallel wires that are used to carry the address of a storage location in the main memory that is to be read or written.
**Address Space** See Process Address Space.
**Alias** See Pseudonym.
**Application Programmer's Interface (API)** The language libraries and system call layer form the application programmer's interface.
**Application Software** Programs that we use to perform various tasks on the computer system, such as word processing, graphing, picture and speech processing, and Web browsing.
**Application user's Interface (AUI)** The application software that a user can use forms the application user's interface.
**Archive** A collection of files contained in a single file in a certain format.
**Array** A named collection of items of the same type stored in contiguous memory locations.
**Array Indexing** The method used to transfer to an array item by using its number. The items in an array are numbered, with the first item numbered 1 (in some languages such as C, the first item is numbered 0).
**Assembler** A program that takes a program in assembly language as input and translates it into object code.
**Assembly Language** See Low-Level Programming language.
**Assignment Statement** A shell command that is used to assign values to one or more shell variables.
**Attributes** The characteristics of a process or file such as its size, the date and time it was created, and the name or ID of its owner.

**Background Process** When a process executes such that it does not relinquish the control of the keyboard, it is said to *execute in background*. The Shell prompt is returned to the user before a background process starts execution, thus allowing the user to use the system (i.e., run commands) while the background processes execute.
**Bash** The Abbreviation for Bourne Again shell.
**Batch Operating System** An operating system that does not allow you to interact with your processes is known as a batch operating system. UNIX and LINUX also allow programs to be executed in the batch mode, with programs executing in the background.
**Bistate Devices** The devices, such as transistors, that operate in "on" or "off" mode.
**Bit** Stands for binary digit, which can be 0 or 1. It is also the smallest unit of storage and transmission.
**Bit Mask** A sequence of bits (usually a byte or multiple bytes) used to retain values of certain bits in another byte (or multiple bytes), or to set them to 0s or 1s, by using a logical operation such as AND or OR.
**Block-Oriented Devices** The devices such as a disk drive, which perform I/O in terms of blocks of data (e.g., in 512-byte chunks). Also see Cluster.
**Block Special Files** The LINUX files that correspond to block-orientated devices. (see Block-Oriented Devices). These files are located in the /dev directory.
**Break Point** A program statement where the execution of the program stops while using a symbolic debugger such as `gdb`.
**Byte** In contemporary literature, a byte refers to 8 bits. For example, 10101100 is a byte. Because of this, a byte is also called an octet. A storage location that can store 8 bits is also known as a byte. In not-so-recent literature, the term byte also referred to 9 bits.

**Central Processing Unit (CPU)** Also known as the brain of the computer system, the CPU executes a program by reading the program instruction from the main memory. It also interacts with the I/O devices in the computer system.

**Character-Oriented Devices** The devices, such as a keyboard, that perform I/O in terms of one byte at a time.

**Character Special Files** The LINUX files that correspond to character-oriented devices. These files are located in the /dev directory.

**Character User Interface (CUI)** See Command Line Interface.

**Child Process** A process created on behalf of another process. In LINUX, the fork system call has to create a child process. The child process is an exact copy of the process executing fork (see parent Process).

**Client Software** In a client-server software model, the client software, when executed, takes the user commands and sends them to the server process. The server process computes the responses for requests and sends them to the client, who handles them according to the semantics of the command. All Internet applications are based on the client-server model of computing.

**Clock Tick** A clock in a computer system ticks as frequently as dictated by the frequency of the clock (ticks per second). For system clocks that are dependent on the frequency of the power line signals (50 or 60 per second), it ticks every 1/50 (or 1/60) of a second.

**Cluster** The minimum unit of disk I/O, which is one or more sectors.

**Coding Rules** A set of rules used by programmers for writing programs. Such rules are usually designed to enhance the readability of programs and to keep consistency in the "look" of the source programs produced by an organization or a coding team. The use of coding rules helps a great deal during the maintenance phase of the product.

**Command Grouping** Specifying two or more commands in such a manner that the shell executes them all as one process.

**Command Interpreter** A program that starts running after you log on to allow you to type commands that it tries to interpret and run. In LINUX, the command is also known as a shell.

**Command Line** A line that comprises a command with its arguments and is typed at a shell prompt. You must hit the <Enter<> key before the command is executed by a shell.

**Command Line Arguments** The arguments that a command needs for its proper execution, which are specified in the command line. For example, in the command cp f1 f2, f1 and f2 are command line arguments. Within a shell script, you can refer to these arguments by using positional parameters *1* through *$9*.

**Command Line User Interface (CUI)** If you use a keyboard to issue commands to a computer's operating system, the computer is said to have command line user interface.

**Command Substitution** A shell feature that allows the substitution of a command by its output. To do so, you enclose a command in back quotes (grave accents). Thus in the echo `date` command, the output of the date command substitutes for the date command, which is then displayed on the display screen. In Bash, $(date) performs the same task.

**Comments** Short notes placed in a program source code to explain segments of code. Comments must be distinguished so they are not executed as program commands (statements). A comment in a shell script must start with a # sign.

**Communication Channel** See Physical Communication Medium.

**Compiler** A program that takes a program written in a high-level language and translates it into an assembly language program. Almost all C and C++ compilers also perform the tasks of preprocessing, assembly, and linking by default.

**Computer Network** An interconnection of two or more computing devices. A device on a network is commonly called a *host*.

**Configuration File** A file that contains the definitions of various environment variables to setup your environment while you use a shell. Every shell has one or more startup configuration files in your home directory that are executed when that shell starts running (e.g., .bashrc Bash shell).

**Control Bus** A set of parallel wires that are used to carry control information from the CPU to the main memory or an I/O device. For example, it carries the "read" or "write" instruction from the CPU to the main memory.

**Controllers** The electronic part of an I/O device, which communicates with the CPU or other devices.

**Control Unit** The part of a CPU that interacts with the devices in a computer system (memory, disk, display screen, etc.) via controllers (see Controllers) in these devices. It also fetches a program instruction from the main memory, decodes it to determine whether the instruction is valid, and then passes it on to the execution unit (see Execution Unit) for its execution.

**C Preprocessor** A program that takes a C program as input and processes all the statements that start with the # sign. It produces output that is taken by the C compiler as input to produce the assembly code. A typical C compiler performs all the tasks necessary to produce the executable code for a C program. These steps are preprocessing, compilation, assembly, and linking.

**CPU Scheduling** A mechanism that is used to multiplex a CPU in a computer system among several processes. This results in all processes making progress in a fair manner and increased utilization of hardware resources in the system.

**CPU Usage** The percentage of the time the CPU in a computer system has been used since the system has been up.

**Csh** The abbreviation of the C shell.

**Current Directory** See Present Working Directory.

**Current Job** The job (process) that is presently being executed by the CPU.

**Cursor** The point that tells you which part of the screen you are interacting with at a given time.

**Daemon** A system process executing in the background to provide a service such as Web browsing. In a typical LINUX system, the lpd daemon provides the printing service, the httpd daemon provides the Web browsing service, and fingerd provides the finger service.

**Data Bus** A set of parallel wires that are used to carry data from the CPU to a subsystem (memory or I/O device), and vice versa.

**Decryption** The process of converting an encrypted file (see Encryption) to its original version.

**Desktop Manager** A software system that provides a graphical method of interacting with the operating system.

**Directory Stack** The storage structure used to maintain the pathnames of recently used directories in a last-in-first-out basis.

**Disk Scheduling** In a time-sharing system, several requests can come to the operating system for reading or writing files on a disk. The disk scheduling code in the operating system decides which request should be served first.

**Domain Name System (DNS)** A distributed database that can be used to convert the domain name of a host to its IP address. In LINUX, you can use the `nslookup` command to perform this task.

**Dotted Decimal Notation (DDN)** The notation in which IPv4 addresses are such as 192.140.30.10.

**Dot File** See Hidden File.

**Dynamic Analysis** The analysis of a software as it executes. The analysis comprises debugging, tracing, and performance monitoring of the software, including testing it against product requirements.

**Edge Flipping** The ability to move between tiles of the virtual desktop by moving the cursor to the edge of one of the virtual screen tiles.

**Editor Buffer** While editing a file, the part of the file that is displayed on the screen is stored in an area in the main memory called the editor buffer. The changes that you make to the file are stored in this buffer and saved in the file (on disk) only when you use the editor command to do so.

**Encryption** The process of converting a file's contents to a completely different form by using a process that is reversible, thereby allowing recovery of the original file.

**End-of-File (EOF) Marker** Every operating system puts a marker (one or more characters) at the end of a file, called the end-of-file (EOF) marker.

**Environment Variables** The shell variables (see Shell Variables) whose values control your environment while you use the system. For example, it dictates which shell process starts running and what directory you are put into when you log on.

**Ethernet** the most famous protocol for physically connecting hosts on local area networks.

**Execute Permission** A LINUX access privilege that must be set for a file to be executed by using the file as a command. When set for a directory, it allows the directory to be searched.

**Execution Unit** Also called the datapath, it executes instructions in a program delivered to it by the control unit.

**Exit Status** A value returned by a process, indicating whether it exited successfully or unsuccessfully. In LINUX, a process returns a status of 0 on success and a non-0 value on failure.

**External Command** A shell command for which the service code is in a file and not part of the shell process. When a user runs and external command, the code in a corresponding file must be executed by the shell. The file may contain binary code or a shell script.

**External Signal** A signal whose source is not the CPU. For example, pressing <Ctrl-C> on the keyboard sends an external signal, also called keyboard interrupt, to the process running in the foreground.

**FCFS** See First-come, First-serve Mechanism.

**FIFO** First-in-first-out order.

**File Compression** The process of shrinking the size of a file.

**File Descriptor** A small positive integer associated with every open file in LINUX. It is used by the kernel to access the inode for an open file and determine its attributes, such as the file's location on the disk.

**File Descriptor Table** A per-process table maintained by the LINUX system that is indexed by using a file descriptor to access the file's inode.

**Filesystem** A filesystem is a directory hierarchy with its own root stored on a disk or disk partition, mounted under (glued to) a directory. The files and directories in the filesystem are accessed through the directory under which they are mounted.

**File System Standard** Every LINUX system contains a set of specific files and directories organized according to a standard proposed in 1994, known as the File System Standard (FSSTND).

**File System Structure** The structure that shows how files and directories in a computer system are organized (as viewed by a user). On most contemporary systems, including LINUX, the files and directories are organized in a hierarchical (tree-like) fashion.

**File Table** A table maintained by the LINUX operating system to keep track of all open files in the system.

**File Transfer Protocol** An application protocol in the TCP/IP protocol suite that allows you to transfer files from a remote host to your host, or vice versa. The LINUX `ftp` command can be used to access this Internet service.

**Filter** A LINUX term for a command that reads input from a standard input, processes it in some fashion, and sends it to standard output. Examples of LINUX filters are `sort`, `pr`, and `tr`.

**First-Come, First-Serve Mechanism** A scheme that allows the print requests (or any other requests) on the basis of their arrival time, serving the first request first.

**First-Come, First-Serve (FCFS) Scheduling Algorithm** A method of prioritizing value. In this method, the process that enters the system first is asigned the highest priority and gets to use the CPU first.

**Folder** Also known as a direcory, it is a place on the disk that contains files and other folders arranged in some organized and logical fashion.

**Foreground Process** A process that keeps control of the keyboard when it executes, i.e., the process whose standard input is attached to the keyboard. Only one foreground process can run on a system at a given time.

**FTP** See File Transfer Protocol.

**Full Screen Display Editor** An editor that displays a portion of the file being edited in the console window or terminal screen. Popular LINUX full screen editors are `vi`, `emacs`, `pico`, and `xemacs`.

**Full Screen Display E-Mail Systems** E-mail systems that allow you to edit any text you see on a single screen display, as you would on a word processor.

**Fully Parameterized Client** A client software that has the flexibility of allowing identification of a particular port number where a server runs. Telnet is an example of a fully parameterized client, because, although the telnet server normally runs on the well-known port 23, you can run telnet server on another port and connect to it by specifying the port number as a command line perimeter with the telnet command. For example, in the `telnet foo.foobar.org 5045` command, the telnet client will try to connect the server running on port 5045.

**Fully Qualified Domain Name (FQDN)** The name of a host that includes the host name and the network domain on which it is connected. For example, www.up.edu is FQDN for the host whose name is www.

**Function** A series of commands that are given a name. The commands in a function are executed when the function is invoked (called).

**Function Body** The series of commands in a function.

**Gateway** See Router.

**Gcc** A popular GNU C compiler for UNIX and LINUX. The command for using this compiler is `gcc`.

**General Purpose Buffer** An area in the main memory maintained by an editor, it contains your most recent cut and copied text.

**Getty Process** At the system bootup time, the LINUX system starts running a process on each working terminal attached to the system. This process runs in the superuser mode and sets terminal attributes such as baud rate as specified in the /etc/ termcap file. Finally it displays the login: prompt and waits for a user to log on. The process name is mingetty on LINUX and getty in UNIX.

**Global Variable** A variable that can be accessed by children of the process (executing shell script) in which it is defined.

**GNU Midnite Commander (GMC)** The GNOME file manager.

**GNU Network Object Model (GNOME)** A popular graphical desktop environment for many LINUX systems, including Red Hat.

**Graphical Server** A terminal that can display graphics or change them by accepting requests from a graphical client. Tektronix's Xterminal is a prime example of a graphical server.

**Graphical User Interface (GUI)** If you use a point-and-click device, such as a mouse, to issue commands to its operating system, a computer is said to have a graphical user interface.

**Grave Accents** Refers to backquotes or left-leaning accent marks, as in the `` `date` `` command.

**Group** In LINUX, every user of the computer system belongs to a collection of users known as the User's group.

**Hard Link** A mechanism that allows file sharing by creating a directory entry in a directory to allow access to a file (or directory) via the directory. Loosely applied, it is a pointer to the inode of a file to be accessed via multiple path names. The ln command is used to create a hard link to a file.

**Head** Refers to the beginning portion of a file. It may be useful to view it in determining the type of data stored in the file. The LINUX `head` command can be used to display the head of a file, which is first 10 lines by default.

**Header file** A file that contains definitions and/or declarations of various items (e.g., constants, variables, and function prototypes) to be used in the program in the C, C++, or Java programming language.

**Here Document** A Bourne and C shell feature that allows you to redirect standard input of a command in a script and attach it to data in the script.

**Hidden File** Files that are not listed when you list the contents of a directory by using the `ls` command. Since the names of hidden files start with the dot (.) character, therefore, they are also called dot files. Some commonly used hidden files are .bashrc (start-up file for Bash), .cshrc (start up file for C shell), and .profile (executed when you log on). All of these files reside in your home directory. Some applications and tools use hidden files as well.

**History Expansion** A feature in Bash and TC shells that allows you to take words from the history list (a list of previously executed commands under the shell) and insert them into the current command line. It makes it easy for you to repeat previously executed commands and or make changes in them and re-execute them.

**Home Directory** See Login Directory.

**Home Page** The contents of a file displayed on the screen (the actual contents can be multiple screens long) for an Internet site.

**Host** A hardware resource, usually a computer system, on a network.

**I-list** A list (array) of inodes on the disk in the LINUX system. See Inode.

**Indexed Buffer** A buffer used by a text editor that allows you to store more than one temporary string.

**Index Node** See Inode.

**Index Screen** The user interface in full-screen-display email systems. It usually consists of three areas: one that contains the message number, sender's email address, date received, size of the message in bytes, and subject line; a second that contains a list of possible commands; and third, a command area where your typed commands are displayed. These screens vary from one system to another.

**Infinite Loop** See Non-Terminating Loop.

**Init Process** The first user process that is created when you boot up the LINUX system. It is the granddaddy of all user processes.

**Inode** An element of an array on disk (called an I-list) allocated to every unique file at the time it is created. It contains files attributes such as file size (in bytes). When a file is opened for an operation (e.g. read), the file's inode is copied from disk to a slot in a table kept the main memory, called the inode table, so that the file's attributes can be assessed quickly.

**Inode Number** A 4-byte index value for the i-list used to access the inode for a file.

**Inode Table** A table (array) of inodes in the main memory that keeps inodes for all open files. The inode number for a file is used to index this array in order to access the attributes of an open file.

**Insert Mode of Operation** Mode that allows you to input text to be inserted in the document being edited.

**Instruction Set** The language that a CPU understands. A CPU can understand instructions only in its own instruction set, which is usually a superset of its predecessors made by the same company.

**Interactive Operating System** An operating system that allows you to interact with your processes. Almost all contemporary operating systems, such as LINUX, UNIX, and Windows are interactive.

**Internal (built-in) Command** A shell command for which the service code is part of the shell process.

**Internal Signal (trap)** An interrupt generated by the CPU. This may be caused, for example, when a process tries to access a memory location that it is not allowed to access. (See Process Address Space.)

**Internet** See Internetwork.

**Internet Domain Name System** A distributed database of domain name and IP address mappings. It is maintained by hosts called name servers. Every site on the internet must have at least one computer that acts as a name server.

**Internet Protocol (IP)** The network layer protocol in the TCP/IP protocol suite that routes packets (known as datagrams in the TCP/IP terminology) from the source (sender) host to the destination (receiver) host.

**Internetwork** A network of computer networks. The ubiquitous internet is called the Internet.

**Internetworking** Making a network of networks. In terms of software, it usually refers to writing client-server programs that allow processes on various hosts on the Internet to communicate with each other.

**Interpreted Program** A program that is executed one statement (or command) at a time by an interpreter.

**Interpreter** A program that executes statements (or commands) in a program one by one. An example of an interpreter is a LINUX shell that reads commands from a keyboard or a shell script and executes them one by one.

**Interprocess Communication (IPC) Mechanisms** Facilities (channels and operations on them) provided by an operating system that allow processes to communicate with each other. LINUX has several channels for IPC including pipes, FIFOs, and BSD sockets. These Channels are created by using LINUX systems called pipe, mkfifo (mknod in older systems), and socket.

**Intranet** A network of computer networks in an organization that is accessible to people in the organization only.

**I/O Bound Process** A process that spends most of its time performing I/O operations, as opposed to performing some calculations by using the CPU.

**IP Address** A 32-bit positive integer (in IPv4) to uniquely identify a host on the Internet. In IPv6, it is a 128-bit positive integer.

**Iteration** A single execution of the piece of code in a loop. (See Loop.)

**Job** A job is a print request or a process running in the background.

**Job ID** A number assigned to a print job. On some systems, it is preceded by the name of the printer.

**Job Number** A small integer number assigned to a background process.

**K Desktop Environment (KDE)** A popular graphical desktop environment for many LINUX systems.

**Kernel** The operating system kernel is that part of an operating system software where the real work is done. It performs all those tasks that deal with input and output devices, such as a disk drive.

**Keyboard interrupt** An event generated when you press <Ctrl-C> that causes the termination of the foreground process.

**Keyboard Macro** A collection of keystrokes that can be recorded and then accessed at any time. This capability allows you to define repetitive multiple keystroke operations as a single command and then execute that command at anytime—as many times as you want.

**Keystroke Command** A command that corresponds to pressing one or more keys.

**Kill Ring** Text held in a buffer by killing it.

**Kpackage** A KDE application for package installation.

**KWM** The default window manager for KDE.

**Language Libraries** A set of pre-written and tested functions for various languages that can be used by application programmers instead of having to write their own.

**Latency Time** The time taken by a disk to spin in order to bring the right sector under the read/write head is called the latency time for the disk. It is dictated by the rotation speed of the disk.

**Lazy Locking** In version control systems that allow multiple users to check out a file for editing, lazy locking does not lock the file until the file contents are changes by a user. The Concurrent Versions System (CVS) uses this file locking scheme.

**Legacy Code** Program written long ago that has no written documentation describing the purpose of various parts of the program.

**Lempel-Ziv Coding** A coding technique used by the `gzip` and `gunzip` (and other related) commands for compressing and decompressing files.

**Library** A set of prewritten and pretested functions in various languages (e.g., C, C++, Java) available to programmers for use with the software they develop.

**Librarian** A nickname used for LINUX `ar` utility that allows you to archive your object files into a single library file and manipulate the archive file in various ways.

**Line Display E-mail System** Email system that allows you to edit one line at a time when you are composing an email message. The LINUX mail utility is a prime example of such a system.

**Link** A link is a way to connect a file to a directory so that the file can be accessed as a child of the directory. The actual file may be in another directory.

**Link File** A file in LINUX that contains the pathname for a file. A link file, therefore, "points to" another file. The type of such a file is line (denoted by `l` in the output of the `ls -l` command). (See Symbolic Link.)

**Literal Constants** Constant values such as digits, letters, and string. For example 103, "A", "x", and "Hello".

**Loader Program** An operating system program that reads an application from a disk, loads it into the main memory, and sets the CPU state so that it can start program execution.

**Local Area Network (LAN)** Multiple computing devices interconnected form a LAN if the distance between these devices is small. LANs are used to connect computing devices in small to medium size organizations such as universities and colleges.
**Local File System** File system used for organizing files and directories of a single computer system. By using a local file system on a computer system, you can access files and directories on that system only. (A remote file system allows you to access files on the remote computers on a local network.)
**Local Host Computer System** The computer system that you are logged on to.
**Local Variable** A variable that is not accessible outside the executing shell (or shell script) in which it is defined.
**Login Directory** The directory that you are placed in when you log on.
**Login Name** See Username.
**Login Process** A process created by the getty process (mingetty) that accepts your password, checks for its validity, and allows you to log on by running your login shell process.
**Login Prompt** A character or character string displayed by an operating system to inform you that you need to enter your login name and password in order to use the system. In the LINUX system, the getty process displays the login prompt.
**Login Shell** The shell process that starts execution when you log on.
**Lpd** The line printer daemon. (See Printer Daemon.)

**Machine Cycle** A CPU continuously fetches the next program instruction from the main memory, decodes it to verify if the instruction is valid, and then executes it. This process of fetching, decoding, and executing instructions is known as the CPU cycle.
**Machine Language** The instruction set of a CPU denoted in the form of 0s and 1s.
**Machine Programs** The programs written in a CPU's machine language.
**Main Buffer** Also known as the editing buffer, or the work buffer, it is the main repository for the body of the text that you are trying to create or modify from some previous permanently archived file on disk.
**Mainframe** See Mainframe Computer.
**Mainframe Computer** A computer system that has powerful processing and input/output capabilities and allows hundreds of users to use the system simultaneously.
**Make Rules** The rules that are used by the LINUX `make` utility to compile and link multiple modules of a software product.
**Mark** A place holder in the buffer.
**Message Body** The message text of an email message.
**Message Header** An important structural part of an email message that usually appears at the top of the message text. It normally contains information such as sender and receiver's addresses, subject, date, time the message was sent, attachments, and email addresses of the people who received carbon copies of the mail message.
**Millisecond** One thousandth of a second.
**Minicomputer** A midrange computer that is more powerful than a PC but less powerful than mainframe computers. Like Mainframe computers, the minicomputer also allows multiple users to access the system at the same time.
**Multimedia Internet Mail Standard (MIME)** An email standard that defines various multimedia content types for attachments. In particular, digital images, audio clips, and movie files can be transmitted via email attachments, even on dissimilar email systems, if the systems are MIME-compliant.
**Multi-Port Router** A router that can interconnect more than two networks.
**Mulitprogramming** In a computer system, the mechanism that allows the execution of multiple processes by multiplexing the CPU. Under multiprogramming, when the process currently using the CPU needs to perform some I/O operation, the CPU is assigned to another process that is ready to execute.

**Named Pipes** Communication channels that can be used by unrelated LINUX processes on the same computer to communicate with each other. The LINUX system call mkfifo (mknod in older systems) is used to create a named pipe.
**Name Server** A computer system on an Internet site that helps in mapping a domain name to an IP address or vice versa. Name servers implement the DNS.
**Nanosecond** One billionth of a second.

**Network File System (NFS)** Client server software, commonly used on network LINUX machines, that allows you to access your files and directories from any computer transparently.

**Network Interface Card** Also known as NIC, it is a circuit board in a computer system that has a link level protocol implemented in it. For example, a network card with Ethernet protocol implemented in it (also referred to as the Ethernet card).

**Nice Value** An integer value used in calculating the priority number of a LINUX process. The greater the nice value for a process, the lower its priority.

**Nonterminating Loop** A loop that does not have the proper termination condition, and therefore, does not terminate. This is usually caused by bad programming, but there are certain applications, such as Internet servers, that must use infinite loops to offer the intended service.

**Null Command** The Bourne shell command **:**. It does not do anything except for returning true. When used in a C shell script, this command causes the C shell to execute the remaining script under the Bourne shell.

**Null String** The string that contains no value. When displayed on the screen it results in a blank line.

**Object Code** A program generated by the assembler program. It is in the machine language of the CPU in the computer but is not executable.

**Open Software System** A software whose source code is freely available to the community of users so they can modify it as they wish. An example of such a system is the LINUX operating system.

**Operating System** Software that manages the resources in a computer system and provides an interface for users to use application software.

**Others** In LINUX, when we talk about a user's access permissions for a file, the *others* refers to everyone except the owner of the file and the users in the owner's group.

**Package** Useful application software.

**Packet** A term used for a fixed-sized message (containing data and control information) in the networking terminology. A TCP packet is called a segment, and a UDP or IP packet is called a datagram.

**Parallel Execution** Simultaneous execution of multiple commands with the help of CPU scheduling. The process corresponding to all the commands in the common line are executed in the background.

**Parent Process** A process that creates one or more children processes.

**Password** A sequence of characters that every user of a timesharing computer system must have in order for him/her to use the system. (See Username.)

**Pathname** The specification of the location of a file (or a directory) in a system with a hierarchical file system.

**Physical communication medium** The medium used to connect the hardware resources on a network. It includes telephone lines, coaxial cable, glass fiber, a microwave link, and a satellite link.

**Point and-Click Device** Under a graphical user interface, a device is needed to point to an icon, button, window or any other part of a window and press(click) a button on the device to perform an operation such as executing a program. Joysticks and mouses are examples of a point-and-click device.

**Pop** Operation to take an item off the stack.

**Portability** The ability to move the source code (see Source Code) for a software easily and without major modifications from one hardware platform to another.

**Port Number** A 16-bit integer number associated with every Internet service, such as Telnet. Port numbers are maintained by TCP and UDP. Well-known services such as http, ftp, and telnet have well-known ports associated with them. The port numbers for some well-known services are: 80 for http, 21 for ftp, and 23 for telnet.

**Positional Arguments** See Command Line Arguments.

**Postamble** With reference to brace expansion, it is a sequence of characters before the comma-separated strings enclosed in braces.

**Preamble** With reference to brace expansion, it is a sequence of characters after the comma-separated strings enclosed in braces.

**Present Working Directory** The directory that you are in at a given time while using a computer system is known as your current directory. In LINUX, the `pwd` command can be used to display the absolute pathname of your current directory.

**Print Queue** A queue associated with every printer where incoming print requests are queued if the printer is busy printing, and printed one by one as the printer becomes available.

**Printer Daemon** See Printer Spooler.

**Printer Spooler** A system process running in the background that receives print requests and sends them to the appropriate printer for printing. If the printer is busy, its request is put in printer's print queue.

**Process** An executing program.

**Process Address Space** The main memory space allocated to a process for its execution. When a process tries to access any location outside its address space, the operating system takes over the control, terminates the process, and displays an error message that informs the user of the problem.

**Processor Scheduler** A piece of code in an operating system that implements a CPU scheduling algorithm.

**Program Control Flow Commands** See Program Control Flow Statements.

**Program Control Flow Statements** The shell commands that allow the control of a shell script to go from one place in the program to another. Examples of these statements are if-then-else-fi and case.

**Program Generation Tools** Software tools and utilities that can be used by application programmers to generate program and executable files. Examples of such tools are editors, compilers, and the `make` utility.

**Program Header** Important notes at the top of a program file that include information like file name, date the program was written and last modified, author's name, purpose of the program, and a very brief description of the main algorithm used in the program.

**Protocol** A set of rules used by computers—network protocols in the operating system software or network applications—to communicate with each other. Some of the commonly used protocols in the networking world are ATM, Ethernet, FTP, HTTP, IP, SMTP, TCP, Telnet, and UDP.

**Pseudo Devices** Files in the /dev directory that simulate physical devices.

**Pseudonym** Also known as an alias, a nickname given to a command or email address.

**Push** Operation used to put an item on the stack.

**Quantum** In a time-sharing system, a quantum is the amount of time a process uses the CPU before it is given to another process.

**Random Access Memory (RAM)** A storage place inside a computer system that is divided into fixed size locations where each location is identified by a unique integer address and any location can be accessed by specifying its address. Although there are RAMs in various I/O devices, RAM is normally used for main memory in a computer system, which is also a read-write memory.

**RCS** See Revision Control System.

**Readline Library** An interface which provides useful commandline editing facilities.

**Read Permission** The read permission on a LINUX file allows a user to read the file. The read permission on a directory allows us to read the names of files and directories in the directory.

**Real-Time Computer System** A real-time computer system is one that must generate output for a command within a specified interval of time, or else output is useless.

**Redirection Operator** An operator used in a LINUX shell for attaching standard imput, standard output, and standard error of a process to a desired file. (See Standard Files.)

**Region** The area defined by the Mark and Point settings, and the area in which cut and paste commands are executed in an editor.

**Registers** Temporary storage locations inside a CPU that are used by it as scratch pads.

**Regular Expression** A set of rules that can be used to specify one or more items in a single character string (sequence of characters). Many LINUX tools such as `awk`, `egrep`, `fgrep`, `grep`, `sed`, and `vi` support regular expressions.

**Resource Manager** The operating system is also known as the resource manager because it allocates and deallocates the computer resources in an efficient, fair, orderly, and secure manner.

**Resource Utilization** The resource utilization of a resource (usually a hardware resource, such as CPU) is the percentage of the time it has been in use since the computer system has been running.

**Revision Control System** A LINUX tool for revision control.

**Root** The login name of the superuser in a LINUX system.

**Root Directory** The directory under which hang all files and directories in a computer system with a hierarchical file system. Thus, it is the granddaddy of all the files and directories.

**Root Window** The window under which all other windows are opened as its children.

**Round Robin Scheduling Algorithm** A CPU Scheduling Algorithm in which a process gets to use the CPU for one quantum and then the CPU is given to another process. This algorithm is commonly used in time-sharing systems like UNIX and LINUX for scheduling multiple processes on a single CPU.

**Route** The sequence of routers that a packet goes through before it reaches its destination.

**Router** A special host on an Internet that interconnects two or more networks and performs routing packets (called datagrams in the TCP/IP terminology) from the sender host to the receiver host. Routers are also called gateways.

**Rsh** A LINUX network protocol that allows you to execute a command on another computer on a local area network.

**Sawfish** The most popular window manager for GNOME.

**Search Path** A list of directories that your shell searches to find the location of the executable file (binary or shell script) to be executed when you type an external command at the shell prompt and hit the <Enter<> key.

**Sector** Disks are read and written in terms of blocks of data, known as sectors. Typical sector size is 512 bytes.

**Seek Time** Time taken by the read/write head of a disk drive to move laterally to the desired track (cylinder) before a read or write operation can take place.

**Sequential Execution** One-by-one execution of commands; one command finishes its execution and only then does the execution of the second command start.

**Server Process** In a client-server software model, the server process computers the response for a client request and sends it to the client, who handles it according to the semantics of the command. All Internet services are implemented on the basis of a client-server software model. Some popular Internet server processes are FTP server, mail (SMTP) server, Telnet server, and Web (HTTP) server.

**Session** The execution of a shell process.

**Session Leader** The login shell process.

**Set-group-ID (SGID) Bit** A special file protection bit which, when set for an executable file, allows you to execute the file on the behalf of the file's group. Thus you execute the file with group privileges.

**Set-User-ID (SUID) Bit** A special file protection bit which, when set for an executable file, allows you to execute the file on the behalf of the file's owner. Thus you execute the file with the owner's privileges.

**Shell** A computer program that starts execution when the computer system is turned on, or the user logs on. Its purpose is to capture user commands and execute them.

**Shell Environment Variables** Shell variables used to customize the environment in which your shell runs and for proper execution of shell commands.

**Shell Metacharacters** Most of the characters other than letters and digits, have special meaning to a shell, and are known as shell metacharacters. They are treated specially and therefore can not be used in shell commands as literal characters without specifying them in a particular way.

**Shell Prompt** A character or character string displayed by a shell process to inform you that it is ready to accept your command. The default shell prompt for Bash is `$` and TC shell is `%`. You can change the prompt for your shell to any character or character string.

**Shell Script** A program consisting of shell commands.

**Shell Start-Up Files** Files that are executed when a shell process starts. These files are usually located in the /etc or your home directories. For example, ~/.bashrc and ~/.tcshrc are start-up files for Bash and TC shells.

**Shell Variable** A memory location that is given a name which can then be used to read or write the memory location.

**Signal** See Software Interrupt.

**Single Stepping** A feature in symbolic debuggers that allows you to stop program execution after every instruction execution. The next instruction is executed by using a command. This is sometimes called *tracing program execution.*

**SMTP** It stands for Simple Mail Transfer Protocol, which is the protocol used in all email systems (e.g., `elm`, `mail`, and `pine`) running on the Internet.

**Socket** In a client-server model that uses the Socket Interface (see below), a socket is a communication endpoint between a client and server.

**Socket Interface** A popular UNIX and LINUX API for TCP/IP network programming, first written for the BSD UNIX.

**Soft Link** See Symbolic Link.

**Software Interrupt** A Mechanism used in LINUX to inform a process of some event, such as the user pressing <Ctrl-C>, or logging out.

**Sorting** Arranging a set of items in ascending or descending order by using a sort key.

**Sort Key** A field, or portion of an item, used to arrange items in sorted order (see Sorting). For example, the Social Security number can be used as the sort key for sorting employee records in an organization.

**Source Code** A computer program written in a programming language to implement the solution for a problem.

**Special Character** A character that when used in a command is not treated literally by the command. An example of such a character is * in a file name in a shell command, which stands for zero or more characters. Similarly, the \ character is a special character (known as the escape character) that can be used to escape the special meaning of a special character so that it is treated literally.

**Stack** The storage structure that maintains items on last-in-first-out (LIFO) basis.

**Standalone Connection** Refers to a computer not hooked up to a LAN, intranet, or the Internet, nor is it dedicated to a single user that logs on to use LINUX on that hardware platform only.

**Standard Error** See Standard Files.

**Standard Files** The files where the input of a process comes from and its output and error messages go to. The standard file where a process reads its input is called standard input. The process output goes to standard output, and the error messages generated by a process go to standard error. By default, the standard input comes from your keyboard, and standard output and standard error are sent to the display screen.

**Standard Input** See Standard Files

**Standard Output** See Standard Files

**Start-up Files** A file that is executed when you log on or when you start a new shell process. These files belong to a class of files called, dot or hidden files, as their names start with a dot (.) and they are not listed when you list the contents of a directory by using the ls command. Some commonly used start-up files are .bashrc (start-up file for Bash), .cshrc (start-up file for C shell), .profile (executed when you log on to a LINUX system), and .tcshrc (start-up file for TC shell). All of these files reside in your home directory.

**States** The states (conditions) a process can be in, such as, running, waiting, ready, and swapped.

**Static Analysis** The static analysis of a software involves analyzing its structure and properties without executing it.

**Sticky Bit** When an executable file with stickybit is executed, the LINUX kernel keeps it in the memory for as long as it can so that the time taken to load it from the disk can be saved when the file is executed the next time. When such a file has to be taken out of the main memory, it is saved on the swap space, thus resulting in less time to load it into memory once again.

**Subshell** A child shell executed under another shell.

**Supercomputer** The name used for most powerful computers that typically have many CPUs in them and are used to solve scientific problems that would take a long time to complete on smaller computers. Supercomputers are used in NASA and various U.S. national laboratories.

**Superuser** There is a special user in every LINUX system who can access any file or directory on the system. This user is the system administrator, commonly known as the *superuser* on the system.
**Sure Kill** Sending signal number 9 to a process is known as the sure kill as this signal cannot be intercepted by the process and is terminated for sure.
**Swap Space** An area set aside on the disk at the system boot time where processes can be saved temporarily in order to be reloaded into the memory at a later time. The activity of saving processes on the swap space is called *swap out,* and of bringing them back into the main memory is known as *swap in.* The time taken to load a process from the swap space into main memory is less than the time taken to load a file from the disk when it is stored in the normal fashion.
**Swapper Process** A process that swaps in a process from the swap space into the main memory, or swaps out a process from the main memory to the swap space. See Swap Space.
**Symbolic Constant** A constant value that is given to a name so that the name can be used to refer to the value.
**Symbolic Link** When a symbolic link to a shared file is created in a directory, a link file is created that contains a pathname of the shared file. The link therefore "points to" the shared file. The `ln -s` command is used to create a symbolic link.
**System Bus** A set of parallel wires used to take bits from the CPU to a device, or vice versa.
**System Call** A system call is an entry point into the operating system kernel code. System calls can be used by application programmers to have the kernel perform the tasks that need access to a hardware resource, such as reading a file on a hard disk.
**System Mailbox File** A file that contains all of the e-mail messages that the system has received for you. It is usually under the /usr/spool/mail directory, in a file with your login name.

**Tail** Refers to the last portion of a file. It is useful if you need to see the end of a file that is growing. In LINUX, you can display the tail of a file (last ten lines by default) by using the `tail` command.
**TCP/IP** See Transport Control Protocol/Internet Protocol.
**TCP/IP Protocol Suite** See Transport Control Protocol/Internet Protocol.
**Tee** The tee command reads standard input and sends it to both standard output and to one or more file arguments.
**Telnet** An application level Internet protocol that allows you to log on to a remote host on the internet.
**Text-Based Interface** A user interface to an application software or operating system in which the primary input device is the keyboard (i.e., user enters commands from the keyboard).
**Text-Driven Operating System** An operating system that takes commands to be executed from the keyboard.
**Throughput** The number of processes finished in a computer system in unit time.
**Time-Sharing System** A multiuser, multiprocess, and interactive operating system is known as the time-sharing system. UNIX and LINUX are prime examples of the time-sharing system.
**Topology** The physical arrangement of hosts in a network. Some commonly used topologies are bus, ring, mesh, and general graph.
**Transport Control Protocol/Internet Protocol** The suite of communication and routing protocols that are the basis of the Internet. They include many protocols such as FTP, ICMP, IP, TCP, Telnet, and UDP.
**Trusted Host** This term is in conjunction with the transferring of files from one host to another. If the rcp command fails, it is because the remote host does not trust your local host. The name of your local host must be in the /etc/hosts.equiv file on the remote machine for it to be "trusted."

**Universal Resource Locator** Protocol://IP_address/pathname or protocol://FQDN/pathname. The "protocol" field is usually http, but can be ftp, or telnet as well. "FQDN" is the fully qualified domain name such as mit.edu. The "pathname" field is used to identify the location of a file on the host. URLs are commonly used to identify the location of a Web page to be displayed on your screen. An example of a URL is http://www.up.edu/~johndoe/index.html. In this example the protocol is http, the FQDN is www.up.edu, and the pathname is ~/johndoe/index.html.

**URL** See Universal Resource Locator.

**User** In LINUX jargon, this term is used for the owner of a file when we talk about file access privileges.

**User-Defined Variables** These shell variables are used within shell scripts as temporary storage places whose values can be changed when the script executes.

**Username** A name by which a user of a multiuser computer system is known to it. Before you can use the computer system, you must enter your username at the login prompt and hit the <Enter> key, followed by entering your password and hitting the <Enter> key.

**Uudecode** The command for transforming a uuencoded ASCII file to the corresponding binary file.

**Uuencode** The command for transforming a binary file to an ASCII file.

**Virtual Connection** A virtual connection is said to be established between client and server processes when the two have made an initial contact to exchange each other's location (usually IP address and protocol port number). The connection request is almost always initiated by the client process. After the virtual connection has been established, the server process understands that it will receive service request(s) from the client process. The virtual connection is broken when the client process has received the response to its last request and initiates a request for closing the virtual connection.

**Virtual machine** The operating system software isolates you from the complications of the hardware resources, such as a disk drive, and is said to provide you a virtual machine that is much easier to use than the real machine.

**Web Browser** An Internet application that allows you to surf the web by allowing users to, among other things, view web pages.

**Wide Area Network (WAN)** Also known as a long haul network, it is a network that connects computing resources that are thousands of kilometers apart, typically spanning over several states, countries, and continents.

**Window Manager** A particular implementation of the functionality provided by a Window system.

**Window System** A graphical system that provides the generic features of a GUI.

**Write Permission** The write permission on a LINUX file allows a user to write to the file, thus allowing the insertion or deletion of its contents and its removal from the system. The write permission on a directory allows us to create a new file or directory, under another file.

**X Window System** A graphical intermediary between you and LINUX operating system. It was developed at MIT in 1983 as part of the Athena Project and is the defacto LINUX GUI.

**Zombie** A dying LINUX process is known as a zombie process. It is usually created when a process's parent terminates before it finishes execution. Such processes have finished their work but still have some system resources allocated to them, thus resulting is wastage of system resources.

# GNU General Public License

GNU GENERAL PUBLIC LICENSE—Version 2, June 1991



*Preamble*

The licenses for most software are designed to take away your freedom to share and change it. By contrast, the GNU General Public License is intended to guarantee your freedom to share and change free software—to make sure the software is free for all its users. This General Public License applies to most of the Free Software Foundation's software and to any other program whose authors commit to using it. (Some other Free Software Foundation software is covered by the GNU Library General Public License instead.) You can apply it to your programs, too.

When we speak of free software, we are referring to freedom, not price. Our General Public Licenses are designed to make sure that you have the freedom to distribute copies of free software (and charge for this service if you wish), that you receive source code or can get it if you want it, that you can change the software or use pieces of it in new free programs; and that you know you can do these things.

To protect your rights, we need to make restrictions that forbid anyone to deny you these rights or to ask you to surrender the rights. These restrictions translate to certain responsibilities for you if you distribute copies of the software, or if you modify it.

For example, if you distribute copies of such a program, whether gratis or for a fee, you must give the recipients all the rights that you have. You must make sure that they, too, receive or can get the source code. And you must show them these terms so they know their rights.

We protect your rights with two steps: (1) copyright the software, and (2) offer you this license which gives you legal permission to copy, distribute and/or modify the software.

Also, for each author's protection and ours, we want to make certain that everyone understands that there is no warranty for this free software. If the software is modified by someone else and passed on, we want its recipients to know that what they have is not the original, so that any problems introduced by others will not reflect on the original authors' reputations.

Finally, any free program is threatened constantly by software patents. We wish to avoid the danger that redistributors of a free program will individually obtain patent licenses, in effect making the program proprietary. To prevent this, we have made it clear that any patent must be licensed for everyone's free use or not licensed at all.

The precise terms and conditions for copying, distribution and modification follow.

TERMS AND CONDITIONS FOR COPYING, DISTRIBUTION AND MODIFICATION

0. This License applies to any program or other work which contains a notice placed by the copyright holder saying it may be distributed under the terms of this General Public License. The "Program", below, refers to any such program or work, and a "work based on the Program" means either the Program or any derivative work under copyright law: that is to say, a work containing the Program or a portion of it, either verbatim or with modifications and/or translated into another language. (Hereinafter, translation is included without limitation in the term "modification".) Each licensee is addressed as "you".

Activities other than copying, distribution and modification are not covered by this License; they are outside its scope. The act of running the Program is not restricted, and the output from the Program is covered only if its contents constitute a work based on the Program (independent of having been made by running the Program). Whether that is true depends on what the Program does.

1. You may copy and distribute verbatim copies of the Program's source code as you receive it, in any medium, provided that you conspicuously and appropriately publish on each copy an appropriate copyright notice and disclaimer of warranty; keep intact all the notices that refer to this License and to the absence of any warranty; and give any other recipients of the Program a copy of this License along with the Program.

You may charge a fee for the physical act of transferring a copy, and you may at your option offer warranty protection in exchange for a fee.

2. You may modify your copy or copies of the Program or any portion of it, thus forming a work based on the Program, and copy and distribute such modifications or work under the terms of Section 1 above, provided that you also meet all of these conditions:

* a) You must cause the modified files to carry prominent notices stating that you changed the files and the date of any change.

* b) You must cause any work that you distribute or publish, that in whole or in part contains or is derived from the Program or any part thereof, to be licensed as a whole at no charge to all third parties under the terms of this License.

* c) If the modified program normally reads commands interactively when run, you must cause it, when started running for such interactive use in the most ordinary way, to print or display an announcement including an appropriate copyright notice and a notice that there is no warranty (or else, saying that you provide a warranty) and that users may redistribute the program under these conditions, and telling the user how to view a copy of this License. (Exception: if the Program itself is interactive but does not normally print such an announcement, your work based on the Program is not required to print an announcement.)

These requirements apply to the modified work as a whole. If identifiable sections of that work are not derived from the Program, and can be reasonably considered independent and separate works in themselves, then this License, and its terms, do not apply to those sections when you distribute them as separate works.

But when you distribute the same sections as part of a whole which is a work based on the Program, the distribution of the whole must be on the terms of this License, whose permissions for other licensees extend to the entire whole, and thus to each and every part regardless of who wrote it.

Thus, it is not the intent of this section to claim rights or contest your rights to work written entirely by you; rather, the intent is to exercise the right to control the distribution of derivative or collective works based on the Program.

In addition, mere aggregation of another work not based on the Program with the Program (or with a work based on the Program) on a volume of a storage or distribution medium does not bring the other work under the scope of this License.

3. You may copy and distribute the Program (or a work based on it, under Section 2) in object code or executable form under the terms of Sections 1 and 2 above provided that you also do one of the following:

* a) Accompany it with the complete corresponding machine-readable source code, which must be distributed under the terms of Sections 1 and 2 above on a medium customarily used for software interchange; or,

* b) Accompany it with a written offer, valid for at least three years, to give any third party, for a charge no more than your cost of physically performing source distribution, a complete machine-readable copy of the corresponding source code, to be distributed under the terms of Sections 1 and 2 above on a medium customarily used for software interchange; or,

* c) Accompany it with the information you received as to the offer to distribute corresponding source code. (This alternative is allowed only for noncommercial distribution and only if you received the program in object code or executable form with such an offer, in accord with Subsection b above.)

The source code for a work means the preferred form of the work for making modifications to it. For an executable work, complete source code means all the source code for all modules it contains, plus any associated interface definition files, plus the scripts used to control compilation and installation of the executable. However, as a special exception, the source code distributed need not include anything that is normally distributed (in either source or binary form) with the major components (compiler, kernel, and so on) of the operating system on which the executable runs, unless that component itself accompanies the executable.

If distribution of executable or object code is made by offering access to copy from a designated place, then offering equivalent access to copy the source code from the same place counts as distribution of the source code, even though third parties are not compelled to copy the source along with the object code.

4. You may not copy, modify, sublicense, or distribute the Program except as expressly provided under this License. Any attempt otherwise to copy, modify, sublicense or distribute the Program is void, and will automatically terminate your rights under this License. However, parties who have received copies, or rights,

from you under this License will not have their licenses terminated so long as such parties remain in full compliance.

5. You are not required to accept this License, since you have not signed it. However, nothing else grants you permission to modify or distribute the Program or its derivative works. These actions are prohibited by law if you do not accept this License. Therefore, by modifying or distributing the Program (or any work based on the Program), you indicate your acceptance of this License to do so, and all its terms and conditions for copying, distributing or modifying the Program or works based on it.

6. Each time you redistribute the Program (or any work based on the Program), the recipient automatically receives a license from the original licensor to copy, distribute or modify the Program subject to these terms and conditions. You may not impose any further restrictions on the recipients' exercise of the rights granted herein. You are not responsible for enforcing compliance by third parties to this License.

7. If, as a consequence of a court judgment or allegation of patent infringement or for any other reason (not limited to patent issues), conditions are imposed on you (whether by court order, agreement or otherwise) that contradict the conditions of this License, they do not excuse you from the conditions of this License. If you cannot distribute so as to satisfy simultaneously your obligations under this License and any other pertinent obligations, then as a consequence you may not distribute the Program at all. For example, if a patent license would not permit royalty-free redistribution of the Program by all those who receive copies directly or indirectly through you, then the only way you could satisfy both it and this License would be to refrain entirely from distribution of the Program.

If any portion of this section is held invalid or unenforceable under any particular circumstance, the balance of the section is intended to apply and the section as a whole is intended to apply in other circumstances.

It is not the purpose of this section to induce you to infringe any patents or other property right claims or to contest validity of any such claims; this section has the sole purpose of protecting the integrity of the free software distribution system, which is implemented by public license practices. Many people have made generous contributions to the wide range of software distributed through that system in reliance on consistent application of that system; it is up to the author/donor to decide if he or she is willing to distribute software through any other system and a licensee cannot impose that choice.

This section is intended to make thoroughly clear what is believed to be a consequence of the rest of this License.

8. If the distribution and/or use of the Program is restricted in certain countries either by patents or by copyrighted interfaces, the original copyright holder who places the Program under this License may add an explicit geographical distribution limitation excluding those countries, so that distribution is permitted only in

or among countries not thus excluded. In such case, this License incorporates the limitation as if written in the body of this License.

9. The Free Software Foundation may publish revised and/or new versions of the General Public License from time to time. Such new versions will be similar in spirit to the present version, but may differ in detail to address new problems or concerns.

Each version is given a distinguishing version number. If the Program specifies a version number of this License which applies to it and "any later version", you have the option of following the terms and conditions either of that version or of any later version published by the Free Software Foundation. If the Program does not specify a version number of this License, you may choose any version ever published by the Free Software Foundation.

10. If you wish to incorporate parts of the Program into other free programs whose distribution conditions are different, write to the author to ask for permission. For software which is copyrighted by the Free Software Foundation, write to the Free Software Foundation; we sometimes make exceptions for this. Our decision will be guided by the two goals of preserving the free status of all derivatives of our free software and of promoting the sharing and reuse of software generally.

NO WARRANTY

11. BECAUSE THE PROGRAM IS LICENSED FREE OF CHARGE, THERE IS NO WARRANTY FOR THE PROGRAM, TO THE EXTENT PERMITTED BY APPLICABLE LAW. EXCEPT WHEN OTHERWISE STATED IN WRITING THE COPYRIGHT HOLDERS AND/OR OTHER PARTIES PROVIDE THE PROGRAM "AS IS" WITHOUT WARRANTY OF ANY KIND, EITHER EXPRESSED OR IMPLIED, INCLUDING, BUT NOT LIMITED TO, THE IMPLIED WARRANTIES OF MERCHANTABILITY AND FITNESS FOR A PARTICULAR PURPOSE. THE ENTIRE RISK AS TO THE QUALITY AND PERFORMANCE OF THE PROGRAM IS WITH YOU. SHOULD THE PROGRAM PROVE DEFECTIVE, YOU ASSUME THE COST OF ALL NECESSARY SERVICING, REPAIR OR CORRECTION.

12. IN NO EVENT UNLESS REQUIRED BY APPLICABLE LAW OR AGREED TO IN WRITING WILL ANY COPYRIGHT HOLDER, OR ANY OTHER PARTY WHO MAY MODIFY AND/OR REDISTRIBUTE THE PROGRAM AS PERMITTED ABOVE, BE LIABLE TO YOU FOR DAMAGES, INCLUDING ANY GENERAL, SPECIAL, INCIDENTAL OR CONSEQUENTIAL DAMAGES ARISING OUT OF THE USE OR INABILITY TO USE THE PROGRAM (INCLUDING BUT NOT LIMITED TO LOSS OF DATA OR DATA BEING RENDERED INACCURATE OR LOSSES SUSTAINED BY YOU OR THIRD PARTIES OR A FAILURE OF THE PROGRAM TO OPERATE WITH ANY OTHER PROGRAMS), EVEN IF SUCH HOLDER OR OTHER PARTY HAS BEEN ADVISED OF THE POSSIBILITY OF SUCH DAMAGES.

END OF TERMS AND CONDITIONS

# Index

## D

## I



## J



## K



## L



## M

**R**

SYSTEM REQUIREMENTS

* PU Intel Pentium and compatible processors (PentiumI/MMX/Pro/Celeron/III, AMD K6/K6-2, Cyrix 6x86/M-II).
* RAM: 32MB required, 64MB recommended for X Window System
* Disk space 500MB minimum, 1BG+ recommended
* CD-ROM Drive